Lecture Notes in Computer Science　　11099

Commenced Publication in 1973
Founding and Former Series Editors:
Gerhard Goos, Juris Hartmanis, and Jan van Leeuwen

More information about this series at http://www.springer.com/series/7410

Javier Lopez · Jianying Zhou
Miguel Soriano (Eds.)

Computer Security

23rd European Symposium
on Research in Computer Security, ESORICS 2018
Barcelona, Spain, September 3–7, 2018
Proceedings, Part II

 Springer

Editors
Javier Lopez
Department of Computer Science
University of Malaga
Málaga, Málaga
Spain

Miguel Soriano
Universitat Politècnica de Catalunya
Barcelona
Spain

Jianying Zhou
Singapore University of Technology
  and Design
Singapore
Singapore

ISSN 0302-9743   ISSN 1611-3349 (electronic)
Lecture Notes in Computer Science
ISBN 978-3-319-98988-4   ISBN 978-3-319-98989-1 (eBook)
https://doi.org/10.1007/978-3-319-98989-1

Library of Congress Control Number: 2018951097

LNCS Sublibrary: SL4 – Security and Cryptology

This Springer imprint is published by the registered company Springer Nature Switzerland AG
The registered company address is: Gewerbestrasse 11, 6330 Cham, Switzerland

Preface

This book contains the papers that were selected for presentation and publication at the 23rd European Symposium on Research in Computer Security — ESORICS 2018 – which was held in Barcelona, Spain, September 3–7, 2018. The aim of ESORICS is to further the progress of research in computer, information, and cyber security and in privacy, by establishing a European forum for bringing together researchers in these areas, by promoting the exchange of ideas with system developers, and by encouraging links with researchers in related fields.

In response to the call for papers, 283 papers were submitted to the conference. These papers were evaluated on the basis of their significance, novelty, and technical quality. Each paper was reviewed by at least three members of the Program Committee. The Program Committee meeting was held electronically, with intensive discussion over a period of two weeks. Finally, 56 papers were selected for presentation at the conference, giving an acceptance rate of 20%.

ESORICS 2018 would not have been possible without the contributions of the many volunteers who freely gave their time and expertise. We would like to thank the members of the Program Committee and the external reviewers for their substantial work in evaluating the papers. We would also like to thank the general chair, Miguel Soriano, the organization chair, Josep Pegueroles, the workshop chair, Joaquin Garcia-Alfaro, and all workshop co-chairs, the publicity chairs, Giovanni Livraga and Rodrigo Roman, and the ESORICS Steering Committee and its chair, Sokratis Katsikas.

Finally, we would like to express our thanks to the authors who submitted papers to ESORICS. They, more than anyone else, are what makes this conference possible.

We hope that you will find the program stimulating and a source of inspiration for future research.

June 2018

Javier Lopez
Jianying Zhou

ESORICS 2018

23rd European Symposium on Research in Computer Security
Barcelona, Spain
September 3–7, 2018

Organized by Universitat Politecnica de Catalunya - BarcelonaTech, Spain

General Chair

Miguel Soriano   Universitat Politecnica de Catalunya, Spain

Program Chairs

Javier Lopez   University of Malaga, Spain
Jianying Zhou   SUTD, Singapore

Workshop Chair

Joaquin Garcia-Alfaro   Telecom SudParis, France

Organizing Chair

Josep Pegueroles   Universitat Politecnica de Catalunya, Spain

Publicity Chairs

Giovanni Livraga   Università degli studi di Milano, Italy
Rodrigo Roman   University of Malaga, Spain

Program Committee

Gail-Joon Ahn   Arizona State University, USA
Cristina Alcaraz   University of Malaga, Spain
Elli Androulaki   IBM Research - Zurich, Switzerland
Vijay Atluri   Rutgers University, USA
Michael Backes   Saarland University, Germany
Carlo Blundo   Università degli Studi di Salerno, Italy
Levente Buttyan   BME, Hungary
Jan Camenisch   IBM Research - Zurich, Switzerland
Alvaro Cardenas   University of Texas at Dallas, USA
Aldar C-F. Chan   University of Hong Kong, SAR China
Liqun Chen   University of Surrey, UK

Ivan Martinovic	University of Oxford, UK
Sjouke Mauw	University of Luxembourg, Luxembourg
Catherine Meadows	Naval Research Laboratory, USA
Weizhi Meng	Technical University of Denmark, Denmark
Chris Mitchell	RHUL, UK
Haralambos Mouratidis	University of Brighton, UK
David Naccache	Ecole Normale Superieure, France
Martín Ochoa	Universidad del Rosario, Colombia
Eiji Okamoto	University of Tsukuba, Japan
Rolf Oppliger	eSECURITY Technologies, Switzerland
Günther Pernul	Universität Regensburg, Germany
Joachim Posegga	University of Passau, Germany
Christina Pöpper	NYU Abu Dhabi, UAE
Indrajit Ray	Colorado State University, USA
Giovanni Russello	University of Auckland, New Zealand
Mark Ryan	University of Birmingham, UK
Peter Y. A. Ryan	University of Luxembourg, Luxembourg
Rei Safavi-Naini	University of Calgary, Canada
Pierangela Samarati	Universitá degli studi di Milano, Italy
Damien Sauveron	XLIM, France
Steve Schneider	University of Surrey, UK
Einar Snekkenes	Gjovik University College, Norway
Willy Susilo	University of Wollongong, Australia
Pawel Szalachowski	SUTD, Singapore
Qiang Tang	LIST, Luxembourg
Juan Tapiador	University Carlos III, Spain
Nils Ole Tippenhauer	SUTD, Singapore
Aggeliki Tsohou	Ionian University, Greece
Jaideep Vaidya	Rutgers University, USA
Serge Vaudenay	EPFL, Switzerland
Luca Viganò	King's College London, UK
Michael Waidner	Fraunhofer SIT, Germany
Cong Wang	City University of Hong Kong, SAR China
Lingyu Wang	Concordia University, Canada
Edgar Weippl	SBA Research, Austria
Christos Xenakis	University of Piraeus, Greece
Kehuan Zhang	Chinese University of Hong Kong, SAR China
Sencun Zhu	Pennsylvania State University, USA

Organizing Committee

Oscar Esparza
Marcel Fernandez
Juan Hernandez
Olga Leon

Isabel Martin
Jose L. Munoz
Josep Pegueroles

Additional Reviewers

Akand, Mamun
Al Maqbali, Fatma
Albanese, Massimiliano
Amerini, Irene
Ammari, Nader
Avizheh, Sepideh
Balli, Fatih
Bamiloshin, Michael
Bana, Gergei
Banik, Subhadeep
Becerra, Jose
Belguith, Sana
Ben Adar-Bessos, Mai
Berners-Lee, Ela
Berthier, Paul
Bezawada, Bruhadeshwar
Biondo, Andrea
Blanco-Justicia, Alberto
Blazy, Olivier
Boschini, Cecilia
Brandt, Markus
Bursuc, Sergiu
Böhm, Fabian
Cao, Chen
Caprolu, Maurantonio
Catuogno, Luigi
Cetinkaya, Orhan
Chang, Bing
Charlie, Jacomme
Chau, Sze Yiu
Chen, Rongmao
Cheval, Vincent
Cho, Haehyun
Choi, Gwangbae
Chow, Yang-Wai
Ciampi, Michele
Costantino, Gianpiero
Dai, Tianxiang
Dashevskyi, Stanislav
Del Vasto, Luis
Diamantopoulou, Vasiliki
Dietz, Marietheres
Divakaran, Dinil

Dong, Shuaike
Dupressoir, François
Durak, Betül
Eckhart, Matthias
El Kassem, Nada
Elkhiyaoui, Kaoutar
Englbrecht, Ludwig
Epiphaniou, Gregory
Fernández-Gago, Carmen
Fojtik, Roman
Freeman, Kevin
Fritsch, Lothar
Fuchsbauer, Georg
Fuller, Ben
Gabriele, Lenzini
Gadyatskaya, Olga
Galdi, Clemente
Gassais, Robin
Genc, Ziya A.
Georgiopoulou, Zafeiroula
Groll, Sebastian
Groszschaedl, Johann
Guan, Le
Han, Jinguang
Hassan, Fadi
Hill, Allister
Hong, Kevin
Horváth, Máté
Hu, Hongxin
Huh, Jun Ho
Iakovakis, George
Iovino, Vincenzo
Jadla, Marwen
Jansen, Kai
Jonker, Hugo
Judmayer, Aljosha
Kalloniatis, Christos
Kambourakis, Georgios
Kannwischer, Matthias Julius
Kar, Diptendu
Karamchandani, Neeraj
Karati, Sabyasach
Karati, Sabyasachi

Karegar, Farzaneh
Karopoulos, Georgios
Karyda, Maria
Kasra, Shabnam
Kohls, Katharina
Kokolakis, Spyros
Kordy, Barbara
Krenn, Stephan
Kilinç, Handan
Labrèche, François
Lai, Jianchang
Lain, Daniele
Lee, Jehyun
Leontiadis, Iraklis
Lerman, Liran
León, Olga
Li, Shujun
Li, Yan
Liang, Kaitai
Lin, Yan
Liu, Shengli
Losiouk, Eleonora
Lykou, Georgia
Lyvas, Christos
Ma, Jack P. K.
Magkos, Emmanouil
Majumdar, Suryadipta
Malliaros, Stefanos
Manjón, Jesús A.
Marktscheffel, Tobias
Martinez, Sergio
Martucci, Leonardo
Mayer, Wilfried
Mcmahon-Stone, Christopher
Menges, Florian
Mentzeliotou, Despoina
Mercaldo, Francesco
Mohamady, Meisam
Mohanty, Manoranjan
Moreira, Jose
Mulamba, Dieudonne
Murmann, Patrick
Muñoz, Jose L.
Mykoniati, Maria
Mylonas, Alexios
Nabi, Mahmoodon

Nasim, Tariq
Neven, Gregory
Ngamboe, Mikaela
Nieto, Ana
Ntantogian, Christoforos
Nuñez, David
Oest, Adam
Ohtake, Go
Oqaily, Momen
Ordean, Mihai
P., Vinod
Panaousis, Emmanouil
Papaioannou, Thanos
Paraboschi, Stefano
Park, Jinbum
Parra Rodriguez, Juan D.
Parra-Arnau, Javier
Pasa, Luca
Paspatis, Ioannis
Perillo, Angelo Massimo
Pillai, Prashant
Pindado, Zaira
Pitropakis, Nikolaos
Poh, Geong Sen
Puchta, Alexander
Pöhls, Henrich C.
Radomirovic, Sasa
Ramírez-Cruz, Yunior
Raponi, Simone
Rial, Alfredo
Ribes-González, Jordi
Rios, Ruben
Roenne, Peter
Roman, Rodrigo
Rubio Medrano, Carlos
Rupprecht, David
Salazar, Luis
Saracino, Andrea
Schindler, Philipp
Schnitzler, Theodor
Scotti, Fabio
Sempreboni, Diego
Senf, Daniel
Sengupta, Binanda
Sentanoe, Stewart
Sheikhalishahi, Mina

Shirani, Paria
Shrishak, Kris
Siniscalchi, Luisa
Smith, Zach
Smyth, Ben
Soria-Comas, Jordi
Soumelidou, Katerina
Spooner, Nick
Stergiopoulos, George
Stifter, Nicholas
Stojkovski, Borce
Sun, Menghan
Sun, Zhibo
Syta, Ewa
Tai, Raymond K. H.
Tang, Xiaoxiao
Taubmann, Benjamin
Tian, Yangguang
Toffalini, Flavio
Tolomei, Gabriele
Towa, Patrick
Tsalis, Nikolaos
Tsiatsikas, Zisis
Tsoumas, Bill
Urdaneta, Marielba
Valente, Junia
Venkatesan, Sridhar
Veroni, Eleni
Vielberth, Manfred
Virvilis, Nick
Vizár, Damian

Vukolic, Marko
Wang, Daibin
Wang, Ding
Wang, Haining
Wang, Jiafan
Wang, Jianfeng
Wang, Juan
Wang, Jun
Wang, Tianhao
Wang, Xiaolei
Wang, Xiuhua
Whitefield, Jorden
Wong, Harry W. H.
Wu, Huangting
Xu, Jia
Xu, Jun
Xu, Lei
Yang, Guangliang
Yautsiukhin, Artsiom
Yu, Yong
Yuan, Lunpin
Zamyatin, Alexei
Zhang, Lei
Zhang, Liang Feng
Zhang, Yangyong
Zhang, Yuexin
Zhao, Liang
Zhao, Yongjun
Zhao, Ziming
Zuo, Cong

Contents – Part II

Applied Crypto (I)

Privacy (II)

Multi-party Computation

SDN Security

Applied Crypto (II)

Contents – Part I

Attacks

Malware and Vulnerabilities

Protocol Security

Mobile Security

Workflow-Aware Security of Integrated Mobility Services

Prabhakaran Kasinathan[1,2(✉)] and Jorge Cuellar[1,2]

[1] Siemens AG, CT, IT Security, Munich, Germany
{prabhakaran.kasinathan,jorge.cuellar}@siemens.com
[2] University of Passau, Passau, Germany

Abstract. The Connected Mobility Lab (CML) is a mobility solution created in collaboration between Siemens and BMW. The CML provides a multi-tenant cloud infrastructure where entities – mobility providers, financial service providers, users – might know each other or might be complete strangers. The CML encapsulates core services from different stakeholders and exposes an integrated, comprehensive, and innovative mobility service to its users. The different owners may have different security goals and impose their own rules and workflows on entities interacting with their services. Thus, there is a need to negotiate in order to reach mutually acceptable compromises, and inter-operate services within the CML. Especially, when different services collaborate to fulfill a *purpose* it is important to allow only authorized entities to execute the required tasks. To enforce such tasks to be executed in a particular order we need *a workflow specification and enforcement method.*

This paper presents a workflow specification and enforcement framework that guarantees the process integrity (for instance, a technical process) by enforcing an access control method that restricts the entities to do only what is allowed in the specified workflow. The framework also supports dynamic workflows that adapt to error conditions, and a method to support accountability. We evaluate our proposed framework on a CML business mobility use case. We extend the Petri Nets based workflow specification and enforcement framework proposed in [2] to achieve our goals.

Keywords: Workflow · Process integrity · Security · Petri nets
Mobility services

1 Introduction

The Connected Mobility Lab (CML) has been developed within the scope of a public funded project (see [1]) to enable smart mobility applications by seamlessly exchanging data and analytics. The CML integrates the services from

P. Kasinathan—This research work was partially supported by the Zentrum Digitilisierung Bayern (ZD.B) [1] by project IUK 1504-003 IUK474/002.

J. Lopez et al. (Eds.): ESORICS 2018, LNCS 11099, pp. 3–19, 2018.
https://doi.org/10.1007/978-3-319-98989-1_1

different stakeholders – such as mobility, financial and IT services – to provide comprehensive mobility solutions to its users. Figure 1 shows how the CML core services such as security, accounting, data management and identity management enable the integration of data and processes from different mobility providers (partners) to provide the CML mobility services. The CML mobile application (CML App) runs on mobility assistant devices such as smart phone and touch points as shown in Fig. 1; the users can access the CML App and use the comprehensive CML mobility solution.

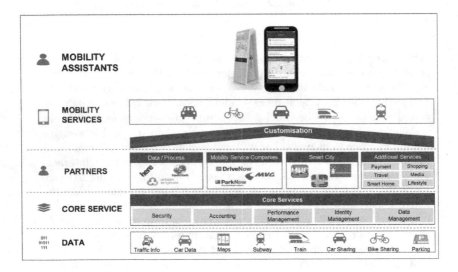

Fig. 1. The Connected Mobility Lab (CML) solution [1]

The users of CML can be private persons or employees of a company that has a service agreement with the CML. A user may wish to use different mobility services to complete one single journey. Each stakeholder enforces his own business processes on the customers (CML users) who use his services, therefore CML must integrate different stakeholders' processes.

A process is a set of interrelated activities or tasks that must be carried out to accomplish a goal [3]. A business process is also called a workflow, but we use the two words as synonymous. A workflow must be executed as it is specified, and only using the available information it has, i.e., no one is able to change, add additional steps or skip steps, etc. and the workflow should not use any interface that he is not allowed do use. This property is called *"process integrity"*. During the execution of the workflow, the participants may exchange each other documents, information, see [4].

For instance, a user might use a carsharing service from his home to the main train station, then park the car in one of available the parking lots and take a train to reach the final destination. During the trip, the user must obey the rules and conditions specified by that particular mobility provider. The CML provides a global workflow for the trip that enforces each stakeholder's processes that must be executed by the user in order to complete the journey.

The CML users execute the workflow to consume the services offered by the CML. When users execute any task that involve accessing a service it is important to enforce strict access control. We enforce a *least privilege* principle for task authorizations within each workflow. The least privilege principle is a security concept where every computer module (such as a process, user, or program, depending on the subject) may be able to access only the information and resources that are necessary for its legitimate purpose. As a particular case, the principle "Need to Know" is a confidentiality policy which states that no subject should be able to read objects unless reading them is necessary for that subject to perform its functions [3]. What we need is a similar policy, but regarding integrity. We might call this principle "Need to Access": it states that no subject should be able to *write or change* objects unless it is necessary to complete the required task of a process or workflow at that particular state. By enforcing the need to access principle, an entity can get privileges to execute a task only at the required step of the workflow. This provides workflow driven (wokflow-aware) access control.

The first main motivation of our work is to provide an access control that restricts the entities to do only what is allowed in the workflow, and to guarantee the process integrity. The second main objective of our framework is to support dynamic workflows which adapts to error conditions by, for instance, allowing services to create on the fly sub-workflows without changing the main workflow. Note that protecting the integrity of the processes and allowing the creation of dynamic workflows may be competing goals: it must be assured that the creation of the workflow can be done only by an "authorized" entity, and any misuse must be penalized. Thus, our framework must have a workflow driven access control in contrast to the commonly used mandatory (MAC), discretionary (DAC), or role-based access control (RBAC), which have been well-studied in the literature, see [5]. In addition, we need a system to log all actions of each participant executing the workflow for auditing purpose. As CML consists of different partners it is important to have an auditing system without assuming a central authority.

Summarizing the CML requirements, the main goal of this paper is to develop a framework that:

- supports the specification of processes as workflows that can be created in a step wise manner using standard software engineering processes and tools.
- constrain an entity using an application/services to obey a prescribed workflow with fine-grained authorization constraints (least privilege and need to access) and provides a formal background to guarantee process integrity.
- allows entities participating in a workflow to have a choice for example, to accept (or reject) "*contracts*" or conditions,
- allows services and entities executing a workflow to handle error conditions by supporting creation of dynamic workflows, and
- provides accountability without assuming a central authority.

To achieve the goals described above, we contribute and extend our *Petri Nets and Transition Contracts* framework presented in [2] by:

- Using SysML activity diagram to model the business or technical process of stakeholders.
- Introducing open Petri Net places to exchange information between workflows.
- Using timeout transitions that can trigger a transition, fire a timeout token after a predefined time expires.
- Using of PNML to write and exchange Petri Net workflows between entities and users.
- Introducing a private blockchain network for accountability purposes without assuming the central trusted authority.

The rest of the paper is structured as the follows: Sect. 2 presents our previous framework, Sect. 3 describes the contributions of this paper, extensions to existing framework and how we adapt it for the CML with a prototype implementation, Sect. 4 presents how our framework can solve a CML use case, Sect. 5 presents related work and at the end, Sect. 6 presents the conclusion and future work.

2   Background Work

In this section, we introduce Petri Nets based workflow specification and enforcement presented in [2].

2.1   Petri Nets for Workflow Specification

Petri Nets enable us to create workflows with properties like deadlock-free, guaranteed termination, separation-of-duties, etc. Properties of Petri Nets such as reachability, liveness (deadlock-free), and coverability [6–8] can be verified. Hierarchical Petri Nets can simplify the process of creating complex workflows by breaking them into smaller partial workflows.

In traditional Petri Nets (PN) (see [9]) there are places, tokens and transitions. A place in a traditional Petri Net can hold one or more tokens (Markings) of same type. Colored Petri Nets (CPN) (see [10]) is an extension of Petri Nets, and in CPN different types of tokens can exist in the same place. A transition may have one or more input places, and a place may have one or several tokens. A transition fires if its input places have sufficient tokens and as a result it produces tokens in output places. Entities executing the Petri Net workflow change their state from one place to another via a transition firing. Extensions of Petri Nets such as colored Petri Nets have enabled Petri Nets to represent different types of tokens in one place.

In our Petri Net model for workflows presented in [2], we extend Colored Petri Nets (CPN) by introducing the following additional concepts:

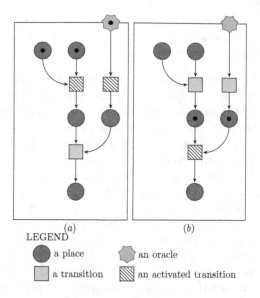

LEGEND

(a) (b)

🔴 a place   ⭐ an oracle

🔲 a transition   ▨ an activated transition

Fig. 2. (a) shows the initial state of a Petri Net workflow specification and (b) shows the state of the Petri Net after the first two transitions have fired.

- A *Token* in our Petri Nets can be a representation of permissions, endorsements, money (crypto coins), signature, or any information that is required for the workflow execution. We will use explicit token names (for example, oauth token) and explain their purpose wherever necessary to avoid confusion between different types of tokens used in use cases.
- A special type of Petri Net place (called an *oracle*) that can receive tokens (information) from an external source and it is represented as star shape (filled with green color) in our Petri Nets. The Fig. 2 shows a simple workflow specified as a Petri Net. The oracle is represented as a star and all other places are represented as circles. A place that contains or holds a token is marked with a small black circle. The transitions waiting for tokens are presented as squares without patterns, and activated transitions ready for firing are shown as patterned squares. The Fig. 2(a) shows that the first two transitions are enabled (ready to fire) because the input places have tokens, and the Fig. 2(b) shows that those two transitions have fired and as a result produced tokens in the output places. An oracle is drawn usually on the boundary of a Petri Net to represent that the information is from an external source. Note: the term oracle is used in different computer science fields including cryptography, blockchain and smart contracts, etc. Our concept of an Oracle is similar to the Oracles introduced in Ethereum blockchain, i.e., it is used to receive external information into the workflow. An Oracle in our method need not be a contract that is accessed by other contracts as to get external information as described in [11,12]. If a blockchain implementation is used then an external service can push some information into the blockchain, later

an oracle is used to query that information. In other instances, an oracle in our Petri Net can have a predefined URL, and by querying that URL the Oracle may get the required information.

Workflows can be specified using Petri Nets, but we need a mechanism to enforce conditions that are written in the transitions of Petri Nets. For this purpose, we proposed to use *smart contracts*. Smart Contracts introduced in [13], have become popular with the advancements in blockchain technology. Smart contracts are often written to ensure fairness between participating entities even when one entity may attempt to cheat the other entity in arbitrary ways (see [14]). Ethereum [15], which has popularized the use of smart contracts defines a smart contract as "/a computer code that defines certain parts of an agreement and can self-execute if terms are met/". Bitcoins uses a simple stack (or non-Turing complete language) language to express the rules and conditions for a successful transaction i.e., how new coins are produced and consumed. Ethereum uses a Turing complete language (Solidity [16]) to express complex contractual terms and conditions. Luu et al. [17] studied the security of running smart contracts based on Ethereum, and presented the problems in Ethereum's smart contract language solidity; they also show some ways to enhance the operational semantics of Ethereum to make smart contracts less vulnerable. For our requirements both Bitcoin and Ethereum languages are not suitable. Bitcoin's stack language is not flexible therefore, we cannot express workflow conditions on it. Ethereum's solidity language could be vulnerable (see [17]), and we cannot verify such contracts. Therefore, a smart contract language that is flexible to specify conditions and at the same time verifiable is required. Some transitions within our Petri Net workflow have additionally a *transition contract* as shown in Fig. 3.

2.2 Transition Contracts

In traditional Petri Nets a transition fires when its input places has sufficient tokens. To implement a workflow driven access control system in Petri Nets, the transitions should be able to verify conditions and evaluate information encoded in the tokens. The conditions written on a single transition using a simple smart contract language is called a *transition contract*. We propose to use a simple guarded command (a conditionally executed statement) language (similar to [18]) to write transition contracts.

The Fig. 3 shows a simple Petri Net where two transitions (*T1 and T2*) have a pointer to the transition contracts (*TC (a) and TC (b)*) respectively. Note: smart contracts do not always have to run on blockchain, they can also be implemented between two or more parties without blockchain technology.

The properties (or rules) for each transition may be seen as small smart contracts that restrict the choices of the participants of the workflow for this step, or they impose additional conditions. The combination of few transition contracts allow us to create *multi-step smart contracts*: say, the first transition creates a token based on some conditions (which may verify authentication or

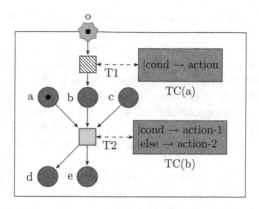

Fig. 3. Smart contract: Petri Net with transition contracts

authorization status of participants), and then the second transition produces an oauth token that can only be used in a subsequent transition in a particular way. The allowed actions, permissions of workflow participants are determined by the Petri Net and the next transition contracts. We propose to use the combination of Petri Nets and transition contracts to specify, enforce sequences of atomic transitions (transactions), and properties that must be satisfied in a workflow.

A transition performs three steps before firing:

- First, it takes tokens from the input places (could be a normal place, open place or an oracle).
- Next, it verifies the validity, properties of input tokens.
- Finally, it evaluates the conditions described (as guarded commands) in the transition contract, and produces the output tokens in output places (could be a normal place, open place or an oracle).

An output produced by the transition contract can be a token representing information or a workflow for one or more entities.

3 Specifying and Enforcing Workflows in CML

In CML, services or applications may have been developed by different service providers, have different specifications and implement "equivalent" tasks differently. In addition, it is important to guarantee the process integrity, and provide workflow driven access control. This implies that the workflows must be specified at a higher layer, abstracting away from implementation details. For this purpose, first we need a high level workflow specification language to express a process in a given context as a workflow. The workflow specification language should be amenable to lightweight formal methods, so that the different parties can reason locally about them. Petri Nets as the workflow specification language is a used for the above mentioned reasons. In our previous work [2], we focused on applying our framework to the constrained devices of Internet of Things (IoT). The CML App is installed in devices such as smart phones and touch points, therefore we apply our framework in CML without any problems.

The integrity of the workflow is guaranteed without requiring a central enforcement authority or workflow engine. Instead, the owner of each CML provider enforces his own conditions on users to access his services by verifying that the user has the necessary tokens, including ones which demonstrate the successful completion of previous steps in the workflow. This service then also provides a token to the user which he can present to the service in the next interaction.

We believe that the way to secure a reliable, consistent and predictable set of rules in complex environments is using formal methods. This is also one reason for choosing Petri Nets as a specification language. Since some transactions have some further logic depending on the values of the tokens presented, we propose to specify Smart Transition Contracts (presented in Sect. 2) in a simple declarative language.

It is a complex task to design a process from scratch that uses different services from various providers. The general accepted method is to refine the specification in a step wise manner using software engineering tools such as the object management group (OMG) system modeling language's (SysML) activity diagram presented in [19]. The OMG SysML is a general purpose graphical modeling language for specifying, analyzing, designing and verifying complex systems. In particular, it provides a semantic foundation for modeling system requirements, and the SysML's activity diagram can be transformed intuitively into a Petri Nets model.

A workflow should handle error conditions to an extent, and we propose to use dynamic workflows. Dynamic workflows are created to handle special and error conditions, user choices, etc., by authorized entities (of the main workflow) without changing the goal or purpose of the main workflow. Note that protecting the integrity of the processes and allowing the creation of dynamic workflows may be competing goals: it must be assured that the creation of the workflow can be done only by an "authorized" entity, and any misuse must be penalized. Therefore, we also need a system to account (save or log) all activities performed by the participants of the workflow. To enable dynamic workflows and guarantee the process integrity within CML, we introduce to two extensions to our existing framework.

First, we propose to use Open Petri Nets (see [20]), which provide entry and exit points (via Open Petri Net places) to exchange information between workflows. Open Petri Nets [20] enable two or more workflows to exchange information in the form of tokens. For instance, Fig. 4 shows that WF (a) and WF (b) exchanging tokens via the open place (oa and ob). An open place exists on the boundary of the workflow, and the equivalence (=) sign identifies the entry and exit places between two workflows. The open place (oa) is an exit place for WF (a) and entry place for WF (b). The main difference between an oracle and an open place is: an oracle can receive information from external sources whereas,

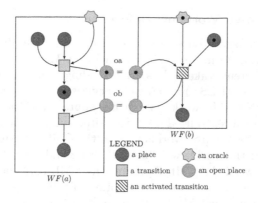

Fig. 4. WF (a) and (b) exchange information using Open Petri Net places.

the open places are mainly used to exchange tokens between workflows. Open petri net places are particularly useful when creating the main workflow would like to create a dynamic workflow and exchange information with it.

Sometimes, a user or an entity may fail to complete a task in a workflow that is expected to be completed within a certain time. This could lead into an error condition (for example, a transition may wait forever to get a token in a required place). To solve this problem, we propose to use timeouts in Petri Net transitions i.e., after a predefined time expires, the transition executes set of predefined conditions and fire a timeout token. We call these transitions as *timeout transitions*. Timeouts in transitions should be used only when necessary, and timeout transitions can be triggered by a token in one of the input places. For example, consider a task (tsk1) that should be completed within 10 min, and this task can be initiated after transition (t1) produces a token in the place (a). The next transition (t2)'s is implemented as a timeout transition that is triggered when a token appears in place (a) i.e. the countdown starts and default conditions are executed to produce a token when the time expires after 10 min.

The CML is a centralized system but our framework uses a distributed blockchain network for accountability purposes. A private blockchain is used to set access control restrictions i.e., who is allowed to participate in the blockchain. For instance, the users when executing the workflow publishes status of every task that they are executing – i.e., status of transitions of the Petri Net workflow – in the private blockchain. The stakeholders will verify and approve the transactions in the blockchain, and this provides transparency and accountability in an immutable database without assuming a trusted centralized entity.

Finally, we need a standard method to exchange Petri Net workflows between users and CML entities. Weber et al. in [21] introduced Petri Net Markup Language (PNML) which is based on XML, and in this work we propose to use the PNML for writing, exchanging Petri Net workflows between different entities and users of CML.

3.1   Petri Net Based Workflow Enforcement

Our prototype implementation also demonstrates the feasibility of using Petri Nets to enforce workflows in a real system such as CML.

Assume that different stakeholders are providing their services as Representational State Transfer (REST) based web services through CML core services. The workflows are created by workflow experts, approved by the stakeholders and made available within a centralized CML repository. A participant can download the CML App and the required workflow from the CML repository, and then he may start executing the workflow. The CML front-end provides the communication interface between the CML App and the CML core services – standard security protocols are used to protect the communication channel. How participants authenticate with the CML front-end application is out of scope here. The enforcement of the Petri Net workflows is integrated with the CML App. The workflows being executed within the CML App run within a Trusted Execution Environment (TEE) and may contain secret material; we assume that the participants are not able to extract or modify any secrets from the workflow. For instance, to authenticate against a CML service the shared secret material can be used by a transition of the workflow.

The Python library called "SNAKES", presented in [22] by Pommereau, is used to execute the Petri Nets workflows written in Petri Net Markup language (PNML). The SNAKES library is extended to support different types of Petri Net places such as oracles and open places, and to evaluate transitions with external conditions and produce the necessary tokens that will be required for subsequent transitions. In current implementation, the transition contracts are expressed with limited features of SNAKES library's arc notations, expressions that can use native python functions to evaluate input tokens and produce required tokens.

4   A CML Use Case

A typical commuter in a cosmopolitan city has several transportation options such as flights, train network for intercity travel, public transport, car and bike sharing services including parking facilities within the city, and so on. The CML envisions to integrate mobility services, and provide a mobile/web application to its users with an objective to provide a comprehensive mobility service.

We describe a business mobility use case scenario of the CML where a company can enforce project specific travel restrictions, special conditions – such as on what situation an employee can take business class trips – on its employees.

Let us consider that two companies A and B work on a public-funded project, and due to the nature of the project the team members need to travel between two companies frequently. The companies A and B decide to use mobility services offered by CML to its team members. The CML's workflow specification and enforcement module – described in the Sect. 3.1 – supports to enforce Petri Net based workflows.

The CML business mobility use case requirements are:

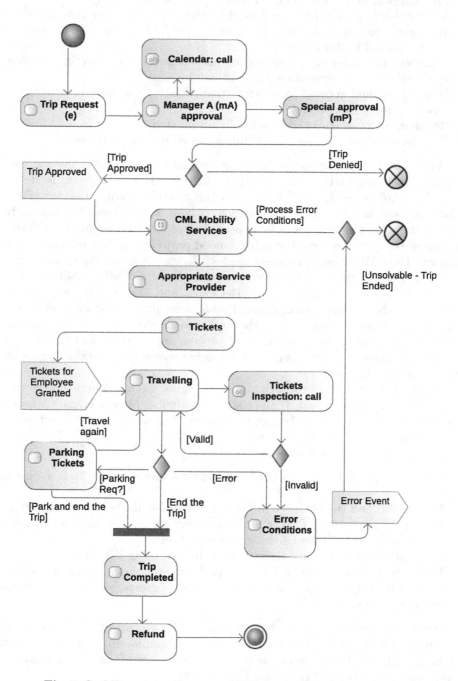

Fig. 5. SysML activity diagram of CML business mobility use case

- Companies A and B can enforce travel restrictions on employees.
- All travel activities must be approved by the respective managers of participating companies, and in special cases the public funding project manager (mP) approval is also required.
- Managers may specify special conditions whenever necessary in workflow specification i.e. decentralized decisions can be made.
- Workflow should recover from error conditions for instance, re-booking or canceling should be possible.
- Reimbursement of travel cost should be automated.
- Data immutability should be available in an immutable database.

As the first step, the requirement engineering experts model the use case requirements using OMG SysML's activity diagram. The open source modeling tool "Modelio" is used, and Fig. 5 shows the SysML activity diagram of the CML business mobility use case workflow: where an employee (e) is able to make a travel request which can be approved or rejected by his manager (mA), and in case of special request the public funded project manager (mP) must also approve. The CML calendar service provides information about the meeting such as location, time, etc. If the trip is approved, then the CML mobility service provides tickets to the employee via the CML app. The employee (traveler) may choose the transportation means (public transport, carsharing, etc), and accordingly the tickets are given to the employee via the CML app. Finally, the trip comes to an end; the reimbursement process begins after the trip has been completed successfully. Thanks to the CML core services, it is possible to provide such services to the users.

The business mobility process and conditions are discussed between the participating companies (A and B) and the public funding project manager. Later, workflow experts transform the SysML activity diagram into a Petri Net workflow specification as shown in Fig. 6.

Let us consider the following:

- The CML app has access to CML core services including the CML calendar service.
- The WF (a) and (b) as shown in Fig. 6 are available in the central repository and can be accessed by CML app i.e. the users are able to use the CML app to download required workflows and execute them.
- The participants can make travel request by executing WF (a).
- The CML services (such as mobility, parking, etc) provide tickets, parking lot information, visiting passes for authorized requests (similar to an oauth resource request).

Below, we describe step by step process of WF (a). In Fig. 6 the places and transitions are marked with identifier such as e (employee), mA (manager of Company A), mP (manager of the public funded project), cal (CML calendar service) and at1 (WF (a) transition 1), bt1 respectively.

- A project meeting invitation with an identifier (mID) is generated by the project manager of company B (mB) in the CML calendar service, and the

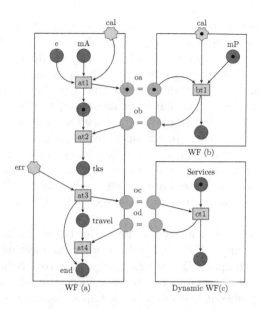

Fig. 6. Business mobility use case Petri Net workflows

identifier is required by the employee (e) of company A to initiate the travel request using the CML app.

- The employee (e) from Company A places a request as a token in the place (e) to travel to Company B for the meeting (mID). When a travel request is raised, the CML app starts to execute WF (a) as show in Fig. 6 WF (a).
- The manager of Company A provides his approval in place (mA) with mID. The oracle place (cal) performs a GET request with meeting mID to the CML calendar service's REST interface URL to retrieve event information such as location, time, etc.
- The first transition (at1) of WF (a) evaluates the information token from the oracle (cal) and tokens from places (e and mA). In particular at1 evaluates whether the mID, employee email address and approval from his manager are valid or not. As this trip is a special trip, it requires additional approval from the public funding manager (mP). Given this special case, the transition (at1) fires a token in the Petri Net place (oa and in the next place of WF (a).
- The CML workflow enforcement engine processes the token from the WF (a)'s open place (oa) and downloads the workflow WF (b) from CML repository to be executed in special cases. The project manager (mP) approves or rejects the trip request. WF (b)'s transition contract (bt1) evaluates the input tokens if valid, bt1 produces output tokens that instructs, provides the secret (similar to an oauth access-token) required by the transition at2 via the open place (ob).
- When transition at2 receives the required secret information, it queries the respective CML mobility service to get the tickets.

- In case of unforeseen circumstances (delay in public transportation, or due to illness) the traveler is able to request an alternative transportation option to the CML mobility service or cancel the existing trip via the CML app by placing a token in the oracle place (err). The transition (at3) evaluates the error token, if the traveler wants to end the trip, then it places a token in place (end) and places a cancellation request in open place (oc).
- If the traveler requests alternative tickets, then transition (at3) places an error token to request new tickets in the open place (oc), this token is processed by dynamically created WF (c)'s transition (ct1). If the error conditions are acceptable (may require human intervention), then new tickets are delivered via the open place (od). Note: Fig. 6 shows the workflow only until this stage, the rest of the workflow steps can be executed with more transitions and places.
- Thanks to the transition contracts in Petri Net based workflows, fine-grained access – such as, temporary access valid during the meeting period – can be granted to enter company B (for example, access to meeting rooms), reimbursements can be automated i.e., after a successful trip a waiting time is introduced using timeout transition, if the trip is not successful then a default process is initiated.
- At the end, the organizer of the meeting is able to confirm the attendees through his CML mobile app, therefore the payment transition is activated such that payment to mobility providers, reimbursements to the employees can be handled appropriately.

A private blockchain is used in the CML for accountability reasons every Petri Net transitions' input and output tokens are recorded as transactions on the blockchain. This feature provides data immutability and opportunity for future auditing in case of any fraud without a centralized trusted entity. There are several advantages for companies to enforce such business mobility conditions on its employees. The companies could restrict its employees from using transportation service for private purposes. Further, the employees can only use the cost effective transportation available. By automating this process, the overhead for the employees and its managers are reduced. The companies can satisfy regional policies such as reducing the carbon footprint.

5   Related Work

In the literature, we can find extensive work on the specification and enforcement of workflows; in particular, Bertino et al. in [23] studied how to model and enforce workflow authorization constraints such as separation-of-duties in workflows, but using a centralized workflow management system. Workflow based access control is also well-known (Knorr in [24] calls them "Dynamic access control"), but this requires a centralized WF enforcement engine. Basin et al. in [25] model the business process activities as workflows with a special focus on optimizing the authorizations permissions.

Petri Nets (see [9]) provide a graphical modeling tool used to describe processes performing an orchestrated activity, or in other words, a workflow (see [7]). Petri Nets have the advantage that many properties such as liveness (deadlock-freeness), reachability are easy to verify. (see [6, 8, 26]). Atluri et al. [27, 28] studied how to model workflows using Petri Nets, but did not describe the implementation details. Huang et al. [29] presented a web-enabled workflow management system, and Compagna et al. [30] presented an automatic enforcement of security policies based on workflow driven web application, but both works presented a centralized architecture. Heckel in [20] showed how open Petri Nets are suitable for modeling workflows spanning different enterprises.

In OAuth-2.0 [31] context an authorization server provides an oauth token (representing a permission) to the client to access a resource in the server. We have similar requirements in our method, for example, an authority of an entity in a given context can create, pass tokens to another; but, for the purposes of workflows, we need further types of tokens (not just permissions).

Linhares et al. in [32] presented an empirical evaluation of OMG SysML's to model an industrial automation unit using the open source modeling tool Modelio[1] but not in the context of modeling workflows.

6   Conclusion and Future Work

In this paper we demonstrate an extension of [2] to enforce workflow-aware security in the Connected Mobility Lab (CML). We showed that our framework can support and handle the integrated business mobility use cases (where different mobility services work loosely coupled) to achieve a common goal. The extensions presented in this paper enable the main workflow to handle error conditions and exchange information between workflows. In many business applications, securing the integrity of processes is the most important security requirement. We demonstrated that our framework provides workflow-aware access control and also enforce the integrity of processes.

We believe that access control permissions should be granted to users in the form: "*You are allowed to execute this task in this workflow*" instead of "You are authorized to access this service during this period of time". The permission to execute a step in a workflow depends on having executed the required previous steps.

We mention some future directions of this work: a simple verifiable language required to write transition contracts and a tool that can transform SysML activity diagrams into Petri Net workflows.

---

[1] http://www.modelio.org/.

References

1. Krebs, B.: BMW: Connected Mobility Lab - center digitization.bayern (2017). https://zentrum-digitalisierung.bayern/connected-mobility-lab
2. Kasinathan, P., Cuellar, J.: Securing the integrity of workflows in IoT. In: International Conference on Embedded Wireless Systems and Networks (EWSN), pp. 252–257. ACM Digital Library (2018)
3. Bishop, M.: Computer Security: Art and Science. Addison-Wesley, Boston (2002)
4. WfMC: Workflow Management Coalition (2009). http://www.wfmc.org
5. Sandhu, R.S., Samarati, P.: Access control: principles and practice. IEEE Commun. Mag. **32**(9), 40–48 (1994)
6. Murata, T.: Petri nets: properties, analysis and applications. Proc. IEEE **77**(4), 541–580 (1989)
7. van der Aalst, W.M.P.: Verification of workflow nets. In: Azéma, P., Balbo, G. (eds.) ICATPN 1997. LNCS, vol. 1248, pp. 407–426. Springer, Heidelberg (1997). https://doi.org/10.1007/3-540-63139-9_48
8. Esparza, J.: Decidability and complexity of Petri net problems — an introduction. In: Reisig, W., Rozenberg, G. (eds.) ACPN 1996. LNCS, vol. 1491, pp. 374–428. Springer, Heidelberg (1998). https://doi.org/10.1007/3-540-65306-6_20
9. Petri, C.A.: Communication with automata (1966). http://edoc.sub.uni-hamburg. de/informatik/volltexte/2010/155/pdf/diss_petri_engl.pdf
10. Jensen, K.: Coloured petri nets. In: Brauer, W., Reisig, W., Rozenberg, G. (eds.) ACPN 1986. LNCS, vol. 254, pp. 248–299. Springer, Heidelberg (1987). https://doi.org/10.1007/978-3-540-47919-2_10
11. Zhang, F., Cecchetti, E., Croman, K., Juels, A., Shi, E.: Town crier. In: Proceedings of the 2C, pp. 270–282. ACM Press, New York (2016)
12. Bartoletti, M., Pompianu, L.: An empirical analysis of smart contracts: platforms, applications, and design patterns. In: Brenner, M., et al. (eds.) FC 2017. LNCS, vol. 10323, pp. 494–509. Springer, Cham (2017). https://doi.org/10.1007/978-3-319-70278-0_31
13. Szabo, N.: Smart Contracts: Building Blocks for Digital Markets Copyright, p. 16 (1996). alamut.com
14. Delmolino, K., Arnett, M., Kosba, A.E., Miller, A., Shi, E.: Step by Step Towards Creating a Safe Smart Contract: Lessons and Insights from a Cryptocurrency Lab. IACR Cryptology ePrint Archive **2015**, 460 (2015)
15. Ethereum: What Are Smart Contracts - EthereumWiki. http://www.ethereumwiki.com/ethereum-wiki/smart-contracts/
16. Ethereum: Solidity – Solidity. https://solidity.readthedocs.io/en/develop/
17. Luu, L., Chu, D.H., Olickel, H., Saxena, P., Hobor, A.: Making smart contracts smarter. In: Proceedings of the 2016 ACM SIGSAC Conference on Computer and Communications Security - CCS 2016, pp. 254–269. ACM Press, New York (2016)
18. Dijkstra, E.W.: Guarded commands, nondeterminacy and formal derivation of programs. Commun. ACM **18**(8), 453–457 (1975)
19. The Official OMG SysML site: What Is OMG SysML? (2012)
20. Heckel, R.: Open petri nets as semantic model for workflow integration. In: Ehrig, H., Reisig, W., Rozenberg, G., Weber, H. (eds.) Petri Net Technology for Communication-Based Systems. LNCS, vol. 2472, pp. 281–294. Springer, Heidelberg (2003). https://doi.org/10.1007/978-3-540-40022-6_14

21. Weber, M., Kindler, E.: The petri net markup language. In: Ehrig, H., Reisig, W., Rozenberg, G., Weber, H. (eds.) Petri Net Technology for Communication-Based Systems. LNCS, vol. 2472, pp. 124–144. Springer, Heidelberg (2003). https://doi.org/10.1007/978-3-540-40022-6_7

22. Pommereau, F.: SNAKES: a flexible high-level petri nets library (tool paper). In: Devillers, R., Valmari, A. (eds.) PETRI NETS 2015. LNCS, vol. 9115, pp. 254–265. Springer, Cham (2015). https://doi.org/10.1007/978-3-319-19488-2_13

23. Bertino, E., Ferrari, E., Atluri, V.: The specification and enforcement of authorization constraints in workflow management systems. ACM Trans. Inf. Syst. Secur. **2**(1), 65–104 (1999)

24. Knorr, K.: Dynamic access control through Petri net workflows. In: Proceedings - Annual Computer Security Applications Conference, ACSAC 2000, pp. 159–167 (2000)

25. Basin, D., Burri, S.J., Karjoth, G.: Optimal workflow-aware authorizations. In: ACM Symposium on Access Control Models and Technologies (SACMAT), pp. 93–102 (2012)

26. Reisig, W.: Petri Nets: An Introduction. Springer, Heidelberg (1985). https://doi.org/10.1007/978-3-642-69968-9

27. Atluri, V., Huang, W.-K.: An authorization model for workflows. In: Bertino, E., Kurth, H., Martella, G., Montolivo, E. (eds.) ESORICS 1996. LNCS, vol. 1146, pp. 44–64. Springer, Heidelberg (1996). https://doi.org/10.1007/3-540-61770-1_27

28. Atluri, V., Huang, W.K.: A Petri net based safety analysis of workflow authorization models. J. Comput. Secur. **8**(2/3), 209 (2000)

29. Huang, W.K., Atluri, V.: SecureFlow: a secure web-enabled workflow management system. In: Proceedings of the Fourth ACM Workshop on Role-Based Access Control - RBAC 1999, pp. 83–94 (1999)

30. Compagna, L., dos Santos, D.R., Ponta, S.E., Ranise, S.: Aegis: automatic enforcement of security policies in workflow-driven web applications. In: Proceedings of ACM on Conference on Data and Application Security and Privacy - CODASPY 2017, pp. 321–328 (2017)

31. Hardt, D.: The OAuth 2.0 Authorization Framework (2012)

32. Linhares, M.V., da Silva, A.J., de Oliveira, R.S.: Empirical evaluation of SysML through the modeling of an industrial automation unit. In: 2006 IEEE Conference on Emerging Technologies and Factory Automation, pp. 145–152. IEEE, September 2006

Emulation-Instrumented Fuzz Testing of 4G/LTE Android Mobile Devices Guided by Reinforcement Learning

Kaiming Fang and Guanhua Yan[(✉)]

Department of Computer Science, Binghamton University,
State University of New York, Binghamton, USA
{kfang2,ghyan}@binghamton.edu

Abstract. The proliferation of 4G/LTE (Long Term Evolution)-capable mobile devices calls for new techniques and tools for assessing their vulnerabilities effectively and efficiently. Existing methods require significant human efforts, such as manual examination of LTE protocol specifications or manual analysis of LTE network traffic, to identify potential vulnerabilities. In this work, we investigate the possibility of automating vulnerability assessment of 4G/LTE mobile devices based on AI (Artificial Intelligence) techniques. Towards this end, we develop LEFT (LTE-Oriented Emulation-Instrumented Fuzzing Testbed), which perturbs the behavior of LTE network modules to elicit vulnerable internal states of mobile devices under test. To balance exploration and exploitation, LEFT uses reinforcement learning to guide behavior perturbation in an instrumented LTE network emulator. We have implemented LEFT in a laboratory environment to fuzz two key LTE protocols and used it to assess the vulnerabilities of four COTS (Commercial Off-The-Shelf) Android mobile phones. The experimental results have shown that LEFT can evaluate the security of 4G/LTE-capable mobile devices automatically and effectively.

1 Introduction

The last decade has witnessed rapid advancement of mobile technologies, evolving from the 2G/GSM systems to the 3G/UMTS systems and then to the current 4G/LTE systems. The GSMA Intelligence estimates that the number of 4G/LTE connections will increase from 500 million at the end of 2014 to 2.8 billion by 2020 worldwide [12]. Currently, the majority of LTE-capable mobile devices run on Android, which has dominated the mobile OS market with a market share of 87.7% in the second quarter of 2017 [5]. The security risks posed by vulnerable mobile devices have been revealed in a number of reports, including SMS flooding attacks [18], man-in-the-middle attacks [26], and botnet attacks [13,14].

Existing research on LTE network security has mainly focused on manual analysis of potential attacks against 4G/LTE networks [28,29] or manually constructing abstract models from 3GPP standards to validate 4G/LTE protocol

© Springer Nature Switzerland AG 2018
J. Lopez et al. (Eds.): ESORICS 2018, LNCS 11099, pp. 20–40, 2018.
https://doi.org/10.1007/978-3-319-98989-1_2

implementations with model checkers [20,31]. Although shedding lights on the vulnerabilities of a small number of 4G/LTE mobile devices, the level of human efforts required in these works makes it difficult, if not impossible, to perform device-specific vulnerability assessment at a large scale. As there have been more than 24,000 distinct Android devices from over 1000 brands [3], there is necessity for new techniques that can automate vulnerability assessment of various 4G/LTE Android mobile devices.

Against this backdrop, we develop a testbed called LEFT (*LTE-Oriented Emulation-Instrumented Fuzzing Testbed*) for fuzz testing COTS (Commercial-Off-The-Shelf) 4G/LTE Android mobile devices. LEFT uses high-fidelity LTE network emulation to create an immersive environment for testing these devices. By perturbing the behavior of the emulated LTE network according to a user-provided threat model, LEFT elicits unexpected sequences of messages from the LTE network that, hopefully, can expose vulnerable internal states of the mobile device under test. Moreover, different from most existing fuzzers which are based upon evolutionary algorithms, LEFT uses reinforcement learning (RL) to train a fuzzer agent that not only balances its vulnerability discovery efforts between exploration and exploitation but also avoids the undesirable crashes of the LTE network emulator due to inconsistent process states after behavior perturbation.

In a nutshell, our key contributions are summarized as follows:

- We have developed three novel fuzzing methodologies, emulation-instrumented fuzzing, threat-model-aware fuzzing, and RL-guided fuzzing in LEFT to assess the vulnerabilities in LTE-capable mobile devices;
- We have implemented LEFT in a laboratory environment based on an open-source LTE network emulator and commodity SDR (Software-Defined Radio)-based devices. To achieve full automation, we adopt both a systematic approach to recover from process failures by catching OS (Operating System)-level signals and an algorithmic approach that can train the fuzzer agent to avoid actions likely to cause emulator crashes.
- Using LEFT, we have fuzzed the behavior of two key LTE protocols, one responsible for managing the connections between end devices and base stations and the other providing mobility services to end devices by the core network. The experimental results on four COTS Android mobile phones have demonstrated that LEFT is capable of discovering LTE protocol vulnerabilities automatically and effectively.

The remainder of the paper is organized as follows. Section 2 summarizes the related work. Section 3 discusses the background and methodology of this work. Section 4 presents the design of LEFT and Sect. 5 its implementation. We show the evaluation results of LEFT in Sect. 6 and draw concluding remarks in Sect. 7.

2 Related Work

LTE Network Security. Due to the rising popularity of 4G/LTE services, a number of previous works have been dedicated to analyzing and improving their security. A comprehensive survey was given in [16] on the vulnerabilities in LTE networks at different levels; it also offered suggestions on how to address these vulnerabilities. The work in [22] surveyed possible attacks against the availability of LTE networks, including DoS (Denial of Service) attacks, DDoS (Distributed Denial of Service) attacks, and insider attacks. In [31], six types of vulnerabilities in cellular networks were reported due to problematic protocol interactions. Another recent survey summarizes the security challenges in different generations of mobile communication networks based on a variety of root causes, including specification issues, implementation issues, protocol context discrepancy, and wireless channel [27]. A theoretical security architecture was proposed in [23] to thwart smart jamming attacks in LTE networks. The work in [25] investigated the vulnerabilities of 4G/LTE modem implementations by several manufacturers. The work [32] addresses the issue of open transmission of IMSIs (International Mobile Subscriber Identities) with Pseudo Mobile Subscriber Identifiers. Our work has been motivated by the work in [29], which demonstrated practical attacks against privacy and availability in 4G/LTE networks. The work in [20] proposed LTEInspector, which combines symbolic model checking and cryptographic protocol verifier to identify vulnerabilities in LTE network protocols. A semi-automated framework was proposed in [28] to evaluate the implementation compliance of the security procedures of LTE devices.

Our contributions in this work differ from the existing works on 4G/LTE network security. *First*, it relies on fuzzing to reveal vulnerabilities automatically, which differs from the verification-based methods used in [20,31,32]. Protocol security verification requires significant efforts in developing accurate abstraction models of the protocols based on their specifications and cannot reveal implementation-specific vulnerabilities; verification based on model checking is also time consuming and thus may not be applicable to analysis of complex security protocols. *Second*, although the works in [20,25,28,29] also use an emulated LTE network environment for security evaluation, they used emulation to validate the vulnerabilities found instead of using it to fully automate the process of vulnerability discovery. Our work, instead, instruments an LTE network emulator to support perturbation of network protocol behavior. *Finally but not least*, our work explores a new direction in applying AI-based methods to search for vulnerabilities in LTE networks automatically.

Network Protocol Fuzzing. Fuzzing is a technique widely used to evaluate security protocols. Fuzzing was used to assess the security of IKE (Internet Key Exchange) implementations [30] and the security of TLS (Transport Layer Security) implementations [15,17]. The work in [21] developed T-Fuzz, a model-based fuzzing framework to assess the robustness of telecommunication protocols, and used it to fuzz a simplified state machine of a key protocol in LTE. T-Fuzz is useful for testing a protocol at its design phase but cannot be used directly to test the security of a COTS system. Our work has explored a new direction in network protocol fuzzing: it leverages the protocol implementation of an existing network emulator and instruments it to support fuzzing capabilities. As such implementation code provides more low-level details than abstract models derived from protocol specifications, it can be used to reveal fine-grained protocol implementation vulnerabilities in COTS systems.

3   Background and Methodology

The architecture of a typical 4G/LTE network, which is shown in Fig. 1(1), consists of three key components:

- **UE (User Equipment):** A UE is a mobile device (e.g., a cell phone) used by an end user to communicate through the LTE network.
- **E-UTRAN (Evolved Universal Terrestrial Radio Access Network):** The E-UTRAN consists of base stations called eNobeBs in LTE parlance.
- **EPC (Evolved Packet Core):** The EPC is an LTE system's packet-only core network. Its S-GW (Serving Gateway) is responsible for handoffs among different eNodeBs and data transfer of packets across the u-plane of LTE. The P-GW (PDN Gateway) acts as a middleman between the LTE network and other packet data networks such as the Internet. The MME (Mobility Management Entity) is the key control node of an LTE system, performing functionalities such as initiating paging and authentication of mobile devices, location tracking and radio resource management. The HSS (Home Subscriber Server) is a database that stores users' subscription information. Finally, the PCRF (Policy and Charging Rules Function) module supports flow-based charging and enforces policy rules on users' data flows.

The LTE protocol specification defined by the 3GPP organization is complex, covering thousands of pages [1], and as illustrated in Fig. 1(2), it describes the rules and conventions at multiple protocol layers in each LTE module. Clearly, it is a daunting task to verify whether a COTS 4G/LTE mobile device has a security vulnerability due to its non-conformance with the 3GPP standards. Moreover, vendors usually do not reveal the details on how their Modem firmware implement the LTE protocols, making it difficult for white-hat security researchers to find vendor-specific security bugs. Finally but not least, as evidenced by previous security analysis of LTE protocols [20,31], the LTE protocol specification itself may have design flaws that can pose serious security risks to the mobile users.

In the design of LEFT – a testbed dedicated to assessing the vulnerabilities of COTS 4G/LTE-capable Android mobile devices – we adopt three novel fuzzing methodologies to overcome the aforementioned challenges:

(1) **Emulation-instrumented blackbox fuzzing:** Due to the difficulty of knowing the LTE implementation specifics in a mobile device under test, we treat it as a blackbox when assessing its vulnerabilities. To this end, we create an immersive environment in which the test device can interact with an emulated LTE network. By instrumenting the emulation code, we perturb the behavior of the emulated LTE network, hoping that the reply packets from the network are unexpected by the LTE protocol implementation of the test device and thus elicit its vulnerable internal states.

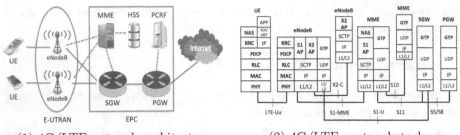

(1) 4G/LTE network architecture   (2) 4G/LTE protocol stacks

Fig. 1. The architecture and protocol stacks of an LTE network. Its key protocols include: NAS (Non-Access Stratum), RRC (Radio Resource Control), PDCP (Packet Data Convergence Protocol), and RLC (Radio Link Control).

(2) **Threat-model-aware fuzzing:** In a network environment, there can be a wide spectrum of threat vectors, who may have different capabilities and attack goals. By differentiating threat models, we are able to design customized fuzzing strategies aimed at specific attack scenarios to improve fuzzing efficiency. For instance, an attack scenario aimed at compromising confidentiality may differ significantly from that targeting availability.

(3) **RL-guided fuzzing:** Inspired by the success of RL in solving real-world problems (e.g., playing against professional go players), we use RL-guided fuzzers to balance efforts on exploring new regions in the fuzzing space and exploiting previous fuzzing experiences. One hurdle we face in perturbing the behavior of the emulated LTE network is that it constantly causes the LTE emulator to crash due to inconsistent process states after behavior perturbation. When the LTE emulator crashes, we have to restart the LTE emulator from a clean state, which incurs significant computational overhead. Using reinforcement learning, we train the fuzzer to avoid actions that are likely to cause emulator crashes.

4 Design

The high-level architecture of LEFT is illustrated in Fig. 2. It requires a user-provided threat model, which defines the security goal of the attacker (e.g., information leakage) as well as his prior knowledge. Based on the threat model, a configuration file is generated to set up the testbed. The hardware needed by the testbed includes the 4G/LTE Android device under test, a combination of USRP B210 boards and LTE antennae that enable SDR-based communications between the UE and the emulated LTE network, and workstations that are used to emulate the LTE network and perform fuzzing. The LEFT software adopts a client-server structure which includes:

– **Client:** The client interacts with the 4G/LTE Android device under test through ADB (Android Debug Bridge). The client can execute ADB commands to elicit responses from the device, and has a sensor that parses these

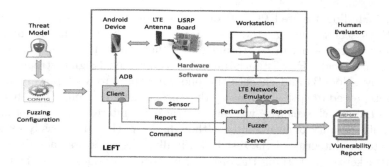

Fig. 2. The architecture of LEFT

responses to infer its internal states. The client reports these inferred states to the server and also accepts commands from it.

- **Server:** The controller of the server is a fuzzer that perturbs the behavior of an emulated LTE network. The LTE network emulator is instrumented to take a perturbation action requested by the fuzzer for each incoming message from the test device. It also includes sensors that can assess the vulnerabilities based on the messages received.

The output of a fuzzing campaign is a list of vulnerabilities in the test device that are exploitable under the threat model assumed. The vulnerability report is sent to a human evaluator for further examination.

4.1   Threat Model

Due to the integrated emulation functionality within LEFT, it can be used to construct a variety of attack scenarios. For each attack scenario, the LEFT user needs to specify the following:

- **Knowledge:** Does the attacker know the victim UE's authentication credential, such as the secret key stored in its SIM card?
- **Security goal:** What security goal does the attacker want to compromise (e.g., confidentiality, integrity, or availability)?
- **Capability:** Can the attacker emulate a malicious LTE network or UE?
- **Protocol:** What is the specific LTE protocol, as illustrated in Fig. 1(2), that the attacker would like to focus on?
- **Action:** What kind of actions can the attacker take? There are two options for fuzzing protocol messages, *bit-level* and *order-level*. Most network protocol fuzzers implement bit-level message fuzzing, which randomly flips the bits in a protocol message. In contrast, order-level message fuzzing perturbs the order of protocol messages to find logic flaws in the protocol implementation.

Focus of This Work. As the attack surface in an LTE network is so large that it cannot be tackled all at once within a single work, this study focuses on a practical threat model where the attacker is able to emulate a malicious LTE

network, including its core EPC network and eNodeBs, but knows nothing about
the victim's secrets such as the keys stored in the SIM card. The malicious
eNodeB can force a victim UE to make a connection to itself with high signal
power, as a typical UE constantly measures the received signal strengths from
neighboring eNodeBs and chooses the one with the strongest power during a
hand-over procedure [24]. Moreover, the threat model assumed in this work
considers the attack scenarios where the attacker is interested in compromising
either confidentiality or availability, although the work can be easily extended
to evaluate the integrity of the test UE. Finally, this work assumes the actions
of the attacker as perturbing the order of protocol messages, so its focus is to
find logic-level vulnerabilities in the LTE protocol implementation of the test
UE instead of its low-level software vulnerabilities such as buffer overflow or
use-after-free bugs.

4.2   Sensors

To evaluate the security status of the victim UE, we deploy two types of sensors:

- **Client-side sensors:** A client-side sensor parses the UE's responses to ADB
  commands and infers its status. For example, the client can issue an ADB
  shell ping to test the UE's network connectivity. Its responses can be used to
  assess the availability of the network to the UE.
- **Server-side sensors:** On the server side, we instrument the code of an LTE
  network emulator and place a sensor at each protocol layer to infer leakage
  of sensitive data without proper encryption. As a protocol layer only parses
  a certain portion of an incoming message, its corresponding sensor detects if
  there exists any sensitive data unencrypted at that layer. If it is true *and* no
  other sensor at any lower layer on the protocol stack detects that the payload
  has been decrypted by the protocol on that layer, an information leakage
  compromising confidentiality occurs.

It is noted that to compromise confidentiality, the attacker can sniff LTE
packets in the air and parse them with tools such as Wireshark [11]. Although it
is possible to use passive packet sniffers along with sensors to detect information
leakage, their deployment requires additional computational resources and incurs
unnecessary communication latency between the sensors associated with the
sniffers and the fuzzer. As the LTE network emulator needs to parse the messages
anyway, we can place the sensors *inside* the network emulator in a non-intrusive
manner to infer the possible leakage of sensitive information.

4.3   RL-Guided Fuzzing

The key component of LEFT is its fuzzer, which decides how to perturb the
behavior of the LTE network emulator based on the reports collected from the
various sensors deployed. Due to the No-Free-Lunch-Theorem [33], there is no
optimal fuzzing strategy suitable for all situations. As LEFT is aimed at discovering vulnerabilities in a variety of 4G/LTE Android mobile devices, we design

the fuzzer inside the server to be an intelligent agent that can balance exploring test scenarios with unsure results and exploiting those close to the expectation based on its previous experiences. Such a tradeoff between exploration and exploitation is well studied within the RL framework, which is built upon the Markov decision process (MDP) model (S, A, P, R, γ):

- **S**: a finite set of states, including both environment states and agent states;
- **A**: a finite set of actions that can be taken by the agent;
- **P**: $P_a(s, s')$ gives the transition probability from state s to s' after the agent takes action a;
- **R**: $R_a(s, s')$ is the immediate reward received by the agent after taking action a, which leads to state transition from s to s';
- γ: $\gamma \in [0, 1]$ is a per-step discount of the reward.

An important concept in RL is its value functions, including state values $V(s)$ and state-action values $Q(s, a)$, which reflect the agent's long-term returns of entering state s and taking action a at state s, respectively. To apply RL for perturbing the behavior of the LTE network emulator, we need to extract a MDP model from its emulation code. Network protocols are usually developed from FSM (Finite State Machine) specifications, and as a result, they are often implemented in an event-driven programming style. Hence, when an incoming message is received by a protocol layer, the event is processed by the emulator based on the message type and sometimes a few internal state variables. Accordingly, in the MDP model, we use the collection of message types as its state set S. The action set of the agent A includes all possible cases dealing with the different types of incoming messages. In some cases, the emulator's action depends upon an internal state variable. For example, after receiving the same type of messages, the emulator does a if an internal state c is true, or does a' otherwise. Then, both actions a and a' are added to the agent's action set A.

In the RL framework, the fuzzer agent works by demanding the LTE emulator to choose a certain action $a \in A$ when a message of type $s \in S$ is received. This action a may not be the proper one according to the LTE protocol specification. Our hope is that, by choosing nonconforming actions on the LTE network side, it returns unexpected messages to the victim UE that can reveal its vulnerabilities.

The key challenge in applying RL-guided fuzzing is the *delayed reward issue*, which manifests itself for both confidentiality and availability:

- **Confidentiality:** For state-action pair (s, a), action a in state s may induce a message M, which is sent to the victim UE by the LTE network emulator; after the UE receives this packet, it sends back another one M' to the LTE network emulator according to its LTE implementation. The reward of state-action pair (s, a) is calculated by a sensor inside the LTE network emulator after it receives message M'. Hence, there is a round-trip delay before the agent can collect its reward.
- **Availability:** Consider the case where the security goal is to assess whether the victim UE is able to connect to a benign LTE network (which is emulated separately from the malicious one being perturbed) after the attack. The

agent, however, cannot assess the UE's loss of network connectivity directly; instead, it sends a command to the client (see Fig. 2), which further sends an ADB command to the UE to test its network connectivity with a benign LTE network. The sensor located inside the client reports the test result to the agent in the server for calculating its reward. Different from the case of confidentiality, the fuzzer agent cannot calculate its reward after each state-action pair (s, a) because this requires the victim UE to test its network connectivity with a benign LTE network after every message it has received.

With the delayed reward issue in mind, we develop the RL-guided fuzzing algorithm as illustrated in Algorithm 1. In parlance of RL, an *episode* consists of a sequence of states and actions: $(s_0, a_0, s_1, a_1, ..., a_{n-1}, s_n)$ where s_n is a terminal state. In LEFT, a terminal state is defined as one of the following three cases:

- $S_{timeout}$: After taking action a_{n-1}, the LTE network emulator has not heard from the UE after τ seconds. This indicates either the end of a normal protocol procedure or a preemptive termination action by the test UE.
- S_{limit}: To prevent an episode from running indefinitely without revealing any vulnerability, we set an upper bound δ on the number of steps in each episode. If the length of an episode exceeds the limit, it is forced to terminate.
- S_{crash}: Perturbing the behavior of the LTE network emulator may crash the process due to inconsistent internal states of the emulator process. When the emulator crashes, the current episode terminates.

Table 1. Notations used in Algorithm 1 and their meanings

Notation	Meaning	Default value
goal	Security goal (CONFIDENTIALITY or AVAILABILITY)	User-provided
N	Order of the UE being tested	0
Q_c^{avg}	Average Q-table for evaluating confidentiality	0
Q_a^{avg}	Average Q-table for evaluating availability	0
Q_c	Q-table for evaluating the current UE's confidentiality	Q_c^{avg}
Q_a	Q-table for evaluating the current UE's availability	Q_a^{avg}
δ	Maximum number of steps in an episode	50
τ	Timeout for waiting the UE's messages	10 s
α	Learning rate	0.1
γ	Reward discount per step	0.9
ϵ_{min}	Minimum probability of exploration per step	0.1
β^{crash}	Agent's reward if the emulator crashes	−100
β_c^{leak}	Agent's reward if there is an information leakage	100
β_a^{loss}	Agent's reward if the UE loses network connectivity	100
episodes	Number of episodes performed for the current UE	0
steps	Number of steps performed within the current episode	0
L	List of state-action pairs in the current episode	$\emptyset$

Algorithm 1. RL_GUIDED_FUZZING($goal$, Q_c^{avg}, Q_a^{avg}, N)

1:   $\alpha \leftarrow 0.1$, $\epsilon_{min} \leftarrow 0.1$, $\delta \leftarrow 50$, $\gamma \leftarrow 0.9$, $\tau \leftarrow 10$
2:   $\beta^{crash} \leftarrow -100$, $\beta_c^{leak} \leftarrow 100$, $\beta_a^{loss} \leftarrow 100$
3:   initialize Q_c and Q_a to be Q_c^{avg} and Q_a^{avg}, respectively
4:   $episodes \leftarrow 0$
5:   **for** each episode **do**
6:       $episodes \leftarrow episodes + 1$, $(s, a) \leftarrow (null, null)$, $steps \leftarrow 0$, $L \leftarrow []$
7:       restart the LTE network emulator, command the client to restart the UE
8:       **for** each new message M received from the victim UE **do**
9:          **if** M leads to information leakage **then**
10:             $r_c \leftarrow \beta_c^{leak}$
11:          **else**
12:             $r_c \leftarrow 0$
13:          **end if**
14:          append state-action pair (s, a) to list L
15:          $s' \leftarrow$ the type of message M
16:          **if** $goal =$ CONFIDENTIALITY **then**
17:             $Q = Q_c$
18:          **else if** $goal =$ AVAILABILITY **then**
19:             $Q = Q_a$
20:          **else**
21:             error
22:          **end if**
23:          $a' \leftarrow \epsilon\text{-greedy}(s', Q, \max\{1/episodes, \epsilon_{min}\})$
24:          $Q_c(s, a) \leftarrow Q_c(s, a) + \alpha(r_c + \gamma \max_{a''}(Q_c(s', a'') - Q_c(s, a)))$
25:          $steps \leftarrow steps + 1$
26:          **if** $steps > \delta$ **then** break **end if**
27:          let the LTE network emulator take action a'
28:          **if** the emulator crashes **then**
29:             $Q_c(s', a') \leftarrow \beta^{crash}$, $Q_a(s', a') \leftarrow \beta^{crash}$
30:             append state-action pair (s', a') to list L
31:             break
32:          **end if**
33:          $(s, a) \leftarrow (s', a')$
34:          schedule a timer which fires after τ seconds
35:          wait for a new incoming message or the firing of the timer
36:          **if** the timer fires **then** break **else** cancel the timer **end if**
37:       **end for**
38:       send a command to client to test the UE's network connectivity
39:       wait for the report from the client
40:       **if** the client reports that the UE has good network connectivity **then**
41:          $r_a \leftarrow 0$
42:       **else**
43:          $r_a \leftarrow \beta_a^{loss}$
44:       **end if**
45:       **for** the i-th state-action pair (s_i, a_i) on list L where $1 \leq i \leq |L|$ **do**
46:          $Q_a(s_{i-1}, a_{i-1}) \leftarrow Q_a(s_{i-1}, a_{i-1}) + \alpha(\frac{1/2^{(|L|-i+1)}}{1-1/2^{|L|}} \cdot r_a + \gamma \max_{a''}(Q_a(s_i, a'') - Q_a(s_{i-1}, a_{i-1})))$
47:       **end for**
48:   **end for**
49:   $N \leftarrow N + 1$, $Q_c^{avg} \leftarrow Q_c^{avg} + \frac{1}{N}(Q_c - Q_c^{avg})$, $Q_a^{avg} \leftarrow Q_a^{avg} + \frac{1}{N}(Q_a - Q_a^{avg})$

Table 1 summarizes the notations used in Algorithm 1 and their meanings. In Algorithm 1, function ϵ-greedy(s, Q, ϵ) returns a random action with probability ϵ (i.e., exploration) and argmax$_a Q(s, a)$ with probability $1 - \epsilon$ (i.e., exploitation).

Algorithm 1 is called when a new UE needs to be tested for a user-provided security goal, either confidentiality or availability. Assuming that this UE is the N-th one tested, the average Q-tables for both confidentiality and availability calculated over the previous $N - 1$ UEs are used to initialize the Q-tables for evaluating the current UE. In RL, these Q-tables are crucial to the agent's decision-making as each entry (s, a) stores the agent's estimated long-term value of taking action a at state s. By initializing the current UE's Q-tables as the Q-tables averaged over the previous ones tested, it is assumed at the very beginning that there is nothing special about this new UE, which should have similar vulnerabilities as the ones tested.

It is, however, possible that the new UE may be different from the ones previously tested (e.g., a new model just released to the market). We thus update the Q-tables associated with this UE dynamically based on its test results, hoping that they can lead to an optimal policy in generating test cases (by perturbing the behavior of the LTE network emulator) for revealing its vulnerabilities. After the evaluation of this UE, its Q-tables are used to update the average Q-tables in an incremental manner (see Line 49 in Algorithm 1).

As no explicit MDP model is needed in Algorithm 1, it adopts a model-free approach to reinforcement learning. This is desirable because in practice it is usually difficult to derive an accurate yet efficient environment model such as its state transition probabilities. Model-free control samples the environment by repeating test episodes (see Line 5 in Algorithm 1). Algorithm 1 uses Q-learning, a popular model-free off-policy RL technique, to update its Q-tables (Lines 24 and 46). For confidentiality, the agent knows the reward of its previous action at each step of an episode (when it receives a new message from the UE). Hence, the agent can use its reward received to update its Q_c-table immediately without waiting for the episode to terminate (see Line 24 of Algorithm 1). For availability (i.e., network connectivity), the agent needs to test if the UE is able to connect to the benign LTE network after each episode finishes; hence, the corresponding Q_a-table is updated after an episode finishes (see Line 46 of Algorithm 1).

There is a subtle issue when assessing the UE's vulnerabilities related to network connectivity. Consider a complete episode $(s_0, a_0, ..., s_{n-1}, a_{n-1}, s_n)$, which ends due to either a timeout ($s_n = S_{timeout}$), the limit on the episode length ($s_n = S_{limit}$), or a crash of the LTE network emulator ($s_n = S_{crash}$). Suppose that after the episode, through the client, it is found that the UE cannot connect to a benign LTE network any more. The overall reward for this episode is β_a^{loss}, but we need to assign the credits among the state-action pairs in it, which is a classical problem in reinforcement learning. In Algorithm 1, we use an exponential credit assignment scheme based on the assumption that later state-actions in the episode should be given more credits than the previous ones: the credit assigned to each state-pair (s_i, a_i) is half of that of (s_{i+1}, a_{i+1}), which leads to the equation on Line 46 in the algorithm.

Different from a standard RL algorithm, Algorithm 1 updates two Q-tables, Q_c for confidentiality and Q_a for availability. As seen among Lines 16–23, the security goal (i.e., the *goal* parameter of Algorithm 1) decides which Q-table should be used to generate the next action for perturbing the emulator's behavior (*on-goal learning*), while the other one is updated in an offline fashion (*off-goal learning*). It is noted that on/off-goal learning should *not* be confused with *on/off-policy learning* in RL parlance because the Q-learning technique, which belongs to the category of off-policy learning, is used for updating both Q_c and Q_a (Lines 24 and 46). The purpose of combining both on-goal and off-goal learning is to improve efficiency: although the LEFT user specifies one security goal in her threat model, the fuzzing experiments performed may reveal a different type of vulnerabilities in the UE. By incorporating these findings into the corresponding average Q-table, they can benefit later experiments aimed at finding the same type of vulnerabilities.

Algorithm 1 can be easily extended for finding multiple fine-grained types of UE vulnerabilities. For example, sensitive information of a UE includes its IMSI, its exact location, and the user's voice data. At the cost of maintaining a separate Q-table for each vulnerability type, it may be useful to learn a separate policy for perturbing the LTE emulator's behavior for revealing each fine-grained type of information leakage. With the aforementioned off-goal learning approach, we can use the same set of experiments to update the multiple Q-tables maintained for different types of vulnerabilities.

5 Implementation

The software component of LEFT adopts a client/server architecture, as seen in Fig. 2. The client is written in around 280 lines of Python code, and on the server side, the RL-guided fuzzing algorithm is written in around 350 lines of C code embedded within the OpenAirInterface LTE network emulator [8]. The fuzzer agent uses the same process as the network emulator, but replaces its control flow with Algorithm 1.

5.1 Emulator Instrumentation

There are multiple open-source LTE network emulators, such as LENA [7], OpenAirInterface [8], openLTE [9], and srsLTE [19]. After surveying these different emulators, we decide to use OpenAirInterface for the LTE network emulator in LEFT because it offers the most comprehensive functionalities with emulation code for all the key LTE network elements. The drawback of this choice, however, is that the codebase of OpenAirInterface is complex, making it a daunting task to understand and revise its source code. Another challenge in incorporating the OpenAirInterface emulator into LEFT is that some of its documentation has become outdated due to its active development. As illustrated in Fig. 1(1), an LTE network consists of a variety of network elements.

The OpenAirInterface LTE network emulator separates them into two different modules, `openair-cn` and `openairinterface5G`. The `openair-cn` module emulates the LTE core network (i.e., its EPC), including its MME, HSS, S-GW, and P-GW, while `openairinterface5G` focusing on emulation of UEs and eNodeBs. The current implementation of LEFT builds upon the development branch of `openairinterface5G` downloaded on November 14, 2017 and the `nas_pdn_type_ipv6_handle` branch of `openair-cn` downloaded on July 28, 2017 from their respective github pages.

To reveal the protocol-level vulnerabilities of a test UE, we need to instrument the emulation code of the corresponding protocol in the OpenAirInterface emulator by supporting the perturbation functionality. There are various protocols involved in LTE communications, as seen from Fig. 1(2). In this work, we focus two of them, *RRC* and *EMM* (EPS (Evolved Packet System) Mobility Management), both of which play a key role in LTE network security.

RRC: The RRC protocol is responsible for controlling the air interface between the UE and the E-UTRAN, and its functions include broadcast of system information for both the non-access and the access strata, establishment, maintenance and release of RRC connections between the UE and the E-UTRAN and radio bearers, RRC connection mobility functions, paging, control of ciphering, RRC message integrity protection, UE measurement reporting, and so on [2]. The RRC protocol is implemented by the `openairinterface5G` module. In file `openairinterface5g/openair2/RRC/LITE/rrc_eNB.c`, function `rrc_enb_task(void* args_p)` contains a message processing loop, which uses the message type of an incoming message `msg_p` (i.e., `ITTI_MSG_ID(msg_p)`) to decide how to process the message. The loop contains 16 switch cases, including the default one, and each of these cases defines a respective action. Hence, we have 16 states and 16 actions defined for the purpose of RL.

EMM: EMM is a NAS-stratum protocol dealing with mobility over an E-UTRAN access in the control plane between the UE and the MME module in the core network. The 3GPP organization specifies three types of EMM procedures: *common procedures* include GUTI (Global Unique Temporary ID) reallocation, authentication, security mode control, identification, and EMM information, *specific procedures* define mechanisms for attaching to the EPC and detaching from it, and *connection management procedures* manage UEs' connections with the core network such as service request, paging procedure, and transport of NAS messages. The EMM protocol is implemented within the `openair-cn` module as it deals with functionalities of the LTE core network.

In `openair-cn`, message processing by the EMM protocol is done in two functions in file `openair-cn/SRC/NAS/EMM/SAP/emm_as.c`: `_emm_as_recv()`, which decodes and processes normal EMM messages, and `_emm_as_establish_req()`, which processes connection establishment requests for EMM access stratum SAP (Service Access Point). In function `_emm_as_recv()`, there are 12 switch cases for the message type (`emm_msg->header.message_type`), each representing a unique state in RL. In nine of these 12 cases, the emulator's action further depends on a Boolean variable, `emm_cause`; hence, we define 21 separate actions.

In function _emm_as_establish_req(), there are five switch cases for the message type (emm_msg->header.message_type), but two of them are identical as in function _emm_as_recv(). As processing one of these five cases does not depend on variable emm_cause, function _emm_as_establish_req() introduces five new actions. In total, there are 15 states and 26 actions defined for the purpose of RL.

5.2   Testbed Automation

An important goal of LEFT is to minimize human efforts in assessing vulnerabilities of 4G/LTE Android mobile devices. A key challenge in testbed automation is to prevent emulator crashes. As we perturb the behavior of the LTE network emulator, it is possible that the action taken by the emulator results in a faulty internal state and thus causes it to crash or freeze. In Algorithm 1, we use a negative reward β^{crash} to discourage the fuzzer agent from taking an action that causes the emulator to crash at a certain state. However, the network emulator may still crash or freeze due to an inappropriate action taken by the agent working in an exploration mode.

The fuzzer agent's internal states, such as its Q-tables and reward tables, are declared as global variables of the network emulator. To prevent loss of these states after the emulator crashes, we modify the emulator's handler of its logging timer, which fires every 30 s, and periodically save these states onto persistent storage. Moreover, LEFT applies two techniques deployed at different places to detect if the network emulator crashes or freezes:

- On the server side, we add sensors inside the LTE network emulator to catch certain Linux signals that indicate system failures. These signals include SIGTERM (process termination), SIGSEGV (invalid memory reference), SIGABRT (abort), and SIGFPE (floating point exception). When a sensor catches such a signal, it saves the fuzzer's internal states, as well as the last state-action pair retrieved from the crashed network emulator, onto persistent storage. When the fuzzer agent recovers, it collects a reward for the last state-action pair as β^{crash}.
- For the rare cases where some faulty situations are not caught by the Linux signal handlers, LEFT uses heartbeat messages communicated between the client and the server every two seconds. If the client has not received the heartbeat message from the server after 20 s, the client restarts the server. Since the client does not know the exact state-action pair that causes the emulator to crash, the fuzzer agent, after it is restarted, *cannot* collect a negative reward for its last action (we do not save every state-action pair onto persistent storage due to its high overhead). In this case, the RL algorithm cannot prevent the agent from taking the same action that has caused the network emulator to crash or freeze in the future.

At the end of each episode, the client clears the test UE's internal state by toggling its airplane mode with appropriate ADB shell commands.

6   Evaluation

We perform experiments to evaluate the effectiveness of LEFT in assessing both confidentiality and availability. We configure LEFT to emulate two LTE networks, one benign and the other malicious:

- **Benign LTE network:** Its EPC is emulated with a Lenovo ThinkCenter mini-workstation (CPU: Intel i7 6700T, RAM: 16 GB, and Ubuntu 16.04 with kernel 4.13) and its eNodeB is emulated with a Dell Inspiron 5000 laptop (CPU: Intel i7 6500U, RAM: 8G, and Ubuntu 16.04 with low-latency kernel 4.13). The communications between the test UE and the benign eNodeB are supported by a set of USRP B210 board and LTE antenna. The benign LTE network is assumed to know each test UE's authentication credentials.
- **Malicious LTE network:** A single commodity desktop PC (CPU: Intel i7 4790, RAM 32G, and Archlinux with kernel 4.15) is used to emulate both the malicious LTE network's EPC and eNodeB. The EPC is emulated within a VirtualBox VM (Virtual Machine) configured to have 4G RAM and run Ubuntu 16.04 with kernel 4.10, and the eNodeB within another VirtualBox VM configured similarly, except that it uses a low-latency kernel. A different set of USRP B210 board and LTE antenna is used for the communications between the UE and the malicious eNodeB. The malicious LTE network can be configured based on the user-provided threat model (see Sect. 4.1).

The parameters of Algorithm 1 in LEFT are configured with their default values, which have been shown in Table 1. We use LEFT to assess the vulnerabilities of four COTS Android mobile phones, `Samsung Note II` (unknown LTE Cat 4 Modem), `LG G5` (Snapdragon X12 LTE Modem), `Huawei Honor 8` (Balong 720 chipset), and `BLU LifeOne X2` (Snapdragon X6 LTE Modem). Each of these phones uses a sysmoUSIM-SJS1 SIM card [6] recommended by the OpenAirInterface developers.

We consider two sets of experiments: fuzzing the RRC protocol to compromise confidentiality and fuzzing the EMM protocol in NAS to compromise availability (see Fig. 1(2)). As it is trivial to catch the IMSIs in the air [32], such vulnerabilities are thus ignored from our experiments. For checking network connectivity, we let the test UE ping any machine on the Internet through the benign LTE network, and if the ping test fails after 30 s, the UE is deemed to lose the LTE network connectivity.

6.1   Perturbation Sequences with Vulnerabilities Discovered

We first assess the performance of LEFT in discovering the vulnerabilities in the four test UEs individually without off-goal learning. In each experiment, we evaluate one test UE for 200 episodes, with either confidentiality or availability as the goal. All experiments are performed independently. After each experiment, we collect the unique *perturbation sequences* that have led to the compromise of the pre-defined security goal, where a perturbation sequence is defined as the sequence of state-action pairs observed in an episode.

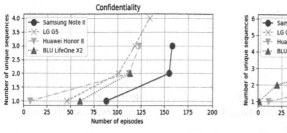
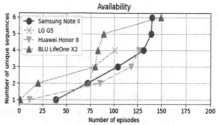

(1) Confidentiality, RRC fuzzing   (2) Availability, EMM fuzzing

Fig. 3. Number of unique perturbation sequences with vulnerabilities discovered

Figure 3 shows the number of unique perturbation sequences with vulnerabilities discovered throughout an evaluation experiment for each phone. We observe that for each phone tested, there are two to four unique perturbation sequences that have revealed a confidentiality vulnerability, and four to six unique perturbation sequences that lead to loss of network connectivity.

To verify whether each vulnerability discovered is correct, we present in Table 3 the list of state-action pairs in each unique perturbation sequence that has revealed a confidentiality vulnerability in LG G5. Common to each perturbation sequence is a measurement report received from the test UE in a `Connection Reconfiguration Complete` message. According to 3GPP standard, the measurement report from a UE may include detailed location information (e.g., GNSS (Global Navigation Satellite System) location information), physical cell identity of the logged cell, and cell identities and carrier frequencies of neighboring cells [4], which presents a confidentiality risk. This vulnerability has been reported in the work in [29] but our work discovers it automatically through fuzzing.

In Table 3, we show the six perturbation sequences that cause loss of network connectivity for Samsung Note II. Common to these sequences are responses with `TAU reject` or `attach reject`. As neither `TAU reject` nor `attach reject` messages are integrity-protected, for certain rejection causes, the UE may not only lose the connectivity with the malicious eNodeB but also with the benign one [10,29]. Hence, the vulnerabilities automatically found by LEFT are indeed exploitable by an adversary under the assumed threat model.

On average, for each phone it takes 253 min to finish a confidentiality test of 200 episodes, and 277 min an availability test of 200 episodes – *without any human supervision*. It may seem unintuitive that an availability test needs only slightly more time than a confidentiality test, because it requires testing the network connectivity with the benign LTE network and if the network connectivity is lost the UE has to wait for 30 s of ping tests. Actually the fraction of episodes with lost network connectivity is small, which explains why the execution times for a confidentiality test and an availability test are comparable.

Table 2. Perturbation sequences leading to location leakage (each tuple shows the type of message received and the type of message by which it is processed)

No	Perturbation sequence
1	(RRC Connection Request, RRC Connection Setup), (RRC Connection Setup Complete, RRC Connection Reconfiguration), (RRC Connection Reconfiguration Complete + Measurement Report, RRC Connection Release)
2	(RRC Connection Request, RRC Connection Setup), (RRC Connection Setup Complete, RRC Connection Reconfiguration), (RRC Connection Reconfiguration Complete + Measurement Report, Security Mode Command), (Security Mode Reject, RRC Connection Release)
3	(RRC Connection Request, RRC Connection Setup), (RRC Connection Setup Complete, RRC Connection Reconfiguration), (RRC Connection Reconfiguration Complete + Measurement Report, RRC Connection Release)
4	(RRC Connection Request, RRC Connection Setup), (RRC Connection Setup Complete, RRC Connection Reconfiguration), (RRC Connection Reconfiguration Complete + Measurement Report, RRC Connection Reconfiguration)

Table 3. Perturbation sequences leading to loss of network connectivity (each tuple has the same meaning as in Table 2)

No	Perturbation sequence
1	(TAU request, TAU reject)
2	(TAU request, detach request), (detach accept, paging), (attach request, attach reject (with random cause))
3	(TAU request, TAU reject), (attach request, identity request), (identity response, detach request (reattach required)), (detach accept, paging), (attach request, attach reject (with random cause))
4	(TAU request, TAU reject), (attach request, attach reject (with random cause))
5	(TAU request, TAU reject), (attach request, authentication request), (authentication response, authentication reject)
6	(TAU request, TAU reject), (attach request, authentication request), (authentication failure, identity request), (identity response, detach request), (detach accept, paging), (attach request, attach reject (with random cause))

Note: TAU stands for Track Area Update.

6.2   Prevention of Emulator Crashes

The RL-guided fuzzing algorithm shown in Algorithm 1 assigns a negative reward to discourage the fuzzer agent from taking actions that may lead to emulator crashes. To show its effect, we compare the numbers of emulator crashes with and without using a negative reward when the emulator crashes. The results are illustrated in Fig. 4. In the case of confidentiality with RRC fuzzing, using a negative reward, after 200 episodes the number of emulator crashes has been reduced by 39.47%, 43.18%, 40.00%, and 31.70% for Samsung Note II, LG G5, Huawei Honor 8, and BLU LifeOne X2, respectively, and the average reduction rate over the four phones is 38.59%. Similarly in the case of availability with EMM fuzzing, using a negative reward reduces the number of emulator crashes by 34.88%, 39.02%, 48.89%, and 51.06%, respectively, for these same phones after 200 episodes, leading to an average reduction rate of 43.47%. Clearly, the fuzzer agent benefits significantly from exploiting its previous crash experiences to avoid crash-causing actions.

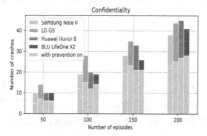
(1) Confidentiality, RRC fuzzing

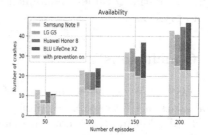
(2) Availability, EMM fuzzing

Fig. 4. Number of emulator crashes

6.3   Cross-Device Learning

In addition to using a negative reward to avoid actions likely to crash the emulator process, the fuzzer agent can also exploit the experiences with previous test UEs. Recall that in Algorithm 1, for each of confidentiality and availability, an average Q-table is maintained over all the UEs tested. We next perform a set of experiments to evaluate the effects of using such an average Q-table to bootstrap the Q-table when evaluating a new UE. In each experiment, we use Huawei Honor 8 as the target phone (always evaluated last). To calculate the average Q-table, we choose zero to three phones from Samsung Note II, LG G5, and BLU LifeOne X2 in the same order and evaluate them sequentially. When a security goal is specified for the target phone, the remaining phones can be tested either on goal (using the same security goal) or off goal (using a different security goal).

Figure 5 confirms the advantages of cross-device learning. When the target phone is evaluated first without any previous experiences for guiding vulnerability discovery, the fuzzer agent needs more episodes to find the same number of

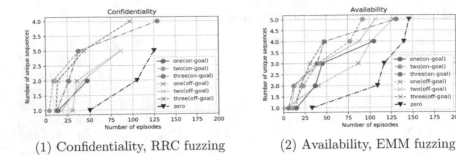

(1) Confidentiality, RRC fuzzing   (2) Availability, EMM fuzzing

Fig. 5. Effects of cross-device learning

unique perturbation sequences with vulnerabilities discovered, regardless of the security goal. Moreover, the differences between on-goal and off-goal learning are small, suggesting that we can improve the efficiency of security evaluation by updating the Q-tables maintained for different security goals with the same set of episodes.

7   Conclusions

This work explores a new direction of using AI-based techniques to assess vulnerabilities of LTE-capable Android mobile phones. We have developed LEFT, a testbed adopting three novel fuzzing methodologies, emulation-instrumented blackbox fuzzing, threat-model-aware fuzzing, and RL-guided fuzzing to assess vulnerabilities of 4G/LTE Android mobile phones. We have demonstrated that LEFT can be used to discover automatically the vulnerabilities in four COTS Android mobile phones, which may be exploited to compromise confidentiality or availability. In our future work, we plan to extend the capabilities of LEFT to discover new types of vulnerabilities in LTE networks automatically.

Acknowledgments. We acknowledge the Critical Infrastructure Resilience Institute, a Department of Homeland Security Center of Excellence, for supporting this work. We also thank anonymous reviewers for their valuable comments.

References

1. 3GPP. http://www.3gpp.org/
2. 3GPP TS 25.331 version 12.4.0 Release 12. http://www.etsi.org/deliver/etsi_ts/125300_125399/125331/12.04.00_60/ts_125331v120400p.pdf
3. Android Fragmentation, August 2015. http://opensignal.com/reports/2015/08/android-fragmentation/
4. ETSI TS 137 320 V11.2.0, February 2013. http://www.etsi.org/deliver/etsi_ts/137300_137399/137320/11.02.00_60/ts_137320v110200p.pdf

5. Global mobile OS market share in sales to end users from 1st quarter 2009 to 2nd quarter 2017. https://www.statista.com/statistics/266136/global-market-share-held-by-smartphone-operating-systems/
6. http://sysmocom.de
7. LENA: LTE-EPC Network simulAtor. http://networks.cttc.es/mobile-networks/software-tools/lena/
8. OpenAirInterface. http://www.openairinterface.org/
9. openLTE. https://github.com/osh/openlte
10. http://www.sharetechnote.com/html/Handbook_LTE_AttachReject.html
11. Wireshark. https://www.wireshark.org
12. GSMA - mobile spectrum: data demand explained. Technical report (2015). http://www.gsma.com/spectrum/wp-content/uploads/2015/06/GSMA-Data-Demand-Explained-June-2015.pdf
13. Hacked cameras, DVRs powered today's massive internet outage. Technical report (2016). https://krebsonsecurity.com/2016/10/hacked-cameras-dvrs-powered-todays-massive-internet-outage/
14. Antonakakis, M., April, T., Bailey, M., et al.: Understanding the mirai botnet. In: Proceedings of USENIX Security Symposium (2017)
15. Beurdouche, B., et al.: A messy state of the union: taming the composite state machines of TLS. In: Proceedings of IEEE Symposium on Security and Privacy, pp. 535–552. IEEE (2015)
16. Cao, J., Ma, M., Li, H., Zhang, Y., Luo, Z.: A survey on security aspects for LTE and LTE-A networks. IEEE Commun. Surv. Tutor. 16(1), 283–302 (2014)
17. De Ruiter, J., Poll, E.: Protocol state fuzzing of TLS implementations. In: USENIX Security Symposium, pp. 193–206 (2015)
18. Enck, W., Traynor, P., McDaniel, P., La Porta, T.: Exploiting open functionality in SMS-capable cellular networks. In: Proceedings of the 12th ACM Conference on Computer and Communications Security (2005)
19. Gomez-Miguelez, I., Garcia-Saavedra, A., Sutton, P.D., Serrano, P., Cano, C., Leith, D.J.: srsLTE: an open-source platform for LTE evolution and experimentation. arXiv preprint arXiv:1602.04629 (2016)
20. Hussain, S.R., Chowdhury, O., Mehnaz, S., Bertino, E.: LTEInspector: a systematic approach for adversarial testing of 4G LTE. In: Proceedings of the Network and Distributed System Security Symposium (2018)
21. Johansson, W., Svensson, M., Larson, U.E., Almgren, M., Gulisano, V.: T-fuzz: model-based fuzzing for robustness testing of telecommunication protocols. In: Proceedings of the Seventh IEEE International Conference on Software Testing, Verification and Validation, pp. 323–332. IEEE (2014)
22. Jover, R.P.: Security attacks against the availability of LTE mobility networks: overview and research directions. In: Proceedings of the 16th International Symposium on Wireless Personal Multimedia Communications. IEEE (2013)
23. Jover, R.P., Lackey, J., Raghavan, A.: Enhancing the security of LTE networks against jamming attacks. EURASIP J. Inf. Secur. 2014(7) (2014). https://jis-eurasipjournals.springeropen.com/track/pdf/10.1186/1687-417X-2014-7
24. Karandikar, A., Akhtar, N., Mehta, M.: Mobility Management in LTE Networks. In: Karandikar, A., Akhtar, N., Mehta, M. (eds.) Mobility Management in LTE Heterogeneous Networks, pp. 13–32. Springer, Singapore (2017). https://doi.org/10.1007/978-981-10-4355-0_2
25. Michau, B., Devine, C.: How to not break LTE crypto. In: Proceedings of the ANSSI Symposium sur la sécurité des Technologies de l'information et des Communications (2016)

26. Onwuzurike, L., De Cristofaro, E.: Danger is my middle name: experimenting with SSL vulnerabilities in android apps. In: Proceedings of the 8th ACM Conference on Security & Privacy in Wireless and Mobile Networks (2015)

27. Rupprecht, D., Dabrowski, A., Holz, T., Weippl, E., Pöpper, C.: On security research towards future mobile network generations. IEEE Commun. Surv. Tutor. (2018). https://ieeexplore.ieee.org/stamp/stamp.jsp?tp=&arnumber=8329226

28. Rupprecht, D., Jansen, K., Pöpper, C.: Putting LTE security functions to the test: a framework to evaluate implementation correctness. In: Proceedings of USENIX Workshop on Offensive Technologies (2016)

29. Shaik, A., Borgaonkar, R., Asokan, N., Niemi, V., Seifert, J.-P.: Practical attacks against privacy and availability in 4G/LTE mobile communication systems. In: Proceedings of the Network and Distributed System Security Symposium (2015)

30. Tsankov, P., Dashti, M.T., Basin, D.: SECFUZZ: fuzz-testing security protocols. In: Proceedings of the 7th International Workshop on Automation of Software Test, pp. 1–7. IEEE (2012)

31. Tu, G.-H., Li, Y., Peng, C., Li, C.-Y., Wang, H., Lu, S.: Control-plane protocol interactions in cellular networks. ACM SIGCOMM Comput. Commun. Rev. **44**(4), 223–234 (2015)

32. van den Broek, F., Verdult, R., de Ruiter, J.: Defeating IMSI catchers. In: Proceedings of the 22nd ACM SIGSAC Conference on Computer and Communications Security, pp. 340–351. ACM (2015)

33. Wolpert, D.H., Macready, W.G.: No free lunch theorems for optimization. IEEE Trans. Evol. Comput. **1**(1), 67–82 (1997)

PIAnalyzer: A Precise Approach
for PendingIntent Vulnerability Analysis

Sascha Groß$^{(\boxtimes)}$ ⓘ, Abhishek Tiwari ⓘ, and Christian Hammer ⓘ

University of Potsdam, Potsdam, Germany
{saschagross,tiwari}@uni-potsdam.de, hammer@cs.uni-potsdam.de

Abstract. PendingIntents are a powerful and universal feature of
Android for inter-component communication. A PendingIntent holds a
base intent to be executed by another application with the creator's permissions and identity without the creator necessarily residing in memory.
While PendingIntents are useful for many scenarios, e.g., for setting an
alarm or getting notified at some point in the future, insecure usage of
PendingIntents causes severe security threats in the form of denial-of-
service, identity theft, and privilege escalation attacks. An attacker may
gain up to SYSTEM privileges to perform the most sensitive operations,
e.g., deleting user's data on the device. However, so far no tool can detect
these PendingIntent vulnerabilities.

In this work we propose PIAnalyzer, a novel approach to analyze
PendingIntent related vulnerabilities. We empirically evaluate PIAnalyzer on a set of 1000 randomly selected applications from the Google
Play Store and find 1358 insecure usages of PendingIntents, including
70 severe vulnerabilities. We manually inspected ten reported vulnerabilities out of which nine correctly reported vulnerabilities, indicating a
high precision. The evaluation shows that PIAnalyzer is efficient with an
average execution time of 13 seconds per application.

Keywords: Android · Intent analysis · Information flow control
Static analysis

1   Introduction

The usage of mobile devices is rapidly growing with Android being the most
prevalent mobile operating system (global market share of 74.39% as of January 2018 [23]). Android phones are used for a plenitude of highly security
critical tasks, and a lot of sensitive information—including session tokens of
online services—are saved on these devices. As the official Google Play Store
and other alternative Android app marketplaces are not strongly regulated, the
main defense against malware that aims to steal sensitive information is the
Android sandbox and permission system.

In our study we discover that the Android permission system can be cir-
cumvented in many cases in the form of denial-of-service, identity theft, and

© Springer Nature Switzerland AG 2018
J. Lopez et al. (Eds.): ESORICS 2018, LNCS 11099, pp. 41–59, 2018.
https://doi.org/10.1007/978-3-319-98989-1_3

privilege escalation attacks. By exploiting vulnerable but benign applications that are insecurely using PendingIntents, a malicious application *without any permissions* can perform many critical operations, such as sending text messages (SMS) to a premium number. PendingIntents are a widespread Android callback mechanism and reference token. While the concept of PendingIntents is flexible and powerful, insecure usage can lead to severe vulnerabilities. Yu et al. [25] report a PendingIntent vulnerability in Android's official Settings app, which made a privilege escalation attack up to SYSTEM privileges possible for every installed application. Thus, given the severe security implications, the official Android documentation on PendingIntents [12] now warns against insecure usage. However, to the best of our knowledge, to-date no analysis tool detects the described PendingIntent vulnerabilities. Thus, an automated analysis tool is envisioned that scales to a large number of applications.

In this work we propose a novel approach to detect PendingIntent related vulnerabilities in Android applications. We implemented our approach in a tool called PIAnalyzer. In multiple analysis steps, PIAnalyzer computes the relevant information of the potentially vulnerable code based on program slicing [26]. PIAnalyzer is fully automated and does not require the source code of the application under inspection. PIAnalyzer assists human analysts by computing and presenting vulnerability details in easily understandable log files. We evaluated PIAnalyzer on 1000 randomly selected applications from the Google Play Store. We discover 435 applications that wrap at least one implicit base intent with a PendingIntent object, out of which 1358 insecure usages of PendingIntents arise. These include 70 PendingIntent vulnerabilities leading up to the execution of critical operations from unprivileged applications. We manually investigate multiple findings and inspect reports on examples known to be vulnerable. Our investigation show that PIAnalyzer is highly precise and sound. Technically, we provide the following contributions:

- *PendingIntent analysis.* We propose a novel method based on program slicing for the detection of PendingIntent related vulnerabilities.
- *Implementation.* We implemented a program slicer for SMALI intermediate code and the proposed PendingIntent analysis in a tool called *PIAnalyzer*.
- *Evaluation of PIAnalyzer.* We empirically evaluate PIAnalyzer on a set of 1000 randomly selected applications from the Google Play Store and find 1358 insecure usages of PendingIntents. These include 70 severe vulnerabilities. We find critical vulnerabilities in widely used libraries such as, *TapJoy* and *Google Cloud Messaging.* PIAnalyzer is efficient and only takes 13 seconds per application on average.
- *Validation of PIAnalyzer.* We manually validated multiple reports of PIAnalyzer. Our validation confirms PIAnalyzer's high precision and recall.

2   Background

Android applications are written in Kotlin [3], Java and C++. From an architectural point of view they may consist of four types of components: Activities,

Services, Broadcast Receivers, and Content Providers. Each of these components acts as an entry point through which a user or the system can interact. Activities are a single screen with a user interface, e.g., the login screen in a banking application. Services run in the background without a user interface, and are intended to perform long-term operations, e.g., Internet downloads. Broadcast receivers are components that receive system or application events to be notified, e.g., when an external power source has been connected. Finally, Content Providers dispense data to applications via various storage mechanisms.

Each component in an Android application is defined in a mandatory manifest file, *AndroidManifest.xml*. The manifest file proclaims essential information about the application, e.g., permissions that are required by the application.

Android applications are compiled from source code to Dalvik bytecode [11], which is specially designed for Android. Finally, the compiled classes along with additional metadata are compressed into an *Android Package* (APK). APKs are made available in different marketplaces such as the official Google Play Store.

As Dalvik bytecode is complex and non-human-readable, a widely used intermediate representation has become the de-facto standard to analyze Android applications: Smali [9] improves code readability and eases the analysis.

2.1   Intents

Android promotes communication between different components via a message passing mechanism: Intents are messages sent from one component to another to invoke a certain functionality, e.g., to start an Activity of another component. Intents can be sent from the system to applications or vice versa, from one application to another (inter-app communication) or even from one component to another within the same application (intra-app-communication) [10].

Central pieces of information associated with intents are a *target component*, an *intent action* and *extra data*. The intent action represents the general action to be performed by the receiving component, e.g., *ACTION_MAIN* is used to launch the home screen. The extra data contains additional information similar to parameters, which can be used by the receiving component, such as passing user input data from one component to another.

Depending on the target component or action, one distinguishes *explicit* from *implicit* intents. An *explicit* intent defines a target component and thus is only delivered to the specified component. Conversely, an *implicit* intent can be delivered to all components that register a matching intent filter in their manifest file. An implicit intent gives an user flexibility to choose among different supported components, e.g., users can opt among different browsers to open a specific webpage. In the event of multiple components registering the same intent filter, the intent resolution asks the user to select, e.g., between multiple browsers to open a particular webpage. In contrast, a *broadcast intent* is broadcast to every registered component instead of only one. Lastly, Android offers *PendingIntents*. A PendingIntent is intended for another application to perform a certain action in the context of the sending application. The usage and security implications of PendingIntents are discussed in the following.

Listing 1.1. A simple PendingIntent Usage

```
1  //Component A: Create the base Intent with a target component
2    Intent baseIntent = new Intent("TARGET_COMPONENT");
3  //Create a PendingIntent object wrapping the base Intent
4    PendingIntent pendingIntent = PendingIntent.getActivity(this, 1,
        baseIntent, PendingIntent.FLAG_UPDATE_CURRENT);
5  //Component B (may be in another application or within a system
        manager):
6  //Execute the PendingIntent (internally launches the base intent)
7    try {
8        pendingIntent.send();
9    } catch (PendingIntent.CanceledException e) {}
```

2.2   PendingIntent

A PendingIntent is a special kind of intent which stores a base intent that is to be executed at some later point in time by another component/application, but with the original app's identity and permissions. The point is that the original app is not required to be in memory or active at that point of time, as the receiver will execute it as if executed by the original application. Thus Pending-Intent is applicable in cases where normal intents are not. "A PendingIntent itself is simply a reference to a token maintained by the system describing the original data used to retrieve it. This means that even if its owning application's process is killed, the PendingIntent itself will remain usable from other processes that have been given it" [12]. A possible usage scenario for PendingIntent is a notification. If an application wishes to get notified by the system at a later point of time, it can create a PendingIntent and pass this PendingIntent to the Notification Manager. The Notification Manager will trigger this PendingIntent in the future, and so a predefined component of the application will be notified and gets executed.

Programmatically, the usage of a PendingIntent is a three step process (List-ing 1.1). First, the so called *base intent* is created. The base intent is an ordinary intent which defines the action to be performed on the execution of the Pending-Intent. The PendingIntent object wraps the base intent using the factory meth-ods *getActivity()*, *getActivities()*, *getBroadcast()* or *getService()*. These factory methods define the nature of the base intent, e.g., *PendingIntent.getBroadcast()* will launch the base intent as a broadcast intent. The PendingIntent object returned by these methods can be passed to another application or system com-ponent, e.g., it can be embedded in another intent object (the wrapping intent) as extra data to make it available to other applications. It is also common to pass a PendingIntent object to a system component, e.g., the AlarmManager, for callback purposes.

Security Implications: Whenever a PendingIntent is triggered, the associated base intent is executed in the context (with the same privileges and name) of the application that created it. However, the three main pieces of data of the base intent may be changed even after the PendingIntent has been handed to

Listing 1.2. App A - Vulnerable Activity

```
1  protected void onCreate(Bundle savedInstanceState) {
2    super.onCreate(savedInstanceState);
3    setContentView(R.layout.activity_main_vuln);
4    Intent baseIntent = new Intent();
5    PendingIntent pendingIntent = PendingIntent.getActivity(this, 1,
         baseIntent, PendingIntent.FLAG_UPDATE_CURRENT);
6    Intent implicitWrappingIntent = new Intent(Intent.ACTION_SEND);
7    implicitWrappingIntent.putExtra("vulnPI", pendingIntent);
8    sendBroadcast(implicitWrappingIntent);
9  }
```

another component, which may alter the semantics of the base intent that is to be executed with the original app's identity and permissions. While the Target Component or Action of the base Intent cannot be overridden by an attacker if already defined by the sender, an undefined Action or Target Component may be defined after handing it to the receiver. Finally, extra data, which is effectively a key-value store, can always be added after the fact. The implications include that an implicit intent (with no target component defined) can be altered by the receiving app to target any component it desires (and with the original app's permission support), including system features like wiping the phone.

As a consequence, the Android documentation of PendingIntent [12] explicitly warns about potential vulnerabilities caused by misusage: "By giving a PendingIntent to another application, you are granting it the right to perform the operation you have specified as if the other application was yourself (with the same permissions and identity) (but just for a predefined piece of code). As such, you should be careful about how you build the PendingIntent: almost always, for example, the base Intent you supply should have the component name explicitly set to one of your own components, to ensure it is ultimately sent there and nowhere else". In fact, if a malicious application can retrieve a PendingIntent from another application with an implicit base intent, it may perform a restricted form of *arbitrary code execution* in the context of the application that created the PendingIntent object: As many (but not all) permission-clad functionalities are accessible via intents, the attacker can reroute the base intent to such functions. The next section will exemplify the attack opportunities via PendingIntents.

3 Motivation

3.1 A Potential Vulnerable Example

We demonstrate PendingIntent-related vulnerabilities and exploitation via a simplified example (Listings 1.2 and 1.3). In this example, the vulnerable application has the permission to perform phone calls, while the malicious application does not. In Listing 1.2, the vulnerable application creates an empty base intent (line 4), wraps it into a PendingIntent (line 5), and sends it as an extra of

Listing 1.3. App B - Malicious Activity

```
1  public void onReceive(Context context, Intent intent) {
2    Bundle extras = intent.getExtras();
3    PendingIntent pendingIntent = (PendingIntent) extras.get("vulnPI");
4    Intent vunlnIntent = new Intent(Intent.ACTION_CALL,
        Uri.parse("tel:" + "0900123456789"));
5    try {
6      pendingIntent.send(context, 2, vunlnIntent, null, null);
7    } catch (PendingIntent.CanceledException e) { e.printStackTrace(); }
8  }
```

the broadcast intent *implicitWrappingIntent* (line 6, 7, 8). Any application that defines a corresponding intent filter in their manifest file can receive *implicitWrappingIntent*. In Listing 1.3, a malicious application which is capable of receiving *implicitWrappingIntent*, extracts the PendingIntent (line 3) and creates a new intent (with the motivation to manipulate the base intent) (line 4) such that it triggers a phone call to some arbitrary number, e.g., to a premium number. On line 6, an invocation of the *send* method of this PendingIntent object causes the execution of the base intent but with all empty properties updated to the values specified in *vulnIntent*, which results in calling the premium number.

While this example is simplified for better understanding, PendingIntent vulnerabilities can occur in various forms and lead to different types of severe security implications. In our study we find that at least 435 out of 1000 applications wrap at least one implicit base intent into a PendingIntent object. The vulnerable application can accidentally send the PendingIntent object in numerous ways. Instead of broadcasting, it can also be sent out via an implicit wrapping intent. If more than one application has a matching intent filter, the user will be asked to choose a destination. This case can be abused by an intent phishing application. In the majority of the cases the PendingIntent is not sent out by wrapping it into another intent, but by passing it to system components such as the AlarmManager or the NotificationManager. These components will eventually call the *send* method of the PendingIntent object, which triggers the base intent. A malicious app can register a component to retrieve the base intent to perform a denial of service attack, as these intents are then not passed to the intended component.

This situation becomes even more critical when the described PendingIntent vulnerability occurs in system components. Tao et al. [25] found this type of vulnerability in the Android Settings application. In the following subsection we elaborate on the details of this vulnerability.

3.2   A Real-World PendingIntent Vulnerability

For all subversions of Android 4, the *Settings* application triggered a PendingIntent with an empty base intent [25]. In February 2018, 17.4% of all Android devices still run such an Android version [13], rendering them vulnerable to a privilege escalation attack up to system privileges. This vulnerability occurred

Listing 1.4. Android Settings: AddAccountSettings.java

```
1   private void addAccount(String accountType) {
2     Bundle addAccountOptions=new Bundle();
3     mPendingIntent=PendingIntent.getBroadcast(this, 0, new Intent(), 0);
4     addAccountOptions.putParcelable(KEY_CALLER_IDENTITY,
          mPendingIntent);
5     addAccountOptions.putBoolean(EXTRA_HAS_MULTIPLE_USERS,
          Utils.hasMultipleUsers(this));
6     AccountManager.get(this).addAccount( accountType, null,
7       /* authTokenType */ null, /* requiredFeatures */
          addAccountOptions,
8       null, mCallback, null /* handler */);
9     mAddAccountCalled = true;
10  }
```

Listing 1.5. Malicious Application A: Activity 1

```
1   Intent intent = new Intent();
2   intent.setComponent(new ComponentName("com.android.settings",
      "com.android.settings.accounts.AddAccountSettings"));
3   intent.setAction(Intent.ACTION_RUN);
4   intent.setFlags(Intent.FLAG_ACTIVITY_NEW_TASK);
5   String authTypes[] = {AccountGeneral.ACCOUNT_TYPE};
6   intent.putExtra("account_types", authTypes);
7   startActivity(intent);
```

due to unawareness of the PendingIntent security implications. The fix in Android version 5.0 makes the base intent explicit.

Listing 1.4 shows the code snippet of the corresponding vulnerable method *addAccount*. In this method a PendingIntent object, *mPendingIntent*, is created (line 3) with an empty base intent. Whenever an application requests to add an account of the requested (custom) type, the *addAccount* method gets invoked and the vulnerable PendingIntent (*mPendingIntent*) is returned to this application if it registers to receive `android.accounts.AccountAuthenticator` intents (see Listing 1.6). As this application executes *mPendingIntent* in the context of the *Settings* application (with *SYSTEM* level permissions), it can maliciously overwrite the (empty) action and extra data in the base intent.

Listings 1.5 and 1.6 describe the code snippets of a malicious application *A*, targeting the vulnerability of the *Settings* application. In Listing 1.5, *A* initiates an intent to add an account type (line 7). Upon reception of this intent, the *Settings* application invokes the *addAccount* method (cf. Listing 1.4) and sends *mPendingIntent* out. As *A* has registered as *AccountAuthenticator*, it receives this PendingIntent (line 2 of Listing 1.6). On line 3, it creates an intent *vulnIntent* to perform a Factory Reset[1]. Later it triggers the PendingIntent with *vulnIntent* as the updated base intent (line 5). As *A* executes the Pending-

---

[1] A factory reset resets the device to its factory setting, i.e., deletes all data.

Listing 1.6. Malicious Application A: Activity 2

```
1  public Bundle addAccount(AccountAuthenticatorResponse response,
        String accountType, String authTokenType, String[]
        requiredFeatures, Bundle options) throws NetworkErrorException {
2  PendingIntent pi =
        (PendingIntent)options.getParcelable("pendingIntent");
3  Intent vulnIntent = new Intent("android.intent.action.MASTER_CLEAR");
4  try {
5    pi.send(mContext, 0, vulnIntent, null, null);
6  } catch (CanceledException e) { e.printStackTrace(); }
```

Intent in the same context as the *Settings* application (with *SYSTEM* level permissions), a Factory Reset is performed.

As previously described, the key cause of this type of vulnerability is the usage of implicit base intents for PendingIntents. Therefore, in this work we provide a novel analysis mechanism which detects implicit base intents in PendingIntents, analyzes their usage and gives a security warning in case of an actual vulnerability.

4 Methodology

4.1 SMALI and SMALI Slicing

PIAnalyzer analyzes the SMALI intermediate representation (IR) of the Dex bytecode extracted from an APK. SMALI is an intermediate representation of Dalvik bytecode that improves readability and analyzability. As background information, Listing A.1 (in the appendix) shows a simplified example of the creation of an Intent object in SMALI code. Similar to Dalvik bytecode, SMALI is register based. As known from assembly languages, registers are universally used for holding values. For example, on line 15 the register $v3$ is used to store a String variable, while on line 18 an Intent object is saved in the register $v0$. Please consider the comments in the listing for a more detailed explanation of the code.

PIAnalyzer transforms the bytecode of an APK to its SMALI IR using APK-Tool [19]. The core of the analysis of PIAnalyzer is performed through program slicing [26] the SMALI representation. Conceptually, a slice is a list of statements that influence a statement (backward slice), or get influenced by a statement (forward slice). For this purpose we design a SMALI slicer. Our SMALI slicer can create both forward and backward slices that are required for the analysis of PIAnalyzer. As registers are SMALI's universal storage mechanism for holding any kind of values, our SMALI slicer is register based. The SMALI slicer is initialized with an arbitrary start position in the code as well as with a set of relevant registers. After completion it returns a set of influencing statements. For example, in Listing A.1 the backward slice of the registers $v0$ and $v3$, starting from line 21 will return the statements on lines 15, 18 and 21 as backward

Fig. 1. The workflow of PIAnalyzer

slice. We would like to stress that the PendingIntent analysis described in the following is just one usage of our developed slicer. In fact, our slicer is universal and can be used for various program analysis purposes. The software architecture of PIAnalyzer is designed in a modular way that facilitates the extension by further analysis approaches. Similar to the analysis of PendingIntents, these approaches can easily make use of our generic SMALI slicer.

4.2   PendingIntent Analysis

PIAnalyzer is designed for the efficient analysis of a large number of APKs and therefore accepts as input an arbitrarily large set of APKs. Figure 1 depicts the workflow of PIAnalyzer per APK. The analysis of PIAnalyzer consists of the following steps.

PendingIntent Extraction. PIAnalyzer decompiles the DEX bytecode of a given APK to the SMALI IR using APKTool [19]. It then parses the content of each SMALI file together with the application's manifest. PendingIntents can only be created by four methods: *getActivity()*, *getActivities()*, *getBroadcast()* and *getService()* [12]. PIAnalyzer searches in the parsed SMALI files for calls to these methods, leading to a complete list of all PendingIntent creations in the application.

Base Intent Analysis. In the next step PIAnalyzer extracts the base Intent object used for creating the PendingIntent. It builds the backward slice from the PendingIntent creation site to the creation site(s) of the base Intent leveraging our universal SMALI slicer. Based on this backward slice, PIAnalyzer determines whether the base Intent is potentially implicit, meaning no target component was definitely set. For determining whether an Intent may be implicit, PIAnalyzer first confirms that an implicit constructor, i.e., a constructor without a specified target component was used to create the base Intent. It then examines whether an explicit transformation method was invoked on the base Intent object. Explicit transformation methods set the target component of an Intent object after it has been constructed, transforming an implicit Intent into an explicit one. To the best of our knowledge only five explicit transformation functions exist at the time of this writing: *setClass()*, *setClassName()*, *setComponent() setPackage()* and *setSelector()*. If an Intent has been created by an implicit constructor and no explicit transformation has definitely been invoked on the Intent, it is considered implicit. In the following steps, PIAnalyzer only considers occurrences of PendingIntents with implicit base Intents, as only these can lead to the described security issues (see discussion in Sect. 2.2).

PendingIntent Analysis. The severity of the vulnerability depends on the usage of the PendingIntent. Concretely, it depends on the sink functions to which the PendingIntent object is passed. A PendingIntent can either be sent to a trusted system component, e.g. Alarm manager, or wrapped into another Intent. PIAnalyzer therefore computes the forward slice from the creation of the PendingIntent object to either of the mentioned APIs, using our universal SMALI slicer.

WrappingIntent Analysis. The most dangerous class of attacks can occur if the PendingIntent object itself is intercepted by a malicious application. This can happen if the PendingIntent is wrapped in another intent (referred to in the sequel as *wrapping Intent*) as Intent extra data. If the wrapping Intent is implicit it can be received by a malicious application to extract its wrapped PendingIntent and manipulate the base Intent. To detect this particularly dangerous class of vulnerabilities, PIAnalyzer examines all wrapping Intents whether they are implicit, as only in this case they can be received by a malicious application. To that end, PIAnalyzer creates the backward slice for all wrapping Intents using our universal SMALI slicer. From the resulting slice it determines whether the wrapping Intent is implicit (in analogy to the base Intent analysis phase), in which case it reports a vulnerability.

Call Graph Generation. PIAnalyzer is designed to facilitate the analysis of human security experts. PIAnalyzer assists human investigation of a reported vulnerability via a generated the call graph, which leads to the method in which it has been detected. Thus human experts may determine the events that lead to the execution of the vulnerable code spot. The generated call graph can track control flow between the main application and its used libraries. Additionally, it handles recursive functions.

Reporting. In the last phase, PIAnalyzer logs the results of the analysis. PIAnalyzer creates two types of log files: For each detected vulnerability, it creates a vulnerability log file that reports details of that vulnerability. Additionally, it creates a summary log file that summarizes the findings in the whole APK batch and gives general statistics:

- *Vulnerability Log File.* This file contains the slice from the creation of the base intent, over the creation of the PendingIntent object, to the final sink function. Additionally, each vulnerability log file contains the slice from the base Intent to the PendingIntent, as well as the PendingIntent forward slice. Finally, the call graph to the method containing the vulnerability is logged.
- *Summary Log File.* For each batch of APKs one summary log file is created. Apart from some hardware specifications, this summary log file contains the total number of warnings and vulnerabilities, as well as some statistics over the batch of APKs.

4.3   Vulnerability Severity Levels

PIAnalyzer distinguishes the following levels of severity (in increasing order):

- *Secure.* PendingIntents with explicit base Intents are considered secure as a known and apparently trusted component is invoked. We respect this trust relation and create no report for these cases.
- *Warning.* If a PendingIntent with an implicit base Intent is created, but this PendingIntent is only passed to System managers that are supposed to be benign, it is considered a *Warning*. As a System manager will not redefine the base Intent of the PendingIntent, the only possible attack scenario in this case is a denial of service attack if a malicious application catches the implicit base Intent after the System manager has triggered the *send()* method of the PendingIntent.
- *Vulnerability.* PIAnalyzer reports a *Vulnerability* if a PendingIntent has been created with an implicit base Intent and the PendingIntent has been wrapped in another implicit WrappingIntent. In this scenario a malicious application can receive the PendingIntent, and redefine its base Intent resulting in a privilege escalation attack.

5 Evaluation

We applied PIAnalyzer to 1000 randomly selected applications from the Google Play Store. All experiments were performed on a MacBook Pro with MacOS High Sierra 10.13.3 installed, a 2.9 GHz Intel Core i7 processor and 16 GB DDR3 RAM.

PIAnalyzer reports 70 PendingIntent vulnerabilities and 1288 PendingIntent warnings[2]. We statistically analyzed the distribution of vulnerabilities and warnings among the inspected applications. Table 1 depicts the distribution ratios. In the vast majority of the cases a vulnerability does not occur more than once per application. However, the situation is different for warnings. Our findings show that it is likely for an application to include more than one warning. Pending-Intents are thus more likely to be delivered to system components (e.g., Alarm-Manager).

Table 1. Distribution of vulnerabilities and warnings

# vuln.	0	1	2	4
# apps	938	56	5	1

# warn.	0	1	2	3	4	5	6	7	8	9	10	13
# apps	565	104	101	96	61	33	16	16	2	2	3	1

Additionally, we analyzed the proportion of vulnerabilities and warnings that were contained in third party libraries. Remarkably, we find that 80% of the reported vulnerabilities and 98% of the reported warnings occur in third party libraries. Third party libraries thereby act as a multiplier for vulnerabilities, as they are used by a large number of applications. We therefore would like to stress the importance of PIAnalyzer for library developers. Table 2 provides a

---

[2] For explanations of the severity levels please refer to Sect. 4.3.

list of these libraries along with their contribution to the number of vulnerable apps. Libraries are included as the dependencies in the *build.gradle* file[3]. As this file is not compiled into the APKs, we could not find the exact version of the library. A tedious way to find the exact version of the library is to match the app's intermediate code with the intermediate code of the each version of the library. We find that these versions of libraries are still in use in the recent versions of applications. Thus, instead of providing the exact version of libraries we provide their year of appearance in an application (in 1000 applications from our experiment).

Table 2. Libraries contribution to number of vulnerabilities

Library	Description	App vuln.	Year
Google messaging library	Cloud messaging	39	2017
Cloud to device messaging	Cloud messaging	8	2016
TapJoy	Marketing and automation	3	2016
MixPlane	Push notification & in app messaging	4	2016
LeanPlum	Messaging, variable, analytics & testing	2	2017

As mentioned, an attacker can escalate a PendingIntent vulnerability into a privilege escalation attack and leverage the permissions of the vulnerable applications. We therefore analyzed the permissions of the applications for which PIAnalyzer reported vulnerabilities. We find that 279 dangerous permissions [14] and 273 normal permissions are used by these vulnerable applications. As dangerous permissions are required for performing critical operations on the device, an attacker may act maliciously in many of these instances, e.g., call a premium number.

Table 3 provides a list of ten vulnerable applications (randomly selected) along with their category and used dangerous permission groups. The permission groups contain permissions organized into a device's capabilities or features, e.g., *PHONE* group includes the *CALL_PHONE* permission. 35% of the vulnerable applications belong to the *Business, Entertainment, or Education* category.

In our experiment with 1000 real-world applications, the average execution time of PIAnalyzer is close to 13 s with a minimum of 10 s and the maximum time of 21 s. This time performance strongly demonstrates the efficiency of PIAnalyzer and proves that it can easily be applied to a large number of real-world applications.

To evaluate the precision and the soundness of PIAnalyzer, we manually inspected the reported results of ten applications (out of 70 vulnerable applications). Manual inspection is time consuming as it requires analysis of many SMALI code files. Out of ten applications, we find that nine times PIAnalyzer reports correct vulnerabilities/warnings, indicating a high precision. In one case,

---

[3] https://developer.android.com/studio/build/index.html.

Table 3. Vulnerable applications with dangerous permissions

App name	App category	Dangerous permission group
SandWipPlus	Communication	Contacts, Phone, Sms, Storage
Reason	News & Magazines	Contacts, Location, Phone, Storage
Santa Dance Man	News & Magazines	Phone, Storage
SmartInput Keyboard	Personalization	Phone
drift15house	Entertainment	Calendar, Contacts, Location, Phone, Storage
Fishermens	Entertainment	Contacts, Camera, Location, Microphone, Phone, Storage
Derek Carroll	Photography	Camera, Location, Microphone, Phone, Photography, Sms, Storage
ElleClub	Business	Camera, Contacts, Location, Microphone, Phone, Sms, Storage
Chat Locator	Productivity	Location, Storage
Deptford Mall	Lifestyle	Calendar, Contacts, Location, Microphone, Phone, Sms, Storage

the base intent was manipulated dynamically and thus PIAnalyzer conservatively overapproximated it as implicit intent.

In addition, we applied PIAnalyzer to the vulnerability in the *Settings* app (described in the Sect. 3.2) that led to privilege escalation to SYSTEM privileges. PIAnalyzer correctly reports the vulnerability and so PIAnalyzer could have prevented the discussed vulnerability. Finally, we applied PIAnalyzer to multiple self-written demo examples that included PendingIntent vulnerabilities. PIAnalyzer correctly reports each of them, indicating high recall.

5.1 Case Study: Vulnerability in the Google Cloud Messaging (GCM) Library

PIAnalyzer finds a vulnerability in an outdated version of the Google Cloud Messaging (GCM) Library, which is part of the Google Messaging Library and still in use by many applications, e.g., Table Tennis 3D [17] or the Android Device Manager. Among 1000 analyzed applications, we find that 37 out of 39 (cf. Table 2) applications still use this version of GCM. The vulnerability exists in the file *GoogleCloudMessaging.java* of the GCM Library. Listing 1.7 shows the code snippet of the vulnerable method *send*. On line 4, an implicit intent named *localIntent* is created. On line 6, *localIntent* is passed to a method *c*. Listing 1.8 shows the code snippet for the method *c*. In this method, a PendingIntent with an empty base intent is created (line 4). On line 5, this PendingIntent is stored as extra data to the input parameter *paramIntent*. Later in method *send* (Listing 1.7), *localIntent* is broadcast to all registered receivers. Any Broadcast Receiver, declaring this intent filter (*com.google.android.gcm.intent.SEND*) in

Listing 1.7. Vulnerable Method

```
1    public void send(String paramString1, String paramString2,
2            long paramLong, Bundle paramBundle) {
3      // ...
4      Intent localIntent = new Intent("com.google.android.gcm.intent.SEND");
5      localIntent.putExtras(paramBundle);
6      c(localIntent);
7      localIntent.putExtra("google.to", paramString1);
8      localIntent.putExtra("google.message_id", paramString2);
9      localIntent.putExtra("google.ttl", Long.toString(paramLong));
10     this.eh.sendOrderedBroadcast(localIntent, null);
11   }
```

Listing 1.8. PendingIntent with an empty base intent

```
1    void c(Intent paramIntent) {
2      try {
3        if (this.xg == null)
4          this.xg = PendingIntent.getBroadcast(this.eh, 0, new Intent(),
               0);
5        paramIntent.putExtra("app", this.xg);
6      } finally {}
7    }
```

its manifest file, can receive this Intent and can easily extract the associated PendingIntent. In this case the permissions of the attacker application are escalated to the permissions of applications that use GCM. In our experiments, we are able to intercept *localIntent* and to extract the associated PendingIntent. As the base intent in the associated PendingIntent is blank, we set any arbitrary action/component and trigger it with the same identity as the vulnerable application. This enables us to perform arbitrary actions with the identity of the vulnerable application, e.g., sending a malicious message to a different component of the vulnerable application and making it believe it was sent from within the application (i.e. identity theft). In the worst case scenario, if this GCM version were used by a system application with system permissions (GCM is an official Google library), a malicious application could for example factory reset the device (deleting all data). We tested several versions (4–7) of system APKs from Google without such inclusions found. However, due to lacking availability we could not check system APKs from other vendors.

5.2   Discussion

PIAnalyzer is a static analysis tool which shares common limitations with other static analysis approaches. As the program behavior can depend on dynamic input, every static analysis tool cannot be completely sound and precise. The slicing analysis of PIAnalyzer is affected by these limitations. In theory, it is possible to make an Intent implicit or explicit depending on external runtime input. This could happen either by making the constructor used for intent creation or the usage of explicit transformation methods depend on external input.

When it is not clear at compile time whether an Intent is implicit or explicit, PIAnalyzer conservatively assumes that it is implicit. Analogously, the slices computed by PIAnalyzer are, by their nature, conservative approximations of the actual control flow at runtime. In theory, it is also possible to make use of Intents in Reflection or native code. PIAnalyzer neither supports reflection, nor native code. We would like to stress that while the above mentioned cases are possible in theory, they are rare in the real world and we could not observe a single instance of these cases during inspection of many applications. Some of the operations that require permissions cannot be performed directly via Intents to system interfaces, e.g., the retrieval of a precise location. Thus an application with only these permissions may not be vulnerable to PendingIntent related attacks.

6   Related Work

To the best of our knowledge, there exists no approach that precisely detects the described PendingIntent vulnerabilities at the time of this writing. In a concurrent effort Trummer and Dalvi [7] developed QARK, an Android vulnerability scanner that also detects PendingIntent based vulnerabilities described in this work. However, QARK ignores the flow of PendingIntents with implicit base intents, so even PendingIntents that are never sent anywhere will be reported a vulnerability. In our tool such a case would only be considered a vulnerability if it flows there via another implicit intent. Additionally, they do not consider whether an implicit intent is transformed to an explicit intent via further API calls. In summary this leads to imprecise results as demonstrated in our evaluation, where we observed that these cases are highly relevant and frequently occur in real-world applications. Their work [7] contains no result other than the prototype tool, particularly no evaluation of their technique.

Bugiel et al. [4] proposed XManDroid, a reference monitor to prevent privilege escalation attacks. Their approach is focused on application permissions and policies to model the desired application privileges. In contrast to our approach, XManDroid only regards PendingIntents as vehicle for inter-component communication and does not consider the peculiarities and vulnerabilities of PendingIntents.

SAAF [1], proposed by Hoffmann et al., is a tool to statically analyze SMALI code. It recovers String constants from backward slices of method calls in order to detect suspicious behavior. However, as it could not produce the expected results in our experiments with current APKs we re-implemented a SMALI slicer.

Li et al. [16] analyzed vulnerabilities in Google's GCM and Amazon's ADM mobile-cloud services. They discovered a critical logical flaws, concerning both of these services. Additionally, they discovered a PendingIntent vulnerability in GCM. Unlike our approach, they discovered this vulnerability by manual code analysis and they do not provide an automated approach for discovering PendingIntent vulnerabilities.

Apart from work considering PendingIntents, there is an extensive body of work on general Intent analysis. One line focuses on Intent fuzzers for finding

Intent related vulnerabilities. For example, Yang et al. [27] developed an Intent fuzzer for the detection of capability leaking vulnerabilities in Android applications. JarJarBinks, proposed by Maji et al. [18], is a fuzzing tool for Android intents. By sending a large number of requests, the authors found robustness vulnerabilities in the Android runtime environment. Sasnauskas and Regher [22] created an Intent Fuzzer. Their approach is based on static analysis and generates random test-cases based on the analysis results. In contrast to our approach, their approaches do not consider PendingIntent related vulnerabilities.

Other work focuses on Intent based test case generation. For example, Jha et al. [15] proposed a model that abstracts Android inter-component communication. From this model the authors derived test cases that facilitates the software engineering process. Salva and Zafimiharisoa [21] proposed APSET, a tool that implements a model-based testing approach for Android applications. The proposed approach generates test cases that check for the leakage of sensitive information. In contrast, our approach is focused on the security perspective of PendingIntents.

As Intents are extensively used by malware, some approaches use Intent analysis as a feature for malware detection. Feizollah et al. [8] proposed Andro-Dialysis, a tool that uses Intents as indicating feature for Android malware. Tam et al. [24] proposed CopperDroid, a monitor system which tracks events via virtual machine introspection. CopperDroid considers PendingIntent as vehicle for Inter Process Communication. In contrast, our approach is intended for finding PendingIntent related vulnerabilities in benign applications.

Several approaches use various static information flow techniques for Intent analysis. Sadeghi et al. [20] proposed COVERT, a static analysis tool for the analysis of Intents. It computes information flows by static taint analysis. Using COVERT, the authors discovered hundreds of vulnerabilities in applications from the Google Play Store and other sources. Yang et al. [28] proposed AppIntent, an analysis tool for finding leakage of sensitive information via Intents. The key idea of their approach is to distinguish intended information leakage from unintended leakage considering user interface actions. The authors leverage the Android execution model to perform an efficient symbolic execution analysis. Unlike ours, both approaches do not consider PendingIntent related vulnerabilities. Arzt et al. [2] proposed FlowDroid, a taint analysis tool for the static analysis of Android applications. It achieves precise and sound results by appropriately modeling the Android lifecycle and maintaining context, flow, field and object-sensitivity. While FlowDroid is intended for detecting unwanted information flows for the sake of confidentiality and integrity, PIAnalyzer focuses on the detection of vulnerabilities that arise by the wrong usage of PendingIntent and that can not be detected by FlowDroid.

Chin et al. [6] proposed ComDroid, a tool for detecting inter-component related vulnerabilities, e.g., Intent spoofing or Service Hijacking. Chan et al. [5] proposed an approach to detect privilege escalation attacks in Android applications. As their approach does not include any kind of information flow control, it overapproximates possible attacks leading to reduced precision. Again, both do not detect security vulnerabilities caused by PendingIntents.

7   Conclusion

We described the first approach to analyze and detect PendingIntent-related vulnerabilities. We implemented our approach together with a generic SMALI slicer in a tool called PIAnalyzer. PIAnalyzer is fully automated and does neither require the source code of the applications under inspection, nor any effort by the analyst. We evaluated PIAnalyzer on 1000 randomly selected applications from the Google Play Store to assess the runtime performance, precision and soundness of PIAnalyzer. PIAnalyzer takes on average only approximately 13 seconds per application, which scaled up well to large test sets. PIAnalyzer discovers 1288 warnings and 70 PendingIntent vulnerabilities. We manually investigated some of the reports and elaborated on a privilege escalation vulnerability caused by the usage of a prevalent Google library.

Acknowledgements. This work was supported by the German Federal Ministry of Education and Research (BMBF) through the project SmartPriv (16KIS0760).

A   Appendices

A.1   Simplified SMALI Code Example

```
1    .method protected onCreate(Landroid/os/Bundle;)V
2        # 5 local registers are used in this method
3        .locals 5
4
5        # Declaration of a parameter register with a given name
6        .param p1, "savedInstanceState" # Landroid/os/Bundle;
7
8        # End of the method prologue. Start of the actual code.
9        .prologue
10
11       # A call to a super constructor
12       invoke-super {p0, p1},
           Landroid/support/v7/app/AppCompatActivity;->onCreate(Landroid/os/Bundle;)V
13
14       # Declaration of a String in register v3
15       const-string v3, "android.intent.action.CALL"
16
17       # Creation of an Intent object in register v0
18       new-instance v0, Landroid/content/Intent;
19
20       # Invocation of the constructor of the intent object
21       invoke-direct {v0, v3}, Landroid/content/Intent;-><init>(Ljava/lang/String;)V
22
23       # Return of the method with no return value
24       return-void
25
26   .end method
```

References

1. Hoffmann, J., Ussath, M., Holz, T., Spreitzenbarth, M.: Slicing droids: program slicing for smali code. In: Proceedings of the ACM Symposium on Applied Computing, SAC. ACM, New York (2013)
2. Arzt, S., et al.: Flowdroid: precise context, flow, field, object-sensitive and lifecycle-aware taint analysis for android apps. ACM SIGPLAN Not. **49**(6), 259–269 (2014)
3. Brains, J.: Kotlin. https://kotlinlang.org
4. Bugiel, S., Davi, L., Dmitrienko, A., Fischer, T., Sadeghi, A.R.: XManDroid: a new android evolution to mitigate privilege escalation attacks. Technische Universität Darmstadt, Technical report TR-2011-04 (2011)
5. Chan, P.P., Hui, L.C., Yiu, S.: A privilege escalation vulnerability checking system for android applications. In: 2011 IEEE 13th International Conference on Communication Technology (ICCT), pp. 681–686. IEEE (2011)
6. Chin, E., Felt, A.P., Greenwood, K., Wagner, D.: Analyzing inter-application communication in android. In: Proceedings of the 9th International Conference on Mobile Systems, Applications, and Services, pp. 239–252. ACM (2011)
7. Trummer, T., Dalvi, T.: QARK: Quick Android Review Kit. DefCon 23, August 2015. https://github.com/linkedin/qark
8. Feizollah, A., Anuar, N.B., Salleh, R., Suarez-Tangil, G., Furnell, S.: Androdialysis: analysis of android intent effectiveness in malware detection. Comput. Secur. **65**, 121–134 (2017)
9. Freke, J.: Baksmali. https://github.com/JesusFreke/smali
10. Google: Android Intent Documentation. https://developer.android.com/reference/android/content/Intent.html. Accessed May 2017
11. Google: Dalvik bytecode documentation. https://source.android.com/devices/tech/dalvik/dalvik-bytecode. Accessed May 2017
12. Google: Pending intent documentation. https://developer.android.com/reference/android/app/PendingIntent.html
13. Google: Android OS Statistics, February 2018. https://developer.android.com/about/dashboards/index.html#Screens
14. Google: Android permissions, April 2018. https://developer.android.com/guide/topics/permissions/overview.html
15. Jha, A.K., Lee, S., Lee, W.J.: Modeling and test case generation of inter-component communication in android. In: Proceedings of the Second ACM International Conference on Mobile Software Engineering and Systems, pp. 113–116. IEEE Press (2015)
16. Li, T., et al.: Mayhem in the push clouds: understanding and mitigating security hazards in mobile push-messaging services. In: Proceedings of the 2014 ACM SIGSAC Conference on Computer and Communications Security, pp. 978–989. ACM (2014)
17. Table Tennis 3D. Google Play Store, April 2014
18. Maji, A.K., Arshad, F.A., Bagchi, S., Rellermeyer, J.S.: An empirical study of the robustness of inter-component communication in android. In: 2012 42nd Annual IEEE/IFIP International Conference on Dependable Systems and Networks (DSN), pp. 1–12. IEEE (2012)
19. Ryszard Wiśniewski, C.T.: Apktool. https://ibotpeaches.github.io/Apktool/
20. Sadeghi, A., Bagheri, H., Malek, S.: Analysis of android inter-app security vulnerabilities using covert. In: 2015 IEEE/ACM 37th IEEE International Conference on Software Engineering (ICSE), vol. 2, pp. 725–728. IEEE (2015)

21. Salva, S., Zafimiharisoa, S.R.: Data vulnerability detection by security testing for android applications. In: Information Security for South Africa, pp. 1–8. IEEE (2013)
22. Sasnauskas, R., Regehr, J.: Intent fuzzer: crafting intents of death. In: Proceedings of the 2014 Joint International Workshop on Dynamic Analysis (WODA) and Software and System Performance Testing, Debugging, and Analytics (PERTEA), pp. 1–5. ACM (2014)
23. Statcounter.com: Operating system market share worldwide, January 2018. http://gs.statcounter.com/os-market-share/mobile/worldwide
24. Tam, K., Khan, S.J., Fattori, A., Cavallaro, L.: CopperDroid: automatic reconstruction of android malware behaviors. In: NDSS (2015)
25. Tao, W., Zhang, D., Yu, W.: Android settings pendingintent leak, November 2014. https://packetstormsecurity.com/files/129281/Android-Settings-Pendingintent-Leak.html
26. Weiser, M.: Program slicing. IEEE Trans. Softw. Eng. **10**(4), 352–357 (1984)
27. Yang, K., Zhuge, J., Wang, Y., Zhou, L., Duan, H.: Intentfuzzer: detecting capability leaks of android applications. In: Proceedings of the 9th ACM Symposium on Information, Computer and Communications Security, pp. 531–536. ACM (2014)
28. Yang, Z., Yang, M., Zhang, Y., Gu, G., Ning, P., Wang, X.S.: Appintent: analyzing sensitive data transmission in android for privacy leakage detection. In: Proceedings of the 2013 ACM SIGSAC Conference on Computer & Communications Security, pp. 1043–1054. ACM (2013)

Investigating Fingerprinters
and Fingerprinting-Alike Behaviour
of Android Applications

Christof Ferreira Torres[1,2(✉)] and Hugo Jonker[3,4]

[1] Fraunhofer AISEC, Munich, Germany
[2] SnT, University of Luxembourg, Luxembourg, Luxembourg
christof.torres@uni.lu
[3] Open University of the Netherlands, Heerlen, Netherlands
hugo.jonker@ou.nl
[4] Radboud University, Nijmegen, Netherlands

Abstract. Fingerprinting of browsers has been thoroughly investigated. In contrast, mobile phone applications offer a far wider array of attributes for profiling, yet fingerprinting practices on this platform have hardly received attention.

In this paper, we present the first (to our knowledge) investigation of Android libraries by commercial fingerprinters. Interestingly enough, there is a marked difference with fingerprinting desktop browsers. We did not find evidence of typical fingerprinting techniques such as canvas fingerprinting. Secondly, we searched for behaviour resembling that of commercial fingerprinters. We performed a detailed analysis of six similar libraries. Thirdly, we investigated ~30,000 apps and found that roughly 19% of these apps is using one of the these libraries. Finally, we checked how often these libraries were used by apps subject to the *Children's Online Privacy Protection Act* (i.e. apps targeted explicitly at children), and found that these libraries were included 21 times.

1 Introduction

Fingerprinting is a side-channel approach to identifying devices.Instead of using an explicitly defined identifier (e.g. an HTTP cookie), fingerprinting relies on determining a set of characteristics that together are uniquely identifying. This can be used for user tracking as well as fraud prevention (e.g. preventing logins from devices with unknown fingerprints). For desktop internet browsers, Eckersley found [3] that even a small set of attribute values such as screen resolution, browser version, and operating system version is typically sufficient to reliably re-identify a browser and, thereby, a user.

In comparison to desktop browsers, smartphone platforms facilitate fingerprinting better. Smartphones possess a large array of sensors (e.g. accelerometer, GPS, etc.), antennas (e.g. WiFi, Bluetooth, GSM, etc.) and internal characteristics (phone number, contact list, installed apps, etc.), which together provide

© Springer Nature Switzerland AG 2018
J. Lopez et al. (Eds.): ESORICS 2018, LNCS 11099, pp. 60–80, 2018.
https://doi.org/10.1007/978-3-319-98989-1_4

a large fingerprintable surface. The extent to which these data can be accessed without privileges is far greater than on desktop browsers (e.g. JavaScript access to sensor APIs like the Android device motion API). Moreover, unlike desktop browsers where third-party cookies can be used to track users across sites, the Android API does not provide any features for sharing state between apps. Any cross-app tracking is therefore forced to develop its own approach to re-identification, which, in absence of an explicit identification mechanism, must rely on side channels, i.e. fingerprinting. Moreover, currently Android offers several globally unique identifiers (e.g., MAC address, ANDROID_ID, advertising ID etc.). However, their use for tracking is reducing as newer versions of Android take privacy measures to precisely prevent this. In other words: unique identifiers seem not to be future-proof. In contrast, fingerprinting is easy to realize with few permissions, can result in a large set of identifying data, serves cross-app and cross-device tracking, and is more future-proof than relying on identifiers. This provides a strong incentive for using fingerprinting in mobile apps. Unlike browser fingerprinting, mobile device fingerprinting in practice has, to the best of our knowledge, received scant attention.

In this paper, we investigate the extent to which the rich fingerprinting opportunities offered by Android smartphones are being taken advantage of. The results are surprising. A large amount of companies is collecting data that could be potentially used for profiling/identification of users (besides unique identifiers). We show evidence that companies are not just collecting identifiers but much more data. These results are uncovered by a scanning tool: *FP-Sherlock*. This is a static scanner, designed to quickly identify potential fingerprinting apps from a large corpus, reducing the search space sufficiently to make manual inspection feasible.

Contributions. We reverse engineer two commercial fingerprinting libraries and analyse and discuss their workings. Based on this, we design *FP-Sherlock*, a static scanner that can find fingerprinting-alike behaviour in APK files. We apply FP-Sherlock to a corpus of ~30,000 top apps, which identifies a number of libraries that exhibit such behaviour. We reverse engineer the six most similar libraries and discuss their workings and their occurrence rates within our corpus. Finally, we check how many apps in our corpus include such libraries while being age-restricted, i.e., subject to the *Children's Online Privacy Protection Act* (COPPA), which strictly regulates profiling of children.

2   Background and Related Work

Eckersley [3] was the first to investigate browser fingerprinting. He computed the entropy for various browser attributes, and found that about 90% of desktop browsers were unique in his data set (about 470,000 fingerprints). Commercial fingerprinters were first identified by Mayer et al. [7], identifying (amongst others) Iovation as a company that offers browser fingerprinting services to websites. This triggered research aimed at detecting commercial as well as non-commercial fingerprinters. Nikiforakis et al. [9] investigated the workings of three commercial browser fingerprinters. A work by Acar et al. [1] uncovered a new commercial fingerprinter (ThreatMetrix).

Browser fingerprinting has also been investigated on mobile phones. Spooren et al. [12], Hupperich et al. [4], and Laperdrix et al. [6] all investigated browser fingerprinting on mobile devices. While Laperdrix et al. were positive by using canvas fingerprinting [8], the other two studies reported negative results. Remark that none of these studies leverage the far richer attribute surface of mobile devices, and so are ill-suited for investigating real-life data gathering practices in the mobile domain. Hupperich et al. proposed to break away from browser fingerprinting for mobile device fingerprinting. They introduce four classes of attributes (browser, system, hardware and behaviour) and set up an experiment using 45 attributes over these four classes. Their experiments illustrate the feasibility of fingerprinting mobile devices, as well as the strong reliance dependence of their re-identification process on two attributes in particular. Others have also looked beyond browser fingerprinting into mobile device fingerprinting.

Kurtz et al. [5] investigate device fingerprinting for iOS devices. They manually evaluated the iOS SDK to find fingerprintable attributes, identifying 29 attributes as such, including last played songs, list of installed applications, etc. They created an iOS application to fingerprint devices based on these 29 attributes, and found that in their test set of 8,000 different devices, each device had a unique fingerprint. Wu et al. [15] provide a similar study focused on the Android operating system. They construct a fingerprinting mechanism that does not require permissions, relying on 38 attributes. Wu et al. investigate the entropy of these 38 attributes, finding the list of currently installed applications and wallpapers to be the most revealing.

In summary, the many developments that occurred to desktop browser fingerprinting are not directly applicable to mobile fingerprinting. While Wu et al. [15] demonstrated the possibility of fingerprinting users on Android devices, there is insufficient data available on the entropy of attributes to label determine whether a specific set of gathered attribute values could serve as a fingerprint. Remark that Wu et al. only investigated 38 attributes that served their purpose. In contrast, we seek to find out what attributes are being used by actual fingerprinters in practice, and the extent to which other apps engage in similar behaviour. To the best of our knowledge, we are the first to study whether or not mobile fingerprinting occurs in practice.

3 Investigating Known Fingerprinters

Previous works [1,7,9] had identified three companies behind commercial browser fingerprinting: *BlueCava*, *Iovation* and *ThreatMetrix*. We used the ICSI Haystack Panopticon project [14] to check whether any of these companies' names or their domain names occurred in applications scanned by the project. The ICSI Haystack Panopticon project gathers data communication between mobile applications and trackers, and offers an online interface[1] to search for tracking activity on the collected dataset. We found eleven applications communicating with ThreatMetrix, but none that communicated with either BlueCava or Iovation. We downloaded these eleven applications and disassembled them in order to verify that these applications actually included a library or code that would communicate with ThreatMetrix. Via a thorough manual examination of the source code, we identified the presence of a ThreatMetrix library with the package name "`com.threatmetrix.TrustDefenderMobile`" in each application. Moreover, after gradually de-obfuscating each piece of code, we were able to confirm that the library is indeed performing fingerprinting by gathering a large amount of information about the device and transmitting it to their back-end. From this, we learned how the fingerprinting library communicates to its back-end servers.

To find fingerprinting libraries by Iovation and BlueCava, we downloaded all top free apps for each of the 62 categories on the Google Play Store (about 600 per category). This resulted in a dataset containing a total of 30,696 apps, collected in mid-July 2017. We scanned their source code for the string "*iovation*" and "*bluecava*", respectively, which uncovered ten applications including Iovation. Upon manual investigation and de-obfuscation, we found they were indeed using a fingerprinting library by Iovation with the package name "`com.iovation.mobile.android`". We also found that Iovation's fingerprinting library avoids detection by the ICSI Haystack project because communication with Iovation's back-end is handled by the developer's back-end and not by the library itself (cf. Sect. 5.3).

Through reverse engineering, we found that unlike desktop browser fingerprinting, the identified libraries do not engage in side channel techniques to establish an identifier. That is, we did not find canvas fingerprinting or other similar techniques that are common to browser fingerprinters. Moreover, to our surprise we discovered that, except for the JavaScript based plugin enumeration performed by ThreatMetrix, the libraries did not reuse code from their already existing browser fingerprinting libraries. Instead, the libraries seem to focus on the Android environment and to have been created independently to collect a large set of different attributes.

Note that there are several attributes on mobile phones that provide a globally unique identifier. Any of these would suffice as a way to identify a user without using fingerprinting. Hence, an app or library that goes beyond these and engages in promiscuous collection of diverse attribute data is thus suspect of performing fingerprinting.

4 FP-Sherlock: Hunting for Unknown Fingerprinters

To identify unknown fingerprinters, a definition of what constitutes a fingerprinter is needed. However, there is no agreed-upon definition of fingerprinting.

---

[1] https://haystack.mobi/panopticon/index.html, providing data from 2015.

Fingerprint-detecting tools such as FPDetective focus on detecting use of specific techniques, e.g. font list probing or canvas fingerprinting. In contrast, we aim to create a tool that can detect siphoning of large quantities of attributes that together constitute a fingerprint (as shown by Eckersley [3]). However, in the mobile domain there is no equivalent to the work of Eckersley. Previous studies focused on a subset of attributes (e.g. [15]), which only have a very limited overlap with attributes used by actual fingerprinters. This means we cannot determine whether a given set of attributes constitutes a unique fingerprint in the mobile domain. Thus we have to approach detection of fingerprinters differently. Instead of looking for a library that is fingerprinting, we look for fingerprinting behaviour: is the app collecting attributes commonly used by fingerprinters, and is this accumulation due to one single library?

Based on previous studies in browser fingerprinting [1,3,9,13], studies in mobile fingerprinting [4,5,12,15] as well as our findings from analysing mobile fingerprinters (cf. Sect. 3), we find that all fingerprinters share two characteristics:

Diversity: measures how many different attributes are accessed by a library.
Accumulation: determines whether the attributes identified by the diversity measure are all collected at one point in the library.

Both diversity and accumulation are necessary characteristics of fingerprinters, but they are not sufficient to positively identify a fingerprinter. Therefore, any approach based on them requires post-processing, e.g. manual inspection of found candidate fingerprinters.

To concretise the notion of diversity, we set out to construct a taxonomy of attributes. Diversity could then be based not on the amount of attributes itself, but on the amount of groups in the taxonomy accessed by the suspect library. We chose an initial set of classes of attributes based on the classifications proposed by Wu et al. [15], expanding it to incorporate the results of our analysis on the commercial fingerprinting libraries by Iovation and ThreatMetrix (cf. Table 5). To concretise the notion of accumulation, we examine the call graph (a directed graph) of a library. This allows us to perform flow analysis, determining whether there is a single point in the suspect library where attribute values could be accumulated. We thus arrive at the following concretisation:

δ-**diversity:** there must be at least one node in the call graph of the library that accesses attributes (either directly or accumulated) from at least δ different categories listed in Table 5,
α-**accumulation:** a node inherits the attributes accessed by its children, iff:
1. there exists a calling relationship between the two nodes (e.g. the parent node calls a subroutine of the child node)
2. the child node accesses at least one of the attributes listed in Table 5
3. the similarity between the class names of the parent and the child is at least α

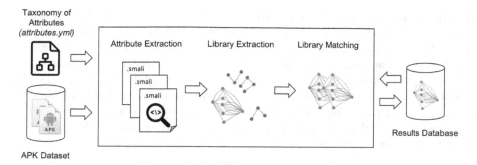

Fig. 1. FP-Sherlock's main steps and workflow.

4.1   System Design

FP-Sherlock is a static analysis tool for Android applications that uncovers fingerprinting libraries. As FP-Sherlock is based on static analysis, it is quick in comparison to approaches based on dynamic analysis. This enables large scale scanning of applications. The tool is based on our characterisation of fingerprinting: *accumulation* and *diversity*. As mentioned, this characterisation is sound but not complete. FP-Sherlock is intended to be used to scan a large set and identify a much smaller set of candidates, which is then investigated by other, more time-consuming analysis methods (e.g. manual analysis or dynamic analysis). By updating the list of attributes covered and setting rates for α-accumulation and δ-diversity, FP-Sherlock can easily be adopted to other studies. FP-Sherlock's workflow in evaluating a single application is as follows (cf. Fig. 1):

1. **Attribute Extraction:** the application is disassembled and the source code is examined for methods and fields that occur in the attribute taxonomy. In addition, FP-Sherlock keeps track of all call relationships between classes.
2. **Library Extraction:**
    (a) a partial call graph is generated, taking only call relations into account between classes that share a similar class name and that call on attributes. *(accumulation)*
    (b) we extract all connected components from the call graph. Each connected component represents a library and is only considered relevant if the overall categories of its attributes are sufficiently distinctive. *(diversity)*
3. **Library Matching:** every extracted library is matched with previously stored libraries, possibly exposing the un-obfuscated class names of obfuscated libraries. Eventually, the library is stored in a database for subsequent matches.

The remainder of this section explains each of the three main steps of FP-Sherlock in more detail.

Attribute Extraction. As input, FP-Sherlock takes a set of Android applications to be analysed and a taxonomy of attributes to look for in these applications. We created a taxonomy of 120 attributes, mapping all the smali methods and fields that we came across during our reverse engineering of Iovation's and ThreatMetrix's libraries (see Sect. 5) to our own representation of attributes. We stored our taxonomy using YAML, a human-readable data serialization language commonly used for configuration files. In the attribute representation, we store class name, method name, field name and parameters separately. For example, the following smali method invocation:

```
const−string  v1 ,  ”http_proxy”

invoke−virtual  {v0 ,  v1 },  Landroid/provider/Settings$Secure;−>getString
(Ljava/lang/String ;) Ljava/lang/String ;
```

is mapped to the subsequent YAML description:

```
- className: Landroid/provider/Settings$Secure
  methodName: getString
  parameters: [http_proxy]
  category: "Proxies"
  description: "HTTP Proxy Settings (Secure)"
```

We separate these in order to easily search for occurrences and overcome simple Java reflection, where methods of a class are retrieved by passing the name of the method as a string.

Every attribute contains a description and a category. We grouped the 120 attributes into 10 different categories (see Table 5 for more details). Our classification is based on the classification of 38 attributes by Wu et al. [15] (*Hardware, Operating System*, and *Settings*), which we expanded further to account for the attributes collected by ThreatMetrix and Iovation. We grouped attributes with similar purpose into one class, and separate classes based on perceived use. For example, unlike Wu et al., we distinguish a class *Localisation* as separate from *Settings*. This ensures that applications that access localisation information but no other settings score lower than apps that gather both localisation attributes and other settings. Similarly, we distinguish the class *Device* from *Hardware* and *Network* from *Carrier*. In addition, we identify a class *Applications* whose attributes pertain to infer installed applications. Finally, we consider the class *WebView*, which governs attributes accessed via JavaScript inside a Webview.

The analysis of an application starts by disassembling its bytecode using *baksmali*, a tool that translates DEX bytecode into a more human readable representation called *smali*. As a next step, we iterate over all method definitions. To boost performance, we slightly modified *baksmali* in order to keep the smali representation of a method definition in memory as a string, instead of writing it to a file. Afterwards, we use a regular expression (`const-string.*? v.+?, (".*?")`) to extract all the string constants contained inside the method definition. In addition, we keep track of calling relations between methods and classes, (deliberately ignoring system libraries, e.g. classes that start with

Landroid/, Lcom/android/ or Lcom/google/), by using another regular expression ("invoke .+? {.+?}, (.+?;)"), that extracts all method invocations. Finally, for every attribute, we search for occurrences of its class name and method name (or field name) within the method definition. Analogous, for the parameters of a method, we loop through the string constants and search for strings that match the given parameters. If the current class contains any occurrences of attributes, we create new node in the call graph labeled by the name of that class, and add all the matched attributes to it. Please note that the call graph is only a partial call graph as it only contains class nodes that hold attributes.

Library Extraction. In the previous step we extracted the attributes and added nodes to the call graph. A node represents a class and contains a list of attributes that have been found in the method definitions of the class. However, the previous step does not connect any of these nodes. In this step, we iterate over the pairs of the previously extracted call relations by solely considering pairs where the callee node contains at least one attribute and adding a connection to the call graph if the class names of the nodes are different, yet share at least a similarity score of α. The similarity between two class names is computed using fuzzy string matching. We use the JavaWuzzy[2] implementation. JavaWuzzy uses the Levenshtein Distance to determine the similarity between two strings. This metric determines the similarity of two strings by looking at the minimum number of edits required for two strings to be equivalent. However, this approach does not work for pair of nodes with short obfuscated class names, as these will not fulfil the similarity score of at least α. Hence, for such pairs we perform a less precise matching, where we check whether the token set ratio and the token set partial ratio of their class names are equivalent, and whether both class names share a non-empty longest common starting substring. We then add a connection between a pair of nodes, if these two properties are fulfilled. JavaWuzzy computes the token set ratio by tokenising the strings and comparing their intersection and remainder. The partial token set ratio is identical to the token set ration, except that the partial token set ratio matches based on the best substrings (e.g. the best partial match from a set of matching tokens), whereas the token set ratio matches based on pure Levenshtein Distance.

Finally, after adding the connections to the call graph, we extract the connected components. The connected components of a graph are the set of largest subgraphs of which every subgraph is connected, where connected means that there is a path from any point in the graph to any other point in the graph. As a result, a connected component represents a library, e.g. a subgraph that is connected and yet independent from the other subgraphs, similar to the concept of a library included inside an Android application. For every connected component we compute the cardinality-based cosine set similarity between the set of all possible categories and the set of categories for the node of the connected component with the highest number of attributes (including its children's

---

[2] https://github.com/xdrop/fuzzywuzzy.

attributes). The cardinality-based cosine set similarity is computed as follows, where A and B are sets of categories:

$$cos(A, B) = \frac{|A \cap B|}{\sqrt{|A| \times |B|}}$$

A connected component must have a cosine set similarity score of at least δ in order to be considered as a library with potential fingerprinting-alike behaviour. *Limitations.* Obviously, as FP-Sherlock is a static analysis tool that relies on comparing strings, it inherits certain limitations such as dynamic code loading or string encryption. Although, none of the studied fingerprinting libraries made use of such techniques at the time of writting.

Library Matching. In this last step, we compare the extracted libraries with previously analysed libraries in order to search for identical libraries. This can be useful in order to match obfuscated with non-obfuscated libraries and extract their non-obfuscated class names. We use a greedy library matching algorithm (see Algorithm 1) in order to compare two libraries. As previously stated, libraries are represented as connected components, hence graphs. The algorithm matches libraries by matching nodes. We match nodes based on attributes, the attributes of both nodes' parents and the attributes of both nodes children. We did not consider graph isomorphism as we want to preserve permutation between nodes. If a graph matches a previously analysed graph, we extract the longest common starting substring amongst the class names of its nodes and append it to the list of candidate names for that particular graph. If there is no match, we store the graph and create a new list of candidates names for that particular graph, appending its longest common starting substring as a first candidate. We store the graphs and the lists of candidate names in a MongoDB database for subsequent analysis.

4.2   Experiment: Scanning 30,000 Applications

As mentioned above, we downloaded a set of free top-rated applications from the Google Play store ($\sim$30,000 apps) as of July 2017. We scanned this corpus with FP-Sherlock, using $\delta = 0.75$ and $\alpha = 0.75$. We ran a single instance of FP-Sherlock on a customer grade computer with a dual core CPU and 16 GB of RAM. With these settings we were able to scan our corpus in approximately 8 hours ($\sim$1 second per app). We uncovered 150 candidate fingerprinting libraries. Of these, we analysed the six most popular ones in terms of occurrences in our corpus: *Amazon Mobile Ads, Chartboost, INFOnline, Kochava, Kontagent* and *Tapjoy.* More details about these six libraries, are condensed in Table 1.

Algorithm 1. A greedy library matching algorithm

```
 1: function MATCHGRAPHS(G_1, G_2)
 2:     if |G_1.nodes()| ≠ |G_2.nodes()| or |G_1.edges()| ≠ |G_2.edges()| then
 3:         return False
 4:     matched ← {}
 5:     for every node n_1 ∈ G_1.nodes() do
 6:         found ← False
 7:         for every node n_2 ∈ G_2.nodes() do
 8:             if n_2 ∉ visited and n_1.attributes() = n_2.attributes() then
 9:                 if MATCHNODELIST(n_1.parents(), n_2.parents()) and
10:                     MATCHNODELIST(n_1.children(), n_2.children()) then
11:                         matched ← matched ∪ {n_2}
12:                         found ← True
13:                         break
14:         if not found then
15:             return False
16:     return True

17: function MATCHNODELIST(N_1, N_2)
18:     if |N_1| ≠ |N_2| then
19:         return False
20:     matched ← {}
21:     for every node n_1 ∈ N_1 do
22:         found ← False
23:         for every node n_2 ∈ N_2 do
24:             if n_2 ∉ matched and n_1.attributes() = n_2.attributes() then
25:                 matched ← matched ∪ {n_2}
26:                 found ← True
27:                 break
28:         if not found then
29:             return False
30:     return True
```

Table 1. List of most popular libraries and their package names.

Library	Category	Package name
Amazon (AZ)	Ads/Analytics	com.amazon.device.ads
Chartboost (CB)	Ads/Analytics	com.chartboost.sdk
INFOnline (IN)	Ads/Analytics	de.infonline.lib
Kochava (KC)	Ads/Analytics	com.kochava.android
Kontagent (KA)	Ads/Analytics	com.kontagent.fingerprint
Tapjoy (TJ)	Ads/Analytics	com.tapjoy.connect

Table 2. Permissions required by the analysed libraries.

Permission	Protection	IO	TM	TJ	AZ	IN	CB	KA	KC
INTERNET	*Normal*	✓	✓	✓	✓	✓	✓	✓	✓
READ_PHONE_STATE	*Dangerous*	✓	✓	✓	✓	✓	✓	✓	✓
ACCESS_WIFI_STATE	*Normal*	✓		✓	✓	✓	✓	✓	
ACCESS_NETWORK_STATE	*Normal*			✓	✓	✓	✓		
ACCESS_COARSE_LOCATION	*Dangerous*	✓	✓		✓				✓
ACCESS_FINE_LOCATION	*Dangerous*	✓	✓		✓				✓
BLUETOOTH	*Normal*	✓							
GET_ACCOUNTS	*Dangerous*	✓							

5   Analysis of Fingerprinting-Alike Libraries

We manually analysed the source code of every library using JADX[3], a DEX to Java decompiler with a GUI. For each of the analysed libraries, both those by fingerprinters as well as those uncovered by FP-Sherlock, we determined which permissions are necessary (cf. Table 2). Note that permissions with protection level "normal" are automatically granted by the system, whereas those with protection level "dangerous" must be actively granted by the user.

Once a library is called upon to gather a fingerprint, it typically operates in two or three phases, as shown below. The remainder of this section is structured along these three phases.

1. An optional initialisation phase, during which additional configuration may be loaded from a remote server;
2. A collection phase during which attribute values are collected; and
3. A submission phase, during which the accumulated fingerprint is transmitted back to a designated collection point, typically a server of the party that developed the library.

5.1   Initialization Phase

The ThreatMetrix library is the sole library (of those investigated) that contacts an external server before gathering attributes. It requests an XML file containing configuration information. This seems to be a way to include experimental attributes, such as novel checks for packages which indicate if the device has been rooted or to test for emulators by giving a list of phone numbers and IMEI numbers (a per-device unique number) known to be used in emulators.

---

[3] https://github.com/skylot/jadx.

5.2 Collection Phase

This section discusses our findings on the collection of attributes by the eight studied libraries and compares them to Wu et al.'s permissionless fingerprinter [15], which was based on implicit identifiers. The attributes collected by the libraries are shown in Table 5.

Inclusion of Other Fingerprinting Libraries. During our manual analysis of Tapjoy's source code, we noticed that Tapjoy includes the ThreatMetrix fingerprinting library and combines it together with its own fingerprint.

Collection of Explicit Identifiers. Wu et al. [15] focused on implicit identifiers and therefore did not consider explicit identifiers. However, as one can see in Table 5, known fingerprinting companies such as Iovation and ThreatMetrix make extensive use of identifiers such as the Android ID, IMEI, Bluetooth and WiFi MAC addresses, etc. Note that not all explicit identifiers necessarily require a permission. For example, ThreatMetrix, Tapjoy and Amazon obtain the device hardware serial via `android.os.Build.SERIAL`, whereas access to this identifier does not require any permission while it can be used as a unique device identifier.

Attributes Relevant for Cross-Device Tracking. Of particular interest is Iovation's access to certain attributes: WiFi's SSID (network name), BSSID (MAC address of the base station), list of user accounts, phone number, subscriber ID and SIM serial number. Especially user account information may contain personally identifiable information (PII), such as username, that may link the device to external accounts (such as Facebook, Google, etc.). Obviously, all this information together can be used for cross-device tracking.

Context Checks. Iovation and ThreatMetrix have some checks that consider the integrity and the environment of its hosting application. For instance, Threat-Metrix gathers some attributes in two different ways (via Java API and JNI) enabling them to detect inconsistencies. Both libraries check if the device is rooted or running inside an emulator by checking for instance the existence of installed binaries such as `/system/xbin/su`. Interestingly enough, Iovation search for installed applications that have the ACCESS_MOCK_LOCATION permission. This permission allows an application to override the current location with a fake location. Moreover, Iovation checks the signature on the hosting application. If this was re-signed, this probably indicates the hosting application has been potentially modified. Also, Iovation checks the `isUserAMonkey()` method. This method returns *true* if the user interface is undergoing structured testing by a program (e.g. a 'monkey'). Finally, Iovation checks wether the hosting application has the debug flag set, which should not occur in production runs.

Location Fallback Methods. In Table 5 we see that Iovation requests the cell ID and the location area code (*Localisation*: GSM/CDMA CID & LAC). Combined with the locale country and operator name, these attributes allow Iovation to derive a so-called "Global Cell-ID". This ID determines the specific cell in which a mobile device is located world-wide, without relying on GPS.

Device Uptime. Iovation and ThreatMetrix derive the timestamp when the device was last booted, by subtracting the device's uptime from the current time. We suspect that this is because these companies found the timestamp of the last boot to have a high entropy. Note that we cannot verify this suspicion, since to the best of our knowledge, none of the published works on attribute entropy in Android devices consider device uptime.

Browser Properties. ThreatMetrix gathers a list of installed browser plugins and mime-types via Javascript injected inside a WebView. This is rather bizarre as we suspect WebViews to have no browser plugins installed and to share the same set of mime-types.

Inference of Installed Applications. Iovation abuses a method intended as an easter egg by Google (i.e. `UserManager.isUserAGoat()`) in order to check if a specific goat simulator package is installed. ThreatMetrix scans every 60 seconds for newly installed non-system applications on the device as well as a list of running processes. Tapjoy checks whether two alternative application markets are installed on the device: Gfan (a Chinese application market) and SK Telekom (a South Korean application market). Tapjoy also checks for the presence of four specific social sharing applications: Facebook, Twitter, Google+ and LinkedIn, thus inferring in which social networks the user is present.

Proxy Detection. Iovation tries to detect if the user is using a proxy for FTP, HTTP, and HTTPS. It does so by calling the method `ProxySelector.getDefault().select(<url>).toString()`, for the three URLs: ftp://www.example.com/, http://www.example.com/ and https://www.example.com/.

Font Enumeration. ThreatMetrix attempts to get the list of system fonts, first via JNI, failing that, via Java, looking in the `/system/fonts` directory for all files having the `.ttf` extension. Note that this is not equivalent to font list probing – in desktop browsers, the font list is not directly accessible, but may be partially determined by checking whether specific fonts are present. Conversely, on Android systems, the list of fonts is directly accessible. Moreover, Wu et al. found that the lists of fonts in Android devices does not provide a great amount of entropy, in contrast to font lists on desktop computers.

Storage Capacity. Similar to Wu et al., Iovation and ThreatMetrix compute the capacity of the internal and external storage by multiplying block size with block count. ThreatMetrix goes further by also computing the available space left on the internal storage.

Battery Characteristics. Iovation gathers information about the current battery level and whether the device is currently plugged to a power source. Olejnik et al. [10] have shown that the HTML5 Battery Status API exposes a fingerprint-able surface that can be used to track web users in short time intervals.

CPU and Memory Characteristics. Iovation and ThreatMetrix, both gather information about the CPU and Memory by reading `/proc/cpuinfo` and `/proc/meminfo` respectively. Moreover, Threatmetrix extracts the BogoMips value per CPU core. The BogoMips (from 'bogus' and MIPS) is an unscientific measurement of CPU speed made during boot.

Camera Characteristics. Iovation gathers characteristics of all built-in cameras. In particular, it gathers the values of INFO_SUPPORTED_ HARDWARE_ LEVEL and SENSOR_CALIBRATION_TRANSFORM1 for every camera.

5.3   Submission Phase

After collection, the gathered data is sent back to the back-end. Thankfully, all studied libraries make use of HTTPS to submit the gathered data. Nikiforakis et al. [9] found two scenarios for communicating browser fingerprints: by an included third party without involvement of the first party, or explicitly upon the request of the first party. In our analysis, we find exactly the same two scenarios in the mobile domain. While the top six investigated libraries do not require interaction with the host application developer, the libraries by ThreatMetrix and Iovation take a different approach. These two libraries operate on the explicit request of the hosting application, and provide the gathered user identity to the hosting application. In contrast, the top six libraries are advertising and analytics libraries that do not offer explicit identification services to applications, and therefore do not have to communicate an identity back to the developer. In the remainder of the submission section, we thus focus on the submission processes of Iovation and ThreatMetrix.

Iovation. Iovation is the odd library out, as it does not explicitly submit the fingerprint to its own back-end, but leaves this to the app developers. These thus have to set up and maintain a back-end server which gathers and forwards the fingerprints to Iovation's back-end. This also explains why Iovation was not in the ICSI Panopticon dataset. Iovation's fingerprinting library encrypts its fingerprints (using AES in CBC mode without padding) via a hard-coded key that is identical across all applications that include Iovation. Moreover, Iovation uses a random initialisation vector, which is concatenated in clear to the AES output. The input to AES is a concatenation of all the collected attributes, starting with the magic number "0500". In order to collect a fingerprint, the hosting application typically calls Iovation's method `DevicePrint.getBlackbox()`. This method returns a base64 encoded version of the encrypted string. Application developers explicitly do not know about the AES encryption, nor about the key used for encryption. Thus, app developers must submit the collected fingerprints back to Iovation if they are to be used. This delivery mechanism not only permits Iovation to hide their implementation details and to bill their customers, but this also allows Iovation to remain undetected towards traffic analysis tools such as the ICSI Panopticon.

ThreatMetrix. In contrast to Iovation's fingerprinting library, ThreatMetrix communicates its fingerprint directly to its back-end servers. The fingerprint is submitted via a web beacon, a 1 × 1 pixel image hosted at https://h.online-metrix.net/fp/clear.png. ThreatMetrix follows the same approach to submit fingerprints via its browser fingerprinting scripts. The body of the request contains the fingerprint, as the parameter "ja". The fingerprint is "encrypted" by XOR'ing it with the session_id. The HTTP Referer header contains the package name of the host application. In addition to submitting the fingerprint, ThreatMetrix also submits an HTTP cookie (thx_guid) to its own back-end servers. This cookie includes a unique identifier that is based on the Android ID of the mobile device. The developer can request any information about the user from ThreatMetrix's back-end servers via the session_id.

6   Adoption of Investigated Libraries

We investigated the adoption of the investigated libraries across popular Android applications. Fingerprinting-alike behaviour turns out to be much more common in Android applications than on the web (see e.g. Acar et al.'s study [1]) We found 5.917 unique applications that include at least one of the eight studied libraries, hence 19% of our dataset. Our findings are summarised in Table 3. Using the classification from the Google Play Store, we state that the majority of the investigated fingerprinting libraries can be found inside games with the following categories: *Action, Casino, Casual, Racing* and *Games*, whereas the five app categories with the least library occurrences are: *Events, Art & Design, Business, Maps and Navigation* and *Libraries & Demo.*

Table 3. Prevalence of fingerprinting-alike libraries in popular applications from the Google Play Store.

Library	# Apps	# Installs			
		[0, 10K)	[10K, 100K)	[100K, 1M)	[1M, +∞)
Chartboost	4493	188	633	1564	2108
Amazon	1428	85	204	492	647
Tapjoy	1204	42	132	350	680
ThreatMetrix	471	3	22	123	323
Kochava	221	4	12	49	156
INFOnline	220	18	66	78	58
Kontagent	54	0	0	15	39
Iovation	12	0	1	1	10
	5917 *unique*				

Table 4. Prevalence of identified libraries in applications subject to COPPA.

Library	# Apps subject to COPPA
Chartboost	13
Tapjoy	6
Kochava	5
Amazon mobile ads	3
ThreatMetrix	2
INFOnline	0
Iovation	0
Kontagent	0
	21 *unique*

Adoption Amongst Apps Targeted at Children. Collecting children's personal information without parental consent is illegal in the USA under the *Children's Online Privacy Protection Act* (COPPA) [2]. In particular, collection of personally identifiable information of children is mostly prohibited, and exceptions are only allowed under "verifiable parental consent". Where a recent study by Reyes et al. [11] searched for any COPPA violations in their data set, we explicitly limit ourselves to the previously analysed libraries. Therefore, we do not need to encode COPPA regulations into a scanner.

We identified 21 applications from Play Store categories *5 & Under* and *6–8* (both clearly subject to COPPA) that used one or more of the analysed libraries. Only three of the eight investigated libraries were not present (cf. Table 4).

The question of whether or not the observed behaviour is a violation of COPPA is a legal matter beyond the scope of this paper. That notwithstanding, we hold the view that apps explicitly aimed at children should sidestep this question by not engaging in fingerprinting-alike behaviour at all.

7 Conclusions and Future Work

We reverse-engineered two commercial fingerprinting libraries for Android apps and analysed their behaviour. We expected these libraries to reuse techniques that their creators apply for fingerprinting browsers but, to our surprise, we did not encounter this. We also expected to find typical fingerprinting techniques such as canvas fingerprinting, but found no such techniques. These commercial authentication libraries apparently do not need such techniques to be certain about a user's identity – collecting a large set of attribute values and some unique identifiers apparently suffices. This implies that there is quite some authenticating information to be gleaned from the collected attribute values.

With this in mind, we set out to identify other libraries that gather similar amounts of attribute values. We designed and implemented *FP-Sherlock*, a static scanner for fingerprint-alike behaviour. FP-Sherlock is based on the notions of *diversity* and *accumulation*, which provide a necessary but incomplete characterisation of fingerprint behaviour.

We applied FP-Sherlock to a corpus of ~30,000 applications and found several candidate fingerprinters. Of these, we reverse-engineered the six most popular libraries (i.e., with the highest usage rate in our corpus). We were able to establish a lower bound on mobile device fingerprinting-alike behaviour that is vastly higher than browser fingerprinting: 5,917 out of 30,695 or 19.28%. In contrast, recent studies into browser fingerprinting prevalence find between 0.4% and 1.4% adoption rate amongst popular websites. While the found behaviour lacks the telltale signs of fingerprinting present in browser fingerprinters, the amount of data gathered by these libraries is clearly unwarranted and exceeds the bounds of reason. We believe that neither users nor app developers are aware of this data gathering, let alone of the scale of this.

Moreover, we investigated how many apps targeted at children include one of the studied libraries. Tracking children is (in general) subject to stricter legal restrictions than tracking adults. In our dataset, we found 21 apps targeted at children that included one or more of the studied libraries. Two of the used libraries explicitly fingerprint, and thus definitely should fall under tracking restrictions.

Future Work. Future work focuses on three aspects. First of all, we are currently developing a framework to repeat Eckersley's study of attribute entropy [3] for mobile devices. Secondly, we are looking to improving and automating the detection of fingerprinters, using machine learning techniques. Thirdly, countering fingerprinters seems more challenging than for web browsers, as some fingerprinters piggyback on the first-party. Solution approaches based on guided randomization at level of the Android API should be further investigated.

A   A Detailed Taxonomy of Attributes Used by Fingerprinting-Alike Libraries

Table 5. A detailed taxonomy comparing all the attributes used by the studied libraries.

Category	Attribute	Authentication			Advertising/analytics					
		[15]	IO	TM	TJ	AZ	IN	CB	KA	KC
Applications	List of installed applications	✓	✓	✓ (JAVA/JNI)	✓					✓
	App/package name		✓	✓	✓	✓	✓	✓	✓	✓
	App/package version		✓		✓	✓	✓	✓	✓	✓
	App/package hash			✓	✚					
	App/package signatures		✓							
	Debug flag		✓							
	Is user a goat/monkey		✓							
	List of special files & Properties			✓ (JAVA/JNI)	✚					
	List of running processes			✓ (JAVA/JNI)	✚					
	Usage of alternative app markets				✓					
	List of social sharing services				✓					

(continued)

Table 5. (*continued*)

Category	Attribute	Authentication			Advertising/analytics					
		[15]	IO	TM	TJ	AZ	IN	CB	KA	KC
Carrier	SIM operator name (P)		✓				✓	✓		
	SIM operator country (P)		✓	✓	✛		✓			
	Network operator name (P)		✓	✓	✓	✓	✓	✓	✓	✓
	Network operator country (P)		✓		✓			✓		
	MSISDN (phone number) (P)		✔							
	IMSI (subscriber ID) (P)		✔							
	SIM serial number (P)		✔							
Device	Manufacturer	✓	✓	✓	✓	✓	✓	✓		
	Brand		✓	✓	✛		✓			✓
	Model	✓	✓	✓	✓	✓	✓	✓	✓	✓
	Product		✓	✓	✛		✓	✓		
	Device build		✓	✓	✛		✓		✓	
	IMEI (device ID) (P)		✔	✔	✔		✔			
	Uptime		✓	✓	✛					
Hardware	Screen resolution	✓	✓	✓	✓	✓	✓	✓	✓	✓
	Screen orientation		✓		✓	✓	✓	✓		
	Internal storage capacity	✓	✓	✓	✛					
	External storage capacity	✓	✓							
	Available internal storage			✓	✛					
	Battery information		✓							
	Proximity sensor		✓							
	CPU information		✓	✓	✛					
	RAM information		✓	✓	✛					
	Hardware build							✓		
	Hardware serial		✔		✔	✔				
	Camera information		✓							
Identifiers	**Android ID**		✔	✔	✔	✔	✔	✔	✔	✔
	Google play advertising ID (P)				✔	✔	✔	✔	✔	✔
	Facebook attribution ID								✔	✔
Localisation	Locale country			✓	✓	✓	✓	✓		
	Locale currency		✓							
	Locale language	✓	✓	✓	✓	✓	✓	✓	✓	
	Timezone	✓	✓	✓	✛			✓		
	Time & date format	✓								
	Geolocation (P)		✓	✓	✛	✓				✓
	GSM/CDMA CID & LAC (P)		✓							
Network	Local IP addresses		✓					✓		
	Local hostname		✓							
	Connection type (P)				✓	✓	✓	✓		
	WiFi MAC address (P)		✔		✔	✔	✔	✔	✔	

(*continued*)

Table 5. (*continued*)

Category	Attribute	Authentication			Advertising/analytics					
		[15]	IO	TM	TJ	AZ	IN	CB	KA	KC
	WiFi SSID (P)		✓							
	WiFi BSSID (P)		✓							✓
	Bluetooth MAC address (P)		✔							
	List of available proxies		✓							
Operating system	OS name		✓	✓	✓	✓	✓	✓	✓	✓
	OS version		✓	✓	✓	✓	✓	✓		✓
	Root status	✓	✓ (JNI)	✓ (JAVA/JNI)	+		✓			
	Is an emulator		✓		✓		✓			
	Kernel information	✓	✓							
	API level		✓						✓	
	Build ID		✓							
	Build display		✓	✓						
	Build fingerprint		✓							
	Build host		✓							
	Build time		✓							
	User-agent	✓		✓ (JAVA/JS)	+	✓				✓
	System storage structure	✓								
	Root directory structure	✓								
	Input methods	✓								
	System font size	✓								
	List of system fonts	✓		✓ (JAVA/JNI)	+					
Settings	Automatic time sync	✓								
	Automatic timezone selection	✓								
	Time of screen locking	✓								
	Notify WiFi availability	✓								
	Policy of WiFi sleeping	✓								
	Lock pattern enabled/visible	✓								
	Phone unlocking vibration	✓								
	Sound effects enabled	✓								
	Show password in text editors	✓								
	Screen brightness mode	✓								
	Is device orientation locked	✓								
	Current wallpaper	✓								
	List of default ringtones	✓	✓							
	Install non market apps		✓							
	Granted permissions		✓		✓					✓
	List of user accounts (P)		✓							
	HTTP proxy settings		✓							
	System volume									✓

(*continued*)

Table 5. (*continued*)

		Authentication			Advertising/analytics					
Category	Attribute	[15]	IO	TM	TJ	AZ	IN	CB	KA	KC
Web view	List of Plugins			✔ (JS)	✛					
	List of mime-types			✔ (JS)	✛					

✔: Explicit identifier that by itself is sufficient to uniquely identify a device.
✛: Attribute collaterally called via the ThreatMetrix SDK.
(P): Attribute requires a permission in order to be retrieved.
(JS): Value retrieved via JavaScript Interface (allowing calls to JavaScript objects).
(JNI): Value retrieved via Java Native Interface (allowing calls to native methods written in C/C++).
(JAVA/JNI): Value retrieved via Java and Java Native Interface.
(JAVA/JS): Value retrieved via Java and JavaScript Interface.

References

1. Acar, G., Juarez, M., Nikiforakis, N., Diaz, C., Gürses, S., Piessens, F., Preneel, B.: FPDetective: dusting the web for fingerprinters. In: Proceedings of the 2013 ACM SIGSAC Conference on Computer and Communications Security (CCS 2013), pp. 1129–1140. ACM (2013)
2. Children's Online Privacy Protection Act of 1998 (COPPA). United States federal law, 15 U.S.C. §§ 6501–6506, Pub.L. 105–277, 112 Stat. 2681-728, enacted October 21, 1998
3. Eckersley, P.: How unique is your web browser? In: Atallah, M.J., Hopper, N.J. (eds.) PETS 2010. LNCS, vol. 6205, pp. 1–18. Springer, Heidelberg (2010). https://doi.org/10.1007/978-3-642-14527-8_1
4. Hupperich, T., Maiorca, D., Kührer, M., Holz, T., Giacinto, G.: On the robustness of mobile device fingerprinting: can mobile users escape modern web-tracking mechanisms? In: Proceedings of the 31st Annual Computer Security Applications Conference (ACSAC 2015), pp. 191–200. ACM (2015)
5. Kurtz, A., Gascon, H., Becker, T., Rieck, K., Freiling, F.: Fingerprinting mobile devices using personalized configurations. Proc. Priv. Enhanc. Technol. (PETS) **2016**(1), 4–19 (2016)
6. Laperdrix, P., Rudametkin, W., Baudry, B.: Beauty and the beast: diverting modern web browsers to build unique browser fingerprints. In: Proceedings of the 2016 IEEE Symposium on Security and Privacy (S&P 2016), pp. 878–894. IEEE (2016)
7. Mayer, J.R., Mitchell, J.C.: Third-party web tracking: policy and technology. In: Proceedings of the 2012 IEEE Symposium on Security and Privacy (S&P 2012), pp. 413–427. IEEE (2012)
8. Mowery, K., Shacham, H.: Pixel perfect: fingerprinting canvas in HTML5. In: Proceedings of 2012 Workshop on Web 2.0 Security and Privacy (W2SP 2012), pp. 1–12. IEEE (2012)
9. Nikiforakis, N., Kapravelos, A., Joosen, W., Kruegel, C., Piessens, F., Vigna, G.: Cookieless monster: exploring the ecosystem of web-based device fingerprinting. In: Proceedings of the 2013 IEEE Symposium on Security and privacy (S&P 2013), pp. 541–555. IEEE (2013)

10. Olejnik, Ł., Acar, G., Castelluccia, C., Diaz, C.: The leaking battery. In: Garcia-Alfaro, J., Navarro-Arribas, G., Aldini, A., Martinelli, F., Suri, N. (eds.) DPM/QASA -2015. LNCS, vol. 9481, pp. 254–263. Springer, Cham (2016). https://doi.org/10.1007/978-3-319-29883-2_18

11. Reyes, I., Wijesekera, P., Reardon, J., On, A.E.B., Razaghpanah, A., Vallina-Rodriguez, N., Egelman, S.: "Won't somebody think of the children?" Examining coppa compliance at scale. PoPETs **2018**(3), 63–83 (2018)

12. Spooren, J., Preuveneers, D., Joosen, W.: Mobile device fingerprinting considered harmful for risk-based authentication. In: Proceedings of the Eighth European Workshop on System Security (EuroSec 2015), pp. 6:1–6:6. ACM (2015)

13. Torres, C.F., Jonker, H., Mauw, S.: *FP-Block*: usable web privacy by controlling browser fingerprinting. In: Pernul, G., Ryan, P.Y.A., Weippl, E. (eds.) ESORICS 2015. LNCS, vol. 9327, pp. 3–19. Springer, Cham (2015). https://doi.org/10.1007/978-3-319-24177-7_1

14. Vallina-Rodriguez, N., Sundaresan, S., Razaghpanah, A., Nithyanand, R., Allman, M., Kreibich, C., Gill, P.: Tracking the trackers: towards understanding the mobile advertising and tracking ecosystem. CoRR abs/1609.07190 (2016)

15. Wu, W., Wu, J., Wang, Y., Ling, Z., Yang, M.: Efficient fingerprinting-based android device identification with zero-permission identifiers. IEEE Access **4**, 8073–8083 (2016)

Database and Web Security

Towards Efficient Verifiable Conjunctive Keyword Search for Large Encrypted Database

Jianfeng Wang[1], Xiaofeng Chen[1](✉), Shi-Feng Sun[2,3], Joseph K. Liu[2], Man Ho Au[4], and Zhi-Hui Zhan[5]

[1] State Key Laboratory of Integrated Service Networks (ISN), Xidian University, Xi'an, China
{jfwang,xfchen}@xidian.edu.cn
[2] Faculty of Information Technology, Monash University, Melbourne, Australia
{shifeng.sun,joseph.liu}@monash.edu
[3] Data 61, CSIRO, Melbourne, Australia
shifeng.sun@data61.csiro.au
[4] Department of Computing, The Hong Kong Polytechnic University, Hong Kong, China
csallen@comp.polyu.edu.hk
[5] School of Computer Science and Engineering, South China University of Technology, Guangzhou, China
cszhanzhh@scut.edu.cn

Abstract. Searchable Symmetric Encryption (SSE) enables a client to securely outsource large encrypted database to a server while supporting efficient keyword search. Most of the existing works are designed against the honest-but-curious server. That is, the server will be curious but execute the protocol in an honest manner. Recently, some researchers presented various verifiable SSE schemes that can resist to the malicious server, where the server may not honestly perform all the query operations. However, they either only considered single-keyword search or cannot handle very large database. To address this challenge, we propose a new verifiable conjunctive keyword search scheme by leveraging accumulator. Our proposed scheme can not only ensure verifiability of search result even if an empty set is returned but also support efficient conjunctive keyword search with sublinear overhead. Besides, the verification cost of our construction is independent of the size of search result. In addition, we introduce a sample check method for verifying the completeness of search result with a high probability, which can significantly reduce the computation cost on the client side. Security and efficiency evaluation demonstrate that the proposed scheme not only can achieve high security goals but also has a comparable performance.

Keywords: Searchable encryption · Verifiable search · Conjunctive keyword search · Accumulator

1 Introduction

Cloud computing, as a promising computing paradigm, offers seemly unbounded data storage capability and computation resource in a pay-as-you-go manner.

© Springer Nature Switzerland AG 2018
J. Lopez et al. (Eds.): ESORICS 2018, LNCS 11099, pp. 83–100, 2018.
https://doi.org/10.1007/978-3-319-98989-1_5

More and more resource-constrained users trend to move their own data into the cloud so that they can enjoy superior data storage services without data maintenance overheads locally. Despite its tremendous benefits, data outsourcing suffers from some security and privacy concerns [10,12,23]. One main challenge is the secrecy of outsourced data [11]. That is, the cloud server should not learn any useful information about the private data. For example, it has been reported recently that up to 87 million users' private information in Facebook is leaked to the Cambridge Analytica firm [26]. Although traditional encryption technology can guarantee the confidentiality of outsourced data, it heavily impedes the ability of searching over outsourced data [22].

A promising solution, called Searchable Symmetric Encryption (SSE), has attracted considerable interest from both academic and industrial community. SSE enables a data owner to outsource encrypted data to the cloud server while reserving searchability. Specifically, the data owner encrypts data with his private key before outsourcing and then stores the ciphertext associated with some metadata (e.g., indices) into the cloud server. Upon receiving a search token, the server performs the search operation and returns all the matched results to the user. The primitive of SSE has been widely studied [5,7,13,16,18,20,28]. Note that the above works only consider single-keyword search. To enhance the search availability, SSE supporting conjunctive keyword search has been extensively studied [3,6,17,27]. However, those schemes either suffer from low search efficiency or leak too much information on the queried keyword. Recently, Cash et al. [8] presented the first sublinear SSE scheme with support for conjunctive keyword search, named OXT. In their construction, the search complexity is linear with the matched document of the least frequent keyword, which makes it adaptable to the large database setting. There are different extensions of OXT subsequently. Sun et al. [29] extended this scheme to a multi-user setting, in which any authorized user can submit a search query and retrieve the matched documents. Following that, a fast decryption improvement has been given in [34]. Another multi-user scheme has been proposed in [19] by using a threshold approach. Zuo et al. [35] gave another extension supporting general Boolean queries. Note that all the above works are constructed in the honest-but-curious cloud model, where the cloud server is assumed to honestly perform all search operations.

In practice however, the cloud server may be malicious, since it may return an incorrect and/or incomplete search result for selfish reasons. According to Veritas [31], 28% of organizations admit to suffering from permanent data loss in the past three years. Thus, in order to resist to malicious server, verifiable SSE attracted more and more attention [2,4,9,25,30]. Azraoui et al. [2] proposed a publicly verifiable conjunctive keyword search scheme by integrating Cuckoo hashing and polynomial-based accumulators. The main idea is that the server performs search for each individual keyword and then computes the intersection of all the matched document subsets. The drawback of this method is that the search cost increases linear with the entire database size and reveals more intra-query leakage information, such as access pattern on each distinct keyword in a conjunction query. Recently, Bost et al. [4] proposed an efficient verifiable

SSE scheme by using verifiable hash table. Nevertheless, their solution can just support verifiable single keyword search. To our best knowledge, how to simultaneously achieve verifiability of the search result and efficient conjunctive keyword search on large database remains a challenge problem.

1.1 Our Contribution

In this paper, we focus on verifiable conjunctive keyword search scheme for large encrypted database. Our contribution can be summarized as follows:

- We propose a new verifiable conjunctive keyword search scheme based on accumulator, which can ensure correctness and completeness of search result even if an empty set is returned. The search cost of the proposed scheme depends on the number of documents matching with the least frequent keyword, which is independent of the entire database.
- The proposed scheme can achieve verifiability of the search result with constant size communication overhead between the client and server. That is, the server returns a constant size proof (i.e., *witness*) of the search result, and the client is able to check the correctness of the search result with a constant computation overhead. In addition, we introduce a sample check method to check the completeness of search result, which can achieve low false-positive by checking only a fraction of the search result and reduce the computation overhead on the client side.
- We present a formal security analysis of our proposed construction and also provide a thorough implementation of it on a real-world dataset. The experiment results demonstrate that our proposed construction can achieve the desired property with a comparable computation overhead.

1.2 Related Work

Song et al. [28] proposed the first SSE scheme, in which the document is encrypted word by word. As a result, the search cost grows linear with the size of database. Goh [16] constructed a search index for each document to improve the search efficiency. However, the search complexity is linear with the number of documents. Curtmola et al. [13] introduced the first sublinear SSE scheme, in which an inverted index is generated based on all distinct keyword. Kamara et al. [18] extended [13] to support dynamic search. Subsequently, a line of research focused on dynamic search [5,7,20]. In order to enrich query expressiveness, Golle et al. [17] presented the first secure conjunctive keyword search scheme. The search complexity is linear with the number of documents in the whole database. Later, some work [3,6,27] are proposed to enhance the search efficiency. However, those solutions can only support search on the structured data. In 2013, Cash et al. [8] proposed the first sublinear SSE scheme supporting conjunctive keyword search, which can be used to perform search on structured data as well as free text. The search complexity is only linear in the number of documents which contain the least frequency keyword among the queried keywords. Thus, it is suitable to deploy in large-scale database setting. Recently, Sun et al. [29] extended this scheme to multi-user setting. That is, it not only support for the data owner but also an arbitrary authorized user to perform search.

Chai et al. [9] first considered verifiable search in malicious server model and presented a verifiable keyword search scheme based on the character tree. However, the proposed scheme can only support the exact keyword search in plaintext scenario. Kurosawa and Ohtaki [21] proposed the first verifiable SSE scheme to support the verifiability of the correctness of search result. Wang et al. [33] presented a verifiable fuzzy keyword search scheme, which can simultaneously achieve fuzzy keyword search and verifiability query. Recently, plenty of works [4,25,32] were dedicated to give a valid proof when the search result is an empty set. That is, when the search query has no matched result, the client can verify whether there is actually no matched result or it is a malicious behavior. Note that all the above-mentioned solutions are focused on single keyword search. Sun et al. [30] proposed a verifiable SSE scheme for conjunctive keyword search based on accumulator. However, their construction cannot work when the server purposely returned an empty set. Similarly, Azraoui et al. [2] presented a verifiable conjunctive keyword search scheme which support public verifiability of search result.

1.3   Organization

The rest of this paper is organized as follows. We present some preliminaries in Sect. 2. The verifiable conjunctive-keyword search scheme is proposed in Sect. 3. Section 4 presents the formal security analysis of the proposed construction. Its performance evaluation is given in Sect. 5. Finally, the conclusion is given in Sect. 6.

2   Preliminaries

In this section, we first present some notations (as shown in Table 1) and basic cryptographic primitives that are used in this work. We then present the formal security definition.

2.1   Bilinear Pairings

Let $\mathbb{G}$ and $\mathbb{G}_T$ be two cyclic multiplicative groups of prime order p, and g be a generator of $\mathbb{G}$. A bilinear pairing is a mapping $e : \mathbb{G} \times \mathbb{G} \rightarrow \mathbb{G}_T$ with the following properties:

1. Bilinearity: $e(u^a, v^b) = e(u, v)^{ab}$ for all $u, v \in \mathbb{G}$, and $a, b \in \mathbb{Z}_p$;
2. Non-degeneracy: $e(g, g) \neq 1$, where 1 represents the identity of group $\mathbb{G}_T$;
3. Computability: there exists an algorithm to efficient compute $e(u, v)$ for any $u, v \in \mathbb{G}$.

Table 1. Notations.

Notations	Meaning
λ	Security parameter of the system
ind_i	Identifier of the i-th file
W_i	Keyword list of ind_i
$\mathrm{W} = \cup_{i=1}^{T} \mathrm{W}_i$	Keyword set of the whole database
$\mathrm{DB} = (\mathrm{ind}_i, \mathrm{W}_i)_{i=1}^{T}$	The representation of the whole database
$F : \{0,1\}^\lambda \times \{0,1\}^\lambda \mapsto \{0,1\}^\lambda$	A pseudo-random function
$F_p : \{0,1\}^\lambda \times \{0,1\}^\lambda \mapsto Z_p^*$	A pseudo-random function mapped into group Z_p^*
stag_w	Trapdoor of a given keyword w
Stag	Trapdoors of all the keywords in a search query
$\mathbf{e}_w$	File identifiers contain keyword w
$Acc(S)$	Accumulator value for the set S
$\mathrm{W}_{x,S}$	The proof of membership of element x for set S
$\hat{\mathrm{W}}_{x,S}$	The proof of non-membership of element x for set S
Td	The user's search token with a set of keywords
R_{w_1}	Search result contain the keyword w_1
R	Final result satisfied the search criteria
proof	The evidence of search result, i.e., Witness

2.2 Complexity Assumptions

Decisional Diffie-Hellman (DDH) Assumption. Let $a, b, c \in_R \mathbb{G}$ and g be a generator of $\mathbb{G}$. We say that the DDH assumption holds if there no probabilistic polynomial time algorithm can distinguish the tuple (g, g^a, g^b, g^{ab}) from (g, g^a, g^b, g^c) with non-negligible advantage.

q-Strong Diffie-Hellman (q-SDH) Assumption. Let $a \in_R \mathbb{Z}_p$ and g be a generator of $\mathbb{G}$. We say that the q-SDH assumption holds if given a $q + 1$-tuple $(g, g^a, g^{a^2}, \ldots, g^{a^q})$, there no probabilistic polynomial time algorithm can output a pair $(g_1^{1/a+x}, x)$ with non-negligible advantage, where $x \in \mathbb{Z}_p^*$.

2.3 Security Definitions

Similar to [8,29], we present the security definition of our VSSE scheme by describing the leakage information $\mathcal{L}_{\mathrm{VSSE}}$, which refers to the maximum information that is allowed to learn by the adversary.

Let $\Pi = (\mathsf{VEDBSetup}, \mathsf{KeyGen}, \mathsf{TokenGen}, \mathsf{Search}, \mathsf{Verify})$ be a verifiable symmetric searchable encryption scheme, VEDB be the encrypted version database, $\mathcal{A}$ be an polynomial adversary and $\mathcal{S}$ be a simulator. Assuming that PK/MK be the public key/system master key, SK be the private key for a given authorized user. We define the security via the following two probabilistic experiments:

- **Real**$_{\mathcal{A}}^{\Pi}(\lambda)$: $\mathcal{A}$ chooses a database DB, then the experiment runs $\mathsf{VEDBSetup}(\lambda,$ DB) and returns (VEDB, PK) to $\mathcal{A}$. Then, $\mathcal{A}$ generates the authorized private key SK by running KeyGen(MK, **w**) for the authorized keywords **w** of a given client, adaptively chooses a conjunctive query $\bar{w}$ and obtains the search token Td by running TokenGen(SK, $\bar{w}$). The experiment answers the query by running Search(Td, VEDB, PK) and Verify(R_{w_1}, R, {proof$_i$}$_{i=1,2}$, VEDB)), then gives the transcript and the client output to $\mathcal{A}$. Finally, the adversary $\mathcal{A}$ outputs a bit $b \in \{0, 1\}$ as the output of the experiment.

- **Ideal**$_{\mathcal{A},\mathcal{S}}^{\Pi}(\lambda)$: The experiment initializes an empty list **q** and sets a counter $i = 0$. Adversary $\mathcal{A}$ chooses a database DB, the experiment runs $\mathcal{S}(\mathcal{L}_{\text{VSSE}}(\text{DB}))$ and returns (VEDB, PK) to $\mathcal{A}$. Then, the experiment insert each query into **q** as **q**[i], and outputs all the transcript to $\mathcal{A}$ by running $\mathcal{S}(\mathcal{L}_{\text{VSSE}}(\text{DB}, \mathbf{q}))$. Finally, the adversary $\mathcal{A}$ outputs a bit $b \in \{0, 1\}$ as the output of the experiment.

We say the Π is $\mathcal{L}$-semantically secure verifiable symmetric searchable encryption scheme if for all probabilistic polynomial-time adversary $\mathcal{A}$ there exist an simulator $\mathcal{S}$ such that:

$$| \Pr[\mathbf{Real}_{\mathcal{A}}^{\Pi}(\lambda) = 1] - \Pr[\mathbf{Ideal}_{\mathcal{A},\mathcal{S}}^{\Pi}(\lambda)]| \leq negl(\lambda)$$

2.4 Leakage Function

The goal of searchable symmetric encryption is to achieve efficient search over encrypted data while revealing as little as possible private information. Following with [13,29], we describe the security of our VSSE scheme with leakage function $\mathcal{L}_{\text{VSSE}}$.

For the sake of simplicity, given $\mathbf{q} = (\mathbf{s}, \mathbf{x})$ represent a sequence of query, where $\mathbf{s}(\mathbf{x})$ denotes *sterm* (*xterm*) array of the query **q**. The i-th query is expressed as $\mathbf{q}[i] = (\mathbf{s}[i], \mathbf{x}[i])$. On input DB and **q**, the leakage function $\mathcal{L}_{\text{VSSE}}$ consists of the following leakage information:

- $K = \cup_{i=1}^{T} W_i$ is the total number of keywords in the DB.
- $N = \sum_{i=1}^{T} |W_i|$ is the total number of keyword/document identifier pairs in DB.
- $\bar{\mathbf{s}} \in \mathbb{N}^{|q|}$ is the equality pattern of the *sterm* set **s**, where each distinct *sterm* is assigned by an integer according to its order of appearance in **s**. i.e., if $\mathbf{s} = (a, b, c, b, a)$, then $\bar{\mathbf{s}} = (1, 2, 3, 2, 1)$.
- SP is the size pattern of the queries, which is the number of document identifiers matching the *sterm* in each query, i.e., SP$[i] = |\text{DB}(\mathbf{s}[i])|$. In addition, we define SRP$[i] = \text{DB}(\mathbf{s}[i])$ as the search result associated with the *sterm* of the i-th query, which includes the corresponding proof.
- RP is the result pattern, which consists of all the document identifiers matching the query **q**[i]. That is, the intersection of the *sterm* with all *xterm* in the same query.
- IP is the conditional intersection pattern, which represents a matrix satisfies the following condition:

$$\text{IP}[i, j, \alpha, \beta] = \begin{cases} \text{DB}(\mathbf{s}[i]) \cap \text{DB}(\mathbf{s}[j]), & \text{if } \mathbf{s}[i] \neq \mathbf{s}[j] \text{ and } \mathbf{x}[i, \alpha] = \mathbf{x}[j, \beta] \\ \emptyset, & \text{otherwise} \end{cases}$$

3   Verifiable Conjunctive Keyword Search Scheme Based on Accumulator

In this section, we firstly introduce some building blocks adopted in the proposed construction. Then, we present the proposed verifiable conjunctive keyword search scheme in detail.

3.1   Building Block

Bilinear-Map Accumulators. We briefly introduce the accumulator based on bilinear maps supporting non-membership proofs [14]. It can provide a short proof of (non)-membership for any subset that (not) belong to a given set. More specifically, given a prime p, it can accumulates a given set $S = \{x_1, x_2, \cdots, x_N\} \subset \mathbb{Z}_p$ into an element in $\mathbb{G}$. Given the public parameter of the accumulator PK $= (g^s, \ldots, g^{s^t})$, the corresponding private key is $s \in \mathbb{Z}_p$. The accumulator value of S is defined as

$$Acc(S) = g^{\prod_{i=1}^{N}(x_i+s)}$$

Note that $Acc(S)$ can be reconstructed by only knowing set S and PK in polynomial interpolation manner. The proof of membership for a subset $S_1 \subseteq S$ is the witness $W_{S_1,S} = g^{\prod_{x \in S-S_1}(x+s)}$, which shows that a subset S_1 belongs to the set S.

Using the witness $W_{S_1,S}$, the verifier can determine the membership of subset W_{S_1} by checking the following equation $e(W_{S_1,S}, g^{\prod_{x \in S_1}(x+s)}) = e(Acc(S), g)^1$.

To verify some element $x_i \notin S$, the witness consists of a tuple $\hat{W}_{x_i,S} = (w_{x_i}, u_{x_i}) \in \mathbb{G} \times \mathbb{Z}_p^*$ satisfying the following requirement:

$$u_x \neq 0$$

$$(x_i + s) \mid [\prod_{x \in S}(x + s) + u_{x_i}]$$

$$w_x^{x_i+s} = Acc(S) \cdot g^{u_{x_i}}$$

In particular, let $f_S(s)$ denote the product in the exponent of $Acc(S)$, i.e., $f_S(s) = \prod_{x \in S}(x + s)$, any $y \notin S$, the unique non-membership witness $\hat{W}_{x_i,S} = (w_y, u_y)$ can be denoted as:

$$u_y = -f_S(-y) \mod p = -\prod_{x \in S}(x - y) \mod p$$

$$w_y = g^{[f_S(s)-f_S(-y)]/(y+s)}.$$

The verification algorithm in this case checks that

$$e(w_y, g^y \cdot g^s) = e(Acc(S) \cdot g^{u_y}, g)$$

---

[1] Particularly, for a given element x, the corresponding witness is $W_{x,S} = g^{\prod_{\hat{x} \in S: \hat{x} \neq x}(\hat{x}+s)}$, the verifier can check that $e(W_{x,S}, g^x \cdot g^s) = e(Acc(S), g)$.

3.2   The Concrete Construction

In this section, we present a concrete verifiable SSE scheme which mainly consists of five algorithms $\Pi = (\mathsf{VEDBSetup}, \mathsf{KeyGen}, \mathsf{TokenGen}, \mathsf{Search}, \mathsf{Verify})$. We remark that each keyword w should be a prime in our scheme. This can be easily facilitated by using a hash-to-prime hash function such as the one used in [29]. For simplicity, we omit this "hash-to-prime" statement in the rest of this paper and simply assume that each w is a prime number. The details of the proposed scheme are given as follows.

- $\mathsf{VEDBSetup}(1^\lambda, \mathsf{DB})$: the data owner takes as input of security parameter λ, a database $\mathsf{DB} = (\mathrm{ind}_i, \mathrm{W}_i)_{i=1}^T$, and outputs the system master key MK, public key PK and the Verifiable Encrypted Database (VEDB). As shown in the following Algorithm 1.

Algorithm 1. $\mathsf{VEDBSetup}(\lambda, \mathsf{DB})$

Input: $\mathsf{DB} = (\mathrm{ind}_i, \mathrm{W}_i)_{i=1}^T$
Output: VEDB, MK, PK
1: The data owner selects two big primes p, q, random keys K_X, K_I, K_Z for PRF F_P, K_s for PRF F, and computes $n = pq$.
2: The data owner randomly selects $g \xleftarrow{R} \mathbb{G}$, $g_1, g_2, g_3 \xleftarrow{R} \mathbb{Z}_n^*$ and secret key $sk = s$, then computes $pk = (g^s, \ldots, g^{s^t})$, where t is an upper bound on the number of the cardinality. The system public/master key pair are defined as: MK $\leftarrow$ $\{K_X, K_I, K_Z, K_S, p, q, s\}$, PK $\leftarrow \{n, g, pk\}$.
3: $\mathrm{TSet}, \mathrm{XSet}, \mathrm{Stag} \leftarrow \phi$;
4: **for** $w \in \mathrm{W}$ **do**
5:     $\mathbf{e}_w \leftarrow \phi$; $c \leftarrow 1$
6:     $K_e \leftarrow F(K_S, w)$; $\mathrm{stag}_w \leftarrow F(K_S, g_1^{1/w} \bmod n)$
7:     $\mathrm{Stag} \leftarrow \mathrm{Stag} \cup \{\mathrm{H}(\mathrm{stag}_w)\}$, where $\mathrm{H}(\cdot)$ is a secure hash function, i.e., SHA-256.
8:     **for** $\mathrm{ind} \in \mathsf{DB}(w)$ **do**
9:         $\mathrm{xind} \leftarrow F_p(K_I, \mathrm{ind})$; $z \leftarrow F_p(K_Z, g_2^{1/w} \bmod n \parallel c)$
10:        $l \leftarrow F(\mathrm{stag}_w, c)$; $e \leftarrow \mathrm{Enc}(K_e, \mathrm{ind})$; $y \leftarrow \mathrm{xind} \cdot z^{-1}$
11:        $\mathrm{TSet}[l] = (e, y)$; $\mathbf{e}_w \leftarrow \mathbf{e}_w \cup \{e\}$;
12:        $\mathrm{xtag}_w \leftarrow g^{F_p(K_X \cdot g_3^{1/w} \bmod n) \cdot \mathrm{xind}}$; $\mathrm{XSet} \leftarrow \mathrm{XSet} \cup \{\mathrm{xtag}_w\}$
13:        $c \leftarrow c + 1$
14:     **end for**
15:     $l \leftarrow F(\mathrm{stag}_w, 0)$
16:     $Acc(\mathbf{e}_w) \leftarrow g^{\prod_{e_i \in \mathbf{e}_w}(e_i + s)}$
17:     $\mathrm{TSet}[l] = (Acc(\mathbf{e}_w), \mathrm{H}(K_e, Acc(\mathbf{e}_w)))$
18: **end for**
19: Compute accumulator values:
    - $Acc(\mathrm{XSet}) \leftarrow g^{\prod_{\mathrm{xtag} \in \mathrm{XSet}}(\mathrm{xtag} + s)}$
    - $Acc(\mathrm{Stag}) \leftarrow g^{\prod_{\mathrm{stag} \in \mathrm{Stag}}(\mathrm{stag} + s)}$
20: Set VEDB $\leftarrow \{\mathrm{TSet}, \mathrm{XSet}, \mathrm{Stag}, Acc(\mathrm{Stag}), Acc(\mathrm{XSet})\}$
21: **return** $\{\mathrm{VEDB}, \mathrm{MK}, \mathrm{PK}\}$

- KeyGen(MK, **w**): Assume that an authorized user is allowed to perform search over an authorized keywords $\mathbf{w} = \{w_1, w_2, \ldots, w_N\}$, the data owner computes $sk_{\mathbf{w}}^{(i)} = (g_i^{1/\prod_{j=1}^{N} w_j} \bmod n)$ for $i \in \{1, 2, 3\}$ and generates search key $sk_{\mathbf{w}} = (sk_{\mathbf{w}}^{(1)}, sk_{\mathbf{w}}^{(2)}, sk_{\mathbf{w}}^{(3)})$, then sends the authorized private key SK $= (K_S, K_X, K_Z, K_T, sk_{\mathbf{w}})$ to the authorized user.

Algorithm 2. TokenGen(SK, $\bar{w}$)

Input: SK, $\bar{w}$
Output: Td
1: Td, xtoken $\leftarrow \phi$
2: stag $\leftarrow F(K_S, (sk_{\bar{w}}^{(1)})^{\prod_{w \in kw \setminus w_1} w} \bmod n) = F(K_S, g_1^{1/w_1} \bmod n)$
3: **for** $c = 1, 2, \ldots$ until the server stops **do**
4:     **for** $i = 2, \ldots, d$ **do**
5:        xtoken$[c, i] \leftarrow g^{F_p(K_Z, (sk_{\bar{w}}^{(2)})^{\prod_{w \in \bar{w} \setminus w_1} w} \bmod n \| c) \cdot F_p(K_X, (sk_{\bar{w}}^{(3)})^{\prod_{w \in \bar{w} \setminus w_i} w}) \bmod n} =$
       $g^{F_p(K_Z, g_2^{1/w_1} \bmod n \| c) \cdot F_p(K_X, g_3^{1/w_i} \bmod n)}$
6:     **end for**
7:     xtoken$[c] = $ xtoken$[c, 2], \ldots,$ xtoken$[c, d]$
8: **end for**
9: Td $\leftarrow$ (stag, xtoken$[1]$, xtoken$[2]$, ...)
10: **return** the search token Td

- TokenGen(SK, $\bar{w}$): Suppose that an authorized user wants to perform a conjunctive query $\bar{w} = (w_1, \ldots, w_d)$, where $d \leq N$. Let *sterm* be the least frequent keyword in a given search query. Without loss of generality, we assume that the *sterm* of the query $\bar{w}$ is w_1, then the search token *st* of the query is generated with Algorithm 2 and sent to the cloud server.
- Search(Td, VEDB, PK): Upon receiving the search token Td, the cloud server firstly performs a single keyword search with stag, and then returns all the document identities that matching the search criteria along with the corresponding proof. The detail is shown in Algorithm 3.
- Verify(R_{w_1}, R, $\{\mathsf{proof}_i\}_{i=1,2}$, VEDB)): To verify the integrity of search result, the user checks the validity in terms of both correctness and completeness. At the end of the verification, it outputs *Accept* or *Reject* that represents the server is honest or malicious. Precisely, the algorithm is performed according to the following cases:

Case 1: When R_{w_1} is an empty set, it implies that there is no matched tuples in the TSet. The server returns the corresponding verification information $(\mathsf{proof}_1, Acc(\mathrm{Stag}))$. Let $f_{\mathrm{Stag}}(s)$ denote the product in the exponent of $Acc(\mathrm{Stag})$, that is $f_{\mathrm{Stag}}(s) = \prod_{x \in \mathrm{Stag}}(x + s)$. The non-membership witness $\hat{W}_{stag_{w_1}, \mathrm{Stag}} = \mathsf{proof}_1 = (w_{stag_{w_1}}, u_{stag_{w_1}})$ can be denoted as:

$$u_{stag_{w_1}} = -f_{\mathrm{Stag}}(-stag_{w_1}) \mod p = -\prod_{x \in \mathrm{Stag}}(x - stag_{w_1}) \mod p$$

$$w_{stag_{w_1}} = g^{[f_{\mathrm{Stag}}(s) - f_{\mathrm{Stag}}(-stag_{w_1})]/(stag_{w_1}+s)}.$$

Algorithm 3. Search(Td, VEDB, PK)

Input: Td, VEDB, PK
Output: R_{w_1}, R, proof
1: R_{w_1}, R, B $\leftarrow \phi$; proof $\leftarrow NULL$
    Phase 1 :
2: $l \leftarrow F(stag_{w_1}, 0)$; $(Acc(\mathbf{e}_w), H(K_e, Acc(\mathbf{e}_w))) \leftarrow \mathrm{TSet}[l]$
3: **for** $c = 1, 2, \cdots$ **do**
4:      $l \leftarrow F(stag_{w_1}, c)$; $(e_c, y_c) \leftarrow \mathrm{TSet}[l]$; $R_{w_1} \leftarrow R_{w_1} \cup \{e_c\}$
5: **end for**
6: **if** $R_{w_1} = \phi$ **then**
7:      proof$_1 \leftarrow \hat{\mathrm{W}}_{stag_{w_1}, \mathrm{Stag}}$ // Refer to Case 1 below
8: **return** (proof$_1$, $Acc(\mathrm{Stag})$) and exit
9: **else**
10:     proof$_1 \leftarrow \mathrm{W}_{R_{w_1}, \mathrm{Stag}}$ // Refer to Case 2 and 3 below
11:
12: **end if**
    Phase 2 :
13: **for** $c = 1, \cdots, |R_{w_1}|$ **do**
14:     **for** $i = 2, \cdots, d$ **do**
15:         $b[c, i] \leftarrow \mathrm{xtoken}[c, i]^{y_c}$
16:     **end for**
17:     **if** $\forall i = 2, ..., d : b[c, i] \in \mathrm{XSet}$ **then**
18:         R $\leftarrow$ R $\cup \{e_c\}$; B $\leftarrow$ B $\cup \{b[c, i]\}$
19:     **end if**
20: **end for**
21: **if** R $\neq \phi$ **then**
22:     proof$_2 \leftarrow \mathrm{W}_{B, \mathrm{XSet}}$ // Refer to Case 3 below
23:
24: **end if**
25: **proof** $\leftarrow \{Acc(\mathrm{Stag}), Acc(\mathrm{XSet}), \{\mathrm{proof}_i\}_{i=1,2}\}$
26: **return** (R_{w_1}, R, proof)

The user checks the equalities $u_{stag_{w_1}} \neq 0$ and $e(w_{stag_{w_1}}, g^{stag_{w_1}} \cdot g^s) = e(Acc(\mathrm{Stag}) \cdot g^{u_{stag_{w_1}}}, g)$. If pass, the process terminates and outputs *Accept*.

Case 2: When R_{w_1} is not an empty set and R is an empty one, the cloud claims that there is no tuple satisfied the query condition. To verify the correctness of the search result, the user firstly verifies the integrity of R_{w_1}. Then the user randomly selects some elements from the R_{w_1} and requires the cloud to feedback the corresponding non-member proof for the query condition. The detail of the process is described as follows:

Step 1: The user checks the integrity of R_{w_1} with the following equality:

$$e(\mathrm{W}_{R_{w_1}, \mathrm{Stag}}, g^{\prod_{x \in R_{w_1}} (x+s)}) = e(Acc(\mathrm{Stag}), g)$$

If it holds, then go to Step 2.

Step 2: The user randomly selects k elements from R_{w_1} and checks the membership with the query condition. The detail is as shown in Algorithm 4.

Case 3: When both R_{w_1} and R are non-empty set, the verifications of R_{w_1} and R is very similar to that of Case 2. The difference is that the user randomly selects k elements from $R_{w_1} \setminus R$. For the detail of verifying process, please refer to the Case 2.

Algorithm 4. $\mathrm{Verify}(R_{w_1}(R), \bar{w}, \mathrm{XSet})$

Input: $(\mathbf{R}_{w_1}(R), \bar{w}, \mathrm{XSet})$
Output: *Accept* or *Reject*

1: User side :
2: The user randomly selects $\{\mathrm{ind}_1, \cdots, \mathrm{ind}_k\} \in R_{w_1}$
3: **for** $i = 1, \cdots, k$ **do**
4:      $\mathrm{xtag}[i] \leftarrow \phi$
5:      $\mathrm{xind} \leftarrow F_p(K_I, \mathrm{ind}_i)$
6:      **for** $j = 2, \cdots, d$ **do**
7:          $\mathrm{xtag}[i, j] \leftarrow g^{F_p(K_X, \vartheta_3^{1/w_j} \bmod n) \cdot \mathrm{xind}}$
8:          $\mathrm{xtag}[i] \leftarrow \mathrm{xtag}[i] \cup \mathrm{xtag}[i, j]$
9:      **end for**
10: **end for**
11: The user sends the $\mathrm{xtag} \leftarrow \{\mathrm{xtag}[1], \cdots, \mathrm{xtag}[k]\}$ to the cloud.
    Cloud side :
12: **for all** $\mathrm{xtag}[i] \in \mathrm{xtag}$ **do**
13:      **for** $j = 2, \cdots, d$ **do**
14:          **if** $\mathrm{xtag}[i, j] \notin \mathrm{XSet}$ **then**
15:              $\mathrm{proof}[i] \leftarrow \hat{W}_{\mathrm{xtag}[i,j], \mathrm{XSet}}$ **and break**
16:          **end if**
17:      **end for**
18:      $\mathrm{proof} \leftarrow \mathrm{proof} \cup \{\mathrm{proof}[i]\}$
19: **end for**
    User side :
20: **for all** $\mathrm{proof}[i] \in \mathrm{proof}$ **do**
21:      **if** $\mathrm{proof}[i]$ holds **then**
22:          **return** *Accept*
23:      **else**
24:          **return** *Reject*
25:      **end if**
26: **end for**

Remark 1. Note that we accumulate all $ind \in \mathrm{DB}[w]$ into a accumulator value $Acc(\mathbf{e}_w)$, it can be used to ensure the completeness of search result. In order to associate with the corresponding $stag$, it is assigned into TSet indexed by $l = F(stag, 0)$. More precisely, a tuple consisting of $(Acc(e_w), H(K_e, Acc(e_w)))$

is stored in TSet$[l]$, where $K_e = F(K_S, w)$. The integrity of $Acc(e_w)$ can be verified by reconstructing the keyed-hash value.

Remark 2. Inspired by [1], we introduce a sample check method to verify the completeness of search result. We determine the completeness of search result by randomly choosing a fraction of the matched documents. More specifically, we just randomly choose k element in $R_{w_1} \setminus R$ for completeness checking. Let P_X be the probability that the user detects the misbehavior of the server. We have $P_X = 1 - \frac{n-t}{n} \cdot \frac{n-1-t}{n-1} \cdot \frac{n-2-t}{n-2} \cdot \ldots \cdot \frac{n-k+1-t}{n-k+1}$, where n is the size of $R_{w_1} \setminus R$, t is the missed documents of search result. Since $\frac{n-i-t}{n-i} \geq \frac{n-i-1-t}{n-i-1}$, P_X satisfies that $1 - (\frac{n-t}{n})^k \leq P_X \leq 1 - (\frac{n-k+1-t}{n-k+1})^k$. Similar to scheme [1], once the percentage of the missed documents is determined, the misbehavior can be detected with a certain high probability by checking a certain number of documents that is independent of the size of the dataset. For example, in order to achieve a 99% probability, 65, 21 and 7 documents should be checked when $t = 10\% \cdot n$, $t = 20\% \cdot n$ and $t = 50\% \cdot n$, respectively.

Note that the server can generate a non-membership proof for each document. So we need to perform multiple times non-membership verification to ensure completeness of the search result. Although the sample check method can greatly reduce the verification overhead at the expense of low false positive, it remains a drawback in our proposed scheme. Thus, one interesting question is whether there is an efficient way to achieve non-membership verification in a batch manner.

4   Security and Efficiency Analysis

4.1   Security Analysis

In this section, we present the security of our proposed VSSE scheme with simulation-based approach. Similar to [8,29], we first provide a security proof of our VSSE scheme against non-adaptive attacks and then discuss the adaptive one.

Theorem 1. *The proposed scheme is $\mathcal{L}$-semantically secure VSSE scheme where $\mathcal{L}_{\text{VSSE}}$ is the leakage function defined as before, assuming that the q-SDH assumption holds in $\mathbb{G}$, that F, F_P are two secure PRFs and that the underlying (Enc, Dec) is an IND-CPA secure symmetric encryption scheme.*

Theorem 2. *Let $\mathcal{L}_{\text{VSSE}}$ be the leakage function defined as before, the proposed scheme is $\mathcal{L}$-semantically secure VSSE scheme against adaptive attacks, assuming that the q-SDH assumption holds in $\mathbb{G}$, that F, F_P are two secure PRFs and that the underlying (Enc, Dec) is an IND-CPA secure symmetric encryption scheme.*

Due to space constraints, we will provide the detailed proofs in our full version.

4.2 Comparison

In this section, we compare our scheme with Cash et al.'s scheme [8] and Sun et al.'s scheme [29]. Firstly, all of the three schemes can support conjunctive keyword search. In particular, Our scheme can be seen as an extension from Cash et al. scheme and Sun et al. scheme, which supports verifiability of conjunctive query based on accumulator. All the three schemes have almost equal computation cost in search phase. Secondly, our scheme and Sun et al.'s scheme support the authorized search in multi-user setting. Note that our scheme can support verifiability of search result. Although it requires some extra computation overhead to construct verifiable searchable indices, we remark that the work is only done once.

To achieve the verification functionality in our scheme, the server requires to generate the corresponding proofs for the search result. Here we assume that the search result R is not empty. In this case, the proofs contain three parts. The first part is used to verify both the correctness and completeness of the search result for the sterm R_{w_1}. The second part and the third part are used to verify the correctness and completeness of the conjunctive search result R, respectively. The proofs generation are related to the size of database, but they can be done in parallel on the powerful server side. In contrast, it is efficient for the client to verify the corresponding proofs.

Table 2. Performance comparison

Schemes	Scheme [8]	Scheme [29]	Our scheme
Query-type	Conjunctive	Conjunctive	Conjunctive
Multi-user	No	Yes	Yes
Verification	No	No	Yes
EDBSetup	$|DB|E$	$(|DB| + 2|W|)E$	$(|DB| + 3|W| + 2)E$
TokenGen	$|R_{w_1}|(d-1)E$	$(|R_{w_1}|(d-1) + (d+1))E$	$(|R_{w_1}|(d-1) + (d+1))E$
Search	$|R_{w_1}|(d-1)E$	$|R_{w_1}|(d-1)E$	$|R_{w_1}|(d-1)E$
Verify (Server)	-	-	$(|DB| - |R| - 1)E + k(|DB| - 2)E$
Verify (User)	-	-	$2E + 4P + k(2E + 2P)$

Table 2 provides the detailed comparison of all the three schemes. For the computation overhead, we mainly consider the expensive operations, like exponentiation and pairing operations. We denote by E an exponentiation, P a computation of pairing, $|R_{w_1}|$ the size of search result for *sterm* w_1, $|DB|$ the number of whole keyword-document pairs, $|R|$ the size of conjunctive search results, d the number of queried keywords, k the number of selected identifiers which are used for completeness verification.

5   Performance Evaluation

In this section, we present an overall performance evaluation of the proposed scheme. First, we give a description of the prototype to implement the VEDB generation, the query processing and proof verification. Here the biggest challenge is how to generate the VEDB. Second, we analyze the experimental results and compare them with [8,29].

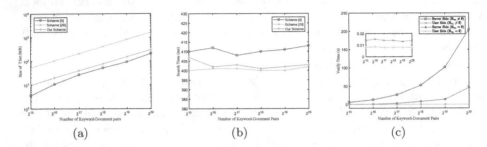

(a)   (b)   (c)

Fig. 1. The performance comparison among three schemes. (a) Storage cost of VEDBSetup. (b) Time cost of Search. (c) Time cost of Verify

Prototype. There are three main components in the prototype. The first and most important one is for VEDB generation. The second one is for query processing and the last one is for the verification of the search result. We leverage OpenSSL and PBC libraries to realize the cryptographic primitives. Specifically, we use Type 1 pairing function in PBC library for pairing, HMAC for PRFs, AES in CTR model to encrypt the indices in our proposed scheme and in scheme [8], ABE to encrypt the indices in Sun et al.'s scheme [29].

In order to generate the VEDB efficiently, we use four LINUX machines to establish a distributed network. Two of them are service nodes with Intel Core I3-2120 processors running at 3.30 GHz, 4G memory and 500G disk storage. The other two are compute nodes with Intel Xeon E5-1603 processors running at 2.80 GHz, 16G memory and 1T disk storage. One of the service nodes is used for storing the whole keyword-document pairs. To enhance the retrieving efficiency, the pairs are stored in a key-value database, i.e., Redis database. The other service node is used to store the VEDB which is actually in a MySQL database. In order to improve the efficiency of generating VEDB, both of the two compute nodes are used to transform the keyword-document pairs to the items in VEDB. The experiments of server side is implemented on a LINUX machine with Intel Core I3-2120 processors running at 3.30 GHz, 4G memory and 500G disk storage. In order to improve the search efficiency, the TSet is transformed to a Bloom Filter [24], which can efficiently test membership with small storage. The verification on the user side is also implemented on a LINUX machine with Intel Core I3-2120 processors running at 3.30 GHz, 4G memory and 500G disk storage.

Experimental Results. We implement the three compared schemes on the real-world dataset from Wikimedia Download [15]. The number of documents, distinct keywords and distinct keyword-document pairs are $7.8 * 10^5$, $4.0 * 10^6$ and $6.2 * 10^7$, respectively.

As shown in Fig. 1, we provide the detailed evaluation results by comparing the proposed scheme with [7] and [29]. In the phrase of system setup, we mainly focus on the size of TSet(As the XSet is almost the same in all three schemes). The size of TSet in our scheme is slightly larger than that of [8], because the TSet in our scheme contains the accumulators of each keywords, $\{Acc(\mathbf{e}_w)\}_{w \in W}$. However, the size of TSet in [29] is larger than both of our scheme and Cash et al.'s scheme as the document identities are encrypted by the public encryption scheme (i.e., ABE) in [29]. The search complexity of all the three schemes depends only on the least frequent keyword, i.e., *sterm*. It is slightly inefficient for the scheme [8] because of the different structure of TSet. In addition, we measure the verification cost for our scheme in two cases, $\mathsf{R}_{w_1} = \emptyset$ and $\mathsf{R}_{w_1} \neq \emptyset$. Obviously, it is very efficient for the client to verify the proofs given by the server. Although the proof generation on the server side is not so efficient, it can be generated in parallel for the powerful server. Besides, it is unnecessary for the server to give the search result with the proofs at the same time. Alternatively, the server can send the proofs slightly behind the search result. The experimental results show that the proposed scheme can achieve security against malicious server while maintaining a comparable performance.

6   Conclusion

In this paper, we focus on the verifiable conjunctive search of encrypted database. The main contribution is to present a new efficient verifiable conjunctive keyword search scheme based on accumulator. Our scheme can simultaneously achieve verifiability of search result even when the search result is empty and efficient conjunctive keyword search with search complexity proportional to the matched documents of the least frequent keyword. Moreover, the communication and computation cost of client is constant for verifying the search result. We provide a formal security proof and thorough experiment on a real-world dataset, which demonstrates our scheme can achieve the desired security goals with a comparable efficiency. However, our scheme needs to perform non-membership verification for each document individually. How to design a variant of accumulator that can provide a constant non-membership proof for multiple elements is an interesting problem.

Acknowledgement. This work is supported by National Key Research and Development Program of China (No. 2017YFB0802202), National Natural Science Foundation of China (Nos. 61702401, 61572382, 61602396 and U1636205), China 111 Project (No. B16037), China Postdoctoral Science Foundation (No. 2017M613083), Natural Science Basic Research Plan in Shaanxi Province of China (No. 2016JZ021), the Research Grants Council of Hong Kong (No. 25206317), and the Australian Research Council (ARC) Grant (No. DP180102199).

References

1. Ateniese, G., et. al.: Provable data possession at untrusted stores. In: Proceedings of the 14th ACM Conference on Computer and Communications Security, CCS 2007, pp. 598–609. ACM (2007)
2. Azraoui, M., Elkhiyaoui, K., Önen, M., Molva, R.: Publicly verifiable conjunctive keyword search in outsourced databases. In: Proceedings of 2015 IEEE Conference on Communications and Network Security, CNS 2015, pp. 619–627. IEEE (2015)
3. Ballard, L., Kamara, S., Monrose, F.: Achieving efficient conjunctive keyword searches over encrypted data. In: Qing, S., Mao, W., López, J., Wang, G. (eds.) ICICS 2005. LNCS, vol. 3783, pp. 414–426. Springer, Heidelberg (2005). https://doi.org/10.1007/11602897_35
4. Bost, R., Fouque, P., Pointcheval, D.: Verifiable dynamic symmetric searchable encryption: optimality and forward security. IACR Cryptology ePrint Archive, p. 62 (2016). http://eprint.iacr.org/2016/062
5. Bost, R., Minaud, B., Ohrimenko, O.: Forward and backward private searchable encryption from constrained cryptographic primitives. In: Proceedings of the 24th ACM Conference on Computer and Communications Security, CCS 2017, pp. 1465–1482. ACM (2017)
6. Byun, J.W., Lee, D.H., Lim, J.: Efficient conjunctive keyword search on encrypted data storage system. In: Atzeni, A.S., Lioy, A. (eds.) EuroPKI 2006. LNCS, vol. 4043, pp. 184–196. Springer, Heidelberg (2006). https://doi.org/10.1007/11774716_15
7. Cash, D., et al.: Dynamic searchable encryption in very-large databases: data structures and implementation. In: Proceedings of the 21st Annual Network and Distributed System Security Symposium, NDSS 2014. The Internet Society (2014)
8. Cash, D., Jarecki, S., Jutla, C., Krawczyk, H., Roşu, M.-C., Steiner, M.: Highly-scalable searchable symmetric encryption with support for Boolean queries. In: Canetti, R., Garay, J.A. (eds.) CRYPTO 2013. LNCS, vol. 8042, pp. 353–373. Springer, Heidelberg (2013). https://doi.org/10.1007/978-3-642-40041-4_20
9. Chai, Q., Gong, G.: Verifiable symmetric searchable encryption for semi-honest-but-curious cloud servers. In: Proceedings of IEEE International Conference on Communications, ICC 2012, pp. 917–922. IEEE (2012)
10. Chen, X., Li, J., Ma, J., Tang, Q., Lou, W.: New algorithms for secure outsourcing of modular exponentiations. IEEE Trans. Parallel Distrib. Syst. **25**(9), 2386–2396 (2014)
11. Chen, X., Li, J., Weng, J., Ma, J., Lou, W.: Verifiable computation over large database with incremental updates. In: Kutyłowski, M., Vaidya, J. (eds.) ESORICS 2014. LNCS, vol. 8712, pp. 148–162. Springer, Cham (2014). https://doi.org/10.1007/978-3-319-11203-9_9
12. Chu, C., Zhu, W.T., Han, J., Liu, J.K., Xu, J., Zhou, J.: Security concerns in popular cloud storage services. IEEE Pervasive Comput. **12**(4), 50–57 (2013)
13. Curtmola, R., Garay, J.A., Kamara, S., Ostrovsky, R.: Searchable symmetric encryption: improved definitions and efficient constructions. In: Juels, A., Wright, R.N., di Vimercati, S.D.C. (eds.) Proceedings of the 13th ACM Conference on Computer and Communications Security, CCS 2006, pp. 79–88. ACM (2006)
14. Damgård, I., Triandopoulos, N.: Supporting non-membership proofs with bilinear-map accumulators. IACR Cryptology ePrint Archive 2008/538 (2008). http://eprint.iacr.org/2008/538

15. Wikimedia Foundation: Wikimedia downloads. https://dumps.wikimedia.org. Accessed 18 Apr 2018
16. Goh, E.: Secure indexes. IACR Cryptology ePrint Archive 2003/216 (2003). http://eprint.iacr.org/2003/216
17. Golle, P., Staddon, J., Waters, B.: Secure conjunctive keyword search over encrypted data. In: Jakobsson, M., Yung, M., Zhou, J. (eds.) ACNS 2004. LNCS, vol. 3089, pp. 31–45. Springer, Heidelberg (2004). https://doi.org/10.1007/978-3-540-24852-1_3
18. Kamara, S., Papamanthou, C., Roeder, T.: Dynamic searchable symmetric encryption. In: Yu, T., Danezis, G., Gligor, V.D. (eds.) Proceedings of the 19th ACM Conference on Computer and Communications Security, CCS 2012, pp. 965–976. ACM (2012)
19. Kasra Kermanshahi, S., Liu, J.K., Steinfeld, R.: Multi-user cloud-based secure keyword search. In: Pieprzyk, J., Suriadi, S. (eds.) ACISP 2017. LNCS, vol. 10342, pp. 227–247. Springer, Cham (2017). https://doi.org/10.1007/978-3-319-60055-0_12
20. Kim, K.S., Kim, M., Lee, D., Park, J.H., Kim, W.: Forward secure dynamic searchable symmetric encryption with efficient updates. In: Proceedings of the 24th ACM Conference on Computer and Communications Security, CCS 2017, pp. 1449–1463. ACM (2017)
21. Kurosawa, K., Ohtaki, Y.: UC-secure searchable symmetric encryption. In: Keromytis, A.D. (ed.) FC 2012. LNCS, vol. 7397, pp. 285–298. Springer, Heidelberg (2012). https://doi.org/10.1007/978-3-642-32946-3_21
22. Liu, J.K., Au, M.H., Susilo, W., Liang, K., Lu, R., Srinivasan, B.: Secure sharing and searching for real-time video data in mobile cloud. IEEE Netw. **29**(2), 46–50 (2015)
23. Liu, J.K., Liang, K., Susilo, W., Liu, J., Xiang, Y.: Two-factor data security protection mechanism for cloud storage system. IEEE Trans. Comput. **65**(6), 1992–2004 (2016)
24. Nikitin, A.: Bloom filter scala. https://alexandrnikitin.github.io/blog/bloom-filter-for-scala/. Accessed 10 Apr 2018
25. Ogata, W., Kurosawa, K.: Efficient no-dictionary verifiable searchable symmetric encryption. In: Kiayias, A. (ed.) FC 2017. LNCS, vol. 10322, pp. 498–516. Springer, Cham (2017). https://doi.org/10.1007/978-3-319-70972-7_28
26. Ruvic, R.D.: Facebook says up to 87M people affected in Cambridge Analytica data-mining scandal. http://www.abc.net.au/news/2018-04-05/facebook-raises-cambridge-analytica-estimates/9620652. Accessed 10 Apr 2018
27. Ryu, E., Takagi, T.: Efficient conjunctive keyword-searchable encryption. In: Proceedings of the 21st International Conference on Advanced Information Networking and Applications, AINA 2007, pp. 409–414. IEEE (2007)
28. Song, D.X., Wagner, D.A., Perrig, A.: Practical techniques for searches on encrypted data. In: 2000 IEEE Symposium on Security and Privacy, S&P 2000, pp. 44–55. IEEE (2000)
29. Sun, S.-F., Liu, J.K., Sakzad, A., Steinfeld, R., Yuen, T.H.: An efficient non-interactive multi-client searchable encryption with support for Boolean queries. In: Askoxylakis, I., Ioannidis, S., Katsikas, S., Meadows, C. (eds.) ESORICS 2016. LNCS, vol. 9878, pp. 154–172. Springer, Cham (2016). https://doi.org/10.1007/978-3-319-45744-4_8
30. Sun, W., Liu, X., Lou, W., Hou, Y.T., Li, H.: Catch you if you lie to me: efficient verifiable conjunctive keyword search over large dynamic encrypted cloud data. In: Proceedings of 2015 IEEE Conference on Computer Communications, INFOCOM 2015, pp. 2110–2118. IEEE (2015)

31. Veritas: Accelerating digital transformation through multi-cloud data management. https://manufacturerstores.techdata.com/docs/default-source/veritas/360-data-management-suite-brochure.pdf?sfvrsn=2. Accessed 15 Apr 2018

32. Wang, J., Chen, X., Huang, X., You, I., Xiang, Y.: Verifiable auditing for outsourced database in cloud computing. IEEE Trans. Comput. **64**(11), 3293–3303 (2015)

33. Wang, J., et al.: Efficient verifiable fuzzy keyword search over encrypted data in cloud computing. Comput. Sci. Inf. Syst. **10**(2), 667–684 (2013)

34. Wang, Y., Wang, J., Sun, S.-F., Liu, J.K., Susilo, W., Chen, X.: Towards multi-user searchable encryption supporting boolean query and fast decryption. In: Okamoto, T., Yu, Y., Au, M.H., Li, Y. (eds.) ProvSec 2017. LNCS, vol. 10592, pp. 24–38. Springer, Cham (2017). https://doi.org/10.1007/978-3-319-68637-0_2

35. Zuo, C., Macindoe, J., Yang, S., Steinfeld, R., Liu, J.K.: Trusted Boolean search on cloud using searchable symmetric encryption. In: 2016 IEEE Trustcom/BigDataSE/ISPA, pp. 113–120. IEEE (2016)

Order-Revealing Encryption: File-Injection Attack and Forward Security

Xingchen Wang[1,2,3] and Yunlei Zhao[1,2,3(✉)]

[1] Shanghai Key Laboratory of Data Science, School of Computer Science,
Fudan University, Shanghai, China
{xingchenwang16,ylzhao}@fudan.edu.cn
[2] State Key Laboratory of Integrated Services Networks,
Xidian University, Xi'an, China
[3] State Key Laboratory of Cryptology,
Beijing, China

Abstract. Order-preserving encryption (OPE) and order-revealing encryption (ORE) are among the core ingredients for encrypted databases (EDBs). In this work, we study the leakage of OPE and ORE and their forward security.

We propose generic yet powerful file-injection attacks (FIAs) on OPE/ORE, aimed at the situations of possessing *order by* and range queries. Our FIAs only exploit the *ideal* leakage of OPE/ORE (in particular, no need of data denseness or frequency). We executed some experiments on real datasets to test the performance, and the results show that our FIAs can cause an extreme hazard on most of the existing OPEs and OREs with high efficiency and 100% recovery rate.

We then formulate forward security of ORE, which is of independent of interest, and propose a practical compilation framework for achieving forward secure ORE in order to resist the perniciousness of FIA. The compilation framework can transform most of the existing OPEs/OREs into forward secure OREs, with the goal of minimizing the extra burden incurred on computation and storage. We also execute some experiments to analyze its performance.

Keywords: Order-revealing encryption
Order-preserving encryption · File-injection attack · Forward security

This work is supported in part by National Key Research and Development Program of China under Grant No. 2017YFB0802000, National Natural Science Foundation of China under Grant Nos. 61472084 and U1536205, Shanghai Innovation Action Project under Grant No. 16DZ1100200, Shanghai Science and Technology Development Funds under Grant No. 6JC1400801, and Shandong Provincial Key Research and Development Program of China under Grant Nos. 2017CXG0701 and 2018CXGC0701.

© Springer Nature Switzerland AG 2018
J. Lopez et al. (Eds.): ESORICS 2018, LNCS 11099, pp. 101–121, 2018.
https://doi.org/10.1007/978-3-319-98989-1_6

1   Introduction

In recent years, many property-preserving encryption (PPE) schemes and property-revealing encryption (PRE) schemes have been proposed with increased efficiency or/and security. This condition promotes the occurrence of encrypted database (EDB) systems. CryptDB [22] has been proposed by Popa et al. as the first practical EDB system for executing data manipulations on encrypted data. Because of its onion encryption model and its proxy architecture, CryptDB supports most of the basic operations on ciphertexts with acceptable efficiency.

As a kind of PPE, order-preserving encryption (OPE) has been gaining more and more attention and studies because of its applications on EDB. OPE was first proposed for numeric data by Agrawal et al. [3], where the order of plaintexts can be obtained by comparing their ciphertexts directly. Later, order-revealing encryption (ORE) was proposed by Boneh et al. [6] as the generalization of OPE, where the ciphertexts reveal their order by a special algorithm rather than comparing themselves directly.

Even though OPE and ORE aim at leaking nothing other than the order of ciphertexts, many attacks have been proposed against OPE and ORE in recent years. Naveed et al. [20] proposed several inference attacks against the deterministic encryption (DTE) and OPE in CryptDB. Durak et al. [10] showed that some ORE schemes, whose security is discussed on uniform inputs, could make the plaintext recovery of some known attacks more accurate on nonuniform data. They also proposed an attack, aiming at multiple encrypted columns of correlated data, which reveals more information than prior attacks against columns individually. Grubbs et al. [13] proposed new leakage-abuse attacks that achieve high-correctness recovery on OPE-encrypted data. They also presented the first attack on frequency-hiding OPE proposed in [16].

1.1   Our Contributions

In this paper, we first demonstrate the power of file-injection attacks (FIAs) on OPE/ORE, by developing two categories of FIA schemes (to the best of our knowledge, the first such attacks) against OPE/ORE. (The underlying assumptions and work flows of FIAs are briefly described in Sect. 3.1). Our FIA attacks are generic and powerful, in the sense that they only exploit the *ideal* leakage of OPE/ORE. Specifically, for our FIA attacks to work, the adversary only possesses the plaintext space, some old *order by* or range queries and the corresponding cipher result sets returned from EDB. In particular, the adversary does not need either the ability of comparing ciphertexts with the ORE comparison algorithm, or that of obtaining the ciphertexts outside of the result sets for *order by* and range queries.

In comparison with other attacks against OPE/ORE proposed in recent years, our FIA attacks rely upon less demanding conditions, and are more effective (particularly for attacking systems, like encrypted email systems, with the function of data sharing or transferring). For example, compared with the attacks against OPE/ORE proposed in [13, 20], our FIA attacks have the following features simultaneously: (1) no need of data denseness or frequency, and (2) generic against any OPE/ORE with *ideal* leakage. Furthermore, as shown in Appendix A, we compare and clarify in detail the advantages of our attacks over the chosen-plaintext attack (CPA) and the inference attack (IA). We present more details and experiments in the extended version [25] of this paper. Moreover, the experiment results show that our FIAs can cause an extreme hazard on most of the existing OPE and ORE schemes with high efficiency and 100% recovery rate.

The strong security property against FIA is forward security, which ensures that the previous data manipulations do not cause any leakage of the newly inserted data. In other words, it is infeasible for the server to produce a correct response when applying an old query to newly inserted ciphertexts encrypted by a forward secure scheme. To the best of our knowledge, no OPE/ORE construction offered the forward security to thwart FIAs up to now.

In this work, we give the formal definition of forward security for OPE/ORE, which might be of independent interest. Then, we propose a compilation framework for achieving forward secure ORE schemes against FIA attacks. Specifically, the compilation framework is applicable to most of the existing OPE/ORE schemes to transform them into forward secure ones. The resultant forward secure schemes leak nothing about newly inserted data that match the previous *order by* or range queries. Moreover, the compilation framework is constructed with the goal of minimizing the extra burden incurred on computation and storage. In particular, the compilation only uses some simple cryptographical tools like pseudo-random function (PRF), keyed hash function and trapdoor permutation (TDP). Finally, we execute some experiments to analyze the additional cost caused when applying our compilation framework to some prominent OPE/ORE schemes developed in recent year.

1.2 Related Work

Order-Preserving Encryption (OPE). Agrawal et al. [3] first proposed an OPE scheme for numeric data. Afterwards, OPE was formally studied by Boldyreva et al. [4], where, in particular, two leakage profiles were introduced. Boldyreva et al. [5] analyzed the one-wayness security of OPE, and showed that any OPE scheme must have immutable large ciphertexts if the scheme is constructed for leaking only order and frequency information. Popa et al. [21] proposed an OPE scheme in order tree structure, which is the first OPE scheme achieving the security of IND-OCPA (indistinguishability under ordered chosen-plaintext attack). Kerschbaum [16] proposed a frequency-hiding OPE scheme, which supports the security of IND-FA-OCPA (indistinguishability under frequency-analyzing ordered chosen-plaintext attack) for the first time. Later, a partial order preserving encryption (POPE), with a method for frequency-hiding, was developed by Roche et al. [23].

Order-Revealing Encryption (ORE). ORE was first generalized from OPE by Boneh et al. [6]. Their ORE scheme is built upon multilinear maps, which provides better security but at the cost of worse efficiency. Chenette et al. [9] proposed the first practical ORE, which achieves a simulation-based security w.r.t. some leakage functions that precisely quantify what is leaked by the scheme. Recently, Cash et al. [8] presented a general construction of ORE with reduced leakage as compared to [9], but at the cost of using a new type of "property-preserving" hash function based on bilinear maps.

File-Injection Attack on SSE. As a kind of query-recovery attack, Islam et al. [15] initiated the study of FIA attack against searchable symmetric encryption (SSE), by showing that a curious service provider can recover most of the keywords-search queries with high accuracy. Cash et al. [7] further improved the power of the attack initiated in [15], by assuming less knowledge about the files of clients even in a larger plaintext space. Except the encrypted email systems like Pmail [2], they also discussed how their active attacks (e.g., query recovery attacks, partial plaintext recovery attacks, FIAs) might be used to break through other systems such as the systems in [14,17]. Zhang et al. [26] showed that FIA can recover the keywords-search queries with just a few injected files even for SSE of low leakage. Their attacks outperform the attacks proposed in [7,15] in efficiency and in the prerequisite of adversary's prior knowledge.

2 Preliminaries

In this section we introduce some fundamental knowledge of TDP, ORE and OPE. We use standard notations and conventions below for writing probabilistic algorithms, experiments and protocols. If $\mathcal{D}$ denotes a domain, $x \xleftarrow{\$} \mathcal{D}$ is the operation of picking an element uniformly at random from $\mathcal{D}$. If $\mathbf{S}$ is a set, then for any k, $0 \leq k \leq |\mathbf{S}| - 1$, $\mathbf{S}[k]$ denotes the $(k+1)$-th element in $\mathbf{S}$. If α is neither an algorithm nor a set, then $x \leftarrow \alpha$ is a simple assignment statement. If A is a probabilistic algorithm, then $A(x_1, x_2, \cdots ; r)$ is the result of running A on inputs $x_1, x_2, \cdots$ and coins r. We let $A(x_1, x_2, \cdots) \rightarrow y$ denote the experiment of picking r at random and letting y be $A(x_1, x_2, \cdots ; r)$. By $\mathbb{P}[R_1; \cdots ; R_n : E]$ we denote the probability of event E, after the ordered execution of random processes $R_1, \cdots, R_n$.

Definition 1 (Trapdoor Permutation). *A tuple of polynomial-time algorithms (KeyGen, Π, Inv) over a domain $\mathcal{D}$ is a family of trapdoor permutations (or, sometimes, a trapdoor permutation informally), if it satisfies the following properties:*

- *KeyGen(1^λ) $\rightarrow$ (I, td). On input a secure parameter λ, the parameter generation algorithm outputs a pair of parameters (I, td). Each pair of the parameters defines a set $\mathcal{D}_I = \mathcal{D}_{\text{td}}$ with $|I| \geqslant \lambda$. Informally, I (resp., td) is said to be the public key (resp., secret key) of TDP.*
- *KeyGen$_1$(1^λ) $\rightarrow$ I. Let KeyGen$_1$ be the algorithm that executes KeyGen and returns I as the only result. Then (KeyGen$_1$, Π) is a family of one-way permutations.*

– $\mathsf{Inv}_{\mathsf{td}}(y) \to x$. Inv *is a deterministic inverting algorithm such that, for every pair of* (I, td) *output by* $\mathsf{KeyGen}\,(1^\lambda)$ *and any* $x \in \mathcal{D}_{\mathsf{td}} = \mathcal{D}_I$ *and* $y = \Pi_I(x)$, *it holds* $\mathsf{Inv}_{\mathsf{td}}(y) = x$. *For presentation simplicity, we also write the algorithm* $\mathsf{Inv}_{\mathsf{td}}$ *as* Π_{td}^{-1}, *and denoted by* $\Pi_I^k(x) = \overbrace{\Pi_I(\Pi_I(\cdots \Pi_I(x) \cdots))}^{k\ \text{TDPs}}$ *for some integer* $k \geq 1$.

2.1 Definition of ORE

Definition 2 (Order-Revealing Encryption). *A secret-key encryption scheme is an order-revealing encryption (ORE), if the scheme can be expressed as a tuple of algorithms* $\mathsf{ORE} = (\mathsf{ORE.Setup}, \mathsf{ORE.Encrypt}, \mathsf{ORE.Compare})$ *which is defined over a well-ordered domain* $\mathcal{M}$.

– $\mathsf{ORE.Setup}(1^\lambda) \to (pp, sp)$. *On input of a secure parameter* λ, *the setup algorithm outputs the set of public parameters* pp *and the set of secret parameters* sp *which includes the secret key for encryption algorithm.*
– $\mathsf{ORE.Encrypt}(pp, sp, m, \sigma_1) \to c$. *On input of* pp, sp *and a set* σ_1 *of other auxiliary parameters (that are not generated in the setup algorithm), the encryption algorithm encrypts the input plaintext* $m \in \{0, 1\}^*$ *to a ciphertext* c *that can reveal the correct order with other ciphertexts.*
– $\mathsf{ORE.Compare}(pp, sp, c_1, c_2, \sigma_2) \to b$. *On input of* pp, sp, *two ciphertexts* c_1, c_2, *and the set* σ_2 *of other auxiliary parameters, the comparison algorithm returns a bit* $b \in \{0, 1\}$ *as the result of order.*

The ORE definition in other literature is simple and only remains the necessary parameters. Our definition above is more complex, and the additional parameters are used for better describing the latter framework. With the above formulation, we aim for a generic and basic definition of ORE, where σ_1 and σ_2 may depend upon and vary with the concrete implementations of ORE. As a consequence, we do not introduce many details (that may vary with different implementations) and components like clients for interactive queries (as our FIAs are w.r.t. the generic OPE/ORE structure).

Leakage Profiles. The *ideal* leakage profile, the *random order-preserving function* profile, the *most significant-differing bit* profile, the *RtM* profile and the *MtR* profile are five leakage profiles that have been proposed in the literature. The first two were described by Boldyreva et al. [4], and the others were described by Chenette et al. [9].

We remark that, in Sect. 3, our FIAs are generic in the sense that they are constructed only with the *ideal* leakage profile. The *ideal* leakage profile just reveals the order and the frequency of the plaintexts. More precisely, only the leakage of order is necessary for our FIAs.

An adversary is said to be adaptive, if it is allowed to adaptively select data to be encrypted by the clients and then stored back to the server. Roughly speaking, an ORE scheme is said to be $\mathcal{L}$-adaptively-secure, if any probabilistic polynomial-time (PPT) adaptive adversary cannot learn more than the leakage as described according to the leakage profile $\mathcal{L}$.

2.2 Definition of OPE

Order-preserving encryption (OPE) is a simplified case of ORE. The ciphertext domain $\mathcal{C}$ of OPE needs to be well-ordered exactly as the plaintext domain $\mathcal{M}$.

Definition 3 (Order-Preserving Encryption). *A secret-key encryption scheme is an order-preserving encryption (OPE), if the scheme can be expressed as a tuple of algorithms OPE = (OPE.Setup, OPE.Encrypt), which is defined over a well-ordered plaintext domain $\mathcal{M}$ and a well-ordered ciphertext domain $\mathcal{C}$.*

- OPE.Setup(1^λ) → (pp, sp). *On input of a secure parameter λ, the setup algorithm outputs the set of public parameters pp and the set of secret parameters sp which includes the secret key for encryption algorithm.*
- OPE.Encrypt(pp, sp, m, σ_1) → c. *On input of pp, sp, and a set σ_1 of other auxiliary parameters, the encryption algorithm encrypts the input plaintext m to a ciphertext c that preserves the correct order with other ciphertexts.*

3 File-Injection Attacks on OPE/ORE

3.1 Assumptions and Basic Workflow

File injection attack has the following five assumptions: (1) The target system has a dependable component used for data-sharing or data-transmitting; (2) The adversary possesses the plaintext space of the target ciphertexts, and can store correct ciphertexts by sending some forged data to the client without suspicion; (3) The adversary possesses some old encrypted queries and can obtain the correct result sets from the server; (4) The adversary can only get the ciphertexts included in the result sets. (If the plaintext injected by the adversary does not match the queries, the corresponding ciphertext will not be known to it;) (5) The adversary is unable to forge queries or execute any PPE/PRE algorithm.

The basic workflow of FIA is briefly described as following:

- First, the adversary forges some data and sends them to the client from the server. After being encrypted by the client, the resultant ciphertexts of the forged data are sent back to the server for storing.
- Second, the adversary replays some old queries and infers the responses from the database management system (DBMS) with the leakage of newly inserted data.
- Third, the adversary adaptively executes the first two steps repeatedly. And the data will be recovered successfully when the adversary obtains enough leakage.

In some application scenarios like encrypted email system (e.g., Pmail [2]) or the systems in [14,17], FIA can be easily executed. Assuming that the server has already responded many email-order requests and recorded many encrypted data manipulation statements, the adversary can forge some emails and send to the client. When the new emails are encrypted and sent back to the DBMS, the adversary can take advantage of the entire set of ciphertexts, as well as the old queries, to collect more leakage and infer the corresponding plaintexts.

Unlike the FIA attacks against SSE, our FIA attacks against OPE/ORE are data-recovery attacks, which are more powerful. Moreover, the forged data are less likely to be detected because of the smaller forged part. Furthermore, by extending the concept of FIA, with our FIA attacks files do not only represent the data elements in NoSQL database, but can also be any kind of data which fit the target system.

Table 1. Notations in Sect. 3

Notation	Meaning
m, c	Instance variables of plaintext, ciphertext
$\mathcal{M}, \mathcal{C}$	Ordered spaces of plaintexts and ciphertexts
$\mathbf{M}, \mathbf{C}$	Set of plaintexts and set of ciphertexts
ω	Adversary makes at most ω file-injections
$q, \mathbf{Q}$	Instance variable of query and set of queries
ϕ	The flag variable which shows whether the plaintext of the target ciphertext has been recovered
i	The record of counter that is used for efficiency analysis in our experiments

3.2   Notations

Table 1 lists the meaning of some simple notations, which is helpful to comprehend the two FIA algorithms against *ideal*-secure OPEs/OREs presented in Sect. 3. Let $\mathbf{R}_q^i$ and $\mathbf{R}_q$ denote the result set of query q before the $(i + 1)$-th file-injection and the current result set of query q. Let $c \xleftarrow{\textit{file injection}} m$ denote the process in which the adversary sends the forged plaintext m from the server to the client and the resultant ciphertext c is sent back (by client) and stored in the EDB. Let a and b denote the indices of data which show their locations in their domains or their sets. Let $\mathsf{mid}(a, b)$ denote an arbitrary scheme for efficient median calculation, regardless of the round-off method. Let $\mathbf{d}$ and $\mathbf{dqueue}$ denote a structural body contains two indices (a, b) and a queue of the structural body. Let m_l and m_r (resp., $q.c_l$ and $q.c_r$) denote the left plaintext (resp., ciphertext) and right plaintext (resp., ciphertext) boundary values of range condition in a range query q. We use the composite notation to represent the main part which is related to the additional part. Hence, we let m_c denote the plaintext of the ciphertext c, let $\mathcal{M}_{a,b}$ denote the plaintext space between a and b, let $\mathbf{d}.a$ and $\mathbf{d}.b$ denote the parameters a and b in the structural body $\mathbf{d}$. Let $\mathcal{M}[\mathsf{mid}(a, b)]$ denotes the $(k + 1)$-th element in $\mathcal{M}$ for $k = \mathsf{mid}(a, b)$.

3.3   Binary Search

The two FIA algorithms presented below are based on a common algorithm – binary search. The difference between the two FIA algorithms lies in the search

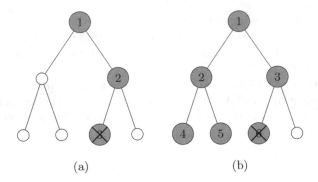

(a)   (b)

Fig. 1. Depth first binary search (a) and breadth first binary search (b). (Color figure online)

types they employ: one uses the traditional binary search like the depth first traversal, and another uses the breadth first traversal. The traditional binary search is a kind of (depth-first like) search algorithm, which finds the position of a target value within a sorted array by testing the order of the target value and the median value. In this work, we import the idea of breadth first traversal in the second FIA algorithm, with which we can get the relatively near data (around the target) that does not match the range condition.

We show two types of binary search in Fig. 1, where the colored nodes are the passed nodes with their order marked, and the crosses mark the target nodes. In the second FIA algorithm, our FIA attacker, with the range query determined by (m_l, m_r), needs to find a value m_1 matching the range condition, and a pair of relatively near unmatched values (m_2, m_3) in the file-injected dataset, such that $m_2 < m_l < m_1 < m_r < m_3$. The details are presented in Sect. 3.5.

3.4   Basic FIA with *order by* Query

Our FIA attacks use two kinds of order queries respectively: *order by* queries and range queries. The *order by* query (e.g., *select * from table_1 order by column_1*, which ensures that the result data are ordered, is one of two Data Manipulation Languages (DMLs) that are based on the order of data. And the other one is the range query with relational operators like "<", ">" and so on. In Sects. 3.4 and 3.5, we present the attack models and the FIA algorithms, assuming the attacker possesses these two kinds of order queries respectively.

The attack model of basic FIA, with *order by* queries, consists of the adversarial information (i.e., leakage) and the adversarial goal. As to the adversarial information, we limit the power of adversaries in order for more practical attacks in practice. Specifically, the adversary only possesses, as adversarial information, the plaintext space $\mathcal{M}$, the set $\mathbf{Q}$ of old *order by* queries, and the result sets of those queries with forged data. In particular, they do not have any information about the data not in the result sets of the old queries. About the adversarial goal, we partition it into two types: recovering the plaintext of a single ciphertext, and recovering the plaintexts of all the ciphertexts in the result sets. This partition facilitates the discussion of time complexity as we show later. We formalize the attack model as following:

Leakage: $\mathcal{L}(\mathcal{M}, \mathbf{Q}, \mathbf{R_Q} = \{ \bigcup_{q \in \mathbf{Q}, 0 \leq i \leq \omega} \mathbf{R}^i_{q|\text{ordered}} \})$

Goal: $m_c \ (c \in \mathbf{R}^0_{q|\text{ordered}}, \ q \in \mathbf{Q}) \ or \ \mathbf{M_C} \ (\mathbf{C} = \bigcup_{q \in \mathbf{Q}} \mathbf{R}_q)$

where $\mathbf{R}^i_{q|\text{ordered}}$ denotes the *ordered* result set for *order by* query q before the $(i+1)$-th file-injection, $\mathbf{R}^0_{q|\text{ordered}}$ denotes the original *ordered* result set for *order by* query q, $\mathbf{M_C} \ (\mathbf{C} = \bigcup_{q \in \mathbf{Q}} \mathbf{R}_q)$ denotes the plaintext set $\mathbf{M_C}$ corresponding to the ciphertext set $\mathbf{C}$ in the current result sets for all the queries in $\mathbf{Q}$. Here, $\mathbf{M_C}$ can also be expressed as a mapping relation precisely, denoted $\mathcal{T}_{(\mathbf{M},\mathbf{C})}$, between all the ciphertexts in $\mathbf{C}$ (which includes all the original and forged data) and their corresponding plaintexts in $\mathbf{M_C}$.

Algorithm 1.
$\quad m_c \leftarrow \mathsf{FIA\_Orderby}(\mathcal{M}, c \in \mathbf{R}^0_{q|\text{ordered}}, q)$

1: $a \leftarrow -1, \ \phi \leftarrow 0, \ b \leftarrow |\mathcal{M}|$
2: **for** $i \leftarrow 1$ **to** ∞ **do**
3: $\quad$ $c_i \xleftarrow{\textit{file injection}} \mathcal{M}[\text{mid}(a, b)]$
4: $\quad$ **if** $(\mathsf{Comp}(c_i, c) = 0)$
5: $\quad\quad$ $\phi \leftarrow 1,$ **break**
6: $\quad$ **else if** $(\text{mid}(a, b) = a$ **or** $\text{mid}(a, b) = b)$ **break**
7: $\quad$ **else if** $(\mathsf{Comp}(c_i, c) = 1)$
8: $\quad\quad$ $b \leftarrow \text{mid}(a, b)$
9: $\quad$ **else** $a \leftarrow \text{mid}(a, b)$
10: $\quad$ **end if**
11: **end for**
12: **if** $(\phi = 1)$ **return** $m_c \leftarrow \mathcal{M}[\text{mid}(a, b)]$
13: **else return** $\bot$

For ease of comprehension, Algorithm 1 describes the elementary FIA based on utilizing a single *order by* query over an entire dataset. The adversary will continually detect the plaintext of the target ciphertext c with an old query q by file-injections. We use $\mathsf{Comp}(c_i, c)$ to express the order result of query q about the target ciphertext c and the i-th injected ciphertext c_i, where the result expresses as following:

$$\mathsf{Comp}(c_i, c) = \begin{cases} 0 & c_i = c \\ 1 & c_i > c \\ -1 & c_i < c. \end{cases}$$

Time Complexity. The time complexity of Algorithm 1 is $O(\log|\mathcal{M}|)$ obviously in the worst condition for recovering one plaintext. When the adversarial goal is to recover all the N nonrepetitive ciphertexts in the entire result set, the time complexity is $O(N\log|\mathcal{M}| - N\log N)$ in the worst case. This means, in this case, the average time complexity of recovering a single ciphertext becomes smaller because the order of a ciphertext can be used for both sides. In other words, a file-injection for a target will reveal some order information about other target ciphertexts as well.

In Algorithm 1, we only take advantage of the leakage $\mathcal{L}_1(\mathcal{M}, q, \mathbf{R}'_q)$, where $\mathbf{R}'_q = \mathbf{R}_q \setminus \mathbf{R}^0_q$ is the result set after file-injections excluding the original result set. Because the leakage of the original result set $\mathbf{R}^0_q$ is in the *ideal* leakage profile, we can only get some order information between the target ciphertext c_{target} and other ciphertexts. In other words, we can rewrite the original result set as

$$\mathbf{R}^0_q = \{\mathbf{C}^-_{\text{ordered}}, c_{\text{target}}, \mathbf{C}^+_{\text{ordered}}\}$$

where $\mathbf{C}^-_{\text{ordered}}$ is the set of ordered ciphertexts which are smaller than the target, and $\mathbf{C}^+_{\text{ordered}}$ is the set of ordered ciphertexts which are greater than the target. Under the assumption of knowing nothing about the original ciphertexts except their order information, we can only take advantage of $|\mathbf{C}^-_{\text{ordered}}|$ and $|\mathbf{C}^+_{\text{ordered}}|$ to curtail the plaintext space. We delete the first $|\mathbf{C}^-_{\text{ordered}}|$ plaintexts and the last $|\mathbf{C}^+_{\text{ordered}}|$ plaintexts from the ordered plaintext space $\mathcal{M}$, and then we get a smaller new plaintext space $\mathcal{M}'$ for the target c_{target}. Thus, the time complexity of recovering a single ciphertext becomes $O(\log|\mathcal{M}'|)$ which is even smaller now. In this way, the adversary can adaptively curtail the plaintext space according to the number of ciphertexts on both sides after each file-injection.

Moreover, an improved method with hierarchical idea is presented in the extended version [25] of this paper.

3.5   FIA with Range Queries

The attack model of FIA with range queries also consists of the adversarial information and the adversarial goal. As to the adversarial information, the adversary just has the plaintext space $\mathcal{M}$, the old range queries in $\mathbf{Q}$, and the result sets of those queries without inner order. In this condition, the leakage is less than that with *order by* queries, because the adversary only knows the result set matching the range conditions without knowing the inner order. As to the adversarial goal, the adversary needs to recover the boundary plaintexts of the range conditions as well as all the plaintexts matching the range conditions. We formalize the attack model as following:

$$\textbf{Leakage:} \quad \mathcal{L}(\mathcal{M}, \mathbf{Q}, \mathbf{R_Q} = \{ \bigcup_{q\in\mathbf{Q}, 0\leq i\leq\omega} \mathbf{R}^i_q\})$$

$$\textbf{Goal:} \quad \mathbf{M}_l, \mathbf{M}_r, \mathbf{M_C} \ (\mathbf{C} = \{c \mid q.c_l < c < q.c_r, q \in \mathbf{Q}\})$$

where $\mathbf{M_C}$ can be expressed as a mapping relation precisely, denoted $\mathcal{T}_{(\mathbf{M},\mathbf{C})}$, between all the ciphertexts in $\mathbf{C}$ (which includes all the original and forged data) and their plaintexts in $\mathbf{M_C}$, $\mathbf{R}^i_q$ is not ordered, $\mathbf{M}_l$ and $\mathbf{M}_r$ contain all the boundary plaintexts of the range queries in $\mathbf{Q}$. In our construction, we design 3 steps to achieve the goal as following:

- First, the adversary must find a plaintext matching the range condition, whether its ciphertext is in the original EDB or not.
- Second, the adversary recovers the boundary plaintexts using Algorithm 1.
- Third, the adversary recovers all the plaintexts of the ciphertexts matching the range condition by several file-injections.

Here, to describe the FIA scheme briefly, Algorithm 2 is based on utilizing a single range query without any *order by* operation. In the following descriptions, q denotes the range query with the boundary ciphertexts denoted $q.c_l$ and $q.c_r$ respectively. $\mathbf{M_{R_q}}$ denotes the plaintext set corresponding to the cipher result set $\mathbf{R_q}$ for query q.

In Algorithm 2, we adopt the breadth first search, because under the assumption of FIA the adversary does not know the order between file-injected data and the boundary ciphertexts in case the file-injected data do not match the range condition. With this limitation, the breadth first search is beneficial to find a plaintext matching the condition, and to get the relatively near unmatching plaintexts that are necessary for recovering the boundary plaintexts. Then, the boundary plaintexts m_l and m_r are recovered by calling Algorithm 1. Finally, the plaintext set $\mathbf{M_{R_q}}$ is recovered by several file-injections over the entire plaintext set matching the condition.

Algorithm 2.

$\quad m_l,\ m_r,\ \mathbf{M_{R_q}} \leftarrow \mathsf{FIA\_Rangequery}(\mathcal{M},\ q)$

1: $a \leftarrow -1,\ b \leftarrow |\mathcal{M}|,\ \mathbf{d} \leftarrow (a,\ b)$
2: insert $\mathbf{d}$ into the queue **dqueue**
3: **while dqueue** $\neq \emptyset$
4: $\quad$ take out the first $\mathbf{d}$ in **dqueue**, $a \leftarrow \mathbf{d}.a,\ b \leftarrow \mathbf{d}.b$
5: $\quad c \xleftarrow{\ file\ injection\ } \mathcal{M}[\mathsf{mid}(a,\ b)]$
6: $\quad$ **if** $|\mathbf{R_q^0}| \neq |\mathbf{R_q}|$ **break**
7: $\quad$ **if** $(\mathsf{mid}(a,\ \mathsf{mid}(a,\ b)) \neq a$ **and** $\mathsf{mid}(a,\ \mathsf{mid}(a,\ b)) \neq \mathsf{mid}(a,\ b))$
8: $\quad\quad \mathbf{d} \leftarrow (a,\ \mathsf{mid}(a,\ b))$, insert $\mathbf{d}$ into **dqueue**
9: $\quad$ **end if**
10: $\quad$ **if** $(\mathsf{mid}(\mathsf{mid}(a,\ b),\ b) \neq b$ **and** $\mathsf{mid}(\mathsf{mid}(a,\ b),\ b) \neq \mathsf{mid}(a,\ b))$
11: $\quad\quad \mathbf{d} \leftarrow (\mathsf{mid}(a,\ b),\ b)$, insert $\mathbf{d}$ into **dqueue**
12: $\quad$ **end if**
13: $m_l \leftarrow \mathsf{FIA\_Orderby}(\mathcal{M}_{a,\mathsf{mid}(a,b)},\ q.c_l,\ q)$
14: $m_r \leftarrow \mathsf{FIA\_Orderby}(\mathcal{M}_{\mathsf{mid}(a,b),b},\ q.c_r,\ q)$
15: $\mathbf{M_{R_q}} \leftarrow$ do file-injections from m_l to m_r and get their mapping table or corresponding plaintext set briefly
16: **return** $m_l,\ m_r,\ \mathbf{M_{R_q}}$

Most of the boundary values are very special in practice. For instance, the numbers, which are the multiple of $10^\gamma (\gamma = 0, 1, 2...)$, are frequently used for range query over numerical data; and the 26 letters are used for the same purpose over string data usually. Based on the different frequency of the plaintexts which are between every two adjacent common boundary plaintexts, the adversary may recover them more rapidly by several file-injections instead of the first step.

For space limitation, the analysis of time complexity, the discussions on FIA with both *order by* Queries and Range Queries, the description of our experiments and the FIA against Frequency-Hiding OPE are presented in the extended version [25] of this paper.

4   Formulating Forward Secure ORE

Forward security is a strong property of the dynamic SSE leakage profile. For a dynamic SSE scheme, its forward security means that: the previous data manipulations do not cause any leakage of the newly inserted data. Stefanov et al. [24] proposed this notion informally. Stefanov et al. [24] also proposed the concept of backward security, which ensures that the previous data manipulations do not leak any information about the newly deleted data. In this work, we extend this concept from SSE to OPE/ORE. Specifically, we give the definitions of forward security and backward security informally, as following:

Definition 4 (Forward/Backward Security). *An $\mathcal{L}$-adaptively-secure ORE scheme is forward (resp., backward) secure if the leakage profile, denoted $\mathcal{L}_{update}$, of update operation for* update = add *(resp.,* update = delete*) can be described as following:*

$$\mathcal{L}_{update}(\text{update}, \mathbf{W}_{update}) = (\text{update}, \mathbf{IND}_{update})$$

where add *(resp.,* delete*) denotes the addition (resp., deletion) of data.* $\mathbf{W}_{update}$ *is the data set of the update operations, in which the data have their own data storage structure, indices, and constraints according to the database.* $\mathbf{IND}_{update}$ *is a set that only describes the modified column (in SQL database) or the document (in NoSQL database) and the indices of updated data.*

Informally, a forward secure ORE ensures that the previous data order manipulations do not leak any information about the newly inserted data. Meanwhile, the new data order manipulations can be executed normally, and can correctly leak the order information about the newly inserted data. And in a forward secure ORE scheme, $\mathbf{W}_{update}$ of a simple insertion can be briefly described as $\mathbf{W}_{add} = (m, s)$, where s denotes the order space of the related data on which order queries may be executed. For SQL databases, s can represent a column of a table. And for NoSQL databases, s can represent a set of documents. $\mathbf{IND}_{update}$ of a simple insertion can be briefly described as $\mathbf{IND}_{add} = (j, s)$, where the incremental timestamp j is initially set to be 0 and is shared by all the manipulations.

Let e denote the intermediate ciphertext without forward security. Let $\mathbf{op}(s)$ denote the order pattern of an order space s, which lists all the timestamps of the order queries. $\mathbf{Hist}(s)$ contains all the data-updating histories of s as well as the index $index_s$ of s. Here, we only use it to list all the data-addition histories over the time. More formally, they can be defined as:

$$\mathbf{op}(s) = \{j : (j, s, \mathsf{order}) \in \mathbf{List_{SQL}}\}$$

$$\mathbf{Hist}(s) = \{index_s, (j, \mathsf{add}, e) : (j, s, \mathsf{add}, e) \in \mathbf{List_{SQL}}\}$$

where add denotes the addition manipulation, order denotes the ordering manipulation, $\mathbf{List_{SQL}}$ denotes the list of data-manipulations. And we give the formal definition of forward secure ORE below.

Definition 5 (Forward Secure ORE). *Let the algorithm tuple*

$$\Gamma = (\mathsf{ORE\_Setup}, \mathsf{ORE\_Encrypt}, \mathsf{ORE\_Compare})$$

be an ORE scheme. Let $\mathcal{A}$ denote a PPT adaptive adversary. Define a real security game $\mathbf{FS\text{-}ORE\text{-}R}_{\mathcal{A}}^{\Gamma}(\lambda)$, in which $\mathcal{A}$ gets the public parameters output by $\mathsf{ORE\_Setup}(\lambda)$ and gets access to the encryption oracle and the comparison oracle adaptively. Based on the given public parameters and all the answers received from the oracles, $\mathcal{A}$ outputs a bit as the result of the game. Define an ideal security game $\mathbf{FS\text{-}ORE\text{-}I}_{\mathcal{A},\mathcal{S},\mathcal{L}_{\Gamma}}^{\Gamma}(\lambda)$, in which a PPT simulator $\mathcal{S}$ only takes the leakage profile $\mathcal{L}_{\Gamma}$ as input. $\mathcal{L}_{\Gamma}$ has two parts as following:

$$\mathcal{L}_{\mathsf{update}}(\mathsf{add}, (m, s)) = (\mathsf{add}, (j, s))$$

$$\mathcal{L}_{\mathsf{compare}}(c_1, c_2, s) = (\mathbf{op}(s), \mathbf{Hist}(s))$$

The simulator $\mathcal{S}$ will output a bit as the result of the ideal game. The scheme Γ is said to be forward secure, if the following equation holds for any sufficient large λ:

$$|\mathbb{P}[\mathbf{FS\text{-}ORE\text{-}R}_{\mathcal{A}}^{\Gamma}(\lambda) = 1] - \mathbb{P}[\mathbf{FS\text{-}ORE\text{-}I}_{\mathcal{A},\mathcal{S},\mathcal{L}_{\Gamma}}^{\Gamma}(\lambda) = 1]| \leq \mathrm{negl}(\lambda)$$

where $\mathrm{negl}(\lambda)$ denotes a negligible function.

5   A Compilation Framework for Forward Secure ORE

To the best of our knowledge, all the existing OPE and ORE schemes in the literature do not have forward security *precisely*. Here, we use *"precisely"* with only the special case of POPE [23]. In [23], there is not any statement about whether the interactive processes need a client authorization or not. For the common application scenarios of OPE/ORE in practice, there is not any client authorization for querying. However, if the client authorization is mandated, POPE has forward security.

In the general case, the ciphertexts in EDB do not cover the entire ciphertext space. In other words, the ciphertexts in EDB are not dense usually. Thus, it is difficult to recover all the stored ciphertexts correctly with the limited leakage of

OPE/ORE. However, according to our FIA constructions and experiments, FIA schemes are powerful and effective in recovering data encrypted by OPE/ORE without forward security in practice. Though forward security can be achieved with oblivious RAM (ORAM) [11,12] in general, it incurs massive overburden of performance [19] (large bandwidth consumption, multiple data round-trips, and/or large client storage complexity). Thus, it is desirable to have practical forward secure OPE/ORE schemes.

Table 2. Notations in Sect. 5

Notation	Meaning
e	Instance of intermediate ciphertext output by the original ORE or OPE scheme in EDB
$\Pi, \mathsf{KeyGen}, sk, pk$	A TDP scheme, its key-generation algorithm and its secret key, public key
PRF, H	A pseudo-random function and a keyed hash function
$\mathrm{OT}, \mathbf{OT}, \mathcal{OT}$	Instance of order token, map of order token stored on the client and domain of order token
i	The counter of order tokens, which is equal to the number of order tokens minus one
s	Instance of order space, which ensures that the data in different order spaces cannot be ordered

In this section, we present a practical compilation framework that transforms most of the existing OPE/ORE schemes into forward secure ones. To ease the understanding of the framework, we first give the meaning of some notations in Table 2.

5.1 Basic Ideas

With forward security, the *add* operation should leak nothing to server. In other words, the server should not distinguish between the ciphertexts output by a forward secure ORE and the ciphertexts encrypted by a perfect encryption scheme, when they are just inserted to the database before undergoing any search operation. In order to realize this goal, the ciphertext e generated by original OPE/ORE should be salted in our compilation framework. And we use TDP to link the salts to reduce the bandwidth consumption.

The salt is a hash value of an order token OT in our construction. To insert a new datum to EDB (say, the $(i + 1)$-th insertion, $i \geq 0$), the client generates an order token OT_i based on the TDP scheme Π, its secret key sk, and the last order token OT_{i-1}. If OT_i ($i = 0$) is the first order token in the order space, it will be randomly selected from the domain of order token $\mathcal{OT}$. In order to reduce the client storage, the client only stores the latest order token OT_i and the corresponding counter i in our basic construction. When an order query needs to be executed, the client sends the current order token OT_i and the counter i to the server. The server can then calculate all the order tokens with the public key pk, and gets the original OPE/ORE ciphertexts by desalting operations. At last, the client will receive the correct comparison result which is calculated with the comparison algorithm of the original OPE/ORE by the server.

5.2 The Compilation Framework

Given any OPE or ORE scheme, denoted Γ = (ORE_Setup, ORE_Encrypt, ORE_Compare), the compiled ORE scheme is described in Algorithm 3, which is denoted by Γ_{fp} = (Setup, Encrypt, Compare). In Algorithm 3, the parts of the original OPE/ORE are only briefly described.

Algorithm 3. Γ_{fp}

Setup(1^λ)
1: $(pp, sp) \leftarrow$ ORE_Setup(1^λ)
2: $\mathbf{OT} \leftarrow$ empty map
3: $(sk, pk) \leftarrow$ KeyGen(1^λ)
4: $k_0 \xleftarrow{\$} \{0,1\}^\lambda$
5: **return** $((pk, pp), (sk, sp, k_0, \mathbf{OT}))$

Encrypt($pp, (sk, sp, k_0, \mathbf{OT}), m, (\mathsf{add}, s, \sigma_1)$)
      Client :
1: $k_s \leftarrow$ PRF$_{k_0}[s]$
2: $(OT_i, i) \leftarrow \mathbf{OT}[s]$
3: **if** $(OT_i, i) = \perp$ $\{i \leftarrow -1, \ OT_{i+1} \xleftarrow{\$} \mathcal{OT}\}$
4: **else** $OT_{i+1} \leftarrow \Pi_{sk}^{-1}(OT_i)$
5: **end if**
6: $\mathbf{OT}[s] \leftarrow (OT_{i+1}, i+1)$
7: $c_{i+1} \leftarrow$ ORE_Encrypt($pp, sp, m, (\mathsf{add}, s, \sigma_1)$) $\oplus$ H(k_s, OT_{i+1})
8: Send c_{i+1} to server.
      Server :
9: Insert c_{i+1} into EDB.

Compare($(pk, pp), (sp, k_0, \mathbf{OT}), c_{s_\alpha}, c_{s_\beta}, (s, \sigma_2)$)
      Client :
1: $k_s \leftarrow$ PRF$_{k_0}[s]$
2: $(OT_i, i) \leftarrow \mathbf{OT}[s]$
3: **if** $(OT_i, i) = \perp$ **OR** $i = 0$ **return** $\emptyset$
4: Send (OT_i, i, k_s) to server.
      Server :
5: $e_{s_\alpha} \leftarrow c_{s_\alpha} \oplus$ H($k_s, \Pi_{pk}^{i-\alpha}(OT_i)$)
6: $e_{s_\beta} \leftarrow c_{s_\beta} \oplus$ H($k_s, \Pi_{pk}^{i-\beta}(OT_i)$)
7: $b \leftarrow$ ORE_Compare($pp, sp, e_{s_\alpha}, e_{s_\beta}, (s, \sigma_2)$)
8: Send the result b to client

In our construction, we let λ denote the secure parameter. Let k_0 denote the main key of our compilation framework. For each order space s, the key k_s of keyed hash function H is calculated by pseudo-random function $\mathsf{PRF}_{k_0}[s]$. Let add denote the addition/insertion of data. The order tokens are calculated with TDP one by one in sequence, and the hash values of these tokens will xor the original OPE/ORE ciphertexts to generate the final ciphertexts without extra storage consumption at the server side. The salt of the final ciphertext is of λ bits, and will be desalted in the comparison algorithm. In the comparison algorithm, we let c_{s_α} and c_{s_β} denote two ciphertexts to be compared in the order space s with their indices α and β respectively. We let e_{s_α} and e_{s_β} denote their intermediate ciphertexts output by the original OPE/ORE respectively.

For space limitation, the methods of data deletion and batch encryption is postponed to Appendix B.

5.3 Analysis of Forward Security

In our framework, the ciphertexts output by the original OPE/ORE xor the one-way generated salts. Hence, the newly inserted data leak nothing to the server if they have not been queried. Once the data have been queried and desalted, the ciphertexts turn into the security level of the original OPE/ORE scheme for the adversary with continuous monitoring. Hence, the security of the composite forward secure ORE cannot be weaker than that of the original OPE/ORE. On the other hand, our compilation framework is powerful against FIAs, because the forged data will not leak any information with the old queries. The data need a new credible order query from the client to desalt.

For space limitation, the formal proof of forward security is presented in the extended version [25] of this paper. Moreover, the description of our experiments is postponed to Appendix C.

6   Conclusion and Future Work

In this work, we study the leakage of OPE and ORE. We propose generic yet devastating FIA attacks which only exploit the *ideal* leakage of OPE/ORE. We also propose various improved methods to further boost the efficiency. Compared with existing attacks against OPE/ORE, our FIA attacks rely upon less demanding conditions, and can be more effective. We executed some experiments on real datasets to test the performance, and the results show that our FIA attacks can cause an extreme hazard on most of the existing OPE and ORE schemes with high efficiency and 100% recovery rate.

We then formulate forward-secure ORE, which may be of independent interest. In order to resist the disastrous effectiveness of FIA, we propose a practical compilation framework for transforming most existing OPE/ORE schemes into forward-secure ones. Finally, we execute experiments on some prominent OPE/ORE schemes developed in recent years, and the results show that our compilation framework is practical and useful for most of the systems.

Our compilation framework does not fit the OPE/ORE schemes which store the inserted data in order trees. Achieving forward security for these OPE/ORE schemes is an interesting direction for future research.

Acknowledgement. We thank the anonymous reviewers for their insightful comments. We are grateful to Yuan Li and Hongbing Wang for many helpful discussions.

A   Comparison Among FIA and Other Generic Attacks Against OPE/ORE

Known- and chosen-plaintext attacks (CPAs) have been considered in many OPE/ORE works. To the best of our knowledge, the latest discussion of CPA is in [13]. Besides these attacks against OPE/ORE, inference attack (IA) is also a kind of powerful generic attack which has been described in [20] detailedly. In this subsection, we make brief comparisons among FIA, CPA and IA.

About the adversarial prerequisite, these three attacks all need an unbroken auxiliary dataset as the plaintext space, but only IA needs the data-frequency statistics. About the source of leakage information, CPA only utilizes the data which are chosen by the adversary and encrypted by the encryption scheme in the system; IA only utilizes the original ciphertexts in the EDB; but FIA can utilize both the main forged data (which are chosen by the adversary and encrypted by the system) and the secondary original ciphertexts in the EDB. Specially, the leakage information in FIA is obtained through old queries. In other words, the ciphertexts, which are not included in the result sets of the old queries, are not required in the adversarial prerequisite. As for the comparison algorithm, CPA and IA must use it; FIA only calls it normally through the old queries. About the performance, 100% accuracy can be achieved easily with either CPA or FIA, but it is difficult to achieve with IA. Additionally, CPA and FIA can attack the frequency-hiding OPE, but IA cannot do this without the decline of accuracy and applicability.

Overall, FIA and CPA require less auxiliary information, while IA needs more auxiliary information. CPA needs more adversarial abilities, but FIA/IA need less adversarial abilities. Because of the utilization rate of leakage, FIA is more efficient than CPA, while the efficiency of IA depends on the size of plaintext space overly.

B   The Methods of Data Deletion and Batch Encryption

For data deletion, the first method is to store the deleted data in another EDB. Then a checking procedure should be added into the comparison algorithm to ensure that the ordered data have not been deleted. When the computing and bandwidth resource are sufficient and the server does not receive any query, the system can execute a **refresh** operation, which deletes all the deleted data from both EDB and recalculate all the order tokens and ciphertexts in sequence for curtailing storage and lifting efficiency. In this case, the scheme also achieves backward security. The second method is to insert the sequence numbers into EDB when inserting data. Then, for the situation where some data have been deleted, the server can calculate the salts of the remaining data by executing TDP exact times according to the interval leaked by sequence numbers. For space limitation, the analysis of storage and computational complexity is presented in the extended version [25] of this paper.

For batch encryptions, we can simply arrange all the elements in random order, and run the Encrypt algorithm in sequence. If batch encryptions are common in the system, we can add an extra batch index in the database for each datum, and use the same calculated order token for salting all the intermediate ciphertexts in a batch. This solution reduces the average computational complexity at the expense of leaking some information (e.g. equality) of the elements in the same batch.

C   Applicability and Experiments

Our compilation framework can be applied to all the OPE/ORE schemes except the OPE schemes (like the *ideal*-secure schemes proposed in [16,21]) that store the ciphertexts in order trees. These OPE schemes [16,21] leak all the ciphertext order from the tree structure. Hence, the salting of our framework is useless in this case.

In the experiments, we combined the OPE/ORE schemes in [4] and [9] with our forward secure framework. The experiments are implemented in C/C++,

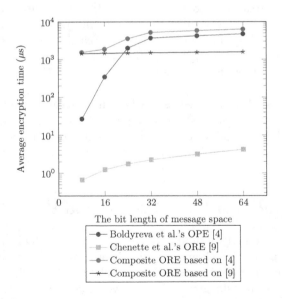

Fig. 2. The comparison of average encryption time between two existing OPE/ORE schemes and the composite forward secure ORE schemes with our compilation framework.

and our experiments were performed using a single core on a machine with an Intel Pentium G2020 2.9 GHz CPU and 4 GB available RAM. We operate at 128-bits of security. We use HMAC as the PRF and the keyed hash function, and we use the RSA implementation (with 2048 bits RSA keys) in OpenSSL's BigNum library as the TDP. We use Blake2b as the underlying hash function. For our basic implementation of Boldyreva et al.'s OPE scheme, we use the C++ implementation from CryptDB [22], and for the implementation of Chenette et al.'s ORE scheme, we use the C-implemented FastORE mentioned in [18]. We use the California public employee payroll data from 2014 [1] as the experimental plaintext sets.

Figure 2 shows the comparison results of the average encryption time between the original schemes and the composite schemes. We respectively used 100000 data for testing each of the points in Fig. 2 and calculated the average results.

About the additional average encryption time, the composite forward secure ORE schemes demand about 1.5 ms for each datum encryption. Moreover, as to the additional average comparison time, the composite forward secure ORE schemes demand about 47 μs. Because we chose two of the most practical OPE/ORE schemes as the contrasts, the composite forward secure ORE schemes seem slower. However, the additional comparison time is still at the microsecond level. Hence, our scheme is still practical and useful for the most common systems.

References

1. California Public Employee Payroll Data (2014). http://transparentcalifornia.com/downloads/
2. Pmail (2014). https://github.com/tonypr/Pmail
3. Agrawal, R., Kiernan, J., Srikant, R., Xu, Y.: Order preserving encryption for numeric data. In: ACM SIGMOD International Conference on Management of Data, pp. 563–574. ACM, Paris (2004)
4. Boldyreva, A., Chenette, N., Lee, Y., O'Neill, A.: Order-preserving symmetric encryption. In: Joux, A. (ed.) EUROCRYPT 2009. LNCS, vol. 5479, pp. 224–241. Springer, Heidelberg (2009). https://doi.org/10.1007/978-3-642-01001-9_13
5. Boldyreva, A., Chenette, N., O'Neill, A.: Order-preserving encryption revisited: improved security analysis and alternative solutions. In: Rogaway, P. (ed.) CRYPTO 2011. LNCS, vol. 6841, pp. 578–595. Springer, Heidelberg (2011). https://doi.org/10.1007/978-3-642-22792-9_33
6. Boneh, D., Lewi, K., Raykova, M., Sahai, A., Zhandry, M., Zimmerman, J.: Semantically secure order-revealing encryption: multi-input functional encryption without obfuscation. In: Oswald, E., Fischlin, M. (eds.) EUROCRYPT 2015. LNCS, vol. 9057, pp. 563–594. Springer, Heidelberg (2015). https://doi.org/10.1007/978-3-662-46803-6_19
7. Cash, D., Grubbs, P., Perry, J., Ristenpart, T.: Leakage-abuse attacks against searchable encryption. In: Proceedings of the 22nd ACM SIGSAC Conference on Computer and Communications Security, pp. 668–679. ACM, Denver (2015)
8. Cash, D., Liu, F.H., O'Neill, A., Zhang, C.: Reducing the leakage in practical order-revealing encryption. Cryptology ePrint Archive, Report 2016/661 (2016). http://eprint.iacr.org/2016/661

9. Chenette, N., Lewi, K., Weis, S.A., Wu, D.J.: Practical order-revealing encryption with limited leakage. In: Peyrin, T. (ed.) FSE 2016. LNCS, vol. 9783, pp. 474–493. Springer, Heidelberg (2016). https://doi.org/10.1007/978-3-662-52993-5_24

10. Durak, F.B., DuBuisson, T.M., Cash, D.: What else is revealed by order-revealing encryption? In: Proceedings of the 2016 ACM SIGSAC Conference on Computer and Communications Security, pp. 1155–1166. ACM, Vienna (2016)

11. Garg, S., Mohassel, P., Papamanthou, C.: TWORAM: Efficient Oblivious RAM in Two Rounds with Applications to Searchable Encryption. In: Robshaw, M., Katz, J. (eds.) CRYPTO 2016. LNCS, vol. 9816, pp. 563–592. Springer, Heidelberg (2016). https://doi.org/10.1007/978-3-662-53015-3_20

12. Goldreich, O., Ostrovsky, R.: Software protection and simulation on oblivious RAMs. J. ACM (JACM) 43(3), 431–473 (1996)

13. Grubbs, P., Sekniqi, K., Bindschaedler, V., Naveed, M., Ristenpart, T.: Leakage-abuse attacks against order-revealing encryption. In: 2017 IEEE Symposium on Security and Privacy (SP), pp. 655–672. IEEE (2017)

14. He, W., Akhawe, D., Jain, S., Shi, E., Song, D.: Shadowcrypt: encrypted web applications for everyone. In: Proceedings of the 2014 ACM SIGSAC Conference on Computer and Communications Security, pp. 1028–1039. ACM, Scottsdale (2014)

15. Islam, M.S., Kuzu, M., Kantarcioglu, M.: Access pattern disclosure on searchable encryption: ramification, attack and mitigation. In: 19th Annual Network and Distributed System Security Symposium, vol. 20, p. 12. The Internet Society, San Diego (2012)

16. Kerschbaum, F.: Frequency-hiding order-preserving encryption. In: Proceedings of the 22nd ACM SIGSAC Conference on Computer and Communications Security, pp. 656–667. ACM, Denver (2015)

17. Lau, B., Chung, S.P., Song, C., Jang, Y., Lee, W., Boldyreva, A.: Mimesis aegis: a mimicry privacy shield-a system's approach to data privacy on public cloud. In: Proceeding of the 23rd USENIX conference on Security Symposium, pp. 33–48. USENIX Association, San Diego (2014)

18. Lewi, K., Wu, D.J.: Order-revealing encryption: new constructions, applications, and lower bounds. In: Proceedings of the 2016 ACM SIGSAC Conference on Computer and Communications Security, pp. 1167–1178. ACM, Vienna (2016)

19. Naveed, M.: The fallacy of composition of oblivious ram and searchable encryption. Cryptology ePrint Archive, Report 2015/668 (2015). http://eprint.iacr.org/2015/668

20. Naveed, M., Kamara, S., Wright, C.V.: Inference attacks on property-preserving encrypted databases. In: Proceedings of the 22nd ACM SIGSAC Conference on Computer and Communications Security, pp. 644–655. ACM, Denver (2015)

21. Popa, R.A., Li, F.H., Zeldovich, N.: An ideal-security protocol for order-preserving encoding. In: 2013 IEEE Symposium on Security and Privacy (SP), pp. 463–477. IEEE, San Francisco (2013)

22. Popa, R.A., Redfield, C., Zeldovich, N., Balakrishnan, H.: Cryptdb: protecting confidentiality with encrypted query processing. In: Proceedings of the 23rd ACM Symposium on Operating Systems Principles, pp. 85–100. ACM, Cascais (2011)

23. Roche, D.S., Apon, D., Choi, S.G., Yerukhimovich, A.: Pope: partial order preserving encoding. In: Proceedings of the 2016 ACM SIGSAC Conference on Computer and Communications Security, pp. 1131–1142. ACM, Vienne (2016)

24. Stefanov, E., Papamanthou, C., Shi, E.: Practical dynamic searchable encryption with small leakage. In: 21st Annual Network and Distributed System Security Symposium, vol. 71, pp. 72–75. The Internet Society, San Diego (2014)

25. Wang, X., Zhao, Y.: Order-revealing encryption: file-injection attack and forward security. Cryptology ePrint Archive, Report 2017/1086 (2017). http://eprint.iacr.org/2017/1086
26. Zhang, Y., Katz, J., Papamanthou, C.: All your queries are belong to us: the power of file-injection attacks on searchable encryption. In: Proceeding of the 25th USENIX conference on Security Symposium, pp. 707–720. USENIX Association, Austin (2016)

SEISMIC: SEcure In-lined Script Monitors for Interrupting Cryptojacks

Wenhao Wang[(✉)], Benjamin Ferrell, Xiaoyang Xu, Kevin W. Hamlen, and Shuang Hao

The University of Texas at Dallas, Richardson, TX, USA
{wenhao.wang,benjamin.ferrell,xiaoyang.xu,hamlen,shao}@utdallas.edu

Abstract. A method of detecting and interrupting unauthorized, browser-based cryptomining is proposed, based on semantic signature-matching. The approach addresses a new wave of cryptojacking attacks, including XSS-assisted, web gadget-exploiting counterfeit mining. Evaluation shows that the approach is more robust than current static code analysis defenses, which are susceptible to code obfuscation attacks. An implementation based on in-lined reference monitoring offers a browser-agnostic deployment strategy that is applicable to average end-user systems without specialized hardware or operating systems.

Keywords: Web security · WebAssembly · Cryptomining
Intrusion detection · In-lined reference monitors

1 Introduction

Cryptojacking—the unauthorized use of victim computing resources to mine and exfiltrate cryptocurrencies—has recently emerged as one of the fastest growing new web cybersecurity threats. Network-based cryptojacking attacks increased 600% in 2017, with manufacturing and financial services as the top two targeted industries, according to IBM X-Force [31]. Adguard reported a 31% surge in cryptojacking attacks in November 2017 alone [32]. The Smominru botnet is estimated to be earning its owners about $8,500 each week via unauthorized Monero[1] mining, or an estimated $2.8–3.6 million total as of January 2018 [19].

The relatively recent escalation of cryptojacking threats can be traced to several converging trends, including the emergence of new mining-facilitating technologies that make cryptojacking easier to realize, next-generation cryptocurrencies that are easier to mine and offer greater anonymity to criminals, and the rising value of cryptocurrencies [23]. Among the chiefs of these new technologies is WebAssembly (Wasm),[2] a new bytecode language for web browsers that affords faster and more efficient computation than previous web scripting languages, such as JavaScript (JS). By implementing cryptomining algorithms

---

[1] https://cointelegraph.com/news/monero.
[2] http://webassembly.org.

© Springer Nature Switzerland AG 2018
J. Lopez et al. (Eds.): ESORICS 2018, LNCS 11099, pp. 122–142, 2018.
https://doi.org/10.1007/978-3-319-98989-1_7

in Wasm, legitimate miners can make more efficient use of client computing resources to generate greater revenue, and attackers can covertly establish illicit mining operations on browsers around the world with only average hardware and computing resources, thereby achieving the mass deployment scales needed to make cryptojacking profitable. For this reason, a majority of in-browser coin miners currently use Wasm [35].

Unfortunately, this availability of transparent cryptomining deployment models is blurring distinctions between legitimate, legal cryptomining and illegitimate, illegal cryptojacking. For example, in 2015, New Jersey settled a lengthy lawsuit against cryptomining company Tidbit, in which they alleged that Tidbit's browser-based Bitcoin mining software (which was marketed to websites as a revenue-generation alternative to ads) constituted "access to computers... without the computer owners' knowledge or consent" [36]. The definition and mechanism of such consent has therefore become a central issue in protecting users against cryptojacking attacks. For example, numerous top-visited web sites, including Showtime [28], YouTube [11], and The Pirate Bay [17], have come under fire within the past year for alleged cryptojacking attacks against their visitors. In each case, cryptocurrency-generation activities deemed consensual by site owners were not deemed consensual by users.

In order to provide end-users an enhanced capability to detect and consent to (or opt-out of) browser-based cryptomining activities, this paper investigates the feasibility of *semantic signature-matching* for robustly detecting the execution of browser-based cryptomining scripts implemented in Wasm. We find that top Wasm cryptominers exhibit recognizable computation signatures that differ substantially from other Wasm scripts, such as games. To leverage this distinction for consent purposes, we propose and implement SEcure In-lined Script Monitors for Interrupting Cryptojacks (SEISMIC). SEISMIC automatically modifies incoming Wasm binary programs so that they self-profile as they execute, detecting the echos of cryptomining activity. When cryptomining is detected, the instrumented script warns the user and prompts her to explicitly opt-out or opt-in. Opting out halts the script, whereas opting in continues the script without further profiling (allowing it to execute henceforth at full speed).

This semantic signature-matching approach is argued to be more robust than syntactic signature-matchers, such as n-gram detectors, which merely inspect untrusted scripts syntactically in an effort to identify those that might cryptomine when executed. Semantic approaches ignore program syntax in favor of monitoring program behavior, thereby evading many code obfuscation attacks that defeat static binary program analyses.

Instrumenting untrusted web scripts at the Wasm level also has the advantage of offering a browser-agnostic solution that generalizes across different Wasm virtual machine implementations. SEISMIC can therefore potentially be deployed as an in-browser plug-in, a proxy service, or a firewall-level script rewriter. Additional experiments on CPU-level instruction traces show that semantic signature-matching can also be effective for detection of non-Wasm cryptomining implementations, but only if suitable low-level instruction tracing facilities become more widely available on commercial processors.

To summarize, this paper makes the following contributions:

- We conduct an empirical analysis of the ecosystem of in-browser cryptocurrency mining and identify key security-relevant components, including Wasm.
- We introduce a new proof-of-concept attack that can hijack mining scripts and abuse client computing resources to gain cryptocurrency illicitly.
- We develop a novel Wasm in-line script monitoring system, SEISMIC, which instruments Wasm binaries with mining sensors. SEISMIC allows users to monitor and consent to cryptomining activities with acceptable overhead.
- We apply SEISMIC on five real-world mining Wasm scripts (four families) and seven non-mining scripts. Our results show that mining and non-mining computations exhibit significantly different behavioral patterns. We also develop a classification approach and achieve $\geq 98\%$ accuracy to detect cryptomining activities.

The remainder of the paper is structured as follows. Sections 2 and 3 begin with an overview of technologies of rising importance in web cryptomining, and a survey of the cryptomining ecosystem, respectively. Section 4 presents a new cryptojacking attack that demonstrates how adversaries can bypass current security protections in this ecosystem to abuse end-user computing resources and illicitly mine cryptocurrencies. Section 5 introduces our defense strategy based on semantic signature-detection and in-lined reference monitoring, and Sect. 6 evaluates its effectiveness. Finally, Sect. 7 summarizes related work and Sect. 8 concludes.

2 Background

2.1 Monero

Monero (XMR) is a privacy-focused cryptocurrency launched in April 2014. The confidentiality and untraceability of its transactions make Monero particularly popular on darknet markets. Monero's mining process is egalitarian, affording both benign webmasters and malicious hackers new funding avenues.

The core of Monero involves the CryptoNight proof-of-work hash algorithm based on the CryptoNote protocol [48]. CryptoNight makes mining equally efficient on CPU and GPU, and restricts mining on ASIC. This property makes Monero mining particularly feasible on browsers. A majority of current browser-based cryptocurrency miners target CryptoNight, and miner web script development has become an emerging business model. Page publishers embed these miners into their content as an alternative or supplement to ad revenue.

2.2 WebAssembly

Wasm [14] is a new bytecode scripting language that is now supported by all major browsers [7]. It runs in a sandbox after bytecode verification, where it aims to execute nearly as fast as native machine code.

Wasm complements and runs alongside JS. JS loads Wasm scripts, whereupon the two languages share memory and call each other's functions. Wasm is

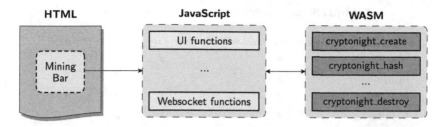

Fig. 1. Browser-based mining workflow

typically compiled from high-level languages (e.g., C, C++, or Rust). The most popular toolchain is Emscripten,[3] which compiles C/C++ to a combination of Wasm, JS glue code, and HTML. The JS glue code loads and runs the Wasm module.

Browsers can achieve near-native speeds for Wasm because it is designed to facilitate fast fetching, decoding, JIT-compilation, and optimization of Wasm bytecode instructions relative to JS. Wasm does not require reoptimization or garbage collection. These performance advantages make Wasm attractive for computationally intensive tasks, leading most browser-based cryptocurrency miners to use Wasm.

3   Ecosystem of Browser-Based Cryptocurrency Mining

Although cryptomining is technically possible on nearly any browser with scripting support, efficient and profitable mining with today's browsers requires large-scale deployment across many CPUs. Webmasters offering services that attract sufficient numbers of visitors are therefore beginning to adopt cryptomining as an alternative or supplement to online ads as a source of revenue. This has spawned a secondary business model of cryptomining web software development, which markets mining implementations and services to webmasters.

Thus, although mining occurs on visitors' browsers, miner developers and page publishers play driving roles in the business model. As more miner developers release mining libraries and more page publishers adopt them, a browser-based cryptocurrency mining ecosystem forms. To better understand the ecosystem, we here illustrate technical details of browser-based mining.

Page publishers first register accounts with miner developers. Registration grants the publisher an asymmetric key pair. Publishers then download miner code from the miner developer and customize it to fit their published pages, including adding their public keys. The miner developer uses the public key to attribute mining contributions and deliver payouts to page publishers.

Figure 1 illustrates the resulting workflow. After publishers embed the customized miner into their pages, it is served to client visitors and executes in their browsers. The HTML file first loads into the client browser, causing the mining bar to trigger supporting JS modules, which share functionalities with

---

[3] http://kripken.github.io/emscripten-site.

Table 1. Security-related features of popular miners

	Wasm	Domain whitelisting	Opt-In	CPU throttle
Adless	✓	✗	✗	✓
Coinhive	✓	✗	✓	✓
CoinImp	✓	✗	✗	✓
Crypto-Loot	✓	✗	✗	✓
JSECoin	✓	✓	✗	✓
WebMinePool	✓	✗	✗	✓

Wasm modules. The Wasm code conducts computationally intensive tasks (e.g., `cryptonight_hash`), whereas UI and I/O interactions (e.g., Websocket communications) are implemented in JS. The code framework is typically created and maintained by miner developers.

Table 1 summarizes security-related features of top web miner products:

- *Wasm:* Most miners use Wasm for performance. For example, Coinhive mines Monera via Wasm, and has about 65% of the speed of a native miner.[4]
- *Domain Whitelisting:* To help deter malicious mining, some miner developers offer domain name whitelisting to webmasters. If miner developers receive mining contributions from unlisted domains, they can withhold payouts.
- *Opt-In Tokens:* To support ad blockers and antivirus vendors, some miner products generate opt-in tokens for browsers. Mining can only start after an explicit opt-in from the browser user. The opt-in token is only valid for the current browser session and domain.
- *CPU Throttling:* Using all the client's computing power tends to draw complaints from visitors. Miner developers therefore advise page publishers to use only a fraction of each visitor's available computing power for mining. Webmasters can configure this fraction.

4   Counterfeit Mining Attacks

To underscore the dangers posed by many browser-based mining architectures, and to motivate our defense, we next demonstrate how the ecosystem described in Sect. 3 can be compromised through *counterfeit mining*—a new cryptojacking attack wherein third-party adversaries hijack mining scripts to work on their behalf rather than for page publishers or page recipients.

Our threat model for this attack assumes that miner developers, page publishers, and page recipients are all non-malicious and comply with all rules of the cryptomining ecosystem in Sect. 3, and that mining scripts can have an unlimited variety of syntactic implementations. Specifically, we assume that miner developers and webmasters agree on a fair payout rate, publishers notify visitors that

---

[4] https://coinhive.com.

```
1  <script src="https://authedmine.com/lib/simple-ui.min.js" async></script>
2  <div class="coinhive-miner"
3     style="width:256px;height:310px"
4     data_key="YOUR_SITE_KEY">
5     <em>Loading...</em>
6  </div>
```

Listing 1.1. Embedded miner HTML code

pages contain miners, and mining only proceeds with visitor consent. Despite this compliance, we demonstrate that malicious third-parties can compromise the ecosystem by abusing the miner software, insecure web page elements, and client computing resources to mine coins for themselves illegitimately.

To understand the attack procedure, we first illustrate how publishers embed miners into their web pages. Listing 1.1 shows the HTML code publishers must typically add. Line 1 imports the JS library maintained by miner developer. Line 3 specifies the dimensions of the miner rendered on the page. Line 4 identifies the publisher to the miner developer. To receive revenue, publishers must register accounts with miner developers, whereupon each publisher receives a unique data key. This allows miner developers to dispatch payroll to the correct publishers.

Our attack is predicated on two main observations about modern web pages: First, cross-site scripting (XSS) vulnerabilities are widely recognized as a significant and pervasive problem across a large percentage of all web sites [13,52]. Thus, we realistically assume that some mining pages contain XSS vulnerabilities. Second, although some XSS mitigations can block injection of executable scripts, they are frequently unsuccessful at preventing all injections of non-scripts (e.g., pure HTML). Our attack therefore performs purely HTML XSS injection to hijack miners via web gadgets [24]—a relatively new technique whereby existing, non-injected script code is misused to implement web attacks.

Examining the JS library called in line 1 reveals several potentially abusable gadgets, including the one shown in Listing 1.2. This code fragment selects all `div` elements of class `.coinhive-miner` on the page, and renders a miner within each. Unfortunately, line 1 is exploitable because it cannot distinguish publisher-provided `div` elements from maliciously injected ones. This allows an adversary to maliciously inject a `div` element of that class but with a different data key, causing the recipient to mine coins for the attacker instead of the publisher. We emphasize that in this attack, the exploited gadget is within the miner software, not within the publisher's page. Therefore *all web pages that load the miner* are potentially vulnerable, creating a relatively broad surface for criminals to attack.

To verify our counterfeit miner attack, we deploy two proof-of-concept attacks. Since the attacks begin with XSS exploits, we give two demonstrations: one using a reflected XSS vulnerability and one with a stored XSS vulnerability. The reflected XSS attack crafts a URL link containing the injected HTML code, where the injected code is a `div` element similar to Listing 1.1. After enticing visitors to click the URL link (e.g., via phishing), the visitor's browser loads and

```
1 var elements = document.querySelectorAll('.coinhive-miner');
2 for (var i = 0; i < elements.length; i++) {
3     new Miner(elements[i])
4 }
```

Listing 1.2. JavaScript gadget

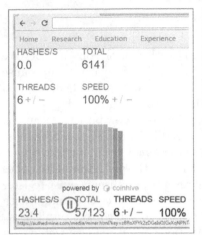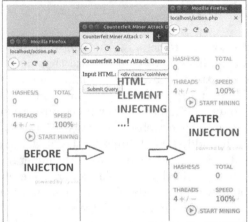

Fig. 2. Reflected (left) and stored (right) counterfeit mining attacks

executes the counterfeit miner. The left of Fig. 2 shows a snapshot of the infected page, in which the counterfeit miner is visible at the bottom.

The stored XSS attack involves a page that reads its content from a database, to which visitors can add insufficiently sanitized HTML elements. In this scenario, injecting the malicious miner HTML code into the database causes the counterfeit miner to permanently inhabit the victim page. The right of Fig. 2 illustrates the attack procedure. The three screenshots show sequential phases of the attack.

Counterfeit mining attacks illustrate some of the complexities of the cryptomining consent problem. In this case, asking users to consent to mining in general on affected web pages does not distinguish between the multiple miners on the compromised pages, some of which are working for the page publisher and others for a malicious adversary. The next section therefore proposes an automated, client-side consent mechanism based on in-lined reference monitoring that is per-script and is page- and miner-agnostic. This allows users to detect and potentially block cryptomining activities of individual scripts on a page, rather than merely the page as a whole.

Fig. 3. Antivirus detection of CryptoNight before and after function renaming

5   Detection

In light of the dangers posed by counterfeit and other cryptomining attacks, this section proposes a robust defense strategy that empowers page recipients with a more powerful detection and consent mechanism. Since cryptojacking attacks ultimately target client computing resources, we adopt a strictly client-side defense architecture; supplementary publisher- and miner developer-side mitigations are outside our scope.

Section 5.1 begins with a survey of current static approaches and their limitations. Section 5.2 then proposes a more dynamic strategy that employs semantic signature detection, and presents experimental evidence of its potential effectiveness. Finally, Sect. 5.3 presents technical details of our defense implementation.

5.1   Current Methods

Antivirus engines detect browser mining primarily via script file signature databases. The most popular Wasm implementation of the CryptoNight hashing algorithm [48] is flagged by at least 21 engines. A few of these (e.g., McAfee) go a step further and detect cryptomining implementations based on function names or other recognized keywords and code file structures.

Unfortunately, these static approaches are easily defeated by code obfuscations. For example, merely changing the function names in the CryptoNight Wasm binary bypasses all antivirus engines used on VirusTotal. Figure 3 shows detection results for the original vs. obfuscated CryptoNight binary.

Web browsers also have some detection mechanisms in the form of plug-ins or extensions, but these have similar limitations. The No Coin [21] Chrome extension enforces a URL blacklist, which prevents miners from contacting their proxies. However, criminals can bypass this by setting up new proxies not on

Table 2. Execution trace average profiles

	i32.add	i32.and	i32.shl	i32.shr_u	i32.xor
A-Star	86.78	4.71	5.52	0.44	2.54
Asteroids	89.67	4.33	5.10	0.44	0.42
Basic4GL	75.78	8.43	13.75	1.78	0.27
Bullet(1000)	84.42	3.55	11.30	0.20	0.51
CoinHive	19.90	17.90	22.60	17.00	22.60
CoinHive_v0	20.20	17.50	22.70	17.00	22.70
CreaturePack	54.70	0.52	44.27	0.21	0.40
FunkyKarts	77.89	8.68	12.28	0.44	0.71
HushMiner	62.53	6.45	17.87	6.23	6.93
NFWebMiner	28.00	15.80	20.40	15.30	20.40
Tanks	61.90	12.29	22.27	2.02	1.51
YAZECMiner	57.99	4.37	30.75	3.26	3.63

the blacklist. MinerBlock[5] statically inspects scripts for code features indicative of mining. For instance, it detects CoinHive miners by searching for functions named `isRunning` and `stop`, and variables named `_siteKey`, `_newSiteKey`, and `_address`. These static analyses are likewise defeated by simple code obfuscations.

5.2   Semantic Signature-Matching

A common limitation of the aforementioned detection approaches is their reliance on syntactic features (*viz.*, file bytes and URL names) that are easily obfuscated by attackers. We therefore focus on detection via semantic code features that are less easy to obfuscate because they are fundamental to the miner's computational purpose. Our proposed solution monitors Wasm scripts as they execute to derive a statistical model of known mining and non-mining behavior. Profiling reveals a distribution of Wasm instructions executed, which we use at runtime to distinguish mining from non-mining activity.

Using Intel Processor Tracing (PT), we first generated native code instruction counts for Wasm web apps. We recorded native instruction counts for 1-second computation slices on Firefox, for web apps drawn from: 500 pages randomly selected from Alexa top 50K, 500 video pages from YouTube, 100 Wasm embedded game or graphic pages, and 102 browser mining pages. Detailed results are presented in Appendix A. The traces reveal that cryptomining Wasm scripts rely much more upon packed arithmetic instructions from the MMX, SSE, and SSE2 instruction sets of CISC processors than do other Wasm scripts, like games.

Although PT is useful for identifying semantic features of possible interest, it is not a good basis for implementing detection on average client browsers since

---

[5] https://github.com/xd4rker/MinerBlock.

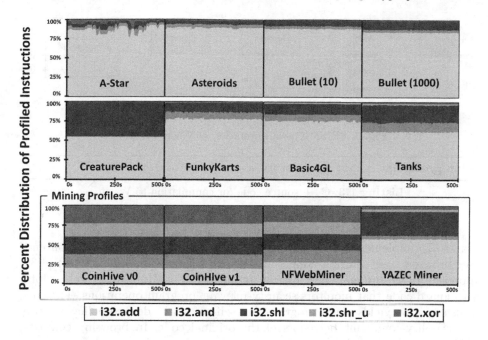

Fig. 4. Semantic profiles for mining vs. non-mining Wasm apps

PT facilities are not yet widely available on average consumer hardware and OSes. We therefore manually identified the top five Wasm bytecode instructions that JIT-compile to the packed arithmetic native code instructions identified by the PT experiments. These five instructions are the column labels of Table 2.

We next profiled these top-five Wasm instructions at the Wasm bytecode level by instrumenting Wasm binary scripts with self-profiling code. We profiled four mining apps plus one variant, and seven non-mining apps. The non-mining apps are mostly games (which is the other most popular use of Wasm), and the rest are graphical benchmarks. For each app, we executed and interacted with them for approximately 500 real-time seconds to create each profile instance. For each app with configurable parameters, we varied them over their entire range of values to cover all possible cases.

Figure 4 displays the resulting distributions. There is a clear and distinct stratification for the two CoinHive variants and NFWebMiner, which are based on CryptoNight. YAZEC (Yet Another ZEC) Miner uses a different algorithm, and therefore exhibits slightly different but still distinctive profile. Table 2 displays an average across the 100 distributions for all of the profiled applications.

5.3   SEISMIC In-lined Reference Monitoring

Our profiling experiments indicate that Wasm cryptomining can potentially be detected by semantic signature-matching of Wasm bytecode instruction

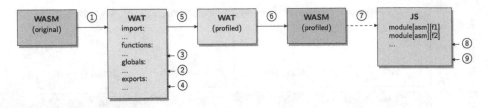

Fig. 5. SEISMIC transformation of Wasm binaries

```
1 int pythag(int a, int b) { return a * a + b * b; }
```

Listing 1.3. C++ source code for compilation to Wasm

---

counts. To implement such a detection mechanism that is deployable on end-user browsers, our solution adopts an *in-lined reference monitor* (IRM) [8,39] approach. IRMs automatically instrument untrusted programs (e.g., web scripts) with guard code that monitors security-relevant program operations. The code transformation yields a new program that self-enforces a desired policy, yet preserves policy-compliant behaviors of the original code. In browsing contexts, IRM formalisms have been leveraged to secure other scripting languages, such as JS and Flash (cf., [37]), but not yet Wasm. In this scenario, our goal is to design and implement an IRM system that automatically transforms incoming Wasm binaries to dynamically compute their own semantic features and match them to a given semantic signature.

Wasm scripts are expressed in binary or human-readable textual form. Each can be translated to the other using the Wasm Binary Toolkit (WABT). Typically scripts are distributed in binary form for size purposes, but either form is accepted by Wasm VMs. The programs are composed of *sections*, which are each lists of section-specific content. Our automated transformation modifies the following three Wasm section types:

- Functions: a list of all functions and their code bodies
- Globals: a list of variables visible to all functions sharing a thread
- Exports: a list of functions callable from JS.

Figure 5 shows a high-level view of our Wasm instrumentation workflow. We here explain a workflow for a single Wasm binary file, but our procedure generalizes to pages with multiple binaries. As a running example, Listing 1.3 contains a small C++ function that computes the sum of the squares of its two inputs. Compiling it yields the Wasm bytecode in Listing 1.4.

Our prototype implementation of SEISMIC first parses the untrusted binary to a simplified abstract syntax tree (AST) similar to the one in Listing 1.4 using `wasm2wat` from WABT with the `--fold-exprs` flag (①). It next injects a fresh global variable of type i64 (64-bit integer) into the globals section for each Wasm instruction opcode to be profiled (②). The JS-Wasm interface currently does not support the transfer of 64-bit integers, so to allow JS code to read these

```
1  (module (table 0 anyfunc) (memory $0 1)
2  (export "memory" (memory $0))
3  (export "pythag" (func $pythag))
4  (func $pythag (; 0 ;) (param $0 i32) (param $1 i32) (result i32)
5   (i32.add (i32.mul (get_local $1) (get_local $1))
6            (i32.mul (get_local $0) (get_local $0)))))
```

Listing 1.4. Original Wasm compiled from C++

```
1  (module (table 0 anyfunc) (memory $0 1)
2  (export "memory" (memory $0))
3  (export "pythag" (func $pythag))
4  (export "_getAddsLo" (func $_getAddsLo))
5  ...
6  (export "_reset" (func $_reset))

8  (func $pythag (; 0 ;) (param $0 i32) (param $1 i32) (result i32)
9   (i32.add (set_global 0 (i64.add (get_global 0) (i64.const 1)))
10   (i32.mul (set_global 1 (i64.add (get_global 1) (i64.const 1)))
11    (get_local $1) (get_local $1))
12   (i32.mul (set_global 1 (i64.add (get_global 1) (i64.const 1)))
13    (get_local $0) (get_local $0))))

15 (func $_getAddsLo (; 1 ;) (result i32) (return (i32.wrap/i64 (get_global 0))))
16 ...
17 (func $_reset (; 5 ;) (set_global 0 (i64.const 0)) (set_global 1 (i64.const 0)))
18 (global (;0;) (mut i64) (i64.const 0))
19 (global (;1;) (mut i64) (i64.const 0)))
```

Listing 1.5. Instrumented Wasm

counters, 32-bit accessor functions getInstLo and getInstHi are added (③). An additional reset function that resets all the profile counters to zero is also added, to allow the security monitor to separately profile different time slices of execution. All three functions are added to the binary's exports (④).

The transformation algorithm next scans the bodies of all Wasm functions in the script and in-lines counter-increment instructions immediately after each instruction to be profiled (⑤). Our prototype currently takes the brute-force approach of in-lining the counter-increment guard code for each profiled instruction, but optimizations that improve efficiency by speculatively increasing counters by large quantities in anticipation of an uninterruptable series of signature-relevant operations are obviously possible.

The modified Wasm text file is now ready to be translated to binary form, which we perform by passing it to wat2wasm from WABT (⑥). At this point, we redirect the JS code that loads the Wasm binary to load the new one (⑦). This can be done either by simply using the same name as the old file (i.e., overwriting it) or by modifying the load path for the Wasm file in JS to point to the new one.

```
1  function wasmProfiler() {
2   if (Module["asm"] != null && typeof _reset === "function") {
3     console.log(_getAddsHi() * 2³² + _getAddsLo() + "␣adds");
4     console.log(_getMulsHi() * 2³² + _getMulsLo() + "␣multiplies");
5     _reset();
6   } else { console.log("Wasm␣not␣loaded␣yet"); }
7   setTimeout(wasmProfiler, 5000);
8  }
9  wasmProfiler();
10 ...
11 Module["asm"] = asm;
12 var _getAddsLo = Module["_getAddsLo"] = function() {
13   return Module["asm"]["_getAddsLo"].apply(null, arguments) };
14 ...
```

Listing 1.6. SEISMIC JavaScript code

Listing 1.5 shows the results of this process when profiling Wasm instructions i32.add and i32.mul. Lines 4–6 export the IRM helper functions defined in lines 15–17. Lines 18 and 19 define global counter variables to profile i32.add and i32.mul instructions, respectively. The two i32.mul instructions are instrumented on lines 10 and 12, and the single i32.add instruction is instrumented on line 9.

SEISMIC's instrumentation procedure anticipates an attack model in which script authors and their scripts might be completely malicious, and adversaries might know all details of SEISMIC's implementation. For example, adversaries might craft Wasm binaries that anticipate the instrumentation procedure and attempt to defeat it. We therefore designed our instrumentation in accordance with secure IRM design principles established in the literature [15,29,39]. In particular, the Wasm bytecode language does not include unrestricted computed jump instructions, allowing our transformation to implement uncircumventable basic blocks that pair profiling code with the instructions they profile. Moreover, Wasm is type-safe [14], affording the implementation of incorruptible state variables that track the profiling information. Type-safety ensures that malicious Wasm authors cannot use pointer arithmetic or untyped references to corrupt the IRM's profiling variables (cf., [40,41]). These language properties are the basis for justifying other Wasm security features, such as control-flow integrity [50].

To start the enforcement, Listing 1.6 instantiates a JS timer that first executes at page-load and checks whether Wasm code has been loaded and compiled (⑧). If so, all Wasm instruction counters are queried, reset, and logged to the console. The timer profiles another slice of computation time every 5000 ms. This affords detection of scripts that mine periodically but not continuously.

6   Evaluation

To evaluate our approach, we instrumented and profiled the web apps listed in Table 2. The majority of Wasm code we profiled was identifiable as having been compiled with Emscripten, an LLVM-based JS compiler that yields a JS-Wasm pair of files for inclusion on web pages. The JS file contains an aliased list of exported functions, where we insert our new entries for the counters (⑨). The remaining Wasm programs we profiled have a similar structure to the output of Emscripten, so they can be modified in a similar manner.

We profiled every instruction used in the CoinHive worker Wasm, which is a variant of the CryptoNight hashing algorithm, and determined the top five byte-code instructions used: `i32.add`, `i32.and`, `i32.shl`, `i32.shr_u`, and `i32.xor`. Normalized counts of how many times these instructions execute constitute feature vectors for our approach.

Table 3. Mining overhead

	Vanilla	Profiled
CoinHive v1	36 hash/s	18 hash/s
CoinHive v0	40 hash/s	19 hash/s
NFWebMiner	38 hash/s	16 hash/s
HushMiner	1.6 sol/s	0.8 sol/s
YAZECMiner	1.8 sol/s	0.9 sol/s

Runtime Overhead. Table 3 reports runtime overheads for instrumented binaries. The data was obtained by running each miner in original and instrumented form over 100 trials, and averaging the results. CoinHive and NFWebMiner were set to execute with 4 threads and their units are in hashes per second. HushMiner and Yet Another ZEC Miner are single-threaded and display units in solutions per second. In general, the miners we tested incurred a runtime overhead of roughly 100%. We deem this acceptable because once mining is explicitly allowed by the user, execution can switch back to the faster original code.

Non-mining code overhead must be calculated in a different way, since most are interactive and non-terminating (e.g., games). We therefore measured overhead for these programs by monitoring their frames-per-second. In all cases they remained at a constant 60 frames-per-second once all assets had loaded. Overall, no behavioral differences in instrumented scripts were observable during the experiments (except when mining scripts were interrupted to obtain user consent). This is expected since guard code in-lined by SEISMIC is implemented to be transparent to the rest of the script's computation.

Robustness. Our approach conceptualizes mining detection as a binary classification problem, where mining and non-mining are the two classes. Features are normalized vectors of the counts of the top five used Wasm instructions. For model selection, we choose Support Vector Machine (SVM) with linear kernel function. We set penalty parameter C to 10, since it is an unbalanced problem

Table 4. SVM stratified 10-fold cross validation

Miner	Fold	Precision	Recall	F_1	Fold	Precision	Recall	F_1
N	1	1.00	0.99	0.99	2	1.00	1.00	1.00
Y		0.96	1.00	0.98		1.00	1.00	1.00
N	3	1.00	1.00	1.00	4	1.00	1.00	1.00
Y		1.00	1.00	1.00		1.00	1.00	1.00
N	5	1.00	1.00	1.00	6	1.00	0.99	0.99
Y		1.00	1.00	1.00		0.96	1.00	0.98
N	7	1.00	1.00	1.00	8	1.00	1.00	1.00
Y		1.00	1.00	1.00		1.00	1.00	1.00
N	9	1.00	1.00	1.00	10	1.00	1.00	1.00
Y		1.00	1.00	1.00		1.00	1.00	1.00

(there are far fewer mining instances than non-mining instances). To evaluate this approach, we use stratified 10-fold cross validation on 1900 instances, which consist of 500 miners and 1400 non-miners.

The results shown in Table 4 are promising. All mining activities are identified correctly, and the overall accuracy (F_1 score) is 98% or above in all cases. SEIS-MIC monitoring exhibits negligible false positive rate due to our strict threshold for detection. Visitors can also manually exclude non-mining pages if our system exhibits a false positive, though the cross-validation results indicate such misclassifications are rare.

7   Related Work

Browser-based cryptocurrency mining is an emerging business model. A recent study has provided preliminary analysis of in-browser mining of cryptocurrencies [9], while we strive to inspect its security issues in depth. In particular, our work is the first to investigate the specific security ramifications of using Wasm for cryptomining.

7.1   Cryptocurrencies

Researchers have conducted a variety of systematic analyses of cryptocurrencies and discussed open research challenges [4]. A comprehensive study of Bitcoin mining malware has shown that botnets generate additional revenue through mining [18]. MineGuard [47] utilizes hardware performance counters to generate signatures of cryptocurrency mining, which are then used to detect mining activities. Other research has focused on the payment part of cryptocurrencies. For example, EZC [1] was proposed to hide the transaction amounts and address balances. Double-spending attacks threaten fast payments in Bitcoin [20]. Bitcoin timestamp reliability has been improved to counter various attacks [46]. Through analysis of Bitcoin transactions of CryptoLocker, prior studies revealed the financial infrastructure of ransomware [27] and reported its economic impact [6]. In contrast, in-browser cryptomining, such as Monero, is less studied in the scholarly literature. In this work, we conducted the first analysis to study Wasm-based cryptomining, and developed new approaches to detect mining activities.

7.2   Cross-Site Scripting

Our counterfeit mining attack (Sect. 4) leverages cross-site scripting (XSS). The attacks and defenses of XSS have been an ongoing cat-and-mouse game for years. One straightforward defense is to validate and sanitize input on the server side, but this places a heavy burden on web developers for code correctness. XSS-GUARD [3] utilizes taint-tracking technology to centralize validation and sanitization on the server-side. Blueprint [30], Noncespaces [12], DSI [34], and CSP [42] adopt the notion of client-side HTML security policies [51] to defend XSS. Large-scale studies have also been undertaken to examine the prevalence of DOM-based XSS vulnerabilities [25] and the security history of the Web's client side [44], concluding that client-side XSS stagnates at a high level. To remedy the shortcomings of string-based comparison methods, taint-aware XSS filtering has been proposed to thwart DOM-based XSS [45]. DOMPurify [16] is an open-source library designed to sanitize HTML strings and document objects from DOM-based XSS attacks. Recently, attacks leveraging script gadgets have been discovered that circumvent all currently existing XSS mitigations [24]. We showed that in-browser crypomining is susceptible to such gadget-powered XSS attacks to hijack Wasm mining scripts.

Although our SEISMIC defense detects and warns users about cryptomining activities introduced through XSS, XSS can still potentially confuse users into responding inappropriately to the warnings. For example, attackers can potentially leverage XSS to obfuscate the provenance of cryptomining scripts, causing users to misattribute them to legitimate page publishers. This longstanding attribution problem is a continuing subject of ongoing study (cf., [38]).

7.3   Related Web Script Defenses

A cluster of research on defense mechanisms is also related to our work. Obliv-iAd [2] is an online behavioral advertising system that aims to protect visitors' privacy. MadTracer [26] leverages decision tree models to detect malicious web advertisements. JStill [54] compares the information from both static analysis and runtime inspection to detect and prevent obfuscated malicious JS code. Analysis of access control mechanisms in the browser has observed that although CSP is a clean solution in terms of access control, XS-search attacks can use timing side-channels to exfiltrate data from even prestigious services, such as Gmail and Bing [10]. Blacklist services provided by browsers to thwart malicious URLs have been shown to be similarly limited [49]. BridgeScope [55] was proposed to precisely and scalably find JS bridge vulnerabilities. Commix [43] automates the detection and exploitation of command injection vulnerabilities in web applications. Our system is orthogonal to these prior defense mechanisms, in that it profiles Wasm execution and helps users detect unauthorized in-browser mining of cryptocurrencies.

7.4   Semantic Malware Detection and Obfuscation

Our semantic signature-matching approach to cryptomining detection is motivated by the widespread belief that it is more difficult for adversaries to obfuscate semantic features than syntactic ones (cf., [5,22]). Prior work has demonstrated that semantic features can nevertheless be obfuscated with sufficient effort, at the cost of reduced performance (e.g., [33,53]). While such semantic obfuscations could potentially evade our SEISMIC monitors, we conjecture that the performance penalty of doing so could make obfuscated cryptojacking significantly less profitable for attackers. Future work should investigate this conjecture once semantically obfuscated cryptojacking attacks appear and can be studied.

8   Conclusion

SEISMIC offers a semantic-based cryptojacking detection mechanism for Wasm scripts that is more robust than current static detection defenses employed by antivirus products and browser plugins. By automatically instrumenting untrusted Wasm binaries in-flight with self-profiling code, SEISMIC-modified scripts dynamically detect mining computations and offer users explicit opportunities to consent. Page-publishers can respond to lack of consent through a JS interface, affording them opportunities to introduce ads or withdraw page content from unconsenting users. Experimental evaluation indicates that self-profiling overhead is unobservable for non-mining scripts, such as games (and is eliminated for miners once consent is granted). Robustness evaluation via cross-validation shows that the approach is highly accurate, exhibiting very few misclassifications.

Acknowledgments. This research was supported in part by NSF award #1513704, ONR award N00014-17-1-2995, AFOSR award FA9550-14-1-0173, and an NSF I/UCRC award from Lockheed-Martin.

A   Processor Tracing Experiments

Table 5 itemizes the 30 most significant opcodes that discriminate between mining and non-mining web contents. Our feature selection process treats all distinct Intel native opcodes as features and their number of occurrences as feature values. We employ forests of trees to evaluate the importance of features. The ranking is based on the feature importance as determined by SVM (see Sect. 6).

Table 5. Top 30 native opcode features that distinguish mining from non-mining

Rank	Opcode	Rank	Opcode
1	SUB	16	LOCK
2	CMOVS	17	CMOVB
3	UNPCKHPS†	18	SETBE
4	DIVSD‡	19	SETNZ
5	SETB	20	ROL
6	MOVQ*	21	MUL
7	MAXPS†	22	SETNLE
8	CMOVNLE	23	CVTTSD2SI‡
9	COMVLE	24	MOVMSKPS†
10	PSUBUSW*	25	CMOVZ
11	CMOVNL	26	TEST
12	UNPCKLPS†	27	CMOVNZ
13	ROUNDSD†	28	ROUNDSS†
14	CMPPS†	29	STMXCSR†
15	MOVLHPS†	30	CMOVNB

* MMX instruction † SSE instruction ‡ SSE2 instruction

References

1. Androulaki, E., Karame, G., Capkun, S.: Hiding transaction amounts and balances in Bitcoin. In: Proceedings of the 7th ACM International Conference on Trust and Trustworthy Computing (TRUST), pp. 161–178 (2014)
2. Backes, M., Kate, A., Maffei, M.: ObliviAd: provably secure and practical online behavioral advertising. In: Proceedings of the 33th IEEE Symposium on Security and Privacy (S&P), pp. 257–271 (2012)
3. Bisht, P., Venkatakrishnan, V.N.: XSS-GUARD: precise dynamic prevention of cross-site scripting attacks. In: Zamboni, D. (ed.) DIMVA 2008. LNCS, vol. 5137, pp. 23–43. Springer, Heidelberg (2008). https://doi.org/10.1007/978-3-540-70542-0_2
4. Bonneau, J., Miller, A., Clark, J., Narayanan, A., Kroll, J.A., Felten, E.W.: SoK: research perspectives and challenges for Bitcoin and cryptocurrencies. In: Proceedings of the 36th IEEE Symposium on Security and Privacy (S&P), pp. 104–121 (2015)
5. Christodorescu, M., Jha, S., Seshia, S.A., Song, D., Bryant, R.E.: Semantics-aware malware detection. In: Proceedings of the 26th IEEE Symposium on Security & Privacy (S&P), pp. 32–46 (2005)
6. Conti, M., Gangwal, A., Ruj, S.: On the economic significance of ransomware campaigns: a Bitcoin transactions perspective (2018). arXiv:1804.01341
7. DeMocker, J.: WebAssembly support now shipping in all major browsers. Mozilla Blog, November 2017

8. Erlingsson, Ú., Schneider, F.B.: SASI enforcement of security policies: a retrospective. In: Proceedings of the New Security Paradigms Workshop (NSPW), pp. 87–95 (1999)
9. Eskandari, S., Leoutsarakos, A., Mursch, T., Clark, J.: A first look at browser-based cryptojacking. In: Proceedings of the 2nd IEEE Security & Privacy on the Blockchain Workshop IEEE (S&B) (2018)
10. Gelernter, N., Herzberg, A.: Cross-site search attacks. In: Proceedings of the 22nd ACM Conference on Computer and Communications Security (CCS), pp. 1394–1405 (2015)
11. Goodin, D.: Now even YouTube serves ads with CPU-draining cryptocurrency miners. Ars Technica, January 2018
12. Gundy, M.V., Chen, H.: Noncespaces: using randomization to defeat cross-site scripting attacks. Comput. Secur. **31**(4), 612–628 (2012)
13. Gupta, S., Gupta, B.: Cross-site scripting (XSS) attacks and defense mechanisms: classification and state-of-the-art. Int. J. Syst. Assur. Eng. Manag. **8**(1), 512–530 (2017)
14. Haas, A., et al.: Bringing the web up to speed with WebAssembly. In: Proceedings of the 38th ACM SIGPLAN Conference on Programming Language Design and Implementation (PLDI), pp. 185–200 (2017)
15. Hamlen, K.W., Morrisett, G., Schneider, F.B.: Computability classes for enforcement mechanisms. ACM Trans. Program. Lang. Syst. (TOPLAS) **28**(1), 175–205 (2006)
16. Heiderich, M., Späth, C., Schwenk, J.: DOMPurify: client-side protection against XSS and markup injection. In: Foley, S.N., Gollmann, D., Snekkenes, E. (eds.) ESORICS 2017. LNCS, vol. 10493, pp. 116–134. Springer, Cham (2017). https://doi.org/10.1007/978-3-319-66399-9_7
17. Hruska, J.: Browser-based mining malware found on Pirate Bay, other sites. ExtremeTech, September 2017
18. Huang, D.Y., et al.: Botcoin: monetizing stolen cycles. In: Proceedings of the 21st Network and Distributed System Security Symposium (NDSS) (2014)
19. Kafeine. Smominru Monero mining botnet making millions for operators. ProofPoint Threat Insight, January 2018
20. Karame, G., Androulaki, E., Capkun, S.: Double-spending fast payments in Bitcoin. In: Proceedings of the 19th ACM Conference on Computer and Communications Security (CCS), pp. 906–917 (2012)
21. Keramidas, R.: Stop coin mining in the browser with No Coin, September 2017. https://ker.af/stop-coin-mining-in-the-browser-with-no-coin
22. Kinder, J., Katzenbeisser, S., Schallhart, C., Veith, H.: Detecting malicious code by model checking. In: Proceedings of the 2nd International Conference on Detection of Intrusions and Malware, and Vulnerability Assessment (DIMVA), pp. 174–187 (2005)
23. Lau, H.: Browser-based cryptocurrency mining makes unexpected return from the dead. Sympantec Threat Intelligence, December 2017
24. Lekies, S., Kotowicz, K., Groß, S., Nava, E.V., Johns, M.: Code-reuse attacks for the web: breaking cross-site scripting mitigations via script gadgets. In: Proceedings of the 24th ACM Conference on Computer and Communications Security (CCS), pp. 1709–1723 (2017)
25. Lekies, S., Stock, B., Johns, M.: 25 million flows later: large-scale detection of DOM-based XSS. In: Proceedings of the 20th ACM Conference on Computer and Communications Security (CCS), pp. 1193–1204 (2013)

26. Li, Z., Zhang, K., Xie, Y., Yu, F., Wang, X.: Knowing your enemy: understanding and detecting malicious web advertising. In: Proceedings of the 19th ACM Conference on Computer and Communications Security (CCS), pp. 906–917 (2012)
27. Liao, K., Zhao, Z., Doupé, A., Ahn, G.-J.: Behind closed doors: measurement and analysis of cryptolocker ransoms in Bitcoin. In: Proceedings of the 11th APWG Symposium on Electronic Crime Research (eCrime), pp. 1–13 (2016)
28. Liao, S.: Showtime websites secretly mined user CPU for cryptocurrency. The Verge, September 2017
29. Ligatti, J., Bauer, L., Walker, D.: Run-time enforcement of nonsafety policies. ACM Trans. Inf. Syst. Secur. (TISSEC) **12**(3), 19 (2009)
30. Louw, M.T., Venkatakrishnan, V.N.: Blueprint: robust prevention of cross-site scripting attacks for existing browsers. In: Proceedings of the 30th IEEE Symposium on Security and Privacy (S&P), pp. 331–346 (2009)
31. McMillen, D.: Network attacks containing cryptocurrency CPU mining tools grow sixfold. IBM X-Force SecurityIntelligence, September 2017
32. Meshkov, A.: Cryptojacking surges in popularity growing by 31% over the past month. AdGuard Research, November 2017
33. Moser, A., Kruegel, C., Kirda, E.: Limits of static analysis for malware detection. In: Proceedings of the 23rd Annual Computer Security Applications Conference (ACSAC), pp. 421–430 (2007)
34. Nadji, Y., Saxena, P., Song, D.: Document structure integrity: a robust basis for cross-site scripting defense. In: Proceedings of the 21st Network and Distributed System Security Symposium (NDSS) (2014)
35. Neumann, R., Toro, A.: In-browser mining: Coinhive and WebAssembly. Forcepoint Security Labs, April 2018. https://blogs.forcepoint.com/security-labs/browser-mining-coinhive-and-webassembly
36. OAG, New Jersey. New Jersey Division of Consumer Affairs obtains settlement with developer of Bitcoin-mining software found to have accessed New Jersey computers without users' knowledge or consent. Office of the Attorney General, Department of Law & Public Safety, State of New Jersey, May 2015
37. Phung, P.H., Monshizadeh, M., Sridhar, M., Hamlen, K.W., Venkatakrishnan, V.: Between worlds: securing mixed JavaScript/ActionScript multi-party web content. IEEE Trans. Dependable Secur. Comput. TDSC **12**(4), 443–457 (2015)
38. Rowe, N.C.: The attribution of cyber warfare. In: Green, J.A. (eds.) Cyber Warfare: A multidisciplinary Analysis, Routledge Studies in Conflict, Security and Technology. Routledge (2015)
39. Schneider, F.B.: Enforceable security policies. ACM Trans. Inf. Syst. Secur. (TISSEC) **3**(1), 30–50 (2000)
40. Sridhar, M., Hamlen, K.W.: ActionScript in-lined reference monitoring in prolog. In: Carro, M., Peña, R. (eds.) PADL 2010. LNCS, vol. 5937, pp. 149–151. Springer, Heidelberg (2010). https://doi.org/10.1007/978-3-642-11503-5_13
41. Sridhar, M., Hamlen, K.W.: Model-checking in-lined reference monitors. In: Barthe, G., Hermenegildo, M. (eds.) VMCAI 2010. LNCS, vol. 5944, pp. 312–327. Springer, Heidelberg (2010). https://doi.org/10.1007/978-3-642-11319-2_23
42. Stamm, S., Sterne, B., Markham, G.: Reining in the web with content security policy. In: Proceedings of the 19th International Conference on World Wide Web WWW, pp. 921–930 (2010)
43. Stasinopoulos, A., Ntantogian, C., Xenakis, C.: Commix: automating evaluation and exploitation of command injection vulnerabilities in web applications. Int. J. Inf. Secur. 1–24 (2018)

44. Stock, B., Johns, M., Steffens, M., Backes, M.: How the web tangled itself: uncovering the history of client-side Web (in)security. In: Proceedings of the 26th USENIX Security Symposium, pp. 971–987 (2017)
45. Stock, B., Lekies, S., Mueller, T., Spiegel, P., Johns, M.: Precise client-side protection against DOM-based cross-site scripting. In: Proceedings of the 23rd USENIX Security Symposium, pp. 655–670 (2014)
46. Szalachowski, P.: Towards more reliable Bitcoin timestamps (2018). arXiv:1803.09028
47. Tahir, R., et al.: Mining on someone else's dime: mitigating covert mining operations in clouds and enterprises. In: Proceedings of the 20th International Symposium on Research in Attacks, Intrusions, and Defenses RAID, pp. 287–310 (2017)
48. van Saberhagen, N.: CryptoNote v 2.0. Technical report, CryptoNote Technology, October 2013
49. Virvilis, N., Mylonas, A., Tsalis, N., Gritzalis, D.: Security busters: web browser security vs. suspicious sites. Comput. Secur. **52**, 90–105 (2015)
50. WebAssembly Community Group. Security (2018). http://webassembly.org/docs/security
51. Weinberger, J., Barth, A., Song, D.: Towards client-side HTML security policies. In: Proceedings of the 6th USENIX Conference on Hot Topics in Security (HotSec), p. 8 (2011)
52. WhiteHat Security. Application security statistics report, vol. 12 (2017)
53. Wu, Z., Gianvecchio, S., Xie, M., Wang, H.: Mimimorphism: a new approach to binary code obfuscation. In: Proceedings of the 17th ACM Conference on Computer and Communications Security (CCS), pp. 536–546 (2010)
54. Xu, W., Zhang, F., Zhu, S.: JStill: mostly static detection of obfuscated malicious JavaScript code. In: Proceedings of the 3rd ACM Conference on Data and Application Security and Privacy (CODASPY), pp. 117–128 (2013)
55. Yang, G., Mendoza, A., Zhang, J., Gu, G.: Precisely and scalably vetting JavaScript bridge in android hybrid apps. In: Dacier, M., Bailey, M., Polychronakis, M., Antonakakis, M. (eds.) RAID 2017. LNCS, vol. 10453, pp. 143–166. Springer, Cham (2017). https://doi.org/10.1007/978-3-319-66332-6_7

Detecting and Characterizing Web Bot Traffic in a Large E-commerce Marketplace

Haitao Xu[1]([⊠]), Zhao Li[2], Chen Chu[2], Yuanmi Chen[2], Yifan Yang[2],
Haifeng Lu[2], Haining Wang[3], and Angelos Stavrou[4]

[1] Arizona State University, Glendale, AZ 85306, USA
hxu@asu.edu
[2] Alibaba Group, Hangzhou, China
{lizhao.lz,chuchen.cc,yuanmi.cym,yifan.yy,haifeng.lhf}@alibaba-inc.com
[3] University of Delaware, Newark, DE 19716, USA
hnw@udel.edu
[4] George Mason University, Fairfax, VA 22030, USA
astavrou@gmu.edu

Abstract. A certain amount of web traffic is attributed to web bots on
the Internet. Web bot traffic has raised serious concerns among website
operators, because they usually consume considerable resources at web
servers, resulting in high workloads and longer response time, while not
bringing in any profit. Even worse, the content of the pages it crawled
might later be used for other fraudulent activities. Thus, it is important
to detect web bot traffic and characterize it. In this paper, we first propose an efficient approach to detect web bot traffic in a large e-commerce
marketplace and then perform an in-depth analysis on the characteristics
of web bot traffic. Specifically, our proposed bot detection approach consists of the following modules: (1) an Expectation Maximization (EM)-
based feature selection method to extract the most distinguishable features, (2) a gradient based decision tree to calculate the likelihood of
being a bot IP, and (3) a threshold estimation mechanism aiming to
recover a reasonable amount of non-bot traffic flow. The detection approach has been applied on Taobao/Tmall platforms, and its detection
capability has been demonstrated by identifying a considerable amount
of web bot traffic. Based on data samples of traffic originating from web
bots and normal users, we conduct a comparative analysis to uncover the
behavioral patterns of web bots different from normal users. The analysis results reveal their differences in terms of active time, search queries,
item and store preferences, and many other aspects. These findings provide new insights for public websites to further improve web bot traffic
detection for protecting valuable web contents.

1 Introduction

Web bots, the programs generating automated traffic, are being leveraged by
various parties for a variety of purposes. Web bots are generating a significant

© Springer Nature Switzerland AG 2018
J. Lopez et al. (Eds.): ESORICS 2018, LNCS 11099, pp. 143–163, 2018.
https://doi.org/10.1007/978-3-319-98989-1_8

volume of web traffic everyday. The 2018 annual report of Distil Networks [2] reveals that web bots account for 42.2% of all website traffic while human traffic makes up the rest 57.8%. The bot landscape is fairly polarized between benign bots and malicious bots [1]. A benign bot mainly refers to a search engine bot that abides by the robot.txt industry opt-in standard and could add value to publishers or advertisers. A malicious bot enables high-speed abuse and attacks on websites. Unsavory competitors and cyber-criminals leverage malicious bots to perform a wide array of malicious activities, such as brute force login, web scraping, adversarial information retrieval, personal and financial data harvesting, and transaction frauds [3,29].

E-commerce portals is among the sites hit hardest by malicious bots: according to the report [3], about 20% of traffic to e-commerce portals is from malicious bots; malicious bots even generated up to 70% of Amazon.com traffic [4]. As one of the largest e-commerce companies in the world, Alibaba also observed a certain amount of malicious bot traffic to its two main subsidiary sites, i.e., Taobao.com and Tmall.com. In this paper, first, we proposed a novel and efficient approach for detecting web bot traffic. We then implemented and deployed the approach on Taobao/Tmall platforms, and it shows that the detection approach performed well on those large websites by identifying a large set of IP addresses (IPs) used by malicious web bots. Second, we conducted an in-deep behavioral analysis on a sample of web bot traffic to better understand the distinguishable characteristics of web bot traffic from normal web traffic initiated by human users.

In particular, we first presented a bot IP detection algorithm, which consists of two steps: (1) we proposed an Expectation Maximization (EM)-based feature selection method to select the features eligible for determining whether an incoming visitor is a bot; and (2) we proposed to employ a decision tree to combine all the selected features to produce an overall value. We computed a threshold to the decision tree result which optimally recovers the non-bot traffic curve over time. In addition, we dissected one-month long malicious web bot traffic sample and examined the unique behavioral patterns of web bots from normal users.

We analyzed interaction logs containing a one-month time window of randomly sampled visits to Taobao or Tmall from more than 99,000 bot IP addresses (BIPs). Note that bots are unlike normal logged-on users and do not have an associated unique user ID. In addition, a bot may change its IP frequently (e.g., within minutes) and it is impossible to establish a one-to-one relationship between a bot and a BIP. Hence, to be accurate, we consider a BIP rather than a bot as the investigated subject in this work. For a comparative analysis, we also obtained a sample set of more than 97,000 normal users and their interaction logs in the same month.

Our analysis results show that BIPs have unique behavioral patterns and different preferences on items and stores in comparison to the normal logged-on users. Specifically, within the same time period, a BIP could generate 10 times more search queries and clicks than a normal user. Also, a BIP tends to visit the same item multiple times within one day probably for the purpose of periodically monitoring the dynamics of the item. A BIP visits more stores daily than a normal user and prefers to visit the stores with middle or lower reputation grades. By characterizing the malicious bot traffic, we are able to provide e-commerce sites with insights of detecting malicious bot traffic and protect valuable web contents on the e-commerce marketplaces.

The remainder of this paper is organized as follows. Section 2 presents our bot IP detection approach and its application on Taobao/Tmall platforms. Section 3 describes our dataset and presents our investigation results about malicious bot traffic. Section 4 discusses limitations and future work. Section 5 surveys the related work, followed by our conclusions in Sect. 6.

2 Bot IP Detection Methodology

Our proposed bot IP detection approach consists of two steps. First, we develop an Expectation-Maximization (EM)-based feature extractor to obtain an abnormal score for each IP, and identify suspicious Bot IPs whose abnormal scores are larger than a threshold (Sect. 2.1). Second, we build a decision tree based on the suspicious label and features of IPs and extract explainable rules from the decision tree (Sect. 2.2). Furthermore, we demonstrate the effectiveness of our detection approach by applying the resulting rules on Taobao/Tmall platforms (Sect. 2.3).

2.1 Using EM-Based Abnormal Score to Generate Labels

In this section, we develop an EM-based approach and define an abnormal score for each IP.

Intuitively we assume that the distribution of any feature in the candidate pool is a mixture of two different distributions that describe normal traffic samples and suspicious traffic ones, respectively. It is reasonable since the normal traffic samples were generated by normal users from normal IPs while the others are not. With this assumption, the EM algorithm is introduced to estimate the parameters of the two distributions [11]. An IP may be suspicious if the distance between the two distributions is large enough. We present the details of our EM-based modeling and feature extraction procedure as follows.

EM-Based Modeling. Suppose we have N IPs, a feature of interest (e.g., click-through rate[1]), and a set of corresponding IP-wise values $X = \{x_1, \cdots, x_N\}$. We randomly sampled the same feature of 1,000 IPs in a normal period and in a abnormal period, respectively. We computed the distributions of 1,000 normal feature values and 1,000 abnormal feature values. As shown in Figs. 1 and 2, the

---

[1] Click-through rate is calculated as the total number of clicks on the product detail webpage divided by the number of impressions of the product information in the Taobao/Tmall search engine return results.

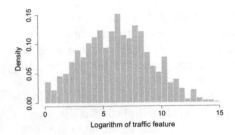

Fig. 1. Distribution of normal traffic of a candidate feature.

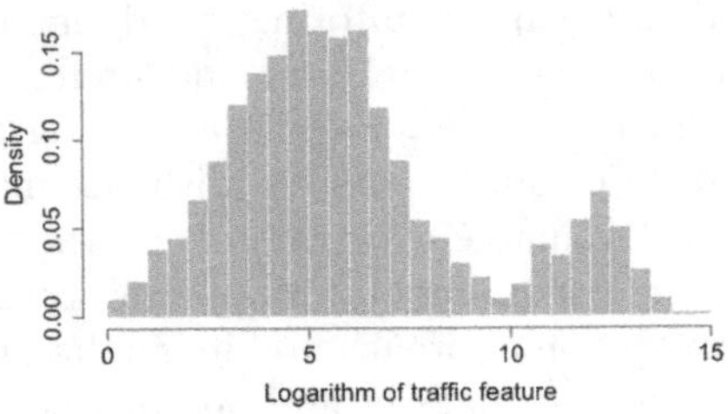

Fig. 2. Distribution of suspicious traffic of a candidate feature.

logarithm of feature values from normal IPs roughly follows a Normal distribution, while the feature values from suspicious IPs nearly follow a mixture of two normal distributions.

We define the mixture of two Normal distributions with the density function $p(x)$:

$$p(x|\Theta) = \alpha_1 p_1(x|\theta_1) + \alpha_2 p_2(x|\theta_2), \tag{1}$$

where $p_i(.|\theta_i)$ is a Gaussian density function with parameter $\theta_i = \{\mu_i, \sigma_i\}$, and α_i denotes the non-negative mixture weight and $\alpha_1 + \alpha_2 = 1$. Under this assumption, x is from a population composed of two Normal-distributed sub-groups, which can not be observed directly. The sub-group indicator $z_i(x)$ is defined as $z_i(x) = 1$ when the sample x is from the i-th distribution, and therefore $z_1(x) + z_2(x) \equiv 1$. Unless explicitly stated, $z_i(x)$ is simplified to z_i in the latter context.

In this model, one p_i represents the distribution of normal customer behavior while the other describes the suspicious one. The nuisance parameter α_i quantifies the probability whether the sample is from suspicious group or not. The product of all probability density functions (PDFs), according to the expression (1), is the full likelihood under the i.i.d. assumption. Equivalently, the following log-likelihood is used:

$$\log L(X, \Theta) = \log \prod_k^N p(x_k|\Theta) = \sum_{k=1}^N \log p(x_k|\Theta) = \sum_{k=1}^N \left(\log \sum_{i=1}^2 \alpha_i p_i(x_k|z_i, \theta_i) \right) \tag{2}$$

This formula could be maximized by the EM algorithm, consisting of three main steps. The EM algorithm repeats the last two steps (i.e., E and M steps) until the convergence criterion is met.

Initialization-Step: starting from an initial estimate of θ_i randomly.

E-Step: Given the parameters of the distributions, calculate the probability that an IP k comes from distribution i. Denote the current parameter values as $\Theta = \{\mu_1, \mu_2, \sigma_1, \sigma_2\}$. Compute the probability $\omega_{k,i}$ for all IPs k, $1 \le k \le N$ and two mixture components $i = 1, 2$ as

$$\omega_{k,i} = p(z_{k,i} = 1 | x_k, \Theta) = \frac{p_i(x_k | z_i, \theta_i) \cdot \alpha_i}{\sum_{m=1}^{2} p_m(x_k | z_m, \theta_m) \cdot \alpha_m} \tag{3}$$

Note that for each IP k, $\omega_{k,1} + \omega_{k,2} = 1$.

M-step: Given the probabilities calculated in E-step, update the distribution parameters. Let $N_i = \sum_{k=1}^{N} \omega_{k,i}, i = 1, 2$, and we have

$$\alpha_i^{new} = \frac{N_i}{N} \tag{4}$$

$$\mu_i^{new} = \left(\frac{1}{N_i}\right) \sum_{k=1}^{N} \omega_{k,i} \cdot x_k \tag{5}$$

$$\sigma_i^{new} = \left(\frac{1}{N_i}\right) \sum_{k=1}^{N} \omega_{k,i} \cdot (x_k - \mu_k^{new})^2 \tag{6}$$

Convergence Criterion: The convergence is generally detected by calculating the value of the log-likelihood after each iteration and halting when it appears not to be changing in a significant manner from one iteration to the next.

Abnormal Score. We consider an IP to be suspicious if the distance between the estimated two distributions is large enough. We define an empirical *abnormal score* of an IP i on feature j as

$$S_{i,j} = \frac{|\mu_{i,j,2}^{\star} - \mu_{i,j,1}^{\star}|}{\max\{|\mu_{i,j,1}^{\star}|, |\mu_{i,j,2}^{\star}|\}} \tag{7}$$

An IP is suspicious if its score $S_{i,j}$ is greater than a certain threshold θ [11].

Threshold Selection. To determine the suspicious threshold θ, we resort to the efforts of human experts. We consider two types of visitor traffic (i.e., not-logged-on) to the Taobao/Tmall platforms: visitor traffic coming through the search engine (SE) of the platforms (termed as SE visitor traffic) and visitor traffic taking other ways to enter the platforms. Normally, the ratio of SE visitor traffic to all visitor traffic received by platforms is quite stable. As shown in Fig. 3[2], SE visitor traffic (represented by the middle red curve) and all visitor traffic (i.e., the top green curve) kept the same pace in growth during consecutive days spanning over a few months in 2015; However, since a changepoint (i.e., a time point, marked as the vertical line T in Fig. 3) in 2015, all visitor traffic decreased, but the SE visitor traffic had a significant increase. Web bot traffic could be the major contributor to the abnormal increase in the SE visitor traffic.

By applying EM-based approach on the data of the whole period of time, we can obtain abnormal score $S_{i,j}$ for each IP i and each feature j. To simplify

---

[2] Both the y-axis and x-axis (denoting the time in 2015) values are deliberately hidden for confidentiality reasons.

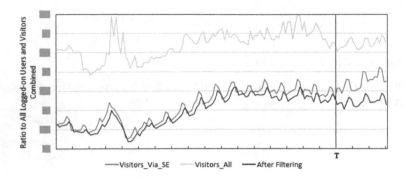

Fig. 3. An abnormally high proportion of unregistered visitors were observed in year 2015. They were then detected and removed by applying our bot detection algorithm on the Alibaba data. (Color figure online)

the threshold selection, we define a score for each IP i: $\bar{S}_i = max_j(S_{i,j})$. And we consider an IP is suspicious if $\bar{S}_i > \theta$. Human experts then choose the best value of θ by manually adjusting the threshold to make sure that the trend of the after-filtering-curve (the bottom black one in Fig. 3) is more similar to all-visitor-curve (the top green one in Fig. 3, especially the end part of that period of time).

2.2 Decision Tree Modeling and Rules' Selection

With the effort of human experts, the EM-based abnormal scores can be used to detect part of the Bot IPs. However, the detection is based on some independent rules, that is, each rule is derived from just one feature. And thus those rules can hardly capture Bot IPs' behaviors. Moreover, the manually-adjusted threshold θ may also result in decrease on the evaluation metric *recall*. We address these problems in three steps:

1. To introduce decision tree, we leverage tens of features to model the suspicious label generated by the EM-based approach.
2. To do feature selection, we conduct cross validation.
3. To generate rules from the resulting decision tree, we adopt the methods introduced in [13].

Following the previous steps, we obtain a list of selected features for the abnormal visitor traffic in 2015, described as follows[3]:

---

[3] When you search a keyword in e-commerce website, the resulting page is the so-called search result page. A search result page view is a page view of search result, for example searching a keyword or going to the next page in search result page.

F_1 : the percentage of visits made by non-login users

F_2 : the percentage of clicking on suggested queries

F_3 : the percentage of HTTP requests with empty referer field

F_4 : the total number of search result page view

F_5 : the total number of distinct query keyword divided by F_4

The consequent rules generated from the resulting decision tree can be described in the form of $R_1 \wedge R_2 \wedge R_3 \wedge (R_4 \vee R_5)$ where,

$$R_1 : F_1 > 0.9$$
$$R_2 : F_2 < 0.1$$
$$R_3 : F_3 > 0.7$$
$$R_4 : F_4 > 50 \wedge F_5 > 0.9$$
$$R_5 : F_4 > 100 \wedge F_5 > 0.7$$

We note that any derived information (e.g., the thresholds shown above) does not represent the true scenarios in Taobao/Tmall platforms.

2.3   Model Validation

To demonstrate the effectiveness of the model, we validate the generated rules using the data labels generated by both the EM-based approach and online test. With the model, we achieve the *precision* of 95.4% and the *recall* of 92%, which implies that the rules are quite effective in detection of bot IPs.

As for the online test, we deploy the rules on Taobao/Tmall platforms. We observe that in Fig. 3 the abnormal increase (represented as the part of red curve since the changepoint T) falls back to the normal black curve after filtering bot IP data.

3   Characterization

3.1   Dataset for Analysis

By broadly sampling the BIPs detected by our bot IP detection approach, we obtained 99,140 BIPs and the associated interaction logs. In addition, we retrieved a sample of 97,109 users and their interaction logs in the same month for comparative analysis. The interaction logs detail the activities conducted by each visitor regardless of whether the visitor is logged on. For a BIP, its activities on an e-commerce site are represented by its search and click behaviors, while a logged-on user may also present transaction-related behaviors such as adding items to cart and checking out.

Loaded on PC or Mobile Devices. An initial examination of the interaction logs reveals that 99.9% (99,089) BIPs were loaded on the PC devices, which contributed to 92.7% searches and 98.7% clicks while 20% BIPs were loaded on

Table 1. Summary of the dataset.

Visitor	Client type (%)	Searches (%)	Clicks (%)
BIP (99,140)	PC (99.9%)	92.7%	98.7%
	Wireless (20.0%)	7.3%	1.3%
User (97,109)	PC (63.4%)	17.6%	10.4%
	Wireless (91.4%)	82.4%	89.6%

the wireless[4] devices, which generated 7.3% searches and 1.3% clicks. Note that some BIPs may be loaded on both PC and wireless devices. Considering the quite scarce activities presented by BIPs on wireless devices, we focus on the 99,089 BIPs presenting search and click behaviors on the PC clients. Additionally, among the 97,109 logged-on users[5], 63.4% (61,521) were logged on the PC devices and generated 17.6% searches and 10.4% clicks while 91.4% users were logged on the wireless devices and launched 82.4% searches and 89.6% clicks. The statistical results shown in Table 1 indicate that most BIPs were loaded on PC devices while normal users preferred to browse the shopping sites on the wireless clients such as smartphones and pads. We focus on three kinds of visitors: BIPs on PC, users on PC, and users on wireless.

Next, we attempt to reveal unique browsing patterns and infer the hidden intents of web bots by characterizing each major step of their browsing activities and making comparisons with normal users.

3.2 Browsing Time and Origin

We first examine how many days a BIP was active in the month, their most active time on a day, the number of MIDs (Machine IDentification numbers) used by BIPs during one month, and their origin countries.

Active Days within One Month. Figure 4 depicts the CDF of the days during which a BIP or a user was observed to generate web traffic in the same month of the changepoint T. It shows that about 88% of BIPs were active for only one or two days and the mean value of active days per BIP is 1.7 days. Different than BIPs, logged-on users were active for more days. About 86% of users on PC were active for more than one day, about 48% were active for at least one week, and about 22% active for more than two weeks. The mean value of active days is 8.8. Users on wireless were more active. About 97% of users on wireless were active for more than one day, about 80% were active for at least one week, about 60% active for more than two weeks, and about 30% active for more than three weeks. The mean value is 15.8 days. The results are consistent with the fact that mobile revenue accounts for 65% of core retail business of Alibaba in the quarter ended December 2015 [5].

---

[4] We use the two terms "wireless" and "mobile" interchangeably.

[5] Note that not all not-logged-on visitors were deemed as bots by Alibaba IT teams. In addition, a user could be logged on both PC and wireless devices.

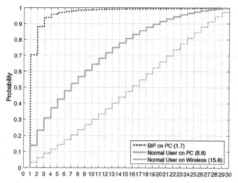
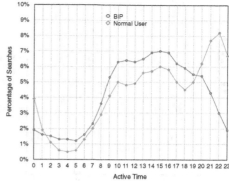

Fig. 4. CDF of active days per BIP and normal user in the same month of the changepoint T. Numbers in parentheses denote the mean values.

Fig. 5. Distribution of search queries launched by BIPs and normal users during the 24 h on one day.

Takeaway: Most BIPs were observed active for at most two days probably due to the fact that web bots change IP addresses frequently to avoid the detection of their brutal crawling activities.

Active Time on One Day. It is interesting to know at which time BIPs and normal users are most active during one day. We measured the degree of being active at a time based on the percentage of search queries made during that time. Figure 5 shows the distribution of search queries made by BIPs and users during 24 h on one day. Evidently, BIPs and normal users presented different patterns. Normal users were most active during hours 20 to 23, consistent with previous reports [6,7], and not so active during the working hours between 9 and 19, while BIPs were not so active during the hours from 20 to 23 but quite active during the working hours.

Takeaway: Web bots are not active in the time period (hours 20 to 23) during which normal users are most active, implying that bot developers only run the bots during their working hours.

Number of MIDs Used within One Month. A website usually creates a cookie string for a newly incoming visitor and stores it in the browser cookie file for session tracking. Alibaba's e-commerce sites generate an MID based on a visitor's cookie string for identifying her in the interaction logs. Each time the cookie is deleted by a visitor, the sites would generate a new MID when she returns back. The boxplot in Fig. 6 depicts the number of MIDs used per BIP and normal user in the same month of the changepoint T. For each box in the figure, its bottom corresponds to the number of MIDs on the 25th percentile, its top corresponds to the value on the 75th percentile, and the line across the box corresponds to the median value. On average, a BIP was corresponding to up to 401 MIDs within just one month. Given the results shown in Fig. 4 that a BIP was observed active in one month for only 1.7 days, we speculate that a BIP

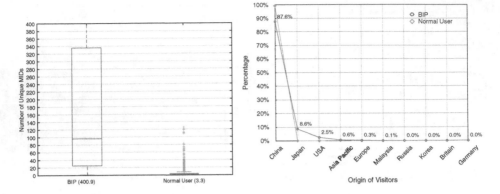

Fig. 6. Number of MIDs used per BIP and normal user within one month. Numbers in parentheses in the x-axis labels denote the mean values.

Fig. 7. Distribution of origin countries of BIPs and normal users.

may clear its cookies up to hundreds of times each day for evading tracking by the e-commerce sites. By contrast, a normal user was associated with only 3.3 MIDs on average although she was observed active for 8 to 15 days within one month on average, as shown in Fig. 4. The result makes sense since a persistent cookie only remains valid during the configured duration period and a new MID would be generated for the user when her cookie becomes invalid.

Takeaway: A BIP may clear its cookies up to hundreds of times a day to avoid tracking.

Origin Country of Visitors. We also compared the origin countries of BIPs to those of normal users in an attempt to identify the origin countries of web bots. Figure 7 depicts the distribution of the origin countries for both BIPs and users. It shows that 99.4% of users were from China, 0.04% were from Japan, and 0.06% from USA. The result makes sense since currently Alibaba keeps its focus on China and Chinese shoppers constitute the majority of its consumers. For the BIPs, 87.6% were from China, 8.6% were from Japan, and 2.5% from USA. Comparatively, the percentages of Japan and USA have risen up.

Takeaway: China, Japan, and USA are the top three countries where bots were launched.

3.3 Statistics of Searches and Clicks

We present the statistics about the searches and clicks made by BIPs and normal users in the one month we investigated.

Daily Number of Searches in One Month. We examined how many search queries submitted daily by BIPs and users during their active days to pinpoint the difference in behavior patterns. Figure 8 depicts the number of search queries made daily per BIP and normal user in the same month of the changepoint T.

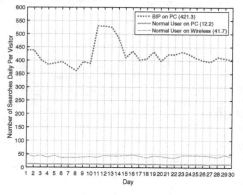

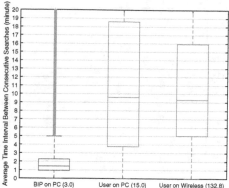

Fig. 8. Number of search queries made daily per BIP and normal user during their active days in the same month of the changepoint T. Numbers in parentheses denote the mean values.

Fig. 9. Average time interval (minutes) between consecutive search queries made by BIPs and normal users. Numbers in parentheses in the x-axis labels denote the mean values.

It shows that BIPs generated an exceptionally large number of search queries on Alibaba e-commerce sites each day. On average, each BIP launched 421.3 search queries daily on the sites. It would be quite unusual if normal users have had made so many queries on Taobao or Tmall for their interested items, since it is quite boring to manually launch hundreds of searches given that each search involves typing keywords and clicking on the search button. In contrast, on average, a normal user on PC generated about 12 search queries daily and a user on wireless made about 42 searches daily, fewer than one tenth of search queries daily made by BIPs. Thus, unlike BIPs, normal users do not search for items excessively. In addition, the result that wireless users made more search queries again confirms that nowadays users prefer online shopping on mobile devices [9].

Takeaway: Bots made about 10 times more search queries daily than normal users.

Time Interval between Consecutive Search Queries. The time interval between consecutive search queries represents the degree of activity. Note that by consecutive search queries, we mean the search queries that happened in sequence on the same day while not necessarily in the same session. Thus the below results represent an upper bound of the time interval between consecutive search queries in one session. Figure 9 depicts the average time interval in minute between consecutive searches made by BIPs and users. Specifically, 25% of BIPs had the time interval of less than 1 min; 50% of BIPs launched the next search query within 1.5 min; and 75% had the time interval of less than 2.2 min. In contrast, for users on PC, the median value of the time interval was 9.5 min, 75% had the time interval of more than 3.8 min, 25% had the interval of more than 18.7 min, and the mean value was 15 min. Users on wireless had much

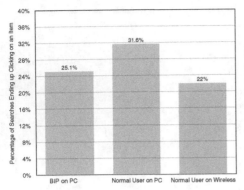

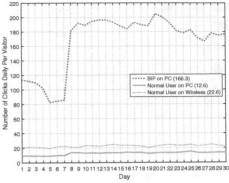

Fig. 10. Percentage of search queries made by BIPs and users that end up clicking on an item.

Fig. 11. Number of clicks generated daily per BIP and normal user during their active days in the same month of the changepoint T. Numbers in parentheses denote the mean values.

longer time intervals than BIPs. 75% had the time interval of more than 5 min, 50% had the time interval of more than 9.2 min and 25% had the time interval of more than 16 min. The mean value was 132.8 min, exceptionally high due to some outliers.

Takeaway: BIPs behaved much aggressively in launching searches. They had much shorter time intervals between consecutive search queries than normal users, about one fifth of that of the latter on average.

Search Queries Ending up Clicking on an Item. When a search query is submitted, the e-commerce search engine will return back all relevant items. Then the visitor could browse the results pages and choose one or more items to click through to the item detail pages. It is interesting to examine the percentage of search queries that finally lead to further clicks on the items. Figure 10 shows that about 25% of search queries launched by BIPs, 31.6% of search queries by users on PC, and 22% of search queries by users on wireless led to further clicks to the item detail pages. Thus, BIPs and users do not present much difference in this metric.

Daily Number of Clicks in One Month. Figure 11 displays the number of clicks made daily per BIP and normal user. On average, a BIP launched 166.3 clicks daily while on average a normal user on PC performed 12.6 clicks daily and a user on wireless generated a bit more clicks with 22.6 clicks daily.

Takeaway: A BIP performed many more clicks daily than a normal user, about 10 times the clicks made by the latter.

Clicks Without Precedent Searches. Normally, a visitor searches in the e-commerce search engine for the desired items and then clicks on one or more items from the results pages to continue browsing their detail pages. Finally, the visitor chooses an item and adds it to the cart. After that, she may continue to

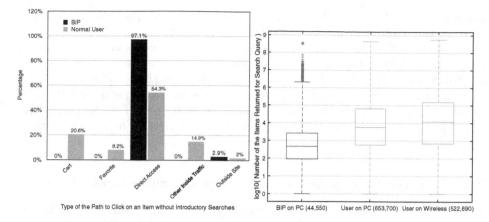

Fig. 12. Breakdown of the paths to the clicks performed by BIPs and users without precedent search queries.

Fig. 13. Number of the items returned for a search query made by BIPs and normal users. Numbers in parentheses in the x-axis labels denote the mean values.

pay online and place an order. Or, she may just leave the platform and return back for checking out several days later, which is also very common. In the latter case, the interaction logs about the visitor for her return would record that the visitor made direct access to the item through her cart or favorite[6] and did not make any precedent search queries.

A statistical analysis of the interaction logs shows that about a half of clicks made by all those three kinds of visitors were not preceded by any search queries. Next we attempt to explore from what path those clicks without precedent search queries were made. Examination of the interaction logs reveals that such clicks were made through one of the following ways: (1) clicking on an item in a cart; (2) clicking on an item in the favorite; (3) direct access to the item detail page through the page URL; (4) access to the item detail page through other traffic directing paths inside the e-commerce site; and (5) access to the item page via advertisements or redirecting from the outside sites. Figure 12 provides a breakdown of the paths to the clicks performed by BIPs and users without precedent search queries. It shows that nearly all (97.1%) of such clicks performed by BIPs were made by direct access to items' detail pages via URLs[7], and the rest clicks (2.9%) originated from the outside sites. Comparatively, 54.3% of such clicks made by normal users were generated by direct access via the detail page URLs, 20.6% of clicks were generated on the carts, 8.2% were generated on the favorites, 14.9% of clicks were the traffic directed by the e-commerce site through

---

[6] Note that the favorite here refers to the favorite feature provided by the e-commerce sites, rather than the bookmark features of modern web browsers.

[7] In essence, a direct click on an item is the same as a direct access to the item's detail page via its URL.

other means, and 2% of clicks originated from outside sites probably by clicking through the advertisements displayed on the outside sites.

Takeaway: The results indicate that web bot designers may first obtain a collection of URLs of the item detail pages and then leverage the bots to automatically crawl each item detail page by following the URLs. The reason why normal users also made direct access to the item detail pages via their URLs for about a half of their clicks could be that many users have the habit of saving the detail page links of the interested items to their web browser bookmarks, rather than adding the items to the favorite of the e-commerce sites.

3.4   Returned Results for Search Queries and Subsequent Clicks

For a search query, Alibaba's built-in search engine usually returns tens of thousands of items. Close scrutiny of the number of returned items, the results pages visited, and click position on a result page may reveal distinct patterns of BIPs.

Number of Returned Items for a Search Query. The number of returned items may reflect whether a search query is elaborately made up. Specific search queries are typically responded with limited but desired results. Figure 13 gives a comparison between BIPs and normal users in terms of the returned items for each of their search queries. It shows that BIPs typically received a much smaller number of returned items for each search query. Specifically, for each search query, BIPs got 91 items returned on the 25th percentile, 462 items in the median, 2,565 items on the 75th percentile, and 44,550 items on average. In comparison, users received much more items returned for their search queries either on PC or on wireless. For each search query made by users on PC clients, the number of returned items is 576 on the 25th percentile, 5,731 in the median, 65,356 on the 75th percentile, and 653,700 in the mean. The search queries submitted by users on wireless clients were returned even more items, with the median value of 11,947 and the 75th percentile of 153,765.

Takeaway: Search queries made by BIPs were often responded with much fewer items, more exactly, about an order of magnitude fewer than the items returned for a search query made by normal users. This result could be attributed to two factors: long and complicated search queries, and searching for unpopular items. Combined with previous findings that BIPs usually launch long search queries and tend to search for not so popular items in the e-commerce search engine, one could conclude that BIPs were indeed using long and elaborately crafted search queries to crawl data on the Alibaba marketplace. However, their intents are still ambiguous and cannot be quickly determined.

Sequence Number of the Results Pages Visited. Among the results pages returned for a search query, choosing which page to visit is an interesting feature to explore. The boxplot in Fig. 14 describes the statistics about the sequence number of the results pages visited by BIPs and normal users. It shows that nearly all BIPs only visited the first results page. Comparatively, in addition to the first results page, normal users may often go further to visit the next pages.

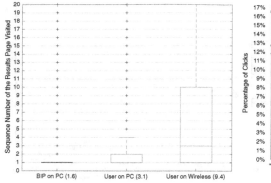

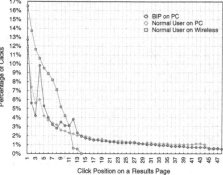

Fig. 14. Sequence number of the results pages visited by BIPs and normal users. Numbers in parentheses in the x-axis labels denote the mean values.

Fig. 15. Distribution of the click traffic on each position of a results page visited by BIPs and normal users.

For normal users on PC, about one third[8] of their navigations were observed beyond the first results page, and for about 20% visits they navigated beyond the second page. Users on wireless demonstrated even much deeper visits. Specifically, the sequence number of results pages visited had the median value of 3, which means that users on wireless browsed the third results page and/or the deeper pages for half of their visits. The sequence number on the 75th percentile was 10, indicating that for about 25% visits, users on wireless browsed the 10th results page and/or the beyond. It makes sense that users on wireless usually navigate to deeper pages since the number of items listed in each results page is only about 10 for mobile devices due to their small screen sizes while each results page could contain about 50 items on PCs. Thus users on wireless had to navigate more pages for the interested items.

Takeaway: Most web bots only browsed the first results page, indicating that web bots were only interested in the items in the top listings.

Click Positions on a Results Page. A results page usually displays tens of items highly relevant to a search query. A visitor typically browses those displayed items and chooses several of them to click on for further review and comparison before making a purchasing decision. We analyzed all clicks made by BIPs and users on the results pages to examine the distribution of click traffic at each position on a results page. Figure 15 depicts such a distribution for BIPs and users. The figure shows that the items at the first position of results pages received the most clicks: 12.7% clicks of BIPs, 11.8% clicks of users on PC, and 16.5% clicks of users on wireless. Overall, the amount of the received click traffic decreased sharply with the larger ranking positions on the results pages, especially compared with that of the top positions. Compared to the click

---

[8] The number was calculated with the dataset and cannot be inferred from Fig. 14.

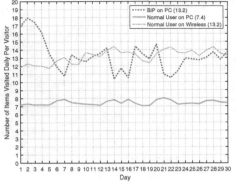
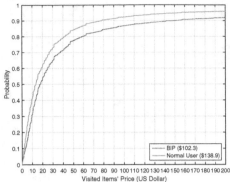

Fig. 16. Number of items visited daily per BIP and normal user. Numbers in parentheses denote the mean values.

Fig. 17. CDF of the price of the items visited by BIPs and normal users. Numbers in parentheses denote the mean values.

traffic to an items at the first position, the clicks received by an items at the second position decreased by 7.1% for BIPs, 4.4% for users on PC, and 2.8% for users on wireless. However, some unusual results were also observed. Nearly 10% click traffic from BIPs were directed to the items at the fourth position, significantly larger than the click traffic received by the items at the third or the second positions. We do not exactly know why but it seems that users on PC also preferred to click on the items at the 4th position than the items at the 3rd position. In addition, since a results page on wireless devices usually contains 10 to 20 items, thus it makes sense that the curve representing users on wireless reaches the x-axis at the position 14.

Takeaway: Both web bots and normal users generated the most clicks on the items at the first position on a results page while web bots were also observed to generate a significant proportion of click traffic to the items at the fourth position.

3.5   Visited Items and Sellers

In this part, we characterize the items whose detail pages were viewed by BIPs and normal users, and the stores which accommodate those items.

Number of Items Visited Daily Per Visitor. We first examined how many items were visited[9] by BIPs and normal users. Figure 16 depicts the number of items visited daily per BIP and normal user in the same month of the change-point T. We found that overall the number of the items visited daily per BIP and normal user is steady. On average, a BIP visited 13.2 items each day, a user on wireless visited the same number of items per day, and a user on PC visited fewer items each day, with 7.4 items visited. Thus, BIPs did not behave

---

[9] An item is deemed visited if its detail page is viewed or retrieved.

abnormally in terms of the number of items visited each day. However, previous results (Fig. 11) show that clicks made daily per BIP was about 10 times the clicks performed daily per normal user. This leads to the conclusion that a BIP may visit one item multiple times per day, more exactly, about 10 times the frequency of a normal user typically visiting an item. And again, users on wireless seem more active than users on PC.

Takeaway: A web bot may visit one item multiple times within one day, probably for monitoring the dynamic of its interested items periodically.

Price of the Items Visited. We also examined the distribution of the price of the items visited by BIPs and normal users, which is depicted in Fig. 17. The two curves follow a similar distribution. Both BIPs and normal users showed great interest in the cheap items, and cheaper items received more visits. Specifically, the items with prices less than 10 US dollars were most visited by both BIPs and users, with the occupation ratio of 30% and 40%, respectively. The items with the prices between 10 and 20 US dollars received 20% and 23% visits from BIPs and users, respectively. About 12% and 13% visits from BIPs and users were for the items with the prices between 20 and 30 US dollars. About 78% items visited by BIPs and 84% by users had the prices less than 50 US dollars.

Takeaway: Overall, the items visited by web bots were a bit more expensive than those visited by normal users. Most items listed on the Alibaba marketplace are very cheap and cheap items are much more popular than the expensive ones.

Number of Sellers Visited Daily Per Visitor. Each item belongs to a store. We also attempted to explore the characteristics of the stores accommodating items. We first examined the number of stores visited daily per BIP and normal user. Figure 18 shows that a BIP visited 12 stores daily on average, about twice the number of stores visited daily per normal user. Specifically, a user on wireless visited about 6 stores per day on average. Considering that a user on wireless visited about 13 items per day on average shown in Fig. 11, we estimate that a user on wireless may view about two items' detail pages in one store per day on average, more than the number of items visited daily per user on the PC client in one store.

Takeaway: A BIP visited twice the number of stores by a normal user daily.

Reputation Grade of the Stores Visited. Based on the trading volume and positive reviews, Alibaba's e-commerce sites Taobao and Tmall divide stores into twenty grades [8], going from one to five stars, then one to five diamonds, then one to five crowns, and lastly one to five red crowns. A high grade often implies the items on the store sell quite well and receive positive customer reviews. Figure 19 provides a breakdown of the reputation grades of the stores ever visited by BIPs and normal users. It shows that the stores visited most by BIPs had diamond or star grades, representing the middle grades or lower. Specifically, about 55% stores had diamond grades and 25.4% had star grades. In contrast, normal users seemed to have preferences for the stores with middle grades or higher. Among the stores visited by them, nearly a half had the crown grades and a third had diamond grades. In addition, BIPs and normal users differed markedly on the

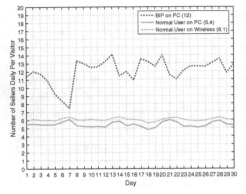

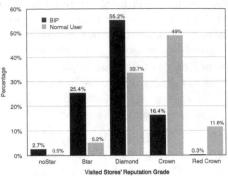

Fig. 18. Number of stores visited daily per BIP and normal user. Numbers in parentheses denote the mean values.

Fig. 19. Breakdown of the reputation grades of the stores ever visited by BIPs and normal users.

stores with the lowest and highest grades. A newly open store or a store without a good sales record usually has a grade of less than one star. The figure shows that such stores occupied 2.7% of all stores visited by BIPs and only 0.5% for normal users. The red crown grades represent the highest grades for the stores on the e-commerce sites. We found that 11.6% stores visited by normal users were with red crown grades while only 0.3% stores visited by BIPs had the highest grades.

Takeaway: Web bots preferred to visit the stores with middle reputation grades or lower.

4   Limitations and Future Work

Our current two-step bot detection approach assumes the logarithm of each candidate feature follows a mixture of two Gaussian distributions. Although it has been successfully applied to realistic log data for bot detection, the assumption may not always hold. In addition, the proposed approach involves human experts to ensure accuracy. In the future work, more general methods such as linear mixture model (LMM) and semi/non-parametric (NP) model could be introduced. The LMM assumes the data follows a mixture of several Gaussians and take into account more covariate features. Meanwhile, deep neural network (DNN) and other deep learning methods are proved much powerful for classification tasks. However, neither LMM nor DNN can be directly applied to our problem since they cannot estimate corresponding parameters and make further inferences without positive and negative IP samples detected by our approach. In addition, we cannot disclose what distinguishable features were trained and used for bot detection in this work because of the data confidentiality policy of our partner e-commerce marketplace.

5   Related Work

Our work is closely related to previous work in the areas of Web traffic characterization and automated traffic detection. Ihm et al. [10] analyzed five years of real Web traffic and made interesting findings about modern Web traffic. Meiss et al. [14] aimed to figure out the statistical properties of the global network flow traffic and found that client-server connections and traffic flows exhibit heavy-tailed probability distribution and lack typical behavior. Lan et al. [15] performed a quantitative analysis of the effect of DDoS and worm traffic on the background traffic and concluded that malicious traffic caused a significant increase in the average DNS and web latency. Buehrer et al. [16] studied automated web search traffic and click traffic, and proposed discriminating features to model the physical indicator of a human user as well as the behavior of automated traffic. Adar et al. [17] explored Web revisitation patterns and the reasons behind the behavior and finally revealed four primary revisitation patterns. Goseva-Popstojanova et al. [18] characterized malicious cyber activities aimed at web systems based on data collected by honeypot systems. They also developed supervised learning methods to distinguish attack sessions from vulnerability scan sessions. Kang et al. [26] proposed a semi-supervised learning approach for classifying automated web search traffic from genuine human user traffic. Weng et al. [11] developed a system for e-commerce platforms to detect human-generated traffic leveraging two detectors, namely EM-based time series detector and graph-based detector. Su et al. [12] developed a factor graph based model to detect malicious human-generated "Add-To-Favorite" behaviors based on a small set of ground truth of spamming activities.

Some other previous work focuses on detecting automated traffic, including web bot traffic. Suchacka et al. [19] proposed a Bayesian approach to detect web bots based on the features related to user sessions, evaluated it with real e-commerce traffic, and computed a detection accuracy of more than 90%. McKenna [20] used honeypots for harvesting web bots and detecting them, and concluded that web bots using deep-crawling algorithms could evade their honeypots-based detection approach. To address the issue of web bots degrading the performance and scalability of web systems, Rude et al. [21, 22] considered it necessary to accurately predict the next resource requested by a web bot. They explored a suite of classifiers for the resource request type prediction problem and found that Elman neural networks performed best. Finally, they introduced a cache system architecture in which web bot traffic and human traffic were served with separate policies. Koehl and Wang [23] studied the impact and cost of the search engine web bots on web servers, presented a practical caching approach for web server owners to mitigate the overload incurred by search engines, and finally validated the proposed caching framework. Gummadi et al. [24] aimed to mitigate the effects of botnet attacks by identifying human-generated traffic and servicing them with higher priority. They identified human-generated traffic by checking whether the incoming request was made within a small amount of time of legitimate keyboard or mouse activity on the client machine.

Jamshed et al. [25] presented another effort on suppressing web bot traffic by proposing deterministic human attestation based on trustworthy input devices, e.g., keyboards. Specifically, they proposed to augment the input devices with a trusted platform module chip. Goseva-Popstojanova et al. [18] characterized malicious cyber activities aimed at web systems based on data collected by honeypot systems. They also developed supervised learning methods to distinguish attack sessions from vulnerability scan sessions. Kang et al. [26] proposed a semi-supervised learning approach for classifying automated web search traffic from genuine human user traffic. Comparatively, we present an EM-based feature selection and rule-based web bot detection approach, which is straightforward but has been evaluated to be effective.

One main goal of web bot traffic to the e-commerce sites could be to infer the reputation system and item ranking rules in use, which could be then manipulated by insincere sellers to attract buyers and gain profits. One work [27] reported the underground platforms which cracked the reputation systems and provided seller reputation escalation as a service through by hiring freelancers to conduct fraud transactions. In addition, Kohavi et al. [28] recommended ten supplementary analyses for e-commerce websites to conduct after reviewing the standard web analytics reports. Identifying and eliminating bot traffic was suggested to be done first before performing any website analysis. This also justifies the value of our work.

6   Conclusion

Web bots contribute to a significant proportion of all traffic to e-commerce sites and has raised serious concerns of e-commerce operators. In this paper, we propose an efficient detection approach of web bot traffic to a large e-commerce marketplace and then perform an in-depth behavioral analysis of a sample web bot traffic. The bot detection approach has been applied to Taobao/Tmall platforms and performed well by identifying a huge amount of web bot traffic. With a sample of web bot traffic and normal user traffic, we performed characteristic analysis. The analytical results have revealed unique behavioral pattens of web bots. For instance, a bot IP address has been found to stay active for only one or two days in one month but generate 10 times more search queries and clicks than a normal user. Our work enables e-commerce marketplace operators to better detect and understand web bot traffic.

Acknowledgement. We would like to thank the anonymous reviewers for their valuable feedback. This work was partially supported by the U.S. NSF grant CNS-1618117 and DARPA XD3 Project HR0011-16-C-0055.

References

1. 'Good' bots are going too far. https://goo.gl/uVjvs3
2. Distil Networks: The 2018 Bad Bot Report. https://goo.gl/Ysmz34

3. Distil Networks: The 2016 Bad Bot Report. https://goo.gl/76T3YQ
4. Distil Networks: The 2015 Bad Bot Report. https://goo.gl/duH5Dy
5. Alibaba Group Quarterly Report. https://goo.gl/LLehdY
6. Taobao Users' Shopping Habits in 24 Hours. https://goo.gl/za6EB2
7. Taobao Online Shoppers Behavior. https://goo.gl/YgiJL1
8. Sellers' Reputation Grade on Alibaba. https://goo.gl/HBQ9MT
9. Alibaba Group's September Quarter 2015 Results. goo.gl/25X7JN
10. Ihm, S., Pai, V.S.: Towards understanding modern web traffic. In: IMC (2011)
11. Weng, H., Li, Z., et al.: Online e-commerce fraud: a large-scale detection and analysis. In: ICDE (2018)
12. Su, N., Liu, Y., et al.: Detecting crowdturfing "add to favorites" activities in online shopping. In: WWW (2018)
13. Quinlan, J.R.: Generating production rules from decision trees. In: IJCAI (1987)
14. Meiss, M., Menczer, F., Vespignani, A.: On the lack of typical behavior in the global web traffic network. In: WWW (2005)
15. Lan, K., Hussain, A., Dutta, D.: Effect of malicious traffic on the network. In: PAM (2003)
16. Buehrer, G., Stokes, J.W., Chellapilla, K.: A large-scale study of automated web search traffic. In: AIRWeb (2008)
17. Adar, E., Teevan, J., Dumais, S.T.: Large scale analysis of web revisitation patterns. In: CHI (2008)
18. Goseva-Popstojanova, K., Anastasovski, G., Dimitrijevikj, A., Pantev, R., Miller, B.: Characterization and classification of malicious web traffic. Comput. Secur. **42**, 92–115 (2014)
19. Suchacka, G., Sobków, M.: Detection of Internet robots using a Bayesian approach. In: IEEE 2nd International Conference on Cybernetics (CYBCONF) (2015)
20. McKenna, S.F.: Detection and classification of Web robots with honeypots. Naval Postgraduate School (2016)
21. Rude, H.N.: Intelligent caching to mitigate the impact of web robots on web servers. Wright State University (2016)
22. Rude, H.N., Doran, D.: Request type prediction for web robot and internet of things traffic. In: ICMLA (2015)
23. Koehl, A., Wang, H.: Surviving a search engine overload. In: WWW (2012)
24. Gummadi, R., Balakrishnan, H., Maniatis, P., Ratnasamy, S.: Not-a-Bot: improving service availability in the face of botnet attacks. In: NSDI (2009)
25. Jamshed, M.A., Kim, W., Park, K.: Suppressing bot traffic with accurate human attestation. In: Proceedings of the First ACM Asia-Pacific Workshop on Workshop on Systems (2010)
26. Kang, H., Wang, K., Soukal, D., Behr, F., Zheng, Z.: Large-scale bot detection for search engines. In: WWW (2010)
27. Xu, H., Liu, D., Wang, H., Stavrou, A.: E-commerce reputation manipulation: the emergence of reputation-escalation-as-a-service. In: WWW (2015)
28. Kohavi, R., Parekh, R.: Ten supplementary analyses to improve e-commerce web sites. In: SIGKDD Workshop (2003)
29. Kolias, C., Kambourakis, G., Stavrou, A., Voas, J.: DDoS in the IoT: Mirai and other botnets. Computer **50**(7), 80–84 (2017)

Cloud Security

Dissemination of Authenticated Tree-Structured Data with Privacy Protection and Fine-Grained Control in Outsourced Databases

Jianghua Liu[1], Jinhua Ma[5], Wanlei Zhou[2], Yang Xiang[3,4], and Xinyi Huang[5(✉)]

[1] School of Information Technology, Deakin University, Burwood, Australia
liujiang@deakin.edu.au
[2] School of Software, University of Technology Sydney, Ultimo, Australia
wanlei.zhou@uts.edu.au
[3] Digital Research and Innovation Capability Platform,
Swinburne University of Technology, Melbourne, Australia
yxiang@swin.edu.au
[4] State Key Laboratory of Integrated Service Networks (ISN), Xidian University,
Xi'an, China
[5] School of Mathematics and Computer Science,
Fujian Normal University, Fuzhou, China
jinhuama55@hotmail.com, xyhuang@fjnu.edu.cn

Abstract. The advent of cloud computing has inspired an increasing number of users outsourcing their data to remote servers to enjoy flexible and affordable data management services. However, storing data in a remote cloud server raises data privacy and security concerns, i.e., the integrity and origin of the query results. Although some solutions have been proposed to address these issues, none of them consider the arbitrary dissemination control of authenticated tree-structured data while disseminating to other users.

To address the above concerns, in this paper, we first propose a novel and efficient redactable signature scheme which features editable homomorphic operation and redaction control on tree-structured data. Subsequently, we prove the security properties of our scheme and conduct extensive theoretical and experimental analyses. The experimental results show that our scheme outperforms the existing solutions in disseminating of authenticated tree-structured data with privacy protection and dissemination control in outsourced database (ODB) model.

1 Introduction

With the rapid development of cloud computing, it has become prevalent for users and enterprises to lease the computing and storage resources to outsource the storage and management of massive data from local to powerful cloud service provider. Under this new IT Paradigm, database outsourcing [8] is considered

© Springer Nature Switzerland AG 2018
J. Lopez et al. (Eds.): ESORICS 2018, LNCS 11099, pp. 167–186, 2018.
https://doi.org/10.1007/978-3-319-98989-1_9

as a promising service model by providing a flexible and affordable solution for resource-constrained users to maintain their database services. There exist several real-world cloud service providers such as Amazon Relational Database, Azure, and Enterprise DB which enable users around the world to share and update their outsourced data anytime.

While enjoying all the benefits, the database outsourcing service poses numerous security challenges which influence the overall performance, usability, and scalability. The reason is that a client stores its data at a remote and potentially untrusted database service provider (DSP) rather than a fully controlled local database. What even worse is the outsourced data often contains some sensitive information that cannot be disclosed. Thus privacy of outsourced data is one of the foremost issues in the outsourced database (ODB) model. Moreover, the dishonest DSP may tamper with the data and return an incorrect or incomplete query result for some economic reasons. Hence, another major security requirement in ODB model is the verifiability of the returned results. The verifiability includes *(1)* the integrity verification of data and *(2)* that the claimed owner is, in fact, the authorized owner of the data. As a result, for the utilization of the outsourced data, the privacy, integrity, and ownership of the disseminated data should be verified from the users' perspective.

Redactable signatures [10], a principle solution, can inherently resolve the above issues in ODB model. In the definition of redactable signature schemes (RSSs), parts of a signed document are allowed to be removed by any party without any help from the original signer while preserving the source and integrity verifiability of the remaining subdocument. What's more, the reserved subdocument and its signature do not reveal any content information about deleted parts. Therefore, RSSs are such a useful primitive that comes in handy in scenarios where only parts of the authenticated data are releasable or required for privacy-preserving, but the origin and integrity authentication of these data must still hold and re-signing is impossible or with striking performance compromise. Nevertheless, the design of RSSs depends on the structure according to which data is organized. Since tree structure is widely used as data organization structure (Extensible Markup Language (XML) is one of today's most prominent example), the specific design of RSSs for data organized according to tree structure is crucial.

Consider the following application scenario taken from [14]. An XML document describes the health-care record of a person and thus contains sensitive information. Assume that such XML is stored in a remote database server. In order to prevent the sensitive information from being accessed by any unauthorized user, the database manager must be able to prune a tree before disseminating. Still, it should be possible to prove the content and structure integrity of the remaining subtree with respect to the original signer, without having to re-sign the document. Therefore, this can in principle be resolved by RSSs for trees [4].

Related Work. The problem of efficiently verifying the integrity and authenticity of the outsourced tree-structured data at an untrusted server has been explored extensively in the literature. The Merkle Hash Tree (MHT) [19] is the most widely used authentication technique for trees and has been exploited for the data dissemination [9,26]. The main problem of this technique is that authentication process does not preserve the confidentiality (hiding) of sensitive information. Therefore, MHT is vulnerable to inference attacks. The searchable encryption schemes [6,28] have been proposed to protect the privacy of the outsourced data. However, these technologies can not ensure the integrity and authenticity of the outsourced data.

Disseminating parts of a document while maintaining the integrity and authenticity of the remaining data is an issue that has been approached. Kundu and Bertino [14] proposed a signature scheme for trees, which assures both confidentiality and integrity efficiently. However, their scheme falls short of providing formal security definitions and proofs. To solve this issue, Brzuska et al. [4] gave rigorous security definitions for redactable signatures for trees, and gave a construction that can be proven secure under standard cryptographic assumptions. However, they did not consider the case when the structure is not separated from content which results in an attack on their proposed scheme. Samelin et al. [22] presented a provably secure RSS for trees which not only supports to redact structure and content independently but also controls consecutive redaction. On top of that, Samelin et al. [23] presented a new attack on the RSS introduced by Kundu and Bertino [14], which is an extension of the works done by Brzuska et al. [4] and Samelin et al. [22]. The secure model is more flexible than the one introduced by Kundu and Bertino [14]. Kundu et al. proposed leakage-free RSSs for trees [12,13] based on secure naming scheme, which is applicable in enabling secure data management in the emerging ODB model as well as in healthcare systems [27].

Motivation. In the definition of conventional RSSs for trees, anyone who possesses the tree-signature pair can execute redaction operation publicly. However, current RSSs for trees are facing with the threat from dishonest redactor or additional redaction because the signature holder can modify the signed trees unrestrictedly. Since the content of each node in a tree can be organized or disseminated in distinct manners, and releasing arbitrary subtrees often makes no sense. Therefore, redaction control is crucial for signers to authorize redactable nodes of authenticated trees. It provides a feasible mechanism for signers to prevent the arbitrary redaction operation of a signed tree from dishonest signature holders, especially in the ODB model where the DSP is untrusted.

In the previous work, Steinfeld et al. [25] introduced $CEAS$ with which signers can specify which portions of the authenticated document is redactable. Afterward, Bull et al. [5] introduced a new hierarchical redaction control policy whose encoding is dramatically smaller. Miyazaki et al. [21] proposed the first authenticated document sanitizing scheme with redaction condition control. However, the signature length of this scheme is relatively long, and the redaction condition reveals the number of sanitized portions. In order to resolve these problems, Miyazaki et al. [20] proposed another authenticated document sanitizing scheme based on bilinear maps. Recently, Ma et al. [16,17] also presented the secure and efficient design of RSSs with subdocument redaction control. At present, although there exist a number of related works that have brought in different methods to prevent unauthorized redaction manipulation, none of them consider the redaction control mechanism in RSSs for trees.

Contributions. To satisfy the aforementioned requirements, in this work, we propose an efficient redactable signature scheme for trees with fine-grained redaction control (RSS-TFRC) which supports the integrity and origin verification of the tree-structured data returned from DSP with privacy preserving and dissemination control. The framework of applying RSS-TFRC in ODB model is described as follows. The data owner generates a redactable signature for a tree and uploads the tree-signature pair to database servers. Since the redactable signature is embedded with a redaction control policy by the data owner, any unauthorized redaction manipulation from attackers or DSP is prohibited. Thus, when data users want to access the data stored on database servers, DSP generates the corresponding redacted tree-signature pair and sends them to users. After receiving the subtree, queries can verify its integrity and origin without obtaining any information of the pruned nodes in the original tree. The main contributions in this paper can be summarized as follows:

- We for the first time propose a practical RSS-TFRC. Our design supports the integrity and origin verification of the released tree-structured data from DSP without revealing any sensitive information.
- We formally define the proposed RSS-TFRC and its security properties in terms of unforgeability, privacy, and transparency. The security properties are proved in a reduction mode.
- We evaluate the performance of our scheme through theoretical comparison and practical implementation, which further validates that the proposed RSS-TFRC is indeed an efficient integrity and origin verification solution for tree-structured data dissemination in ODB model.

Organization of This Paper. The rest of this paper is organized as follows. Section 2 is devoted to the introduction of several cryptographic primitives used in this paper. The definitions of RSS-TFRC and its security properties are described in Sect. 3. Section 4 details our concrete construction of RSS-TFRC and its correctness analysis. We analyze the performance and prove the security of our scheme in Sect. 5. Finally, Sect. 6 concludes this paper.

2   Preliminaries

This section defines the general notations used in the paper, followed by a review of document abstraction, access structure, monotone span program, and linear secret sharing scheme. Finally, the bilinear aggregate signature is introduced.

2.1   General Notations

Let $s \xleftarrow{R} S$ denote the assignment of a uniformly and independently distributed random element from the set S to the variable s. The symbol $\perp \notin \{0,1\}^*$ denotes an error or an exception. We use the notation $\mathrm{Adv}_{\mathsf{exp}}^{\mathsf{Event}}(\lambda)$ to denote the probability of event Event in experiment exp. An integer $\lambda \in \mathbb{N}$ is the security parameter, which allows controlling the security degree of a scheme by controlling the length of the secret key. We say that a scheme achieves the security notion if the success probability for all efficient PPT (probabilistic polynomial time) attackers in breaking the scheme is a negligible function of λ (a function $\epsilon(\lambda)$ is called negligible if for each $\jmath > 0$, there exists λ_0 such that $\epsilon(\lambda) < \frac{1}{\lambda^{\jmath}}$ for all $\lambda > \lambda_0$).

2.2   Document Abstraction

Trees. A *tree* [4] is a connected graph $\Upsilon(V, E)$ which consists of a nonempty finite set V of vertices, a set E of edges and does not contain cycles. The edge between nodes a and b is denoted $l(a, b) \in V \times V$. A node a represents an atomic unit of data, which is always shared as a whole or is not shared at all. A tree Υ_r is rooted if one vertex $r \in V$ (the root) is distinguished from the others. If $l(a_i, b_i)$ is an edge, then the node that is closer to r is called the *parent* of the other node, while the latter is called a *child* of the former. If two vertices have the same parent, then these two vertices are called *siblings*. The vertex with no children is called *leaf*. The root is the only node without parents. A tree is called ordered tree if there is a special order among the children of each vertex. For any vertex a, the content of this node is referred to as c_a. A subtree of tree $\Upsilon(V, E)$ is denoted by $\Upsilon_\delta(V_\delta, E_\delta)$, where $V_\delta \subseteq V$ and $E_\delta \subseteq E$.

Secure Names. As we consider ordered trees, we also have to protect the order of siblings of a node; we do this by assigning a secure name to each node in a tree. The secure naming schemes introduced by Kundu et al. in [12,13] can be used for the purpose of verifying the order between any pair of nodes in a tree without leaking any information of other nodes and their relationship (e.g., whether they are adjacent siblings, how many other siblings are between them, etc.). Their approach follows a bottom-up strategy. Please refer to [12,13] for the definition, concrete construction and security proof of secure naming scheme.

2.3   Access Structure

Definition 1 (Access Structure [1]). *Let $\mathcal{U}$ be a set of parties. An access structure on $\mathcal{U}$ is a collection $\mathbb{A}$ of non-empty sets of parties, i.e., $\mathbb{A} \subseteq 2^{\mathcal{U}} \backslash \{\emptyset\}$. The sets in $\mathbb{A}$ are called the authorized sets and the sets not in $\mathbb{A}$ are called unauthorized sets with respect to $\mathbb{A}$. An access structure $\mathbb{A}$ is called monotone access structure if $\forall B, C \in \mathbb{A} : if\ B \in \mathbb{A}\ and\ B \subseteq C, then\ C \in \mathbb{A}$. A set B satisfies $\mathbb{A}$ (in other words, $\mathbb{A}$ accept B) if and only if B is an authorized set in $\mathbb{A}$, i.e., $B \in \mathbb{A}$.*

In the context of this paper, the role of parties is played by tree node. Thus, the access structure $\mathbb{A}$ contains the authorized subsets of nodes that are not redactable. We restrict our attention to monotone access structure.

2.4   Monotone Span Program

Monotone span program (MSP), a linear algebraic model of computation, constitutes a significant component in realizing our fine-grained redaction control policy. The fine-grained redaction control policy of our construction is depicted by a monotone boolean formula in the first stage, which is the combination of some nodes that are allowed to be disclosed in a tree. We will use monotone span program to represent the monotone boolean formula. In order to represent the monotone boolean formula using monotone span program, we should first convert the monotone boolean formula into an access tree with the method introduced in [7]. The tree here we use is a binary tree: every interior node is either AND or OR gate and each leaf node corresponds to message blocks. An access tree can be converted into an equivalent matrix $\mathbf{E}$ with the technique in [15]. Refer to [7,15] for more details about the construction and operating principle of MSP.

2.5   Linear Secret Sharing Scheme

Definition 2 (Linear Secret-Sharing Scheme (LSSS) [1]). *A secret-sharing scheme $\Pi_{\mathbb{A}}$ for the access structure $\mathbb{A}$ over a set S is called linear (over $\mathbb{Z}_p$) if*

- *The shares of a secret $s \in \mathbb{Z}_p$ for each party form a vector over $\mathbb{Z}_p$.*
- *For each access structure $\mathbb{A}$ on S, there exists a matrix $\mathbf{E}$ with n rows and c columns called the sharing-generating matrix for Π. A function ρ defines each row number i of matrix $\mathbf{E}$ as $\rho(i)$, that labels the rows of $\mathbf{E}$ with elements from S. Let vector $\boldsymbol{\omega} = (s, y_2, \ldots, y_c)^T$, where s is the secret will be shared into n parts, and $y_2, \ldots, y_c$ are chosen in $\mathbb{Z}_p$ randomly. $\mathbf{E}\boldsymbol{\omega}$ is the vector of n shares of s according to Π and each share in $\mathbf{E}\boldsymbol{\omega}$ "belongs" to the party $\rho(i)$. We refer to the pair $(\mathbf{E}, \rho)$ as the policy of the access structure $\mathbb{A}$.*

The existence of an efficient LSSS for tree access structure is equivalent to the existence of a small MSP for the monotone boolean formula of that access structure [1,11]. LSSS enjoys the linear reconstruction property and security requirement. Let $A \in \mathbb{A}$ be an authorized set for the access structure $\mathbb{A}$ encoded by the policy $(\mathbf{E}, \rho)$ and define $I \subset \{1, 2, \ldots, n\}$ as $I = \{i : \rho(i) \in A\}$. The reconstruction requirement asserts that the vector $(1, 0, \ldots, 0)$ is in the span of rows of $\mathbf{E}$ indexed by I. Then, there exist constants $\{\omega_i \in \mathbb{Z}_p\}_{i \in I}$ such that, if $\{\lambda_i = (\mathbf{E}\boldsymbol{\omega})_i\}_{i \in I}$ are valid shares of a secret s according to Π then $s = \sum_{i \in I} \omega_i \lambda_i$.

2.6 Bilinear Aggregate Signature

The first bilinear aggregate signature, introduced by Boneh et al. in [2] (hereafter referred to as the BGLS scheme), is constructed from the short signature scheme based on bilinear maps due to [3]. The basic idea is aggregating signatures generated by different signers on distinct message into one short signature based on elliptic curves and bilinear mappings. The result of this aggregation is an aggregate signature σ whose length is the same as that of any individual signatures. Their scheme is based on Gap Diffie-Hellman groups (GDH) [3] where the Computational Diffie-Hellman (CDH) problem is hard while the Decisional Diffie-Hellman (DDH) problem is easy. Refer to [2,3] for more details about the construction of BGLS scheme and Gap Diffie-Hellman problem.

3 Definitions of RSS-TFRC

The formal scheme and security definitions of RSSs for trees have already been identified by Brzuska et al. in [4]. To prevent arbitrary redaction operations of an authenticated tree from any party in a fine-grained manner, we extend their definitions and first formally define RSS-TFRC. In this section, we will formally define the RSS-TFRC and its security properties via unforgeability, privacy, and transparency.

3.1 The Scheme Definition of RSS-TFRC

In the following, a message is represented by a tree $\Upsilon(V, E)$ which consists of a number of structured message blocks. $\mathcal{P}$ is associated with the encoding of some subtrees of $\Upsilon(V, E)$, which can be used by signer to specify those subsets that the third party is not allowed to redact. The design of $\mathcal{P}$ is specified according to concrete applications. $\Upsilon_{\delta'}(V_{\delta'}, E_{\delta'})$ is used to describe the subtree a redactor intend to redact. $\Upsilon_{\delta}(V_{\delta}, E_{\delta})$ is the subtree after removing subtree $\Upsilon_{\delta'}(V_{\delta'}, F_{\delta'})$ from $\Upsilon(V, E)$ $(\Upsilon_{\delta}(V_{\delta}, E_{\delta}) \leftarrow \Upsilon(V, E) \backslash \Upsilon_{\delta'}(V_{\delta'}, E_{\delta'}))$. $\mathcal{P}(\Upsilon_{\delta}(V_{\delta}, E_{\delta})) = 1$ means that $\Upsilon_{\delta'}(V_{\delta'}, E_{\delta'})$ is a valid redaction description with respect to $\mathcal{P}$ and $\Upsilon(V, E)$, which further indicates that $\Upsilon_{\delta}(V_{\delta}, E_{\delta})$ satisfies $\mathcal{P}$.

Definition 3. *An RSS-TFRC consists of four polynomial time algorithms (*Key-Gen, Sign, Verify, Redact*) such that:*
KeyGen(1^{λ}): *This probabilistic algorithm takes as input a security parameter 1^{λ} and outputs a public key pk for verification and a secret key sk for signing:* $(pk, sk) \leftarrow$ KeyGen(1^{λ}).
Sign($sk, \Upsilon(V, E), \mathcal{P}$): *This algorithm takes as input a secrete key sk, a tree $\Upsilon(V, E)$, and a fine-grained redaction control policy $\mathcal{P}$. It outputs a tree-signature pair $(\Upsilon(V, E), \sigma_{\Upsilon})$: $(\Upsilon(V, E), \sigma_{\Upsilon}) \leftarrow$ Sign($sk, \Upsilon(V, E), \mathcal{P}$). In the simplest case, $\mathcal{P}$ is part of the signature σ_{Υ} and always be recoverable by the third party.*
Verify($pk, \Upsilon(V, E), \sigma_{\Upsilon}$): *This algorithm takes as input a public key pk, a tree $\Upsilon(V, E)$, and a signature σ_{Υ}. It outputs a decision $b \in \{1, 0\}$ verifying that σ_{Υ}*

is a valid redactable signature on a tree $\Upsilon(V, E)$ with respect to a public key pk:
$b \leftarrow \mathsf{Verify}(pk, \Upsilon(V, E), \sigma_\Upsilon)$.

$\mathsf{Redact}(pk, \sigma_\Upsilon, \Upsilon(V, E), \Upsilon_{\delta'}(V_{\delta'}, E_{\delta'}))$: *This algorithm takes as input the public key pk of the signer, a valid signature σ_Υ, an original authenticated tree $\Upsilon(V, E)$, and a redaction subtree $\Upsilon_{\delta'}(V_{\delta'}, E_{\delta'})$. Before the redaction manipulation, it will check if σ_Υ is a valid redactable signature on a tree $\Upsilon(V, E)$ with respect to a public key pk, $V_{\delta'} \subseteq V$, and $E_{\delta'} \subseteq E$. Once the inputs satisfy these requirements, the third party cut the subtree $\Upsilon_{\delta'}(V_{\delta'}, E_{\delta'})$ from $\Upsilon(V, E)$ and updates the signature σ_Υ. Then, it outputs the updated signature σ_{Υ_δ} for the pruned tree $\Upsilon_\delta(V_\delta, E_\delta) \leftarrow \Upsilon(V, E)\backslash\Upsilon_{\delta'}(V_{\delta'}, E_{\delta'})$ (or $\bot$, indicating an error), where $V_\delta = V_\delta \backslash V_{\delta'}$ and $E_\delta = E_\delta \backslash E_{\delta'}$: $(\Upsilon_\delta(V_\delta, E_\delta), \sigma_{\Upsilon_\delta}) \leftarrow \mathsf{Redact}(pk, \Upsilon_{\delta'}(V_{\delta'}, E_{\delta'}), \Upsilon(V, E), \sigma_\Upsilon)$.*

3.2   Correctness of RSS-TFRC

In general, the correctness property of an RSS-TFRC requires that every genuinely generated signature is verified valid by Verify algorithm.

Definition 4 (Signing Correctness). *For any tree $\Upsilon(V, E)$, any security parameter λ, any key pair $(pk, sk) \leftarrow \mathsf{KeyGen}(1^\lambda)$, any fine-grained redaction control policy $\mathcal{P}$, and any signature $(\Upsilon(V, E), \sigma_\Upsilon) \leftarrow \mathsf{Sign}(sk, \Upsilon(V, E), \mathcal{P})$, we have $\mathsf{Verify}(pk, \Upsilon(V, E), \sigma_\Upsilon) = 1$.*

Definition 5 (Redaction Correctness). *For any signature $(\Upsilon(V, E), \sigma_\Upsilon) \leftarrow \mathsf{Sign}(sk, \Upsilon(V, E), \mathcal{P})$ satisfies $\mathsf{Verify}(pk, \Upsilon(V, E), \sigma_\Upsilon) = 1$, any subtree $\Upsilon_{\delta'}(V_{\delta'}, E_{\delta'})$, any subset of vertices $V_{\delta'} \subseteq V$, any subset of edges $E_{\delta'} \subseteq E$ such that $V_\delta = V_\delta \backslash V_{\delta'}$ and $E_\delta = E_\delta \backslash E_{\delta'}$, and any $(\Upsilon_\delta(V_\delta, E_\delta), \sigma_{\Upsilon_\delta}) \leftarrow \mathsf{Redact}(pk, \Upsilon_{\delta'}(V_{\delta'}, E_{\delta'}), \Upsilon(V, E), \sigma_\Upsilon)$ such that $\mathcal{P}(\Upsilon_\delta(V_\delta, E_\delta)) = 1$, we have $\mathsf{Verify}(pk, \Upsilon_\delta(V_\delta, E_\delta), \sigma_{\Upsilon_\delta}) = 1$.*

3.3   Unforgeability of RSS-TFRC

The unforgeability definition of RSS-TFRC is defined analogously to the standard unforgeability definition of conventional digital signature schemes. Informally, it requires that even if signatures on different trees are available by adaptive signature queries, no one should be able to compute a valid signature on a tree Υ^* without having access to the secret key sk provided that Υ^* is neither (A) a subtree of any tree queried to the signing oracle (i.e., $\Upsilon^* \not\subseteq \Upsilon_i$), or (B) is a subtree of a tree Υ_i queried to the signing oracle, but does not satisfy the fine-grained redaction control policy $\mathcal{P}_i$ (i.e., $\Upsilon^* \subsetneq \Upsilon_i$ and $\mathcal{P}_i(\Upsilon^*) \neq 1$).

Definition 6 (Unforgeability). *An RSS-TFRC := (KeyGen, Sign, Verify, Redact) is EUF-CTA (existentially unforgeable under adaptive chosen-tree attacks) if the probability of any PPT adversary $\mathcal{A}$ in winning the following game is a negligible function of the security parameter λ.*
Game 1 : Unforgeability$_\mathcal{A}^{RSS\text{-}TFRC}$

- **Setup:** *The challenger runs* KeyGen *to obtain a public key pk and a private key sk. The adversary $\mathcal{A}$ is given pk.*
- **Query Phase:** *Proceeding adaptively, $\mathcal{A}$ requests signatures with pk on at most q_S trees of his choice $\Upsilon_1, \Upsilon_2, \cdots, \Upsilon_{q_S}$. For each query, the challenger runs $(\Upsilon_i, \sigma_{\Upsilon_i}) \leftarrow$ Sign$(sk, \Upsilon_i, \mathcal{P}_i)$ and forwards $(\Upsilon_i, \sigma_{\Upsilon_i})$ to $\mathcal{A}$. Note that $\mathcal{A}$ is also allowed to choose $\mathcal{P}_i$.*
- **Output:** *Eventually, $\mathcal{A}$ outputs a pair $(\Upsilon^*, \sigma_{\Upsilon^*})$ and wins the above game if (1)* Verify$(pk, \Upsilon^*, \sigma_{\Upsilon^*}) = 1$ *and (2) for all $i = 1, 2, \ldots, q_S$ we have either $\Upsilon^* \not\subseteq \Upsilon_i$ or $\Upsilon^* \subsetneq \Upsilon_i$ but $\mathcal{P}_i(\Upsilon^*) \neq 1$.*

3.4   Privacy of RSS-TFRC

The privacy requirement of RSS-TFRC is to guarantee the confidentiality of the nodes of the tree that were pruned. This is formalized by demanding that, given a subtree with a signature and two possible source trees, it is infeasible for one to decide from which source tree the subtree stems from. The privacy definition for RSS-TFRC is based on the indistinguishability game for encryption schemes: an adversary $\mathcal{A}$ chooses two pairs of trees and subtrees $(\Upsilon_0, \Upsilon_{\delta_0'})$, $(\Upsilon_1, \Upsilon_{\delta_1'})$ such that $\Upsilon_0 \backslash \Upsilon_{\delta_0'} = \Upsilon_1 \backslash \Upsilon_{\delta_1'}$, i.e., removing the subtrees results in isomorphic trees. Furthermore, $\mathcal{A}$ has access to a *left-or-right* oracle, which, given those two trees, consistently either returns a redacted signature for the left pair ($b = 0$) or for the right pair ($b = 1$). The scheme offers privacy if no PPT adversary can decide the origination of received subtree-signature with a non-negligible advantage over $\frac{1}{2}$.

Definition 7 (Privacy). *An RSS-TFRC := (KeyGen, Sign, Verify, Redact) satisfies privacy preserving requirement if for any PPT adversary $\mathcal{A}$, the advantage in wining the following game is a negligible function of the security parameter λ.*
Game 2 : Privacy$_{\mathcal{A}}^{RSS\text{-}TFRC}$

- **Setup:** *The challenger runs $(pk, sk) \leftarrow$ KeyGen(1^λ) and sends pk to $\mathcal{A}$.*
  Phase 1: *The adversary $\mathcal{A}$ can adaptively conduct a polynomially bounded number of queries to the signing oracle. Let $\Upsilon_1, \Upsilon_2, \cdots, \Upsilon_{Q_1}$ denote the Q_1 quires to signing oracle from $\mathcal{A}$. For each query, the challenger runs $(\Upsilon_i, \sigma_{\Upsilon_i}) \leftarrow$ Sign$(sk, \Upsilon_i, \mathcal{P}_i)$ and forwards $(\Upsilon_i, \sigma_{\Upsilon_i})$ to $\mathcal{A}$. Note that $\mathcal{A}$ is also allowed to choose $\mathcal{P}_i$.*
- **Challenge:**
  1. *At the end of **Phase 1**, adversary $\mathcal{A}$ finds two identical tree Υ_0 and Υ_1 besides the difference of redaction subtrees, i.e., $\Upsilon_0 \backslash \Upsilon_{\delta_0'} = \Upsilon_1 \backslash \Upsilon_{\delta_1'}$ with $\Upsilon_{\delta_0'} \neq \Upsilon_{\delta_1'}$. Then, adversary $\mathcal{A}$ sends $(\Upsilon_0, \Upsilon_{\delta_0'})$ and $(\Upsilon_1, \Upsilon_{\delta_1'})$ to challenger. Note that $\mathcal{A}$ is also allowed to choose $\mathcal{P}_0$ and $\mathcal{P}_1$ such that $\Upsilon_0 \backslash \Upsilon_{\delta_0'}$ and $\Upsilon_1 \backslash \Upsilon_{\delta_1'}$ satisfy $\mathcal{P}_0$ and $\mathcal{P}_1$, respectively.*
  2. *The challenger chooses Υ_b randomly by choosing a bit $b \in \{0,1\}$ and computes a redactable signature through $(\Upsilon_b, \sigma_{\Upsilon_b}) \leftarrow$ Sign$(sk, \Upsilon_b, \mathcal{P}_b)$ and $(\Upsilon_{\delta_b}, \sigma_{\Upsilon_{\delta_b}}) \leftarrow$ Redact$(pk, \Upsilon_b, \sigma_{\Upsilon_b}, \Upsilon_{\delta_b'})$, where Υ_{δ_b} satisfies $\mathcal{P}_b$. Then the challenger outputs $(\Upsilon_{\delta_b}, \sigma_{\Upsilon_{\delta_b}})$.*

- **Phase 2**: *In this phase, the adversary $\mathcal{A}$ can proceed again for polynomially bounded number of queries to the signing oracle adaptively in the same way as* **Phase 1**.
- **Guess**: *Finally, a guess b' of b is exported by $\mathcal{A}$. The adversary wins the above game if $b' = b$.*

The $\mathrm{Adv}_{\mathcal{A}}^{\mathrm{Privacy}}(\lambda) = \left| \Pr[b' = b] - \frac{1}{2} \right|$ is defined as the advantage that $\mathcal{A}$ has in the above game. The privacy of RSS-TFRC requires that $\mathrm{Adv}_{\mathcal{A}}^{\mathrm{Privacy}}(\lambda)$ is a negligible function of the security parameter λ, such that $\mathrm{Adv}_{\mathcal{A}}^{\mathrm{Privacy}}(\lambda) \leq \epsilon(\lambda)$.

3.5   Transparency of RSS-TFRC

The above notion of privacy only hides the contents of the deleted nodes, but not necessarily that redaction operation. Transparency is a stronger notion of leakage prevention. It requires that no end-user should be able to infer whether the received tree has been redacted or not. Intuitively, no adversary is able to decide if the given tree-signature pair directly comes from Sign algorithm or Redact algorithm. Let $(\Upsilon_\delta, \sigma_{\Upsilon_\delta}) \leftarrow \mathsf{Redact}(pk, \Upsilon, \sigma_\Upsilon, \Upsilon_{\delta'})$ be a tree-signature pair derived from $(\Upsilon, \sigma_\Upsilon)$ by the application of Redact algorithm, and let $(\Upsilon_\delta, \sigma_{\Upsilon_s}) \leftarrow \mathsf{Sign}(sk, \Upsilon_\delta, \mathcal{P})$ be a tree-signature pair generated from scratch. The task for the adversary is to distinguish both cases.

Definition 8 (Transparency).
An RSS-TFRC := (KeyGen, Sign, Verify, Redact) is transparent if for any PPT adversary $\mathcal{A}$ the advantage in wining the following game is a negligible function of the security parameter λ.
Game 3 : $\mathsf{Transparency}_{\mathcal{A}}^{RSS\text{-}TFRC}$

- **Setup**: *The challenger runs $(pk, sk) \leftarrow \mathsf{KeyGen}(1^\lambda)$ and sends pk to $\mathcal{A}$.*
- **Phase 1**: *The adversary $\mathcal{A}$ can adaptively conduct a polynomially bounded number of queries to the signing oracle. Let $\Upsilon_1, \Upsilon_2, \cdots, \Upsilon_{Q_2}$ denote the Q_2 quires to signing oracle from $\mathcal{A}$. For each query, the challenger runs $(\Upsilon_i, \sigma_{\Upsilon_i}) \leftarrow \mathsf{Sign}(sk, \Upsilon_i, \mathcal{P}_i)$ and forwards $(\Upsilon_i, \sigma_{\Upsilon_i})$ to $\mathcal{A}$. Note that $\mathcal{A}$ is also allowed to choose $\mathcal{P}_i$.*
- **Challenge**:
  1. *At the end of* **Phase 1**, *adversary $\mathcal{A}$ outputs two trees Υ_0 and Υ_1 such that $\Upsilon_0 \subseteq \Upsilon_1$, and a fine-grained redaction control policy $\mathcal{P}$, where $\mathcal{P}(\Upsilon_0) = 1$. Then, $\mathcal{A}$ sends them to the challenger.*
  2. *The challenger randomly chooses a bit $b \in \{0, 1\}$ and computes signature through algorithm $(\Upsilon_b, \sigma_{\Upsilon_b}) \leftarrow \mathsf{Sign}(sk, \Upsilon_b, \mathcal{P})$. If $b = 1$, then the signature for Υ_0 is computed from $\sigma_{\Upsilon_1} : (\Upsilon_0, \sigma_{\Upsilon_0}) \leftarrow \mathsf{Redact}(pk, \Upsilon_1, \sigma_{\Upsilon_1}, \Upsilon_1 \backslash \Upsilon_0)$. Then the challenge $(\Upsilon_0, \sigma_{\Upsilon_0})$ is given to $\mathcal{A}$.*
- **Phase 2**: *In this phase, the adversary $\mathcal{A}$ can continuously have access to the signing, redaction, and verification oracles for polynomially bounded number of queries in the same way as* **Phase 1**.

– **Guess:** *Finally, a guess b' of b is exported by $\mathcal{A}$. The adversary wins the game if $b' = b$.*

The $\text{Adv}_{\mathcal{A}}^{\text{Transparency}}(\lambda) = \left| \Pr[b' = b] - \frac{1}{2} \right|$ is defined as the advantage that $\mathcal{A}$ has in the above game. The transparency of RSS-TFRC requires $\text{Adv}_{\mathcal{A}}^{\text{Transparency}}(\lambda)$ is a negligible function of the security parameter λ, such that $\text{Adv}_{\mathcal{A}}^{\text{Transparency}}(\lambda) \leq \epsilon(\lambda)$.

An RSS-TFRC is secure if no PPT adversary $\mathcal{A}$ can win at least one of the above games with non-negligible advantage.

4   Our Construction

In this section, we propose a construction of efficient RSS-TFRC to support the secure dissemination of authenticated tree-structured data in ODB mode. Our scheme utilizes secure BGLS [2], MSP, LSSS [1] and secure naming scheme [13] as construction primitives. Before outsourcing tree-structured data to DSP, the data owner generates a redactable signature for the data and uploads them to DSP. Once a querier forwards a query to DSP to access parts of the authenticated tree, the DSP executes redaction algorithm and outputs a subtree and its corresponding signature. It should be noticed that the DSP can only generate valid signatures for those subtrees that satisfying the fine-grained redaction control policy defined by the data owner. After receiving the subtree and corresponding signature, the querier can verify the integrity and authenticity of this subtree with the redacted signature and data owner's public key without obtaining any information about the pruned nodes. The concrete construction of this scheme consists of four algorithms: KeyGen, Sign, Verify and Redact.

KeyGen(1^{λ}): This algorithm is identical to the key generation algorithm in BGLS [2]. A signer picks a random $k \xleftarrow{R} \mathbb{Z}_p$ and computes $v \leftarrow g_2^k$. The signer's public key pk is $v \in G_2$ and secret key sk is $k \in \mathbb{Z}_p$.

Sign($sk, \Upsilon(V, E), \mathcal{P}$): This algorithm takes as input a signing secret key sk, a tree $\Upsilon(V, E)$ with n nodes, and a fine-grained redaction control policy $\mathcal{P}$. $\mathcal{P}$ is built upon the monotone span program and linear secret sharing scheme [24] which allows the signer to control what subtrees a third party can distribute. The policy $\mathcal{P}$ is depicted by the monotone boolean formula, where the inputs of this formula are associated with the nodes of $\Upsilon(V, E)$. This policy can be converted into a monotone span program which is a $n \times t$ matrix $\mathbf{M}$. Then, the signer chooses a secret $s \xleftarrow{R} \mathbb{Z}_p$ and constructs a vector $\boldsymbol{\omega} = (s, y_2, \ldots, y_t)^T$ in which $y_i \xleftarrow{R} \mathbb{Z}_p$ and s is the secret to be divided into n shares. For $1 \leq i \leq n$, it calculates $s_i = \mathbf{M} \cdot \boldsymbol{\omega}$, and each share "belongs" to $\rho(i)$, where ρ defines each row number i of matrix $\mathbf{M}$ as $\rho(i)$ that labels the rows of $\mathbf{M}$ with nodes in Υ. After the construction of fine-grained redaction control policy, signer performs the following steps:

1. Let $\theta_{x_i} \xleftarrow{R} \mathbb{Z}_p$ and $\theta_{p_{x_i}} \xleftarrow{R} \mathbb{Z}_p$ be the secure names of node x_i and its parent that are generated through the secure naming scheme in [13].
2. Generate an identity $id \xleftarrow{R} \mathbb{Z}_p$ for tree $\Upsilon(V, E)$, and let m_{x_i} be the content of node x_i in tree $\Upsilon(V, E)$.
3. For all i $(1 \leq i \leq n)$ such that node $x_i \in V$, compute $h_i \leftarrow h(id\|\theta_{p_{x_i}}\|\theta_{x_i}\|m_{x_i})$ and $\sigma_i \leftarrow h_i^k$, where $h : \{0,1\}^* \to G_1$ is a full-domain hash function.
4. Compute $\sigma_0 \leftarrow (g_1^s)^k$ and $z_i \leftarrow g_1^{s_i}$.
5. Compute $\sigma \leftarrow \prod_{i=0}^n \sigma_i$ and $\sigma_S \leftarrow e(\sigma, g_2)$. Note that σ is the aggregate signature for $\sigma_0, \ldots, \sigma_n$.
6. Output $(\Upsilon(V, E), \sigma_\Upsilon)$, where $\sigma_\Upsilon = (\sigma_S, id, \{z_i\}_{x_i \in V}, \{(\theta_{x_i}, \theta_{p_{x_i}})|x_i \in V\})$.

Verify$(pk, \Upsilon(V, E), \sigma_\Upsilon)$: This algorithm takes as input a public key pk, a tree Υ, and a signature σ_Υ. It performs the following steps:

1. For each node $x_i \in V$, compute $h_i \leftarrow h(id\|\theta_{p_{x_i}}\|\theta_{x_i}\|m_{x_i})$.
2. Suppose that $\Upsilon(V, E)$ satisfies the access structure and let $I \subset \{1, 2, \ldots, n\}$ be defined as $I = \{i : x_i \in V\}$. Then, there exist constants $\{\omega_i \in \mathbb{Z}_p\}_{i \in I}$ such that if $\Upsilon(V, E)$ is a tree satisfying the fine-grained redaction policy then $s = \sum_{i \in I} \omega_i s_i$.
3. The verifier ensures $\sigma_S = \prod_{x_i \in V} e(h_i \cdot z_i^{\omega_i}, v)$ holds and rejects otherwise.

Redact$(pk, \Upsilon_{\delta'}(V_{\delta'}, E_{\delta'}), \Upsilon(V, E), \sigma_\Upsilon)$: This algorithm takes as input the public key pk of a signer, a subtree $\Upsilon_{\delta'}(V_{\delta'}, E_{\delta'})$ to be cut, a tree $\Upsilon(V, E)$, and a signature σ_Υ. To redact a subtree $\Upsilon_{\delta'}(V_{\delta'}, E_{\delta'})$, the database service provider executes the redacting operation in the following steps:

1. Check the validity of $(\Upsilon(V, E), \sigma_\Upsilon)$ with Verify algorithm. If the signature is not valid, return $\perp$.
2. If $\Upsilon_{\delta'}(V_{\delta'}, E_{\delta'}) \nsubseteq \Upsilon(V, E)$, return $\perp$.
3. Cut the subtree $\Upsilon_{\delta'}(V_{\delta'}, E_{\delta'})$ from $\Upsilon(V, E)$, the redacted tree is $\Upsilon_\delta(V_\delta, E_\delta)$.
4. Compute $\sigma_F \leftarrow \sigma_S / \prod_{x_i \in V_{\delta'}} e(h_i, v)$ and remove the elements $\{z_i\}_{x_i \in V_{\delta'}}$ and $\{(\theta_{x_i}, \theta_{p_{x_i}})|x_i \in V_{\delta'}\}$ from σ_Υ.
5. Output $(\Upsilon_\delta(V_\delta, E_\delta), \sigma_{\Upsilon_\delta})$, where $\sigma_{\Upsilon_\delta} = (\sigma_F, id, \{z_i\}_{x_i \in V_\delta}, \{(\theta_{x_i}, \theta_{p_{x_i}})|x_i \in V_\delta\})$ and $V_\delta = V \backslash V_{\delta'}$.

The signing correctness of RSS-TFRC is as follows: $\sigma_S = e(\sigma, g_2) = e(\prod_{i \in I} h_i^k \cdot (g_1^s)^k, g_2) = \prod_{i \in I} e(h_i, v) \cdot e(g_1^s, v) = \prod_{i \in I} e(h_i, v) \cdot e(g_1^{\sum_{i \in I} \omega_i s_i}, v) = \prod_{i \in I} e(h_i, v) \cdot e(\prod_{i \in I} g_1^{\omega_i s_i}, v) = \prod_{i \in I} e(h_i, v) \cdot \prod_{i \in I} e(z_i^{\omega_i}, v) = \prod_{i \in I} e(h_i \cdot z_i^{\omega_i}, v)$.

The redaction correctness of RSS-TFRC is as follows: $\sigma_F = \sigma_S / \prod_{i \in L'} e(h_i, v) = \frac{e(\sigma, g_2)}{\prod_{i \in L'} e(h_i, v)} = \frac{e(\prod_{i \in I} h_i^k \cdot (g_1^s)^k, g_2)}{\prod_{i \in L'} e(h_i, v)} = \frac{\prod_{i \in I} e(h_i, v) \cdot e(g_1^s, v)}{\prod_{i \in L'} e(h_i, v)} = \prod_{i \in L} e(h_i, v) \cdot e(g_1^{\sum_{i \in L} \omega_i s_i}, v) = \prod_{i \in L} e(h_i, v) \cdot \prod_{i \in L} e(z_i^{\omega_i}, v) = \prod_{i \in L} e(h_i \cdot z_i^{\omega_i}, v)$, where $L \subset \{1, 2, \ldots, n\}$ is defined as $L = \{i : x_i \in V_\delta\}$ and $L' \subset \{1, 2, \ldots, n\}$ is defined as $L' = \{i : x_i \in V_{\delta'}\}$.

5   Analysis of Our Proposed Scheme

5.1   Security Analysis

In this subsection, we prove the security of our proposed scheme in the aspects of unforgeability, privacy, and transparency. It has been proved that transparency is a stronger notion than privacy [4], which implies privacy. Hence, we only prove the transparency of our scheme. The unforgeability and transparency proofs of our scheme are presented as follows.

Unforgeability of Our Proposed Scheme

Definition 9. *A forger $\mathcal{A}(t, q_S, q_H, \epsilon)$-breaks a signature scheme if $\mathcal{A}$ runs in time at most t, $\mathcal{A}$ makes at most q_S signature queries and at most q_H queries to the hash function, and the probability that $\mathcal{A}$ wins in the above game is at least ϵ, taken over the coin tosses of* KeyGen *and of $\mathcal{A}$. A signature scheme is (t, q_S, q_H, ϵ)-existentially unforgeable under an adaptive chosen-tree attack if no forger (t, q_S, q_H, ϵ)-breaks it.*

Theorem 1. *The proposed scheme is unforgeable, as defined in Definition 6.*

The proof of Theorem 1 is detailed in Appendix A.

Transparency of Our Proposed Scheme

Theorem 2. *Our construction is transparent in the information-theoretical sense, as defined in Definition 8.*

Proof. Our scheme is also transparent in the information-theoretical sense. In another word, the secret bit b is perfectly hidden. Our signing algorithm requires that s is always fresh and chosen uniformly, which results in a uniformly distributed aggregate signature. Removing a random number of individual signatures from the aggregate signature also leads to a uniformly distributed signature again. Hence, even an unbounded adversary is not able to guess the bit better than at random. For the redacted message, if the redacted message would have been signed directly, the distributions are still uniform and it is impossible for any adversary to guess b better than at random. Besides, no information about removed nodes of the originally signed tree remains in the redacted signature. Thus our scheme is transparent in an information theoretic sense.   □

5.2   Performance Analysis

In this subsection, we analyze the efficiency of our scheme and make a comparison in terms of computation, communication cost and functionality with several existing RSSs for trees [4,14,18,22]. The purpose of the comparison is to show that our RSS-TFRC achieves a much more flexible functionality of redaction control without compromising on enormous computation or communication cost.

Theoretical Analysis. We first analyze the efficiency of our proposed scheme from a theoretical view. Table 1 presents the comparison between our scheme and four existing RSSs for trees [4,14,18,22]. As we can see, our scheme is the only one to achieve fine-grained redaction control (FRC) without sacrificing performance obviously, and fully supports non-leaves redaction (NLR) and structural integrity (SI) verification. As for the computation cost, our scheme has slightly higher cost in the signature generation (σ_Υ) than [14,18] but indistinct cost compared with [4,22]. Since it requires one bilinear pairing computation for each node, our scheme has a slightly higher cost in verification than others. Moreover, since our scheme adopted BGLS scheme, it saves substantial communication cost than others. Thus, our scheme is more desirable for ODB model according to the above analysis.

Experimental Analysis. Note that in order to precisely measure the performance of our scheme, we further conduct a thorough experimental evaluation of our scheme. All the experiments are implemented by utilizing the PBC library (version 0.5.14) and GMP library (version 6.1.2). The tests platform is set to be: Intel T8300 Dual Core @2.40 GHz and 4 GiB of RAM, 500 G/5400 rpm hard disk. The OS was Ubuntu 10.10 LTS (64 Bit) with Java version 1.6.0_26-b03. We take the median value of 10 runs for each test result. We evaluate three sizes of curves, i.e. 128 and 256 Bit. Since the scheme proposed in [22] is also based on the bilinear aggregate signature [2], we make a comparison with their experiment result. Table 2 presents the running time of signing algorithm, redaction algorithm, and verification algorithm for trees with 10, 50 and 100 nodes. As shown in Table 2, the signature generation process takes longer time than other two algorithms, and this increases dramatically when the number of nodes changes from 10 to 50 and the size of curves changes from 128 bits to 256 bits. However, redaction operation is negligible in terms of the performance for large trees. Although our scheme is not as efficient as [22], it remains within usable limits. This is because the advanced features of our scheme come at a price: we realize fine-grained redaction control in RSSs for trees which slows the runtime of each algorithm.

In summary, through the performance analysis, we can see that our RSS-TFRC achieves fine-grained redaction control and privacy preservation in authenticated tree-structured data dissemination without introducing a great amount of additional complexity.

Table 1. Efficiency and functionality comparison of RSSs for trees

Scheme	Computation cost		Communication cost		Functionality		
	Generate σ_Γ	Verify σ_Γ	Length of σ_Γ	Length of σ_{Γ_δ}	NLR	SI	FRC
[14]	$\mathcal{O}((n+1)t_S)$	$\mathcal{O}((n+1)t_V + nt_H)$	$(n+1)l_S$	$(n+1-m)l_S$	✓	/	/
[4]	$\mathcal{O}(2nt_S)$	$\mathcal{O}((2n-1)t_V)$	$2nl_S + nl_r$	$(2n-3m)l_S + (n-m)l_r$	/	✓	/
[22]	$\mathcal{O}(2n(t_S + t_H))$	$\mathcal{O}(2nt_H + t_{Pair})$	$2nl_S + nl_r$	$(2n-2m-1)l_S + (n-m)l_r$	/	✓	/
[18]	$\mathcal{O}(t_S)$	$\mathcal{O}((2n-1)t_V)$	$l_S + nl_r$	$l_S + (n-m)l_r$	✓	✓	/
Our	$\mathcal{O}(n(t_S + t_H)) + t_P + t_{Pair})$	$\mathcal{O}(n(t_H + t_{Pair}))$	$l_S + (3n-1)l_r$	$l_S + (3n-3m-1)l_r$	✓	✓	✓

Notations: Let t_S denote the signature generation time, t_V be the signature verification time, t_P be the redaction control policy generation time, t_H be the hashing time, and t_{Pair} be the bilinear pairing computation time. We denote l_S the signature length, l_r the auxiliary parameter length, n the number of nodes in tree, m the number of nodes removed.

Table 2. Median runtime for the schemes in s

Operations		Generation of σ_Γ			Verification of σ_Γ			Redaction		
Nodes		10	50	100	10	50	100	10	50	100
[22]	128	6.350	158.557	615.546	3.675	89.233	338.156	0.003	0.022	0.032
	256	39.313	667.321	2,660.354	20.323	345.360	1,401.178	0.009	0.044	0.083
Our	128	7.432	184.364	785.243	6.251	137.392	597.428	0.004	0.034	0.047
	256	41.364	693.591	2,806.472	33.641	471.243	2,673.580	0.017	0.045	0.098

6   Conclusion

In this paper, we explored the problem of the integrity and origin verification of disseminated tree-structured data with privacy protection and dissemination control in ODB model. To address this problem, we proposed an efficient RSS-TFRC which allows DSP to disseminate partial of authenticated tree-structured data with privacy protection in ODB model. The proposed scheme simultaneously supports the integrity and origin verifications of queried results without disclosing any privacy of data owners, and prevents the dishonest DSP or attackers from returning fake records to the users. Based on the thorough security analysis, we proved the RSS-TFRC is secure against the security threats of signature forgery, privacy disclosure, and information leakage. Finally, the theoretical analysis and experimental results demonstrate that our approach is indeed an efficient and practical solution for the fine-grained dissemination of authenticated trees with privacy protection in ODB model.

It is also important to consider how to design a sort of RSSs for multimedia data sharing, which allow certain types of image modification (e.g. lossy compression and redaction). This kind of RSSs can solve the authenticity and privacy leakage problems in multimedia data sharing. In order to realize the redaction function, signature length of most RSSs has a linear relationship with the number of sub-message blocks, which is impractical in some scenarios with limited communication resources. Therefore, it is urgent to design RSSs with constant signature length by applying aggregate signature schemes, accumulators etc.

We hope that our future work will consider the above issues and develop more practical and functional RSSs to satisfy the security requirements in different scenarios.

Acknowledgment. We thank several anonymous reviewers for their excellent feedback. This work is supported by National Natural Science Foundation of China (61472083, 61771140) and Distinguished Young Scholars Fund of Fujian (2016J06013).

Appendix A Proof for Theorem 1

We will show that if either of the following attackers can succeed in forging a signature for a tree with nonnegligible probability, then we can construct an algorithm $\mathcal{B}$ to solve the co-CDH problem on (G_1, G_2) with nonnegligible probability in the similar method as [3,20].

- There exists an attacker $\mathcal{A}_f$ who generates a valid signature for a tree consisting subtrees of a tree that has never been queried to signing oracle, or
- an attacker $\mathcal{A}_a$ who produces a valid signature for a tree that is a subtree of a tree that has been queried to signing oracle but does not satisfy the redaction control policy.

Attacker 1. Firstly, we will show how to construct a t'-time algorithm $\mathcal{B}_f$ that solves co-CDH problem on (G_1, G_2) with probability at least ϵ' by using the attacker $\mathcal{A}_f$. This will contradict the fact that (G_1, G_2) is a (t', ϵ')-co-CDH group pair.

Proof. Let g_2 be a generator of G_2. Algorithm $\mathcal{B}_f$ is given $g_2, u \in G_2$ and $h \in G_1$, where $u = g_2^a$. Its goal is to output $h^a \in G_1$. Algorithm $\mathcal{B}_f$ simulates the challenger and interacts with forger $\mathcal{A}_f$ as follows.

Setup. Algorithm $\mathcal{B}_f$ starts by giving $\mathcal{A}_f$ the generator g_2 and the public key $v' = u \cdot g_2^r \in G_2$, where r is a random in $\mathbb{Z}_p$.

Hash Queries. At any time algorithm $\mathcal{A}_f$ can query the random oracle H. To respond to these queries, $\mathcal{B}_f$ maintains a list of tuples $\langle M_j, w_j, b_j, c_j \rangle$ as explained below. We refer to this list as the H-list which is initially empty. When $\mathcal{A}_f$ queries the oracle H at a point $M_i \in \{0,1\}^*$, $\mathcal{B}_f$ responds as follows:

1. If the query M_i already appears on the H-list in a tuple $\langle M_i, w_i, b_i, c_i \rangle$ then algorithm $\mathcal{B}_f$ responds with $H(M_i) = w_i \in G_1$.
2. Otherwise, $\mathcal{B}_f$ generates a random coin $c_i \in \{0,1\}$ so that $\Pr[c_i = 0] = 1 - 1/(nq_S + n)$.
3. Algorithm $\mathcal{B}_f$ picks a random $b_i \in \mathbb{Z}_p$ and computes $w_i \leftarrow h^{c_i} \cdot \psi(g_2)^{b_i} \in G_1$.
4. Algorithm $\mathcal{B}_f$ adds the tuple $\langle M_i, w_i, b_i, c_i \rangle$ to the H-list and responds to $\mathcal{A}_f$ by setting $H(M_i) = w_i$.

Note that, either way, w_i is uniformly distributed in G_1 and is independent of $\mathcal{A}_f$'s current view as required.

Signature Queries. Let a tree $\Upsilon(V, E)$ with distribution control policy $\mathcal{P}$ be a signing query issued by $\mathcal{A}_f$ under the challenge public key v'. Algorithm $\mathcal{B}_f$ responds this query as follows:

1. Algorithm $\mathcal{B}_f$ generates secure names θ_{x_i} and $\theta_{p_{x_i}}$ for node x_i and its parent in tree $\Upsilon(V, E)$ and an identity id for $\Upsilon(V, E)$ the same way as in step 1 and step 2 of the signing algorithm of the proposed scheme, respectively.
2. Algorithm $\mathcal{B}_f$ runs the above algorithm for responding to H-queries to obtain a $w_i \in G_1$ such that $H(M_i) = w_i$. Without loss of generality we can assume $\langle M_i, w_i, b_i, c_i \rangle$ to be the tuple on the H-list corresponding to each node x_i.
3. If $c_i = 1$ for all $x_i \in V$, then $w_i = \psi(g_2)^{b_i} \in G_1$. Algorithm $\mathcal{B}_f$ defines $\sigma_i = \psi(u)^{b_i} \cdot \psi(g_2)^{rb_i}$. Observe that $\sigma_i = w_i^{a+r}$ and therefore σ_i is a valid signature on M_i under the public key $u \cdot g_2^r = g_2^{a+r}$. If $c_i = 0$ then $\mathcal{B}_f$ reports failure and terminates.
4. Algorithm $\mathcal{B}_f$ picks a random $s \in \mathbb{Z}_p$ and computes $w_0 \leftarrow h^{c_0} \cdot \psi(g_2)^s \in G_1$. Algorithm $\mathcal{B}_f$ defines $\sigma_0 = \psi(u)^s \cdot \psi(g_2)^{rs}$. Algorithm $\mathcal{B}_f$ defines $z_i = \psi(g_2)^{s_i}$ the same way as the signing algorithm of the proposed scheme. Observe that $\sigma_0 = w_0^{a+r}$ and therefore σ_0 is a valid signature on w_0 under the public key $u \cdot g_2^r = g_2^{a+r}$. Then, algorithm $\mathcal{B}_f$ computes $\sigma \leftarrow \prod_{i=0}^n \sigma_i$. Algorithm $\mathcal{B}_f$ computes $\sigma_S = e(\sigma, g_2)$ and gives σ_Υ to $\mathcal{A}_f$, where $\sigma_\Upsilon = (\sigma_S, id, \{z_i\}_{x_i \in V}, \{(\theta_{x_i}, \theta_{p_{x_i}}) | x_i \in V\})$.

Output. Eventually, $\mathcal{A}_f$ halts. It either concedes failure, in which case so does $\mathcal{B}_f$, or it returns a forged, but valid signature for a tree Υ^* such that no signature query was issued for even one node of tree Υ^*. If there is no tuple on the H-list containing nodes of Υ^* then $\mathcal{B}_f$ issues a hash query itself for each node of Υ^* to ensure that each node in Υ^* has such a tuple. We assume σ_{Υ^*} is a valid signature on Υ^* under the given public key; if it is not, $\mathcal{B}_f$ reports failure and terminates.

Next, algorithm $\mathcal{B}_f$ finds a set of tuple $\{\langle M_i^*, w_i^*, b_i^*, c_i^* \rangle\}_{i \in I}$ on the H-list, where $I \subset \{1, 2, \ldots, n\}$ is defined as $I = \{i : x_i \in V^*\}$. Algorithm $\mathcal{B}_f$ now proceeds only if $c_0^* \neq 0$ and $c_i^* = 0$ $(1 \leq i \leq n)$; otherwise $\mathcal{B}_f$ reports failure and halts. Since $c_0^* = 1$, it follows that $w_0^* = h \cdot \psi(g_2)^{s^*}$. For $1 \leq i \leq n$, since $c_i^* = 0$, it follows that $w_i^* = \psi(g_2)^{b_i^*}$. The aggregate signature σ^* in σ_{Υ^*} must satisfy verification equation, $e(\sigma^*, g_2) = \prod_{x_i \in V} e(w_i^* \cdot z_i^{*\omega_i}, v')$. For each $i \geq 1$, $\mathcal{B}_f$ sets individual signature $\sigma_i^* = \psi(u)^{b_i^*} \cdot \psi(g_2)^{rb_i^*}$. Then $\mathcal{B}_f$ computes the value σ_0^* as $\sigma_0^* \leftarrow \sigma^*/\prod_{i=1}^n \sigma_i^*$. This is a valid signature for w_0^* because $e(\sigma_0^*) = e(\sigma^*, g_2) \cdot \prod_{i=1}^n e(\sigma_i^*, g_2)^{-1} = \prod_{i=0}^n e(w_i^*, v') \cdot \prod_{i=1}^n e(w_i^*, v')^{-1} = e(w_0^*, v')$. Since $w_0^* = h \cdot \psi(g_2)^{s^*}$, this implies that $\sigma_0^* = (h \cdot \psi(g_2)^{s^*})^{a+r}$. Then $\mathcal{B}_f$ calculates and outputs the required h^a as $h^a \leftarrow \sigma_0^*/(h^r \cdot \psi(u)^{s^*} \cdot \psi(g_2)^{rs^*})$.

This completes the description of algorithm $\mathcal{B}_f$. It remains to show that $\mathcal{B}_f$ solves the given instance of the co-CDH problem in (G_1, G_2) with probability at least ϵ'. To do so, we analyze the three events needs for $\mathcal{B}_f$ to succeed:

- ε_1: $\mathcal{B}_f$ does not abort as a result of any of $\mathcal{A}_f$'s signature queries.
- ε_2: $\mathcal{A}_f$ generates a valid tree-signature forgery $(\Upsilon^*, \sigma_{\Upsilon^*})$.
- ε_3: Event ε_2 occurs, and in addition, $c_0^* \neq 0$ and $c_i^* = 0$ $(1 \leq i \leq n)$, where c_i^* is the c-component of the tuple containing M_i^* on the H-list.

$\mathcal{B}_f$ succeeds if all of these events happen. The probability $\Pr[\varepsilon_1 \wedge \varepsilon_3]$ is: $\Pr[\varepsilon_1 \wedge \varepsilon_3] = \Pr[\varepsilon_1] \cdot \Pr[\varepsilon_2 | \varepsilon_1] \cdot \Pr[\varepsilon_3 | \varepsilon_1 \wedge \varepsilon_2]$.

The probability that algorithm $\mathcal{B}_f$ does not abort as a result of $\mathcal{A}_f$'s signature queries is at least $(1 - 1/(nq_S + n))^{nq_S}$, since the c-component of the tuple on the H-list is independent of $\mathcal{A}_f$'s view. Hence, $\Pr[\varepsilon_1] \geq (1 - 1/(nq_S + n))^{nq_S}$.

If the event ε_1 happens, all $\mathcal{A}_f$'s responses to $\mathcal{B}_f$'s signature queries are valid. Since the public key given to $\mathcal{A}_f$ is from the same distribution as public key produced by KeyGen algorithm. Responses to hash queries are as in the real attack since each response is uniformly and independently distributed in G_1. Since $\mathcal{B}_f$ did not abort as a result of $\mathcal{A}_f$'s signature queries, all its responses to those queries are valid. Therefore $\mathcal{B}_f$ will produce a valid signature forgery with probability at least ϵ. Hence $\Pr[\varepsilon_2 | \varepsilon_1] \geq \epsilon$.

If the event ε_1 and ε_2 happen, the forged signature satisfies $c_0^* \neq 0$ and $c_i^* = 0$ $(1 \leq i \leq n)$ with the probability as least $(1 - 1/(nq_S + n))^{n-1} \cdot 1/(nq_S + n)$, since all c_is are independent of one another. Hence, $\Pr[\varepsilon_3 | \varepsilon_1 \wedge \varepsilon_2] \geq (1 - 1/(nq_S + n))^{n-1} \cdot 1/(nq_S + n)$.

Algorithm $\mathcal{B}_f$ produces the correct answer with probability at least $\epsilon' \geq Pr[\varepsilon_1 \wedge \varepsilon_3] \geq (1 - \frac{1}{nq_S + n})^{(nq_S + n - 1)} \cdot \frac{1}{nq_S + n} \cdot \epsilon \geq \frac{\epsilon}{e(nq_S + n)}$, where e is the base of natural logarithms.

This indicates that if the forger algorithm $\mathcal{A}_f$ succeeds in forging a signed tree with nonnegligible probability ϵ, then an algorithm $\mathcal{B}_f$ solving the co-CDH problem on (G_1, G_2) with nonnegligible probability ϵ' exists. Algorithm $\mathcal{B}_f$'s running time is the same as $\mathcal{A}_f$'s running time plus the time it takes to respond to hash queries and signature queries. Each query requires an exponentiation in G_1 which we assume takes time c_{G_1}. The output phase requires at most n additional hash computations, two inversions, two exponentiations, and $n - 1$ multiplications. Hence, the total running time is at most $t + c_{G_1}(q_H + 2q_S + n + 4) + n \leq t'$ as required. This completes the proof of Theorem 1.

Attacker 2. We will show how to construct a t'-time algorithm $\mathcal{B}_a$ that solves co-CDH problem on (G_1, G_2) with probability at least ϵ' by using the attacker $\mathcal{A}_a$. This will contradict the fact that (G_1, G_2) is a (t', ϵ')-co-CDH group pair.

The proof process is analogous to **Attacker 1**. Hence, we omit it for the page limit. $\square$

References

1. Beimel, A.: Secure schemes for secret sharing and key distribution. Ph.D. thesis, Israel Institute of Technology, Technion, Haifa, Israel (1996)
2. Boneh, D., Gentry, C., Lynn, B., Shacham, H.: Aggregate and verifiably encrypted signatures from bilinear maps. In: Biham, E. (ed.) EUROCRYPT 2003. LNCS, vol. 2656, pp. 416–432. Springer, Heidelberg (2003). https://doi.org/10.1007/3-540-39200-9_26

3. Boneh, D., Lynn, B., Shacham, H.: Short signatures from the weil pairing. In: Boyd, C. (ed.) ASIACRYPT 2001. LNCS, vol. 2248, pp. 514–532. Springer, Heidelberg (2001). https://doi.org/10.1007/3-540-45682-1_30

4. Brzuska, C., et al.: Redactable signatures for tree-structured data: definitions and constructions. In: Zhou, J., Yung, M. (eds.) ACNS 2010. LNCS, vol. 6123, pp. 87–104. Springer, Heidelberg (2010). https://doi.org/10.1007/978-3-642-13708-2_6

5. Bull, L., Squire, D.M.G., Zheng, Y.: A hierarchical extraction policy for content extraction signatures. Int. J. Digit. Libr. 4(3), 208–222 (2004)

6. Fu, Z., Ren, K., Shu, J., Sun, X., Huang, F.: Enabling personalized search over encrypted outsourced data with efficiency improvement. IEEE Trans. Parallel Distrib. Syst. 27(9), 2546–2559 (2016)

7. Goyal, V., Pandey, O., Sahai, A., Waters, B.: Attribute-based encryption for fine-grained access control of encrypted data. In: Proceedings of the 13th ACM Conference on Computer and Communications Security, pp. 89–98. ACM (2006)

8. Hacigumus, H., Iyer, B., Mehrotra, S.: Providing database as a service. In: 2002 Proceedings of 18th International Conference on Data Engineering, pp. 29–38. IEEE (2002)

9. Jain, R., Prabhakar, S.: Trustworthy data from untrusted databases. In: 2013 IEEE 29th International Conference on Data Engineering (ICDE), pp. 529–540. IEEE (2013)

10. Johnson, R., Molnar, D., Song, D., Wagner, D.: Homomorphic signature schemes. In: Preneel, B. (ed.) CT-RSA 2002. LNCS, vol. 2271, pp. 244–262. Springer, Heidelberg (2002). https://doi.org/10.1007/3-540-45760-7_17

11. Karchmer, M., Wigderson, A.: On span programs. In: Proceedings of 1993 Eighth Annual Conference on Structure in Complexity Theory, pp. 102–111. IEEE (1993)

12. Kundu, A., Atallah, M.J., Bertino, E.: Efficient leakage-free authentication of trees, graphs and forests. IACR Cryptology ePrint Archive, vol. 2012, p. 36 (2012)

13. Kundu, A., Atallah, M.J., Bertino, E.: Leakage-free redactable signatures. In: Proceedings of the Second ACM Conference on Data and Application Security and Privacy, pp. 307–316. ACM (2012)

14. Kundu, A., Bertino, E.: Structural signatures for tree data structures. Proc. VLDB Endow. 1(1), 138–150 (2008)

15. Liu, J., Huang, X., Liu, J.K.: Secure sharing of personal health records in cloud computing: ciphertext-policy attribute-based signcryption. Future Gener. Comput. Syst. 52, 67–76 (2015)

16. Ma, J., Liu, J., Huang, X., Xiang, Y., Wu, W.: Authenticated data redaction with fine-grained control. IEEE Trans. Emerg. Top. Comput. (2017)

17. Ma, J., Liu, J., Wang, M., Wu, W.: An efficient and secure design of redactable signature scheme with redaction condition control. In: Au, M.H.A., Castiglione, A., Choo, K.-K.R., Palmieri, F., Li, K.-C. (eds.) GPC 2017. LNCS, vol. 10232, pp. 38–52. Springer, Cham (2017). https://doi.org/10.1007/978-3-319-57186-7_4

18. de Meer, H., Pöhls, H.C., Posegga, J., Samelin, K.: Redactable signature schemes for trees with signer-controlled non-leaf-redactions. In: Obaidat, M.S., Filipe, J. (eds.) ICETE 2012. CCIS, vol. 455, pp. 155–171. Springer, Heidelberg (2014). https://doi.org/10.1007/978-3-662-44791-8_10

19. Merkle, R.C.: A certified digital signature. In: Brassard, G. (ed.) CRYPTO 1989. LNCS, vol. 435, pp. 218–238. Springer, New York (1990). https://doi.org/10.1007/0-387-34805-0_21

20. Miyazaki, K., Hanaoka, G., Imai, H.: Digitally signed document sanitizing scheme based on bilinear maps. In: Proceedings of the 2006 ACM Symposium on Information, Computer and Communications Security, pp. 343–354. ACM (2006)

21. Miyazaki, K., Iwamura, M., Matsumoto, T., Sasaki, R., Yoshiura, H., Tezuka, S.: Digitally signed document sanitizing scheme with disclosure condition control. IEICE Trans. Fundam. Electron. Commun. Comput. Sci. **88**(1), 239–246 (2005)

22. Samelin, K., Pöhls, H.C., Bilzhause, A., Posegga, J., de Meer, H.: Redactable signatures for independent removal of structure and content. In: Ryan, M.D., Smyth, B., Wang, G. (eds.) ISPEC 2012. LNCS, vol. 7232, pp. 17–33. Springer, Heidelberg (2012). https://doi.org/10.1007/978-3-642-29101-2_2

23. Samelin, K., Pöhls, H.C., Bilzhause, A., Posegga, J., de Meer, H.: On structural signatures for tree data structures. In: Bao, F., Samarati, P., Zhou, J. (eds.) ACNS 2012. LNCS, vol. 7341, pp. 171–187. Springer, Heidelberg (2012). https://doi.org/10.1007/978-3-642-31284-7_11

24. Shamir, A.: How to share a secret. Commun. ACM **22**(11), 612–613 (1979)

25. Steinfeld, R., Bull, L., Zheng, Y.: Content extraction signatures. In: Kim, K. (ed.) ICISC 2001. LNCS, vol. 2288, pp. 285–304. Springer, Heidelberg (2002). https://doi.org/10.1007/3-540-45861-1_22

26. Wang, Q., Wang, C., Ren, K., Lou, W., Li, J.: Enabling public auditability and data dynamics for storage security in cloud computing. IEEE Trans. Parallel Distrib. Syst. **22**(5), 847–859 (2011)

27. Wu, Z.Y., Hsueh, C.W., Tsai, C.Y., Lai, F., Lee, H.C., Chung, Y.: Redactable signatures for signed CDA documents. J. Med. Syst. **36**(3), 1795–1808 (2012)

28. Xia, Z., Wang, X., Sun, X., Wang, Q.: A secure and dynamic multi-keyword ranked search scheme over encrypted cloud data. IEEE Trans. Parallel Distrib. Syst. **27**(2), 340–352 (2016)

Efficient and Secure Outsourcing of Differentially Private Data Publication

Jin Li[1,3]([✉]), Heng Ye[2], Wei Wang[2], Wenjing Lou[3], Y. Thomas Hou[4],
Jiqiang Liu[2], and Rongxing Lu[5]

[1] School of Computer Science, Guangzhou University,
Guangzhou, Guangdong, China
jinli71@gmail.com
[2] Beijing Key Laboratory of Security and Privacy in Intelligent Transportation,
Beijing Jiaotong University, 3 Shangyuancun, Beijing, China
[3] Department of Computer Science, Virginia Polytechnic Institute
and State University, Falls Church, VA, USA
[4] Department of Electrical and Computer Engineering,
Virginia Polytechnic Institute and State University, Blacksburg, VA, USA
[5] School of Computer Science, University of New Brunswick,
Fredericton, NB, Canada

Abstract. While big data becomes a main impetus to the next generation of IT industry, big data privacy, as an unevadable topic in big data
era, has received considerable attention in recent years. To deal with
the privacy challenges, differential privacy has been widely discussed as
one of the most popular privacy-enhancing techniques. However, with
today's differential privacy techniques, it is impossible to generate a sanitized dataset that can suit different algorithms or applications regardless of the privacy budget. In other words, in order to adapt to various
applications and privacy budgets, different kinds of noises have to be
added, which inevitably incur enormous costs for both communication
and storage. To address the above challenges, in this paper, we propose
a novel scheme for outsourcing differential privacy in cloud computing,
where an additive homomorphic encryption (e.g., Paillier encryption)
is employed to compute noise for differential privacy by cloud servers to
boost efficiency. The proposed scheme allows data providers to outsource
their dataset sanitization procedure to cloud service providers with a low
communication cost. In addition, the data providers can go offline after
uploading their datasets and noise parameters, which is one of the critical requirements for a practical system. We present a detailed theoretical
analysis of our proposed scheme, including proofs of differential privacy
and security. Moreover, we also report an experimental evaluation on real
UCI datasets, which confirms the effectiveness of the proposed scheme.

1 Introduction

There is a general consensus that we are currently in the era of big data, with
tremendous amounts of information being collected by various organizations

J. Lopez et al. (Eds.): ESORICS 2018, LNCS 11099, pp. 187–206, 2018.
https://doi.org/10.1007/978-3-319-98989-1_10

and entities. Often, these data providers may wish to contribute their data to studies involving tasks such as statistical analysis, classification, and prediction. Because cloud service providers (CSPs) offer data providers (owners) great flexibility with respect to computation and storage capabilities, CSPs are presently the most popular avenue, through which data providers can share their data. However, the risk of leaking individuals' private information with the straightforward uploading of data providers' data (which may contain sensitive information such as medical or financial records, addresses and telephone numbers, or preferences of various kinds that the individuals may not want exposed) to CSPs is unacceptable. Usually, data providers protect their data's privacy by using of encryption, but the resulting encrypted data are known to be of poor utility. As an alternative, differential privacy (DP) has been considered as a useful technique not only for protecting the privacy of data but also for boosting the utility of data. As shown in Fig. 1, there are generally two main frameworks that can be used for achieving DP, i.e., the framework with interaction for release, and the framework with no interaction for publication. In this paper, we will focus on the latter, i.e., differentially private publication.

With current techniques, there does not exist an efficient method that allows data to be sanitized only once while still preserving the data's utility for all possible algorithms and applications. When data providers' data need to be shared for uses involving different algorithms, applications, or privacy budgets, different kinds of noise have to be added for privacy protection. Moreover, all of these different noisy datasets must be shared or published. Consequently, the communication overhead will be enormous if the number of different algorithms/applications/privacy budgets is large. Another challenging issue is that when data providers publish their data, public entities must exist somewhere that can store all of the different kinds of datasets with different types of noise, which also inevitably requires considerable storage space.

To overcome these challenges, we propose the notion of outsourcing differentially private data publication in this paper. With the advent of cloud computing, we know an increasing number of storage and computing tasks are moving from local resources to CSPs. In our scheme, the sanitized dataset generation procedure is outsourced to a CSP by the data providers. To protect the privacy of the data, we can use the effective method, i.e., cryptographic techniques, to encrypt the data before outsourcing. However, data sanitization requires the ability to easily modify the data to be sanitized, while encrypted data generally cannot provide such an ability. Using fully homomorphic encryption technique to support ciphertext manipulation is however inefficient and requires enormous amounts of storage space and communication bandwidth. Unlike other schemes, our differentially private data publication requires only addition operations, and such operations can be realized by using the additive homomorphic encryption, which would be much more efficient than the fully homomorphic encryption. Although this approach enables us to add noise to encrypted data, encryption still leads to poor utility or heavy consume of storage/computation in many respects. Therefore, in our scheme, it allows the data evaluator to decrypt the encrypted noisy data, thereby improving the utility of the data as well as the storage cost. In this way, the data providers are not required to be online when their data are requested, which is one of the critical requirements for a practical application system.

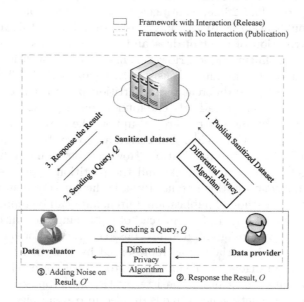

Fig. 1. Frameworks for achieving differential privacy

1.1   Related Work

Differential privacy has been accepted as the main privacy paradigm in recent years, because it is based on purely mathematical calculations and provides a means of quantitative assessment. A large body of work on DP has accumulated due to its support for privacy preserving learning. There are some works which used the cryptographic methods to solve the privacy preserving for data utilization [32,33] before the first work of DP by Dwork in 2006 [9], and the Laplace mechanism for adding noise to achieve ϵ-DP was proposed in the seminal paper. Subsequently, McSherry designed the exponent mechanism [25] and identified the sequential and parallel properties of DP [24].

Generally, DP can be achieved via two main frameworks. In the first framework, the data evaluator's queries are responded under a predetermined privacy budget ϵ; as shown in Fig. 1 with red box. In the framework, we can apply the Laplace [11], Privlet [35], Linear Query [21], and Batch Query [38] techniques, among others, to obtain different responses to these queries that satisfy ϵ-DP. However, this framework demands interaction between the data provider and the data evaluator. For this reason, in this paper, we will focus on the second framework, as depicted in Fig. 1 with the blue dashed box. The second framework not only allows a data provider to immediately publish his data after processing but also does not require any interaction. The main focus of research related to this framework is on how to design efficient and effective noise-adding algorithms to ensure DP while boosting data utility.

Typical publication methods include histogram publication [15,17,36,37], partition publication [5,7,26,28], contingency table publication [1,20], and sanitized dataset publication [8,10,12,14]. A histogram is an intuitive representation of the distribution of a set of data and can be used as a basis for other statistical queries or linear queries. However, histogram publication suffers from problems of redundant noise and inconsistency, meaning that different types of noise should be added for different uses. Partition publication can reduce the amount of noise that must be added. The foundation of partition publication is the careful design of an index structure to support the partitioning of the data. Using this index, the data provider can assign a privacy budget to each partition for noise addition before publication. However, determining how to assign a privacy budget is not a trivial task, and the partition index itself may leak some sensitive information; this potential risk is the core problem that remains to be solved for this method of publication. Often, data can be represented in the form of a contingency table. In fact, instead of publishing the contingency table itself for analysis, data are often published based on the statistical values of the combinations of certain variables, as represented by marginal tables. Directly adding noise to a contingency table introduces too much noise, whereas perturbing the marginal table may cause inconsistency. Qardaji proposed a noise-adding method in which the contingency table is divided into small pieces, called views [29]. This method can reduce the amount of noise introduced, but the questions of how to choose the parameters to be used for division and how to preserve the consistency between the views and the marginal tables remain challenging. The purpose of sanitized dataset publication is to ensure the protection of data privacy after the processing of the original dataset. The question on how to directly publish a sanitized dataset that satisfies DP while allowing the data evaluator to make any necessary inquiries is quite challenging. This method of dataset publication demands considerable calculation and thus is inefficient and difficult to realize. Kasiviswanathan and Blum proved that sanitized dataset publication is possible [3,19]; however, it requires an enormous number of records.

Although the DP model provides frameworks for data evaluators to analyze databases belonging to a single party, the initial frameworks did not consider a multi-party setting. Multi-party DP was first proposed by Manas in 2010 [27], based on the aggregation of multi-party datasets to train a classifier. Subsequently, many works involving multi-party DP publication have been reported, including multi-task learning [13], multi-party deep learning [30], classifier training on private and public datasets [18] and high-dimensional data publication [31]. These works, however, have not considered outsourced computing to relieve the computational burden on data providers.

Outsourced computing is a technique for securely outsourcing expensive computations to untrusted servers, which allows resource-constrained data providers to outsource their computational workloads to cloud servers with unlimited computational resources. Chaum first proposed the notion of wallets, secure hardware installed on a client's computer to perform expensive computations, in 1992 [4]. To protect data providers' privacy, Chevallier presented the first algorithm for the secure delegation of elliptic-curve pairings [6]. In addition, solutions for performing meaningful computations over encrypted data using fully homomorphic encryption have emerged, although they are known to be of poor practicality [2]. Meanwhile, cloud computing using attribute-based encryption appeared, which not only supports ciphertext operation, but also provides fine-grained access control. Some of works that concentrate on privacy preserving in cloud computing have been proposed recently [16,22,23]. Nevertheless, in this paper, we choose additive homomorphic encryption as our basic technique to perform outsourcing computing, which offers a perfect balance of efficiency and security.

1.2 Contributions

In this paper, we propose a novel outsourced DP scheme for cloud computing. Our contributions can be summarized as follows.

- We design an efficient outsourced DP approach using additive homomorphic encryption instead of fully homomorphic encryption. In such a way, data can be efficiently outsourced to a CSP for secure storage and DP supporting noise addition.
- In our scheme, the data provider is not required to be involved in subsequent noise computations and related processing.
- The security of the data against the CSP can be guaranteed under our proposed security model.

1.3 Organization

The rest of this paper is organized as follows. Some preliminary considerations are discussed in Sect. 2. In Sect. 3, the architecture of our scheme and our threat model are introduced. Then, we present the new scheme in Sect. 4. The implementation details and the evaluation of the experimental results are presented in Sect. 5. Finally, we conclude our work in Sect. 6. Also, the security analysis and some related concepts using in this paper are put in the appendix.

2   Preliminaries

2.1   Differential Privacy

DP was introduced by Dwork et al. as a technique for individual privacy protection in data publication. It provides a strong privacy guarantee, ensuring that the presence or absence of an individual will not significantly affect the final output of any function (Table 1).

Table 1. Symbol cross reference table

ϵ	Privacy budget	f	Algorithm for machine learning
m	Plaintext	c	Ciphertext
P	Data provider	$\|m\|$	Ciphertext of m
η	Noise	Δf	Global sensitivity
b	Parameters for distribution	sk_P/pk_P	Secret/public key of P
Sth	Vector of sth		

Definition 1. *(Differential privacy)*
A randomized function $\mathcal{A}$ with a well-defined probability density $\mathcal{P}$ satisfies ϵ-DP if, for any two neighboring datasets D_1 and D_2 that differ by only one record and for any $\mathcal{O} \in range(M)$,

$$\mathcal{P}(\mathcal{A}(D_1) = \mathcal{O}) \leq e^{\epsilon} \cdot \mathcal{P}(\mathcal{A}(D_2) = \mathcal{O}) \tag{1}$$

DP can usually be achieved via one of two standard mechanisms: the Laplace mechanism and the exponential mechanism. Both of them are based on the concept of the sensitivity of a function f. For ease of description, we consider only numeric values in this paper.

Definition 2. *(Global sensitivity)*
Let f be a function that maps a database to a fixed-size vector of real numbers. For all neighboring databases D_l and D_2, the global sensitivity of f is defined as

$$\Delta(f) = \max_{D_1,D_2} \|f(D_1) - f(D_2)\|_1 \tag{2}$$

where $\| \cdot \|_1$ denotes the L_1 norm.

To publish data that satisfy ϵ-DP when a query function f is applied, the principal approach is to perturb the data by adding random noise based on Δf and the privacy budget ϵ. For example, for the Laplace mechanism, let $Lap(\lambda)$ denote the Laplace probability distribution with mean zero and scale λ. The Laplace mechanism achieves DP by adding Laplace noise to an original dataset M.

Definition 3. *(Laplace mechanism)*
Let m be a record in database M ($m \in M$), and let η be a random variable such that $\eta \sim Lap(\Delta f/\epsilon)$. The Laplace mechanism is defined as follows:

$$m' = m + \eta.(\Sigma m = M) \tag{3}$$

3   Architecture

In this section, we formalize our system model, and identify the threat model and security requirements.

3.1   System Model

In our system model, four types of entities are involved in our basic scheme, namely, the trusted authority (TA), the data providers, the cloud service provider (CSP), and the data evaluator. The TA issues credentials for both data providers and data evaluators. The data providers possess data and would like to share those data for purposes such as classification or data analysis. The CSP provides the cloud storage service for the data providers. The data evaluator obtains the sanitized data from the CSP and performs the corresponding data analysis. Each data evaluator may acquire different part of dataset for different usage. However, the same data he got, the same noise the data has.

3.2   Threat Model and Security Requirements

In this work, both the data evaluator and the CSP are assumed to be *honest-but-curious*. The data evaluator needs to protect his trained model against the CSP. Moreover, the data evaluator will follow a specified protocol for building a correct model without obtaining incorrect results. The relationship between CSP and data evaluator is non-cooperative, which means they will not collude with each other (For example, CSP could be Google Inc. and data evaluator is Apple Inc., which is very common in our daily life). Otherwise, even they are honest, data evaluator could give CSP his secret key to get the original dataset. The privacy of the data providers' data needs to be protected against both the CSP and the data evaluator.

For the data owner, the security means that its privacy should be protected against the other entities even if they are curious about the underlying original data. Of course, the CSP and DP are not allowed to collude with each other in our security model.

4   Our Proposed Outsourced Differential Privacy Schemes

In this section, we present several basic outsourced differential privacy (ODP) schemes. During the description, we consider a public key encryption scheme with additive homomorphic properties, i.e., $(Setup, KeyGen, Enc, Dec, Add)$, will be applied in our system.

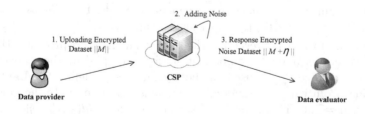

Fig. 2. Single-data-provider scheme

4.1   A Straightforward Scheme

In a straightforward scheme, the typical process of differentially private data publication can be summarized as follows:

- **Setup.** The data evaluator and data provider together establish the privacy budget ϵ.
- **Generation.** The data provider calculates Δf and then uses Δf and ϵ to generate a noisy dataset.
- **Uploading.** The data provider uploads the noisy dataset to the CSP.
- **Analysis.** The data evaluator obtains the noisy dataset from the CSP and analyzes this dataset.

Note that, for different data evaluators and/or different privacy budgets, the above steps should be executed repeatedly, which means more power and bandwidth will be consumed.

To overcome the disadvantages of the above scheme, we show how to provide efficient noise addition with the aid of cloud servers in next sections.

4.2   Our Scheme for Single Data Provider

Initially, we assume that there is a single data provider in the system (Fig. 2). Then, the single-data-provider scheme, as shown in Algorithm 1, is composed of the following steps:

- **Setup.** In this step, the TA generates the public parameters and key pairs involved in the system. Let (pk, sk) be the key pair for the data evaluator, where pk is the public key and sk is the secret key. Note that, the data provider should pre-calculate the possible set of function sensitivities, denoted by $\Delta\mathbf{F} = (\Delta f_1, \Delta f_2, \cdots, \Delta f_m)$, where f_i $(i = 1, \cdots, m)$ are the functions that the data evaluator might use in his evaluations.
- **Data uploading.** The data provider first receives the data evaluator's public key pk from the TA, encrypts his dataset $M = (m_1, m_2, \cdots, m_n)$ using the $Enc(pk, M)$ algorithm, and uploads the resulting ciphertexts $C = (\|m_1\|, \|m_2\|, \cdots, \|m_n\|)$ to the cloud server. Then, the data provider (and perhaps the data evaluator) determines the privacy budget ϵ. Furthermore, the parameter vector $\mathbf{b}$ for noise generation (e.g., for the Laplace mechanism, since the Laplace noise generation depends on $\frac{\Delta\mathbf{F}}{\epsilon}$, $\mathbf{b} = (b_1, b_2, \cdots, b_m) = (\frac{\Delta f_1}{\epsilon}, \frac{\Delta f_2}{\epsilon}, \cdots, \frac{\Delta f_m}{\epsilon}))$ is also sent to the cloud server.
- **Noise addition.** After receiving the data from the data provider, the cloud server generates a noise component η (for example, in the Laplace noise mechanism, $b_i = \frac{\Delta f_i}{\epsilon}$ is used as the parameters to define the Laplace distributions from which to randomly draw noise) and encrypts the noise using $Enc(pk, \eta) = \|\eta\|$. Then, the cloud server uses the $Add(\|M\|, \|\eta\|)$ algorithm to add the noise to the data provider's data (for example, in the case of Paillier encryption, the server multiplies the data provider's encrypted data by the encrypted noise) and sends the resulting noisy data to the data evaluator.

– **Data analysis.** The data evaluator first decrypts the received ciphertexts using $Dec(sk, \|M + \eta\|)$ to obtain all of the noisy data. Based on these data, the data evaluator can successfully perform classification or apply other algorithms to the data.

Algorithm 1. Single data provider scheme for noise addition

Input: Data provider (D): clean dataset
    $M = (m_1, m_2, \cdots, m_n)$.
    Data evaluator (DE): possible functions to be used
    $(f_1, f_2, \cdots, f_m)$.
Output: DE: dataset with noise
    $M + \eta$.
1: D: $\varDelta \mathbf{F} = (\varDelta f_1, \varDelta f_2, \cdots, \varDelta f_m)$, calculates the sensitivities of the possible functions;
2: D: $\epsilon \leftarrow DE$, communicates with DE to establish an appropriate privacy budget;
3: D: $\mathbf{b} = \varDelta \mathbf{F}/\epsilon$, calculates the parameter vector;
4: D: $\{\|M\|, \mathbf{b}\} \rightarrow CSP$, uploads the encrypted dataset and parameter vector;
5: D: $i_0 \leftarrow DE$, obtains which functions DE will use;
6: D: $i_0 \rightarrow CSP$, uploads the number of functions to be used;
7: **for** each $j \in [1, \cdots, n]$ **do**
8:    CSP: $\eta_j \sim Lap(b_{i_0})$, generates noise;
9:    CSP: $\|\eta_j\|_{pk} = Enc(\eta_j, pk)$, encrypts the noise;
10:   CSP: $\|m_j + \eta_j\|_{pk} = Add(\|m_j\|, \|\eta_j\|)$, calculates the noisy dataset;
11: **end for**
12: CSP: sends $\|M + \eta\|$ to DE;
13: DE: $M + \eta = Dec(\|M + \eta\|, sk)$, decrypts the ciphertexts;
14: **return** $M + \eta$.

4.3 A Multi-Data-Provider Scheme

Next, we present the multi-data-provider scheme (similar with Fig. 2, but more data providers). For the ease of description, we assume that each party holds a parallel data set, meaning that there is no overlap between any two parties' databases. Each party P_i hold a portion of D, denoted by D_i, such that $\sum D_i = D$. The scheme, as shown in Algorithm 2, consists of four steps.

– **Setup.** This step is similar to that for a single data provider. The difference is that there are k parties, denoted by $P_1, P_2, \cdots, P_k$, and each user P_i should pre-calculate a set of possible function sensitivities $\varDelta \mathbf{F}_i$.
– **Data uploading.** Each data provider P_i encrypts the dataset $M_i = (m_{i1}, m_{i2}, \cdots, m_{in})$ using the $Enc(pk, M_i)$ algorithm. After the encryption, P_i uploads the ciphertexts $C_i = (\|m_{i1}\|, \|m_{i2}\|, \cdots, \|m_{in}\|)$ to the cloud

server. Then, the users determine the privacy budget ϵ. The parameter vectors $\mathbf{b}_i$ for noise generation are also sent to the cloud server.

– **Noise addition.** Using all the noise parameter vectors $\mathbf{b}_i$ $(i = 1, 2, \cdots, k)$, the cloud server generates the noise η_i for each P_i and encrypts the noise using $Enc(pk, \eta_i) = \|\eta_i\|$. Then, the cloud server uses the $Add(\|M_i\|, \|\eta_i\|)$ algorithm to add the noise to the data providers' data and sends the noisy data to the data evaluator.

– **Data analysis.** This step is the same as that for a single data provider.

Algorithm 2. Multiple-data-provider scheme for noise addition

---

Input: Data providers (D): clean dataset
   $\mathbf{M} = (M_1, M_2, \cdots, M_k)$.
   Data evaluator (DE): possible functions to be used
   $(f_1, f_2, \cdots, f_m)$.
Output: DE: dataset with noise
   $M + \eta$.
 1: D: $\mathbf{\Delta F} = (\Delta \mathbf{F}_1, \Delta \mathbf{F}_2, \cdots, \Delta \mathbf{F}_k)$;
 2: D: $\epsilon \leftarrow DE$;
 3: D: $\mathbf{b} = \Delta \mathbf{F}/\epsilon$;
 4: D: $\{\|M\|, \mathbf{b}\} \rightarrow CSP$;
 5: CSP: generate appropriate noise η under DE's require;
 6: CSP: sends $\|M + \eta\|$ to DE;
 7: DE: $M + \eta = Dec(\|M + \eta\|, sk)$;
 8: **return** $M + \eta$.

4.4   Discussion: How to Add Noise Wisely and Efficiently

In the above schemes, we have assumed that the noise generation is a simple task performed by the CSP. Actually, other noise-adding schemes from other entities are also possible. In the following, we focus on discussing additional methods of noise generation for the single-data-provider schemes. Note that, similar methods can also be applied in the multi-data-provider schemes.

Noise Addition by the Data Provider. Noise can be generated by the data provider; see Fig. 3. In this method, the CSP will have no interaction with the parameter vector $\mathbf{b}$ or the generated noise η. The details of the procedure are shown in Algorithm 3.

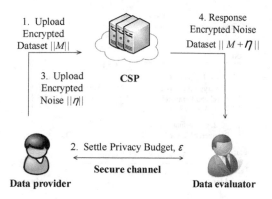

Fig. 3. Noise addition by the data provider

Algorithm 3. Noise addition by the data provider

Input: Data provider (D): clean dataset
 $M = (m_1, m_2, \cdots, m_n)$.
 Data evaluator (DE): function to be used f.
Output: DE: dataset with noise
 $M + \eta$.
1: D: $\Delta f = \max_{M, M'} \|f(M) - f(M')\|_1$
2: D: $\epsilon \leftarrow DE$;
3: D: $b = \Delta f / \epsilon$;
4: D: $\|M\| \rightarrow CSP$;
5: D: sends the new generated noise in encrypted form $\|\eta\|_{pk}$ to the CSP;
6: CSP: $\|M + \eta\|_{pk} = Add(\|M\|, \|\eta\|)$;
7: DE: $M + \eta = Dec(\|M + \eta\|, sk)$;
8: **return** $M + \eta$.

Noise Addition by a Noise Server. Noise addition by the data provider can protect some sensitive parameters from the CSP. However, this scheme does not allow the data provider to go offline. Therefore, we propose a scheme with noise addition by a noise-generating server; see Fig. 4. We assume that there is another server, called the noise-generating server, in our system, i.e., the system now contains five types of entities: the trusted authority (TA), the data provider, the cloud service provider (CSP), the data evaluator and the noise-generating service provider (NSP). The main idea of this design is to separate the noise generation from the rest of the system. The details of the procedure are shown in Algorithm 4.

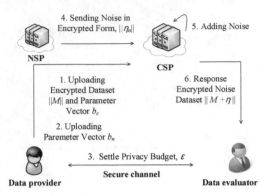

Fig. 4. Noise addition by a noise server

Algorithm 4. Noise addition by a noise server

Input: Data provider (D): clean dataset
$M = (m_1, m_2, \cdots, m_n)$.
Data evaluator (DE): possible functions to be used
$(f_1, f_2, \cdots, f_m)$.
Output: DE: dataset with noise
$M + \eta$.
 1: D: $\mathbf{\Delta F} = (\Delta f_1, \Delta f_2, \cdots, \Delta f_m)$;
 2: D: $\epsilon \leftarrow DE$;
 3: D: $\epsilon = \epsilon_n + \epsilon_c$, divides privacy budget into two parts;
 4: D: $\mathbf{b}_n = \mathbf{\Delta F}/\epsilon_n$, $\mathbf{b}_c = \mathbf{\Delta F}/\epsilon_c$;
 5: D: $\mathbf{b}_n \rightarrow NSP$, uploads a parameter vector to the NSP;
 6: D: $\{\|M\|, \mathbf{b}_c\} \rightarrow CSP$;
 7: NSP: sends encrypted noise $\|\eta_n\|$ to the CSP;
 8: CSP: $\|m_j + \eta_j\|_{pk} = Add(\|m_j\|, \|\eta_{nj}\|, \|\eta_{cj}\|)$;
 9: DE: $M + \eta = Dec(\|M + \eta\|, sk)$;
10: **return** $M + \eta$.

4.5   Discussion: How to Treat High-Dimensional Data

The publication of high-dimensional data can support a wide spectrum of evaluation tasks. However, the problem of how to ensure the privacy of high-
dimensional data is still challenging. Generally speaking, we can handle high-
dimensional data as described below.

View-Based Dimension Reduction. High-dimensional data can be presented in the form of a contingency table [29]. For most types of data evaluations, a k-way marginal contingency table (generally, $k \leq 3$) can be used.
However, directly adding noise to the complete contingency table (all of the
data) to achieve data sanitization will lead to excessive noise. Therefore, determining how to add noise to obtain a high-utility k-way marginal table is the key

to high-dimensional data publication. We use the following basic procedure to reduce the dimensionality of high-dimensional data before publication.

- **Build a contingency table.** In this step, the data provider builds a contingency table based on his high-dimensional dataset.
- **Generate views.** The data provider runs an algorithm to select the best parameters with which to generate views. (For example, suppose that we have an l-column, d-dimensional table, where $d = 8$ and $l = 100$; then, the data provider runs the algorithm to generate $d^2 + l$ sub-contingency tables, which are referred to as views.) The data provider can treat these views in the same way as his original data, following the scheme proposed above (setup, data uploading, noise generation, noise addition). A bloom filter should also be used to assign the attributes to the encrypted views.
- **Reconstruct.** The noisy k-way marginal table is reconstructed based on the encrypted views, and the bloom filter is used to check whether the views can be successfully used to reconstruct the k-way marginal table.

4.6   Discussion: How to Make the Scheme More Practical

In the schemes presented above, each data provider uses the data evaluator's public key to encrypt his own data, which means that the data provider cannot delete his local copy of his dataset to save storage space, because using the data evaluator's public key for encryption causes the data provider to lose the ability to decrypt the dataset stored by the CSP. Inspired by Wang's method [34], we propose our ODP scheme with proxy re-encryption technique; the details of the procedure are shown in Algorithm 5.

Algorithm 5. Using proxy re-encryption during uploading in multi-data-provider scheme

---

Input: Data providers (D): clean dataset
   $M = (M_1, M_2, \cdots, M_k)$.
   Data evaluator (DE): possible functions to be used
   $(f_1, f_2, \cdots, f_m)$.
Output: DE: dataset with noise
   $M + \eta$.
1: D: $\Delta\mathbf{F} = (\Delta\mathbf{F}_1, \Delta\mathbf{F}_2, \cdots, \Delta\mathbf{F}_k)$;
2: D: $\epsilon \leftarrow DE$;
3: D: $\mathbf{b} = \Delta\mathbf{F}/\epsilon$;
4: D: $\{\|M\|, \mathbf{b}\} \rightarrow CSP$;
5: CSP: $(rkey_{P_i} \rightarrow pk_{p_e}) \leftarrow$ TA;
6: CSP: $\|M_i + \eta_i\|_{pk_{P_e}} = ReEnc(rkey_{P_i} \rightarrow pk_{p_e}, \|M_i + \eta_i\|_{pk_{P_i}})$;
7: DE: $M + \eta = Dec(\|M + \eta\|, sk_{P_e})$, decrypts the ciphertexts;
8: **return** $M + \eta$.

---

5   Evaluation

In this section, we evaluate the performance of our scheme in terms of functionality, computational overhead and communication overhead. All experiments were conducted on a PC with a 1.90 GHz AMD A4-3300M APU with Radeon(TM) HD Graphics and 6 GB of RAM. Also, using different kinds of noise addition method only differs nothing but in execution time during noise generation. For simplicity, we choose Laplace mechanism in this evaluation to prove our scheme's feasibility.

5.1   Functionality

We used datasets acquired from the UCI machine learning repository, which can be downloaded from UCI[1], to evaluate our scheme's functionality. To evaluate the classifier performance, we reserved $\frac{1}{10}$ of each dataset to serve as a test dataset, and we chose $\epsilon = 0.1$ for applying the Laplace mechanism to our datasets. Figure 5 shows the accuracies of training KNN and Naive Bayes classifiers for Letter Recognition, EEG Eye State, CPU, and Glass. From the figure, we can see that training a classifier on the sanitized dataset instead of the original dataset exerts little influence on the classifier performance.

5.2   Computational Overhead

We use the Paillier scheme as our homomorphic encryption algorithm. To perform homomorphic addition on ciphertexts, we should treat each attribute as a plaintext input and calculate its related ciphertext. Thus, the total number of encryption operations is counts = records * attributes.

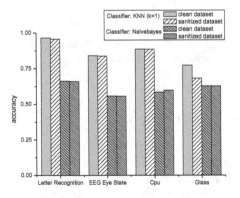

Fig. 5. Functionality

---

[1] http://archive.ics.uci.edu/ml/.

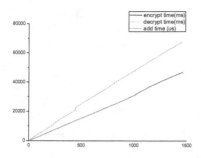

Fig. 6. Computational overhead

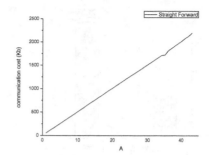

Fig. 7. Communication overhead

As seen in Fig. 6, it takes approximately 30 s to perform 1000 encryption/decryption operations but only 48 ms to perform 1000 addition operations on ciphertexts. In our scheme, data providers can pre-upload their data to the CSP, and the encryption can be executed in the data providers' spare time. Because the cost of ciphertext addition is low, our scheme is acceptable and feasible.

5.3   Communication Overhead

There are two phases that incur main communication costs, including data uploading and data analysis.

In the data uploading phase (see Fig. 7), the size of the message sent in our scheme is $ndc + \frac{k}{1000}$ kb, whereas the message size in the straightforward scheme is $kndp$ kb, where n, d, c, k, and p denote the size of the dataset, the number of attributes, the size of each ciphertext record, the number of types of noise to be added and the size of each plaintext record, respectively. As more different kinds of noise are added, the communication cost grows linearly in the straightforward scheme. Meanwhile, in our scheme, the size of the dataset increases to 88 kb after encryption when the original dataset size is 43 kb, indicating that encryption leads to a ×2 increase. Once there is more than one type of noise to be added, our scheme ensures a lower communication cost.   In the data analysis phase, the total size of the message sent by the CSP is $kndc$, compared with $kndp$ in the straightforward scheme. Generally speaking, therefore, the size of the message sent to the data evaluator in our scheme is approximately twice as large as that in the straightforward scheme. However, as shown in Fig. 8, the storage cost of our scheme is cheaper for both each data provider and the CSP. **Storage cost for a data provider** (see Fig. 8(a)): In our scheme, because the original dataset is uploaded, the data provider is required to store only the secret key for Paillier encryption (approximately 32 kb), which can be used to regain his data. By contrast, in the straightforward scheme, because of the lack of encryption (storage in plaintext poses privacy concerns), the data provider cannot reduce his storage cost for the original dataset. **Storage cost for the CSP** (see Fig. 8(b)): In our scheme, the CSP can store only one copy of the

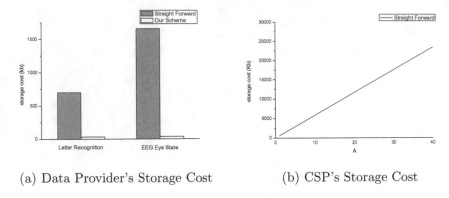

(a) Data Provider's Storage Cost   (b) CSP's Storage Cost

Fig. 8. Storage costs

original dataset in encrypted form and regenerate a noisy dataset every time a data evaluator requests it. However, to preserve confidentiality, the CSP cannot possess the unencrypted original dataset with which to generate noisy datasets using the straightforward scheme; therefore, in this scheme, the CSP must store every noisy dataset, which will lead to a linear increase in storage cost with the number of types of noise to be added.

6   Conclusions

In this paper, we addressed the issues of inefficiency due to adding different types of noise to a dataset for differentially private publication. Specifically, to solve the challenge, we proposed an efficient and secure outsourced differential privacy scheme suitable for all DP algorithms with noise addition operations, including Laplace algorithm, in which the data providers incur reduced communication costs and are not required to be online when the access to their data is requested. We also showed how to use an independant noise server to deal with the differential privacy. The differential privacy for high-dimension data was also discussed. Finally, the experiment showed that the efficiency of our new scheme compared with the basic solutions. In future work, we will consider different kinds of noise-adding methods that can be executed over encrypted data. In addition, we are also interested in researching special encryption algorithms that permit smart and efficient noise addition.

Acknowledgement. This work was supported by Natural Science Foundation of Guangdong Province for Distinguished Young Scholars (2014A030306020), National Natural Science Foundation of China (No. 61472091) and National Natural Science Foundation for Outstanding Youth Foundation (No. 61722203). This work was also supported in part by US National Science Foundation under grants CNS-1446478 and CNS-1443889.

Appendix A: Cryptographic Tools

Additive Homomorphic Encryption. We say that an encryption scheme is additive homomorphic if it conforms to the following definition.

Definition 4. *(Additive homomorphic encryption)*
Let m_1 and m_2 be two plaintexts, let $\mathcal{A}$ be an encryption algorithm that outputs the corresponding ciphertexts $\|m_1\|$ and $\|m_2\|$, and let $\mathcal{B}$ be an operation performed on the two ciphertexts. For any two ciphertexts, additive homomorphic encryption has the following property:

$$\mathcal{B}(\|m_1\|, \|m_2\|) = \mathcal{B}(\mathcal{A}(m_1), \mathcal{A}(m_2)) = \|m_1 + m_2\| \tag{4}$$

In this paper, we discuss an encryption scheme that operates under a public key encryption system and consists of the following algorithms:

- **Setup**(1^l): A trusted authority (TA) uses a security parameter l to generate the public parameters (pp) and the main secret key (msk).
- **KeyGen**(msk, pp, uid): The TA uses a user's identity uid as input to generate a pair of keys (pk, sk) for that user.
- **Enc**(pk, m): The user uses his public key pk to encrypt a plaintext record m, generating the ciphertext $\|m\|$ as output.
- **Dec**$(sk, \|m\|)$: The user uses his secret key sk to decrypt a ciphertext record $\|m\|$ into the corresponding plaintext m.
- **Add**$(\|m_1\|, \|m_2\|)$: Two ciphertexts $\|m_1\|$ and $\|m_2\|$ are inputs, and the result $\|m_1 + m_2\|$ is output.

Due to the simplicity of the Paillier encryption scheme, we choose the Paillier scheme as our additive homomorphic encryption algorithm.

Proxy Re-encryption. Proxy re-encryption is based on the concept that an honest-but-curious proxy uses a re-encryption key to translate a ciphertext encrypted with the data owner's public key into another ciphertext that can be decrypted using another user's private key. The general structure of the proxy re-encryption process can be summarized as follows:

- **Setup**(1^l): The TA uses a security parameter l to generate the public parameters (pp) and the main secret key (msk).
- **KeyGen**(msk, pp, I_{de}): Using a data evaluator's identity I_{de}, msk and pp as input, the TA generates the data evaluator's keys $(pk_{I_{de}}, sk_{I_{de}})$.
- **PrivKeyGen**(pp, uid): The TA generates a pair of keys (pk_{uid}, sk_{uid}) for a user (a data owner) using that user's identity uid and pp.
- **ReKeyGen**$(sk_{uid}, pk_{I_{de}})$: The TA outputs the re-encryption key $rkey_{uid} \rightarrow pk_{I_{de}}$ using the data owner's secret key sk_{uid} and the data evaluator's public key $pk_{I_{de}}$.
- **Enc**(pk_{uid}, m): The data owner uses his public key pk_{uid} to encrypt a plaintext input m, generating the ciphertext $\|m\|$ as output.

- **ReEnc**($rkey_{uid} \rightarrow pk_{I_{de}}, \|m\|$): A cloud server calculates and outputs the re-encrypted ciphertext $\|m\|^R$, using as input the ciphertext $\|m\|$ and the re-encryption key $rkey_{uid} \rightarrow pk_{I_{de}}$.
- **Dec**($sk_{uid}, \|m\|$): The data owner uses his secret key sk_{uid} to decrypt the ciphertext $\|m\|$ into the plaintext m.
- **Dec**($sk_{I_{de}}, \|m\|^R$): The data evaluator uses his secret key $sk_{I_{de}}$ to decrypt the re-encrypted ciphertext $\|m\|^R$ to obtain the plaintext m.

Appendix B: Security Analysis

Clearly, our goals are to protect the data providers' data from any adversary (ADV). In this section, we only present the security proof about data transmission process and noise addition process. Note that, for the data storage process and decryption process, since they depend on the encryption algorithm applied, we will not discuss the security for the two processes here.

According to Fig. 2, the data flows are directed from the data provider to the CSP and from the CSP to the data evaluator. Generally speaking, an ADV may eavesdrop on the communication flow from the data provider to the CSP. However, even if the ADV obtains a message in this way he cannot learn anything from this message without the data evaluator's secret key sk. The data's security depends on the encryption algorithm used (e.g., Paillier). Therefore, we can assert that the ADV cannot access private data even if the communication flow is intercepted. Moreover, even in multi-data-provider schemes, the ADV can collude with some data providers, the ADV cannot reveal the private data of uncompromised data providers. Compromised data providers do not possess the data evaluator's secret key sk_{DE} using in common scheme nor different data providers' secret key sk_{DP} using in proxy encryption scheme, with which to decrypt other providers' messages.

We can treat the noise generated by the data provider, CSP or a noise server as the data provider's private data in transmission process. Thus, the ADV also cannot reveal private data during the noise transmission. Due to the noise addition method, even if the data provider, NSP or CSP discloses the part of the noise that it generates, the data evaluator cannot recover the original data because of the noise addition is performed by CSP and the order after adding will be permutated. It is reasonable to assume that (1) in common schemes, the CSP will not collude with the ADV. (2) in scheme with a NSP, the NSP and CSP will not both disclose their data at the same time and the NSP and CSP will not collude.

References

1. Barak, B., Chaudhuri, K., Dwork, C., Kale, S., Mcsherry, F., Talwar, K.: Privacy, accuracy, and consistency too: a holistic solution to contingency table release, pp. 273–282 (2007)

2. Benjamin, D., Atallah, M.J.: Private and cheating-free outsourcing of algebraic computations, pp. 240–245 (2008)
3. Blum, A., Ligett, K., Roth, A.: A learning theory approach to non-interactive database privacy, pp. 609–618 (2008)
4. Chaum, D., Pedersen, T.P.: Wallet databases with observers. In: Brickell, E.F. (ed.) CRYPTO 1992. LNCS, vol. 740, pp. 89–105. Springer, Heidelberg (1993). https://doi.org/10.1007/3-540-48071-4_7
5. Chen, R., Mohammed, N., Fung, B.C.M., Desai, B.C., Xiong, L.: Publishing set-valued data via differential privacy. Proc. VLDB Endow. **4**, 1087–1098 (2011)
6. Chevallier-Mames, B., Coron, J.-S., McCullagh, N., Naccache, D., Scott, M.: Secure delegation of elliptic-curve pairing. In: Gollmann, D., Lanet, J.-L., Iguchi-Cartigny, J. (eds.) CARDIS 2010. LNCS, vol. 6035, pp. 24–35. Springer, Heidelberg (2010). https://doi.org/10.1007/978-3-642-12510-2_3
7. Cormode, G., Procopiuc, C.M., Srivastava, D., Shen, E., Yu, T.: Differentially private spatial decompositions, pp. 20–31 (2012)
8. Dwork, C., Lei, J.: Differential privacy and robust statistics, pp. 371–380 (2009)
9. Dwork, C., McSherry, F., Nissim, K., Smith, A.: Calibrating noise to sensitivity in private data analysis. In: Halevi, S., Rabin, T. (eds.) TCC 2006. LNCS, vol. 3876, pp. 265–284. Springer, Heidelberg (2006). https://doi.org/10.1007/11681878_14
10. Dwork, C., Naor, M., Reingold, O., Rothblum, G.N., Vadhan, S.: On the complexity of differentially private data release: efficient algorithms and hardness results, pp. 381–390 (2009)
11. Dwork, C., Naor, M., Vadhan, S.: The privacy of the analyst and the power of the state, pp. 400–409 (2012)
12. Dwork, C., Rothblum, G.N., Vadhan, S.: Boosting and differential privacy, pp. 51–60 (2010)
13. Gupta, S.K., Rana, S., Venkatesh, S.: Differentially private multi-task learning. In: Chau, M., Wang, G.A., Chen, H. (eds.) PAISI 2016. LNCS, vol. 9650, pp. 101–113. Springer, Cham (2016). https://doi.org/10.1007/978-3-319-31863-9_8
14. Hardt, M., Rothblum, G.N., Servedio, R.A.: Private data release via learning thresholds, pp. 168–187 (2012)
15. Hay, M., Rastogi, V., Miklau, G., Suciu, D.: Boosting the accuracy of differentially private histograms through consistency. Proc. VLDB Endow. **3**, 1021–1032 (2010)
16. Huang, Z., Liu, S., Mao, X., Chen, K., Li, J.: Insight of the protection for data security under selective opening attacks. Inf. Sci. **412–413**, 223–241 (2017)
17. Jagadish, H.V., Koudas, N., Muthukrishnan, S., Poosala, V., Sevcik, K.C., Suel, T.: Optimal histograms with quality guarantees. Very Large Data Bases, 275–286 (2010)
18. Ji, Z., Jiang, X., Wang, S., Xiong, L., Ohnomachado, L.: Differentially private distributed logistic regression using private and public data. BMC Med. Genomics **7**(1), 1–10 (2014)
19. Kasiviswanathan, S.P., Lee, H.K., Nissim, K., Raskhodnikova, S., Smith, A.: What can we learn privately, pp. 531–540 (2008)
20. Kasiviswanathan, S.P., Rudelson, M., Smith, A., Ullman, J.: The price of privately releasing contingency tables and the spectra of random matrices with correlated rows, pp. 775–784 (2010)
21. Li, C., Hay, M., Rastogi, V., Miklau, G., Mcgregor, A.: Optimizing linear counting queries under differential privacy, pp. 123–134 (2010)
22. Li, P., Li, J., Huang, Z., Gao, C., Chen, W., Chen, K.: Privacy-preserving outsourced classification in cloud computing. Cluster Comput. 1–10 (2017)

23. Li, P., et al.: Multi-key privacy-preserving deep learning in cloud computing. Future Gener. Comput. Syst. **74**, 76–85 (2017)
24. Mcsherry, F.: Privacy integrated queries: an extensible platform for privacy-preserving data analysis. Commun. ACM **53**(9), 89–97 (2010)
25. Mcsherry, F., Talwar, K.: Mechanism design via differential privacy, pp. 94–103 (2007)
26. Mohammed, N., Chen, R., Fung, B.C.M., Yu, P.S.: Differentially private data release for data mining, pp. 493–501 (2011)
27. Pathak, M.A., Rane, S., Raj, B.: Multiparty differential privacy via aggregation of locally trained classifiers, pp. 1876–1884 (2010)
28. Qardaji, W., Yang, W., Li, N.: Differentially private grids for geospatial data, pp. 757–768 (2013)
29. Qardaji, W., Yang, W., Li, N.: Priview: practical differentially private release of marginal contingency tables, pp. 1435–1446 (2014)
30. Shokri, R., Shmatikov, V.: Privacy-preserving deep learning, pp. 1310–1321 (2015)
31. Su, S., Tang, P., Cheng, X., Chen, R., Wu, Z.: Differentially private multi-party high-dimensional data publishing, pp. 205–216 (2016)
32. Vaidya, J., Clifton, C.: Privacy preserving association rule mining in vertically partitioned data, pp. 639–644 (2002)
33. Vaidya, J., Clifton, C.: Privacy-preserving k-means clustering over vertically partitioned data, pp. 206–215 (2003)
34. Wang, B., Li, M., Chow, S.S.M., Li, H.: A tale of two clouds: computing on data encrypted under multiple keys. In: Communications and Network Security, pp. 337–345 (2014)
35. Xiao, X., Wang, G., Gehrke, J.: Differential privacy via wavelet transforms. IEEE Trans. Knowl. Data Eng. **23**(8), 1200–1214 (2011)
36. Xiao, Y., Xiong, L., Yuan, C.: Differentially private data release through multi-dimensional partitioning. In: Jonker, W., Petković, M. (eds.) SDM 2010. LNCS, vol. 6358, pp. 150–168. Springer, Heidelberg (2010). https://doi.org/10.1007/978-3-642-15546-8_11
37. Xu, J., Zhang, Z., Xiao, X., Yang, Y., Yu, G., Winslett, M.: Differentially private histogram publication. Very Large Data Bases **22**(6), 797–822 (2013)
38. Yuan, G., Zhang, Z., Winslett, M., Xiao, X., Yang, Y., Hao, Z.: Low-rank mechanism: optimizing batch queries under differential privacy. Proc. VLDB Endow. **5**(11), 1352–1363 (2012)

Symmetric Searchable Encryption
with Sharing and Unsharing

Sarvar Patel[1][(✉)], Giuseppe Persiano[1,2][(✉)], and Kevin Yeo[1][(✉)]

[1] Google LLC, Mountain View, USA
{sarvar,kwlyeo}@google.com
[2] Università di Salerno, Fisciano, Italy
giuper@gmail.com

Abstract. In this paper, we study Symmetric Searchable Encryption (SSE) in a multi-user setting in which each user dynamically shares its documents with selected other users, allowing sharees also to perform searches. We introduce the concept of a *Symmetric Searchable Encryption with Sharing and Unsharing*, an extension of Multi-Key Searchable Encryption (NSDI '14), that supports dynamic sharing and unsharing of documents amongst users. We also strengthen the security notion by considering a simulation-based notion that does not restrict sharing between honest and compromised users.

We present the notion of *cross-user leakage*, the information leaked about a user's documents and/or queries from the queries of other users, and introduce a novel technique to quantify cross-user leakage. Specifically, we model cross-user leakage by using a graph where nodes correspond to users and the presence of edges between two nodes indicates the existence of cross-user leakage between the two adjacent users. The statistics on the connected components of the cross-user leakage graph provide a quantifiable way to compare the leakage of multi-user schemes which has eluded previous works.

Our main technical contribution is mx-u, an efficient scheme with small cross-user leakage, whose security is based on the decisional Diffie-Hellman assumption. We prove a tight bound on the leakage of mx-u in the presence of an honest-but-curious adversary that colludes with a non-adaptively chosen subset of users. We report on experiments showing that mx-u is efficient and that cross-user leakage grows slowly as queries are performed.

Keywords: Cryptography · Cloud storage · Searchable encryption

1 Introduction

Symmetric Searchable Encryption (SSE), introduced by Song *et al.* [29], has been the object of intensive research in the last several years. The original scenario consists of a certain number of CorpusOwners, each with a distinct *corpus*

The full version of this paper can be found at [26].

© Springer Nature Switzerland AG 2018
J. Lopez et al. (Eds.): ESORICS 2018, LNCS 11099, pp. 207–227, 2018.
https://doi.org/10.1007/978-3-319-98989-1_11

$\mathcal{D}$ of documents. Each CorpusOwner wishes to store his own $\mathcal{D}$ on the Server in encrypted form and be able to subsequently provide the Server with appropriate search tokens to select the ids of (or pointers to) the documents that contain given keywords. In this context, the honest-but-curious Server tries to learn information about the corpus and queries.

Document sharing rises naturally in large organizations where different subsets of members of the organization collaborate on different documents at any give time and, in real-world scenarios, the ability to revoke access is crucial. For example, in organizations with many employees, it is impossible to assume that employees do not shift to different roles, teams and/or projects. As a member changes their responsibilities, organizations would like to revoke that member's access to documents which are no longer relevant as a way to reduce insider risk. Therefore, efficient and secure revocation is an integral functionality to many multiple user settings for searchable encryption.

In this paper, we introduce *Symmetric Searchable Encryption with Sharing and Unsharing* (SSEwSU), an extension of multi-key searchable encryption introduced by Popa and Zeldovich [27], where access is *dynamic* in the sense that a document *shared* with a user can be, subsequently, *unshared* from the same user. For our security notion, we adapt the simulator paradigm used by most previous works. In particular, we prove that a scheme leaks at most some leakage function, $\mathcal{L}$, by showing the existence of a probabilistically polynomial time (PPT) simulator that can compute a view for the adversary that is indistinguishable from the real view of the adversary. In the case of the single-key/single-user schemes, the adversary is the Server. To adapt to our multi-key/multi-user setting, the adversary is assumed to be the Server colluding with a subset of compromised users.

As we have noted above, the simulation-based security proof indicates that the adversary may learn at most $\mathcal{L}$ information about the documents stored in the scheme as well as the queries performed by the users. However, $\mathcal{L}$ is defined as a description of information instead of a quantifiable value. As a result, it is very difficult to compare the leakage profiles of different schemes. Furthermore, the damage that could be inflicted by an adversary that learns such a leakage profile of the documents and queries is not clear.

In this paper, we quantify the phenomenon, that we call *cross-user leakage*, consisting in information about one user's documents and/or queries being learned by the adversary as the result of the actions by another user. Intuitively, a searchable encryption scheme with good security should guarantee that the actions of a single user do not leak too much information about too many other users. We introduce the concept of a *cross-user leakage graph* to have a quantitative measure of the cross-user leakage. Specifically, each node of the cross-user leakage graph is associated with a user and an edge between two nodes indicates the presence of cross-user leakage between the two adjacent users. Immediately after a system has been initialized and no user has performed any action, the cross-user leakage graph has no edges. As actions are performed, edges are added as cross-user leakage appears. Therefore, the cross-user leakage graph describes the growth of leakage as more actions are performed. A connected component is a maximal subgraph such that all pairs of nodes are connected, and we use statistics on the connected components of the cross-user leakage, such as the number of connected components and means and variances on the sizes of all the connected components, as approximations of the total cross-user leakage learned by the adversary. Our description will be pessimistic and assume that cross-user leakage is transitive. That is, if two users belong to the same connected component, then we will assume that cross-user leakage has occurred between the two users even if there is not an edge between the two users.

Our main contribution is mx-u, a searchable encryption scheme with sharing and unsharing. We formally identify the leakage of our construction and show that is an upper bound on the actual leakage by constructing a simulator that simulates the view of the adversarial coalition on input the leakage. Furthermore, we show experimentally by means of the cross-user leakage graph that the growth of cross-user leakage in mx-u is significantly slower than other known schemes with similar efficiency.

Related Work. The notion of *Symmetric Searchable Encryption* was introduced by Song *et al.* [29] and continues to be an active research area. Boneh *et al.* [3] were the first to consider the asymmetric case. The original scenario consists of the CorpusOwner and the Server. In our terminology, the CorpusOwner outsources the storage of an encrypted version of his data on the Server while being able to delegate searches to the Server while protecting the privacy of the data and queries. This basic setting was extended by Curtmola *et al.* [9], which considered the extension of multiple users authorized by the CorpusOwner. The same setting is considered by several subsequent papers such as [8,12,16,19,24,30]. The work by Cash *et al.* [6] was the first to obtain sub-linear search times for conjunctive keyword searches. The recent work of Kamara and Moataz [17] present a scheme that may handle keyword searches for all Boolean formulae in sub-linear time. The work of Cash *et al.* [5] show that a bottleneck in searchable encryption schemes is the lack of locality of server accesses that incur a large number of cache misses and, subsequently, retrievals from secondary storage. Subsequent works [1,2,7,10,11] address the tradeoffs of locality and the time required for searching. Kamara *et al.* [18] consider the tradeoffs of using Oblivious RAM to further suppress the leakage profiles and the increased efficiency costs. In another line of work, several papers have investigated the amount of information that can be extracted from various leakage profiles [4,14,20,22,28,32,33].

In the work described in the previous paragraph, "multiple users" means users (other than the CorpusOwner) can perform searches using tokens provided by the CorpusOwner. However, all users have access to the same set of documents and all users are, typically, considered to be honest. We are interested in allowing different users access to different and dynamically changing subsets of documents as well as protecting against insider threats (adversarial users colluding with the Server). The concept of Multi-key Searchable Encryption, introduced by Popa and Zeldovich [27], is very close in spirit to our work. However, Grubbs *et al.* [14] point out that the security notion considered by Popa and Zeldovich [27] is insufficient in real settings. In addition, the construction proposed in [27] did not support unsharing documents (that is, revocation of sharing) as opposed to ours that allows for efficient sharing and unsharing. A more efficient scheme was presented by Kiayias *et al.* [21] but it suffers from the same security problems of the construction of [27].

In a parallel and independent work to ours, Hamlin *et al.* [15] present two multi-key searchable encryption schemes that consider a stronger security notion similar to ours. Their first construction is based on the existence of PRFs and uses constant-size query tokens. We note that our construction, mx-u, requires query tokens that are linear in the number of the documents accessible to the querying user. On the other hand, the first construction of [15], essentially, duplicates a document for each user granted access while mx-u maintains a single copy of each document for all users and is, thus, more storage efficient. The second construction by Hamlin *et al.* [15] uses software obfuscation to reduce server storage and cannot be considered practical.

2   Key Ideas

We introduce some basic notation that will be used throughout the paper. A document is a tuple $(d, \mathsf{Kw}(d), \mathtt{meta}_d)$ consisting of an id d, a list $\mathsf{Kw}(d)$ of keywords taken from the universe $\mathcal{W}$ of keywords (e.g., English dictionary) and some metadata $\mathtt{meta}_d$ (e.g., title, snippet, creation time). We denote the subset of documents that are accessible to user $u \in \mathcal{U}$ by $\mathsf{Access}(u)$. Similarly, we denote the subset of users with access to document d by $\mathsf{AccList}(d)$. The set $\mathsf{Access}(u)$ of documents shared with user u varies over time as documents can be added/removed. A search for keyword w performed by u returns all pairs $(d, \mathtt{meta}_d)$ such that $w \in \mathsf{Kw}(d)$ and d is in $\mathsf{Access}(u)$ at the time the search is performed. Typically, the user looks at the metadata of the documents returned by the search to determine which document to fully download. A user u should be able to perform queries only on documents in $\mathsf{Access}(u)$ without further intervention of the CorpusOwner. Moreover, sharing and unsharing of documents should be efficient and require only the CorpusOwner and the Server to be active.

We start by describing two constructions, zx-u and lx-u, that are direct extensions of single-user SSE schemes into SSEwSU schemes. zx-u has no cross-user leakage but is extremely inefficient. In contrast, lx-u has very large cross-user leakage but is very efficient.

An Inefficient Construction with no Cross-User Leakage. The first construction we consider, zx-u (for *zero cross-user leakage*), consists in having an independent instance of a single-user SSE supporting addition/deletion of documents for each user. When a document d is shared with user u, d is added to u's instance of the single-user SSE. Similarly, when d is unshared with user u, d is removed from u's instance. zx-u has no cross-user leakage since each user's queries are performed on their independent single-user SSE instance. This construction requires space proportional to $\sum_{u \in \mathcal{U}} \sum_{d \in \mathsf{Access}(u)} |\mathsf{Kw}(d)| = O(|\mathcal{U}| \cdot |\mathcal{D}| \cdot |\mathcal{W}|)$ which is very inefficient.

An Efficient Construction with Large Cross-User Leakage. Following a dual app-roach, lx-u (for *large cross-user leakage*) consists of an independent SSE instance for each document d. We refer to K_d as the private key associated to the SSE instance for document d. K_d is given to all users u with access to d. To search, user u sends the Server a search token for each document $d \in$ Access(u). The per document partition is to ensure proper user access control. The Server stores a list of users with access to each document d in AccList(d). Therefore, mx-u only requires $O(|\mathcal{D}| \cdot |\mathcal{W}| + |\mathcal{D}| \cdot |\mathcal{U}|)$ space.

We show lx-u has large cross-user leakage that increases as queries are being performed. Suppose user u_1 performs a query for keyword w_1 by sending search tokens for each document in Access(u_1). The search tokens sent for a document d are generated by an algorithm using K_d. Any other user $u_2 \neq u_1$ with access to d, $d \in Access(u_2)$, would generate search tokens in an identical manner using the same algorithm and K_d. So, the Server can use these search tokens for all users in AccList(d). The Server infers information for every user $u_2 \neq u_1$ such that $d \in$ Access(u_1)$\cap$Access(u_2). In other words, each query extends the leakage to all users including users that never performed any query. Subsequently, suppose user u_2 searches for w_2. For all documents accessible by both u_1 and u_2 (Access(u_1)$\cap$ Access(u_2)), the Server knows exactly whether each of the documents contain w_1, w_2, both and neither.

Where Does the Problem Come From? The cross-user leakage of lx-u is caused by two factors. First, lx-u is partitioned by documents to allow the Server to enforce access control for each document. Secondly, queries by two different users coincide over documents accessible by both users. We see two contrasting needs fighting here: storing keyword occurrences in documents in a user-independent fashion for efficiency forces the queries of different users over the same document to be identical. In other words, when one user queries, it does so on behalf of all the other users.

To overcome this apparent stalemate, we introduce an intermediate level in which the user-dependent queries are translated to user-independent queries that can be matched with encryptions of keyword-document pairs to perform a search. The intermediate level will be implemented by means of tokens that depend on the user and the document and a token will only be provided by CorpusOwner if the user has access to the document. The introduction of the extra level requires space $O(|\mathcal{D}| \cdot |\mathcal{U}|)$, which is proportional to the size of the original access lists. These ideas lead us to our main contributions.

Our Efficient Construction with Minimal Cross-User Leakage. Our main con-tribution, mx-u, is a construction that has minimal cross-user leakage and can be intuitively described in terms of an abstract primitive that we call *Rewritable Deterministic Hashing* (RDH). RDH is an enhancement of a two-argument hash function H. With slight abuse of terminology, we will denote a *ciphertext* as the value obtained by evaluating H on two arguments, which we refer to as the *plain-texts*. For any two plaintexts A and B, it is possible to construct a *token* $\text{tok}_{A \to B}$ that, when applied to a ciphertext of A, returns a new ciphertext in which A is replaced with B and the other plaintext stays unchanged. Using this abstraction, mx-u can be roughly described as follows. A more formal and precise description that follows this informal blueprint based on RDH is presented in Sect. 4.

During the initialization phase, the CorpusOwner computes $H(w, d)$ for every (w, d) such that $w \in Kw(d)$. We stress that this is done exactly once, independently of the number of users that can access d. In addition, the CorpusOwner produces *authorization* token $tok_{u \to d}$ for every $d \in Access(u)$. All the ciperthexts and the tokens are given to the Server. A user u that wishes to perform a query for keyword w computes the *query* ciphertext $H(u, w)$ and sends it to the server. If u has access to d, the Server has received $tok_{u \to d}$ from the CorpusOwner and the application of $tok_{u \to d}$ to the query ciphertext $H(u, w)$ produces $H(w, d)$ that, if document d contains keyword w, has been given to the Server by the CorpusOwner during the initialization. A more precise description of mx-u can be found in Sect. 4.

The CorpusOwner produces $\sum_d |Kw(d)|$ ciphertexts and $\sum_u |Access(u)|$ tokens. All computed tokens and ciphertexts are stored on the Server for a total space of $O(|\mathcal{D}| \cdot |\mathcal{W}| + |\mathcal{D}| \cdot |\mathcal{U}|)$. This matches the efficiency of lx-u. The rewriting capability of RDH makes it unnecessary to duplicate the pair (w, d) for each user that has access to document d like zx-u. So, mx-u has greatly improved efficiency compared to zx-u. Unlike lx-u, mx-u achieves efficiency with only minimal cross-user leakage. We show that mx-u has cross-user leakage only when two distinct users $u_1 \neq u_2$ who share at least one common document $(Access(u_1) \cap Access(u_2) \neq \emptyset)$ query for the *same* keyword. A formal analysis of mx-u's leakage can be found in Sect. 4.1. In addition to searching, mx-u supports sharing and unsharing of documents very efficiently. Sharing (unsharing) a document d with user u simply adds (removes) the authorization token $tok_{u \to d}$ from storage on the Server. So, sharing and unsharing can be performed in constant time.

We perform extensive experimentation on mx-u and shows that it is practical. We also experimentally show that the cross-user leakage for mx-u accumulates significantly slower compared to lx-u using real world data. Our experiments in Sect. 5 show that mx-u hits the middle ground between the two extremes by providing the same efficiency as lx-u with minimal cross-user leakage like zx-u.

3   Symmetric Searchable Encryption with Sharing and Unsharing

We formally define the concept of a *Symmetric Searchable Encryption with Sharing and Unsharing* (SSEwSU). We provide definitions and algorithms for the case of one CorpusOwner. The extensions to a more complex setting in which several CorpusOwners share documents to a set of users is obtained by considering an independent system for each CorpusOwner. A SSEwSU is a collection of six algorithms: EncryptDoc, Enroll, SearchQuery, SearchReply, AccessGranting, AccessRevoking for three types of players: one CorpusOwner, one Server and several users. The algorithms interact in the following way.

1. CorpusOwner has corpus $\mathcal{D}$ consisting of triplets $(d, \mathsf{Kw}(d), \mathtt{meta}_d)$ of document id d, the set of keywords $\mathsf{Kw}(d)$ in document d, and document metadata $\mathtt{meta}_d$. CorpusOwner computes an encrypted version xSet of $\mathcal{D}$ and a master key K by running algorithm EncryptDoc$(\mathcal{D})$. CorpusOwner sends xSet to Server and keeps K in private memory. CorpusOwner instructs Server to initialize uSet to be empty. Both xSet and uSet are kept private by Server.
2. CorpusOwner executes Enroll to add a new user u to the system. Keys $\mathcal{K}_u$ for u are returned by the algorithm. CorpusOwner stores the pair $(u, \mathcal{K}_u)$ in private memory and sends $\mathcal{K}_u$ to u. When a user is enrolled, they do not have any access rights, that is Access$(u) = \emptyset$.
3. To share document d with user u (that is, Access$(u) :=$ Access$(u) \cup \{d\}$), CorpusOwner executes AccessGranting on input the pair $(u, \mathcal{K}_u)$, document id d and master key K. AccessGranting outputs *authorization token* $U_{u,d}$ for u and d and keys $\mathcal{K}_d$ for document d. $U_{u,d}$ is given to Server for inclusion to uSet and $\mathcal{K}_d$ is given to user u. AccessRevoking is used in a similar way by CorpusOwner to revoke user u's access to document d. Instead, $U_{u,d}$ is given to Server to remove from uSet.
4. To search for all documents d in Access(u) that contain keyword w, user u executes SearchQuery on input w, $\mathcal{K}_u$ and $\{(d, \mathcal{K}_d)\}_{d \in \text{Access}(u)}$ to construct the *query* qSet that is passed onto Server.
5. On input qSet, Server runs SearchReply using xSet and uSet to compute Result, which is returned to u. Using the correct keys, u decrypts Result and obtains the ids and metadata of documents in Access(u) which contain w.

We denote the set of users with access to document d by AccList(d). So, $d \in$ Access(u) if and only if $u \in$ AccList(d). With slight abuse of notation, for a subset $\mathcal{C}$ of users, Access$(\mathcal{C})$ is the union of Access(u) for $u \in \mathcal{C}$.

Our definition is tailored for a static corpus of documents (no document is added and/or edited). This is reflected by the fact that CorpusOwner computes the encrypted version of the corpus by using EncryptDoc at the start. Note that, even though the corpus of documents is static, each document can be dynamically shared and unshared.

Security Notion for SSEwSU. We give our security definition for SSEwSU by following the real vs. simulated game approach. In our trust model, we assume the CorpusOwner to be honest. If this is not the case, since CorpusOwner has access to its whole corpus $\mathcal{D}$, then there is nothing to be protected from compromised users. We assume the Server is honest-but-curious and computes query results as prescribed by SearchReply, stores xSet as received from the CorpusOwner, and updates uSet as instructed by the CorpusOwner. In traditional SSE schemes, the Server is assumed to be curious with access to all observed ciphertexts (in this case, the xSet, the uSet and all queries). In the multi-user setting of SSEwSU, we have to consider that the Server might be colluding with a set of active, compromised users, $\mathcal{C}$. The Server gains access to all private keys of every compromised user in $\mathcal{C}$.

In the real game with a set of users $\mathcal{U}$, we consider the *server view*, sView$^{\mathcal{U},\mathcal{C}}$ where the Server colludes with the non-adaptively chosen subset $\mathcal{C} \subseteq \mathcal{U}$ of users gaining access to all user keys of compromised users, $\{K_u\}_{u \in C}$, and all document keys where the document is accessible by any compromised user, $\{\mathcal{K}_d\}_{d \in \mathsf{Access}(C)}$.

We assume no revocation (unsharing) is made as a curious Server may keep all authorization tokens $U_{u,d}$ provided. All queries are assumed to be performed after all sharing operations as a curious server can always postpone or duplicate the execution of a query. The view is relative to a snapshot of the system (that is xSet and uSet) resulting from a sequence of sharing operations by CorpusOwner whose cumulative effect is encoded in $\mathsf{Access}(u)$ for all $u \in \mathcal{U}$. We define an *instance* of SSEwSU, $\mathcal{I} = \{\mathcal{D}, \{d, \mathsf{Kw}(d), \mathsf{meta}_d\}_{d \in \mathcal{D}}, \{\mathsf{Access}(u)\}_{u \in \mathcal{U}}, \{(u_i, w_i)\}_{i \in [q]}\}$, consisting of: a set of documents $\{d, \mathsf{Kw}(d), \mathsf{meta}_d\}_{d \in \mathcal{D}}$, a collection $\{\mathsf{Access}(u)\}_{u \in \mathcal{U}}$ of subsets of document ids, the set of search queries $Q_i = (u_i, w_i)$, for $i \in [q]$, and the i-th query is performed by user u_i for keyword w_i. We define the view with respect to security parameter λ of the Server colluding with the set, C, of compromised users on instance $\mathcal{I}$ of SSEwSU, as the output of the Real experiment $\mathsf{sView}^{\mathcal{U},C}(\lambda, \mathcal{I})$.

$\mathsf{sView}^{\mathcal{U},C}(\lambda, \mathcal{I})$

1. Set $(\mathsf{xSet}, \mathcal{K}) \leftarrow \mathsf{EncryptDoc}(1^\lambda, \mathcal{D}, \{d, \mathsf{Kw}(d), \mathsf{meta}_d\}_{d \in \mathcal{D}})$;
2. Set $\{K_u\}_{u \in \mathcal{U}} \leftarrow \mathsf{Enroll}(1^\lambda, \mathcal{U})$;
3. Set $(\mathsf{uSet}, \{\{\mathcal{K}_d\}_{d \in \mathsf{Access}(u)}\}_{u \in \mathcal{U}}) \leftarrow \mathsf{AccessGranting}(\{K_u\}_{u \in \mathcal{U}}, \{\mathsf{Access}(u)\}_{u \in \mathcal{U}}, \mathcal{K})$;
4. For each $i \in [q]$
   $\mathsf{qSet}_i \leftarrow \mathsf{SearchQuery}(w_i, K_{u_i}, \{(d, K_d, K_d^{\mathsf{enc}})\}_{d \in \mathsf{Access}(u_i)})$;
   $\mathsf{Result}_i \leftarrow \mathsf{SearchReply}(\mathsf{qSet}_i)$;
5. Output $(K_u, \mathcal{K}_u)_{u \in C}, \mathsf{xSet}, \mathsf{uSet}, (\mathsf{qSet}_i, \mathsf{Result}_i,)_{i \in [q]}$;

We slightly abuse notation by passing a set of values as a parameter to an algorithm instead of a single value. By this, we mean that the algorithm is invoked on each value of the set received and that outputs are collected and returned as a set. For example, "$\mathsf{Enroll}(1^\lambda, \mathcal{U})$" denotes the sequential invocation of algorithm Enroll on input $(1^\lambda, u)$ for all $u \in \mathcal{U}$.

We now present a formal definition of our security notion.

Definition 1. *We say that a SSEwSU is secure with respect to leakage $\mathcal{L}$ if there exists an efficient simulator $\mathcal{S}$ such that for every coalition C and every instance $\mathcal{I}$*

$$\{\mathsf{sView}^{\mathcal{U},C}(\lambda, \mathcal{I})\} \approx_c \{\mathcal{S}(1^\lambda, \mathcal{L}(\mathcal{I}, C))\}.$$

4   SSEwSU Based on Decisional Diffie-Hellman

In this section, we describe mx-u, a concrete construction of SSEwSU based on decisional Diffie-Hellman (DDH) that follows the blueprint based on the concept of a *Rewritable Deterministic Hashing* (RDH) (see Sect. 2 for an informal description). We perform an experimental evaluation of mx-u to evaluate both the leakage and performance in Sect. 5.

We start by describing a simple version that does not offer adequate security. Assume that all document ids (d), user ids (u), and keywords (w) are mapped to group elements. The occurrence of $w \in \mathsf{Kw}(d)$ is encoded by CorpusOwner by computing the x-pair, consisting of the product $w \cdot d$ and of an encryption of meta_d. All x-pairs are given to the Server. The fact that $u \in \mathsf{AccList}(d)$ is encoded by computing *authorization token* d/u and giving it to the Server. The set of all x-pairs and authorization tokens produced by CorpusOwner are called the xSet and uSet respectively. To search for a keyword w in $\mathsf{Access}(u)$, user u produces the *query* consisting of $u \cdot w$. The Server multiplies the query by the corresponding authorization token. If the result appears as a first component of an x-pair, the second component is returned to the user to decrypt. Correctness is obvious but very weak security is offered. Suppose that two users u_1 and u_2 query for the same keyword w thus producing $\mathsf{qct}_1 = u_1 \cdot w$ and $\mathsf{qct}_2 = u_2 \cdot w$. Then the ratio $\mathsf{qct}_1/\mathsf{qct}_2$ can be used to turn an authorization token for u_1 to access document d into an authorization token for user u_2 for the same document. Indeed $d/u_1 \cdot \mathsf{qct}_1/\mathsf{qct}_2 = d/u_2$, so the Server can extend u_2's ability to perform queries to all documents in $\mathsf{Access}(u_1) \cup \mathsf{Access}(u_2)$.

So, we move to a group where DDH is conjectured to hold. Consider x-pairs consisting of an x-*ciphertext* computed as $g^{w \cdot d}$ along with a y-ciphertext that is an encryption of meta_d. Authorization tokens are computed in the same way as before, that is, d/u. A *query* is computed as $g^{u \cdot w}$ as well as pointers to relevant authorization tokens. In performing the search, the Server uses the authorization tokens as an exponent for the query ciphertext (that is, $g^{u \cdot w}$ is raised to the power d/u). The value obtained is looked up as the first component of an x-ciphertext. If found, the associated y-ciphertext is returned. Using the exponentiation one-way function in a group in which DDH is conjectured to hold does not suffice as the set of documents and keywords might be small enough for the Server to conduct dictionary attacks. Instead, we replace document ids, user ids and keywords with their evaluations of pseudorandom functions under the appropriate document and user keys. Document keys are distributed depending on whether a document is shared with a user while each user only has their own user key. The main technical difficulty is to prove that DDH and pseudorandomness are sufficient to limit the leakage obtained by Server that has corrupted a subset of users. This means Server has gained access to the xSet, uSet and all keys from compromised users. Server also knows the patterns of accessing the xSet and uSet when users are performing search queries.

We now formally present the algorithms of mx-u. Both AccessGranting and AccessRevoking will be implemented using a single algorithm AuthComputing. For user u, on input of user keys $K_u, \tilde{K}_u$, document id d, and master keys K_1, K_2, K_3 returns authorization token $U_{u,d}$ allowing u to access document d, pointer (identifier) to the authorization token $\mathsf{uid}_{u,d}$ and the set of keys $\mathcal{K}_d$ for document d. Algorithm AccessGranting is executed by CorpusOwner to grant user u access to document d. It consists in running AuthComputing to obtain $\mathcal{K}_d$, that is sent to user u, and the pair $(\mathsf{uid}_{u,d}, U_{u,d})$ that are sent to the Server for insertion of $U_{u,d}$ at $\mathsf{uSet}[\mathsf{uid}_{u,d}]$. Algorithm AccessRevoking runs AuthComputing and sends $\mathsf{uid}_{u,d}$ to the Server for deletion of $\mathsf{uSet}[\mathsf{uid}_{u,d}]$. Once $U_{u,d}$ has been removed from uSet, user u can still produce a query ciphertext qct_d for document d in the context of searching for keyword w but the Server will not contribute the y-ciphertext to Result even if $w \in \mathsf{Kw}(d)$.

EncryptDoc($1^\lambda, \mathcal{D}$)

Executed by CorpusOwner to encrypt the corpus $\mathcal{D}$.

1. Randomly select $(g, \mathcal{G}) \leftarrow \mathcal{GG}(1^\lambda)$ and initialize $\mathsf{xSet} \leftarrow \emptyset$;
2. Randomly select three master keys $K_1, K_2, K_3 \leftarrow \{0,1\}^\lambda$;
3. For every document d:
   - Set $K_d \leftarrow \mathsf{F}(K_1, d)$;
   - Set $\widetilde{K}_d \leftarrow \mathsf{F}(K_2, d)$;
   - Set $K_d^{\mathrm{enc}} \leftarrow \mathsf{G}(K_3, d)$;
4. For every document d with metadata $\mathtt{meta}_d$ and keyword $w \in \mathsf{Kw}(d)$:
   - Set $X_{w,d} \leftarrow g^{\mathsf{F}(\widetilde{K}_d, d) \cdot \mathsf{F}(K_d, w))}$;
   - Set $Y_{w,d} \leftarrow \mathsf{Enc}(K_d^{\mathrm{enc}}, \mathtt{meta}_d)$;
5. All pairs $(X_{w,d}, Y_{w,d})$ are added in random order to the array xSet;
6. Return $(\mathsf{xSet}, K_1, K_2, K_3)$;

Enroll($1^\lambda, u$)

Executed by CorpusOwner to enroll user u.

1. Randomly select $K_u, \widetilde{K}_u \leftarrow \{0,1\}^\lambda$;
2. Return $(K_u, \widetilde{K}_u)$;

AuthComputing$((u, K_u, \widetilde{K}_u), d, (K_1, K_2, K_3))$

Executed by CorpusOwner to either share or unshare document d with user u.

1. Compute keys $K_d \leftarrow \mathsf{F}(K_1, d)$, $\widetilde{K}_d \leftarrow \mathsf{F}(K_2, d)$, and $K_d^{\mathrm{enc}} \leftarrow \mathsf{G}(K_3, d)$;
2. Set $U_{u,d} \leftarrow \mathsf{F}(\widetilde{K}_d, d)/\mathsf{F}(K_u, d)$;
3. Set $\mathsf{uid}_{u,d} \leftarrow \mathsf{F}(\widetilde{K}_u, d)$;
4. Set $\mathcal{K}_d \leftarrow (d, K_d, K_d^{\mathrm{enc}})$;
5. Return $(\mathsf{uid}_{u,d}, U_{u,d}, \mathcal{K}_d)$;

SearchQuery$(w, (u, K_u, \widetilde{K}_u),$ $\{(d, K_d, K_d^{\mathrm{enc}})\}_{d \in \mathsf{Access}(u)})$

Executed by user u to search for documents with keyword w.

1. For each $(d, K_d, K_d^{\mathrm{enc}})$,
   - Set $\mathsf{uid}_{u,d} \leftarrow \mathsf{F}(\widetilde{K}_u, d)$;
   - Set $\mathsf{qct}_d \leftarrow g^{\mathsf{F}(K_d, w) \cdot \mathsf{F}(K_u, d)}$;
2. All pairs $(\mathsf{uid}_{u,d}, \mathsf{qct}_d)$ are added in random order to the array qSet;
3. Return qSet;

SearchReply(qSet)

Server replying to u's search query consisting of s query ciphertexts.

1. Set $\mathsf{Result} \leftarrow \emptyset$;
2. For each $(\mathsf{uid}_{u,d}, \mathsf{qct}_d) \in \mathsf{qSet}$:
   - Set $\mathsf{ct} \leftarrow \mathsf{qct}_d^{\mathsf{uSet}[\mathsf{uid}_{u,d}]}$;
   - If $(\mathsf{ct}, Y) \in \mathsf{xSet}$, then $\mathsf{Result} \leftarrow \mathsf{Result} \cup \{Y\}$;
3. Return Result;

4.1   The Leakage Function $\mathcal{L}$

In this section, we formally define the leakage $\mathcal{L}(\mathcal{I}, \mathcal{C})$ that Server obtains about instance $\mathcal{I}$ from the view $\mathsf{sView}^{\mathcal{U}, \mathcal{C}}(\lambda, \mathcal{I})$ when corrupting users in $\mathcal{C}$. In the security proof (see the full version [26]), we will show that nothing more than $\mathcal{L}$ is leaked by our construction by giving a simulator that, on input $\mathcal{L}$, simulates the entire view.

A Warm-up Case. We start by informally describing the leakage obtained by Server when no user is compromised ($\mathcal{C} = \emptyset$). Looking ahead, the leakage for $\mathcal{C} = \emptyset$ corresponds to items 0 and 7 in the general case when $\mathcal{C} \neq \emptyset$.

If $\mathcal{C} = \emptyset$, the Server observes xSet, uSet, the query ciphertexts and their interaction with xSet and uSet, including whether each query ciphertext is successful. The size $n := |\mathsf{xSet}|$ leaks the number of pairs (d, w) such that $w \in \mathsf{Kw}(d)$ and the size $m := |\mathsf{uSet}|$ leaks the number of pairs (u, d) such that $d \in \mathsf{Access}(u)$. Note, the xSet by itself does not leak any information about the number of keywords in a document or the number of documents containing a certain keyword (we will see, under the DDH, it is indistinguishable from a set of random group elements). The length of each query ciphertext leaks the number of documents the querier has access to. Note that leakage of (an upper bound on) the size of data is unavoidable.

The interaction of the query ciphertexts with xSet and uSet also leak some information. We set q to be the number of queries, and denote $l := \sum_{i \in [q]} n_{q_i}$ where $l_{q_i} := |\text{qSet}_i|$. A query ciphertext is uniquely identified by the triple (u, w, d) of the user u, the searched keyword w, and the document d for which the query ciphertext is searching.

Roughly speaking, we show that in mx-u, the Server only learns whether two query ciphertexts share two of three components. We assume that no user searches for the same keyword twice and so no two query ciphertexts share all three components. We remind the reader that in lx-u, the Server would learn whether two queries are relative to the same document and this allowed the propagation of cross-user leakage. In contrast, two query ciphertexts of two different users would only leak if they were for the same document and the same keyword in mx-u. In other words, the only way to have cross-user leakage is two users with at least a common document must perform a query for the same keyword.

A useful way to visualize the growth of cross-user leakage is a graph G in which the users are vertices and a query of a user u_1 leaks about the documents of user u_2 if and only if u_1 and u_2 are in the same connected component. The larger the connected components in the graph, the more cross-user leakage each query entails. For both constructions, the graph starts with no edges and edges are added as queries are performed. In lx-u, for every query of user u_1 for keyword w, an edge is added to all vertices of users u_2 that have at least one document in common with u_1, independently of w. In mx-u, an edge is added to all vertices of users u_2 that have at least document in common with u_1 *and* have performed a query for keyword w. Thus, cross-user leakage accumulates for every query in lx-u whereas in mx-u cross-user leakage grows slower and only accumulates across users for queries for repeated keywords.

Let us now explain where the leakage comes from. Consider two query ciphertexts, $(\text{uid}_1, \text{qct}_1)$ and $(\text{uid}_2, \text{qct}_2)$, identified by (u_1, w_1, d_1) and (u_2, w_2, d_2), respectively. Start by observing that if $u_1 = u_2 = u$ and $w_1 = w_2 = w$, then $(\text{uid}_1, \text{qct}_1)$ and $(\text{uid}_2, \text{qct}_2)$ are part of the same query qSet issued by user u for keyword w. Thus, they can be easily identified as such by the Server. Next, consider the case in which $(\text{uid}_1, \text{qct}_1)$ and $(\text{uid}_2, \text{qct}_2)$ are queries from the same user and relative to the same document. That is, $u_1 = u_2 = u$ and $d_1 = d_2 = d$ but $w_1 \neq w_2$. This can be easily identified by the Server since $\text{uid}_1 = \text{uid}_2$. Note the leakage described so far is relative to queries from the same user. Suppose now that $(\text{uid}_1, \text{qct}_1)$ and $(\text{uid}_2, \text{qct}_2)$ are for the same document and the same keyword. That is, $w_1 = w_2 = w$ and $d_1 = d_2 = d$ but $u_1 \neq u_2$. In this case, when qct_1 and qct_2 are coupled with $U_{u_1,d}$ and $U_{u_2,d}$, respectively, they produce the same test value for the xSet (that belongs to the xSet if and only if $w \in \text{Kw}(d)$).

By summarizing, the leakage provides three different equivalence relations, denoted $\approx_d, \approx_w, \approx_u$, over the set $[l]$ of the query ciphertexts defined as follows. Denote by (u_i, w_i, d_i) the components of the generic i-th query:

1. $i \approx_d j$ iff $u_i = u_j$ and $w_i = w_j$; that is the i-th and the j-th query ciphertext only differ with respect to the document; we have q equivalence classes corresponding to the q queries performed by the users;
2. $i \approx_w j$ iff $u_i = u_j = u$ and $d_i = d_j = d$; that is the i-th and the j-th query ciphertext only differ with respect to the keyword. We denote by r the number of the associated equivalence classes $D_1, \ldots, D_r$. Equivalence class D_i can be seen of consisting of pairs of the index of a query ciphertext and the index of an x-ciphertext.
3. $i \approx_u j$ iff $w_i = w_j$ and $d_i = d_j$; that is the i-th and the j-th query ciphertext only differ with respect to the user; we denote by t the number of the associated equivalence classes $E_1, \ldots, E_t$. Equivalence class E_i can be seen of consisting of pairs of the index of a query ciphertext and a token.

Note that the equivalence classes of $\approx_w$ can be deduced from those of $\approx_u$ but we keep the two notions distinct for clarity.

The General Case. We now consider the case where the adversarial Server corrupts a subset $\mathcal{C} \neq \emptyset$ of users. As we shall see, in this case, all information about documents shared to users in $\mathcal{C}$ are leaked to the Server. For documents instead that are not accessible by users in $\mathcal{C}$, we fall back to the case of no corruption and the leakage is the same as described above.

In determining the leakage of our construction, we make the natural assumption that a user u knows all the keywords appearing in all documents $d \in$ Access(u). This is justified by the fact that keywords are taken from a potentially small space and that u could search for all possible keywords in the document d (or u could just download d). If u is corrupted by the Server, then we observe that the Server is able to identify the entry of the xSet relative to (w, d) and the entry of uSet relative to (u, d) (this can be done by constructing an appropriate query ciphertext using the keys in u's possession). From these two entries, and by using the keys $K_u, \widetilde{K}_u, K_d$ and $\widetilde{K}_d$ in u's possession, $\mathsf{F}(\widetilde{K}_d, d)$, $\mathsf{F}(K_d, w), \mathsf{F}(\widetilde{K}_u, d)$ and $\mathsf{F}(K_u, d)$ can be easily derived. Moreover, we assume that the set AccList(d) of users with which d is shared is available to u. In this case, we make the assumption that for all $v \in$ AccList(d), Server can identify the entry of uSet corresponding to $U_{v,d}$ from which the two pseudo-random values contributing to token $U_{v,d}$ can be derived. In general, we make the *conservative assumption* that knowledge of $\mathsf{F}(k, x)$ (or of any expression involving $\mathsf{F}(k, x)$) and k allows the adversarial Server to learn x by means of a dictionary attack. In our construction, the argument x of a PRF is either a keyword or a document id. In both cases, they come from a small space where dictionary attacks are feasible. We stress that these assumptions are not used in our construction (for example, honest parties are never required to perform exhaustive evaluations) but they make the adversary stronger thus yielding a stronger security guarantee. If this assumption is unsupported in a specific scenario, our security guarantees still hold and stronger guarantees can be obtained for the same scenario. We remind the reader that the view of Server when corrupting users in $\mathcal{C}$ for instance $\mathcal{I}$, includes $(K_u, \widetilde{K}_u, D_u)_{u \in \mathcal{C}}$, where D_u is $\{d, K_d, K_d^{\mathsf{Enc}}\}_{d \in \mathsf{Access}(u)}$. Additional the view contains xSet, uSet and the set $(\mathsf{qSet}_i, \mathsf{Result}_i)_{i \in [q]}$ of query ciphertexts and the results for each query. Without loss of generality, we assume that no two queries are identical (that is, from the same user and for the same keyword). First, Server learns from the view n, the number of x-ciphertexts (and y-ciphertexts), m, the number of tokens, q, the number of queries, and l_{q_i}, the number of query ciphertexts for each query $i \in [q]$, and if each query is successful or not.

> 0. n, m, q and $n_{q_i} = |\mathsf{qSet}_i|$ for $i \in [q]$;

In addition, we make the natural assumption that Server learns the following information regarding documents and queries for each user $u \in \mathcal{C}$.

> 1. $\mathsf{Access}(u)$ of documents that have been shared with $u \in \mathcal{C}$;
> 2. $\mathsf{Kw}(d)$ of keywords and the metadata $\mathtt{meta}_d$, for each $d \in \mathsf{Access}(\mathcal{C})$;
> 3. $\mathsf{AccList}(d)$ of users, for each $d \in \mathsf{Access}(\mathcal{C})$;
> 4. (u_i, w_i) for all $i \in [q]$ such that $u_i \in \mathcal{C}$;

Therefore, Server obtains keywords, metadata, and set of users that have access, for all documents that can be accessed by at least one Server corrupted user $u \in \mathcal{C}$. Moreover, Server also knows all queries issued by the corrupted users.

Consider x-ciphertext $X_{w,d} = g^{\mathsf{F}(\bar{K}_d,d) \cdot \mathsf{F}(K_d,w)}$. If $d \in \mathsf{Access}(\mathcal{C})$, then w and d are available to Server by Points 1 and 2 above. Therefore, Server knows exactly all the entries of the xSet corresponding to documents in $\mathsf{Access}(\mathcal{C})$ and nothing more. This implies that if no query is performed, no information is leaked about documents not available to the members of $\mathcal{C}$.

More leakage is derived from the queries. Let us consider a generic query ciphertext,

$$\mathtt{uid}_{u_i,d} = \mathsf{F}(\widetilde{K}_{u_i}, d), \mathtt{qct}_d = g^{\mathsf{F}(K_d, w_i) \cdot \mathsf{F}(K_{u_i}, d)}$$

for document d produced as part of the i-th query qSet_i issued by user u_i for keyword w_i. If $u_i \in \mathcal{C}$, then K_d, K_{u_i} and $\widetilde{K}_{u_i}$ are available to Server and thus (u_i, w_i, d) is leaked. If $u_i \notin \mathcal{C}$ and $d \in \mathsf{Access}(\mathcal{C})$ then K_d is available (whence, by our conservative assumption, w_i is available too) but K_{u_i} and $\widetilde{K}_{u_i}$ are not available. In this case, d and w_i are leaked. We further observe that query ciphertexts from the same user $u_i \notin \mathcal{C}$ and document $d \in \mathsf{Access}(\mathcal{C})$ are easily clustered together since they all share exponent, $\mathsf{F}(K_{u_i}, d)$, and $\mathtt{uid}_{u_i,d}$, $\mathsf{F}(\widetilde{K}_{u_i}, d)$. We define $\hat{u}_i$ to be the smallest index $j \le i$ such that $u_j = u_i$ and $d_j = d$. We say that if $u_i \notin \mathcal{C}$ and $d \in \mathsf{Access}(\mathcal{C})$, then $(\hat{u}_i, w_i, d)$ is leaked.

Suppose $u_i \notin \mathcal{C}$, $d \notin \mathsf{Access}(\mathcal{C})$ but $\mathsf{Access}(u_i) \cap \mathsf{Access}(\mathcal{C}) \ne \emptyset$; that is u_i shares document $d' \ne d$ with $\mathcal{C}$. Then $\mathtt{qct}_{d'}$ leaks w_i (and d' as discussed in the previous point) and this leakage is extended to all the query ciphertexts from the same query. We say $(\hat{u}_i, w_i, \perp)$ is leaked. Notice that identity of $d \notin \mathsf{Access}(\mathcal{C})$ is not leaked.

Finally, let us consider $u_i \notin \mathcal{C}$ and $\mathsf{Access}(u_i) \cap \mathsf{Access}(\mathcal{C}) = \emptyset$, in which case we say that qct_d is a *closed* query ciphertext. This is the case described for the passive case (as in the case all query ciphertexts are closed) and Server can cluster together the closed query ciphertexts that are for the same keyword *and* document and those that are for the same user *and* document. We can thus summarize leakage derived from query ciphertexts as follows.

---

5. For every $\mathsf{qct}_d \in \mathsf{qSet}_i$ (the i-th query for keyword w_i by user u_i);
   (a) If $u_i \in \mathcal{C}$, then (u_i, w_i, d) is leaked; the query is called an *open* query;
   (b) If $u_i \notin \mathcal{C}$ and $d \in \mathsf{Access}(\mathcal{C})$, then $(\hat{u}_i, w_i, d)$ is leaked;
   (c) If $u_i \notin \mathcal{C}$, $d \notin \mathsf{Access}(\mathcal{C})$ and $\mathsf{Access}(u_i) \cap \mathsf{Access}(\mathcal{C}) \neq \emptyset$, then $(\hat{u}_i, w_i, \perp)$ is leaked; the query is called an *half-open* query;
6. Equivalence classes $D_1, \ldots, D_r$ over the set of pairs of closed query ciphertexts and ciphertexts.
7. Equivalence classes $E_1, \ldots, E_t$ over the set of pairs of closed query ciphertexts and tokens.

In what follows we will denote by $\mathcal{L}(\mathcal{I}, \mathcal{C})$ the leakage described in Point 0–7 above. In the next theorem (see the full version [26] for the proof), we show that our construction does not leak any information about an instance $\mathcal{I}$ other than $\mathcal{L}(\mathcal{I}, \mathcal{C})$ where Server corrupts users in $\mathcal{C}$. We do so by showing that there exists a simulator $\mathcal{S}$ for SSEwSU that takes as input a coalition $\mathcal{C}$ of users along with $\mathcal{L}(\mathcal{I}, \mathcal{C})$ and returns a view that is indistinguishable from the real view of Server.

We start by reviewing the DDH Assumption and then state our main result. A *group generator* $\mathcal{GG}$ is an efficient randomized algorithm that on input 1^λ outputs the description of a cyclic group $\mathcal{G}$ of prime order p for some $|p| = \Theta(\lambda)$ along with a generator g for $\mathcal{G}$.

Definition 2. *The Decisional Diffie-Hellman (DDH) assumption holds for group generator $\mathcal{GG}$ if distributions D_λ^0 and D_λ^1 are computational indistinguishable, where $D_\lambda^\xi = \left\{ (g, \mathcal{G}) \leftarrow \mathcal{GG}(1^\lambda); x, y, r \leftarrow \mathbb{Z}_{|\mathcal{G}|} : (g^x, g^y, g^{x \cdot y + \xi \cdot r}) \right\}$.*

Theorem 1. *Under the DDH assumption, $\mathsf{mx\text{-}u}$ is secure with respect to leakage $\mathcal{L}$ as defined in Sect. 4.1.*

For the proof of the theorem above, we will use the following assumption that is equivalent to the DDH Assumption. Let $\mathbf{x} \in \mathbb{Z}_p^{l_0}$, $\mathbf{y} \in \mathbb{Z}_p^{l_1}$. Then, $\mathbf{x} \times \mathbf{y}$ is the $l_0 \times l_1$ matrix whose (i, j)-entry is $x_i \cdot y_j$. For a matrix $A = (a_{i,j})$, we set $g^A = (g^{a_{ij}})$.

Lemma 1. *If DDH holds for $\mathcal{GG}$ then for any l_0, l_1 that are bounded by a polynomial in λ, the distributions $D_{l_0, l_1, \lambda}^0$ and $D_{l_0, l_1, \lambda}^1$ are computational indistinguishable, where*

$$D_{l_0, l_1, \lambda}^\xi = \left\{ (g, \mathcal{G}) \leftarrow \mathcal{GG}(1^\lambda); \mathbf{x}, \leftarrow \mathbb{Z}_{|\mathcal{G}|}^{l_0}, \mathbf{y}, \leftarrow \mathbb{Z}_{|\mathcal{G}|}^{l_1}, \mathbf{r} \leftarrow \mathbb{Z}_{|\mathcal{G}|}^{l_0 \cdot l_1} : (g^{\mathbf{x}}, g^{\mathbf{x}}, g^{\mathbf{x} \times \mathbf{y} + \xi \cdot \mathbf{r}}) \right\}.$$

5   Experiments

In this section, we investigate the costs of mx-u and experimentally evaluate the growth of leakage as queries are being performed. All experiments are conducted on two identical machines, one for the Server and one for the user. The machines used are Ubuntu PC with Intel Xeon CPU (12 cores, 3.50 GHz). Each machine has 32 GB RAM with 1 TB hard disk.

Our experiments will only measure costs associated with mx-u. In practice, mx-u is accompanied by some storage system that allows retrieval of encrypted data. We ignore costs that would be incurred by such a storage system.

All associated programs are implemented using C++ and do not take advantage of the multiple cores available. We use SHA-256-based G and F and AES under Galois Counter Mode for (Enc, Dec). These cryptographic functions implementations are from the BoringSSL library (a fork of OpenSSL 1.0.2). The length of the keys used are 128 bits. All identifiers (document and user) are also 128 bits. We use the NIST recommended Curve P-224 (which has the identifier NID_secp224r1 in OpenSSL) as G. All group exponents are serialized in big-endian form. Elliptic curve points are serialized to octet strings in compressed form using the methods defined by ANSI X9.62 ECDSA.

5.1   Performance

We measure the computation time and bandwidth of uploading and searching documents of mx-u (see Fig. 1(a)–(d)). As expected, the upload and search metrics grow linearly in the number of unique terms and number of owned documents respectively. Furthermore, we note that the amount a user's computational time is much smaller than the server. This is very important as single machine users are more limited in computational power compared to large cloud service providers.

Enron Email Dataset. We consider using mx-u to store the Enron email dataset [13]. We have 150 users and any user that is the sender, recipient, cc'd or bcc'd of an email will be given search access to that email. The sender will be granted access. Every recipient of the email will be given access with $\frac{1}{2}$ probability. The server storage required is 5–6 times the size of the emails being uploaded (see Fig. 1(e)). We remark that SSE might be insecure for emails (e.g., see injection attacks of [33]) and we use the dataset as a means to test practicality.

Ubuntu Chat Corpus. In a separate experiment, we store the Ubuntu Chat Corpus (UCC) [31] with over 700000 users using our scheme. Like emails, the chat logs provide an excellent framework for multi-user searchable schemes. We split the chat corpus into days. That is, each day of history becomes a single file. All users who appear in the chat log for a day will have read rights. Each of the appearing users will also receive write rights with probability $\frac{1}{2}$. For this dataset, we also stem the input for each language and the server storage growth with the number of days considered is found in Fig. 1(f). Stemming removes common words as well as providing pseudonyms.

5.2   Leakage Growth

Figures 1(g)–(i) report the results of experiments in which we compare the rate of leakage growth of lx-u and mx-u as queries are performed[1]. The cross-user leakage graph G for mx-u has a node for each vertex and we have an edge between users u_1 and u_2 means that queries by u_1 or u_2 leak information about documents in Access(u_1)∩Access(u_2). For mx-u, an edge (u_1, u_2) exists iff both users queried for the same keyword w and share at least one document in common. On the other hand, an edge exists in lx-u if both users share at least one document in common and either user ever queried. Furthermore, cross-user leakage is transitive. If two users are in the same component, their queries can leak information about their intersection.

As G becomes more connected, cross-user leakage grows. If G has no edges (and consists of $|\mathcal{U}|$ connected components, one for each user), there is no cross-user leakage, and this is the status of the system before queries have been performed. Conversely, the complete graph has cross-user leakage for every pair of users. The vector of the sizes of the connected components of G at any given point in time describes the current cross-user leakage. The initial vector consists of $|\mathcal{U}|$ 1's (each vertex is in a connected component by itself). We pad with 0's to keep the vector of dimension $|\mathcal{U}|$. We measure how the length of this vector grows as queries are performed by looking at the L_2 norm (the square root of the sum of the squares of component sizes) and the L_∞ norm (the size of the largest component). We also plot the total number of components.

We compute these metrics for both lx-u and mx-u, using 2500 days of UCC data with approximately 55000 users. Keywords are drawn from the global distribution of terms in UCC after stemming. The user that performs the query is drawn uniformly at random from all users. We see that mx-u leakage grows significantly slower than lx-u in all three metrics. In particular, for all three metrics, lx-u approaches a single connected component after about 100 queries. For mx-u, it is possible to perform hundreds of thousands queries before this threshold is reached. In fact, it takes at least 80000 queries to reach 1/3 of the metrics of a single component.

6   Extensions

In the full version of this paper, we discuss several extensions to our results.

---

[1] Note that all considerations about leakage growth apply to mx-u independently of the underlying RDH.

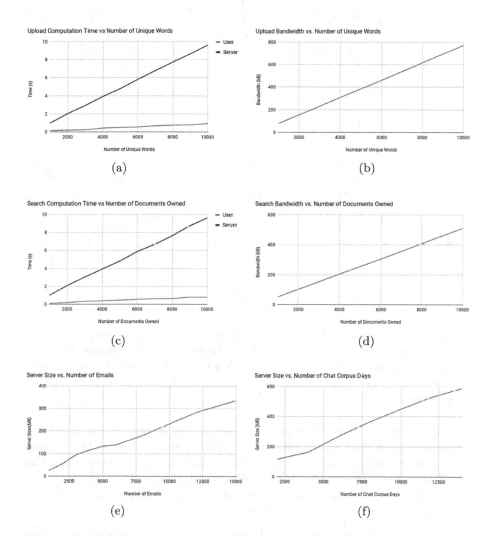

Fig. 1. (a) Upload computation time, (b) Upload bandwidth, (c) Search computation time, (d) Search bandwidth, (e) Enron Email server storage, (f) Ubuntu Chat server storage, (g) Sqrt sum of squares of component sizes, (h) Maximum component size, (i) Number of components.

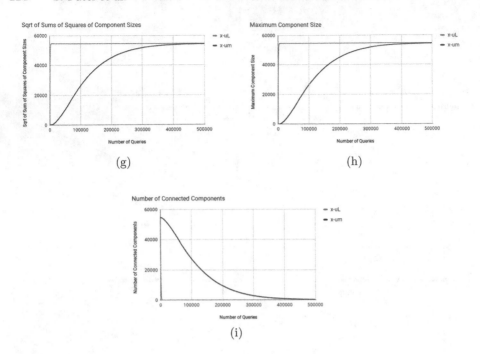

Fig. 1. (*continued*)

Different Access Types. In the above constructions, we simply designate access as *search access* or the ability to search for keywords in documents. We show that the techniques in mx-u can be extended to handle multiple access types (such as ownership or editing). The main idea is to duplicate the uSet for each type of access type that we wish to enforce.

Reducing Leakage using Bilinear Pairings. We present a scheme that uses bilinear pairings which reduces the cross-user leakage compared mx-u in exchange for larger server computation. In particular, we show that cross-user leakage for two different users querying for the same keyword is present if and only if the keyword exists in a document shared by both users. However, the server must now perform computation for all elements in the xSet.

*Sharing by Non-*CorpusOwner *Users.* In mx-u, we only present techniques that CorpusOwner may construct authorization tokens to enable other users to search over documents in CorpusOwner's corpus. We present an algorithm that allows a non-CorpusOwner user that already has access to a document to share with another user without requiring the interaction of CorpusOwner.

Key Rotation by CorpusOwner. We present an efficient key rotation algorithm that can be performed by CorpusOwner for mx-u while simultaneously trying to prevent cross-user leakage accumulation. The goal is to rotate all the keys of ciphertexts in both the uSet and xSet while ensuring that the Server cannot determine whether an old and a new ciphertext contain the same plaintexts under different keys. We will use an oblivious shuffling algorithm [23] to achieve our goal by randomly permuting the elements of the xSet in a manner oblivious to Server. During the shuffle, CorpusOwner will select new keys and replace old RDH evaluations with new RDH evaluations under the new keys. As our shuffling algorithm, we use the K-oblivious shuffling variant of the CacheShuffle [25] which can leverage the fact that some N - K items of the xSet are never involved in searches to improve the efficiency of the shuffling algorithm.

7   Conclusions

In this work, we introduce the concept of *Symmetric Searchable Encryption with Sharing and Unsharing*, which extends previous multi-user definitions by requiring dynamic access allowing both sharing and unsharing. We present the *cross-user leakage graph*, a novel method to bound and quantify the leakage of searchable encryption schemes in multiple user settings. As a result, we are able to quantitatively compare different schemes, which is an important need that previous techniques had yet to achieve. As our main technical contribution, we present mx-u. We directly compare mx-u with previous schemes and show that other schemes are either inefficient or have greater cross-user leakage than mx-u.

References

1. Asharov, G., Naor, M., Segev, G., Shahaf, I.: Searchable symmetric encryption: optimal locality in linear space via two-dimensional balanced allocations. In: Proceedings of the Forty-Eighth Annual ACM Symposium on Theory of Computing, pp. 1101–1114. ACM (2016)
2. Asharov, G., Segev, G., Shahaf, I.: Tight tradeoffs in searchable symmetric encryption. Cryptology ePrint Archive, Report 2018/507 (2018). https://eprint.iacr.org/2018/507
3. Boneh, D., Di Crescenzo, G., Ostrovsky, R., Persiano, G.: Public key encryption with keyword search. In: Cachin, C., Camenisch, J.L. (eds.) EUROCRYPT 2004. LNCS, vol. 3027, pp. 506–522. Springer, Heidelberg (2004). https://doi.org/10.1007/978-3-540-24676-3_30
4. Cash, D., Grubbs, P., Perry, J., Ristenpart, T.: Leakage-abuse attacks against searchable encryption. In: Proceedings of the 22nd ACM SIGSAC Conference on Computer and Communications Security, CCS 2015, pp. 668–679 (2015)
5. Cash, D., et al.: Dynamic searchable encryption in very-large databases: data structures and implementation. In: NDSS, vol. 14, pp. 23–26. Citeseer (2014)
6. Cash, D., Jarecki, S., Jutla, C., Krawczyk, H., Roşu, M.-C., Steiner, M.: Highly-scalable searchable symmetric encryption with support for boolean queries. In: Canetti, R., Garay, J.A. (eds.) CRYPTO 2013. LNCS, vol. 8042, pp. 353–373. Springer, Heidelberg (2013). https://doi.org/10.1007/978-3-642-40041-4_20
7. Cash, D., Tessaro, S.: The locality of searchable symmetric encryption. In: Nguyen, P.Q., Oswald, E. (eds.) EUROCRYPT 2014. LNCS, vol. 8441, pp. 351–368. Springer, Heidelberg (2014). https://doi.org/10.1007/978-3-642-55220-5_20

8. Chase, M., Kamara, S.: Structured encryption and controlled disclosure. In: Abe, M. (ed.) ASIACRYPT 2010. LNCS, vol. 6477, pp. 577–594. Springer, Heidelberg (2010). https://doi.org/10.1007/978-3-642-17373-8_33. Also Cryptology ePrint Archive, Report 2006/210

9. Curtmola, R., Garay, J., Kamara, S., Ostrovsky, R.: Searchable symmetric encryption: improved definitions and efficient constructions. In: Proceedings of the 13th ACM Conference on Computer and Communications Security, pp. 79–88 (2006). Also Cryptology ePrint Archive, Report 2006/210

10. Demertzis, I., Papadopoulos, D., Papamanthou, C.: Searchable encryption with optimal locality: achieving sublogarithmic read efficiency. Cryptology ePrint Archive, Report 2017/749 (2017). https://eprint.iacr.org/2017/749

11. Demertzis, I., Papamanthou, C.: Fast searchable encryption with tunable locality. In: Proceedings of the 2017 ACM International Conference on Management of Data, pp. 1053–1067. ACM (2017)

12. Dong, C., Russello, G., Dulay, N.: Shared and searchable encrypted data for untrusted servers. In: Atluri, V. (ed.) DBSec 2008. LNCS, vol. 5094, pp. 127–143. Springer, Heidelberg (2008). https://doi.org/10.1007/978-3-540-70567-3_10

13. EDRM (EDRM.net): Enron data set. http://www.edrm.net/resources/data-sets/edrm-enron-email-data-set

14. Grubbs, P., McPherson, R., Naveed, M., Ristenpart, T., Shmatikov, V.: Breaking web applications built on top of encrypted data. In: Proceedings of the 2016 ACM SIGSAC Conference on Computer and Communications Security, pp. 1353–1364. ACM (2016)

15. Hamlin, A., Shelat, A., Weiss, M., Wichs, D.: Multi-key searchable encryption, revisited. Cryptology ePrint Archive, Report 2018/018 (2018). https://eprint.iacr.org/2018/018

16. Kamara, S., Lauter, K.: Cryptographic cloud storage. In: Sion, R., et al. (eds.) FC 2010. LNCS, vol. 6054, pp. 136–149. Springer, Heidelberg (2010). https://doi.org/10.1007/978-3-642-14992-4_13

17. Kamara, S., Moataz, T.: Boolean searchable symmetric encryption with worst-case sub-linear complexity. In: Coron, J.-S., Nielsen, J.B. (eds.) EUROCRYPT 2017. LNCS, vol. 10212, pp. 94–124. Springer, Cham (2017). https://doi.org/10.1007/978-3-319-56617-7_4

18. Kamara, S., Moataz, T., Ohrimenko, O.: Structured encryption and leakage suppression. Cryptology ePrint Archive, Report 2018/551 (2018). https://eprint.iacr.org/2018/551

19. Kamara, S., Papamanthou, C., Roeder, T.: Dynamic searchable symmetric encryption. In: Proceedings of the 2012 ACM Conference on Computer and Communications Security, pp. 965–976. ACM (2012)

20. Kellaris, G., Kollios, G., Nissim, K., O'Neill, A.: Generic attacks on secure outsourced databases. In: Proceedings of the 2016 ACM SIGSAC Conference on Computer and Communications Security, pp. 1329–1340. ACM (2016)

21. Kiayias, A., Oksuz, O., Russell, A., Tang, Q., Wang, B.: Efficient encrypted keyword search for multi-user data sharing. In: Askoxylakis, I., Ioannidis, S., Katsikas, S., Meadows, C. (eds.) ESORICS 2016. LNCS, vol. 9878, pp. 173–195. Springer, Cham (2016). https://doi.org/10.1007/978-3-319-45744-4_9

22. Naveed, M., Kamara, S., Wright, C.V.: Inference attacks on property-preserving encrypted databases. In: Proceedings of the 22nd ACM SIGSAC Conference on Computer and Communications Security, pp. 644–655. ACM (2015)

23. Ohrimenko, O., Goodrich, M.T., Tamassia, R., Upfal, E.: The melbourne shuffle: improving oblivious storage in the cloud. In: Esparza, J., Fraigniaud, P., Husfeldt, T., Koutsoupias, E. (eds.) ICALP 2014. LNCS, vol. 8573, pp. 556–567. Springer, Heidelberg (2014). https://doi.org/10.1007/978-3-662-43951-7_47

24. Pappas, V., et al.: Blind seer: a scalable private DBMS. In: Proceedings of the 2014 IEEE Symposium on Security and Privacy, SP 2014, pp. 359–374. IEEE Computer Society (2014)

25. Patel, S., Persiano, G., Yeo, K.: CacheShuffle: an oblivious shuffle algorithm using caches. arXiv preprint arXiv:1705.07069 (2017)

26. Patel, S., Persiano, G., Yeo, K.: Symmetric searchable encryption with sharing and unsharing. Cryptology ePrint Archive, Report 2017/973 (2017). https://eprint.iacr.org/2017/973

27. Popa, R.A., Zeldovich, N.: Multi-key searchable encryption. Cryptology ePrint Archive, Report 2013/508 (2013)

28. Pouliot, D., Wright, C.V.: The shadow nemesis: inference attacks on efficiently deployable, efficiently searchable encryption. In: Proceedings of the 2016 ACM SIGSAC Conference on Computer and Communications Security, CCS 2016, pp. 1341–1352 (2016)

29. Song, D.X., Wagner, D., Perrig, A.: Practical techniques for searches on encrypted data. In: Proceedings of the 2000 IEEE Symposium on Security and Privacy, pp. 44–55 (2000)

30. Stefanov, E., Papamanthou, C., Shi, E.: Practical dynamic searchable encryption with small leakage. In: NDSS, vol. 71, pp. 72–75 (2014)

31. Uthus, D.: Ubuntu chat corpus. http://daviduthus.org/UCC/

32. Van Rompay, C., Molva, R., Önen, M.: A leakage-abuse attack against multi-user searchable encryption. Proc. Priv. Enhanc. Technol. 2017(3), 168–178 (2017)

33. Zhang, Y., Katz, J., Papamanthou, C.: All your queries are belong to us: the power of file-injection attacks on searchable encryption. Cryptology ePrint Archive, Report 2016/172 (2016). http://eprint.iacr.org/2016/172

Dynamic Searchable Symmetric Encryption Schemes Supporting Range Queries with Forward (and Backward) Security

Cong Zuo[1,2], Shi-Feng Sun[1,2(✉)], Joseph K. Liu[1], Jun Shao[3],
and Josef Pieprzyk[2,4]

[1] Faculty of Information Technology, Monash University, Clayton 3168, Australia
{cong.zuo1,shifeng.sun,joseph.liu}@monash.edu
[2] Data61, CSIRO, Melbourne/Sydney, Australia
josef.pieprzyk@data61.csiro.au
[3] School of Computer and Information Engineering, Zhejiang Gongshang University,
Hangzhou 310018, Zhejiang, China
chn.junshao@gmail.com
[4] Institute of Computer Science, Polish Academy of Sciences,
01-248 Warsaw, Poland

Abstract. Dynamic searchable symmetric encryption (DSSE) is a useful cryptographic tool in encrypted cloud storage. However, it has been reported that DSSE usually suffers from file-injection attacks and content leak of deleted documents. To mitigate these attacks, forward security and backward security have been proposed. Nevertheless, the existing forward/backward-secure DSSE schemes can only support single keyword queries. To address this problem, in this paper, we propose two DSSE schemes supporting range queries. One is forward-secure and supports a large number of documents. The other can achieve both forward security and backward security, while it can only support a limited number of documents. Finally, we also give the security proofs of the proposed DSSE schemes in the random oracle model.

Keywords: Dynamic searchable symmetric encryption
Forward security · Backward security · Range queries

1 Introduction

Searchable symmetric encryption (SSE) is a useful cryptographic primitive that can encrypt the data to protect its confidentiality while keeping its searchability. Dynamic SSE (DSSE) further provides data dynamics that allows the client to update data over the time without losing data confidentiality and searchability. Due to this property, DSSE is highly demanded in encrypted cloud. However, many existing DSSE schemes [8,14] suffer from file-injection attacks [7,22], where

© Springer Nature Switzerland AG 2018
J. Lopez et al. (Eds.): ESORICS 2018, LNCS 11099, pp. 228–246, 2018.
https://doi.org/10.1007/978-3-319-98989-1_12

the adversary can compromise the privacy of a client query by injecting a small portion of new documents to the encrypted database. To resist this attack, Zhang et al. [22] highlighted the need of forward security that was informally introduced by Stefanov et al. [19]. The formal definition of forward security for DSSE was given by Bost [5] who also proposed a concrete forward-secure DSSE scheme. Furthermore, Bost et al. [6] demonstrated the damage of content leak of deleted documents and proposed the corresponding security notion–backward security. Several backward-secure DSSE schemes were also presented in [6].

Nevertheless, the existing forward/backward-secure DSSE schemes only support single keyword queries, which are not expressive enough in data search service [12,13]. To solve this problem, in this paper, we aim to design forward/backward-secure DSSE schemes supporting range queries. Our design starts from the regular binary tree in [13] to support range queries. However, the binary tree in [13] cannot be applied directly to the dynamic setting. It is mainly because that the keywords in [13] are labelled according to the corresponding tree levels that will change significantly in the dynamic setting. A naïve solution is to replace all old keywords by the associated new keywords. This is, however, not efficient. To address this problem, we have to explore new approaches for our goal.

Our Contributions. To achieve above goal, we propose two new DSSE constructions supporting range queries in this paper. The first one is forward-secure but with a larger client overhead in contrast to [13]. The second one is a more efficient DSSE which achieves both forward and backward security at the same time. In more details, our main contributions are as follows:

- To make the binary tree suitable for range queries in the dynamic setting, we introduce a new binary tree data structure, and then present the first forward-secure DSSE supporting range queries by applying it to Bost's scheme [5]. However, the forward security is achieved at the expense of suffering from a large storage overhead on the client side.
- To reduce the large storage overhead, we further propose another DSSE scheme supporting range queries by leveraging the Paillier cryptosystem [17]. With its homomorphic property, this construction can achieve not only forward security, but also backward security. Notably, due to the limitation of the Paillier cryptosystem, it cannot support large-scale database consisting a large number of documents. Nevertheless, it suits well for certain scenarios where the number of documents is moderate. The new approach may give new lights on designing more efficient and secure DSSE schemes.
- Also, the comparison with related works in Table 1 and detailed security analyses are provided, which demonstrate that our constructions are not only forward (and backward)-secure but also with a comparable efficiency.

Table 1. Comparison with existing DSSE schemes

Scheme	Client computation		Client storage	Range queries	Forward security	Backward security	Document number
	Search	Update					
[13]	w_R	-	$O(1)$	✓	✗	✗	Large
[5]	-	$O(1)$	$O(W)$	✗	✓	✗	Large
Ours A	w_R	$\lceil log(W) \rceil + 1$	$O(2W)$	✓	✓	✗	Large
Ours B	w_R	$\lceil log(W) \rceil + 1$	$O(1)$	✓	✓	✓	Small

W is the number of keywords in a database, w_R is the number of keywords for a range query (we map a range query to a few different keywords).

1.1 Related Works

Song et al. [18] were the first using symmetric encryption to facilitate keyword search over the encrypted data. Later, Curtmola et al. [11] gave a formal definition for SSE and the corresponding security model in the static setting. To make SSE more scalable and expressive, Cash et al. [9] proposed a new scalable SSE supporting Boolean queries. Following this construction, many extensions have been proposed. Faber et al. [13] extended it to process a much richer collection of queries. For instance, they used a binary tree with keywords labelled according to the tree levels to support range queries. Zuo et al. [23] made another extension to support general Boolean queries. Cash et al.'s construction has also been extended into multi-user setting [15,20,21]. However, the above schemes cannot support data update. To solve this problem, some DSSE schemes have been proposed [8,14].

However, designing a secure DSSE scheme is not an easy job. Cash et al. [7] pointed out that only a small leakage leveraged by the adversary would be enough to compromise the privacy of clients' queries. A concrete attack named file-injection attack was proposed by Zhang et al. [22]. In this attack, the adversary can infer the concept of a client queries by injecting a small portion of new documents into encrypted database. This attack also highlights the need for forward security which protects security of new added parts. Accordingly, we have backward security that protects security of new added parts and later deleted. These two security notions were first introduced by Stefanov et al. [19]. The formal definitions of forward/backward security for DSSE were given by Bost [5] and Bost et al. [6], respectively. In [5], Bost also proposed a concrete forward-secure DSSE scheme, it does not support physical deletion. Later on, Kim et al. [16] proposed a forward-secure DSSE scheme supporting physical deletion. Meanwhile, Bost et al. [6] proposed a forward/backward-secure DSSE to reduce leakage during deletion. Unfortunately, all the existing forward/backward-secure DSSE schemes only support single keyword queries. Hence, forward/backward-secure DSSE supporting more expressive queries, such as range queries, are quite desired.

Apart from the binary tree technique, order preserving encryption (OPE) can also be used to support range queries. The concept of OPE was proposed by

Agrawal et al. [1], and it allows the order of the plaintexts to be preserved in the ciphertexts. It is easy to see that this kind of encryption would lead to the leakage in [2,3]. To reduce this leakage, Boneh et al. [4] proposed another concept named order revealing encryption (ORE), where the order of the ciphertexts are revealed by using an algorithm rather than comparing the ciphertexts (in OPE) directly. More efficient ORE schemes were proposed later [10]. However, ORE-based SSE still leaks much information about the underlying plaintexts. To avoid this, in this paper, we focus on how to use the binary tree structure to achieve range queries.

1.2 Organization

The remaining sections of this paper are organized as follows. In Sect. 2, we give the background information and building blocks that are used in this paper. In Sect. 3, we give the definition of DSSE and its security definition. After that in Sect. 4, we present a new binary tree and our DSSE schemes. Their security analyses are given in Sect. 5. Finally, Sect. 6 concludes this work.

2 Preliminaries

In this section, we describe cryptographic primitives (building blocks) that are used in this work.

2.1 Trapdoor Permutations

A trapdoor permutation (TDP) Π is a one-way permutation over a domain D such that (1) it is "easy" to compute Π for any value of the domain with the public key, and (2) it is "easy" to calculate the inverse Π^{-1} for any value of a co-domain $\mathcal{M}$ only if a matching secret key is known. More formally, Π consists of the following algorithms:

- $\mathsf{TKeyGen}(1^\lambda) \to (\mathsf{TPK}, \mathsf{TSK})$: For a security parameter 1^λ, the algorithm returns a pair of cryptographic keys: a public key TPK and a secret key TSK.
- $\Pi(\mathsf{TPK}, x) \to y$: For a pair: public key TPK and $x \in D$, the algorithm outputs $y \in \mathcal{M}$.
- $\Pi^{-1}(\mathsf{TSK}, y) \to x$: For a pair: a secret key TSK and $y \in \mathcal{M}$, the algorithm returns $x \in D$.

One-wayness. We say Π is one-way if for any probabilistic polynomial time (PPT) adversary $\mathcal{A}$, an advantage

$$\mathsf{Adv}_{\Pi,\mathcal{A}}^{\mathsf{OW}}(1^\lambda) = \Pr[x \leftarrow \mathcal{A}(\mathsf{TPK}, y)]$$

is negligible, where $(\mathsf{TSK}, \mathsf{TPK}) \leftarrow \mathsf{TKeyGen}(1^\lambda)$, $y \leftarrow \Pi(\mathsf{TPK}, x)$, $x \in D$.

2.2 Paillier Cryptosystem

A Paillier cryptosystem $\Sigma = (\texttt{KeyGen}, \texttt{Enc}, \texttt{Dec})$ is defined by following three algorithms:

- $\texttt{KeyGen}(1^\lambda) \rightarrow (\texttt{PK}, \texttt{SK})$: It chooses at random two primes p and q of similar lengths and computes $n = pq$ and $\phi(n) = (p-1)(q-1)$. Next it sets $g = n+1$, $\beta = \phi(n)$ and $\mu = \phi(n)^{-1} \bmod n$. It returns $\texttt{PK} = (n, g)$ and $\texttt{SK} = (\beta, \mu)$.
- $\texttt{Enc}(\texttt{PK}, m) \rightarrow c$: Let m be the message, where $0 \leq m < n$, the algorithm selects an integer r at random from $\mathbb{Z}_n$ and computes a ciphertext $c = g^m \cdot r^n \bmod n^2$.
- $\texttt{Dec}(\texttt{SK}, c) \rightarrow m$: The algorithm calculates $m = L(c^\beta \bmod n^2) \cdot \mu \bmod n$, where $L(x) = \frac{x-1}{n}$.

Semantically Security. We say Σ is semantically secure if for any probabilistic polynomial time (PPT) adversary $\mathcal{A}$, an advantage

$$\texttt{Adv}_{\Sigma, \mathcal{A}}^{\text{IND-CPA}}(1^\lambda) = |\Pr[\mathcal{A}(\texttt{Enc}(\texttt{PK}, m_0)) = 1] - \Pr[\mathcal{A}(\texttt{Enc}(\texttt{PK}, m_1)) = 1]|$$

is negligible, where $(\texttt{SK}, \texttt{PK}) \leftarrow \texttt{KeyGen}(1^\lambda)$, $\mathcal{A}$ chooses m_0, m_1 and $|m_0| = |m_1|$.

Homomorphic Addition. Paillier cryptosystem is homomorphic, i.e.

$$\texttt{Dec}(\texttt{Enc}(m_1) \cdot \texttt{Enc}(m_2)) \bmod n^2 = m_1 + m_2 \bmod n.$$

We need this property to achieve forward security of our DSSE.

2.3 Notations

The list of notations used is given in Table 2.

3 Dynamic Searchable Symmetric Encryption (DSSE)

We follow the database model given in the paper [5]. A database is a collection of (index, keyword set) pairs denoted as $\texttt{DB} = (ind_i, \mathbf{W}_i)_{i=1}^d$, where $ind_i \in \{0,1\}^\ell$ and $\mathbf{W}_i \subseteq \{0,1\}^*$. The set of all keywords of the database $\texttt{DB}$ is $\mathbf{W} = \cup_{i=1}^d \mathbf{W}_i$, where d is the number of documents in $\texttt{DB}$. We identify $W = |\mathbf{W}|$ as the total number of keywords and $N = \Sigma_{i=1}^d |\mathbf{W}_i|$ as the number of document/keyword pairs. We denote $\texttt{DB}(w)$ as the set of documents that contain a keyword w. To achieve a sublinear search time, we encrypt the file indices of $\texttt{DB}(w)$ corresponding to the same keyword w (a.k.a. inverted index[1]).

A DSSE scheme Γ consists of an algorithm **Setup** and two protocols **Search** and **Update** as described below.

---

[1] It is an index data structure where a word is mapped to a set of documents which contain this word.

Table 2. Notations (used in our constructions)

W	The number of keywords in a database DB
BDB	The binary database which is constructed from a database DB by using our binary tree BT
m	The number of values in the range $[0, m-1]$ for our range queries
v	A value in the range $[0, m-1]$ where $0 \leq v < m$
n_i	The i-th node in our binary tree which is considered as the keyword
root_o	The root node of the binary tree before update
root_n	The root node of the binary tree after update
ST_c	The current search token for a node n
$\mathcal{M}$	A random value for ST_0 which is the first search token for a node n
UT_c	The current update token for a node n
T	A map which is used to store the encrypted database EDB
N	A map which is used to store the current search token for n_i
NSet	The node set which contains the nodes
TPK	The public key of trapdoor permutation
TSK	The secret key of trapdoor permutation
PK	The public key of Paillier cryptosystem
SK	The secret key of Paillier cryptosystem
f_i	The i-th file
PBT	Perfect binary tree
CBT	Complete binary tree
VBT	Virtual perfect binary tree
ABT	Assigned complete binary tree

- $(\text{EDB}, \sigma) \leftarrow \textbf{Setup}(\text{DB}, 1^\lambda)$: For a security parameter 1^λ and a database DB. The algorithm outputs an encrypted database EDB for the server and a secret state σ for the client.
- $(\mathcal{I}, \perp) \leftarrow \textbf{Search}(q, \sigma, \text{EDB})$: The protocol is executed between a client (with her query q and state σ) and a server (with its EDB). At the end of the protocol, the client outputs a set of file indices $\mathcal{I}$ and the server outputs nothing.
- $(\sigma', \text{EDB}') \leftarrow \textbf{Update}(\sigma, op, in, \text{EDB})$: The protocol runs between a client and a server. The client input is a state σ, an operation $op = (add, del)$ she wants to perform and a collection of $in = (ind, \mathbf{w})$ pairs that are going to be modified, where add, del mean the addition and deletion of a document/keyword pair, respectively, and ind is the file index and $\mathbf{w}$ is a set of keywords. The server input is EDB. **Update** returns an updated state σ' to the client and an updated encrypted database EDB' to the server.

3.1 Security Definition

The security definition of DSSE is formulated using the following two games: $\text{DSSEREAL}_{\mathcal{A}}^{\Gamma}(1^{\lambda})$ and $\text{DSSEIDEAL}_{\mathcal{A},\mathcal{S}}^{\Gamma}(1^{\lambda})$. The $\text{DSSEREAL}_{\mathcal{A}}^{\Gamma}(1^{\lambda})$ is executed using DSSE. The $\text{DSSEIDEAL}_{\mathcal{A},\mathcal{S}}^{\Gamma}(1^{\lambda})$ is simulated using the leakage of DSSE. The leakage is parameterized by a function $\mathcal{L} = (\mathcal{L}^{Stp}, \mathcal{L}^{Srch}, \mathcal{L}^{Updt})$, which describes what information is leaked to the adversary $\mathcal{A}$. If the adversary $\mathcal{A}$ cannot distinguish these two games, then we can say there is no other information leaked except the information that can be inferred from the leakage function $\mathcal{L}$. More formally,

- $\text{DSSEREAL}_{\mathcal{A}}^{\Gamma}(1^{\lambda})$: On input a database DB, which is chosen by the adversary $\mathcal{A}$, it outputs EDB by using **Setup**$(1^{\lambda}, \text{DB})$ to the adversary $\mathcal{A}$. $\mathcal{A}$ can repeatedly perform a search query q (or an update query (op, in)). The game outputs the results generated by running **Search**(q) (or **Update**(op, in)) to the adversary $\mathcal{A}$. Eventually, $\mathcal{A}$ outputs a bit.
- $\text{DSSEIDEAL}_{\mathcal{A},\mathcal{S}}^{\Gamma}(1^{\lambda})$: On input a database DB which is chosen by the adversary $\mathcal{A}$, it outputs EDB to the adversary $\mathcal{A}$ by using a simulator $\mathcal{S}(\mathcal{L}^{Stp}(1^{\lambda}, \text{DB}))$. Then, it simulates the results for the search query q by using the leakage function $\mathcal{S}(\mathcal{L}^{Srch}(q))$ and uses $\mathcal{S}(\mathcal{L}^{Updt}(op, in))$ to simulate the results for update query (op, in). Eventually, $\mathcal{A}$ outputs a bit.

Definition 1. *A DSSE scheme Γ is $\mathcal{L}$-adaptively-secure if for every PPT adversary $\mathcal{A}$, there exists an efficient simulator $\mathcal{S}$ such that*

$$|\Pr[\text{DSSEREAL}_{\mathcal{A}}^{\Gamma}(1^{\lambda}) = 1] - \Pr[\text{DSSEIDEAL}_{\mathcal{A},\mathcal{S}}^{\Gamma}(1^{\lambda}) = 1]| \leq negl(1^{\lambda}).$$

4 Constructions

In this section, we give two DSSE constructions. In order to process range queries, we deploy a new binary tree which is modified from the binary tree in [13]. Now, we first give our binary tree used in our constructions.

4.1 Binary Tree for Range Queries

In a binary tree BT, every node has at most two children named *left* and *right*. If a node has a child, then there is an edge that connects these two nodes. The node is the parent *parent* of its child. The root *root* of a binary tree does not have parent and the leaf of a binary tree does not have any child. In this paper, the binary tree is stored in thew form of linked structures. The first node of BT is the root of a binary tree. For example, the root node of the binary tree BT is BT, the left child of BT is BT.*left*, and the parent of BT's left child is BT.*left.parent*, where BT = BT.*left.parent*.

In a complete binary tree CBT, every level, except possibly the last, is completely filled, and all nodes in the last level are as far left as possible (the leaf level may not full). A perfect binary tree PBT is a binary tree in which all internal nodes (not the leaves) have two children and all leaves have the same depth or same level. Note that, PBT is a special CBT.

4.2 Binary Database

In this paper, we use binary database BDB which is generated from DB. In DB, keywords (the first row in Fig. 1(c)) are used to retrieve the file indices (every column in Fig. 1(c)). For simplicity, we map keywords in DB to the values in the range $[0, m-1]$ for range queries[2], where m is the maximum number of values. If we want to search the range $[0, 3]$, a naïve solution is to send every value in the range (0, 1, 2 and 3) to the server, which is not efficient. To reduce the number of keywords sent to the server, we use the binary tree as shown in Fig. 1(a). For the range query $[0, 3]$, we simply send the keyword n_3 (the minimum nodes to cover value 0, 1, 2 and 3) to the server. In BDB, every node in the binary tree is the keyword of the binary database, and every node has all the file indices for its decedents, as illustrated in Fig. 1(d).

As shown in Fig. 1(a), keyword in BDB corresponding to node i (the black integer) is n_i (e.g. the keyword for node 0 is n_0.). The blue integers are the keywords in DB and are mapped to the values in the range $[0, 3]$. These values are associated with the leaves of our binary tree. The words in red are the file indices in DB. For every node (keyword), it contains all the file indices in its descendant leaves. Node n_1 contains f_0, f_1, f_2, f_3 and there is no file in node n_4 (See Fig. 1(d)). For a range query $[0, 2]$, we need to send the keywords n_1, n_4 (n_1 and n_4 are the minimum number of keywords to cover the range $[0, 2]$.) to the server, and the result file indices are f_0, f_1, f_2 and f_3.

Bit String Representation. We parse the file indices for every keyword in BDB (e.g. every column in Fig. 1(d)) into a bit string, which we will use later. Suppose there are $y - 1$ documents in our BDB, then we need y bits to represent the existence of these documents. The highest bit is the sign bit (0 means positive and 1 means negative). If f_i contains keyword n_j, then the i-th bit of the bit string for n_j (every keyword has a bit string) is set to 1. Otherwise, it is set to 0. For update, if we want to add a new file index f_i (which also contains keyword n_j) to keyword n_j, we need a positive bit string, where the i-th bit is set to 1 and all other bits are set to 0. Next, we add this bit string to the existing bit string associated with n_j [3]. Then, f_i is added to the bit string for n_j. If we want to delete file index f_i from the bit string for n_j, we need a negative bit string (the most significant bit is set to 1), the i-th bit is set to 1 and the remaining bits are set to 0. Then, we need to get the complement of the bit string [4]. Next, we add the complement bit string as in the add operation. Finally, the f_i is deleted from the bit string for n_j.

---

[2] In different applications, we can choose different kinds of values. For instance, audit documents of websites with particular IP addresses. we can search the whole network domain, particular host or application range.

[3] Note that, in the range queries, the bit strings are bit exclusive since a file is corresponded to one value only.

[4] In a computer, the subtraction is achieved by adding the complement of the negative bit string.

For example, in Fig. 1(b), the bit string for n_0 is 000001, and the bit string for n_4 is 000000. Assume that we want to delete file index f_0 from n_0 and add it to n_4. First we need to generate bit string 000001 and add it to the bit string (000000) for n_4. Next we generate the complement bit string 111111 (the complement of 100001) and add it to 000001 for n_0. Then, the result bit strings for n_0 and n_4 are 000000 and 000001, respectively. As a result, the file index f_0 has been moved from n_0 to n_4.

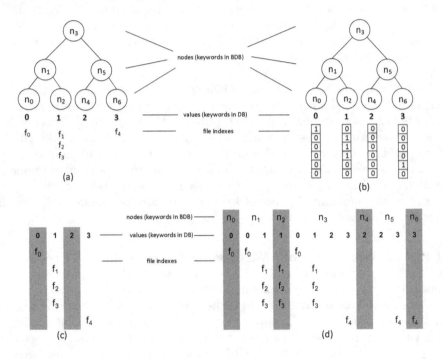

Fig. 1. Architecture of our binary tree for range query (Color figure online)

Binary Tree Assignment and Update. As we use the binary tree to support data structure needed in our DSSE, we define the following operations that are necessary to manipulate the DSSE data structure.

TCon(m): For an integer m, the operation builds a complete binary tree CBT. CBT has $\lceil log(m) \rceil + 1$ levels, where the root is on the level 0, and the leaves are on the level $\lceil log(m) \rceil$. All leaves are associated with the m consecutive integers from left to right.

TAssign(CBT): The operation takes a CBT as an input and outputs an assigned binary tree ABT, where nodes are labelled by appropriate integers. The operation applies **TAssignSub** recursively. Keywords then are assigned to the node integers.

TAssignSub(c, CBT): For an input pair: a counter c and CBT, the operation outputs an assigned binary tree. It is implemented as a recursive function. It starts from 0 and assigns to nodes incrementally. See Fig. 2 for an example.

Algorithm 1. Our Binary Tree

TCon(m)

Input integer m

Output complete binary tree CBT

1: Construct a CBT with $\lceil log(m) \rceil + 1$ levels.
2: Set the number of leaves to m.
3: Associate the leaves with m consecutive integers $[0,m\text{-}1]$ from left to right.
4: **return** CBT

TAssign(CBT)

Input complete binary tree CBT

Output assigned binary tree ABT

1: Counter $c - 0$
2: **TAssignSub**(c, CBT)
3: **return** ABT

TAssignSub(c, CBT)

Input CBT, counter c

Output Assigned binary tree ABT

1: **if** CBT.$left \neq \perp$ **then**
2:     **TAssignSub**(c, CBT.$left$)
3: **end if**
4: Assign CBT with counter c.
5: $c = c + 1$
6: **if** CBT.$right \neq \perp$ **then**
7:     **TAssignSub**(c, CBT.$right$)
8: **end if**
9: Assign CBT with counter c.
10: $c = c + 1$
11: **return** ABT

TGetNodes(n, ABT)

Input node n, ABT

Output NSet

1: NSet $\leftarrow$ Empty Set
2: **while** $n \neq \perp$ **do**
3:     NSet $\leftarrow$ NSet $\cup$ n
4:     $n = n.parent$
5: **end while**
6: **return** NSet

TUpdate(add, v, CBT)

Input op= add, value v, CBT

Output updated CBT

1: **if** CBT $= \perp$ **then**
2:     Create a node.
3:     Associate value $v = 0$ to this node.
4:     Set CBT to this node.
5: **else if** CBT is PBT or CBT has one node **then**
6:     Create a new root node root$_n$.
7:     Create a VBT $=$ CBT
8:     CBT.$parent$=VBT.$parent$=root$_n$
9:     CBT $=$ root$_n$
10:     Associate v to the least virtual leaf and set this leaf and its parents as real.
11: **else**
12:     Execute line 10.
13: **end if**
14: **return** CBT

TGetNodes(n, ABT): For an input pair: a node n and a tree ABT, the operation generates a collection of nodes in a path from the node n to the root node. This operation is needed for our update algorithm if a client wants to add a file to a leaf (a value in the range). The file is added to the leaf and its parent nodes.

TUpdate(add, v, CBT): The operation takes a value v and a complete binary tree CBT and updates CBT so the tree contains the value v. For simplicity, we consider the current complete binary tree contains values in the range $[0, v-1]$[5].

---

[5] Note that, we can use **TUpdate** many times if we need to update more values.

Depending on the value of v, the operation is executed according to the following cases:

- $v = 0$: It means that the current complete binary tree is null, we simply create a node and associate value $v = 0$ with the node. The operation returns the node as CBT.
- $v > 0$: If the current complete binary tree is a perfect binary tree PBT or it consists of a single node only, we need to create a virtual binary tree VBT, which is a copy of the current binary tree. Next, we merge the virtual perfect binary tree with the original one getting a large perfect binary tree. Finally, we need to associate the value v with the least virtual leaf (the leftmost virtual leaf without a value) of the virtual binary tree and set this leaf and its parents as real. For example, in Fig. 2(a), $v = 4$, the nodes with solid line are real and the nodes with dot line are virtual which can be added later. Otherwise, we directly associate the value v to the least virtual leaf and set this leaf and its parents as real [6]. In Fig. 2(b), $v = 5$.

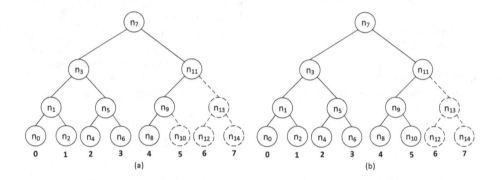

Fig. 2. Example of update operation

Note that, in our range queries, we need to parse a normal database DB to its binary form BDB. First, we need to map keywords of DB to integers in the range $[0, |W| - 1]$, where $|W|$ is the total number of keywords in DB. Next, we construct a binary tree as described above. The keywords are assigned to the nodes of the binary tree and are associated with the documents of their descendants. For example, In Fig. 1a, the keywords are $\{n_0, n_1, \cdots, n_6\}$ and $\mathrm{BDB}(n_0) = \{f_0\}$, $\mathrm{BDB}(n_1) = \{f_0, f_1, f_2, f_3\}$.

4.3 DSSE Range Queries - Construction A

In this section, we apply our new binary tree to the Bost [5] scheme to support range queries. For performing a ranger query, the client in our scheme first determine a collection of keywords to cover the requested range. Then, she generates

---

[6] Only if its parents were virtual, then we need to convert them to real.

the search token corresponding to each node (in the cover) and sends them to the sever, which can be done in a similar way as [5]. Now we are ready to present the first DSSE scheme that supports range queries and is forward-secure. The scheme is described in Algorithm 2, where F is a cryptographically strong pseudorandom function (PRF), H_1 and H_2 are keyed hash functions and Π is a trapdoor permutation.

Setup(1^λ): For a security parameter 1^λ, the algorithm outputs (TPK, TSK, K, $\mathbf{T}, \mathbf{N}, m$), where TPK and TSK are the public key and secret keys of the trapdoor permutation, respectively, K is the secret key of function F, $\mathbf{T}, \mathbf{N}$ are maps and m is the maximum number of the values in our range queries. The map $\mathbf{N}$ is used to store the pair keyword/(ST_c, c) (current search token and the counter c, please see Algorithm 2 for more details.) and is kept by the client. The map $\mathbf{T}$ is the encrypted database EDB that used to store the encrypted indices which is kept by the server.

Search($[a, b], \sigma, m$, EDB): The protocol is executed between a client and a server. The client asks for documents, whose keywords are in the range $[a, b]$, where $0 \leq a \leq b < m$. The current state of EDB is σ and the integer m describes the maximum number of values. Note that knowing m, the client can easily construct the complete binary tree. The server returns a collection of file indices of requested documents.

Update(add, v, ind, σ, m, EDB): The protocol is performed jointly by a client and server. The client wishes to add an integer v together with a file index ind to EDB. The state of EDB is σ, the number of values m. There are following three cases:

- $v < m$: The client simply adds ind to the leaf, which contains value v and its parents (See line 9–24 in Algorithm 2). This is a basic update, which is similar to the one from [5].
- $v - m$: The client first updates the complete binary tree to which she adds the value v. If a new root is added to the new complete binary tree, then the server needs to add all file indices of the old complete binary tree to the new one. Finally, the server needs to add ind to the leaf, which contains value v and its parents.
- $v > m$: The client uses **Update** as many times as needed. For simplicity, we only present the simple case $v = m$, i.e., the newly added value v equals the maximum number of values of the current range $[0, m - 1]$, in the description of Algorithm 2.

The DSSE supports range queries at the cost of large client storage, since the number of search tokens is linear in the number of all nodes of the current tree instead of only leaves. In [5], the number of entries at the client is $|W|$, while it would be roughly $2|W|$ in this construction. Moreover, communication costs is heavy since the server needs to return all file indices to the client when the binary tree is updated with a new root. To overcome the weakness, we give a new construction with lower client storage and communication costs in the following section.

Algorithm 2. Construction A

Setup(1^λ)

Input security parameter 1^λ

Output (TPK, TSK, K, **T**, **N**, m)

  1: $K \leftarrow \{0,1\}^\lambda$

  2: (TSK, TPK) $\leftarrow$ TKeyGen(1^λ)

  3: **T**, **N** $\leftarrow$ empty map

  4: $m = 0$

  5: **return** (TPK, TSK, K, **T**, **N**, m)

Search($[a,b], \sigma, m$, EDB)

Client:

Input $[a,b], \sigma, m$

Output (K_n, ST_c, c)

  1: CBT $\leftarrow$ **TCon**(m)

  2: ABT $\leftarrow$ **TAssign**(CBT)

  3: RSet $\leftarrow$ Find the minimum nodes to cover $[a,b]$ in ABT

  4: **for** $n \in$ RSet **do**

  5:    $K_n \leftarrow F_K(n)$

  6:    $(ST_c, c) \leftarrow$ **N**[n]

  7:    **if** $(ST_c, c) \neq \perp$ **then**

  8:       Send (K_n, ST_c, c) to the server.

  9:    **end if**

10: **end for**

Server:

Input (K_n, ST_c, c), EDB

Output (ind)

11: Upon receiving (K_n, ST_c, c)

12: **for** $i = c$ to 0 **do**

13:    $UT_i \leftarrow H_1(K_n, ST_i)$

14:    $e \leftarrow$ **T**[UT_i]

15:    $ind \leftarrow e \oplus H_2(K_n, ST_i)$

16:    Output the ind

17:    $ST_{i-1} \leftarrow \Pi(\text{TPK}, ST_i)$

18: **end for**

Update(add, v, ind, σ, m, EDB)

Client:

Input add, v, ind, σ, m

Output (UT_{c+1}, e)

  1: CBT $\leftarrow$ **TCon**(m)

  2: **if** $v = m$ **then**

  3:    CBT$\leftarrow$**TUpdate**(add, v, CBT)

  4:    $m \leftarrow m + 1$

  5:    **if** CBT added a new root **then**

  6:       $(ST_c, c) \leftarrow$ **N**[root_o]

  7:       **N**[root_n] $\leftarrow (ST_c, c)$

  8:    **end if**

  9:    Get the leaf n_v of value v.

10:    ABT $\leftarrow$ **TAssign**(CBT)

11:    NSet $\leftarrow$ **TGetNodes**(n_v, ABT)

12:    **for** every node $n \in$ NSet **do**

13:       $K_n \leftarrow F_K(n)$

14:       $(ST_c, c) \leftarrow$ **N**[n]

15:       **if** $(ST_c, c) = \perp$ **then**

16:          $ST_0 \leftarrow \mathcal{M}, c \leftarrow -1$

17:       **else**

18:          $ST_{c+1} \leftarrow \Pi^{-1}(\text{TSK}, ST_c)$

19:       **end if**

20:       **N**[n] $\leftarrow (ST_{c+1}, c+1)$

21:       $UT_{c+1} \leftarrow H_1(K_n, ST_{c+1})$

22:       $e \leftarrow ind \oplus H_2(K_n, ST_{c+1})$

23:       Send (UT_{c+1}, e) to the Server.

24:    **end for**

25: **else if** $v < m$ **then**

26:    Execute line 9-24.

27: **end if**

Server:

Input (UT_{c+1}, e), EDB

Output EDB

28: Upon receiving (UT_{c+1}, e)

29: Set **T**[UT_{c+1}] $\leftarrow e$

4.4 DSSE Range Queries - Construction B

In this section, we give the second construction by leveraging the Paillier cryptosystem [17], which significantly reduce the client storage and communication costs compared with the first one. With the homomorphic addition property of the Paillier cryptosystem, we can add and delete the file indices by parsing them into binary strings, as illustrated in Sect. 4.2. Next we briefly describe our second

DSSE, which can not only support range queries but also achieve both forward and backward security. The scheme is described in Algorithm 3.

Setup(1^λ): For a security parameter 1^λ, the algorithm returns $(\text{PK}, \text{SK}, K, \mathbf{T}, m)$, where PK and SK are the public and secret keys of the Paillier cryptosystem, respectively, K is the secret key of a PRF F, m is the maximum number of values which can be used to reconstruct the binary tree and the encrypted database EDB is stored in a map $\mathbf{T}$ which is kept by the server.

Search$([a, b], \sigma, m, \text{EDB})$: The protocol is executed between a client and a server. The client queries for documents, whose keywords are in the range $[a, b]$, where $0 \le a \le b < m$. σ is the state of EDB, and integer m specifies the maximum values for our range queries. The server returns encrypted file indices e to the client, who can decrypt e by using the secret key SK of Pailler Cryptosystem and obtain the file indices of requested documents.

Update$(op, v, ind, \sigma, m, \text{EDB})$: The protocol runs between a client and a server. A requested update is named by the parameter op. The integer v and the file index ind specifies the tree nodes that need to be updated. The current state σ, the integer m and the server with input EDB. If $op = add$, the client generates a bit string as prescribed in Sect. 4.2. In case when $op = delete$, the client creates the complement bit string as given in Sect. 4.2. The bit string bs is encrypted using the Paillier cryptosystem. The encrypted string is denoted by e. There are following three cases:

- $v < m$: The client sends the encrypted bit string e with the leaf n_v containing value v and its parents to server. Next the server adds c with the existing encrypted bit strings corresponding to the nodes specified by the client. See line 11–23 in Algorithm 3 which is similar to the update in Algorithm 2.
- $v = m$: The client first updates the complete binary tree to which she adds the value v. If a new root is added to the new complete binary tree, then the client retrieves the encrypted bit string of the root (before update). Next the client adds it to the new root by sending it with the new root to the server. Finally, the client adds e to the leaf that contains value v and its parents as in $v < m$ case.
- $v > m$: The client uses **Update** as many times as needed. For simplicity, we only consider $v = m$, where m is the number of values in the maximum range.

In this construction, it achieves both forward and backward security. Moreover, the communication overhead between the client and the server is significantly reduced due to the fact that for each query, the server returns a single ciphertext to the client at the cost of supporting small number of documents. Since, in Paillier cryptosystem, the length of the message is usually small and fixed (e.g. 1024 bits).

This construction can be applied to applications, where the number of documents is small and simultaneously the number of keywords can be large. The reason for this is the fact that for a given keyword, the number of documents which contain it is small. Consider a temperature forecast system that uses a database, which stores records from different sensors (IoT) located in different

---

Algorithm 3. Construction B

Setup(1^λ)

Input security parameter 1^λ

Output (PK, SK, K, **T**, m)

1: $K \leftarrow \{0,1\}^\lambda$
2: (SK, PK) $\leftarrow$ KeyGen(1^λ)
3: **T** $\leftarrow$ empty map
4: $m = 0$
5: **return** (PK, SK, K, **T**, m)

Search($[a,b], \sigma, m$, EDB)

Client:

Input $[a,b], \sigma, m$

Output (UT_n)

1: CBT $\leftarrow$ **TCon**(m)
2: ABT $\leftarrow$ **TAssign**(CBT)
3: **RSet** $\leftarrow$ Find the minimum nodes to cover $[a,b]$ in ABT
4: **for** $n \in$ **RSet do**
5:     $UT_n \leftarrow F_K(n)$
6:     Send UT_n to the server.
7: **end for**

Server:

Input (UT_n), EDB

Output (e)

8: Upon receiving UT_n
9: $e \leftarrow$ **T**$[UT_n]$
10: Send e to the Client.

Update(op, v, ind, σ, m, EDB)

Client:

Input op, v, ind, σ, m

Output (UT_n, e)

1: CBT $\leftarrow$ **TCon**(m)
2: **if** $v = m$ **then**
3:     CBT $\leftarrow$ **TUpdate**(add, v, CBT)
4:     $m \leftarrow m + 1$

5: **if** CBT added a new root **then**
6:     $UT_{\text{root}_o} \leftarrow F_K(\mathbf{root}_o)$
7:     $UT_{\text{root}_n} \leftarrow F_K(\mathbf{root}_n)$
8:     $e \leftarrow$ **T**$[UT_{\text{root}_o}]$
9:     **T**$[UT_{\text{root}_n}] \leftarrow e$
10: **end if**
11: Get the leaf n_v of value v.
12: ABT $\leftarrow$ **TAssign**(CBT)
13: **NSet** $\leftarrow$ **TGetNodes**(n_v, ABT)
14: **if** $op = add$ **then**
15:     Generate the bit string bs as state in Bit String Representation of Sect. 4.2.
16: **else if** $op = del$ **then**
17:     Generate the complement bit string bs as state in Bit String Representation of Sect. 4.2.
18: **end if**
19: **for** every node $n \in$ **NSet do**
20:     $UT_n \leftarrow F_K(n)$
21:     $e \leftarrow$ **Enc**(PK, bs)
22:     Send (UT_n, e) to the server.
23: **end for**
24: **else if** $v < m$ **then**
25:     Execute line 11-23.
26: **end if**

Server:

Input (UT_n, e), EDB

Output EDB

1: Upon receiving (UT_n, e)
2: $e' \leftarrow$ **T**$[UT_n]$
3: **if** $e' \neq \perp$ **then**
4:     $e \leftarrow e \cdot e'$
5: **end if**
6: **T**$[UT_n] \leftarrow e$

---

cities across Australia. In the application, the cities (sensors) can be considered as documents and temperature measurements can be considered as the keywords. For example, Sydney and Melbourne have the temperature of 18°C. Adelaide and Wollongong have got 17°C and 15°C, respectively. If we query for cities, whose temperature measurements are in the range from 17 to 18°C, then the outcome includes Adelaide, Sydney and Melbourne. Here, the number of cities (documents) is not large. The number of different temperature measurements (keywords) can be large depending on requested precision.

5   Security Analysis

In our constructions, we parse a range query into several keywords. Then, following [5], the leakage to the server is summarized as follows:

- search pattern $\mathtt{sp}(w)$, the repetition of the query w.
- history $\mathtt{Hist}(w)$, the history of keyword w. It includes all the updates made to $\mathtt{DB}(w)$.
- contain pattern $\mathtt{cp}(w)$, the inclusion relation between the keyword w with previous queried keywords.
- time $\mathtt{Time}(w)$, the number of updates made to $\mathtt{DB}(w)$ and when the update happened.

Note that, contain pattern $\mathtt{cp}(w)$ is an inherited leakage for range queries when the file indices are revealed to the server. If a query w' is a subrange of query w, then the file index set for w' will also be a subset of the file index set for w.

5.1   Forward Security and Backward Security

Forward security means that an update does not leak any information about keywords of updated documents matching a query we previously issued. A formal definition is given below:

Definition 2. *([5]) A $\mathcal{L}$-adaptively-secure DSSE scheme Γ is forward-secure if the update leakage function $\mathcal{L}^{Updt}$ can be written as*

$$\mathcal{L}^{Updt}(op, in) = \mathcal{L}'(op, (ind_i, \mu_i))$$

where (ind_i, μ_i) is the set of modified documents paired with number μ_i of modified keywords for the updated document ind_i.

Backward security means that a search query on w does not leak the file indices that previously added and later deleted. More formally, we use the level I definition of [6] with modifications which leaks less information. It leaks the encrypted documents currently matching w, when they were updated, and the total number of updates on w.

Definition 3. *A $\mathcal{L}$-adaptively-secure DSSE scheme Γ is insertion pattern revealing backward-secure if the the update leakage function $\mathcal{L}^{Srch}$, $\mathcal{L}^{Updt}$ can be written as $\mathcal{L}^{Updt}(op, w, ind) = \mathcal{L}'(op)$, $\mathcal{L}^{Srch}(w) = \mathcal{L}''(\mathbf{Time}(w))$.*

5.2   Construction A

Since the first DSSE construction is based on [5], it inherits security of the original design. Adaptive security of the construction A can be proven in the Random Oracle Model and is a modification of the security proof of [5]. Due to page limitation, we give a sketch proof here, and refer the reader to the full version [24] for the full proof.

Theorem 1. *(Adaptive forward security of A). Let* $\mathcal{L}_{\Gamma_A} = (\mathcal{L}_{\Gamma_A}^{Srch}, \mathcal{L}_{\Gamma_A}^{Updt})$, *where* $\mathcal{L}_{\Gamma_A}^{Srch}(n) = (sp(n), Hist(n), cp(n))$, $\mathcal{L}_{\Gamma_A}^{Updt}(add, n, ind) = \perp$. *The construction A is* $\mathcal{L}_{\Gamma_A}$-*adaptively forward-secure.*

Proof. (Sketch) Compared with [5], this construction additionally leaks the contain pattern cp as described in Sect. 3.1. Other leakages are exactly the same as [5]. Since the server executes one keyword search and update one keyword/file-index pair at a time. Note that the server does not know the secret key of the trapdoor permutation, so it cannot learn anything about the pair even if the keyword has been searched by the client previously.

5.3   Construction B

The adaptive security of second DSSE construction relies on the semantic security of Paillier cryptosystem. All file indices are encrypted using the public key of Paillier cryptosystem. Without the secret key, the server cannot learn anything from the ciphertext. Due to page limitation, we give a sketch proof here and refer the reader to the full version [24] for the full proof.

Theorem 2. *(Adaptive forward security of B). Let* $\mathcal{L}_{\Gamma_B} = (\mathcal{L}_{\Gamma_B}^{Srch}, \mathcal{L}_{\Gamma_B}^{Updt})$, *where* $\mathcal{L}_{\Gamma_B}^{Srch}(n) = (sp(n))$, $\mathcal{L}_{\Gamma_B}^{Updt}(op, n, ind) = (Time(n))$. *Construction B is* $\mathcal{L}_{\Gamma_B}$-*adaptively forward-secure.*

Proof. (Sketch) In construction B, for the update, we only leak the number of updates corresponding to the queried keywords n. Since all cryptographic operations are performed at the client side where no keys are revealed to the server, the server can learn nothing from the update, given that the Paillier cryptosystem scheme is IND-CPA secure. We can simulate the DSSEREAL as in Algorithm 3 and simulate the DSSEIDEAL by encrypting all 0's strings for the EDB. The adversary $\mathcal{A}$ can not distinguish the real ciphertext from the ciphertext of 0's. Then, $\mathcal{A}$ cannot distinguish DSSEREAL from DSSEIDEAL. Hence, our Construction B achieves forward security.   □

Theorem 3. *(Adaptive backward security of B). Let* $\mathcal{L}_{\Gamma_B} = (\mathcal{L}_{\Gamma_B}^{Srch}, \mathcal{L}_{\Gamma_B}^{Updt})$, *where* $\mathcal{L}_{\Gamma_B}^{Srch}(n) = (sp(n), Hist(n))$, $\mathcal{L}_{\Gamma_B}^{Updt}(op, n, ind) = (Time(n))$. *Construction B is* $\mathcal{L}_{\Gamma_B}$-*adaptively backward-secure.*

Proof. (Sketch) The construction B does not leak the type of update (either add or del) on encrypted file indices since it has been encrypted. Moreover, it does not leak the file indices that previously added and later deleted. The construction B is backward-secure. Since the leakage is same as Theorem 2, then the simulation is same as Theorem 2.   □

6   Conclusion

In this paper, we give two secure DSSE schemes that support range queries. The first DSSE construction applies our binary tree to the scheme from [5] and is forward-secure. However, it incurs a large storage overhead in the client and a large communication costs between the client and the server. To address these problems, we propose the second DSSE construction with range queries that uses Paillier cryptosystem. It achieves both the forward and backward security. Although the second DSSE construction cannot support large number of documents, it can still be very useful in certain applications. In the future, we would like to construct more scalable DSSE schemes with more expressive queries.

Acknowledgment. The authors thank the anonymous reviewers for the valuable comments. This work was supported by the Natural Science Foundation of Zhejiang Province [grant number LZ18F020003], the National Natural Science Foundation of China [grant number 61472364] and the Australian Research Council (ARC) Grant DP180102199. Josef Pieprzyk has been supported by National Science Centre, Poland, project registration number UMO-2014/15/B/ST6/05130.

References

1. Agrawal, R., Kiernan, J., Srikant, R., Xu, Y.: Order preserving encryption for numeric data. In: Proceedings of the 2004 ACM SIGMOD Ninternational Conference on Management of Data, pp. 563–574. ACM (2004)
2. Boldyreva, A., Chenette, N., Lee, Y., O'Neill, A.: Order-preserving symmetric encryption. In: Joux, A. (ed.) EUROCRYPT 2009. LNCS, vol. 5479, pp. 224–241. Springer, Heidelberg (2009). https://doi.org/10.1007/978-3-642-01001-9_13
3. Boldyreva, A., Chenette, N., O'Neill, A.: Order-preserving encryption revisited: improved security analysis and alternative solutions. In: Rogaway, P. (ed.) CRYPTO 2011. LNCS, vol. 6841, pp. 578–595. Springer, Heidelberg (2011). https://doi.org/10.1007/978-3-642-22792-9_33
4. Boneh, D., Lewi, K., Raykova, M., Sahai, A., Zhandry, M., Zimmerman, J.: Semantically secure order-revealing encryption: multi-input functional encryption without obfuscation. In: Oswald, E., Fischlin, M. (eds.) EUROCRYPT 2015. LNCS, vol. 9057, pp. 563–594. Springer, Heidelberg (2015). https://doi.org/10.1007/978-3-662-46803-6_19
5. Bost, R.: Σ οφος: forward secure searchable encryption. In: Proceedings of the 2016 ACM SIGSAC Conference on Computer and Communications Security, pp. 1143–1154. ACM (2016)
6. Bost, R., Minaud, B., Ohrimenko, O.: Forward and backward private searchable encryption from constrained cryptographic primitives. In: Proceedings of the 2017 ACM SIGSAC Conference on Computer and Communications Security, pp. 1465–1482. ACM (2017)
7. Cash, D., Grubbs, P., Perry, J., Ristenpart, T.: Leakage-abuse attacks against searchable encryption. In: Proceedings of the 22nd ACM SIGSAC Conference on Computer and Communications Security, pp. 668–679. ACM (2015)
8. Cash, D., et al.: Dynamic searchable encryption in very-large databases: data structures and implementation. In: NDSS, vol. 14, pp. 23–26. Citeseer (2014)
9. Cash, D., Jarecki, S., Jutla, C., Krawczyk, H., Roşu, M.-C., Steiner, M.: Highly-scalable searchable symmetric encryption with support for boolean queries. In: Canetti, R., Garay, J.A. (eds.) CRYPTO 2013. LNCS, vol. 8042, pp. 353–373. Springer, Heidelberg (2013). https://doi.org/10.1007/978-3-642-40041-4_20

10. Chenette, N., Lewi, K., Weis, S.A., Wu, D.J.: Practical order-revealing encryption with limited leakage. In: Peyrin, T. (ed.) FSE 2016. LNCS, vol. 9783, pp. 474–493. Springer, Heidelberg (2016). https://doi.org/10.1007/978-3-662-52993-5_24

11. Curtmola, R., Garay, J., Kamara, S., Ostrovsky, R.: Searchable symmetric encryption: improved definitions and efficient constructions. In: Proceedings of the 13th ACM Conference on Computer and Communications Security, pp. 79–88. ACM (2006)

12. Demertzis, I., Papadopoulos, S., Papapetrou, O., Deligiannakis, A., Garofalakis, M.: Practical private range search revisited. In: Proceedings of the 2016 International Conference on Management of Data, pp. 185–198. ACM (2016)

13. Faber, S., Jarecki, S., Krawczyk, H., Nguyen, Q., Rosu, M., Steiner, M.: Rich queries on encrypted data: beyond exact matches. In: Pernul, G., Ryan, P.Y.A., Weippl, E. (eds.) ESORICS 2015. LNCS, vol. 9327, pp. 123–145. Springer, Cham (2015). https://doi.org/10.1007/978-3-319-24177-7_7

14. Kamara, S., Papamanthou, C., Roeder, T.: Dynamic searchable symmetric encryption. In: Proceedings of the 2012 ACM Conference on Computer and Communications Security, pp. 965–976. ACM (2012)

15. Kasra Kermanshahi, S., Liu, J.K., Steinfeld, R.: Multi-user cloud-based secure keyword search. In: Pieprzyk, J., Suriadi, S. (eds.) ACISP 2017. LNCS, vol. 10342, pp. 227–247. Springer, Cham (2017). https://doi.org/10.1007/978-3-319-60055-0_12

16. Kim, K.S., Kim, M., Lee, D., Park, J.H., Kim, W.H.: Forward secure dynamic searchable symmetric encryption with efficient updates. In: Proceedings of the 2017 ACM SIGSAC Conference on Computer and Communications Security, pp. 1449–1463. ACM (2017)

17. Paillier, P.: Public-key cryptosystems based on composite degree residuosity classes. In: Stern, J. (ed.) EUROCRYPT 1999. LNCS, vol. 1592, pp. 223–238. Springer, Heidelberg (1999). https://doi.org/10.1007/3-540-48910-X_16

18. Song, D.X., Wagner, D., Perrig, A.: Practical techniques for searches on encrypted data. In: Proceedings 2000 IEEE Symposium on Security and Privacy. S&P 2000, pp. 44–55. IEEE (2000)

19. Stefanov, E., Papamanthou, C., Shi, E.: Practical dynamic searchable encryption with small leakage. In: NDSS, vol. 71, pp. 72–75 (2014)

20. Sun, S.-F., Liu, J.K., Sakzad, A., Steinfeld, R., Yuen, T.H.: An efficient non-interactive multi-client searchable encryption with support for boolean queries. In: Askoxylakis, I., Ioannidis, S., Katsikas, S., Meadows, C. (eds.) ESORICS 2016. LNCS, vol. 9878, pp. 154–172. Springer, Cham (2016). https://doi.org/10.1007/978-3-319-45744-4_8

21. Wang, Y., Wang, J., Sun, S.-F., Liu, J.K., Susilo, W., Chen, X.: Towards multi-user searchable encryption supporting boolean query and fast decryption. In: Okamoto, T., Yu, Y., Au, M.H., Li, Y. (eds.) ProvSec 2017. LNCS, vol. 10592, pp. 24–38. Springer, Cham (2017). https://doi.org/10.1007/978-3-319-68637-0_2

22. Zhang, Y., Katz, J., Papamanthou, C.: All your queries are belong to Us: the power of file-injection attacks on searchable encryption. In: USENIX Security Symposium, pp. 707–720 (2016)

23. Zuo, C., Macindoe, J., Yang, S., Steinfeld, R., Liu, J.K.: Trusted boolean search on cloud using searchable symmetric encryption. In: Trustcom/BigDataSE/ISPA, 2016 IEEE, pp. 113–120. IEEE (2016)

24. Zuo, C., Sun, S.F., Liu, J.K., Shao, J., Pieprzyk, J.: Dynamic searchable symmetric encryption schemes supporting range queries with forward (and backward) security. IACR Cryptology ePrint Archive (2018). http://eprint.iacr.org/

Applied Crypto (I)

Breaking Message Integrity of an End-to-End Encryption Scheme of LINE

Takanori Isobe[1(✉)] and Kazuhiko Minematsu[2]

[1] University of Hyogo, Kobe, Japan
takanori.isobe@ai.u-hyogo.ac.jp
[2] NEC Corporation, Kawasaki, Japan
k-minematsu@ah.jp.nec.com

Abstract. In this paper, we analyze the security of an end-to-end encryption scheme (E2EE) of LINE, a.k.a Letter Sealing. LINE is one of the most widely-deployed instant messaging applications, especially in East Asia. By a close inspection of their protocols, we give several attacks against the message integrity of Letter Sealing. Specifically, we propose forgery and impersonation attacks on the one-to-one message encryption and the group message encryption. All of our attacks are feasible with the help of an end-to-end adversary, who has access to the inside of the LINE server (e.g. service provider LINE themselves). We stress that the main purpose of E2EE is to provide a protection against the end-to-end adversary. In addition, we found some attacks that even do not need the help of E2E adversary, which shows a critical security flaw of the protocol. Our results reveal that the E2EE scheme of LINE do not sufficiently guarantee the integrity of messages compared to the state-of-the-art E2EE schemes such as Signal, which is used by WhatApp and Facebook Messenger.

Keywords: E2EE · LINE · Key exchange · Group message
Authenticated encryption

1 Introduction

1.1 Background

An end-to-end encryption (E2EE) is a secure communication scheme for messaging applications where the only people who are communicating can send and read the messages, i.e. no other party, even service providers of communication system, cannot access to the cryptographic keys needed to encrypt the message, and decrypt the ciphertexts. After Snowden's revelation, the E2EE receives a lot of attentions as a technology to protect a user privacy from mass interception and surveillance of communications carried out by governmental organizations such as NSA (National Security Agency).

Apple first supported an E2EE scheme in their widely-deployed messaging application, iMessage, where a message that is compressed by gzip is encrypted

© Springer Nature Switzerland AG 2018
J. Lopez et al. (Eds.): ESORICS 2018, LNCS 11099, pp. 249–268, 2018.
https://doi.org/10.1007/978-3-319-98989-1_13

by a sender's secret key and distributed with a digital signature for the guarantee of the integrity to the recipient. Unfortunately, several security flaws of the initial iMessage are pointed out in 2016 [20]. A Signal is a new E2EE protocol for instant messaging. The core of the Signal protocol has been adopted by WhatsApp, Facebook Messenger, and Google Allo. A novel technology called ratcheting key update structure enables advanced security properties such as perfect forward secrecy and so-called post-compromise security [17]. Since Signal is an open-source application and its source code for Android and iOS are available on Github [25], its security has been studied well from the cryptographic community [15, 16, 26].

LINE is one of the most widely-deployed messaging applications, especially in East Asia. The number of monthly active users of four key countries, namely Japan, Taiwan, Thailand and Indonesia is about 217 million in January 2017. Their market is still growing, and at the same time their applications are expanding such as banking, payment, shopping, music services. Indeed, it is currently a key platform for any IT services in these countries. For example, Japanese government recently launched a portal cite for management of Japanese social security number, called "My number"or "Individual number", in cooperation with LINE [7]. In fact, LINE dominates the market of mobile messaging application in Japan. It is estimated that more than 85% smartphone users in Japan are regularly using LINE in 2017 [8].

In 2015, LINE announced their new E2EE scheme, called *Letter Sealing*, for a pairwise secure communication between the end users [6]. It became a default feature in 2016, and was also deployed for the group messaging service. While the specification of Letter Sealing was initially not public, after some details were revealed by the reverse engineering [18], a whitepaper describing the high-level specification was published in 2016 [23]. Letter Sealing consists of key generation and registration, client-to-client key exchange, and message encryption phases. To the best of our knowledge, there is only one result of its security analysis by Espinoza et al. [19] which pointed out the lack of forward secrecy and the feasibility of reply attack.

1.2 Our Contribution

In this paper, we show several attacks on the E2EE scheme of LINE by a close inspection of their protocols described in the whitepaper [23] and some reverse engineering results publicly available [18, 19].

Impersonation and Forgery Attacks on Group Message Encryption.
We show impersonation and forgery attacks on the group message encryption scheme by a *malicious group member*, who is a legitimate member of a target group but aims to break the integrity of the message sent by an honest group member. These attacks exploit a vulnerability of the key derivation phase in the group message encryption such that any group member, even a malicious member, is able to derive an encryption key of another member for a group

messaging without any knowledge of a target member's secret. By exploiting this vulnerability, a malicious member is able to send a message to a group as if it was from an honest member, that is, an impersonation attack. Moreover, if a malicious member colludes with an *E2E adversary*, who bypasses client-to-server encryption (e.g. LINE themselves) or if a malicious member herself is the E2E adversary, she freely modifies a message sent by an honest member without being noticed by the other members about the fact that it was tampered, that is, a forgery attack.

Malicious Key Exchange Attacks. We propose a malicious key exchange of the one-to-one E2EE to mount impersonation attacks by a *malicious user* who is a legitimate member of a target group but aims to break the integrity of the message in the other sessions. Exploiting vulnerabilities both of the key exchange and the message encryption phases, a malicious user C establishes a malicious E2EE session with a victim B in which a shared secret between C and B is the same as the one used in a different E2EE session between B and another victim A. Then, the malicious user C is able to impersonate victims A and B. More specifically, the malicious user C is able to

- send a message, that is originally sent to C from B, to A as a message from B (impersonation attack 1),
- send a message, that is originally sent to B from A, to B as a message from C (impersonation attack 2).

Our impersonation attacks are possible by a malicious user who has a trusted relationship with one of the two victims between which a pairwise secure channel is already established. For example, a victim A and the malicious user C are B's friend in the real world, or are company's accounts that B can trust, while the victim A does not need to trust C, and might even not know C. Importantly, even a normal user, who is *not* an E2E adversary (LINE), is able to perform the impersonation attack 1 as long as the above assumption holds. We think that these situations can happen in the real-world use cases of LINE. On the other hand, for the impersonation attack 2, a malicious user needs to collude with E2E adversary (LINE) to bypass the server-client encryption.

Forgery Attack on Authenticated Encryption Scheme. Finally, we evaluate the security of an authenticated encryption (AE) scheme used in the message encryption phase, which combines AES-256 and SHA-256 in a non-standard way. We show that the E2E adversary is able to mount a forgery attack, i.e. the adversary made a forgery message which is accepted as valid by the recipient. Compared to the previous attacks, this forgery attack does not require the assumption that the adversary has a trusted relation to the victim in advance. Thus, any user in the one-to-one and group message encryptions could be the victim of this attack. Furthermore, we give a rigorous security analysis of AE in LINE as a general-purpose authenticated encryption.

This attack is not much practical in terms of the time complexity of the attack, because it needs 2^b offline computation and 2^d online computation for $b + d = 128$, implying **64-bit security**. The popular AE schemes using 128-bit block cipher also have 64-bit security, however, this is about the online data complexity (i.e. it is secure if one key is used with data smaller than 2^{64}). Thus, the implications are quite different. For example, AE in LINE can be broken with 2^{80} offline computation plus 2^{40} online computation, which is not the case of generic composition of CBC mode using AES-256 plus HMAC-SHA-256, as used by Signal.

The attack with 2^b offline computation and 2^d online computation for $b + d = 128$ may be within reach by powerful national organizations such as NSA.

Table 1. Comparison with previous [19] and our attacks: *E2E* is an adversary who has access to the inside of the LINE server. *Malicious member* is a legitimate member of a target group but tries to break the integrity of the message sent by an honest member. *Malicious user* is an end user who is trusted by the victim B where the victim A and B have a pairwise secure connection which is an attack target by the malicious user.

Target	Attack type	Adversary	Reference
One-to-one encryption	Replay	E2E	[19]
Group encryption	Impersonation	Malicious member	Sect. 4.1
	Forgery	Malicious member w/E2E	Sect. 4.2
One-to-one encryption	Impersonation 1	Malicious user	Sect. 5.2
	Impersonation 2	Malicious user w/E2E	Sect. 5.3
One-to-one and group encryption	Forgery	E2E	Sect. 6

Summary. Table 1 summarizes our results. All of our attacks are possible for the E2E adversary, which is the original target adversary of the E2EE scheme, and more powerful than the previous one [19] as impersonation and forgery attacks violate the integrity of the message, which is one of the fundamental security properties. Some of our attacks are performed by not only the E2E adversary but also weaker adversaries such as a malicious group member and a malicious user.

Responsible Disclosure. In December 2017, we delivered our results in this paper to LINE Corporation via the LINE security bug bounty program. They acknowledged that *all of our attacks are feasible with the help of E2E adversary*, and officially recognized our findings as a vulnerability of *encryption break* in the bug bounty program. LINE Corporation told us (and granted us to make it public) that they have a plan to change the key exchange protocol, the group messaging scheme, and the authenticated encryption scheme to improve the security of Letter Sealing in the near future.

On the other hand, they told us that our attacks by a malicious member (Sect. 4.1) and a malicious user (Sect. 5.2) not colluding with LINE Corporation (i.e. E2E adversary) can be mitigated by certain server-side countermeasures. For instance, a malicious key exchange can be prevented by checking the duplication of public keys in the LINE key server. Since they hope to keep the details of their server-side countermeasures secret, we will not explain them here. We consider that it seems difficult to directly apply our attacks without the help of the E2E adversary after we informed LINE Corporation in December 2017. That is, these attacks are now applicable only with the help of E2E adversary who can bypass the server-side countermeasures.

2   Specification of E2EE Scheme of LINE

In this section, we give a high-level description of the E2EE scheme of LINE, called Letter Sealing. The whitepaper published by LINE Corporation [23] describes two types of E2EE schemes: a one-to-one message encryption and a one-to-N group message encryption.

2.1   One-to-One Message Encryption

The one-to-one message encryption scheme of LINE consists of key generation and registration, client-to-client key exchange, and message encryption phases.

Key Generation and Registration Phase. When a LINE application is launched at the first time, each client application generates a key pair of (sk, pk) for the key exchange, where sk and pk are a secret key and a public key for Elliptic curve Diffie–Hellman (ECDH) based on Curve25519 [12], respectively. The client stores the secret key sk into application's private storage area, and registers the public key pk with a LINE messaging server. The server associates the public key pk with the currently authenticated client and sends back a unique key ID to the client. Each key ID is bound to a user and includes the version information of the key.

Client-to-Client Key Exchange Phase. To start a session for exchanging messages between a client and a recipient, the client shares the key called *SharedSecret* with the recipient as follows.

1. Retrieve the recipient public key pk_r from a LINE messaging server.
2. Generate a shared secret *SharedSecret* from the public key pk_r and a client secret key sk_c by ECDH over Curve25519 as

$$SharedSecret = \text{ECDH}_{\text{Curve25519}}(sk_c, pk_r),$$

where $\text{ECDH}_{\text{Curve25519}}$ is a key exchange function (see [12] for details).

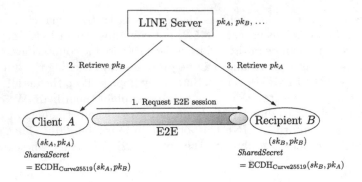

Fig. 1. Key exchange phase based on ECDH over Curve25519

At the same time, the recipient generates the same *SharedSecret* with the recipient secret key sk_r and the client public key pk_c as

$$SharedSecret = \text{ECDH}_{\text{Curve25519}}(sk_r, pk_c).$$

Figure 1 illustrates this key exchange phase.

To make sure that the retrieved public key is a correct one, the fingerprint of a recipient's public key can be displayed in the device. Users can verify it out-of-band.

Message Encryption Phase. A message is encrypted by a unique pair of a 256-bit key K_e and a 128-bit IV (Initialization Vector) IV_e, generated for each message. K_e and IV_e are derived from *SharedSecret* and a randomly-chosen 8-byte *salt* as follows.

$$K_e = \text{SHA}_{256}(SharedSecret \parallel salt \parallel \textsf{Key}), \tag{1}$$

$$IV_{\text{pre}} = \text{SHA}_{256}(SharedSecret \parallel salt \parallel \textsf{IV}), \tag{2}$$

$$IV_e = IV_{\text{pre}}^{\text{left}} \oplus IV_{\text{pre}}^{\text{right}}. \tag{3}$$

Here, $\text{SHA}_{256}(\cdot)$ denotes SHA-256 hash function that outputs a 256-bit digest from an arbitrary-length input [5], and IV_{pre} is a 256-bit variable, and $IV_{\text{pre}}^{\text{left}}$ and $IV_{\text{pre}}^{\text{right}}$ are left and right 128-bit values of IV_{pre}, respectively, i.e. $IV_{\text{pre}} = IV_{\text{pre}}^{\text{left}} \parallel IV_{\text{pre}}^{\text{right}}$. The constants $\textsf{Key}$ and $\textsf{IV}$ denote the corresponding ASCII strings in base64 [18].

A message M is encrypted with K_e and IV_e, and a ciphertext C is obtained as

$$C = \text{CBC}[E](K_e, IV_e, M),$$

where $\text{CBC}[E](K, IV, M)$ denotes CBC encryption mode with AES-256 that takes a 256-bit key K and a 128-bit IV IV, and an arbitrary-length message M as inputs, and outputs a ciphertext C. See [1,2] for details of AES-256 and CBC

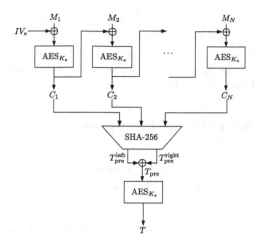

Fig. 2. Authenticated encryption scheme of LINE

mode. A padding scheme is needed in case the bit length of M is not a multiple of 128, however it is not described in the whitepaper.

Next, the ciphertext C is hashed by a variant of SHA_{256} called SHA'_{256} defined as

$$V = \mathrm{SHA}_{256}(C), \quad \text{and } T_{\mathrm{pre}} = V_{\mathrm{pre}}^{\mathrm{left}} \oplus V_{\mathrm{pre}}^{\mathrm{right}},$$

where V is a 256-bit value, and $V_{\mathrm{pre}}^{\mathrm{left}}$ and $V_{\mathrm{pre}}^{\mathrm{right}}$ are left and right 128-bit values of V, and T_{pre} is a 128-bit variable. Then, a 128-bit message authentication tag T is computed by

$$T = E(K_e, T_{\mathrm{pre}}),$$

where $E(K, M)$ denotes an encryption of 128-bit M using AES-256 with 256-bit key K. Figure 2 shows the overview of the authenticated encryption scheme of LINE.

Finally, the client sends the packet D including the ciphertext C and the tag T with associated data (AD). The form of packet D is as follows.

$$D = \text{version} \parallel \text{content type} \parallel salt \parallel C \parallel T \parallel$$
$$\text{sender key ID} \parallel \text{recipient key ID.} \tag{4}$$

Here, AD consists of version, content type, sender key ID and recipient key ID. The first two fields serve to identity the Letter Sealing version used to create the message. The recipient uses the sender key ID to retrieve the public key used to encrypt the message. The recipient key ID value helps to verify that the message can be decrypted using the current local private key. Messages that are processed by a previous key pair (such as one used before migrating to the current device) cannot be decrypted. To facilitate a device migration, the client automatically requests the recent messages processed by a previous key pair to be resent. Once the recipient received the packet D from the client, he derives the same key K_e, and IV IV_e from the shared secret *SharedSecret* as described above. Next, he calculates the tag T from the received ciphertext C, and compares it with the tag value included in the message. If they match, the contents of the message M is decrypted and displayed. Otherwise, the message is discarded.

2.2   One-to-N Group Message Encryption

In the one-to-N group messaging, a group key K_g is shared with all group members via one-to-one message encryption channels. The first member who starts a end-to-end group messaging generates K_g and shares it with all group members as follows.

1. Generate a pair of a secret key sk_g and a public key pk_g for ECDH over Curve25519, where sk_g is used as a group key K_g.
2. Retrieve public keys of all group members from the LINE server, and calculate N shared secrets *SharedSecret* for all members from own private key and a public key of each member to establish a one-to-one message encryption to each member.
3. Broadcast k_g to all members via one-to-one message encryption channels.

Whenever members join or leave the group, K_g is renewed and shared with the group.

Once K_g is shared with all members, a member A who wants to send a message to the group derives a 256-bit encryption key K_e^A and a 128-bit IV IV_e^A from K_g and A's public key pk_A as follows.

$$SharedSecret_g^A = \text{ECDH}_{\text{Curve25519}}(K_g, pk_A), \tag{5}$$

$$K_e = \text{SHA}_{256}(SharedSecret_g^A \,\|\, salt \,\|\, \text{Key}), \tag{6}$$

$$IV_{\text{pre}} = \text{SHA}_{256}(SharedSecret_g^A \,\|\, salt \,\|\, \text{IV}), \tag{7}$$

$$IV_e = IV_{\text{pre}}^{\text{left}} \oplus IV_{\text{pre}}^{\text{right}}. \tag{8}$$

The message data is encrypted and formatted as described in the one-to-one message encryption with the only difference that the recipient key ID field is replaced with the key ID of the group's shared key.

3   Security Model of E2EE

In this section, we explain adversary models and security requirements of E2EE.

3.1   Adversary Model

In a E2EE scheme, no one except a client and a recipient can be trusted, i.e. there is no any trusted third party, and even a service provider (e.g., LINE) is a potential adversary. In this setting, the client-to-server transport encryption (cf. Sect. 3 in [23]) is useless, as the adversary can control the LINE server which stores the secret key for the client-to-server transport encryption. We call such an adversary *E2E adversary*.

Definition 1 (E2E adversary). *An E2E adversary is able to intercept, read and modify any messages sent over the network, and has full access to the messaging server, i.e. bypasses the client-to-server encryption.*

Generally, the E2E adversary is assumed to have a very strong computational power to capture the powerful national organizations for intelligence, such as NSA and GCHQ (Government Communications Headquarters), because one of the objectives of E2EE is to protect user privacy from the mass interception and surveillance of communications against such organizations. In addition, we define a weaker adversary, *malicious user*.

Definition 2 (Malicious User). *An malicious user is a legitimate of one-to-one E2EE but she tries to break one of the subsequently defined security goals of the other E2EE session by maliciously manipulating the protocol.*

A malicious user is much weaker than the original targeted adversary of the E2E adversary, because any user is potentially a malicious user. We will show that even such a weaker adversary than the original target of E2EE can attack the E2EE protocol of LINE.

The existence of *malicious group member* in One-to-N group message encryption must be taken into consideration, as already discussed in some recent papers [15, 26].

Definition 3 (Malicious group member). *A malicious group member, who is a legitimate group member and possesses a shared group key, tries to break the subsequently defined security goals by deviating from the protocol.*

Note that a malicious user and a malicious group member can collude with the E2E adversary in the security model of E2EE, or the E2E adversary herself can be a malicious user and a malicious group member.

3.2 Security Goals

We explain the following two fundamental security goals of E2EE.

Definition 4 (Confidentiality). *Only the two participants of pair-wise messaging or legitimate group member of group messaging can see the message plaintext.*

Definition 5 (Integrity). *If a message is received and successfully validated, then it was indeed sent by the given sender, i.e., other users cannot plant messages into it and they can not modify it.*

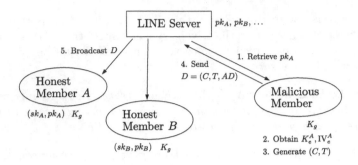

Fig. 3. Impersonation attack

We remark that more advanced security properties of E2EE can be found in the literature, such as forward secrecy, post-compromise security, and traceable delivery [15–17, 26]. Still, an E2EE scheme should guarantee at least the confidentiality and the integrity against the E2E adversary. Since a malicious user and a malicious group member are weaker than the E2E adversary, a secure E2EE scheme should also be secure against any attack by them.

Since a malicious member has a group shared key K_g for the group message encryption, she is able to decrypt any group message. Thus, it is natural to assume that her purpose is to break the integrity.

4   Impersonation and Forgery Attacks on Group Message

This section gives impersonation and forgery attacks on the group message encryption by a malicious group member. Both attacks exploit a following vulnerability of the key derivation phase in the group message encryption.

Vulnerability 1 (Key Derivation of Group Message). *The key and IV for the symmetric-key encryption are derived from a group-shared key K_g and sender's public information.*

A group member A, who wants to send a message to a group, first computes a shared secret $SharedSecret_g^A$ from a group key K_g and sender's public key pk_A. Since a malicious member also possesses K_g and is able to retrieve sender's public key pk_A from the LINE server, she can compute $SharedSecret_g^A$ by which, thus is able to derive K_e^A and IV_e^A as shown in Eqs. (6) and (8). Hence, a malicious member is able to compute any group member's key and IV for the group message.

4.1   Impersonation Attack

Exploiting Vulnerability 1, a malicious group member impersonates an honest member A in the group message encryption as follows.

1. Retrieve A's public key pk_A from the LINE server.
2. Derive K_e^A and IV_e^A from a group-shared key K_g, pk_A and a randomly-generated *salt*.
3. Generate a ciphertext C and a tag T of the message M that the malicious group member chooses.
4. Prepare a packet D following the Eq. (4) by properly choosing AD where sender key ID is set to the victim A's one.
5. Broadcast D to all members via the LINE server.

Figure 3 shows the overview of our impersonation attack. Since the tag T is generated by the valid key of the member A, group members except A do not notice that it is created by the malicious member. When A sees this fake message, A should notice, however, there is no formal way to refute. Therefore, this attack reveals that *the group message encryption of LINE does not provides the authenticity of the message against a malicious member.*

Furthermore, if the malicious member colludes with the LINE server (E2E adversary), it is possible to broadcast D, made by the malicious member, to all members except the victim A. Then, the victim A does not notice that such a attack is mounted by the malicious member.

4.2 Forgery Attack

If a malicious member intercepts a group message that the honest member A sends, she is able to mount a forgery attack as follows (see also Fig. 4).

1. Intercept a packet D sent by the member A, by watching the communication between the victim A and the LINE server.
2. Compute K_e^A and IV_e^A from a group key K_g and a public key pk_A, and *salt* which is derived from D.
3. Decrypt it with K_e^A and IV_e^A and modify the message M of the victim A.
4. Re-encrypt the modified message M' with K_e^A and IV_e^A to generate a new ciphertext C' and a tag T'.
5. Broadcast D' including C', T' and associated data to all members except A, and send the original D to the victim A via the LINE server.

To mount the above attack, a malicious member (C) must intercept packet D between the victim A and the server before it is sent to all members by the LINE server. Since this channel is protected by the client-to-server transport encryption, the malicious member is not able to get D that is encrypted by only K_e^A and IV_e^A. Recall that the E2E adversary is able to bypass the client-to-server transport encryption. If the malicious member colludes with the E2E adversary or the malicious member herself is the E2E adversary, this forgery attack is successful. Furthermore, since the E2E adversary sends unmodified packet D to only the victim A, the victim A does not notice the forgery attack is mounted. Thus, this attack shows that *the E2EE of group messages of LINE does not satisfies the integrity of the message when a malicious member colludes with the E2E adversary.*

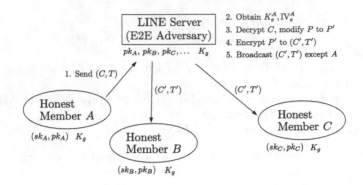

Fig. 4. Forgery attack on the group message

4.3 Discussion

The specification of LINE currently allows a group of up to 500 members (as of April 2018), and the applications of the group messaging service are rapidly expanding, from private to business, banking, advertising, payments, and social network service. In some use cases, it is hard to strictly check the identity of group members, e.g. an online group for common interest and hobby. We believe that there is a significant risk that a group member is malicious. Furthermore if the LINE official account is involved in the target group, the scenario of the forgery attack, i.e., malicious member collude with the E2E adversary, is easily realized. In this case, the impersonation attack is also feasible.

5   Malicious Key Exchange Attack on One-to-One Message Encryption

This section presents a malicious key exchange of the one-to-one message encryption, which leads to an impersonation attack. Our attacks exploit the following vulnerabilities of the key exchange and the message encryption phases.

Vulnerability 2 (No key confirmation). *In the client-to-client key exchange phase, there is no key confirmation.*

In the client-to-client key exchange phase, after individually computing a shared secret *SharedSecret* in both client and recipient sides, there is no key confirmation phase between the client and the recipient. Thus, even if *SharedSecret* is not correctly shared between the client and the recipient, the client is not able to confirm that the recipient possess a shared secret, and vice versa.

Vulnerability 3 (Integrity of packet). *In the message encryption phase, the integrity of the elements of associated data in a packet D, such as* sender key ID *and* recipient key ID, *is not guaranteed.*

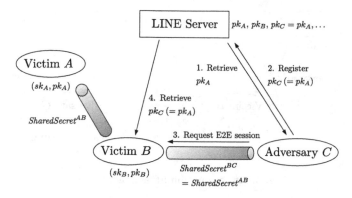

Fig. 5. Malicious key exchange

When computing a message authentication tag, T, $\text{SHA}'_{256}(\cdot)$ takes a ciphertext C as a sole input, and the associated data is just appended to the ciphertext C and the tag T. Hence, the recipient is unable to verify the integrity of associated data. This vulnerability has been pointed out in the previous works [18,19], and used for replay attacks.

5.1 Malicious Key Exchange

Our malicious key exchange is a variant of unknown key share attack [13]. An adversary (malicious user) C shares a secret key with a victim B where the shared secret key is the same as one used in a different session between victims A and B, while the victim A does not know the fact. Our attack is performed under the following assumptions.

Assumption 1. *Two victims A and B have already established a pairwise E2EE session.*

Assumption 2. *An adversary (malicious user) C is able to establish another E2EE session with B which has not been established yet.*

In other words, a victim B trusts both a victim A and a malicious user C, e.g. A and C are B's friend in the real world, or are company's accounts that B can trust, while the victim A does not need to trust C and might even not know the adversary C. Under these assumptions, C attacks on the E2EE session between A and B. Specifically, C tries to establish a fake E2EE session with B where the key and IV are the same as those used in the A-B session.

To establish this fake session, C performs the following procedures in the key generation and registration phases by exploiting Vulnerability 2 (see Fig. 5).

1. Retrieve a public key pk_A from the LINE server.
2. Registers pk_A in the LINE messaging server as C's public key.
3. Request a new E2EE session with B.

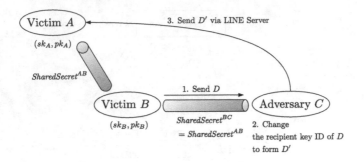

Fig. 6. Impersonation attack against B

After that, the victim B computes a shared secret $SharedSecret^{BC}$ for the one-to-one, E2EE between B and C as

$$SharedSecret^{BC} = \text{ECDH}_{\text{Curve25519}}(sk_B, pk_A).$$

which is the same as the shared secret between A and B. Here, C does not know the value of $SharedSecret^{BC}$, because she does not know sk_A. Nevertheless, due to the lack of the key confirmation (Vulnerability 2), the protocol will not abort, and an E2E session will be established between B and C.

5.2 Impersonation Attack 1: Impersonating B

After the malicious key exchange, the malicious user C is able to send a packet to A which was originally sent from B to C by impersonating B.

1. Receive a packet D which is sent from B to C.
2. Create a new packet D' where recipient key ID is modified from C to A.
3. Send the packet D' to A as a message from the malicious user C via the LINE server.

Figure 6 shows the overview of impersonation attack against B. Due to the lack of the integrity check for recipient key ID in the associated data (Vulnerability 3), the victim A believes that the message is sent from B instead of C while B believes that the message is sent to C and does not notice the message is sent to A.

5.3 Impersonation Attack 2: Impersonating A

The malicious user C can also send a message to B by impersonating A.

1. Intercept a packet D which is sent from A to B.
2. Create a new packet D' where sender key ID is modified from A to C.
3. Send the packet D' to B as a message from the adversary C.

If the adversary colludes with an E2E adversary or she herself is an E2E adversary, she can bypass the client-to-server encryption, and intercept a packet D. Indeed, a packet D is sent to B from A via the LINE server (Fig. 7).

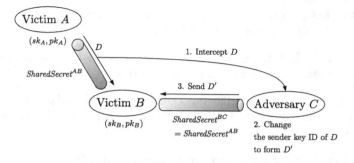

Fig. 7. Impersonation attack against A

5.4 Discussion

Our impersonation attack 1 is feasible as long as the Assumptions 1 and 2 hold. This implies that even a normal user, who is *not* an E2E adversary, is able to mount the attack. Suppose that the victim B sends a very personal request (e.g. asking for debt) to the malicious user C, then C can send a request to the victim A by impersonating B. Then, B's sensitive information is *unintentionally* disclosed to A as a valid message from B. It is a significant problem of privacy.

The impersonation attack 2 is feasible if the Assumptions 1 and 2 hold and the client-to-server encryption is bypassed. For example, if the LINE official account is an E2E adversary, this account is able to mount the impersonation attack 2.

6 Security Evaluation of Message Encryption Scheme

This section evaluates the security of the authenticated encryption scheme in the message encryption phase (hereafter, we call it LINE-AE), and presents a forgery attack by the E2E adversary. Our forgery attack exploits the vulnerability of LINE-AE, which is an original authenticated encryption scheme, i.e. it is not a standard scheme such as generic composition of an encryption and a message authentication code (MAC), e.g. CBC mode and HMAC, or dedicated schemes (modes) such as GCM [4] and CCM [3].

Compared to the previous attacks in Sect. 5, this forgery attack does not require the assumption that the adversary has a trusted relation to the victim in advance. Thus, any user in the one-to-one and group message encryptions could be the victim of this attack.

6.1 Authenticated Encryption: LINE-AE

As shown by Sect. 2.1, LINE-AE first encrypts a message by CBC mode with AES-256, and generates a ciphertext C. After that, a tag T for the ciphertext C is computed as follows: the ciphertext C is hashed by $\text{SHA}'_{256}(C)$, and then T_{pre}, which is an output of $\text{SHA}'_{256}(C)$, is encrypted by ECB mode with AES-256.

Let LINE-MAC denote the tag generation function, that is, $E(K_e,$ $\mathrm{SHA}'_{256}(C))$. Our attack exploits the following vulnerabilities of LINE-AE.

Vulnerability 4 (LINE-MAC). *A 128-bit intermediate value T_{pre} of LINE-MAC is computable without any secret information.*

In LINE-MAC, $\mathrm{SHA}'_{256}(\cdot)$ is a public function for which anyone is able to evaluate. A set of input/output pairs of $\mathrm{SHA}'_{256}(\cdot)$ can be computed by the adversary without any knowledge of the 256-bit key.

Vulnerability 5 (Same Key in encryption and LINE-MAC). *In the CBC encryption and LINE-MAC, the same key K_e is used for AES-256.*

For each message encryption, a 256-bit key K_e is given to not only AES-256 for CBC mode but also AES-256 ECB mode for LINE-MAC. This vulnerability was already pointed out in the previous works [18,19], though they did not find any actual attacks based on it.

6.2   Forgery Attacks

We propose a forgery attack on LINE-AE. Assuming the E2E session between victim A and B, an E2E adversary collect the data between A and B and tries to create a forgery message for this session.

In the offline phase, the adversary precomputes a set of pairs of input/output of $(X, Y(= \mathrm{SHA}'_{256}(X)))$ in LINE-MAC by exploiting Vulnerability 4. In the online phase, she obtains the packets and extracts the sets of C, T and associated data sent by a victim, and she computes pairs of $(T_{\mathrm{pre}}(= \mathrm{SHA}'_{256}(C)), T)$ which are pairs of input/output of one-block AES-256. If T_{pre} matches with Y computed in the offline phase, a new valid pair of input and output of LINE-MAC is obtained as $(X, T(= E(K, \mathrm{SHA}'_{256}(X))))$ without knowing a 256-bit key K. If the adversary sends the pair of (X, T) with properly-chosen associated data, the victim A or B is not able to detect whether it is made by the adversary. Our attack consists of offline and online phases, see Fig. 8. The detailed procedures are as follows.

Offline Phase

1. Compute 2^b pairs of input/output of $(X, Y(= \mathrm{SHA}'_{256}(X)))$ in LINE-MAC.
2. Store these results into a table indexed by values of Y.

Online Phase

1. Get 2^d sets of C, T and associated data sent by a victim.
2. Compute T_{pre} $(= \mathrm{SHA}'_{256}(C))$ from a set of C, T and additional data.
3. Check whether T_{pre} collides with Y in the table created in the offline phase. If a collision exists, obtain a new valid pair $(X, T(= E(K, \mathrm{SHA}'_{256}(X))))$ of LINE-MAC.
4. Repeat Steps 2 to 3 for all 2^d sets of C, T and additional data .

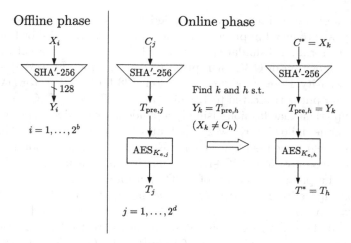

Fig. 8. Forgery attack

Evaluation. The offline phase requires 2^b hash computations and 2^b memory. The online phase requires 2^d data and 2^d hash computations. The success probability of our forgery attack is estimated as $2^{-128+b+d}$. The whole time complexity (Time) is $2^b + 2^d$ and data complexity (Data) is 2^d. Thus if Data $\cdot$ Time $\geq 2^{128}$, our attack is successful with a high probability. We remark that the order of the offline and online can be changed. If the online phase is first, the memory consumption for storing $(T_{\text{pre}}(= \text{SHA}'_{256}(C)), T)$ is 2^d, and the offline phase does not requires memory.

This attack is not much practical in terms of the time complexity of the attack, because it needs 2^b offline computation and 2^d online computation for $b + d = 128$, thus 64-bit security. The popular AE schemes using 128-bit block cipher also have 64-bit security in terms of online data complexity (i.e. it is secure if one key is used with data smaller than 2^{64}), however, the implications are quite different. For example, AE in LINE can be broken with 2^{80} offline computation plus 2^{40} online computation, which is not the case of generic composition of CBC mode using AES-256 plus HMAC-SHA-256, as used by Signal.

6.3   LINE-AE as a General-Purpose Authenticated Encryption

If we take LINE-AE as a general-purpose AE, we expect it to have a sufficient level of security in terms of standard AE security notions, i.e., privacy and authenticity [10,11]. In this respect, except the lack of authenticity of associated data (Vulnerability 3), the most significant shortage of LINE-AE is its short salt. Apparently, 64-bit salt would collide after 2^{32} encryptions, which leads to a break in the privacy notion (confidentiality of plaintext) of AE. Besides, as mentioned at Sect. 2.1 the whitepaper [23] does not specify the padding scheme needed for CBC. Hence, depending on the actual padding scheme, there might be a risk of padding-oracle attack introduced by Vaudenay [27], which exploits the weakness of the padding scheme applied to CBC. Padding-oracle attack is notoriously hard to avoid in practice, as shown by POODLE [14] or Lucky13 [9].

Due to the structural similarity, it may make sense to compare LINE-AE with a generic composition of CBC encryption using AES-256 and HMAC-SHA-256 in terms of security. Here, we assume a random 128-bit initial vector (IV) or salt, and HMAC output is truncated to 128 bits, and CBC and HMAC are composed in the encrypt-then-mac fashion, using independent keys. Given the composition is correctly done, following Krawczyk [22] and Namprempre et al. [24], and the standard cryptographic assumptions on AES and (the compression function of) SHA-256, the composition CBC+HMAC has 64-bit security for privacy, which comes from the provable security of CBC encryption (where 64-bit security of CBC is from the collision probability among the inputs to AES), and 128-bit for authenticity from the security of HMAC [21]. The privacy bound of LINE-AE is 32 bits, and if the salt was 128 bits, it seems not hard to derive 64-bit privacy bound, which is largely equivalent to CBC+HMAC. On the contrary, it seems less trivial to derive the authenticity bound. We expect it is possible to derive one assuming the second preimage resistance of the 128-bit SHA'-256 hash function. Our attack of Sect. 6.2 supports this observation, since it essentially breaks the second preimage resistance of SHA'-256 using 2^d targets.

However, we stress that our attack against LINE-AE allows treading-off of offline and online computations, and needs only single forgery attempt to have a sufficiently high success probability. At the extreme case, we can attack LINE-AE using 2^{128} offline computation with single ciphertext and single forgery attempt, which seems not possible with CBC+HMAC using 256-bit keys.

7   Conclusion

In this paper, we have evaluated the security of the E2EE scheme of LINE, one of the popular messaging applications in East Asia, and proposed several practical attacks. We first showed impersonation and forgery attacks on the group messaging scheme by a malicious group member. Next, we presented the malicious key exchange attack on the one-to-one messaging scheme. Then, we evaluated the security of the authenticated encryption scheme used in the message encryption phase, and presented the forgery attack against the the authenticated encryption scheme by the E2E adversary. We discussed practicality and feasibility of our attacks by considering the use cases of LINE. As a result, we conclude that the E2EE scheme of LINE do not provide a sufficient level of security compared to the start-of-the-art E2EE schemes such as Signal, which is used by WhatApp and Facebook Messenger, and Apple's iMessage.

Acknowledgments. The authors would like to thank the anonymous referees for their insightful comments and suggestions. We are also grateful to LINE corporation for the fruitful discussion and feedback about our findings.

References

1. FIPS PUB 197: Advanced Encryption Standard (AES). U.S. Department of Commerce/National Institute of Standards and Technology (2001)
2. NIST SP 800–38A: Recommendation for Block Cipher Modes of Operation. U.S. Department of Commerce/National Institute of Standards and Technology (2001)
3. NIST SP 800–38C: Recommendation for Block Cipher Modes of Operation: the CCM Mode for Authentication and Confidentiality. U.S. Department of Commerce/National Institute of Standards and Technology (2007)
4. NIST SP 800–38D: Recommendation for Block Cipher Modes of Operation: Galois/Counter Mode (GCM) and GMAC. U.S. Department of Commerce/National Institute of Standards and Technology (2007)
5. FIPS PUB 180–4: Secure Hash Standard. U.S. Department of Commerce/National Institute of Standards and Technology (2015)
6. New generation of safe messaging: Letter Sealing. LINE Blog (2015). https://engineering.linecorp.com/en/blog/detail/65
7. LINE Enters Agreement with Japan's CAO for Mynaportal Interconnectivity (2017). https://linecorp.com/en/pr/news/en/2017/1771
8. Line Will Top 50 Million Users in Japan This Year. eMarketer (2017). https://www.emarketer.com/Article/Line-Will-Top-50-Million-Users-Japan-This-Year/1016207
9. Al Fardan, N.J., Paterson, K.G.: Lucky thirteen: breaking the TLS and DTLS record protocols. In: 2013 IEEE Symposium on Security and Privacy, SP 2013, pp. 526–540. IEEE Computer Society (2013)
10. Bellare, M., Namprempre, C.: Authenticated encryption: relations among notions and analysis of the generic composition paradigm. J. Cryptol. **21**(4), 469–491 (2008)
11. Bellare, M., Rogaway, P., Wagner, D.: The EAX mode of operation. In: Roy, B., Meier, W. (eds.) FSE 2004. LNCS, vol. 3017, pp. 389–407. Springer, Heidelberg (2004). https://doi.org/10.1007/978-3-540-25937-4_25
12. Bernstein, D.J.: Curve25519: new diffie-hellman speed records. In: Yung, M., Dodis, Y., Kiayias, A., Malkin, T. (eds.) PKC 2006. LNCS, vol. 3958, pp. 207–228. Springer, Heidelberg (2006). https://doi.org/10.1007/11745853_14
13. Blake-Wilson, S., Menezes, A.: Unknown key-share attacks on the station-to-station (STS) protocol. In: Imai, H., Zheng, Y. (eds.) PKC 1999. LNCS, vol. 1560, pp. 154–170. Springer, Heidelberg (1999). https://doi.org/10.1007/3-540-49162-7_12
14. Möller, B., Duong, T., Kotowicz, K.: This POODLE Bites: Exploiting The SSL 3.0 Fallback (2016)
15. Cohn-Gordon, K., Cremers, C., Garratt, L., Millican, J., Milner, K.: On Ends-to-Ends Encryption: Asynchronous Group Messaging with Strong Security Guarantees. Cryptology ePrint Archive, Report 2017/666 (2017). http://eprint.iacr.org/2017/666
16. Cohn-Gordon, K., Cremers, C.J.F., Dowling, B., Garratt, L., Stebila, D.: A formal security analysis of the signal messaging protocol. In: 2017 IEEE European Symposium on Security and Privacy, EuroS&P 2017, pp. 451–466. IEEE (2017)
17. Cohn-Gordon, K., Cremers, C.J.F., Garratt, L.: On post-compromise security. In: IEEE 29th Computer Security Foundations Symposium, CSF 2016, pp. 164–178. IEEE Computer Society (2016)

18. Curtis, T.: Encryption out of LINE Reverse engineering end-to-end encrypted messaging. Ekoparty 2016 (2016)
19. Espinoza, A.M., Tolley, W.J., Crandall, J.R., Crete-Nishihata, M., Hilts, A.: Alice and Bob, who the FOCI are they?: analysis of end-to-end encryption in the LINE messaging application. In: 7th USENIX Workshop on Free and Open Communications on the Internet (FOCI 17). USENIX Association (2017)
20. Garman, C., Green, M., Kaptchuk, G., Miers, I., Rushanan, M.: Dancing on the lip of the volcano: chosen ciphertext attacks on apple imessage. In: 25th USENIX Security Symposium (USENIX Security 16), pp. 655–672. USENIX Association (2016)
21. Gaži, P., Pietrzak, K., Rybár, M.: The exact PRF-security of NMAC and HMAC. In: Garay, J.A., Gennaro, R. (eds.) CRYPTO 2014. LNCS, vol. 8616, pp. 113–130. Springer, Heidelberg (2014). https://doi.org/10.1007/978-3-662-44371-2_7
22. Krawczyk, H.: The order of encryption and authentication for protecting communications (or: how secure Is SSL?). In: Kilian, J. (ed.) CRYPTO 2001. LNCS, vol. 2139, pp. 310–331. Springer, Heidelberg (2001). https://doi.org/10.1007/3-540-44647-8_19
23. LINE Corporation: LINE Encryption Overview (2016)
24. Namprempre, C., Rogaway, P., Shrimpton, T.: Reconsidering generic composition. In: Nguyen, P.Q., Oswald, E. (eds.) EUROCRYPT 2014. LNCS, vol. 8441, pp. 257–274. Springer, Heidelberg (2014). https://doi.org/10.1007/978-3-642-55220-5_15
25. Open Whisper Systems: Signal Github Repository (2017). https://github.com/WhisperSystems/
26. Rosler, P., Mainka, C., Schwenk, J.: More is less: how group chats weaken the security of instant messengers signal, WhatsApp, and Threema. In: 3rd IEEE European Symposium on Security and Privacy 2018 (2018)
27. Vaudenay, S.: Security flaws induced by CBC padding — applications to SSL, IPSEC, WTLS. In: Knudsen, L.R. (ed.) EUROCRYPT 2002. LNCS, vol. 2332, pp. 534–545. Springer, Heidelberg (2002). https://doi.org/10.1007/3-540-46035-7_35

Scalable Wildcarded Identity-Based Encryption

Jihye Kim[1], Seunghwa Lee[1], Jiwon Lee[2], and Hyunok Oh[2(✉)]

[1] Kookmin University, Seoul, Korea
{jihyek,ttyhgo}@kookmin.ac.kr
[2] Hanyang University, Seoul, Korea
{jiwonlee,hoh}@hanyang.ac.kr

Abstract. Wildcarded identity-based encryption allows a sender to simultaneously encrypt messages to a group of users matching a certain pattern, defined as a sequence of identifiers and wildcards. We propose a new wildcarded identity-based encryption scheme with generalized key delegation, which reduces the ciphertext size to be constant. To the best of our knowledge, our proposal is the first wildcarded identity-based encryption scheme that generates a constant size ciphertext regardless of the depth of the identities. The proposed scheme also improves the decryption time by minimizing the wildcard conversion cost. According to our experiment results, decryption of the proposed scheme is 3, 10, and 650 times faster than existing WIBE, WW-IBE, and CCP-ABE schemes. The proposal also subsumes the generalized key derivation naturally by allowing wildcards in the key delegation process. We prove CPA security of the proposed scheme and extend it to be CCA secure.

Keywords: Wildcard identity based encryption
Constant ciphertext · Key delegation · Pattern

1 Introduction

The advanced information technology has increased the popularity and diversity of embedded systems (or IoT devices) in a variety of applications such as smart city, transport, smart grid, production control, medical, military, and so on. In these distributed settings, messages often need to be securely delivered to a specific group of devices or users for communication and management. Some examples are as follows:

- The official commands or monitoring messages from a commander or sensors deployed to jointly monitor malicious activity for city security must be securely communicated to a specific group or user determined by its region, role, class, function, etc.
- Secure firmware updates in many systems including vehicles are crucial to improve performance and provide fixes for defective software that can lead to

© Springer Nature Switzerland AG 2018
J. Lopez et al. (Eds.): ESORICS 2018, LNCS 11099, pp. 269–287, 2018.
https://doi.org/10.1007/978-3-319-98989-1_14

costly product recalls. The firmware, the intellectual property of a company, must be distributed securely to a distinct group specified by the brand, model, year, device type, version, etc.
- In the military, tactical communications such as real-time video and targeting data need to be securely transmitted according to the access structure determined by the receiver's class, mission, location, etc.

1.1 Related Work

Identity-based encryption (IBE) is one of most powerful building blocks to provide data confidentiality, which encrypts a message without retrieving and verifying the public key separated from the identity. The IBE scheme proposed by Shamir [12] uses an actual user identity (e.g., alice@cs.univ.edu) as a public key for encryption. The first practical IBE scheme construction was presented by using bilinear maps [7,13]. It has advanced to a hierarchical identity-based encryption (HIBE) scheme in [6] where an identity is defined by multiple identity strings in a hierarchy such that keys for each identity string can be generated in a hierarchically distributed way: users at level l can derive keys for their children at level $l + 1$. The advantage of HIBE is to reduce the burden of a trusted key distribution center by distributing key derivation and solving a bottleneck problem.

Motivated by the fact that many email addresses correspond to groups of users rather than single individuals, Abdalla et al. [2] extended HIBE to wildcarded identity-based encryption (WIBE) by combining a concept called wildcard (∗), which can be replaced by any identity string in a sequence of identity strings. A pattern (or an identity) defined as a sequence of multiple identity strings and wildcards efficiently determines a group of identities as well as a single identity. Abdalla et al. proposed three different WIBE constructions by extending the previous HIBE schemes; however, all constructions suffer from comparatively larger ciphertext size which is at least $O(L)$ where L denotes the maximum depth of a pattern (i.e., the maximum number of identity strings). Later, Birkett et al. [5] presented compilation techniques that convert any L-level CPA-secure WIBE scheme into L-level CCA-secure identity-based key encapsulation mechanisms with wildcards (WIB-KEM). They constructed more efficient CCA-secure WIBE variants by applying their compilation techniques to the CPA-secure WIBE schemes from [2]. However, the ciphertext size is still as large as that for the underlying WIBE schemes, i.e., at least $O(L)$ size ciphertext. In [1], Abdalla et al. upgraded the WIBE notion to the WW-IBE notion by combining the generalized key delegation notion in [3] to provide the full security with pattern anonymity. They utilize bilinear groups of composite order to support the full security when the maximum hierarchy depth is a polynomial in the security parameter. Although key delegation is useful to minimize the key management overhead in the distributed setting, the non-scalable ciphertext size in [1] has not been improved and remained an obstacle so far.

There are attribute-based encryption schemes (ABE) that allow more expressive policies than WIBE. Ciphertext-policy attribute-based encryption (CP-

ABE) in [4] associates to each ciphertext an access structure consisting of a logical combination of attribute values using AND and OR gates. A decryption key is given for a set of attributes and can only decrypt a ciphertext whose access structure is satisfied by the set of its attributes. WIBE schemes are a special case of CP-ABE schemes by mapping the identity vector (*, **Tesla**, *, **Model S**) to the access structure (**2**||**Tesla** ∧ **4**||**Model S**) where an identity is concatenated with its position index. The ciphertext size in [4] grows linearly with the number of attributes in the access structure. The authors in [10] proposed a CP-ABE scheme with constant ciphertext size, but, without supporting wildcards in its access policy. Later, the ABE scheme proposed in [14] supports wildcards with a restricted setting of only binary identities. When it is converted into the string-based identity version, the number of attributes grows exponentially to cover all possible identities in a binary notation, which results in an exponential number of public parameters. Otherwise, each attribute should be denoted in a binary format, which increases the the maximum depth of a pattern by the binary string length times.

In general, the ciphertext size is an important issue because the ciphertext is the actual payload that is transmitted via network in real applications. However, the existing schemes [1, 2] produce a non-constant size ciphertext linearly increasing by the maximum depth of a pattern. It is mainly because the ciphertext should include additional information for each wildcard such that wildcards in a pattern can be transformed for every matching key element in WIBE/WW-IBE scheme. With the approach that the ciphertext contains all information required to conversion, it is not clear how to construct a wildcarded identity based encryption scheme with constant size ciphertext.

In this paper, we devise a method to convert the key pattern into matching ciphertext patterns, contrary to the approach by Abdalla et al. [1,2]. In our method, each user stores a conversion key for each non-wildcard identity in order to replace the identity by a wildcard. A pattern with l specific identity strings leads to a secret key with l conversion keys. The number of the conversion keys in a secret key is bounded by the maximum depth L. The benefit of this approach is that the extra conversion keys do not have to be delivered in the ciphertext any more because the keys deal with conversion into matching patterns. The details of the construction are described in Sect. 3.

CONTRIBUTIONS. In this paper, we propose a new wildcarded identity based encryption scheme with constant size ciphertext and with polynomial overhead in every parameter. Our main contributions are summarized as follows:

- We propose a novel scalable wildcarded identity based encryption scheme called SWIBE. To the best of our knowledge, the proposed scheme is the first WIBE (or WW-IBE) scheme that generates a constant size ciphertext regardless of the depth, i.e., the maximum number of attributes; the ciphertext consists of just four group elements, which is comparable even to the HIBE scheme [6] that contains three group elements for its ciphertext.
- The SWIBE scheme also improves decryption performance of WIBE (or WW-IBE). Much of the decryption overhead in the existing wildcarded schemes is

in the conversion operation of wildcards in a ciphertext into identity strings of a user's secret key. While the WIBE and WW-IBE schemes [1,2] convert a ciphertext to another ciphertext for a specific matching identity strings, our scheme replaces any identity string by a wildcard; this method reduces point multiplications (i.e., exponentiations) required in the previous WIBE/WW-IBE and speeds up the decryption.

- The SWIBE scheme allows wildcards in the key delegation process as well as in the encryption procedure, naturally subsuming the generalized key derivation of wicked-IBE [3] and distributing the key management overhead. The SWIBE schemes with and without generalized key delegation correspond to WW-IBE [1] and WIBE [2], respectively.
- We formally prove the selective CPA-security of the proposed scheme under the L-BDHE assumption. We also extend it to be a CCA secure scheme.

Table 1. Comparison of HIBE, WIBE, wicked-IBE, WW-IBE, CCP-ABE, and proposed SWIBE schemes. *cf.* e = *time of scalar multiplication,* p = *time of pairing, and* L = *hierarchy depth,* ID_i *is represented using a q-bit string, size indicates the number of group elements, Enc = Encryption, and Der = Key derivation.*

	HIBE [6]	WIBE [2]	wicked-IBE [3]	WW-IBE [1]	CCP-ABE [14]	SWIBE
pp size	$L+4$	$L+4$	$L+2$	$2L+2$	$2L2^q+1$	$L+4$
SK size	$L+2$	$L+2$	$L+2$	$L+1$	$3L2^q+1$	$2L+3$
CT size	3	$L+3$	3	$3L+2$	2	4
Enc time	$(L+3)e+p$	$(L+3)e+p$	$(L+1)e+p$	$(3L+2)e$	$2L2^qe+p$	$(L+3)e+p$
Dec time	$2p$	$Le+2p$	$Le+2p$	$Le+(2L+1)p$	$2L2^qe+4L2^qp$	$Le+3p$
Wildcard use	None	Enc	Der	Enc & Der	Enc	Enc & Der

Table 1 compares the HIBE scheme [6] (that does not support wildcards as identities), the WIBE scheme [2], HIBE with the generalized key delegation (wicked-IBE) [3], WIBE scheme with generalized key delegation (WW-IBE) [1], constant-size ciphtertext policy attribute-based encryption (CCP-ABE) [14], and the proposed SWIBE scheme subsuming wildcards as identities as well as the generalized key delegation. The table shows the public parameter size (pp size), the user secret key size (SK size), the ciphertext size, the encryption time (Enc time), and the decryption time (Dec time) according to the maximum depth of the pattern (L) where e and p denote the numbers of scalar multiplications and pairings, respectively. It is assumed that each ID is represented using a q-bit string maximally. For the wildcard use, the table specifies whether wildcards are used in an encryption (Enc) algorithm or in an key derivation (Der) algorithm. Note that the SWIBE scheme has $O(L)$ size of the secret key, while it produces a constant-size ciphertext with allowing wildcards in a ciphertext pattern. Note that if each bit in ID representation is regarded as an attribute in CCP-ABE then pp size, SK size, the encryption, and the decryption time are $2Lq+1$, $3Lq+1$, $2Lqe+p$, and $2Lqe+4Lqp$, respectively. In WW-IBE and CCP-ABE, the decryption time is a major hurdle to be used in practical applications since the decryption requires pairing operations of which number is proportional to the maximum depth level L. Especially, in CCP-ABE, the number of pairing operations is dependent on the length of a bit string in each ID, in addition. In experiment, the decryption times in WW-IBE and CCP-IBE are 10 times and 650 times larger than the proposed approach.

This paper is organized as follows: Sect. 2 introduces the definitions and cryptographic assumptions. In Sect. 3, we explain the main idea of the proposed scheme and how to construct it in details. Section 4 formally proves the security of the proposed scheme and Sect. 5 extends it to be CCA secure. In Sect. 6, we show the experimental results and in Sect. 7, we conclude.

2 Definitions and Background

Wildcarded identity based encryption with generalized key delegation (WW-IBE) extends hierarchical identity based encryption (HIBE). In this section, we recall IBE, HIBE, WW-IBE, and the security definition of WW-IBE. The decryption of WIBE is omitted because WW-IBE subsumes the WIBE definition. We also describe mathematical background necessary to understand our proposal.

Identity-Based Encryption: An identity-based encryption (IBE) scheme is a tuple of algorithm $\mathcal{IBE} = (\mathsf{Setup}, \mathsf{KeyDer}, \mathsf{Enc}, \mathsf{Dec})$. A public/master key pair (pp, msk) is generated from Setup by the trusted authority. A user decryption key with identity ID is computed as $d_{ID} \xleftarrow{\$} \mathsf{KeyDer}(msk, ID)$. To encrypt a message m for a user with identity ID, a ciphertext $C \xleftarrow{\$} \mathsf{Enc}(pp, ID, m)$ is computed, which can be decrypted by the user with ID as $\mathsf{m} \leftarrow \mathsf{Dec}(d_{ID}, C)$. We refer to [8] for details on the security definitions for IBE schemes.

Hierarchical IBE: In a hierarchical IBE (HIBE) scheme, users are organized in a tree of depth L, with the root being the master trusted authority. The identity of a user at level $0 \leq l \leq L$ in the tree is given by a vector $ID = (P_1, \ldots, P_l) \in (\{0,1\}^q)^l$. A HIBE scheme is a tuple of algorithms $\mathcal{HIBE} = (\mathsf{Setup}, \mathsf{KeyDer}, \mathsf{Enc}, \mathsf{Dec})$ providing the same functionality as in an IBE scheme, except that a user $ID = (P_1, \ldots, P_l)$ at level l can use its own secret key sk_{ID} to generate a secret key for any of its children $ID' = (P_1, \ldots, P_l, \ldots, P_L)$ via $sk_{ID'} \xleftarrow{\$} \mathsf{KeyDer}(sk_{ID}, ID')$. The secret key of the root identity at level 0 is $sk_\epsilon = msk$. Encryption and decryption are the same as for IBE, but with vectors of bit strings as identities instead of ordinary bit strings. We use the notation $P_{|l-1}$ to denote vector $(P_1, \ldots, P_{l-1})$. We refer to [6] for details on the security definitions for HIBE schemes.

Wildcarded Identity Based Encryption with Generalized Key Delegation: WW-IBE as a wildcarded identity based scheme allows general key delegation and encryption to a group that is denoted by multiple identity strings and wildcards. To make the further description simple and clear, we define the following notations similarly to [2].

Definition 1. *A pattern P is a vector $(P_1, \ldots, P_L) \in (\mathbb{Z}_p^* \cup \{*\})^L$, where $*$ is a special wildcard symbol, p is a q-bit prime number, and L is the maximal depth of the identity strings.*[1]

Definition 2. *A pattern $P' = (P_1', \ldots, P_L')$ belongs to P, denoted $P' \in_* P$, if and only if $\forall i \in \{1, \ldots, L\}, (P_i' = P_i) \vee (P_i = *)$.*

Definition 3. *A pattern $P' = (P_1', \ldots, P_L')$ matches P, denoted $P' \approx P$, if and only if $\forall i \in \{1, \ldots, L\}, (P_i' = P_i) \vee (P_i = *) \vee (P_i' = *)$.*

Notice that a set of matching patterns of P is a super set of belonging patterns of P. For a pattern $P = (P_1, \ldots, P_L)$, we define $W(P)$ is the set containing all wildcard indices in P, i.e. the indices $1 \leq i \leq L$ such that $P_i = *$, and $\overline{W}(P)$ is the set containing all non-wildcard indices. Clearly, $W(P) \cap \overline{W}(P) = \emptyset$ and $W(P) \cup \overline{W}(P) = \{1, \ldots, L\}$.

Definition 4. $W(P)$ *is the set containing all wildcard indices in a pattern P.*

Definition 5. $\overline{W}(P)$ *is the set containing all non-wildcard indices in a pattern P.*

Wildcarded identity-based encryption with generalized key delegation WW-IBE consists of four algorithms:

Setup(L) takes as input the maximal hierarchy depth L. It outputs a public parameter pp and master secret key msk.

KeyDer(sk_P, P_{new}) takes as input a user secret key sk_P for a pattern $P = (P_1, \ldots, P_L)$ and can derive a secret key for any pattern $P_{new} \in_* P$. The secret key of the root identity is $msk = sk_{(*,\ldots,*)}$.

Encrypt(pp, P, m) takes as input pattern $P = (P_1, \ldots, P_L)$, message $m \in \{0, 1\}^*$ and public parameter pp. It outputs ciphertext C_P for pattern P.

Decrypt($sk_P, C_{P'}$) takes as input user secret key sk_P for pattern P and ciphertext C for pattern P'. Any user in possession of the secret key such that $P' \approx P$ decrypts the ciphertext using sk_P, outputting message m. Otherwise, it outputs $\perp$.

Correctness requires that for all key pairs (pp, msk) output by Setup, all messages $m \in \{0, 1\}^*$, and all patterns $P, P' \in (\mathbb{Z}_p^* \cup \{*\})^L$ such that $P \approx P'$, Decrypt(KeyDer(msk, P), Encrypt(pp, P', m)) = m.

Security: We define the security notion of WW-IBE similarly to [1,2]. An adversary is allowed to choose an arbitrary pattern and query its secret key, except the query to the key derivation oracle for any pattern matching with a challenge pattern. The security is defined by an adversary $\mathcal{A}$ and a challenger $\mathcal{C}$ via the following game. Both $\mathcal{C}$ and $\mathcal{A}$ are given the hierarchy depth L and the identity bit-length q as input.

---

[1] We denote pattern P as in $(\mathbb{Z}_p^* \cup \{*\})^L$ instead of $(\{0,1\}^q \cup \{*\})^L$, since $\{0,1\}^q$ can be easily mapped to $\mathbb{Z}_p^*$ with a hash function.

Setup:Challenger $\mathcal{C}$ runs $\mathsf{Setup}(L)$ to obtain public parameter pp and master secret key msk. $\mathcal{C}$ gives $\mathcal{A}$ public parameter pp.

Query phase 1:

- $\mathcal{A}$ issues key derivation queries $q_{K_1}, \ldots, q_{K_m}$ in which a key derivation query consists of a pattern $P' \in (\mathbb{Z}_p^* \cup \{*\})^L$, and challenger $\mathcal{C}$ responds with $sk_{P'} \xleftarrow{\$} \mathsf{KeyDer}(msk, P')$.
- $\mathcal{A}$ issues decryption queries $q_{D_1}, \ldots, q_{D_n}$ in which a decryption query consists of pattern P for sk_P, ciphertext C, and pattern P' for C, next challenger $\mathcal{C}$ responds with $\mathsf{Decrypt}(sk_P, C_{P'})$.

Challenge:$\mathcal{A}$ outputs two equal-length challenge messages $m_0^*, m_1^* \in \{0, 1\}^*$ and a challenge identity $P^* = (P_1^*, \ldots, P_{L^*}^*)$ s.t. $P^* \not\approx P'$ for all queried P'. $\mathcal{C}$ runs algorithm $C^* \xleftarrow{\$} \mathsf{Encrypt}(pp, P^*, m_b^*)$ for random bit b and gives C^* to $\mathcal{A}$.

Query phase 2:

- $\mathcal{A}$ continues to issue key derivation queries $q_{K_{m+1}}, \ldots, q_{q_K}$ as in Query phase 1, except for pattern $P' \not\approx P^*$.
- $\mathcal{A}$ continues to issue decryption queries $q_{D_{n+1}}, \ldots, q_{q_D}$ as in Query phase 1, except for C^*.

Guess:$\mathcal{A}$ outputs its guess $b' \in \{0, 1\}$ for b and wins the game if $b = b'$.

We also define the IND-ID-CPA game similarly with the IND-ID-CCA game, without allowing any decryption query.

Definition 6. *A WW-IBE is $(t, q_K, q_D, \epsilon, L)$ IND-ID-CCA (or IND-ID-CPA) secure if all t-time adversaries making at most q_K queries to the key derivation oracle and at most q_D queries to the decryption oracle have at most advantage ϵ in the IND-ID-CCA game (or the IND-ID-CPA game) described above.*

Selective Security. A selective-identity (sID) security notion IND-sID-CCA (or IND-sID-CPA) is defined analogously to the IND-ID-CCA (IND-ID-CPA) one: every procedure is the same except that the adversary has to commit to the challenge identity at the beginning of the game, before the public parameter is made available.

Definition 7. *A WW-IBE is $(t, q_K, 0, \epsilon, L)$ IND-sID-CCA (IND-sID-CPA) secure if all t-time adversaries making at most q_K queries to the key derivation oracle have at most advantage ϵ in the IND-sID-CCA (or IND-sID-CPA) game.*

Bilinear Groups and Pairings: We review the necessary facts about bilinear maps and bilinear map groups, following the standard notation [8, 11].

1. $\mathbb{G}$ and $\mathbb{G}_1$ are two (multiplicative) cyclic groups of prime order p.
2. g is a generator of $\mathbb{G}$.
3. $e : \mathbb{G} \times \mathbb{G} \to \mathbb{G}_1$ is a bilinear map.

Let $\mathbb{G}$ and $\mathbb{G}_1$ be two groups as above. A bilinear map is a map $e : \mathbb{G} \times \mathbb{G} \to \mathbb{G}_1$ with the following properties:

1. Bilinear: for all $u, v \in \mathbb{G}$ and $a, b \in \mathbb{Z}$, we have $e(u^a, v^b) = e(u, v)^{ab}$
2. Non-degenerate: $e(g, g) \neq 1$.

We say that $\mathbb{G}$ is a bilinear group if the group action in $\mathbb{G}$ can be computed efficiently and there exist a group $\mathbb{G}_1$ and an efficiently computable bilinear map $e : \mathbb{G} \times \mathbb{G} \to \mathbb{G}_1$ as above.

BDHE Assumption [6]: Let $\mathbb{G}$ be a bilinear group of prime order p. Given a vector of $2L + 1$ elements $(h, g, g^\alpha, g^{(\alpha^2)}, \ldots, g^{(\alpha^L)}, g^{(\alpha^{L+2})}, \ldots, g^{(\alpha^{2L})}) \in \mathbb{G}^{2L+1}$ as input, output $e(g, h)^{\alpha^{L+1}} \in \mathbb{G}_1$. As shorthand, once g and α are specified, we use y_i to denote $y_i = g^{\alpha^i} \in \mathbb{G}$. An algorithm $\mathcal{A}$ has advantage ϵ in solving L-BDHE in $\mathbb{G}$ if

$$Pr[\mathcal{A}(h, g, y_1, \ldots, y_L, y_{L+2}, \ldots, y_{2L}) = e(y_{L+1}, h)] \geq \epsilon$$

where the probability is over the random choice of generators g, h in $\mathbb{G}$, the random choice of α in $\mathbb{Z}_p$, and the random bits used by $\mathcal{A}$.

The decisional version of the L-BDHE problem in $\mathbb{G}$ is defined analogously. Let $\boldsymbol{y}_{g,\alpha,L} = (y_1, \ldots, y_L, y_{L+2}, \ldots, y_{2L})$. An algorithm $\mathcal{B}$ that outputs $b \in \{0, 1\}$ has advantage ϵ in solving decisional L-BDHE in $\mathbb{G}$ if

$$|Pr[\mathcal{B}(g, h, \boldsymbol{y}_{g,\alpha,L}, e(y_{L+1}, h)) = 0] - Pr[\mathcal{B}(g, h, \boldsymbol{y}_{g,\alpha,L}, T) = 0]| \geq \epsilon$$

where the probability is over the random choice of generators g, h in $\mathbb{G}$, the random choice of α in $\mathbb{Z}_p$, the random choice of $T \in \mathbb{G}_1$, and the random bits consumed by $\mathcal{B}$.

Definition 8. *We say that the (decisional) (t, ϵ, L)-BDHE assumption holds in $\mathbb{G}$ if no t-time algorithm has advantage at least ϵ in solving the (decisional) L-BDHE problem in $\mathbb{G}$.*

Occasionally we omit the t and ϵ, and refer to the (decisional) L-BDHE in $\mathbb{G}$.

3   The Proposed Scheme

In this section, we describe a scalable WW-IBE scheme called SWIBE. Since our SWIBE is based on the BBG-HIBE scheme proposed by Boneh et al. [6], we briefly overview the BBG-HIBE protocol and explain our idea to allow wildcards as identities in encryption. And then we illustrate our SWIBE protocol.

3.1   Overview

BBG-HIBE [6]: In the BBG-HIBE scheme, the secret key is composed of two types of keys for its purposes: decryption and key delegation. Given $pp = (g, g_1, g_2, g_3, h_1, h_2, \ldots, h_L)$ and $msk = g_2^\alpha$, a secret key for pattern

$P = \{P_1, \cdots, P_l\}$ consists of elements $(a_1 = g_2^{\alpha}(g_3 \cdot h_1^{P_1} \cdots h_l^{P_l})^r, a_2 = g^r, b = \{b_i = h_i^r\}_{i \in [l+1, \cdots, L]})$. The ciphertext encrypted for $P = \{P_1, \cdots, P_l\}$ is composed of $C_P = (g^s, (g_3 \cdot \prod_{i \in [1, \cdots, l]} h_i^{P_i})^s, M \cdot e(g_1, g_2)^s)$. To decrypt a given ciphertext $C_P = (C_1, C_2, C_3)$ with private key $sk_P = (a_1, a_2, b_{l+1}, \cdots, b_L)$, we compute $C_3 \cdot \frac{e(a_2, C_2)}{e(C_1, a_1)} = M$. Notice that the first two elements a_1 and a_2 are used for decryption, while the remaining elements $\{b_i = h_i^r\}_{i \in [l+1, \cdots, L]}$ are used for key delegation. For the easy delivery of description, we first describe our idea focusing on the decryption key without delegation, assuming the maximum depth is l.

Adding Gadgets for Wildcard Conversion: Multiple identity strings in a pattern $P = (P_1, \cdots, P_l)$ are merged into a single element in the decryption key: $a_1 = g_2^{\alpha}(g_3 \cdot h_1^{P_1} \cdots h_l^{P_l})^r$. We observe that given extra gadget values, each identity string of a pattern in a_1 can be replaced by another identity by multiplication. For instance, given $h_1^{(P_1' - P_1)r}$, it is possible to change $a_1 = g_2^{\alpha}(g_3 \cdot h_1^{P_1} \cdots h_l^{P_l})^r$ into $a_1' = g_2^{\alpha}(g_3 \cdot h_1^{P_1'} \cdots h_l^{P_l})^r$.

Step 1: Assume that a wildcard $*$ is mapped to some element $w \in \mathbb{Z}_p^*$. In order to allow a pattern to include a wildcard, we consider a way to include gadgets $\mathbf{d_i} = (h_i^w / h_i^{P_i})^r$ for every identity string P_i in a secret key. Then each identity part $(h_i^{P_i})^r$ can be substituted by $(h_i^w)^r$. The method, however, is not secure yet. From this extra secret key d_i and the values w and P_i, it is possible to compute $h_i^r = \mathbf{d_i}^{1/(w - P_i)}$; this leads to extract the top level secret key: $g_2^{\alpha} g_3^r = a_1 / (h_1^r)^{P_1} \cdots (h_l^r)^{P_l}$. To avoid this attack, the gadgets need to be randomized.

Step 2: We randomize the gadget using an independent random value $t \in \mathbb{Z}_p$. Thus, the extra gadget value is revised as $\mathbf{d_i} = h_i^{wt} / h_i^{P_i r}$ and g^t is additionally appended so that they can be canceled out correctly in decryption. For example, the key $g_2^{\alpha}(g_3 \cdot h_1^{P_1} h_2^{P_2} h_3^{P_3})^r$ for (P_1, P_2, P_3) is changed to $g_2^{\alpha}(g_3 \cdot h_2^{P_2})^r \cdot (h_1^w h_3^w)^t$ for $(*, P_2, *)$ by multiplying $\mathbf{d_1 d_3}$. The encryption needs to be slightly changed to be compatible with this modification. To encrypt a message to $(*, P_2, *)$, the pattern must be divided into non-wildcard and wildcard identity groups so that they can be treated as follows: the encryption for the non-wildcard identities $(\cdot, P_2, \cdot)$ is the same as the BBG-HIBE which generates three elements: $(g^s, (g_3 \cdot h_2^{P_2})^s, M \cdot e(g_1, g_2)^s)$. The encryption for the wildcard identities $(*, \cdot, *)$ is computed as $(h_1^w h_3^w)^s$, which is used to cancel out the gadget part of user's secret key in decryption. As a result, the ciphertext size increases by a single group element to support wildcards in the proposed scheme. The key size increases linearly to the number of identity strings, which is still polynomial to the maximum depth of a pattern.

Generalized Key Delegation: Finally, the key delegation can be subsumed independently to the wildcard support in encryption and our scheme follows the key delegation method of BBG-HIBE. Only difference is that our key delegation is more flexible because it does not have to follow the hierarchical order as in BBG-HIBE.

The complete scheme is described in the following Sect. 3.2 with $w = 1$ and we prove the security of the proposed scheme in Sect. 4.

3.2 Construction

We propose a new WW-IBE scheme called SWIBE with constant size ciphertexts and $O(L)$ size keys.

Setup(L): L indicates the maximum hierarchy depth. The generation of a random initial set of keys proceeds as follows. Select a random integer $\alpha \in \mathbb{Z}_p^*$, and $O(L)$ random group elements $g, g_2, g_3, h_1, h_2, \ldots, h_L \in \mathbb{G}$, and compute $g_1 = g^\alpha$. The public parameter is given by $pp \leftarrow (g, g_1, g_2, g_3, h_1, h_2, \ldots, h_L)$. A master secret key is defined as $msk = g_2^\alpha$.

KeyDer(pp, sk_P, P'): To compute the secret key $sk_{P'}$ for a pattern $P' = (P_1', \ldots, P_L') \in (\mathbb{Z}_p^* \cup \{*\})^L$ from the master secret key, first two randoms $r, t \xleftarrow{\$} \mathbb{Z}_p^*$ are chosen, then secret key $sk_{P'} = (a_1', a_2', a_3', b', c', d')$ for P' is constructed as

$$a_1' = msk(g_3 \cdot \prod_{i \in \overline{W}(P')} h_i^{P_i'})^r, a_2' = g^r, a_3' = g^t, b' = \{b_i' = h_i^r\}_{i \in W(P')},$$

$$c' = \{c_i' = h_i^t\}_{i \in W(P')}, d' = \{d_i' = h_i^t / h_i^{P_i' r}\}_{i \in \overline{W}(P')}$$

In order to generate secret key $sk_{P'}$ for a pattern P' from secret key $sk_P = (a_1, a_2, a_3, b, c)$ for a pattern P such that $P' \in_* P$, simply choose two randoms $r', t' \xleftarrow{\$} \mathbb{Z}_q^*$ and output $sk_{P'} = (a_1', a_2', a_3', b', c', d')$, where

$$a_1' = a_1 \cdot \Big(\prod_{i \in \overline{W}(P') \cap W(P)} b_i^{P_i'} \Big) \cdot (g_3 \prod_{i \in \overline{W}(P')} h_i^{P_i'})^{r'}, a_2' = a_2 \cdot g^{r'}, a_3' = a_3 \cdot g^{t'},$$

$$b' = \{b_i' = b_i \cdot h_i^{r'}\}_{i \in W(P')}, c' = \{c_i' = c_i \cdot h_i^{t'}\}_{i \in W(P')}$$

$$d' = \{d_i' = d_i \cdot \frac{h_i^{t'}}{h_i^{P_i' r'}}\}_{i \in \overline{W}(P') \cap \overline{W}(P)} \cup \{d_i' = \frac{c_i}{b_i^{P_i'}} \cdot \frac{h_i^{t'}}{h_i^{P_i' r'}}\}_{i \in \overline{W}(P') \cap W(P)}$$

Encrypt(pp, P, m): To encrypt a message $m \in \mathbb{G}_1$ to pattern $P = (P_1, \ldots, P_L)$ under pp, choose $s \xleftarrow{\$} \mathbb{Z}_p^*$, and compute $C_P = (C_1, C_2, C_3, C_4)$

$$C_1 = g^s, \quad C_2 = (g_3 \cdot \prod_{i \in \overline{W}(P)} h_i^{P_i})^s, C_3 = m \cdot e(g_1, g_2)^s, C_4 = (\prod_{i \in W(P)} h_i)^s$$

Decrypt(sk_P, $C_{P'}$): Set $C = (C_1, C_2, C_3, C_4)$ and $sk_P = (a_1, a_2, a_3, b, c, d)$. If $P' \approx P$ then compute $a_1' = a_1 \cdot \prod_{i \in \overline{W}(P') \cap W(P)} b_i^{P_i'} \cdot \prod_{i \in W(P') \cap W(P)} c_i \cdot \prod_{i \in W(P') \cap \overline{W}(P)} d_i$ and output

$$C_3 \cdot \frac{e(a_2, C_2) \cdot e(a_3, C_4)}{e(C_1, a_1')} = m.$$

Otherwise, output $\perp$.

The fact that decryption works can be seen as follows. We denote $\mathsf{W}_{P'P} = W(P') \cap W(P)$, $\mathsf{W}_{\overline{P}'P} = \overline{W}(P') \cap W(P)$, $\mathsf{W}_{P'\overline{P}} = W(P') \cap \overline{W}(P)$, and $\mathsf{W}_{\overline{P}'\overline{P}} = \overline{W}(P') \cap \overline{W}(P)$ to simplify notations.

Since $a_1 = g_2^{\alpha} (g_3 \prod_{i \in \overline{W}(P)} h_i^{P_i})^r$, $b_i = h_i^r$, $c_i = h_i^t$, and $d_i = \frac{h_i^t}{h_i^{P_i r}}$,

$$
a_1' = a_1 \cdot \prod_{i \in \mathsf{W}_{\overline{P}'P}} b_i^{P_i'} \cdot \prod_{i \in \mathsf{W}_{P'P}} c_i \cdot \prod_{i \in \mathsf{W}_{P'\overline{P}}} d_i
$$

$$
= g_2^{\alpha} (g_3 \cdot \prod_{i \in \overline{W}(P)} h_i^{P_i})^r \cdot \prod_{i \in \mathsf{W}_{\overline{P}'P}} h_i^{P_i' r} \cdot \prod_{i \in \mathsf{W}_{P'P}} h_i^t \cdot \prod_{i \in \mathsf{W}_{P'\overline{P}}} \frac{h_i^t}{h_i^{P_i r}}
$$

$$
= g_2^{\alpha} (g_3 \cdot \prod_{i \in \overline{W}(P)} h_i^{P_i} \cdot \prod_{i \in \mathsf{W}_{\overline{P}'P}} h_i^{P_i'} \cdot \prod_{i \in \mathsf{W}_{P'\overline{P}}} h_i^{-P_i})^r \cdot \prod_{i \in \mathsf{W}_{P'\overline{P}}} h_i^t \cdot \prod_{i \in \mathsf{W}_{P'P}} h_i^t
$$

$$
= g_2^{\alpha} (g_3 \cdot \prod_{i \in \mathsf{W}_{\overline{P}'\overline{P}}} h_i^{P_i} \cdot \prod_{i \in \mathsf{W}_{\overline{P}'P}} h_i^{P_i'})^r \cdot \prod_{i \in W(P')} h_i^t
$$

$$
= g_2^{\alpha} (g_3 \cdot \prod_{i \in \mathsf{W}_{\overline{P}'\overline{P}}} h_i^{P_i'} \cdot \prod_{i \in \mathsf{W}_{\overline{P}'P}} h_i^{P_i'})^r \cdot \prod_{i \in W(P')} h_i^t \quad (\because P' \approx P)
$$

$$
= g_2^{\alpha} (g_3 \cdot \prod_{i \in \overline{W}(P')} h_i^{P_i'})^r \cdot \prod_{i \in W(P')} h_i^t.
$$

$$
\frac{e(a_2, C_2) \cdot e(a_3, C_4)}{e(C_1, a_1')} = \frac{e(g^r, (g_3 \cdot \prod_{i \in \overline{W}(P')} h_i^{P_i'})^s) \cdot e(g^t, (\prod_{i \in W(P')} h_i)^s)}{e(g^s, g_2^{\alpha} (g_3 \cdot \prod_{i \in \overline{W}(P')} h_i^{P_i'})^r \cdot \prod_{i \in W(P')} h_i^t)}
$$

$$
= \frac{1}{e(g, g_2)^{s\alpha}} = \frac{1}{e(g_1, g_2)^s}.
$$

4 Security Proof

We show an IND-sID-CPA-security of the SWIBE scheme in the standard model and then transform the scheme to achieve IND-ID-CPA-security in the random oracle model.

4.1 Selective Security

Theorem 1. *Let $\mathbb{G}$ be a bilinear group of prime order p. Suppose the decisional (t, ϵ, L)-BDHE assumption holds in $\mathbb{G}$. Then our SWIBE is $(t', q_K, 0, \epsilon, L)$ IND-sID-CPA secure for arbitrary L, and $t' < t - O(L\boldsymbol{e} + \boldsymbol{p})$, where $\boldsymbol{e}$ is a time of scalar multiplication and $\boldsymbol{p}$ is a time of pairing in $\mathbb{G}$.*

Proof is available in Appendix.

4.2 Full Security

Theorem 1 demonstrates that the SWIBE scheme is IND-sID-CPA secure. Therefore, the SWIBE scheme is secure when the attacker in advance commits to the pattern to attempt to attack.

Any HIBE or WIBE scheme that is IND-sID-CPA secure can be transformed into a HIBE or WIBE scheme that is IND-ID-CPA secure in the random oracle model, as described in [2,6] for the case of HIBE schemes and the case of WIBE schemes, respectively, with losing a factor $O(q_H{}^L)$ in reduction tightness. The transformation is as follows:

Let $H : \{0,1\}^* \rightarrow \{0,1\}^d$ be a hash function and let $SWIBE_H$ be a $SWIBE$ scheme where a pattern $P = (P_1, \cdots, P_L)$ is replaced by $P' = (P'_1, \cdots, P'_L)$ with $P'_i = H(P_i)$ if $P_i \neq *$ and $P'_i = *$ if $P_i = *$ before it is used in key generation, encryption and decryption algorithms. Then, if H is collision resistant, $SWIBE_H$ becomes fully secure, but the reduction introduces a loss factor of $O(q_H{}^{dL})$. In the random oracle model, $SWIBE_H$ is fully secure with a reduction loss factor of $O(q_H{}^L)$. Thus, this transformation only works when the hierarchy depth is small enough.

Theorem 2. *[2] Suppose the SWIBE scheme is $(t, q_K, 0, \epsilon, L)$ IND-sID-CPA secure for arbitrary L with a pattern space $|P|$. The $SWIBE_H$ scheme described above is $(t', q'_K, q'_H, 0, \epsilon', L)$ IND-ID-CPA secure in the random oracle model for all*

$$t' \leq t, \ q'_K \leq q_K \ and \ \epsilon' \geq (L+1)(q'_H + 1)^L \cdot \ \epsilon + q'^2_H/|P|.$$

5 Extension to CCA Security

We extend the semantically secure scheme to obtain chosen ciphertext security using the similar technique in [9]. Given a strong one-time signature scheme $(SigKeyGen, Sign, Verify)$, we enable construction of an L-level IND-sID-CCA secure scheme $\Pi = (\mathsf{Setup}, \mathsf{KeyDer}, \mathsf{Encrypt}, \mathsf{Decrypt})$ from the $(L+1)$-level IND-sID-CPA scheme $\Pi' = (\mathsf{Setup}', \mathsf{KeyDer}' \ \mathsf{Encrypt}', \mathsf{Decrypt}')$. The intuition is that $P = (P_1, \cdots, P_L) \in \{\mathbb{Z}_p^* \cup \{*\}\}^L$ in Π is mapped to $P' = (P_1, \cdots, P_L, *) \in \{\mathbb{Z}_p^* \cup \{*\}\}^{L+1}$ in Π' and the $(L+1)$-th identity string is determined by the verification key of one-time signature scheme. When encrypting a message m with $P = (P_1, \cdots, P_L)$ in Π, the sender generates a one-time signature key (K_{sig}, V_{sig}) such that $V_{sig} \in \mathbb{Z}_p^*$ and then encrypts m with $P' = (P_1, \cdots, P_L, V_{sig})$ using $\mathsf{Encrypt}'$ in Π'. We describe how to construct L-level Π with $(L+1)$-level Π' and a one-time signature scheme in the following:

$\mathsf{Setup}(L)$ runs $\mathsf{Setup}'(L+1)$ to obtain (pp', msk'). Given $pp' \leftarrow (g, g_1, g_2, g_3, h_1, \cdots, h_{L+1})$ and msk', the public parameter is $pp \leftarrow pp'$ and the master secret key is $msk \leftarrow msk'$.

$\mathsf{KeyDer}(pp, sk_P, P')$ is the same as the KeyDer' algorithm.

$\mathsf{Encrypt}(pp, P, m)$ runs $SigKeyGen(1^\lambda)$ algorithm to obtain a signature signing key K_{sig} and a verification key V_{sig}. For a given pattern $P = (P_1, \cdots, P_L)$, encode P to $P' = (P_1, \cdots, P_L, V_{sig})$, compute $C \xleftarrow{\$} \mathsf{Encrypt}'(pp', P', m)$ and $\sigma \xleftarrow{\$} Sign(K_{sig}, C)$, and output $CT = (C, \sigma, V_{sig})$

$\mathsf{Decrypt}(sk_P, C_{P'})$: Let $C_{P'} = (C, \sigma, V_{sig})$.

1. Verify that σ is the valid signature of C under the key V_{sig}. If invalid, output $\perp$.
2. If $P \approx P'$ then run $\mathsf{Decrypt}'$ $(sk_P, C_{P'})$ to extract the message. Otherwise, output $\perp$.

Theorem 3. *Let $\mathbb{G}$ be a bilinear group of prime order p. The above SWIBE Π is $(t, q_K, q_D, \epsilon_1 + \epsilon_2, L)$ IND-sID-CCA secure assuming the SWIBE Π' is $(t', q'_K, 0, \epsilon_1, L + 1)$ IND-sID-CPA secure in $\mathbb{G}$ and signature scheme is (t_s, ϵ_2) strongly existentially unforgeable with $q_K < q'_K$, $t < t' - (Le + 3p)q_D - t_s$, where e is exponential time, p is pairing time, and t_s is sum of SigKeyGen, Sign and Verify computation time.*

Proof is available in Appendix.

6 Experiment

In this section, we measure the execution times of encryption and decryption of the proposed SWIBE, WIBE [2], wicked-IBE [3], WW-IBE [1], and CCP-ABE [14]. We have implemented the algorithms based on the PBC (pairing based cryptography) library with a_param and executed them on Intel Edison with a 32-bit Intel Atom processor 500 MHz and ublinux 3.10.17.

Figure 1a illustrates encryption and decryption times of SWIBE, WIBE, and CCP-ABE by varying the maximal hierarchy depth (L) from 5 to 20. Note that in WIBE and CCP-ABE, only a ciphertext can include wildcards, while the proposed SWIBE allows wildcards in both key and ciphertext. While WIBE performs point multiplications to convert a ciphertext to another ciphertext for a specific matching ID, SWIBE computes point additions to replace any ID by a wildcard. In CCP-ABE, each bit in an ID is regarded as an attribute where each pattern (ID) is 32 bit. Since the decryption requires pairing operations of which number is proportional to the number of attributes in CCP-ABE, the decryption is very slow. On the other hand, since point additions is negligible compared with a pairing operation, decryption time of SWIBE remains as constant. SWIBE improves decryption performance by up to 3 times and 650 times compared with WIBE and CCP-ABE.

Figure 1b compares encryption and decryption performance between SWIBE and wicked-IBE. In this case, a private key may include wildcards but no wildcard is allowed in a ciphertext in wicked-IBE. Since a point multiplication is required to decrypt a ciphertext in both SWIBE and wicked-IBE, both schemes show similar encryption and decryption performance even though SWIBE allows wildcards in a ciphertext which is prohibited in wicked-IBE.

Figure 1c compares encryption and decryption performance between SWIBE and WW-IBE. Both SWIBE and WW-IBE allow wildcards in a key and a ciphertext. While a point multiplication is required to decrypt a ciphertext in SWIBE, $2L$ number of pairing operations are required in WW-IBE. SWIBE improves decryption performance by 10 times compared with WW-IBE.

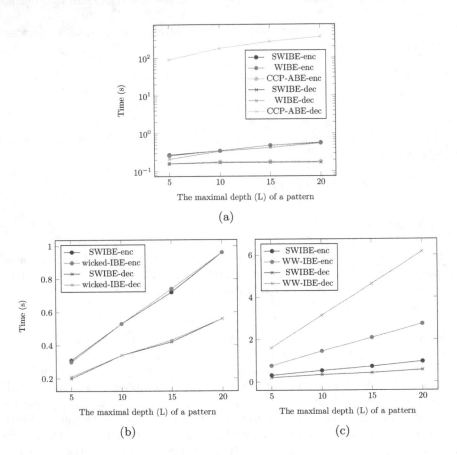

Fig. 1. Encryption and decryption time in (a) SWIBE, WIBE, and CCP-ABE, (b) in SWIBE and wicked-IBE, and (c) in SWIBE and WW-IBE

7   Conclusion

In this paper, we propose a new wildcard identity-based encryption called SWIBE, define appropriate security notions for SWIBE, and provide an efficient provably secure SWIBE construction with constant size ciphertext. Our SWIBE scheme allows wildcards for both key derivation and encryption, and it is the first success on constructing a constant-size ciphertext in a wildcarded identity-based encryption (WIBE) with fast decryption. We prove that our scheme is semantically secure based on L-BDHE assumption. In addition, we extend it to be CCA secure. Experimental results show that the proposed SWIBE improves the decryption performance by 3, 10, and 650 times compared with WIBE, WW-IBE, and CCP-ABE, respectively. It is our future work to construct a fully secure efficient scheme with a decent reduction loss factor in the standard model by considering a different setting such as a composite order group.

Acknowledgement. This work was supported by Institute for Information and communications Technology Promotion (IITP) grant funded by the Korea government (MSIT) (No. 2016-6-00599, A Study on Functional Signature and Its Applications and No. 2017-0-00661, Prevention of video image privacy infringement and authentication technique), by Basic Science Research Program through the National Research Foundation of Korea (NRF) funded by the Ministry of Education (No. 2017R1A2B4009903 and No. 2016R1D1A1B03934545), and by Basic Research Laboratory Program through the National Research Foundation of Korea (NRF) funded by the Ministry of Science, ICT and Future Planning (MSIP) (No. 2017R1A4A1015498).

A   Appendix

Theorem 1. *Let $\mathbb{G}$ be a bilinear group of prime order p. Suppose the decisional (t, ϵ, L)-BDHE assumption holds in $\mathbb{G}$. Then our SWIBE is $(t', q_K, 0, \epsilon, L)$ IND-sID-CPA secure for arbitrary L, and $t' < t - O(Le + p)$, where e is a time of scalar multiplication and p is a time of pairing in $\mathbb{G}$.*

Proof. Suppose $\mathcal{A}$ has advantage ϵ in attacking the SWIBE scheme. Using $\mathcal{A}$, we build an algorithm $\mathcal{B}$ that solves the (decisional) L-BDHE problem in $\mathbb{G}$.

For a generator $g \in \mathbb{G}$ and $\alpha \in \mathbb{Z}_p^*$, let $y_i = g^{\alpha^i} \in \mathbb{G}$. Algorithm $\mathcal{B}$ is given as input a random tuple $(g, h, y_1, \ldots, y_L, y_{L+2}, \ldots, y_{2L}, T)$ that is either sampled from P_{BDHE} (where $T = e(g,h)^{(\alpha^{L+1})}$) or from R_{BDHE} (where T is uniform and independent in $\mathbb{G}_1$). Algorithm $\mathcal{B}$'s goal is to output 1 when the input tuple is sampled from P_{BDHE} and 0 otherwise. Algorithm $\mathcal{B}$ works by interacting with $\mathcal{A}$ in a selective subset game as follows:

Init: The game begins with $\mathcal{A}$ first outputting an identity vector $P^* = (P_1^*, \ldots, P_L^*) \in_* (\mathbb{Z}_p^* \cup \{*\})^L$.

Setup: To generate a public parameter, algorithm $\mathcal{B}$ picks a random γ in $\mathbb{Z}_p$ and sets $g_1 = y_1 = g^\alpha$ and $g_2 = y_L g^\gamma = g^{\gamma + (\alpha^L)}$. Next, $\mathcal{B}$ picks random $\gamma_i \in \mathbb{Z}_p^*$ for $i = 1, \ldots, L$, and sets $h_i = g^{\gamma_i}/y_{L-i+1}$ for $i \in \overline{W}(P^*)$ and $h_i = g^{\gamma_i}$ for $i \in W(P^*)$. Algorithm $\mathcal{B}$ also picks a random δ in $\mathbb{Z}_p^*$ and sets $g_3 = g^\delta \prod_{i \in \overline{W}(P^*)} y_{L-i+1}^{P_i^*}$.

Key derivation queries: Suppose adversary $\mathcal{B}$ makes a key derivation query for pattern $P = (P_1, \ldots, P_L) \in_* (\mathbb{Z}_p^* \cup \{*\})^L$. By the definition of the security experiment, we know that $P^* \not\approx P$. That means that there exists an index $k \in \overline{W}(P^*) \cap \overline{W}(P)$ such that $P_k \neq P_k^*$. We define k to be the smallest one among all possible indices. $\mathcal{B}$ picks two random $\tilde{r}, \tilde{t} \in Z_p^*$ and (implicitly) sets $r \leftarrow -\frac{\alpha^k}{P_k^* - P_k} + \tilde{r}$ and $t \leftarrow r \cdot P_k^* + \tilde{t}$. Secret key $sk_P = (a_1, a_2, a_3, b, c, d)$ for P is constructed as

$$a_1 = g_2^\alpha \cdot (g_3 \prod_{i \in \overline{W}(P)} h_i^{P_i})^r; a_2 = g^r; a_3 = g^t,$$

$$b = \{b_i = h_i^r\}_{i \in W(P)}, c = \{c_i = h_i^t\}_{i \in W(P)}, d = (d_i = h_i^t / h_i^{P_i^* r})_{i \in \overline{W}(P)}$$

We have

$$(g_3 \prod_{i \in \overline{W}(P)} h_i^{P_i})^r = (g^\delta \prod_{i \in \overline{W}(P^*)} y_{L-i+1}^{P_i^*} \prod_{i \in \overline{W}(P)} g^{\gamma_i P_i} y_{L-i+1}^{-P_i})^r$$

$$= (g^{\delta + \sum_{i \in \overline{W}(P)} P_i \gamma_i} \cdot \prod_{i \in \{1, \ldots, k-1, k+1, \ldots, L\}} y_{L-i+1}^{P_i^* - P_i} \cdot y_{L-k+1}^{P_k^* - P_k})^r$$

where let $P_j^* = 0$ for $j \in W(P^*)$ and $P_j = 0$ for $j \in W(P)$.

We split this term up into two factors $A \cdot Z$, where $A = (y_{L-k+1}^{P_k^* - P_k})^r$. It can be checked that Z can be computed by $\mathcal{A}$, i.e. the terms y_i only appear with indices $i \in \{1, \ldots, L\}$. Term A can be expressed as

$$A = g^{\alpha^{L-k+1}(P_k^* - P_k)(-\frac{\alpha^k}{P_k^* - P_k} + \tilde{r})} = y_{L+1}^{-1} \cdot y_{L-k+1}^{(P_k^* - P_k)\tilde{r}}$$

Hence,

$$a_1 = g_2^\alpha \cdot A \cdot Z = y_{L+1} y_1^\gamma \cdot y_{L+1}^{-1} y_{L-k+1}^{(P_k^* - P_k)\tilde{r}} \cdot Z = y_1^\gamma \cdot y_{L-k+1}^{(P_k^* - P_k)\tilde{r}} \cdot Z$$

can be computed by $\mathcal{A}$. Furthermore,

$$g^r = g^{-\frac{\alpha^k}{P_k^* - P_k} + \tilde{r}} = y_k^{-\frac{1}{P_k^* - P_k}} \cdot g^{\tilde{r}}$$

and for each $i \in W(P)$,

$$h_i^r = (g^{\gamma_i} / y_{L-i+1})^{-\frac{\alpha^k}{P_k^* - P_k} + \tilde{r}} = y_k^{-\frac{\gamma_i}{P_k^* - P_k}} y_{L+k-i+1}^{\frac{1}{P_k^* - P_k}} \cdot g^{\gamma_i \tilde{r}} \cdot y_{L-i+1}^{-\tilde{r}}$$

$$h_i^t = (h_i)^{r \cdot P_k^* + \tilde{t}} = h_i^{P_k^* r} \cdot h_i^{\tilde{t}} = y_k^{-\frac{\gamma_i P_k^*}{P_k^* - P_k}} y_{L+k-i+1}^{\frac{P_k^*}{P_k^* - P_k}} \cdot g^{\gamma_i(\tilde{r}P_k^* + \tilde{t})} \cdot y_{L-i+1}^{-(\tilde{r}P_k^* + \tilde{t})}$$

can be computed since $k \notin W(P)$.

And for each $i \in \overline{W}(P)$,

$$h_i^t / h_i^{P_i^* r} = h_i^{rP_k^* + \tilde{t}} / h_i^{P_i^* r} = h_i^{(P_k^* - P_i^*)r + \tilde{t}} = (g^{\gamma_i} / y_{L-i+1})^{(P_k^* - P_i^*)(-\frac{\alpha^k}{P_k^* - P_k} + \tilde{r}) + \tilde{t}}$$

$$= (y_k^{-\frac{\gamma_i}{P_k^* - P_k}} y_{L+k-i+1}^{\frac{1}{P_k^* - P_k}} \cdot g^{\gamma_i \tilde{r}} \cdot y_{L-i+1}^{-\tilde{r}})^{(P_k^* - P_i^*)} \cdot (g^{\gamma_i} / y_{L-i+1})^{\tilde{t}}.$$

If $i = k$, $P_k^* - P_i^* = 0$. So $\mathcal{A}$ can compute it. Otherwise also $\mathcal{A}$ can compute it since $i \neq k$ and y_{L+1} does not appear in the equation.

Challenge: To generate a challenge, $\mathcal{B}$ computes C_1, C_2, and C_4 as h, $h^{\delta + \sum_{i \in \overline{W}(P^*)} (\gamma_i P_i^*)}$, and $h^{\sum_{i \in W(P^*)} \gamma_i}$, respectively. It then randomly chooses a bit $b \in \{0,1\}$ and sets $C_3 = m_b \cdot T \cdot e(y_1, h)^{\gamma}$. It gives $C = (C_1, C_2, C_3, C_4)$ as a challenge to $\mathcal{A}$. We claim that when $T = e(g, h)^{(\alpha^{L+1})}$ (i.e. the input to $\mathcal{B}$ is an L-BDHE tuple) then (C_1, C_2, C_3, C_4) is a valid challenge to $\mathcal{A}$ as in a real attack. To see this, write $h = g^c$ for some (unknown) $c \in \mathbb{Z}_p^*$. Then

$$h^{\delta + \sum_{i \in \overline{W}(P^*)} (\gamma_i P_i^*)} = (g^{\delta + \sum_{i \in \overline{W}(P^*)} (\gamma_i P_i^*)})^c$$

$$= (g^{\delta} \cdot \prod_{i \in \overline{W}(P^*)} y_{L-i+1}^{P_i^*} \prod_{i \in \overline{W}(P^*)} (\frac{g^{\gamma_i}}{y_{L-i+1}})^{P_i^*})^c = (g_3 \prod_{i \in \overline{W}(P^*)} h_i^{P_i^*})^c,$$

$$h^{\sum_{i \in W(P^*)} \gamma_i} = (g^{\sum_{i \in W(P^*)} \gamma_i})^c = (\prod_{i \in W(P^*)} g^{\gamma_i})^c$$

and

$$e(g, h)^{(\alpha^{L+1})} \cdot e(y_1, h)^{\gamma} = e(y_1, y_L)^c \cdot e(y_1, g)^{\gamma \cdot c} = e(y_1, y_L g^{\gamma})^c = e(g_1, g_2)^c.$$

Therefore, by definition, $e(y_{L+1}, g)^c = e(g, h)^{(\alpha^{L+1})} = T$ and hence $C = (C_1, C_2, C_3, C_4)$ is a valid challenge to $\mathcal{A}$. On the other hand, when T is random in $\mathbb{G}_1$ (i.e. the input to $\mathcal{B}$ is a random tuple) then C_3 is just a random independent element in $\mathbb{G}_1$ to $\mathcal{A}$.

Guess: Finally, $\mathcal{A}$ outputs a guess $b' \in \{0,1\}$. Algorithm $\mathcal{B}$ concludes its own game by outputting a guess as follows. If $b = b'$ then $\mathcal{B}$ outputs 1 meaning $T = e(g, h)^{(\alpha^{L+1})}$. Otherwise, it outputs 0 meaning T is random in $\mathbb{G}_1$.

When the input tuple is sampled from P_{BDHE} (where $T = e(g, h)^{(\alpha^{L+1})}$) then $\mathcal{A}$'s view is identical to its view in a real attack game and therefore $\mathcal{A}$ satisfies $|Pr[b = b'] - 1/2| \geq \epsilon$. When the input tuple is sampled from R_{BDHE} (where T is uniform in $\mathbb{G}_1$) then $Pr[b = b'] = 1/2$. Therefore, with g, h uniform in $\mathbb{G}$, α uniform in $\mathbb{Z}_p$, and T uniform in $\mathbb{G}_1$ we have that $|Pr[B(g, h, \boldsymbol{y}_{g,\alpha,L}, e(g, h)^{(\alpha^{L+1})}) = 0] - Pr[B(g, h, \boldsymbol{y}_{g,\alpha,L}, T) = 0]| \geq |(1/2 + \epsilon) - 1/2| = \epsilon$ as required, which completes the proof of the theorem.

Theorem 3. *Let $\mathbb{G}$ be a bilinear group of prime order p. The above SWIBE Π is $(t, q_K, q_D, \epsilon_1 + \epsilon_2, L)$ IND-sID-CCA secure assuming the SWIBE Π' is $(t', q'_K, 0, \epsilon_1, L + 1)$ IND-sID-CPA secure in $\mathbb{G}$ and signature scheme is (t_s, ϵ_2) strongly existentially unforgeable with $q_K < q'_K$, $t < t' - (Le + 3p)q_D - t_s$, where $\boldsymbol{e}$ is exponential time, $\boldsymbol{p}$ is pairing time, and t_s is sum of $SigKeyGen$, $Sign$ and $Verify$ computation time.*

Proof. Suppose there exists a t-time adversary $\mathcal{A}$ breaking IND-sID-CCA security. We build an algorithm $\mathcal{B}$ breaking IND-sID-CPA. Algorithm $\mathcal{B}$ proceeds as follows:

$\mathcal{A}$ announces $P^* = (P_1^*, \cdots, P_L^*)$. $\mathcal{B}$ runs $SigKeyGen(1^{\lambda})$ algorithm to obtain a signature signing key K_{sig}^* and a verification key V_{sig}^*, and announces $P^* = (P_1^*, \cdots, P_L^*, V_{sig}^*)$.

Setup: $\mathcal{B}$ gets the public parameter pp from the challenger and forwards it to $\mathcal{A}$.

Key derivation queries: For a query on $P \not\approx P^*$ from $\mathcal{A}$, $\mathcal{B}$ responds with KeyDer(pp, msk, P).

Decryption queries: Algorithm $\mathcal{A}$ issues decryption queries on $(sk_P, C_{P'})$. Let $C_{P'} = ((C_1, C_2, C_3, C_4), \sigma, V_{sig})$. If $P \not\approx P^*$ then output $\perp$. If $P' = (P_1^*, \cdots, P_L^*, V_{sig}^*)$ then $\mathcal{B}$ aborts. (A *forge* event occurs.) Otherwise, $\mathcal{B}$ queries KeyDer(pp, msk, P), gets sk_P, and decrypts $C_{P'}$ using sk_P.

Challenge: $\mathcal{A}$ gives the challenge (m_0, m_1) to $\mathcal{B}$. $\mathcal{B}$ gives the challenge (m_0, m_1) to $\mathcal{C}$ and gets the challenge (C_b) from $\mathcal{C}$. To generate challenge for $\mathcal{A}$, $\mathcal{B}$ computes C^* as follows:

$$\sigma^* \xleftarrow{\$} Sign(C_b, K_{sig}^*), \quad C^* \xleftarrow{\$} (C_b, \sigma^*, V_{sig}^*)$$

$\mathcal{B}$ replies with C^* to $\mathcal{A}$.

Query phase2: Same as in query phase 1 except decryption query for C* is not allowed.

Guess: The $\mathcal{A}$ outputs a guess $b \in \{0, 1\}$. $\mathcal{B}$ outputs b.

In the above experiment, $\mathcal{A}$ causes an abort by submitting a query that includes an existential forgery under K_{sig}^* on some ciphertexts. Our simulator is able to use this forgery to win the existential forgery game. Note that during the game the adversary makes only one chosen message query to generate the signature needed for the challenge ciphertext. Thus, $Pr[forge] < \epsilon_2$. It now follows that $\mathcal{B}$'s advantage is at least ϵ_1 as required.

References

1. Abdalla, M., Caro, A.D., Phan, D.H.: Generalized key delegation for wildcarded identity-based and inner-product encryption. IEEE Trans. Inf. Forensics Secur. **7**(6), 1695–1706 (2012). https://doi.org/10.1109/TIFS.2012.2213594
2. Abdalla, M., Catalano, D., Dent, A.W., Malone-Lee, J., Neven, G., Smart, N.P.: Identity-based encryption gone wild. In: Bugliesi, M., Preneel, B., Sassone, V., Wegener, I. (eds.) ICALP 2006. LNCS, vol. 4052, pp. 300–311. Springer, Heidelberg (2006). https://doi.org/10.1007/11787006_26
3. Abdalla, M., Kiltz, E., Neven, G.: Generalized key delegation for hierarchical identity-based encryption. In: Biskup, J., López, J. (eds.) ESORICS 2007. LNCS, vol. 4734, pp. 139–154. Springer, Heidelberg (2007). https://doi.org/10.1007/978-3-540-74835-9_10
4. Bethencourt, J., Sahai, A., Waters, B.: Ciphertext-policy attribute-based encryption, pp. 321–334. IEEE Computer Society (2007)
5. Birkett, J., Dent, A.W., Neven, G., Schuldt, J.C.N.: Efficient chosen-ciphertext secure identity-based encryption with wildcards. In: Pieprzyk, J., Ghodosi, H., Dawson, E. (eds.) ACISP 2007. LNCS, vol. 4586, pp. 274–292. Springer, Heidelberg (2007). https://doi.org/10.1007/978-3-540-73458-1_21

6. Boneh, D., Boyen, X., Goh, E.-J.: Hierarchical identity based encryption with constant size ciphertext. In: Cramer, R. (ed.) EUROCRYPT 2005. LNCS, vol. 3494, pp. 440–456. Springer, Heidelberg (2005). https://doi.org/10.1007/11426639_26

7. Boneh, D., Franklin, M.: Identity-based encryption from the weil pairing. In: Kilian, J. (ed.) CRYPTO 2001. LNCS, vol. 2139, pp. 213–229. Springer, Heidelberg (2001). https://doi.org/10.1007/3-540-44647-8_13

8. Boneh, D., Franklin, M.: Identity-based encryption from the weil pairing. SIAM J. Comput. **32**(3), 586–615 (2003)

9. Canetti, R., Halevi, S., Katz, J.: Chosen-ciphertext security from identity-based encryption. In: Cachin, C., Camenisch, J.L. (eds.) EUROCRYPT 2004. LNCS, vol. 3027, pp. 207–222. Springer, Heidelberg (2004). https://doi.org/10.1007/978-3-540-24676-3_13

10. Emura, K., Miyaji, A., Nomura, A., Omote, K., Soshi, M.: A ciphertext-policy attribute-based encryption scheme with constant ciphertext length. In: Bao, F., Li, H., Wang, G. (eds.) ISPEC 2009. LNCS, vol. 5451, pp. 13–23. Springer, Heidelberg (2009). https://doi.org/10.1007/978-3-642-00843-6_2

11. Joux, A.: Multicollisions in iterated hash functions. Application to cascaded constructions. In: Franklin, M. (ed.) CRYPTO 2004. LNCS, vol. 3152, pp. 306–316. Springer, Heidelberg (2004). https://doi.org/10.1007/978-3-540-28628-8_19

12. Shamir, A.: Identity-based cryptosystems and signature schemes. In: Blakley, G.R., Chaum, D. (eds.) CRYPTO 1984. LNCS, vol. 196, pp. 47–53. Springer, Heidelberg (1985). https://doi.org/10.1007/3-540-39568-7_5

13. Waters, B.: Efficient identity-based encryption without random oracles. In: Cramer, R. (ed.) EUROCRYPT 2005. LNCS, vol. 3494, pp. 114–127. Springer, Heidelberg (2005). https://doi.org/10.1007/11426639_7

14. Zhou, Z., Huang, D.: On efficient ciphertext-policy attribute based encryption and broadcast encryption: extended abstract. In: Proceedings of the 17th ACM Conference on Computer and Communications Security, CCS, pp. 753–755 (2010)

Logarithmic-Size Ring Signatures with Tight Security from the DDH Assumption

Benoît Libert[1,2($\boxtimes$)], Thomas Peters[3($\boxtimes$)], and Chen Qian[4($\boxtimes$)]

[1] CNRS, Laboratoire LIP, Lyon, France
[2] ENS de Lyon,
Laboratoire LIP (U. Lyon, CNRS, ENSL, INRIA, UCBL), Lyon, France
benoit.libert@ens-lyon.fr
[3] FNRS & Université catholique de Louvain, Louvain-la-Neuve, Belgium
[4] IRISA, Rennes, France

Abstract. Ring signatures make it possible for a signer to anonymously and, yet, convincingly leak a secret by signing a message while concealing his identity within a flexibly chosen *ring* of users. Unlike group signatures, they do not involve any setup phase or tracing authority. Despite a lot of research efforts in more than 15 years, most of their realizations require linear-size signatures in the cardinality of the ring. In the random oracle model, two recent constructions decreased the signature length to be only logarithmic in the number N of ring members. On the downside, their suffer from rather loose reductions incurred by the use of the Forking Lemma. In this paper, we consider the problem of proving them tightly secure without affecting their space efficiency. Surprisingly, existing techniques for proving tight security in ordinary signature schemes do not trivially extend to the ring signature setting. We overcome these difficulties by combining the Groth-Kohlweiss Σ-protocol (Eurocrypt'15) with dual-mode encryption schemes. Our main result is a fully tight construction based on the Decision Diffie-Hellman assumption in the random oracle model. By full tightness, we mean that the reduction's advantage is as large as the adversary's, up to a constant factor.

Keywords: Ring signatures · Anonymity · Tight security
Random oracles

1 Introduction

As introduced by Rivest, Shamir and Tauman [33], ring signatures make it possible for a signer to sign messages while hiding his identity within an *ad hoc* set of users, called a *ring*, that includes himself. To this end, the signer only needs to know the public keys of all ring members (besides his own secret key) in order to generate an anonymous signature on behalf of the entire ring. Unlike group signatures [16], ring signatures do not require any setup, coordination or registration phase and neither do they involve a tracing authority to de-anonymize

© Springer Nature Switzerland AG 2018
J. Lopez et al. (Eds.): ESORICS 2018, LNCS 11099, pp. 288–308, 2018.
https://doi.org/10.1007/978-3-319-98989-1_15

signatures. Whoever has a public key can be appointed as a ring member without being asked for his agreement or even being aware of it. Moreover, signatures should ideally provide everlasting anonymity and carry no information as to which ring member created them. The main motivation of ring signatures is to enable the anonymous leakage of secrets, by concealing the identity of a source (e.g., a whistleblower in a political scandal) while simultaneously providing guarantees of its reliability.

In this paper, we consider the exact security of ring signatures in the random oracle model [4]. So far, the only known solutions with logarithmic signature length [24,28] suffered from loose reductions: the underlying hard problem could only be solved with a probability smaller than the adversary's advantage by a linear factor in the number of hash queries. Our main result is to give the first construction that simultaneously provides tight security – meaning that there is essentially no gap between the adversary's probability of success and the reduction's advantage in solving a hard problem – and logarithmic signature size in the number of ring members. In particular, the advantage of our reduction is not multiplicatively affected by the number Q_H of random oracle queries nor the number of Q_V of public verification keys in a ring.

OUR CONTRIBUTION. We describe the first logarithmic-size ring signatures with tight security proofs in the random oracle model. The unforgeability of our construction is proved under the standard Decision Diffie-Hellman (DDH) assumption in groups without a bilinear map while anonymity is achieved against unbounded adversaries. Our security proof eliminates *both* the linear gap in the number of random oracle queries *and* the $\Theta(Q_V)$ security loss. It thus features a *fully tight* reduction, meaning that – up to statistically negligible terms – the reduction's advantage as a DDH distinguisher is only smaller than the adversary's forging probability by a factor 2. To our knowledge, our scheme is the first ring signature for which such a fully tight reduction is reported. It is obtained by tweaking a construction due to Groth and Kohlweiss [24] and achieves tight security at the expense of increasing the number of scalars and group elements per signature by a small constant factor. For the same exact security, our reduction allows smaller key sizes which essentially decrease the signature length of [24] by a logarithmic factor n in the cardinality N of the ring and the time complexity by a factor $\omega(n^2)$. For rings of cardinality $N = 2^6$, for example, our signatures can be 36 times faster to compute and 6 times shorter than [24].

OUR TECHNIQUES. Our scheme builds on the Groth-Kohlweiss proof system [24] that allows proving that one-out-of-N commitments opens to 0 with a communication complexity $O(\log N)$. This proof system was shown to imply logarithmic-size ring signatures with perfect anonymity assuming that the underlying commitment scheme is perfectly hiding. At the heart of the protocol of [24] is a clever use of a Σ-protocol showing that a committed value ℓ is 0 or 1, which proceeds in the following way. In order to prove that a commitment $C_\ell \in \{C_i\}_{i=0}^{N-1}$ opens to 0 without revealing the index $\ell \in \{0, \ldots, N-1\}$, the n-bit indexes ℓ_j of the binary representation $\ell_1 \ldots \ell_n \in \{0,1\}^n$ of $\ell \in \{0, \ldots, N-1\}$ are committed to and, for each of them, the prover uses the aforementioned Σ-protocol to prove that $\ell_j \in \{0,1\}$. The response $f_j = a_j + \ell_j x$ of the Σ-protocol is then viewed as a degree-one polynomial in the challenge $x \in \mathbb{Z}_q$ and used to define polynomials

$$P_i[Z] = \prod_{j=1}^{n} f_{j,i_j} = \delta_{i,\ell} \cdot Z^n + \sum_{k=0}^{n-1} p_{i,k} \cdot Z^k \qquad \forall i \in [N],$$

where $f_{j,0} = f_j$ and $f_{f,1} = x - f_j$, which have degree $n = \log N$ if $i = \ell$ and degree $n - 1$ otherwise. In order to prove that one of the polynomials $\{P_i[Z]\}_{i=0}^{N-1}$ has degree n without revealing which one, Groth and Kohlweiss [24] homomorphically compute the commitment $\prod_{i=0}^{N-1} C_i^{P_i(x)}$ and multiply it with $\prod_{k=0}^{n-1} C_{d_k}^{-x^k}$, for auxiliary homomorphic commitments $\{C_{d_k} = \prod_{i=0}^{N-1} C_i^{p_{i,k}}\}_{k=0}^{n-1}$, in order to cancel out the terms of degree 0 to $n - 1$ in the exponent. Then, they prove that the product $\prod_{i=0}^{N-1} C_i^{P_i(x)} \cdot \prod_{k=0}^{n-1} C_{d_k}^{-x^k}$ is indeed a commitment of 0. The soundness of the proof relies on the Schwartz-Zippel lemma, which ensures that $\prod_{i=0}^{N-1} C_i^{P_i(x)} \cdot \prod_{k=0}^{n-1} C_{d_k}^{-x^k}$ is unlikely to be a commitment to 0 if C_ℓ is not.

As an application of their proof system, Groth and Kohlweiss [24] obtained logarithmic-size ring signatures from the discrete logarithm assumption in the random oracle model. While efficient and based on a standard assumption, their scheme suffers from a loose security reduction incurred by the use of the Forking Lemma [32]. In order to extract a discrete logarithm from a ring signature forger, the adversary has to be run $n = \log N$ times with the same random tape (where N is the ring cardinality), leading to a reduction with advantage $\varepsilon' \approx \frac{\varepsilon^n}{Q_V \cdot Q_{\mathcal{H}}}$, where $Q_{\mathcal{H}}$ is the number of hash queries and Q_V is the number of public keys. This means that, if we want to increase the key size so as to compensate for the concrete security gap, we need to multiply the security parameter by a factor $n = \log N$, even without taking into account the factors $Q_{\mathcal{H}}$ and Q_V.

In our pursuit of a tight reduction, a first idea is to apply the lossy identification paradigm [2,27] where the security proofs proceed by replacing a well-formed public key by a so-called lossy public key, with respect to which forging a signature becomes statistically impossible. In particular, the DDH-based instantiation of Katz and Wang [27] appears as an ideal candidate since, somewhat analogously to [24], well-formed public keys can be seen as homomorphic Elgamal encryptions of 0. However, several difficulties arise when we try to adapt the techniques of [2,27] to the ring signature setting.

The first one is that the Groth-Kohlweiss ring signatures [24] rely on perfectly *hiding* commitments in order to achieve unconditional anonymity whereas the Elgamal encryption scheme is a perfectly binding commitment. This fortunately leaves us the hope for computational anonymity if we trade the perfectly hiding commitments for Elgamal encryptions. A second difficulty is to determine which public keys should be replaced by lossy keys in the reduction. At each public key generation query, the reduction has to decide if the newly generated key will be lossy or injective. Replacing all public keys by lossy keys is not possible because of corruptions (indeed, lossy public keys have no underlying secret key) and the reduction does not know in advance which public keys will end up in the target ring $\mathcal{R}^\star$ of the forgery. Only replacing a randomly chosen key by a lossy key does not work either: indeed, in the ring signature setting, having one lossy public key $PK^\dagger$ in the target ring $\mathcal{R}^\star$ does not prevent an unbounded adversary from using the secret key of a well-formed key $PK^\star \in \mathcal{R}^\star \setminus \{PK^\dagger\}$ to create a forgery. Moreover, as long as the reduction can only embed the challenge (injective or lossy) key in one output of the key generation oracle, it remains stuck with an advantage $\Theta(\varepsilon/Q_V)$ if the forger has advantage ε. Arguably, this bound is the best we can hope for by directly applying the lossy identification technique.

To obtain a fully tight reduction, we depart from the lossy identification paradigm [2] in that, instead of tampering with one user's public keys at some step, our security proof embeds a DDH instance in the public parameters pp of the scheme. This allows the reduction to have all users' private keys at disposal and reveal them to the adversary upon request. In the real system, the set pp contains uniformlyrandom group elements $(g, h, \tilde{g}, \tilde{h}, U, V) \in \mathbb{G}^6$ and each user's public key consists of a pair $(X, Y) = (g^\alpha \cdot h^\beta, \tilde{g}^\alpha \cdot \tilde{h}^\beta)$, where $(\alpha, \beta) \in \mathbb{Z}_q^2$ is the secret key. The idea of the security proof is that, if $(g, h, \tilde{g}, \tilde{h}) \in \mathbb{G}^4$ is not a Diffie-Hellman tuple, the public key $PK = (X, Y)$ uniquely determines $(\alpha, \beta) \in \mathbb{Z}_q^2$. In the case $\tilde{h} = \tilde{g}^{\log_g(h)}$, the public key (X, Y) is compatible with q equally likely pairs (α, β) since it only reveals the information $\log_g(X) = \alpha + \log_q(h) \cdot \beta$.

The reduction thus builds a DDH distinguisher by forcing the adversary's forgery to contain a committed encoding $\Gamma = U^\alpha \cdot V^\beta$ of the signer's secret key $(\alpha, \beta) \in \mathbb{Z}_q^2$, which can be extracted using some trapdoor information. So long as (U, V) is linearly independent of (g, h), the encoding $\Gamma = U^\alpha \cdot V^\beta$ is independent of the adversary's view if $(g, h, \tilde{g}, \tilde{h})$ is a Diffie-Hellman tuple. In contrast, this encoding is uniquely determined by the public key if $\tilde{h} \neq \tilde{g}^{\log_g(h)}$. This allows the reduction to infer that $(g, h, \tilde{g}, \tilde{h})$ is a Diffie-Hellman tuple whenever it extracts $\Gamma = U^\alpha \cdot V^\beta$ from the adversary's forgery. To apply this argument, however, we need to make sure that signing queries do not leak any more information about (α, β) than the public key $PK = (X, Y)$ does. For this purpose, we resort to lossy encryption schemes [3] (a.k.a. dual-mode encryption/commitments [25,31]), which can either behave as perfectly hiding or perfectly binding commitments depending on the distribution of the public key. In each signature, we embed a lossy encryption $(T_0, T_1) = (g^{\theta_1} \cdot h^{\theta_2}, U^\alpha \cdot V^\beta \cdot H_1^{\theta_1} \cdot H_2^{\theta_2})$ of $\Gamma = U^\alpha \cdot V^\beta$, which is computed using the DDH-based lossy encryption scheme of [3]. If $(H_1, H_2) \in \mathbb{G}^2$ is linearly independent of (g, h), then (T_0, T_1) perfectly hides Γ. At the same time, the reduction should be able to extract Γ from (T_0, T_1) in the forgery. To combine these seemingly conflicting requirements, we derive (H_1, H_2) from a (pseudo-)random oracle which is programmed to have $(H_1, H_2) = (g^\gamma, h^\gamma)$, for some $\gamma \in_R \mathbb{Z}_q$, in the adversary's forgery and maintain the uniformity of all pairs $(H_1, H_2) \in \mathbb{G}^2$ in all signing queries. By doing so, the witness indistinguishability of the Groth-Kohlweiss Σ-protocol [24] implies that the adversary only obtains a limited amount of information from uncorrupted users' private keys. While the above information theoretic argument is reminiscent of the security proof of Okamoto's identification scheme [29], our proof departs from [29] in that we do not rewind the adversary as it would not enable a tight reduction.

RELATED WORK. The concept of ring signatures was coined by Rivest, Shamir and Tauman [33] who gave constructions based on trapdoor functions and proved their security in the ideal cipher model. They also mentioned different realizations based on proofs of partial knowledge [19]. The latter approach was extended by Abe et al. [1] to support rings containing keys from different underlying signatures and assumptions. Bresson, Stern and Szydlo [11] modified the scheme of Rivest et al. [33] so as to prove it secure in the random oracle model.

In 2006, Bender, Katz and Morselli [7] provided rigorous security definitions and theoretical constructions without random oracles. In the standard model, the first efficient instantiations were put forth by Shacham and Waters [35] in groups with a bilinear map. Brakerski and Tauman-Kalai [10] gave alternative constructions based on lattice assumptions. Meanwhile, Boyen [9] suggested a generalization of the primitive with standard-model instantiations.

The early realizations [11,33] had linear size in the cardinality of the ring. Dodis et al. [20] mentioned constant-size ring signatures as an application of their anonymous ad hoc identification protocols. However, their approach requires a setup phase where an RSA modulus is generated by some trusted entity. Chase and Lysyanskaya [15] suggested a similar construction of constant-size ring signatures from cryptographic accumulators [6]. However, efficiently instantiating their construction requires setup-free accumulators which are compatible with zero-knowledge proofs. The hash-based accumulators of [12,13] would not provide efficient solutions as they would incur proofs of knowledge of hash function pre-images. While the lattice-based construction of [28] relies on hash-based accumulators, its security proof is not tight and its efficiency is not competitive with discrete-logarithm-based techniques. Sander's number-theoretic accumulator [34] is an alternative candidate to instantiate [15] without a setup phase. However, it is not known to provide practical protocols: as observed in [24], it would involve much larger composite integers than standard RSA moduli (besides zero-knowledge proofs for double discrete logarithms). Moreover, it is not clear how it would be compatible with tight security proofs.

Chandran, Groth and Sahai [14] gave sub-linear-size signatures in the standard model, which were recently improved in [23]. In the random oracle model, Groth and Kohlweiss [24] described an elegant construction of logarithmic-size ring signatures based on the discrete logarithm assumption. Libert et al. [28] obtained logarithmic-size lattice-based ring signatures in the random oracle model.

The logarithmic-size ring signatures of [8,24,28] are obtained by applying the Fiat-Shamir heuristic [21] to interactive Σ-protocols. While these solutions admit security proofs under well-established assumptions in the random oracle model, their security reductions are pretty loose. In terms of exact security, they are doomed [30] to lose a linear factor in the number $Q_{\mathcal{H}}$ of random oracle queries as long as they rely on the Forking Lemma [32].

The exact security of digital signatures was first considered by Bellare and Rogaway [5] and drew a lot of attention [2,17,22,26,27] since then.

2 Background

2.1 Syntax and Security Definitions for Ring Signatures

Definition 1. *A ring signature scheme consists of a tuple of efficient algorithms* (Par-Gen, Keygen, Sign, Verify) *with the following specifications:*

Par-Gen(1^λ): *Given a security parameter λ, outputs the public parameters* pp.
Keygen(pp): *Given* pp, *outputs a key pair* (PK, SK) *for the user.*
Sign(pp, $SK, \mathcal{R}, M$)**:** *Given the user's secret key SK, a ring $\mathcal{R}$ and a message M, outputs the signature σ of the message M on behalf of the ring $\mathcal{R}$.*
Verify(pp, $M, \mathcal{R}, \sigma$)**:** *Given the message M, a ring $\mathcal{R}$ and a candidate signature σ, the verification algorithm outputs 0 or 1.*

These algorithms must also verify the correctness, meaning that for all pp $\leftarrow$ Par-Gen(1^λ), $(PK, SK) \leftarrow$ KeyGen(pp), for all M, and for all $\mathcal{R}$ such that $PK \in \mathcal{R}$, we have w.h.p Verify(pp, $M, \mathcal{R},$ Sign(pp, $SK, \mathcal{R}, M$)) = 1.

From a security point of view, Bender *et al.* [7] suggested the following stringent definitions of anonymity and unforgeability.

Definition 2. *A ring signature* (Par-Gen, Keygen, Sign, Verify) *provides statistical* **anonymity** *under* **full key exposure** *if, for any computationally unbounded adversary $\mathcal{A}$, there exists a negligible function $\varepsilon(\lambda)$ such that*

$$| \Pr[\text{pp} \leftarrow \text{Par-Gen}(1^\lambda); (M^\star, i_0, i_1, \mathcal{R}^\star) \leftarrow \mathcal{A}^{\text{Keygen}(\cdot)}; b \xleftarrow{R} \{0, 1\};$$

$$\sigma^\star \leftarrow \text{Sign}(pp, SK_{i_b}, \mathcal{R}^\star, M^\star) : \mathcal{A}(\sigma^\star) = b] - \frac{1}{2}| < \varepsilon(\lambda),$$

where $PK_{i_0}, PK_{i_1} \in \mathcal{R}^\star$ and Keygen *is an oracle that generates a fresh key pair $(PK, SK) \leftarrow$ Keygen(pp) at each query and returns both PK and SK to $\mathcal{A}$.*

Definition 3. *A ring signature* (Par-Gen, Keygen, Sign, Verify) *provides* **unforgeability** *w.r.t* **insider corruption** *if, for any PPT adversary $\mathcal{A}$, there exists a negligible function $\varepsilon(\lambda)$ such that, for any* pp $\leftarrow$ Par-Gen(1^λ), *we have*

$$\Pr[(M, \mathcal{R}, \sigma) \leftarrow \mathcal{A}^{\text{Keygen}(\cdot), \text{Sign}(\cdot), \text{Corrupt}(\cdot)}(\text{pp}) : \text{Verify}(\text{pp}, M, \mathcal{R}, \sigma) = 1] < \varepsilon(\lambda),$$

- Keygen(): *is an oracle that maintains a counter j initialized to 0. At each query, it increments j, generates $(PK_j, SK_j) \leftarrow$ KeyGen(pp) and outputs PK_j.*
- Sign($i, M, \mathcal{R}$) *is an oracle that returns $\sigma \leftarrow$ Sign(pp, $SK_i, \mathcal{R}, M$) if $PK_i \in \mathcal{R}$ and (PK_i, SK_i) has been generated by* Keygen. *Otherwise, it returns $\perp$.*
- Corrupt(i) *returns SK_i if (PK_i, SK_i) was output by* Keygen *and $\perp$ otherwise.*
- $\mathcal{A}$ *is restricted to output a triple $(M, \mathcal{R}, \sigma)$ such that: (i) No query of the form $(\star, M, \mathcal{R})$ has been made to* Sign$(\cdot, \cdot, \cdot)$; *(ii) $\mathcal{R}$ only contains public keys PK_i produced by* Keygen *and for which i was never queried to* Corrupt$(\cdot)$.

2.2   Hardness Assumptions

Definition 4. *The* **Decision Diffie-Hellman** *(DDH) problem in* $\mathbb{G}$*, is to distinguish the distributions* (g^a, g^b, g^{ab}) *and* (g^a, g^b, g^c)*, with* $a, b, c \xleftarrow{R} \mathbb{Z}_q$*. The DDH assumption is the intractability of the problem for any PPT distinguisher.*

2.3   Reminders on Σ-Protocols

Definition 5 ([18])**.** *Let a prover* P *and a verifier* V*, which are PPT algorithms, and a binary relation* $\mathcal{R}$*. A protocol* (P, V) *is a* Σ*-protocol w.r.t.* $\mathcal{R}$*, the challenge set* $\mathcal{C}$*, the public input* u *and the private input* w*, if it satisfies the following:*

- **3-move form:** *The protocol is of the following form:*
  - P *compute commitments* $\{c_i\}_{i=0}^{j}$*, where* $j \in \mathbb{N}$*, and sends* $\{c_i\}_{i=0}^{j}$ *to* V*.*
  - *The verifier* V *generates a random challenge* $x \xleftarrow{R} \mathcal{C}$ *and sends* c *to* P*.*
  - *The prover* P *sends a response* s *to* V*.*
  - *On input of a transcript* $(\{c_i\}_{i=0}^{j}, x, s)$*,* V *outputs 1 or 0.*
- **Completeness:** *If* $(u, w) \in \mathcal{R}$ *and the prover* P *honestly generates the transcript* $(\{c_i\}_{i=0}^{j}, x, s)$ *for a random challenge* $x \xleftarrow{R} \mathcal{C}$ *sent by* V*, there is a negligible function* $\varepsilon(\lambda)$ *such that* V *accepts with probability* $1 - \varepsilon(\lambda)$*.*
- **2-Special soundness:** *There exists a PPT knowledge extractor* $\mathcal{E}$ *that, for any public input* u*, on input of two accepting transcripts* $(\{c_i\}_{i=0}^{j}, x, s)$ *and* $(\{c_i\}_{i=0}^{j}, x', s')$ *with* $x \neq x'$*, outputs a witness* w' *such that* $(u, w') \in \mathcal{R}$*.*
- **Special Honest Verifier Zero-Knowledge (SHVZK):** *There is a PPT simulator* $\mathcal{S}$ *that, given* u *and a random* $x \in \mathcal{C}$*, outputs a simulated transcript* $(\{c_i'\}_{i=0}^{j}, x, s')$ *which is computationally indistinguishable from a real one.*

2.4 Σ-protocol Showing that a Commitment Opens to 0 or 1

We recall the Σ-protocol used in [24] to prove that a commitment opens to 0 or 1. Let $\mathcal{R} = \{(ck, c, (m, r)) \mid c = \mathsf{Com}_{ck}(m, r) \wedge (m, r) \in \{0, 1\} \times \mathbb{Z}_q\}$ the binary relation, where ck is the commitment key generated for the underlying commitment scheme, $u = c$ is the public input and $w = (m, r)$ is the private input. Figure 1 gives us a Σ-protocol (P, V) for $\mathcal{R}$.

Theorem 1 ([24, Theorem 2])**.** *Let* (Setup, Com) *be a perfectly binding, computationally hiding, strongly binding and additively homomorphic commitment scheme. The* Σ*-protocol presented in Fig. 1 for the commitment to 0 or to 1 is perfectly complete, perfectly 2-special sound and perfectly SHVZK.*

2.5 Σ-protocol for One-out-of-N Commitments Containing 0

Groth and Kohlweiss [24] used the Σ-protocol of Sect. 2.4 to build an efficient Σ-protocol allowing to prove knowledge of an opening of one-out-of-N commitments $\{c_i\}_{i=0}^{N-1}$ to $m = 0$. Their protocol outperforms the standard OR-proof

$$
\begin{array}{ll}
\textbf{Prover}(ck, c; m, r) & \textbf{Verifier}(ck, c) \\
a, s, t \xleftarrow{R} \mathbb{Z}_q & \\
c_a = \mathsf{Com}_{ck}(a; s) & \\
c_b = \mathsf{Com}_{ck}(am; t) & \\
\end{array}
$$

$\xrightarrow{\quad (c_a, c_b) \quad}$

$\xleftarrow{\quad x \quad}$ $\qquad x \leftarrow \{0,1\}^\lambda$

$$
\begin{aligned}
f &= mx + a \\
z_a &= rx + s \\
z_b &= r(x - f) + t
\end{aligned}
$$

$\xrightarrow{\quad f, z_a, z_b \quad}$

Accept if and only if
$$c_a, c_b \in \mathcal{C}_{ck}, \ f, z_a, z_b \in \mathbb{Z}_b,$$
$$c^x c_a = \mathsf{Com}_{ck}(f; z_a), \ c^{x-f} c_b = \mathsf{Com}_{ck}(0; z_b)$$

Fig. 1. Σ-protocol for commitment to $m \in \{0,1\}$

$$
\begin{array}{ll}
\textbf{Prover}(ck, (c_0, \ldots, c_{N-1}); (\ell, r)) & \textbf{Verifier}(ck, (c_0, \ldots, c_{N-1})) \\
\end{array}
$$

For $j = 1, \ldots, n$
$$
\begin{aligned}
&r_j, a_j, s_j, t_j, \rho_j \leftarrow \mathbb{Z}_q, \ c_{\ell_j} = \mathsf{Com}_{ck}(\ell_j, r_j) \\
&c_{a_j} = \mathsf{Com}_{ck}(a_j, s_j), \ c_{b_j} = \mathsf{Com}_{ck}(b_j, t_j) \\
&\text{with } b_j = \ell_j \cdot a_j \\
&c_{d_{j-1}} = \prod_{i=0}^{N-1} c_i^{p_{i,j-1}} \cdot \mathsf{Com}_{ck}(0, \rho_{j-1}) \\
&\text{with } p_{i,k} \text{ defined in (1)}
\end{aligned}
$$

$\xrightarrow{\quad \{c_{\ell_j}, c_{a_j}, c_{b_j}, c_{d_{j-1}}\}_{j=1}^n \quad}$

$\xleftarrow{\quad x \quad}$ $\qquad x \xleftarrow{R} \{0,1\}^\lambda$

For $j = 1, \ldots, n$
$$
\begin{aligned}
f_j &= \ell_j x + a_j, \ z_{a_j} = r_j x + s_j \\
z_{b_j} &= r_j(x - f_j) + t_j \\
z_d &= r x^n - \sum_{k=0}^{n-1} \rho_k x^k
\end{aligned}
$$

$\xrightarrow{\quad \{f_j, z_{a_j}, z_{b_j}\}_{j=1}^n, z_d \quad}$

Accept if and only if
$$\{c_{\ell_j}, c_{a_j}, c_{b_j}, c_{d_{j-1}}\}_{j=1}^n \in \mathcal{C}_{ck}, \ \{f_j, z_{a_j}, z_{b_j}\}_{j=1}^n, z_d \in \mathbb{Z}_q$$
For all $j = 1, \ldots, n$
$$c_{\ell_j}^x c_{a_j} = \mathsf{Com}_{ck}(f_j; z_{a_j}), \ c_{\ell_j}^{f_j - x} c_{b_j} = \mathsf{Com}_{ck}(0; z_{b_j})$$
$$\prod_{i=0}^{N-1} c_i^{\prod_{j=1}^n f_{i,i_j}} \cdot \prod_{k=0}^{n-1} c_{d_k}^{-x^k} = \mathsf{Com}_{ck}(0; z_d)$$
with $f_{j,1} = f_j$ and $f_{j,0} = x - f_j$

Fig. 2. Σ-protocol for one of $(c_0, \ldots, c_{N-1})$ commits to 0

approach [19] in that its communication complexity is only $O(\log N)$, instead of $O(N)$. The idea is to see the responses $f = mx + a$ of the basic Σ protocol as degree-1 polynomials in $x \in \mathbb{Z}_q$ and exploit the homomorphism of the commitment.

Theorem 2 ([24, Theorem 3]). *The Σ-protocol of Fig. 2 is perfectly complete. It is (perfectly) $(n+1)$-special sound if the commitment is (perfectly) binding. It is (perfectly) SHVZK if the commitment scheme is (perfectly) hiding.*

In Fig. 2, for each i, $p_{i,0}, \ldots, p_{i,n-1} \in \mathbb{Z}_q$ are the coefficients of the polynomial

$$
P_i[Z] = \prod_{j=1}^n F_{j,i_j}[Z] = \delta_{i,\ell} \cdot Z^n + \sum_{k=0}^{n-1} p_{i,k} \cdot Z^k \qquad \forall i \in \{0, \ldots, N-1\} \tag{1}
$$

obtained by defining $F_{j,1}[Z] = \ell_j \cdot Z + a_j$ and $F_{j,0}[Z] = Z - F_{j,1}[Z]$ for all $j \in [n]$. Note that the equality (1) stems from the fact that, for each index $i = i_1 \ldots i_n \in \{0, \ldots, N - 1\}$, we have $F_{j,i_j}[Z] = \delta_{i_j, \ell_j} \cdot Z + (-1)^{\delta_{0,i_j}} \cdot a_j$ for all $j \in [n]$, so that the coefficient of Z^n in (1) is non-zero if and only if $i = \ell$.

2.6   A Note on the Application to Ring Signatures

In [24], Groth and Kohlweiss obtained a ring signature scheme by applying the Fiat-Shamir paradigm [21] to the above Σ-protocol. In short, key pairs are of the form (c, r) such that $c = \mathsf{Com}(0; r)$ and a ring signature associated with $\mathcal{R} = \{c_0, \ldots, c_N\}$ is simply a proof that the signer knows how to open to 0 one of the N commitments in that ring. In [24], the following theorem states about the security of the resulting construction, denoted $(\mathsf{Setup}, \mathsf{KGen}, \mathsf{Sign}, \mathsf{Vfy})$.

Theorem 3 ([24, Theorem 4]). *The scheme* $(\mathsf{Setup}, \mathsf{KGen}, \mathsf{Sign}, \mathsf{Vfy})$ *is a ring signature scheme with perfect correctness. It has perfect anonymity if the commitment scheme is perfectly hiding. It is unforgeable in the random oracle model if the commitment scheme is perfectly hiding and computationally binding.*

As the security of the ring signature relies on that of the Σ-protocol, it is interesting to take a closer look at the computation of commitments $\{C_{d_{j-1}}\}_{j=1}^n$ in Fig. 2. This part of the Σ-protocol is the only point where the ring signature generation may involve adversarially-generated values. In the anonymity game, the signer's public key may be one of the only two honestly-generated public keys in the ring $\mathcal{R}$. The security proof of [24] argues that, as long as the commitment is perfectly hiding, the fact that each $C_{d_{j-1}}$ contains a (randomizing) factor $\mathsf{Com}(0; \rho_{j-1})$, for some uniformly random ρ_{j-1}, is sufficient to guarantee perfect anonymity. We point out an issue that arises when $\mathcal{R} = \{c_0, \ldots, c_N\}$ contains maliciously generated keys outside the space of honestly generated commitments (even if they are perfectly hiding). In short, multiplying a maliciously generated commitment by a fresh commitment may not fully "clean-up" its distribution.

The following example is a perfectly hiding commitment where re-randomizing does not wipe out maliciously generated commitments components: the setup algorithm outputs generators $ck = (g, h)$ cyclic group $\mathbb{G}$ of prime order q; committing to $m \in \mathbb{Z}_q$ using randomness $\rho = (r, s) \xleftarrow{R} \mathbb{Z}_q^2$ is achieved by computing $\mathsf{Com}_{ck}(m; \rho) = (c_1, c_2, c_3) = (g^m h^r, g^s, h^s) \in \mathbb{G}^3$, which is a perfectly hiding commitment since c_1 is a Pedersen commitment and the Elgamal encryption (c_2, c_3) of 0 is independent of c_1. If we consider the maliciously generated commitment $(c_1^\star, c_2^\star, c_3^\star) = (h^u, g^v, g \cdot h^v)$, multiplying it by any $\mathsf{Com}_{ck}(0; \rho)$ does not bring it back in the range of Com. Therefore, in an instantiation with the above commitment, an unbounded adversary can defeat the anonymity property.

The only missing requirement on behalf of the underlying perfectly hiding commitment is that it should be possible to efficiently recognize elements in the range of the commitment algorithm. This assumption is quite natural and satisfied by schemes like Pedersen's commitment. Hence, this observation does not affect the perfect anonymity of the discrete-log-based instantiation of [24].

3   A Fully Tight Construction from the DDH Assumption

We modify the scheme of [24] so as to prove its unforgeability via a fully tight reduction from the DDH assumption. The advantage of the DDH distinguisher is only smaller than the adversary's advantage by a (small) constant factor.

The price to pay for this fully tight reduction is relatively small since signatures are only longer than in [24] by roughly $2n$ group elements. Moreover, as in [24], our signing algorithm requires $\Theta(N)$ exponentiations if N is the size of the ring.

3.1   Description

We exploit the fact that, in the Σ-protocol of [24], not all first-round messages should be computed using the same commitment scheme as the one used to compute the public key. The second step of the signing algorithm computes perfectly hiding commitments $\{C_{d_k}\}_{k=0}^{n-1}$ which are vectors of dimension 4. They live in a different space than public keys $(X, Y) = (g^\alpha \cdot h^\beta, \tilde{g}^\alpha \cdot \tilde{h}^\beta)$, which are DDH-based lossy encryptions of (and thus perfectly hiding commitments to) 0.

The signer generates a commitment $(T_0, T_1) = (g^{\theta_1} \cdot h^{\theta_2}, \Gamma \cdot H_1^{\theta_1} \cdot H_2^{\theta_2})$ to $\Gamma = U^{\alpha_\ell} \cdot V^{\beta_\ell}$, which encodes his secret key $(\alpha_\ell, \beta_\ell) \in \mathbb{Z}_q^2$. This defines a vector $\boldsymbol{V}_\ell = (X_\ell, Y_\ell, T_0, T_1) \in \mathbb{G}^4$ in the column space of a matrix $\mathbf{M}_H \in \mathbb{G}^{4\times 4}$, which has full rank in the scheme but not in the proof of unforgeability. Then, for each key $\boldsymbol{X}_i = (X_i, Y_i)$ in the ring $\mathcal{R}$, the signer defines $\boldsymbol{V}_i = (X_i, Y_i, T_0, T_1)^\top \in \mathbb{G}^4$ and, by extending the technique of [24], generates a NIZK proof that one of the vectors $\{\boldsymbol{V}_i\}_{i=0}^{N-1}$ is in the column span of $\mathbf{M}_H$. To prove this without revealing which $\boldsymbol{V}_\ell \in \mathbb{G}^4$ is used, the commitments $\{C_{d_{j-1}}\}_{j=1}^n$ are re-randomized by multiplying them with a random vector in the column space of $\mathbf{M}_H$.

Par-Gen(1^λ): Given a security parameter λ, choose a cyclic group $\mathbb{G}$ of prime order q with generators $g, h, \tilde{g}, \tilde{h} \xleftarrow{R} \mathbb{G}$ and $U, V \xleftarrow{R} \mathbb{G}$. Choose hash functions $\mathcal{H}_{\mathsf{FS}} : \{0,1\}^* \to \mathbb{Z}_q$ and $\mathcal{H} : \{0,1\}^* \to \mathbb{G}^2$ which will be modeled as random oracles. Output the common public parameters $\mathsf{pp} = \big(\lambda, \mathbb{G}, g, h, \tilde{g}, \tilde{h}, U, V\big)$.

Keygen(pp): Given pp, choose a secret key is $SK = (\alpha, \beta) \xleftarrow{R} \mathbb{Z}_q^2$ and compute the public key $PK = \boldsymbol{X} = (X, Y) = (g^\alpha \cdot h^\beta, \tilde{g}^\alpha \cdot \tilde{h}^\beta)$.

Sign$(\mathsf{pp}, SK, \mathcal{R}, M)$: To sign $M \in \{0,1\}^*$ on behalf of $\mathcal{R} = \{\boldsymbol{X}_0, \ldots, \boldsymbol{X}_{N-1}\}$ such that $\boldsymbol{X}_i = (X_i, Y_i) \in \mathbb{G}^2$ for each $i \in [N]$, the signer uses $SK = (\alpha, \beta)$ and $PK = \boldsymbol{X} = (X, Y) = (g^\alpha \cdot h^\beta, \tilde{g}^\alpha \cdot \tilde{h}^\beta) \in \mathcal{R}$ as follows. We assume that $N = 2^n$ for some n. Let $\ell \in \{0, \ldots, N-1\}$ the index of $PK = \boldsymbol{X}$ in $\mathcal{R}$ when $\mathcal{R}$ is arranged in lexicographical order and write it as $\ell = \ell_1 \ldots \ell_n \in \{0,1\}^n$.

1. Choose $\theta_1, \theta_2 \xleftarrow{R} \mathbb{Z}_q$. For all $j \in [n]$, choose $a_j, r_j, s_j, t_j, u_j, v_j, w_j, \rho_{j-1} \xleftarrow{R} \mathbb{Z}_q$ and compute $(T_0, T_1) = (g^{\theta_1} \cdot h^{\theta_2}, U^\alpha \cdot V^\beta \cdot H_1^{\theta_1} \cdot H_2^{\theta_2})$, as well as

$$
\begin{aligned}
\boldsymbol{C}_{\ell_j} &= (C_{\ell_j,0}, C_{\ell_j,1}) = \big(g^{r_j} \cdot h^{s_j},\ g^{\ell_j} \cdot H_1^{r_j} \cdot H_2^{s_j}\big) \\
\boldsymbol{C}_{a_j} &= (C_{a_j,0}, C_{a_j,1}) = \big(g^{t_j} \cdot h^{u_j},\ g^{a_j} \cdot H_1^{t_j} \cdot H_2^{u_j}\big) \qquad (2) \\
\boldsymbol{C}_{b_j} &= (C_{b_j,0}, C_{b_j,1}) = \big(g^{v_j} \cdot h^{w_j},\ g^{\ell_j \cdot a_j} \cdot H_1^{v_j} \cdot H_2^{w_j}\big),
\end{aligned}
$$

where $(H_1, H_2) = \mathcal{H}(M, \mathcal{R}, T_0, \{C_{\ell_j,0}, C_{a_j,0}, C_{b_j,0}\}_{j=1}^n) \in \mathbb{G}^2$. Define

$$\mathbf{M}_H = \begin{bmatrix} g & h & 1 & 1 \\ \tilde{g} & \tilde{h} & 1 & 1 \\ 1 & 1 & g & h \\ U & V & H_1 & H_2 \end{bmatrix} \in \mathbb{G}^{4 \times 4} \tag{3}$$

and its corresponding discrete logarithms $\mathbf{L}_h = \log_g(\mathbf{M}_H)$ matrix

$$\mathbf{L}_h = \begin{bmatrix} 1 & \log_g(h) & 0 & 0 \\ \log_g(\tilde{g}) & \log_g(\tilde{h}) & 0 & 0 \\ 0 & 0 & 1 & \log_g(h) \\ \log_g(U) & \log_g(V) & \log_g(H_1) & \log_g(H_2) \end{bmatrix} \in \mathbb{Z}_q^{4 \times 4}. \tag{4}$$

Note that the signer's witnesses $(\alpha, \beta, \theta_1, \theta_2) \in \mathbb{Z}_q^4$ satisfy

$$\log_g \left[X \mid Y \mid T_0 \mid T_1 \right]^\top = \mathbf{L}_h \cdot \left[\alpha \mid \beta \mid \theta_1 \mid \theta_2 \right]^\top. \tag{5}$$

In the following, we will sometimes re-write relation (5) as

$$\begin{bmatrix} X \\ Y \\ T_0 \\ T_1 \end{bmatrix} = \begin{bmatrix} g & h & 1 & 1 \\ \tilde{g} & \tilde{h} & 1 & 1 \\ 1 & 1 & g & h \\ U & V & H_1 & H_2 \end{bmatrix} \odot \begin{bmatrix} \alpha \\ \beta \\ \theta_1 \\ \theta_2 \end{bmatrix}. \tag{6}$$

For each $i \in [N]$, define the vector $\mathbf{V}_i = (X_i, Y_i, T_0, T_1)^\top \in \mathbb{G}^4$. The next step is to prove knowledge of witnesses $(\alpha_\ell, \beta_\ell, \theta_1, \theta_2) \in \mathbb{Z}_q^4$ such that $\mathbf{V}_\ell = (X_\ell, Y_\ell, T_0, T_1)^\top = g^{\mathbf{L}_h \cdot (\alpha_\ell, \beta_\ell, \theta_1, \theta_2)^\top}$, for some $\ell \in [N]$.

2. For each $j \in [n]$, pick $\rho_{j-1,\alpha}, \rho_{j-1,\beta}, \rho_{j-1,\theta_1}, \rho_{j-1,\theta_2} \xleftarrow{R} \mathbb{Z}_q$ and compute

$$\mathbf{C}_{d_{j-1}} = \prod_{i=0}^{N-1} \mathbf{V}_i^{p_{i,j-1}} \cdot g^{\mathbf{L}_h \cdot (\rho_{j-1,\alpha}, \rho_{j-1,\beta}, \rho_{j-1,\theta_1}, \rho_{j-1,\theta_2})^\top} \in \mathbb{G}^4, \tag{7}$$

where, for each $i \in \{0, \ldots, N-1\}$, $p_{i,0}, \ldots, p_{i,n-1}$ are the coefficients of

$$P_i[Z] = \prod_{j=1}^n F_{j,i_j}[Z] = \delta_{i,\ell} \cdot Z^n + \sum_{k=0}^{n-1} p_{i,k} \cdot Z^k \in \mathbb{Z}_q[Z], \tag{8}$$

where $F_{j,1}[Z] = \ell_j \cdot Z + a_j$ and $F_{j,0}[Z] = Z - F_{j,1}[Z]$ for all $j \in [n]$. Note that the coefficient of Z^n in (8) is non-zero if and only if $i = \ell$.

3. Compute $x = \mathcal{H}_{\mathsf{FS}}(M, \mathcal{R}, T_0, T_1, \{C_{\ell_j}, C_{a_j}, C_{b_j}, C_{d_{j-1}}\}_{j=1}^n) \in \mathbb{Z}_q$.

4. For each $j \in [n]$, compute (modulo q) $f_j = \ell_j \cdot x + a_j = F_{j,1}(x)$ and

$$\begin{aligned} z_{r_j} &= r_j \cdot x + t_j, & \bar{z}_{r_j} &= r_j \cdot (x - f_j) + v_j \\ z_{s_j} &= s_j \cdot x + u_j, & \bar{z}_{s_j} &= s_j \cdot (x - f_j) + w_j \end{aligned}$$

and

$$z_{d,\alpha} = \alpha \cdot x^n - \sum_{k=0}^{n-1} \rho_{k,\alpha} \cdot x^k, \qquad z_{d,\beta} = \beta \cdot x^n - \sum_{k=0}^{n-1} \rho_{k,\beta} \cdot x^k$$

$$z_{d,\theta_1} = \theta_1 \cdot x^n - \sum_{k=0}^{n-1} \rho_{k,\theta_1} \cdot x^k, \qquad z_{d,\theta_2} = \theta_2 \cdot x^n - \sum_{k=0}^{n-1} \rho_{k,\theta_2} \cdot x^k$$

Let $\Sigma_j = \left(C_{\ell_j}, C_{a_j}, C_{b_j}, C_{d_{j-1}}, f_j, z_{r_j}, z_{s_j}, \bar{z}_{r_j}, \bar{z}_{s_j} \right)$ for all $j \in [n]$ and output

$$\sigma = \left(\{\Sigma_j\}_{j=1}^n, T_0, T_1, z_{d,\alpha}, z_{d,\beta}, z_{d,\theta_1}, z_{d,\theta_2} \right). \tag{9}$$

Verify$(\mathsf{pp}, M, \mathcal{R}, \sigma)$: Given a ring $\mathcal{R} = \{X_0, \ldots, X_{N-1}\}$ and a pair (M, σ), parse σ as in (9) and define $f_{j,1} = f_j$ and $f_{j,0} = x - f_j$ for each $j \in [n]$.

1. Compute $(H_1, H_2) = \mathcal{H}(M, \mathcal{R}, T_0, \{C_{\ell_j,0}, C_{a_j,0}, C_{b_j,0}\}_{j=1}^n) \in \mathbb{G}^2$ and, for each public key $X_i = (X_i, Y_i) \in \mathbb{G}^2$ in $\mathcal{R}$, set $V_i = (X_i, Y_i, T_0, T_1)^\top \in \mathbb{G}^4$.
2. Let $x = \mathcal{H}_{\mathsf{FS}}(M, \mathcal{R}, T_0, T_1, \{C_{\ell_j}, C_{a_j}, C_{b_j}, C_{d_{j-1}}\}_{j=1}^n)$. If the equalities

$$C_{a_j} \cdot C_{\ell_j}^x = \left(g^{z_{r_j}} \cdot h^{z_{s_j}}, g^{f_j} \cdot H_1^{z_{r_j}} \cdot H_2^{z_{s_j}} \right), \tag{10}$$

$$C_{b_j} \cdot C_{\ell_j}^{x - f_j} = \left(g^{\bar{z}_{r_j}} \cdot h^{\bar{z}_{s_j}}, H_1^{\bar{z}_{r_j}} \cdot H_2^{\bar{z}_{s_j}} \right), \qquad \forall j \in [n]$$

are not satisfied, return 0. Then, return 1 if and only if

$$\prod_{i=0}^{N-1} V_i^{\prod_{j=1}^n f_{j,i_j}} \cdot \prod_{j=1}^n C_{d_{j-1}}^{-(x^{j-1})}$$

$$= \begin{bmatrix} g & h & 1 & 1 \\ \tilde{g} & \tilde{h} & 1 & 1 \\ 1 & 1 & g & h \\ U & V & H_1 & H_2 \end{bmatrix} \odot \begin{bmatrix} z_{d,\alpha} \\ z_{d,\beta} \\ z_{d,\theta_1} \\ z_{d,\theta_2} \end{bmatrix}. \tag{11}$$

Correctness is shown by observing from (8) that $\prod_{i=0}^{N-1} V_i^{\prod_{j=1}^n f_{j,i_j}}$ equals

$$\prod_{i=0}^{N-1} V_i^{P_i(x)} = \prod_{i=0}^{N-1} V_i^{\delta_{i,\ell} \cdot x^n + \sum_{k=0}^{n-1} p_{i,k} \cdot x^k} = V_\ell^{x^n} \cdot \prod_{i=0}^{N-1} V_i^{\sum_{k=0}^{n-1} p_{i,k} \cdot x^k}$$

$$= V_\ell^{x^n} \cdot \prod_{k=0}^{n-1} \left(\prod_{i=0}^{N-1} V_i^{p_{i,k}} \right)^{x^k} = V_\ell^{x^n} \cdot \prod_{k=0}^{n-1} \left(C_{d_k} \cdot g^{-\mathbf{L}_h \cdot (\rho_{k,\alpha}, \rho_{k,\beta}, \rho_{k,\theta_1}, \rho_{k,\theta_2})^\top} \right)^{x^k},$$

where the last equality follows from (7). Since $V_\ell = g^{\mathbf{L}_h \cdot (\alpha_\ell, \beta_\ell, \theta_1, \theta_2)^\top}$, we obtain

$$\prod_{i=0}^{N-1} V_i^{\prod_{j=1}^n f_{j,i_j}} \cdot \prod_{k=0}^{n-1} C_{d_k}^{-x^k} = V_\ell^{x^n} \cdot \prod_{k=0}^{n-1} g^{-\mathbf{L}_h \cdot (\rho_{k,\alpha}, \rho_{k,\beta}, \rho_{k,\theta_1}, \rho_{k,\theta_2})^\top (x^k)},$$

$$= g^{\mathbf{L}_h \cdot (z_{d,\alpha}, z_{d,\beta}, z_{d,\theta_1}, z_{d,\theta_2})^\top}.$$

3.2   Security Proofs

Statistical anonymity is achieved because $\{C_{d_{j-1}}\}_{j=1}^n$ are uniformly distributed. The reason is that the matrices (4) have full rank in the scheme (but not in the proof of unforgeability), so that computing $C_{d_{j-1}}$ as per (7) makes its distribution uniform over $\mathbb{G}^4$. The proof of Theorem 4 is given in the full version of the paper.

Theorem 4. *Any unbounded* **anonymity** *adversary $\mathcal{A}$ has advantage at most* $\mathbf{Adv}_{\mathcal{A}}^{\mathrm{anon}}(\lambda) \leq \frac{2}{q} + \frac{Q_{\mathcal{H}_{\mathsf{FS}}}}{q^2}$*, where $Q_{\mathcal{H}_{\mathsf{FS}}}$ is the number of hash queries to $\mathcal{H}_{\mathsf{FS}}$.*

Theorem 5. *The scheme is* **unforgeable** *under the DDH assumption in the random oracle model. For any adversary $\mathcal{A}$ with running time t and making Q_V queries to the key generation oracle, Q_S signing queries as well as $Q_{\mathcal{H}}$ and $Q_{\mathcal{H}_{\mathsf{FS}}}$ queries to the random oracles $\mathcal{H}$ and $\mathcal{H}_{\mathsf{FS}}$, respectively, there is a DDH distinguisher $\mathcal{B}$ with running time $t' \leq t + \mathsf{poly}(\lambda, Q_S, Q_V, Q_{\mathcal{H}})$ and such that*

$$\mathbf{Adv}_{\mathcal{A}}^{\mathrm{euf-cma}}(\lambda) \leq 2 \cdot \mathbf{Adv}_{\mathcal{B}}^{\mathrm{DDH}}(\lambda) + \frac{Q_S + Q_{\mathcal{H}_{\mathsf{FS}}} \cdot (1 + \log Q_V) + 5}{q} \qquad (12)$$
$$+ \frac{Q_S \cdot (Q_{\mathcal{H}_{\mathsf{FS}}} + 2Q_{\mathcal{H}} + 2Q_S)}{q^2}.$$

Proof. We use a sequence of games where, for each i, W_i stands for the event that the challenger outputs 1 in Game i.

Game 0: This is the real game. At each query $i \in [Q_V]$ to the key generation oracle $\mathsf{Keygen}(\cdot)$, the challenger $\mathcal{B}$ honestly chooses $\alpha_i, \beta_i \xleftarrow{R} \mathbb{Z}_q$ and returns the public key $PK_i = \boldsymbol{X}_i = (X_i, Y_i) = (g^{\alpha_i} \cdot h^{\beta_i}, \tilde{g}^{\alpha_i} \cdot \tilde{h}^{\beta_i})$ and retains $SK_i = (\alpha_i, \beta_i)$ for later use. If $\mathcal{A}$ subsequently submits $\boldsymbol{X}_i = (X_i, Y_i)$ to the corruption oracle, $\mathcal{B}$ reveals $SK_i = (\alpha_i, \beta_i)$. Moreover, all signing queries are answered by faithfully running the signing algorithm. At the end of the game, $\mathcal{A}$ outputs a forgery $(M^\star, \sigma^\star, \mathcal{R}^\star)$, where $\mathcal{R}^\star = \{\boldsymbol{X}_0^\star, \dots, \boldsymbol{X}_{N^\star-1}^\star\}$,

$$\sigma^\star = \left(\{\boldsymbol{\Sigma}_j^\star\}_{j=1}^n, T_0^\star, T_1^\star, z_{d,\alpha}^\star, z_{d,\beta}^\star, z_{d,\theta_1}^\star, z_{d,\theta_2}^\star\right), \qquad (13)$$

with $\boldsymbol{\Sigma}_j^\star = \left(C_{\ell_j}^\star, C_{a_j}^\star, C_{b_j}^\star, C_{d_{j-1}}^\star, f_j^\star, z_{r_j}^\star, z_{s_j}^\star, \bar{z}_{r_j}^\star, \bar{z}_{s_j}^\star\right)$. At this point, $\mathcal{B}$ outputs 1 if and only if $\mathcal{A}$ wins, meaning that: (i) $\sigma^\star$ correctly verifies; (ii) $\mathcal{R}^\star$ only contains uncorrupted public keys; (iii) No signing query involved a tuple of the form $(\cdot, M^\star, \mathcal{R}^\star)$. By definition, we have $\mathbf{Adv}_{\mathcal{A}}^{\mathrm{euf-cma}}(\lambda) = \Pr[W_0]$.

Game 1: This game is like Game 0 but we modify the signing oracle. Note that each signing query triggers a query to the random oracle $\mathcal{H}(.)$ since the challenger $\mathcal{B}$ has to faithfully compute T_0 and $\{C_{\ell_j,0}, C_{a_j,0}, C_{b_j,0}\}_{j=1}^n$ before obtaining $\mathcal{H}(M, \mathcal{R}, T_0, \{C_{\ell_j,0}, C_{a_j,0}, C_{b_j,0}\}_{j=1}^n)$. In Game 1, at each signing query, $\mathcal{B}$ aborts in the event that $\mathcal{H}(\cdot)$ was already defined for the input $(M, \mathcal{R}, T_0, \{C_{\ell_j,0}, C_{a_j,0}, C_{b_j,0}\}_{j=1}^n)$. Since such an input contains uniformly random elements, the probability to abort during the entire game is at most $Q_S \cdot (Q_S + Q_{\mathcal{H}})/q^2$ and we have $|\Pr[W_1] - \Pr[W_0]| \leq Q_S \cdot (Q_S + Q_{\mathcal{H}})/q^2$.

Game 2: We modify the random oracle $\mathcal{H}$ when it is directly invoked by $\mathcal{A}$ (i.e., $\mathcal{H}$-queries triggered by signing queries are treated as in Game 0). At each $\mathcal{H}$-query $\left(M, \mathcal{R}, T_0, \{C_{\ell_j,0}, C_{a_j,0}, C_{b_j,0}\}_{j=1}^n\right)$, the challenger $\mathcal{B}$ returns the previously defined value if it exists. Otherwise, it picks $\gamma \xleftarrow{R} \mathbb{Z}_q$ and defines the hash value as $(H_1, H_2) = \mathcal{H}\left(M, \mathcal{R}, T_0, \{C_{\ell_j,0}, C_{a_j,0}, C_{b_j,0}\}_{j=1}^n\right) = (g^\gamma, h^\gamma)$. Note that $\mathcal{H}(\cdot)$ is no longer a truly random oracle since (g, h, H_1, H_2) is a Diffie-Hellman tuple. Still, under the DDH assumption, this modification has no noticeable effect on $\mathcal{A}$'s winning probability. Lemma 1 describes a DDH distinguisher such that $|\Pr[W_2] - \Pr[W_1]| \leq \mathbf{Adv}_{\mathcal{B}}^{\mathrm{DDH}}(\lambda) + 1/q$.

Since (g, h, H_1, H_2) is a Diffie-Hellman tuple in Game 2, $\gamma \in \mathbb{Z}_q$ can be used as a decryption key for the DDH-based dual-mode encryption scheme. Another consequence of the last transition is that the matrix $\mathbf{L}_h$ of (3) has no longer full rank since its last row is linearly dependent with the first three rows.

Game 3: We introduce a failure event F_3 which causes the challenger $\mathcal{B}$ to output 0. When $\mathcal{A}$ outputs its forgery $\sigma^\star$, $\mathcal{B}$ parses $\sigma^\star$ as in (13) and computes $(H_1^\star, H_2^\star) = \mathcal{H}\left(M^\star, \mathcal{R}^\star, T_0^\star, \{C_{\ell_j,0}^\star, C_{a_j,0}^\star, C_{b_j,0}^\star\}_{j=1}^n\right)$. Event F_3 is defined to be the event that either: (1) The hash value $(H_1^\star, H_2^\star)$ was not defined at any time; (2) It was defined but collides with a pair $(H_1, H_2) = \mathcal{H}(M, \mathcal{R}, T_0, \{C_{\ell_j,0}, C_{a_j,0}, C_{b_j,0}\}_{j=1}^n)$ defined in response to a signing query $(\ell, M, \mathcal{R})$ for some index $\ell \in \{0, \ldots, |\mathcal{R}| - 1\}$, when $\mathcal{R}$ is arranged in lexicographic order. Note that the probability of case (1) cannot exceed $1/q$ because $\mathcal{H}(\cdot)$ is unpredictable as a random oracle. Moreover, since a winning adversary must forge a signature on some $(M^\star, \mathcal{R}^\star)$ that has never been queried for signature, the probability of case (2) is bounded by Q_S/q^2 multiplied by $Q_{\mathcal{H}}$ since we must consider the probability that a tuple (g, h, H_1, H_2) defined in a signing query is accidentally a Diffie-Hellman tuple and collides with the response of a hash query. We find $|\Pr[W_3] - \Pr[W_2]| \leq \Pr[F_3] \leq 1/q + Q_S \cdot Q_{\mathcal{H}}/q^2$.

Game 4: This game is identical to Game 3 with one modification. When the adversary $\mathcal{A}$ outputs its forgery $\sigma^\star$, $\mathcal{B}$ parses $\sigma^\star$ as in (13) and computes $(H_1^\star, H_2^\star) = \mathcal{H}\left(M^\star, \mathcal{R}^\star, T_0^\star, \{C_{\ell_j,0}^\star, C_{a_j,0}^\star, C_{b_j,0}^\star\}_{j=1}^n\right)$. Then, $\mathcal{B}$ recalls the previously defined exponent $\gamma^\star \in \mathbb{Z}_q$ such that $(H_1^\star, H_2^\star) = (g^{\gamma^\star}, h^{\gamma^\star})$ and uses it to decrypt the dual-mode ciphertexts $\{C_{\ell_j}^\star\}_{j=1}^n$. It aborts and outputs 0 if one of these ciphertexts turns out not to encrypt a bit $\ell_j^\star \in \{0,1\}$. Note that, if $\mathcal{B}$ does not abort, it decodes an n-bit string $\ell^\star = \ell_1^\star \ldots \ell_n^\star \in \{0,1\}^n$ from $\{C_{\ell_j}^\star\}_{j=1}^n$. We claim that we have $|\Pr[W_4] - \Pr[W_3]| \leq (1 + Q_{\mathcal{H}_{\mathsf{FS}}})/q$.

The only situation where Game 4 deviates from Game 3 is the event F_4 that either: (i) $\mathcal{A}$ did not query $\mathcal{H}_{\mathsf{FS}}(\cdot)$ on the input that the forgery relates to; (ii) $\mathcal{A}$ manages to break the soundness of the proof system showing that each of the ciphertexts $\{C_{\ell_j}^\star\}_{j=1}^n$ encrypts a bit. Lemma 2 shows that $\Pr[F_4] \leq (1 + Q_{\mathcal{H}_{\mathsf{FS}}})/q$.

Game 5: In this game, we modify the challenger's behavior when $\mathcal{A}$ outputs a forgery $\sigma^\star$. Having decoded the n-bit string $\ell^\star = \ell_1^\star \ldots \ell_n^\star \in \{0,1\}^n$ from the dual-mode ciphertexts $\{C_{\ell_j}^\star\}_{j=1}^n$, $\mathcal{B}$ also runs the decryption algorithm for

$(T_0^\star, T_1^\star)$ to compute $\Gamma^\star = T_1^\star/T_0^{\star\gamma^\star}$. At this point, $\mathcal{B}$ recalls the secret key $SK = (\alpha_{\ell^\star}, \beta_{\ell^\star})$ of the $\ell^\star$-th member of the ring $\mathcal{R}^\star = \{\boldsymbol{X}_0^\star, \ldots \boldsymbol{X}_{N^\star-1}^\star\}$ in lexicographical order. If $\Gamma^\star = U^{\alpha_{\ell^\star}} \cdot V^{\beta_{\ell^\star}}$, $\mathcal{B}$ outputs 1. Otherwise, it outputs 0. Lemma 3 shows that $|\Pr[W_5] - \Pr[W_4]| \leq Q_{\mathcal{H}_{\mathsf{FS}}} \cdot \log(Q_V)/q$.

Game 6: This game is identical to Game 5 except that we change the distribution of $\mathsf{pp} = (\lambda, \mathbb{G}, g, h, \tilde{g}, \tilde{h}, U, V)$. Here, instead of choosing $g, h, \tilde{g}, \tilde{h} \xleftarrow{R} \mathbb{G}$ uniformly, we set $(g, h, \tilde{g}, \tilde{h}) = (g, h, g^\rho, h^\rho)$ for a randomly chosen $\rho \xleftarrow{R} \mathbb{Z}_q$. Clearly, the two distributions of pp are indistinguishable under the DDH assumption and $\mathcal{B}$ can immediately be turned into an efficient DDH distinguisher (the proof is straightforward) such that $|\Pr[W_6] - \Pr[W_5]| \leq \mathbf{Adv}_{\mathcal{B}}^{\mathrm{DDH}}(\lambda)$.

Game 7: This game is like Game 6 except that we now simulate the proof of knowledge of secret keys in all outputs of the signing oracle. On a signing query $(M, \mathcal{R}, \ell)$, where $(0 \leq \ell \leq |\mathcal{R}| - 1)$, the challenger parses $\mathcal{R}$ as $\{\boldsymbol{X}_0, \ldots, \boldsymbol{X}_{N-1}\}$ and returns $\bot$ if $\boldsymbol{X}_\ell$ is not public keys produced by the Keygen(.) oracle. Otherwise, the challenger chooses $x \xleftarrow{R} \mathbb{Z}_q$ as well as $z_{d,\alpha}, z_{d,\beta}, z_{d,\theta_1}, z_{d,\theta_2} \xleftarrow{R} \mathbb{Z}_q$ and $f_j, z_{r_j}, z_{s_j}, \bar{z}_{r_j}, \bar{z}_{s_j} \xleftarrow{R} \mathbb{Z}_q$, for all $j \in [n]$. Then, it picks $T_0 \xleftarrow{R} \mathbb{G}$ as well as $r_j, s_j \xleftarrow{R} \mathbb{Z}_q$ for all $j \in [n]$, and honestly computes $C_{\ell_j, 0} = g^{r_j} \cdot h^{s_j}$ for all $j \in [n]$. It can now compute for all $j \in [n]$,

$$C_{a_j, 0} = g^{z_{r_j}} \cdot h^{z_{s_j}} \cdot C_{\ell_j, 0}^{-x}, \qquad C_{b_j, 0} = g^{\bar{z}_{r_j}} \cdot h^{\bar{z}_{s_j}} \cdot C_{\ell_j, 0}^{f_j - x},$$

and define $(H_1, H_2) = \mathcal{H}(M, \mathcal{R}, T_0, \{(C_{\ell_j, 0}, C_{a_j, 0}, C_{b_j, 0})\}_{j=1}^n)$. Then, it completes the computation of dual-mode commitments as follows. First, it chooses $T_1 \xleftarrow{R} \mathbb{G}$ and computes $C_{\ell_j, 1} = g^{\ell_j} \cdot H_1^{r_j} \cdot H_2^{s_j}$ for all $j \in [n]$. Then, it computes

$$C_{a_j, 1} = \left(g^{f_j} \cdot H_1^{z_{r_j}} \cdot H_2^{z_{s_j}}\right) \cdot C_{\ell_j, 1}^{-x}, \qquad C_{b_j, 1} = \left(H_1^{\bar{z}_{r_j}} \cdot H_2^{\bar{z}_{s_j}}\right) \cdot C_{\ell_j, 1}^{f_j - x},$$

for all $j \in [n]$. Then, for each $j \in \{2, \ldots, n\}$, the challenger faithfully computes $C_{d_{j-1}}$ as per (7) but, for index $j = 1$, it computes

$$C_{d_0} = \prod_{i=0}^{N-1} \boldsymbol{V}_i^{\prod_{j=1}^n f_{j, i_j}} \prod_{j=2}^n C_{d_{j-1}}^{-(x^{j-1})} \left(\mathbf{M}_{\mathcal{H}} \odot \left(-z_{d,\alpha}, -z_{d,\beta}, -z_{d,\theta_1}, -z_{d,\theta_2}\right)^\top\right),$$

where $\boldsymbol{V}_i = (X_i, Y_i, T_0, T_1)^\top$, $f_{j,1} = f_j$ and $f_{j,0} = x - f_j$ for each $j \in [n]$. Finally, the challenger $\mathcal{B}$ programs the random oracle $\mathcal{H}_{\mathsf{FS}}$ to have the equality $x = \mathcal{H}_{\mathsf{FS}}(M, \mathcal{R}, T_0, T_1, \{C_{\ell_j}, C_{a_j}, C_{b_j}, C_{d_{j-1}}\}_{j=1}^n)$. If $\mathcal{H}_{\mathsf{FS}}$ was already defined for this input, $\mathcal{B}$ aborts and outputs 0. If the simulation does not fail, the oracle sets $\boldsymbol{\Sigma}_j = \left(C_{\ell_j}, C_{a_j}, C_{b_j}, C_{d_{j-1}}, f_j, z_{r_j}, z_{s_j}, \bar{z}_{r_j}, \bar{z}_{s_j}\right)$ for all $j \in [n]$ and outputs the signature $\sigma = \left(\{\boldsymbol{\Sigma}_j\}_{j=1}^n, T_0, T_1, z_{d,\alpha}, z_{d,\beta}, z_{d,\theta_1}, z_{d,\theta_2}\right)$, which is distributed exactly as in Game 6 unless (g, h, H_1, H_2) happens to form a Diffie-Hellman tuple. Indeed, although the adversary's signing queries may involve rings $\mathcal{R}$ that contain maliciously generated keys of the form $\boldsymbol{X}_i = (X_i, Y_i) = (X_i, \Omega_i \cdot X_i^{\log_g(\tilde{g})})$, with $\Omega_i \neq 1_{\mathbb{G}}$, this does not prevent the simulated commitments $\{C_{d_{j-1}}\}_{j=1}^{n}$ from having the same distribution as in Game 6. In simulated signatures, we indeed have

$$C_{d_{j-1}} = \prod_{i=0}^{N-1} V_i^{p_{i,j-1}} \cdot g^{\mathbf{L}_h \cdot \rho_j} \qquad \forall j \in \{2, \ldots, n-1\}$$

for random $\rho_2, \ldots, \rho_{n-1} \in_R \mathbb{Z}_q^4$, where $p_{i,0}, \ldots, p_{i,n-1}$ are the coefficients of $\prod_{j=1}^{n} f_{j,i_j} = \delta_{i,\ell} x^n + \sum_{j=1}^{n} p_{i,j-1} x^{j-1}$. Since $\mathbf{V}_\ell = g^{\mathbf{L}_h \cdot (\alpha_\ell, \beta_\ell, \theta_1, \theta_2)^\top}$ and defining $\rho_1 = -(z_{d,\alpha}, z_{d,\beta}, z_{d,\theta_1}, z_{d,\theta_1})^\top - \sum_{j=2}^{n} \rho_j x^{j-1} + (\alpha_\ell, \beta_\ell, \theta_1, \theta_2) \cdot x^n$, we have

$$C_{d_0} = \mathbf{V}_\ell^{x^n} \cdot \prod_{i=0}^{N-1} \mathbf{V}_i^{\sum_{j=1}^{n} p_{i,j-1} x^{j-1}} \cdot \prod_{i=0}^{N-1} \mathbf{V}_i^{-\sum_{j=2}^{n} p_{i,j-1} x^{j-1}}$$

$$\cdot g^{-\mathbf{L}_h \cdot (z_{d,\alpha}, z_{d,\beta}, z_{d,\theta_1}, z_{d,\theta_1})^\top - \mathbf{L}_h \cdot \sum_{j=2}^{n} \rho_j x^{j-1}} = \prod_{i=0}^{N-1} \mathbf{V}_i^{p_{i,0}} \cdot g^{\mathbf{L}_h \cdot \rho_1}$$

Note that the Fiat-Shamir proof does not hide which index $\ell \in \{0,1\}^n$ the signing oracle uses (and it does not have to since $\mathcal{A}$ knows ℓ): indeed, for any signing query, the matrix $\mathbf{L}_h$ has only rank 3 and $\mathbf{X}_\ell$ may be the only key of the ring $\mathcal{R}$ to be in the column span of $\mathbf{M}_H$. However, the same holds in Game 6. As long as the simulation does not fail because of a collision on $\mathcal{H}_{\mathsf{FS}}$ or because (H_1, H_2) accidentally lands in the span of (g, h) at some signing query, the simulated proof is perfectly indistinguishable from a real proof that would be generated as in Game 6. Taking into account the probability that the signing oracle fails at some query, we obtain the inequality $|\Pr[W_7] - \Pr[W_6]| \leq Q_S/q + Q_S \cdot (Q_{\mathcal{H}_{\mathsf{FS}}} + Q_S)/q^2$.

In Game 7, we claim that $\Pr[W_7] = 2/q$. To prove this claim, we recall that $\mathcal{B}$ only outputs 1 if $(T_0^\star, T_1^\star)$ decrypts to $\Gamma^\star = U^{\alpha_{\ell^\star}} \cdot V^{\beta_{\ell^\star}}$. We next argue that, except with probability $1/q$, $\Gamma^\star$ is independent of $\mathcal{A}$'s view in Game 7.

Indeed, since $(g, h, \tilde{g}, \tilde{h})$ is a Diffie-Hellman tuple, the only information that $\mathbf{X}_{\ell^\star} = (X_{\ell^\star}, Y_{\ell^\star}) = (g^{\alpha_{\ell^\star}} \cdot h^{\beta_{\ell^\star}}, \tilde{g}^{\alpha_{\ell^\star}} \cdot \tilde{h}^{\beta_{\ell^\star}})$ reveals about $(\alpha_{\ell^\star}, \beta_{\ell^\star}) \in \mathbb{Z}_q^2$ is $\log_g(X_{\ell^\star}) = \alpha_{\ell^\star} + \log_g(h) \cdot \beta_{\ell^\star}$ since $\log_g(Y_{\ell^\star})$ only provides redundant information. Also, in all outputs of the signing oracle, the pair $(T_0, T_1) \xleftarrow{R} \mathbb{G}^2$ is chosen independently of $U^{\alpha_{\ell^\star}} \cdot V^{\alpha_{\ell^\star}}$. Finally, in Game 7, all signing queries are answered by simulating a NIZK proof without using the witnesses $SK_{\ell^\star} = (\alpha_{\ell^\star}, \beta_{\ell^\star}) \in \mathbb{Z}_q^2$ at any time. This ensures that no information is leaked about $(\alpha_{\ell^\star}, \beta_{\ell^\star})$ whatsoever.

Taking into account the event that (U, V) accidentally falls in the span of (g, h), we find that $\Gamma^\star$ remains independent of $\mathcal{A}$'s view until the forgery stage. In this case, $(T_0^\star, T_1^\star)$ only decrypts to $U^{\alpha_{\ell^\star}} \cdot V^{\beta_{\ell^\star}}$ with probability $1/q$, which implies $\Pr[W_7] = 2/q$. When counting probabilities, we obtain the bound (12). $\square$

Lemma 1. *There exists an efficient DDH distinguisher $\mathcal{B}$ that bridges between Game 1 and Game 2 and such that $|\Pr[W_2] - \Pr[W_1]| \leq \mathbf{Adv}_{\mathcal{B}}^{\mathrm{DDH}}(\lambda) + 1/q$.*

Proof. We consider a DDH instance (g, g^a, g^b, g^{ab+c}) for which $\mathcal{B}$ has to decide if $c = 0$ or $c \in_R \mathbb{Z}_q$. To do this, $\mathcal{B}$ initially defines $h = g^b$ and emulates the random oracle $\mathcal{H}(\cdot)$ at each (direct) query by randomly choosing $\delta_1, \delta_2 \xleftarrow{R} \mathbb{Z}_q$ and setting $(H_1, H_2) = ((g^a)^{\delta_1} \cdot g^{\delta_2}, (g^{ab+c})^{\delta_1} \cdot (g^b)^{\delta_2}) = (g^{a\delta_1 + \delta_2}, g^{(a\delta_1 + \delta_2)b + c\delta_1})$. If $c = 0$, (H_1, H_2) is distributed as in Game 2 for $\gamma = a\delta_1 + \delta_2$. If $c \in_R \mathbb{Z}_q$, we have $c \neq 0$ with probability $1 - 1/q$, so that (H_1, H_2) are uniform over $\mathbb{G}^2$ and independently distributed across distinct queries, exactly as in Game 1. When $\mathcal{A}$ halts, $\mathcal{B}$ outputs 1 if $\mathcal{A}$ creates a valid forgery and 0 otherwise.   □

Lemma 2. *From Game 3 to Game 4, the adversary's winning probabilities differ by at most* $|\Pr[W_4] - \Pr[W_3]| \leq (1 + Q_{\mathcal{H}_{FS}})/q$.

Proof. We bound the probability $\Pr[F_4]$. Recall that F_4 occurs if $\mathcal{A}$ breaks the soundness of the proof that a dual-mode ciphertext encrypts a bit. This implies that $\sigma^\star = (\{\Sigma_j^\star\}_{j=1}^n, T_0^\star, T_1^\star, z_{d,\alpha}^\star, z_{d,\beta}^\star, z_{d,\theta_1}^\star, z_{d,\theta_2}^\star)$ verifies and there exists $k \in [n]$ such that $\Sigma_k^\star = (C_{\ell_k}^\star, C_{a_k}^\star, C_{b_k}^\star, C_{d_{k-1}^\star}, f_k^\star, z_{r_k}^\star, z_{s_k}^\star, \bar{z}_{r_k}^\star, \bar{z}_{s_k}^\star)$ contains a ciphertext $C_{\ell_k}^\star$ that decrypts to $\ell_k \notin \{0, 1\}$. For this index k, $\sigma^\star$ contains a NIZK proof

$$((C_{a_k}^\star, C_{b_k}^\star), x, (f_k^\star, z_{r_k}^\star, z_{s_k}^\star, \bar{z}_{r_k}^\star, \bar{z}_{s_k}^\star)) \tag{14}$$

that $C_{\ell_k}^\star$ encrypts $\ell_k^\star \in \{0, 1\}$. This proof, which is obtained from the Σ-protocol of [24, Fig. 1], is known [24, Theorem 2] to provide special soundness with soundness error $1/q$. Hence, if the statement is false and $C_{\ell_k}^\star$ does not encrypt a bit, for any given pair $(C_{a_k}^\star, C_{b_k}^\star)$, only one challenge value $x \in \mathbb{Z}_q$ admits a response $(f_k^\star, z_{r_k}^\star, z_{s_k}^\star, \bar{z}_{r_k}^\star, \bar{z}_{s_k}^\star)$ that makes (14) into an accepting transcript.

At each query $\mathcal{H}_{FS}(M, \mathcal{R}, T_0, T_1, \{C_{\ell_j}, C_{a_j}, C_{b_j}, C_{d_{j-1}}\}_{j=1}^n)$ such that one of the $\{C_{\ell_j}\}_{j=1}$ does not encrypt a binary value, the probability that oracle $\mathcal{H}_{FS}(\cdot)$ returns the unique "bad" $x \in \mathbb{Z}_q$ for which a correct response exists is exactly $1/q$. Finally, since $\mathcal{H}_{FS}$ is simulated by the challenger $\mathcal{B}$, we may assume that $\mathcal{B}$ makes the query $\mathcal{H}_{FS}(M^\star, \mathcal{R}^\star, T_0^\star, T_1^\star, \{C_{\ell_j}^\star, C_{a_j}^\star, C_{b_j}^\star, C_{d_{j-1}}^\star\}_{j=1}^n)$ for itself in case it was not explicitly made by the time $\mathcal{A}$ terminates. Taking a union bound over all $\mathcal{H}_{FS}$-queries, we obtain $|\Pr[W_4] - \Pr[W_3]| \leq \Pr[F_4] \leq (1 + Q_{\mathcal{H}_{FS}})/q$.   □

Lemma 3. *From Game 4 to Game 5, the adversary's winning probabilities differ by at most* $|\Pr[W_5] - \Pr[W_4]| \leq Q_{\mathcal{H}_{FS}} \cdot \log(Q_V)/q$. *(The proof is Appendix B.1.)*

Acknowledgements. This work was funded in part by the French ANR ALAMBIC project (ANR-16-CE39-0006).

A   Reminders on Commitment Schemes

A non-interactive commitment scheme allows a sender to commit to a message m by sending a commitment string to the receiver. Later on the sender can convince the receiver that the committed value was really m. A commitment scheme must satisfy two security properties called *hiding* and *binding*. The former captures that the commitment hides any partial information about the message.

The latter requires that the sender be unable to open the commitment to two distinct messages. Formally, a non-interactive commitment scheme is a pair of PPT algorithms (Setup, Com). The setup algorithm $ck \leftarrow$ Setup(1^λ) generates a commitment key ck, which specifies a message space $\mathcal{M}_{ck}$, a randomness space $\mathcal{R}_{ck}$ and a commitment space $\mathcal{C}_{ck}$. The commitment algorithm Com defines a function $\text{Com}_{ck} : \mathcal{M}_{ck} \times \mathcal{R}_{ck} \rightarrow \mathcal{C}_{ck}$. On input of $m \in \mathcal{M}_{ck}$, the sender randomly chooses $r \xleftarrow{R} \mathcal{R}_{ck}$ and computes a commitment string $c = \text{Com}_{ck}(m, r) \in \mathcal{C}_{ck}$.

A commitment is *perfectly hiding* if, for any $m \in \mathcal{M}_{ck}$, the distribution $\{\text{Com}_{ck}(m, r) \mid r \xleftarrow{R} \mathcal{R}_{ck}\}$ is statistically independent of m. It is perfectly binding if any element of the commitment space $\mathcal{C}_{ck}$ uniquely determines the message. Groth and Kohlweiss [24] use the following additional properties.

Definition 6. *A commitment scheme* (Setup, Com) *is* **strongly binding** *if, for any PPT adversary* $\mathcal{A}$, *there exists a negligible function* $\varepsilon(\lambda)$ *such that*

$$| \Pr[ck \leftarrow \text{Setup}(1^\lambda); (c, m_1, r_1, m_2, r_2) \leftarrow \mathcal{A}(PK) :$$
$$\text{Com}_{ck}(m_1; r_1) = c \ \wedge \ \text{Com}_{ck}(m_2; r_2) = c \ \wedge \ (m_1, r_1) \neq (m_2, r_2)]| < \varepsilon(\lambda).$$

We consider a prime $q > 2^\lambda$ specified in the commitment key ck. The message space and the randomness space are both $\mathcal{M}_{ck} = \mathcal{R}_{ck} = \mathbb{Z}_q$.

Definition 7. *A commitment scheme* (Setup, Com) *is* **additively homomorphic** *if for all messages* $m_1, m_2 \in \mathcal{M}_{ck}$ *and all random coins* $r_1, r_2 \in \mathcal{R}_{ck}$, *we have* $\text{Com}_{ck}(m_1; r_1) \cdot \text{Com}_{ck}(m_2; r_2) = \text{Com}_{ck}(m_1 + m_2; r_1 + r_2)$.

B   Deferred Proofs for the Fully Tight Construction

B.1   Proof of Lemma 3

Proof. The only situation where Game 5 differs from Game 4 is the event F_5 that extracting $\{C^\star_{\ell_j}\}^n_{j=1}$ leads to a string $\ell^\star \in \{0,1\}^n$ but $(T^\star_0, T^\star_1)$ does not decrypt to an encoding $U^{\alpha_{\ell^\star}} \cdot V^{\beta_{\ell^\star}}$ of the $\ell^\star$-th ring member's secret key. This implies that $V_{\ell^\star} = (X_{\ell^\star}, Y_{\ell^\star}, T^\star_0, T^\star_1)$ is not in the column space of $\mathbf{M}_H$ (as defined in (3)) and we show that this event can only happen with probability $Q_{\mathcal{H}_{FS}} \cdot n/q \le Q_{\mathcal{H}_{FS}} \cdot \log(Q_V)/q$, where $n = \log N^\star$.

Note that (10) implies that $f^\star_j$ equals $f^\star_j = a^\star_j + \ell^\star_j \cdot x^\star$ for all $j \in [n]$, where $a^\star_j \in \mathbb{Z}_q$ is encrypted by $C^\star_{a_j}$. Defining $f^\star_{j,1} = f^\star_j$ and $f^\star_{j,0} = x - f^\star_j$, we know that

$$\prod_{j=1}^n f^\star_{j,i_j} = \delta_{i,\ell^\star} \cdot x^{\star n} + \sum_{k=0}^{n-1} p_{i,k} \cdot x^{\star k} \qquad \forall i \in \lfloor N^\star \rfloor,$$

for some $p^\star_{i,0}, \ldots, p^\star_{i,n-1} \in \mathbb{Z}_q$. This implies

$$\prod_{i=0}^{N-1} V_i^{\prod_{j=1}^n f^\star_{j,i_j}} = \prod_{i=0}^{N-1} V_i^{\delta_{i,\ell^\star} \cdot x^n + \sum_{k=0}^{n-1} p^\star_{i,k} \cdot x^k}$$

$$= V_{\ell^\star}^{x^n} \cdot \prod_{i=0}^{N-1} V_i^{\sum_{k=0}^{n-1} p^\star_{i,k} \cdot x^k} = V_{\ell^\star}^{x^n} \cdot \prod_{k=0}^{n-1} \Big(\prod_{i=0}^{N-1} V_i^{p^\star_{i,k}}\Big)^{x^k}.$$

Moreover, the last verification Eq. (11) implies

$$V_{\ell*}^{x^n} \cdot \prod_{k=0}^{n-1} \cdot \left(\prod_{i=0}^{N-1} V_i^{p_{i,k}^*} \right)^{x^k} \cdot \prod_{k=0}^{n-1} C_{d_k}^{-(x^k)} = g^{\mathbf{L}_h \cdot (z_{d,\alpha}^*, z_{d,\beta}^*, z_{d,\theta_1}^*, z_{d,\theta_2}^*)^\top}. \tag{15}$$

By taking the discrete logarithms $\log_g(\cdot)$ of both members of (15), we get

$$x^n \cdot \mathbf{v}_{\ell*} + \sum_{i=0}^{N-1}\sum_{k=0}^{n-1}(p_{i,k}^* \, x^k) \cdot \mathbf{v}_i - \sum_{k=0}^{n-1} x^k \cdot \mathbf{c}_{d_k} = \mathbf{L}_h \cdot (z_{d,\alpha}^*, z_{d,\beta}^*, z_{d,\theta_1}^*, z_{d,\theta_2}^*)^\top. \tag{16}$$

Since $\mathbf{L}_h$ has rank at most 3 due to the modification introduced in Game 2 and Game 3, assuming that $\mathbf{v}_{\ell*} = \log_g(\mathbf{V}_{\ell*}) \in \mathbb{Z}_q^4$ is not in the column space of $\mathbf{L}_h$, there exists a non-zero vector $\mathbf{t} \in \mathbb{Z}_q^4$ such that $\mathbf{t}^\top \cdot \mathbf{L}_h = \mathbf{0}^{1\times4}$ and $\mathbf{t}^\top \cdot \mathbf{v}_{\ell*} \neq 0$. If we multiply both members of (16) on the left by $\mathbf{t}^\top$, we obtain

$$x^n \cdot (\mathbf{t}^\top \cdot \mathbf{v}_{\ell*}) + \sum_{i=0}^{N-1}\sum_{k=0}^{n-1}(p_{i,k}^* \cdot x^k) \cdot (\mathbf{t}^\top \cdot \mathbf{v}_i) - \sum_{k=0}^{n-1} x^k \cdot (\mathbf{t}^\top \cdot \mathbf{c}_{d_k}) = 0. \tag{17}$$

If $\mathbf{t}^\top \cdot \mathbf{v}_{\ell*} \neq 0$, equality (17) implies that x is a root of a non-zero polynomial of degree n. However, x is uniformly distributed over $\mathbb{Z}_q$ and the Schwartz-Zippel Lemma implies that (17) can only hold with probability $n/q < \log(Q_V)/q$.

In order to bound the probability $\Pr[F_5]$, we have to consider all hash queries $H_{FS}(M, \mathcal{R}, T_0, T_1, \{\mathbf{C}_{\ell_j}, \mathbf{C}_{a_j}, \mathbf{C}_{b_j}, \mathbf{C}_{d_{j-1}}\}_{j=1}^n)$ for which $\mathcal{R}$ only contains honestly generated keys and (T_0, T_1) does not decrypt to an encoding $U^{\alpha_\ell} \cdot V^{\beta_\ell}$ of the ℓ-th key of $\mathcal{R}$, where $\ell \in \{0, \ldots, |\mathcal{R}| - 1\}$ is determined by $\{\mathbf{C}_{\ell_j}\}_{j=1}^n$. Taking a union bound over all hash queries, we obtain $\Pr[F_5] \leq Q_{\mathcal{H}_{FS}} \cdot \log(Q_V)/q$. □

References

1. Abe, M., Ohkubo, M., Suzuki, K.: 1-out-of-n signatures from a variety of keys. In: Zheng, Y. (ed.) ASIACRYPT 2002. LNCS, vol. 2501, pp. 415–432. Springer, Heidelberg (2002). https://doi.org/10.1007/3-540-36178-2_26
2. Abdalla, M., Fouque, P.-A., Lyubashevsky, V., Tibouchi, M.: Tightly-secure signatures from lossy identification schemes. In: Pointcheval, D., Johansson, T. (eds.) EUROCRYPT 2012. LNCS, vol. 7237, pp. 572–590. Springer, Heidelberg (2012). https://doi.org/10.1007/978-3-642-29011-4_34
3. Bellare, M., Hofheinz, D., Yilek, S.: Possibility and impossibility results for encryption and commitment secure under selective opening. In: Joux, A. (ed.) EUROCRYPT 2009. LNCS, vol. 5479, pp. 1–35. Springer, Heidelberg (2009). https://doi.org/10.1007/978-3-642-01001-9_1
4. Bellare, M., Rogaway, P.: Random oracles are practical: a paradigm for designing efficient protocols. In: ACM CCS (1993)
5. Bellare, M., Rogaway, P.: The exact security of digital signatures-how to sign with RSA and Rabin. In: Maurer, U. (ed.) EUROCRYPT 1996. LNCS, vol. 1070, pp. 399–416. Springer, Heidelberg (1996). https://doi.org/10.1007/3-540-68339-9_34

6. Benaloh, J., de Mare, M.: One-way accumulators: a decentralized alternative to digital signatures. In: Helleseth, T. (ed.) EUROCRYPT 1993. LNCS, vol. 765, pp. 274–285. Springer, Heidelberg (1994). https://doi.org/10.1007/3-540-48285-7_24

7. Bender, A., Katz, J., Morselli, R.: Ring signatures: stronger definitions, and constructions without random oracles. In: Halevi, S., Rabin, T. (eds.) TCC 2006. LNCS, vol. 3876, pp. 60–79. Springer, Heidelberg (2006). https://doi.org/10.1007/11681878_4

8. Bootle, J., Cerulli, A., Chaidos, P., Ghadafi, E., Groth, J., Petit, C.: Short accountable ring signatures based on DDH. In: Pernul, G., Ryan, P.Y.A., Weippl, E. (eds.) ESORICS 2015. LNCS, vol. 9326, pp. 243–265. Springer, Cham (2015). https://doi.org/10.1007/978-3-319-24174-6_13

9. Boyen, X.: Mesh signatures. In: Naor, M. (ed.) EUROCRYPT 2007. LNCS, vol. 4515, pp. 210–227. Springer, Heidelberg (2007). https://doi.org/10.1007/978-3-540-72540-4_12

10. Brakerski, Z., Tauman-Kalai, Y.: A framework for efficient signatures, ring signatures and identity based encryption in the standard model. Cryptology ePrint Archive: Report 2010/086 (2010)

11. Bresson, E., Stern, J., Szydlo, M.: Threshold ring signatures and applications to ad-hoc groups. In: Yung, M. (ed.) CRYPTO 2002. LNCS, vol. 2442, pp. 465–480. Springer, Heidelberg (2002). https://doi.org/10.1007/3-540-45708-9_30

12. Buldas, A., Laud, P., Lipmaa, H.: Accountable certificate management using undeniable attestations. In: ACM-CCS (2000)

13. Camacho, P., Hevia, A., Kiwi, M., Opazo, R.: Strong accumulators from collision-resistant hashing. In: Wu, T.-C., Lei, C.-L., Rijmen, V., Lee, D.-T. (eds.) ISC 2008. LNCS, vol. 5222, pp. 471–486. Springer, Heidelberg (2008). https://doi.org/10.1007/978-3-540-85886-7_32

14. Chandran, N., Groth, J., Sahai, A.: Ring signatures of sub-linear size without random oracles. In: Arge, L., Cachin, C., Jurdziński, T., Tarlecki, A. (eds.) ICALP 2007. LNCS, vol. 4596, pp. 423–434. Springer, Heidelberg (2007). https://doi.org/10.1007/978-3-540-73420-8_38

15. Chase, M., Lysyanskaya, A.: On signatures of knowledge. In: Dwork, C. (ed.) CRYPTO 2006. LNCS, vol. 4117, pp. 78–96. Springer, Heidelberg (2006). https://doi.org/10.1007/11818175_5

16. Chaum, D., van Heyst, E.: Group signatures. In: Davies, D.W. (ed.) EUROCRYPT 1991. LNCS, vol. 547, pp. 257–265. Springer, Heidelberg (1991). https://doi.org/10.1007/3-540-46416-6_22

17. Coron, J.-S.: On the exact security of full domain hash. In: Bellare, M. (ed.) CRYPTO 2000. LNCS, vol. 1880, pp. 229–235. Springer, Heidelberg (2000). https://doi.org/10.1007/3-540-44598-6_14

18. Cramer, R.: Modular design of secure, yet practical cryptographic protocols. Ph.D. thesis, University of Amsterdam (1996)

19. Cramer, R., Damgård, I., Schoenmakers, B.: Proofs of partial knowledge and simplified design of witness hiding protocols. In: Desmedt, Y.G. (ed.) CRYPTO 1994. LNCS, vol. 839, pp. 174–187. Springer, Heidelberg (1994). https://doi.org/10.1007/3-540-48658-5_19

20. Dodis, Y., Kiayias, A., Nicolosi, A., Shoup, V.: Anonymous identification in *Ad Hoc* groups. In: Cachin, C., Camenisch, J.L. (eds.) EUROCRYPT 2004. LNCS, vol. 3027, pp. 609–626. Springer, Heidelberg (2004). https://doi.org/10.1007/978-3-540-24676-3_36

21. Fiat, A., Shamir, A.: How to prove yourself: practical solutions to identification and signature problems. In: Odlyzko, A.M. (ed.) CRYPTO 1986. LNCS, vol. 263, pp. 186–194. Springer, Heidelberg (1987). https://doi.org/10.1007/3-540-47721-7_12

22. Goh, E.-J., Jarecki, S.: A signature scheme as secure as the Diffie-Hellman problem. In: Biham, E. (ed.) EUROCRYPT 2003. LNCS, vol. 2656, pp. 401–415. Springer, Heidelberg (2003). https://doi.org/10.1007/3-540-39200-9_25

23. González, A.: A ring signature of size $O(\sqrt[3]{n})$ without random oracles. Cryptology ePrint Archive: Report 2017/905 (2017)

24. Groth, J., Kohlweiss, M.: One-out-of-many proofs: or how to leak a secret and spend a coin. In: Oswald, E., Fischlin, M. (eds.) EUROCRYPT 2015. LNCS, vol. 9057, pp. 253–280. Springer, Heidelberg (2015). https://doi.org/10.1007/978-3-662-46803-6_9

25. Groth, J., Sahai, A.: Efficient non-interactive proof systems for bilinear groups. In: Smart, N. (ed.) EUROCRYPT 2008. LNCS, vol. 4965, pp. 415–432. Springer, Heidelberg (2008). https://doi.org/10.1007/978-3-540-78967-3_24

26. Kakvi, S.A., Kiltz, E.: Optimal security proofs for full domain hash, revisited. In: Pointcheval, D., Johansson, T. (eds.) EUROCRYPT 2012. LNCS, vol. 7237, pp. 537–553. Springer, Heidelberg (2012). https://doi.org/10.1007/978-3-642-29011-4_32

27. Katz, J., Wang, N.: Efficiency improvements for signature schemes with tight security reductions. In: ACM-CCS (2003)

28. Libert, B., Ling, S., Nguyen, K., Wang, H.: Zero-knowledge arguments for lattice-based accumulators: logarithmic-size ring signatures and group signatures without trapdoors. In: Fischlin, M., Coron, J.-S. (eds.) EUROCRYPT 2016. LNCS, vol. 9666, pp. 1–31. Springer, Heidelberg (2016). https://doi.org/10.1007/978-3-662-49896-5_1

29. Okamoto, T.: Provably secure and practical identification schemes and corresponding signature schemes. In: Brickell, E.F. (ed.) CRYPTO 1992. LNCS, vol. 740, pp. 31–53. Springer, Heidelberg (1993). https://doi.org/10.1007/3-540-48071-4_3

30. Paillier, P., Vergnaud, D.: Discrete-log-based signatures may not be equivalent to discrete log. In: Roy, B. (ed.) ASIACRYPT 2005. LNCS, vol. 3788, pp. 1–20. Springer, Heidelberg (2005). https://doi.org/10.1007/11593447_1

31. Peikert, C., Vaikuntanathan, V., Waters, B.: A framework for efficient and composable oblivious transfer. In: Wagner, D. (ed.) CRYPTO 2008. LNCS, vol. 5157, pp. 554–571. Springer, Heidelberg (2008). https://doi.org/10.1007/978-3-540-85174-5_31

32. Pointcheval, D., Stern, J.: Security proofs for signature schemes. In: Maurer, U. (ed.) EUROCRYPT 1996. LNCS, vol. 1070, pp. 387–398. Springer, Heidelberg (1996). https://doi.org/10.1007/3-540-68339-9_33

33. Rivest, R.L., Shamir, A., Tauman, Y.: How to leak a secret. In: Boyd, C. (ed.) ASIACRYPT 2001. LNCS, vol. 2248, pp. 552–565. Springer, Heidelberg (2001). https://doi.org/10.1007/3-540-45682-1_32

34. Sander, T.: Efficient accumulators without trapdoor extended abstract. In: Varadharajan, V., Mu, Y. (eds.) ICICS 1999. LNCS, vol. 1726, pp. 252–262. Springer, Heidelberg (1999). https://doi.org/10.1007/978-3-540-47942-0_21

35. Shacham, H., Waters, B.: Efficient ring signatures without random oracles. In: Okamoto, T., Wang, X. (eds.) PKC 2007. LNCS, vol. 4450, pp. 166–180. Springer, Heidelberg (2007). https://doi.org/10.1007/978-3-540-71677-8_12

RiffleScrambler – A Memory-Hard Password Storing Function

Karol Gotfryd[1], Paweł Lorek[2], and Filip Zagórski[1,3(✉)]

[1] Department of Computer Science, Faculty of Fundamental Problems of Technology,
Wrocław University of Science and Technology, Wrocław, Poland
filip.zagorski@pwr.edu.pl
[2] Faculty of Mathematics and Computer Science, Mathematical Institute,
Wrocław University, Wrocław, Poland
[3] Oktawave, Warsaw, Poland

Abstract. We introduce RiffleScrambler: a new family of directed acyclic graphs and a corresponding data-independent memory hard function with password independent memory access. We prove its memory hardness in the random oracle model.

RiffleScrambler is similar to Catena – updates of hashes are determined by a graph (bit-reversal or double-butterfly graph in Catena). The advantage of the RiffleScrambler over Catena is that the underlying graphs are not predefined but are generated per salt, as in Balloon Hashing. Such an approach leads to higher immunity against practical parallel attacks. RiffleScrambler offers better efficiency than Balloon Hashing since the in-degree of the underlying graph is equal to 3 (and is much smaller than in Ballon Hashing). At the same time, because the underlying graph is an instance of a Superconcentrator, our construction achieves the same time-memory trade-offs.

Keywords: Memory hardness · Password storing · Markov chains
Mixing time

1 Introduction

In early days of computers' era passwords were stored in plaintext in the form of pairs $(user, password)$. Back in 1960s it was observed, that it is not secure. It took around a decade to incorporate a more secure way of storing users' passwords – via a DES-based function **crypt**, as $(user, f_k(password))$ for a secret key k or as $(user, f(password))$ for a one-way function. The first approach (with encrypting passwords) allowed admins to learn a user password while both methods enabled to find two users with the same password. To mitigate that problem, a random **salt** was added and in most systems, passwords are stored as $(user, f(password, salt), salt)$ for a one-way function f. This way, two identical

Authors were supported by Polish National Science Centre contract number DEC-2013/10/E/ST1/00359.

© Springer Nature Switzerland AG 2018
J. Lopez et al. (Eds.): ESORICS 2018, LNCS 11099, pp. 309–328, 2018.
https://doi.org/10.1007/978-3-319-98989-1_16

passwords will with high probability be stored as two different strings (since the salt should be chosen uniformly at random).

Then another issue appeared: an adversary, having a database of hashed passwords, can try many dictionary-based passwords or a more targeted attack [21]. The ideal password should be random, but users tend to select passwords with low entropy instead. Recently, a probabilistic model of the distribution of choosing passwords, based on Zipf's law was proposed [20]. That is why one requires password-storing function to be **"slow"** enough to compute for an attacker and **"fast"** enough to compute for the authenticating server.

To slow-down external attackers two additional enhancements were proposed. Pepper is similar to salt, its value is sampled from uniform distribution and passwords are stored as $(user, f(password, salt, pepper), salt)$ but the value of pepper is not stored – evaluation (and guessing) of a password is slowed down by the factor equal to the size of the space from which pepper is chosen. Garlic is also used to slow down the process of verifying a password – it tells how many times f is called, a password is stored as $(user, f^{garlic}(password, salt, pepper), salt, garlic)$. Using pepper and garlic has one bottleneck – it slows down at the same rate both an attack and the legitimate server. Moreover this approach does not guarantee required advantage over an adversary who can evaluate a function simultaneously using ASICs (Application Specific Integrated Circuit) or clusters of GPUs. The reason is that the cost of evaluation of hash functions like SHA-1, SHA-2 on an ASIC is even several thousands times smaller than on a CPU. For instance Antminer S9 has claimed performance of 14 TH/s [2] (double SHA256) versus about 30 GH/s for the best currently available GPU cards (GeForce GTX 1080TI, Radeon RX Vega 56) and up to 1 GH/s for CPUs. Percival [17] noted that memory cost is more comparable across various platforms than computation time. He suggested a memory-hard functions (MHF) and introduced scrypt [17]. So the right approach in designing a password-storing function is not only to make a function slow, but to make it use relatively large amounts of memory.

One can think about an MHF as a procedure of evaluating a function F which uses some ordering of memory calls. Such a function can be described as a DAG (Directed Acyclic Graph) $G = G_F$. Vertex v represents some internal value, and if evaluating this value requires values at $v_{i_1}, \ldots, v_{i_M}$, then $v_{i_1}, \ldots, v_{i_M}$ are parents of v in G. For example, calculating a function $F = H^N(x) = H(\ldots H(H(x)) \ldots)$ (H computed N times – like PBKDF2 – Password Based Key Derivation Function 2 [13] where $N = 1024$) can be represented by a graph $G = (V, E)$ with vertices $\{v_0, v_1, \ldots, v_{N-1}, v_N\}$ and edges $E = \{(v_i, v_{i+1}), i = 0, \ldots, N-1\}$ (*i.e.*, a path). Initially, the value at vertex v_0 is x, computations yield in value $F(x)$ at vertex v_N.

We can categorize MHFs into two groups: data dependent MHFs (dMHF) and data independent MHFs (iMHF). Roughly speaking, for iMHFs the order of computations (graph G_F) does not depend on a *password* (but it can still depend on a *salt*), whereas the ordering of calculations in dMHFs depends on data (*i.e.*, a *password*). Because dMHFs may be susceptible to various side-channel attacks (via *e.g.*, timing attacks, memory access pattern) the main focus is on designing iMHFs.

Sequential vs Parallel Attacks. Security of memory-hard functions can be analyzed in two models: sequential one and parallel one. In the sequential model, an adversary tries to invert a function by performing computation on a single-core machine while in the parallel model an adversary may use many processors to achieve its goal. The security of a given memory-hard function comes from the properties of the underlying graphs, *e.g.*, if an underlying graph is a *Superconcentrator* (see Definition 3) then a function is memory-hard in the sequential model while if the underlying graph is *depth-robust* then the function is memory-hard in the parallel model.

1.1 Related Work

To compare various constructions, besides iMHF and dMHF distinction, one considers the complexity of evaluation of a given function. The formal definitions of sequential/parallel complexity are stated in Sect. 2 (and are formalized as a pebble-game), here we provide the intuitive motivation behind these definitions. The sequential complexity $\Pi_{st}(G)$ of a directed acyclic graph G is the time it takes to label (pebble/evaluate) the graph times the maximal number of memory cells the best sequential algorithm needs to evaluate (pebble) the graph. In the similar fashion one defines cumulative complexity of parallel pebbling $\Pi_{cc}^{\parallel}(G)$ of G, here this is the sum of the number of used memory cells during labeling (pebbling) the graph by the best parallel algorithm. For detailed discussion on the pebbling game see e.g. [9,11,14,16].

For a graph that corresponds to evaluating PBKDF2 above values are equal to $\Pi_{st}(PBKDF2) = n$ and $\Pi_{cc}^{\parallel}(PBKDF2) = n$ while if a function is memory hard $\Pi_{st}(PBKDF2) = \Omega(n^2)$.

The Password Hashing Competition [1] was announced in 2013 in the quest of a standard function in the area. Argon2i [10] was the winner, while Catena [15], Lyra2 [19], yescript [3] and Makwa [18] were given a special recognition.

Let DFG_n^λ be the Catena Dragonfly Graph, BFG_n^λ be the Catena Butterfly Graph (see [8,15]) and $\mathsf{BHG}_\sigma^\lambda$ be the graph corresponding to evaluating Balloon Hashing [11].

Concerning sequential attacks for DFG_N^λ and $\mathsf{BHG}_\sigma^\lambda$ we have:

Lemma 1. *Any adversary using $S \leq N/20$ memory cells requires T placements such that*

$$T \geq N \left(\frac{\lambda N}{64S} \right)^\lambda$$

for DFG_N^λ.

Lemma 2. *Any adversary using $S \leq N/64$ memory cells, for in-degree $\delta = 7$ and λ rounds requires*

$$T \geq \frac{(2^\lambda - 1)N^2}{32S}$$

placements for $\mathsf{BHG}_\sigma^\lambda$.

Concerning parallel attacks for BFG_n^λ, DFG_λ^n and BHG_σ^λ we have the following

Theorem 1 (Theorem 7 in [8]).

- *If $\lambda, n \in \mathbb{N}^+$ such that $n = 2^g(\lambda(2g-1)+1)$ for some $g \in \mathbb{N}^+$ then*

$$\Pi_{cc}^{||}(BFG_n^\lambda) = \Omega\left(\frac{n^{1.5}}{g\sqrt{g\lambda}}\right)$$

- *If $\lambda, n \in \mathbb{N}^+$ such that $k = n/(\lambda+1)$ is a power of 2 then*

$$\Pi_{cc}^{||}(DFG_n^\lambda) = \Omega\left(\frac{n^{1.5}}{\sqrt{\lambda}}\right)$$

- *If $\tau, \sigma \in \mathbb{N}^+$ such that $n = \sigma \cdot \tau$ then with high probability*

$$\Pi_{cc}^{||}(BHG_\tau^\sigma) = \Omega\left(\frac{n^{1.5}}{\sqrt{\tau}}\right)$$

Alwen and Blocki [6] show that it is possible (in parallel setting) that an attacker may save space for any iMHF (*e.g.,* Argon2i, Balloon, Catena, *etc.*) so the $\Pi_{cc}^{||}$ is not $\Omega(n^2)$ but $\Omega(n^2/\log n)$. The attack is applicable only when the instance of an MHF requires large amount of memory (*e.g.,* >1 GB) while in practice, MHFs would be run so the memory consumption is of the order of just several megabytes (*e.g.,* 16 MB). In order to mount such an attack, a special-purpose hardware must be built (with lots of shared memory and many cores). While Alwen, Blocki and Pietrzak [8] improve these attacks even further, it was still unclear if this type of attack is of practical concern. But recently Alwen and Blocki [7] improved these attacks even more and presented implementation which *e.g.,* successfully ran against the latest version of Argon (Argon2i-B).

1.2   Our Contribution

In this paper (details given in Sect. 3) we introduce RiffleScrambler– a new family of directed acyclic graphs and a corresponding data-independent memory hard function with password independent memory access. We prove its memory hardness in the random oracle model.

For a password x, a salt s and security parameters (integers) g, λ:

1. a permutation $\rho = \rho_g(s)$ of $N = 2^g$ elements is generated using (time reversal of) Riffle Shuffle (see Algorithm 1) and
2. a computation graph $RSG_\lambda^N = G_{\lambda,g,s} = G_{\lambda,g}(\rho)$ is generated.

Evaluation of RiffleScrambler (a function on 2λ stacked RSG^N graphs) with $S = N = 2^g$ memory cells takes the number of steps proportional to $T \approx 3\lambda N$ (the max-indegree of the graph is equal to 3).

Our result on time-memory trade-off concerning *sequential attacks* is following.

Lemma 3. *Any adversary using $S \leq N/20$ memory cells requires T placements such that*

$$T \geq N \left(\frac{\lambda N}{64S}\right)^{\lambda}$$

for the $\mathsf{RSG}_{\lambda}^{N}$.

The above lemma means that (in the sequential model) any adversary who uses S memory cells for which $S \leq N/20$ would spend at least T steps evaluating the function and $T \geq N \left(\frac{\lambda N}{64S}\right)^{\lambda}$ (the punishment for decreasing available memory cells is severe). The result for sequential model gives the same level as for Catena (see Lemma 1) while it is much better than for BallonHashing (see Lemma 2). The main advantage of RiffleScrambler (compared to Catena) is that each salt corresponds (with high probability) to a different computation graph, and there are $N! = 2^g!$ of them (while Catena uses one, *e.g.*, bit-reversal based graph). Moreover it is easy to modify RiffleScrambler so the number of possible computation graphs is equal to $N!^{2\lambda} = (2^g!)^{2\lambda}$ (we can use different – also salt dependent – permutations in each stack).

On the other hand RiffleScrambler guarantees better immunity against parallel attacks than Catena's computation graph. Our result concerning *parallel attacks* is following.

Lemma 4. *For positive integers λ, g let $n = 2^g(2\lambda+1)$ for some $g \in \mathbb{N}^+$. Then*

$$\Pi_{cc}^{\|}(\mathsf{RSG}_{\lambda}^k) = \Omega\left(\frac{n^{1.5}}{\sqrt{g\lambda}}\right).$$

The RiffleScrambler is a password storing method that is immune to cache-timing attacks since memory access pattern is password-independent.

2   Preliminaries

For a directed acyclic graph (DAG) $G = (V, E)$ of $n = |V|$ nodes, we say that the indegree is $\delta = \max_{v \in V} indeg(v)$ if δ is the smallest number such that for any $v \in V$ the number of incoming edges is not larger than δ. Parents of a node $v \in V$ is the set $\mathsf{parents}_G(v) = \{u \in V : (u, v) \in E\}$.

We say that $u \in V$ is a *source* node if it has no parents (has indegree 0) and we say that $u \in V$ is a *sink* node if it is not a parent for any other node (it has 0 outdegree). We denote the set of all sinks of G by $\mathsf{sinks}(G) = \{v \in V : outdegree(v) = 0\}$.

The directed path $p = (v_1, \ldots, v_t)$ is of length t in G if $(\forall i)v_i \in V$, $(v_i, v_{i+1}) \in E$, we denote it by $\mathsf{length}(p) = t$. The *depth* $d = \mathsf{depth}(G)$ of a graph G is the length of the longest directed path in G.

2.1   Pebbling and Complexity

One of the methods for analyzing iMHFs is to use so called *pebbling game*. We will follow [8] with the notation (see also therein for more references on pebbling games).

Definition 1 (Parallel/Sequential Graph Pebbling). *Let $G = (V, E)$ be a DAG and let $T \subset V$ be a target set of nodes to be pebbled. A pebbling config-uration (of G) is a subset $P_i \subset V$. A legal parallel pebbling of T is a sequence $P = (P_0, \ldots, P_t)$ of pebbling configurations of G, where $P_0 = \emptyset$ and which sat-isfies conditions 1 and 2 below. A sequential pebbling additionally must satisfy condition 3.*

1. *At some step every target node is pebbled (though not necessarily simultane-ously).*
$$\forall x \in T \quad \exists z \leq t \quad : \quad x \in P_z.$$

2. *Pebbles are added only when their predecessors already have a pebble at the end of the previous step.*
$$\forall i \in [t] \quad : \quad x \in (P_i \setminus P_{i-1}) \Rightarrow \text{parents}(x) \subset P_{i-1}.$$

3. *At most one pebble is placed per step.*
$$\forall i \in [t] : |P_i \setminus P_{i-1}| \leq 1.$$

We denote with $\mathcal{P}_{G,T}$ and $\mathcal{P}_{G,T}^{\|}$ the set of all legal sequential and parallel peb-blings of G with target set T, respectively.

Note that $\mathcal{P}_{G,T} \subset \mathcal{P}_{G,T}^{\|}$. The most interesting case is when $T = \text{sinks}(G)$, with such a T we write $\mathcal{P}_G$ and $\mathcal{P}_G^{\|}$.

Definition 2 (Time/Space/Cumulative Pebbling Complexity). *The time, space, space-time and cumulative complexity of a pebbling $P = \{P_0, \ldots, P_t\} \in \mathcal{P}_G^{\|}$ are defined as:*

$$\Pi_t(P) = t, \quad \Pi_s(P) = \max_{i \in [t]} |P_i|, \quad \Pi_{st}(P) = \Pi_t(P) \cdot \Pi_s(P), \quad \Pi_{cc}(P) = \sum_{i \in [t]} |P_i|.$$

For $\alpha \in \{s, t, st, cc\}$ and a target set $T \subset V$, the sequential and parallel pebbling complexities of G are defined as

$$\Pi_\alpha(G, T) = \min_{P \in \mathcal{P}_{G,T}} \Pi_\alpha(P), \qquad \Pi_\alpha^{\|}(G, T) = \min_{P \in \mathcal{P}_{G,T}^{\|}} \Pi_\alpha(P).$$

When $T = \text{sinks}(G)$ we write $\Pi_\alpha(G)$ and $\Pi_\alpha^{\|}(G)$.

2.2 Tools for Sequential Attacks

Definition 3 (N-Superconcentrator). *A directed acyclic graph $G = \langle V, E \rangle$ with a set of vertices V and a set of edges E, a bounded indegree, N inputs, and N outputs is called **N-Superconcentrator** if for every k such that $1 \leq k \leq N$ and for every pair of subsets $V_1 \subset V$ of k inputs and $V_2 \subset V$ of k outputs, there are k vertex-disjoint paths connecting the vertices in V_1 to the vertices in V_2.*

By stacking λ (an integer) N-Superconcentrators we obtain a graph called (N, λ)-Superconcentrator.

Definition 4 ((N, λ)-Superconcentrator). *Let $G_i, i = 0, \ldots, \lambda - 1$ be N-Superconcentrators. Let G be the graph created by joining the outputs of G_i to the corresponding inputs of $G_{i+1}, i = 0, \ldots, \lambda - 2$. Graph G is called (N, λ)-Superconcentrator.*

Theorem 2 (Lower bound for a (N, λ)-Superconcentrator [16]). *Pebbling a (N, λ)-Superconcentrator using $S \leq N/20$ pebbles requires T placements such that*

$$T \geq N \left(\frac{\lambda N}{64 S} \right)^{\lambda}.$$

2.3 Tools for Parallel Attacks

We build upon the results from [8], hence we shall recall the definitions used therein.

Definition 5 (Depth-Robustness [8]). *For $n \in \mathcal{N}$ and $e, d \in [n]$ a DAG $G = (V, E)$ is (e, d)-depth-robust if*

$$\forall S \subset V \quad |S| \leq e \Rightarrow depth(G - S) \geq d.$$

For (e, d)-depth-robust graph we have

Theorem 3 (Theorem 4 [8]). *Let G be an (e, d)-depth-robust DAG. Then we have $\Pi_{cc}^{\|}(G) > ed$.*

We can obtain better bounds on $\Pi_{cc}^{\|}(G)$ having more assumptions on the structure of G.

Definition 6 (Dependencies [8]). *Let $G = (V, E)$ be a DAG and $L \subseteq V$. We say that L has a $(z, g)-$dependency if there exist nodes-disjoint paths $p_1, \ldots, p_z$ of length at least g each ending in L.*

Definition 7 (Dispersed Graph [8]). *Let $g \geq k$ be positive integers. A DAG G is called $(g, k)-$dispersed if there exists ordering of its nodes such that the following holds. Let $[k]$ denote last k nodes in the ordering of G and let $L_j = [jg, (j + 1)g - 1]$ be the jth subinterval. Then $\forall j \in [\lfloor k/g \rfloor]$ the interval L_j has a $(g, g)-$dependency. More generally, let $\varepsilon \in (0, 1]$. If each interval L_j only has an $(\varepsilon g, g)-$dependency, then G is called (ε, g, k)-dispersed.*

Definition 8 (Stacked Dispersed Graphs [8]**).** *A DAG* $G \in \mathbb{D}_{\varepsilon,g}^{\lambda,k}$ *if there exist* $\lambda \in \mathbb{N}^+$ *disjoint subsets of nodes* $\{L_i \subseteq V\}$, *each of size* k, *with the following two properties:*

1. *For each* L_i *there is a path running through all nodes of* L_i.
2. *Fix any topological ordering of nodes of* G. *For each* $i \in [\lambda]$ *let* G_i *be the sub-graph of* G *containing all nodes of* G *up to the last node of* L_i. *Then* G_i *is an* (ε, g, k)–*dispersed graph.*

For stacked dispersed graphs we have

Theorem 4 (Theorem 4 in [8]**).** *Let* G *be a DAG such that* $G \in \mathcal{D}_{\varepsilon,g}^{\lambda,k}$. *Then we have*

$$\Pi_{cc}^{||}(G) \geq \varepsilon \lambda g \left(\frac{k}{2} - g\right).$$

3   RiffleScrambler

The RiffleScrambler function uses the following parameters:

- s is a salt which is used to generate a graph G,
- g - garlic, $G = \langle V, E \rangle$, *i.e.*, $V = V_0 \cup \ldots \cup V_{2\lambda g}$, $|V_i| = 2^g$,
- λ - is the number of layers of the graph G.

Let $HW(x)$ denote the Hamming weight of a binary string x (*i.e.*, the number of ones in x), and $\bar{x}$ denotes a coordinate-wise complement of x (thus $HW(\bar{x})$ denotes number of zeros in x).

Definition 9. *Let* $B = (b_0 \ldots b_{n-1}) \in \{0,1\}^n$ *(a binary word of length* n*). We define a rank* $r_B(i)$ *of a bit* i *in* B *as*

$$r_B(i) = |\{j < i : b_j = b_i\}|.$$

Definition 10 (Riffle-Permutation). *Let* $B = (b_0 \ldots b_{n-1})$ *be a binary word of length* n. *A permutation* π *induced by* B *is defined as*

$$\pi_B(i) = \begin{cases} r_B(i) & \text{if } b_i = 0, \\ r_B(i) + HW(\bar{B}) & \text{if } b_i = 1 \end{cases}$$

for all $0 \leq i \leq n - 1$.

Example 1. Let $B = 11100100$, then $r_B(0) = 0, r_B(1) = 1, r_B(2) = 2, r_B(3) = 0,$ $r_B(4) = 1, r_B(5) = 3, r_B(6) = 2, r_B(7) = 3$. The Riffle-Permutation induced by B is equal to $\pi_B = \begin{pmatrix} 0\ 1\ 2\ 3\ 4\ 5\ 6\ 7 \\ 4\ 5\ 6\ 0\ 1\ 7\ 2\ 3 \end{pmatrix}$. For graphical illustration of this example see Fig. 1.

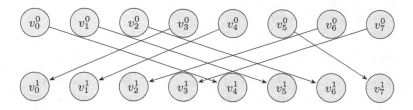

Fig. 1. A graph of Riffle-Permutation induced by $B = 11100100$.

Definition 11 (N-Single-Layer-Riffle-Graph). *Let $\mathcal{V} = \mathcal{V}^0 \cup \mathcal{V}^1$ where $\mathcal{V}^i = \{v_0^i, \ldots, v_{N-1}^i\}$ and let B be an N-bit word. Let π_B be a Riffle-Permutation induced by B. We define N-Single-Layer-Riffle-Graph (for even N) via the set of edges E:*

- *1 edge: $v_{N-1}^0 \to v_0^1$,*
- *N edges: $v_i^0 \to v_{\pi_B(i)}^1$ for $i = 0, \ldots, N-1$,*
- *N edges: $v_i^0 \to v_{\pi_{\bar{B}}(i)}^1$ for $i = 0, \ldots, N-1$.*

Example 2. Continuing with B and π_B from Example 1, the 8-Single-Layer-Riffle-Graph is presented in Fig. 2.

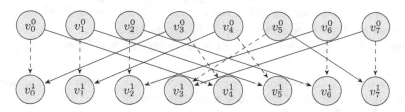

Fig. 2. An 8-Single-Layer-Riffle-Graph (with horizontal edges and edge (v_7^0, v_0^1) skipped) for $B = 11100100$. Permutation π_B is depicted with solid lines, whereas $\pi_{\bar{B}}$ is presented with dashed lines.

Algorithm 3 is responsible for generating an N-Double-Riffle-Graph which is defined in the following way. From now on, we assume that $N = 2^g$.

Definition 12 (N-Double-Riffle-Graph). *Let V denote the set of vertices and E be the set of edges of $G = (V, E)$. Let $B_0, \ldots, B_{g-1}$ be g binary words of the length 2^g each. Then N-Double-Riffle-Graph is obtained by stacking $2g$ Single-Layer-Riffle-Graphs resulting in a graph consisting of $(2g + 1)2^g$ vertices*

- $\{v_0^0, \ldots, v_{2^g-1}^0\} \cup \ldots \cup \{v_0^{2g}, \ldots, v_{2^g-1}^{2g}\}$,

and edges:

- *$(2g + 1)2^g$ edges: $v_{i-1}^j \to v_i^j$ for $i \in \{1, \ldots, 2^g - 1\}$ and $j \in \{0, 1, \ldots, 2^g\}$,*

- $2g$ edges: $v_{2^g-1}^j \rightarrow v_0^{j+1}$ for $j \in \{0, \ldots, 2g-1\}$,
- $g2^g$ edges: $v_i^{j-1} \rightarrow v_{\pi_{B_j}(i)}^j$ for $i \in \{0, \ldots, 2^g-1\}$, $j \in \{1, \ldots, g\}$,
- $g2^g$ edges: $v_i^{j-1} \rightarrow v_{\pi_{B_j}(i)}^j$ for $i \in \{0, \ldots, 2^g-1\}$, $j \in \{1, \ldots, g\}$,

and the following edges for the lower g layers – which are symmetric with respect to the level g (and where we use inverse of permutations induced by $B_j, j \in \{0, \ldots, g-1\}$):

- $g2^g$ edges: $v_{\pi_{B_j}^{-1}(i)}^{2g-j} \rightarrow v_i^{2g-j+1} \rightarrow$ for $i \in \{0, \ldots, 2^g-1\}$, $j \in \{1, \ldots, g\}$,
- $g2^g$ edges: $v_i^{2g-j} \rightarrow v_{\pi_{B_j}^{-1}(i)}^{2g-j+1}$ for $i \in \{0, \ldots, 2^g-1\}$, $j \in \{1, \ldots, g\}$.

Definition 13 $((N, \lambda)$-**Double-Riffle-Graph**$)$. Let $G_i, i = 0, \ldots, \lambda-1$ be N-Double-Riffle-Graphs. The (N, λ)-Double-Riffle-Graph is a graph obtained by stacking λ times N-Double-Riffle-Graphs together by joining outputs of G_i to the corresponding inputs of $G_{i+1}, i = 0, \ldots, \lambda-2$.

One of the ingredients of our main procedure is a construction of (N, λ)-Double-Riffle-Graph using specific binary words $B_0, \ldots, B_{g-1}$. To continue, we have to introduce "trajectory tracing". For given σ – a permutation of $\{0, \ldots, 2^g-1\}$ – let $\mathbf{B}$ be a binary matrix of size $2^g \times g$, whose j-th row is a binary representation of $\sigma(j), j = 0, \ldots, 2^g-1$. Denote by B_i the i-th column of $\mathbf{B}$, i.e., $\mathbf{B} = (B_0, \ldots, B_{2^g-1})$. We call this matrix a binary representation of σ. Then we create a binary matrix $\mathfrak{B} = (\mathfrak{B}_0, \ldots, \mathfrak{B}_{2^g-1})$ (also of size $2^g \times g$) in the following way. We set $\mathfrak{B}_0 = B_0$. For $i = 1, \ldots, 2^g-1$ we set $\mathfrak{B}_i = \pi_{\mathfrak{B}_{i-1}^T}(B_i)$. The procedure TraceTrajectories is given in Algorithm 2.

Roughly speaking, the procedure RiffleScrambler(x, s, g, λ) works in the following way.

- For given salt s it calculates a pseudorandom permutation σ (using inverse Riffle Shuffle), let $\mathbf{B}$ be its binary representation.
- It calculates $\mathfrak{B}$ =TraceTrajectories$(\mathbf{B})$.
- It creates an instance of N-Double-Riffle-Graph $(2g + 1$ rows of 2^g vertices$)$ using $\mathfrak{B}_0^T, \ldots, \mathfrak{B}_{g-1}^T$ as binary words.
- It evaluates x on the graph, calculates values at nodes on last row, i.e., $v_0^{2g+1}, \ldots, v_{2g+1}^{2^g-1}$.
- Last row is rewritten to first one, i.e., $v_i^0 = v_i^{2g+1}, i = 0, \ldots 2^g-1$, and whole evaluation is repeated λ times.
- Finally, the value at $v_{2^g-1}^{2g}$ is returned.

The main procedure RiffleScrambler(x, s, g, λ) for storing a password x using salt s and memory-hardness parameters g, λ is given in Algorithm 4.

Example 3. An example of $(8, 1)$-Double-Riffle-Graph which was obtained from a permutation $\sigma = \begin{pmatrix} 0\,1\,2\,3\,4\,5\,6\,7 \\ 5\,4\,6\,3\,2\,7\,0\,1 \end{pmatrix}$. Its binary representation is the following:

$$\mathbf{B} = (B_0, B_1, B_2), \quad \mathbf{B}^T = \begin{pmatrix} 1\,1\,1\,0\,0\,1\,0\,0 \\ 0\,0\,1\,1\,1\,1\,0\,0 \\ 1\,0\,0\,1\,0\,1\,0\,1 \end{pmatrix}.$$

We obtain trajectories of the elements and we can derive words/permutations for each layer of the graph:

- $\mathfrak{B}_0 = B_0 = (11100100)^T$ (used in the previous examples) – obtained by concatenating first digits of elements, we have $\pi_{B_0} = \begin{pmatrix} 0\,1\,2\,3\,4\,5\,6\,7 \\ 4\,5\,6\,0\,1\,7\,2\,3 \end{pmatrix}$.

- $\mathfrak{B}_1 = \pi_{\mathfrak{B}_0^T}(B_1) = \pi_{\mathfrak{B}_0^T}(11100100) = (11000011)^T$, thus $\pi_{\mathfrak{B}_1} = \begin{pmatrix} 0\,1\,2\,3\,4\,5\,6\,7 \\ 4\,5\,0\,1\,2\,3\,6\,7 \end{pmatrix}$.

- $\mathfrak{B}_2 = \pi_{\mathfrak{B}_1^T}(B_2) = \pi_{\mathfrak{B}_1^T}(10010101) = (01011001)^T$, thus $\pi_{\mathfrak{B}_2} = \begin{pmatrix} 0\,1\,2\,3\,4\,5\,6\,7 \\ 0\,4\,5\,1\,6\,2\,3\,7 \end{pmatrix}$.

- Finally,

$$\mathfrak{B} = (\mathfrak{B}_0, \mathfrak{B}_1, \mathfrak{B}_2), \quad \mathfrak{B}^T = \begin{pmatrix} 1\,1\,1\,0\,0\,1\,0\,0 \\ 1\,1\,0\,0\,0\,0\,1\,1 \\ 0\,1\,0\,1\,1\,0\,0\,1 \end{pmatrix}.$$

The resulting graph is given in Fig. 3.

3.1 Pseudocodes

Algorithm 1. RiffleShuffle$_H(n, s)$

1: $\pi = \langle 1, \ldots, n \rangle$
2: **for** $i = 1$ to n **do**
3:      **for** $j = 1$ to $i - 1$ **do**
4:      | $M[i, j] = 0$
5:      **end for**
6: **end for**
7: **while** $\exists_{1 \leq i \leq n} \exists_{1 \leq j < i} M[i, j] = 0$ **do**
8:      $S_0, S_1 = \emptyset$
9:      **for** $w := 1$ to n **do**
10:      | $b = H(s, w, r)_1$
11:      | $S_b = S_b \uplus \pi[w]$
12:      **end for**
13:      **for** $i \in S_0$ **do**
14:      | **for** $j \in S_1$ **do**
15:      | | $M[\max(i, j), \min(i, j)] = 1$
16:      | **end for**
17:      **end for**
18:      $\pi = S_0 \uplus S_1$
19: **end while**
20: **return** π

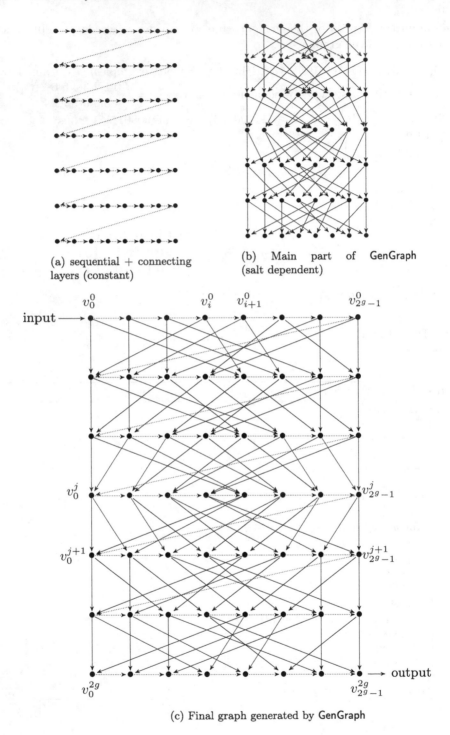

(a) sequential + connecting layers (constant)

(b) Main part of GenGraph (salt dependent)

(c) Final graph generated by GenGraph

Fig. 3. Instance of (8,1)-Double-Riffle-Graph the graph

Algorithm 2. TraceTrajectories($\mathbf{B}$)

Require: : $\mathbf{B} = (B_0, \ldots, B_{g-1})$ {binary matrix of size $2^g \times g$ with columns $B_i, i = 0, \ldots, g-1$}
Ensure: : $\mathfrak{B}$ {binary matrix of size $2^g \times g$ with recalculated trajectories}
1: $\mathfrak{B}_0 = B_0$
2: **for** $i := 1$ to $g-1$ **do**
3: $\quad \mathfrak{B}_i = \pi_{\mathfrak{B}^T_{i-1}}(B_i^T)$ $\qquad$ //Riffle-Permutation induced by B_i^T
4: **end for**
5: **return** $\mathfrak{B} = (\mathfrak{B}_0, \ldots, \mathfrak{B}_{g-1})$

Algorithm 3. GenGraph$_H(g, \sigma)$

1: $N = 2^g$
2: $V = \{v_i^j : i = 0, \ldots, N-1; j = 0, \ldots, 2g\}$
3: $E = \{v_i^j \to v_{i+1}^j : i = 0, \ldots, N-2; j = 0, \ldots, 2g\}$
4: $E = E \cup \{v_{n-1}^j \to v_0^{j+1} : j = 0, \ldots, 2g-1\}$
5: Let $\mathbf{B}$ be a binary representation of σ
6: Calculate $\mathfrak{B} = (\mathfrak{B}_0, \ldots, \mathfrak{B}_{g-1}) =$ TraceTrajectories($\mathbf{B}$). Let $\mathfrak{B}_{2g+1-m} = \mathfrak{B}_m, m = 0, \ldots, g-2$.
$\quad$ Let $\mathfrak{B}_j = \mathfrak{B}_{j,0}\mathfrak{B}_{j,1} \ldots \mathfrak{B}_{j,2^g-1}$
7: **for** $i = 0$ to $2g$ **do**
8: **end for**
9: **for** $j = 0$ to $2g-1$ **do**
10: $\quad$ **for** $i = 0$ to $2^g - 1$ **do**
11: $\quad\quad E = E \cup \{v_i^j \to v_{\pi_{\mathfrak{B}_{j,i}}}^{j+1}\} \cup \{v_i^j \to v_{\pi_{\mathfrak{B}_{j,i}}}^{j+1}\}$
12: $\quad$ **end for**
13: **end for**
14: **return** π

Algorithm 4. RiffleScrambler(n, x, s, g, λ)

Require: s {Salt}, g {Garlic}, x {Value to Hash}, λ {Depth}, H {Hash Function}
Ensure: x {Password Hash}
1: $\sigma = $ RiffleShuffle$_H(2^g, s)$
2: $G = (V, E) = $ GenGraph(g, σ)
3: $v_0^0 \leftarrow H(x)$
4: **for** $i := 1$ to $2^g - 1$ **do**
5: $\quad v_i^0 = H(v_{i-1}^0)$
6: **end for**
7: **for** $r := 1$ to λ **do**
8: $\quad$ **for** $j := 0$ to $2g$ **do**
9: $\quad\quad$ **for** $i = 0$ to $2^g - 1$ **do**
10: $\quad\quad\quad v_i^{j+1} := 0$
11: $\quad\quad\quad$ **for all** $v \to v_i^{j+1} \in E$ **do**
12: $\quad\quad\quad\quad v_i^{j+1} := H(v_i^{j+1}, v)$
13: $\quad\quad\quad$ **end for**
14: $\quad\quad$ **end for**
15: $\quad$ **end for**
16: $\quad$ **for** $i = 0$ to $2^g - 1$ **do**
17: $\quad\quad v_i^0 = v_i^{2g+1}$
18: $\quad$ **end for**
19: **end for**
20: $x := v_{n-1}^{2g}$
21: **return** x

4   Proofs

4.1   Proof of Lemma 3

In this Section we present the security proof of our scheme in the sequential model of adversary. Recall that $N = 2^g$. To prove Lemma 3 it is enough to prove the following theorem (since then the assertion follows from Theorem 2).

Theorem 5. *Let* $\rho = (\rho_0, \ldots, \rho_{2^g-1})$ *be a permutation of* $N = 2^g$ *elements, let* **B** *be its binary representation and let* $\mathfrak{B} = (\mathfrak{B}_0, \ldots, \mathfrak{B}_{g-1}) = TraceTrajectories(\mathbf{B})$. *Let* G *be an* N-*Double-Riffle-Graph using* $\mathfrak{B}$. *Then* G *is an* N-*Superconcentrator.*

Before we proceed to the main part of the proof, we shall introduce some auxiliary lemmas showing some useful properties of the N-Double-Riffle-Graph.

Lemma 5. *Let* ρ *be a permutation of* $N = 2^g$ *elements,* $\rho = (\rho_0, \ldots, \rho_{2^g-1})$ *and let* **B** *be its binary representation. Let* $\mathfrak{B} = TraceTrajectories(\mathbf{B})$. *Let* $\bar{G}$ *be the subgraph of* N-*Double-Riffle-Graph* G *constructed using* $\mathfrak{B}$, *consisting of* $g + 1$ *layers and only of directed edges corresponding to the trajectories defined by* ρ. *Then the index of the endpoint of the directed path from* jth *input vertex* v_j^0 *of* $\bar{G}$ *is uniquely given by the reversal of the bit sequence* $\mathfrak{B}_j^T$. *The input vertex* v_j^0 *corresponds to the output vertex* v_k^g, *where* $k = \mathfrak{B}_j(2^g - 1) \ldots \mathfrak{B}_j(1)\mathfrak{B}_j(0)$.

The above lemma is very closely related to the interpretation of time-reversed Riffle Shuffle process and it follows from a simple inductive argument. Let us focus on the last layer of $\bar{G}$, *i.e.*, the sets of vertices $V_{g-1} = \{v_0^{g-1}, \ldots, v_{2^g-1}^{g-1}\}$, $V_g = \{v_0^g, \ldots, v_{2^g-1}^g\}$ and the edges between them. Let us observe that from the construction of Riffle-Graph, the vertices from V_g with indices whose binary representation starts with 1 are connected with the vertices from V_{g-1} having the last bit of their trajectories equal to 1 (the same applies to 0). Applying this kind of argument iteratively to the preceding layers will lead to the claim.

Let us observe that choosing two different permutations ρ_1 and ρ_2 of 2^g elements will determine two different sets of trajectories, each of them leading to different configurations of output vertices in $\bar{G}$ connected to respective inputs from $V_0 = \{v_0^0, \ldots, v_{2^g-1}^0\}$. Thus, as a simple consequence of Lemma 5 we obtain the following corollary.

Corollary 1. *There is one-to-one correspondence between the set* $\mathbb{S}_2^g$ *of permutations of* 2^g *elements determining the trajectories of input vertices in* N-*Double-Riffle-Graph and the positions of endpoint vertices from* V_g *connected with consecutive input vertices from* V_0 *in the graph* $\bar{G}$ *defined in Lemma 5.*

In order to provide a pebbling-based argument on memory hardness of the RiffleScrambler, we need the result on the structure of N-Double-Riffle-Graph given by the following Lemma 6, which is somewhat similar to that of Lemma 4 from [12].

Lemma 6. *Let G be an N-Double-Riffle-Graph with 2^g input vertices. Then there is no such pairs of trajectories that if in some layer $1 \leq i \leq g$ the vertices v_k^{i-1} and v_l^{i-1} on that trajectories are connected with some $v_{k'}^i$ and $v_{l'}^i$ (i.e., they form a size-1 switch) on the corresponding trajectories, there is no $0 < j < i$ such that the predecessors (on a given trajectory) of v_k^{i-1} and v_l^{i-1} are connected with predecessors of $v_{k'}^i$ and $v_{l'}^i$.*

Proof. Assume towards contradiction that such two trajectories exist and denote by v and w the input vertices on that trajectories. For the sake of simplicity we will denote all the vertices on that trajectories by v^i and w^i, respectively, where i denotes the row of G. Let j and k be the rows such that $v^j, v^{j+1}, w^j, w^{j+1}$ and $v^k, v^{k+1}, w^k, w^{k+1}$ are connected forming two size-1 switches. Without loss of generality, let $j < k$. Define the trajectories of v and w as

- $P_v = b_0^v b_1^v \ldots b_{j-1}^v b b_{j+1}^v \ldots b_{k-1}^v b' b_{k+1}^v \ldots b_g^v$ and
- $P_w = b_0^w b_1^w \ldots b_{j-1}^w \bar{b} b_{j+1}^w \ldots b_{k-1}^w \bar{b'} b_{k+1}^w \ldots b_g^w$.

Consider another two trajectories, namely

- $P_v^* = b_0^v b_1^v \ldots b_{j-1}^v \bar{b} b_{j+1}^w \ldots b_{k-1}^w \bar{b'} b_{k+1}^v \ldots b_g^v$ and
- $P_w^* = b_0^w b_1^w \ldots b_{j-1}^w b b_{j+1}^v \ldots b_{k-1}^v b' b_{k+1}^w \ldots b_g^w$.

Clearly, $P_v \neq P_v^*$ and $P_w \neq P_w^*$. Moreover, one can easily see that P_v and P_v^* move v^0 to v^g, P_w and P_w^* move w^0 to w^g. Since other trajectories are not affected when replacing P_u with P_u^* for $u \in \{v, w\}$, such replacement does not change the order of vertices in g^{th} row. If P_v and P_w differ only on positions j and k, then $P_v = P_w^*$ and $P_w = P_v^*$, what leads to two different sets of trajectories resulting in the same correspondence between vertices from rows 0 and g. This contradicts Corollary 1. Otherwise, there exist another two trajectories $P_x = P_v^*$ and $P_y = P_w^*$. However, in such situation, from Lemma 5 it follows that x^0 and v^0 should be moved to the same vertex $x^g = v^g$, but this is not the case (similar holds for y and w). Thus, the resulting contradiction finishes the proof.

Being equipped with the lemmas introduced above, we can now proceed with the proof of Theorem 5.

Proof. (of Theorem 5). We need to show that for every $k : 1 \leq k \leq G$ and for every pair of subsets $V_{in} \subseteq \{v_0^0, \ldots, v_{2^g-1}^0\}$ and $V_{out} \subseteq \{v_0^{2g}, \ldots, v_{2^g-1}^{2g}\}$, where $|V_{in}| = |V_{out}| = k$ there are k vertex-disjoint paths connecting vertices in V_{in} to the vertices in V_{out}.

The reasoning proceeds in a similar vein to the proofs of Theorems 1 and 2 from [12]. Below we present an outline of the main idea of the proof.

Let us notice that it is enough to show that for any V_{in} of size k there exists k vertex-disjoint paths that connect vertices of V_{in} to the vertices of $V_{middle} \subseteq \{v_0^g, \ldots, v_{2^g-1}^g\}$ with vertices of V_{middle} forming a line, *i.e.,* either:

- $V_{middle} = \{v_i^g, v_{i+1}^g, \ldots, v_{i+k-1}^g\}$ for some i,
- or $V_{middle} = \{v_0^g, \ldots, v_{i-1}^g\} \cup \{v_{2^g-k+i}^g, \ldots, v_{2^g-1}^g\}$.

If the above is shown, we obtain the claim by finding vertex-disjoint paths between V_{in} and V_{middle} and then from V_{middle} to V_{out} from the symmetry of G-Double-Riffle-Graph.

Fix $1 \leq k \leq G$ and let V_{in} and V_{out} be some given size-k subsets of input and output vertices, respectively, as defined above. From Lemma 6 it follows that if some two vertices x and y are connected in i^{th} round forming a size-1 switch then they will never be connected again until round g. Thus, the paths from x and y can move according to different bits in that round, hence being distinguished (they will share no common vertex). Having this in mind, we can construct the nodes-disjoint paths from V_{in} to V_{middle} in the following way. Starting in vertices from V_{in}, the paths will move through the first $t = \lceil \log k \rceil$ rounds according to all distinct t-bits trajectories. Then, after round t, we will choose some fixed $g-t$-sequence τ common for all k paths and let them follow according τ. Lemma 5 implies that the k paths resulting from the construction described above after g steps will eventually end up in some subset V_{middle} of k vertices forming a line, whereas Lemma 6 ensures that the paths are vertex-disjoint.

5 Summary

We presented a new memory hard function which can be used as a secure password-storing scheme. RiffleScrambler achieves better time-memory trade-offs than Argon2i and Balloon Hashing when the buffer size n grows and the number of rounds r is fixed (and the same as Catena-DBG) (Fig. 4).

	BHG_7	BHG_3	Argon2i	Catena BFG	RiffleScrambler
Server - time T (for S = N)	$8\lambda N$	$4\lambda N$	$2\lambda N$	$4\lambda N$	$3\lambda N$
Attacker - time T ($S \leq \frac{N}{64}$)	$T \geq \frac{2^\lambda - 1}{32S} N^2$	$T \geq \frac{\lambda N^2}{32S}$	$T \geq \frac{N^2}{1536S}$	$T \geq (\frac{\lambda N}{64S})^\lambda N$	$T \geq (\frac{\lambda N}{64S})^\lambda N$
Attacker - time T ($\frac{N}{64} \leq S \leq \frac{N}{20}$)	unknown				
Salt-dependent graph	yes	yes	yes	no	yes

Fig. 4. Comparison of the efficiency and security of BalloonHashing (BHG_3 is BalloonHashing with $\delta = 3$ and BHG_7 is BHG graph for $\delta = 7$), Argon2i, Catena (with Butterfly graph) and RiffleScrambler (RSG).

On the other hand, in the case of massively-parallel adversaries the situation of Catena is much worse than RiffleScrambler. In Catena, only double-butterfly graph (Catena-DBG) offered a time-memory trade-off which depends on the number of layers of the graph. Unfortunately, Catena-DBG is just a single graph instance, so in theory an adversary may try to build a parallel hardware to achieve better trade-off. In the case of RiffleScrambler the time-memory trade-off is the same as for the Catena-DBG but for RiffleScrambler, a different salt corresponds (with high probability) to the computation on a different (one from $N!$) graph. So an adversary cannot build just a single device for cracking all passwords (as in the case of Catena).

A   Markov Chains, Mixing Times, Strong Stationary Times

Consider an ergodic Markov chain $\mathbf{X} = \{X_k, k \geq 0\}$ on a finite state space $\mathbb{E}$ with stationary distribution π. Ergodicity implies that $d_{TV}(\mathcal{L}(X_k), \pi) \to 0$ (total variation distance) as $k \to \infty$, where $\mathcal{L}(X_k)$ is the distribution of the chain at step k. Define

$$\tau_{mix}(\varepsilon) = \inf\{k : d_{TV}(\mathcal{L}(X_k), \pi) \leq \varepsilon\},$$

often called total variation *mixing time*.

Perfect Simulation and Strong Stationary Times. *Perfect simulation* refers to the art of converting an algorithm for running a Markov chain into an algorithm which returns an unbiased sample from its stationary distribution. *Coupling from the past* (CFTP) is one of the most known ones. However, it is not applicable to our models. Another method is based on *strong stationary times* (SSTs), a method whose prime application is studying the rate of convergence (of a chain to its stationary distribution).

Definition 14. *A stopping time is a random variable $T \subset \mathbb{N}$ such that the event $\{T = k\}$ depends only on $X_0, \ldots, X_k$. A stopping time T is a **strong stationary time (SST)** if*

$$\forall (i \in \mathbb{E}) P(X_k = i | T = k) = \pi(k).$$

Due to [5], we have

$$d_{TV}(\mathcal{L}(X_k), \pi) \leq Pr(T > k). \tag{1}$$

Remark 1. An SST T can be *non-randomized*, i.e., an event $\{T = k\}$ depends only on on the path $X_0, \ldots, X_k$ and *does not* use any extra randomness (which is the case for *randomized* SST). For non-randomized SST performing perfect simulation is relatively easy: simply run the chain X_k until event T occurs and stop. Then X_T has distribution π.

Obtaining a Random Permutation: SST for Riffle Shuffle. In our applications we will need a random permutation of N elements. We can think of these elements as of cards, and of a chain on permutations as of card shuffling. Consider the following shuffling scheme (one step of a corresponding Markov chain):

> *For each card in the deck, flip a coin and label the back of the card with 0 (if Heads occurred) or with 1 (if Tails occurred). Take all the cards labeled 1 out of the deck and put them on the top keeping their relative ordering.*

This is the *inverse Riffle Shuffle*. The following rule is an SST for this shuffling (due to Aldous and Diaconis [4]):

> *Keep track of assigned bits (storing a sequence of assigned bits for each card). Stop when all the sequences are different.*

Once stopped, we have a permutation obtained from *exactly* uniform distribution (which is the stationary distribution of this chain). On average, this takes $2 \log_2 N$ steps. What we considered was *an idealized model*, in a sense that if we use some shuffling scheme in cryptography, we do not have an infinite sequence of random numbers. In reality we must obtain them in a deterministic way, *e.g.*, from a private key or a salt (depending on applications). In our constructions, it depends on some salt s and some hash function H. The Algorithm 1 called RiffleShuffle$_H(n, s)$ takes as input a salt s, a hash function H and the number of elements n. It performs inverse Riffle Shuffle (with randomness obtained from salt s and hash function H) until above SST event occurs. Thus, its output is a random permutation of $\{1, \ldots, n\}$ (in the random-oracle model).

B   Parallel Attacks

In this section we formulate lemmas which are used to prove Lemma 4.

These lemmas follow directly the proof of parallel security of Catena presented in [8]. The proof technique is exactly the same as in [8] since RSG$_\lambda^k$ is a Superconcentrator. The only difference comes from the fact that each stack of Catena (Butterfly) is built out of $2g - 1$ layers while RSG$_\lambda^k$ is built from $2g$ layers. First, let us collect some observations on RSG$_\lambda^k$.

Lemma 7. *Let $\lambda, n \in \mathbb{N}^+$ such that $n = n'(2c\lambda + 1)$ where $n' = 2^c$ for some $c \in \mathcal{N}^+$. Then the Riffle Shuffle graph RSG$_\lambda^k$ consists of a stack λ sub-graphs such that the following holds.*

1. *The graph RSG$_\lambda^k$ has n nodes in total.*
2. *The graph RSG$_\lambda^k$ is built as a stack of λ sub-graphs $\{G_i\}_{i \in [\lambda]}$ each of which is a Superconcentrator. In the unique topological ordering of RSG$_\lambda^k$ denote the first and final n' nodes of each G_i as $L_{i,0}$ and $L_{i,1}$ respectively. Then there is a path running through all nodes in each $L_{i,1}$.*
3. *Moreover, for any $i \in [\lambda]$ and subsets $S \subset L_{i,0}$ and $T \subset L_{i,1}$ with $|S| = |T| = h \leq n'$ there exist h nodes-disjoint paths $p_1, \ldots, p_h$ of length $2c$ from S to T.*

Using Lemma 7 and following the proof of Lemma 6 in [8] we obtain the following lemma.

Lemma 8. *Let $\lambda, n \in \mathbb{N}^+$ be such that $n = n'(2\lambda c + 1)$ with $n' = 2^c$ for some $c \in \mathcal{N}^+$. Then it holds that RSG$_\lambda^k \in \mathcal{D}_{1,g}^{\lambda,n'}$ for $g = \lceil \sqrt{n'} \rceil$.*

The above Lemma 7 together with Theorem 4 imply Lemma 4.

References

1. Password Hashing Competition. https://password-hashing.net/
2. The Antminer S9 Bitcoin Miner - Bitmain. https://shop.bitmain.com/antminer_s9_asic_bitcoin_miner.htm

3. yescrypt - a Password Hashing Competition submission. Technical report (2014). https://password-hashing.net/submissions/specs/yescrypt-v2.pdf
4. Aldous, D., Diaconis, P.: Shuffling cards and stopping times. Am. Math. Mon. **93**(5), 333–348 (1986). http://www.jstor.org/stable/2323590
5. Aldous, D., Diaconis, P.: Strong uniform times and finite random walks. Adv. Appl. Math. **97**, 69–97 (1987)
6. Alwen, J., Blocki, J.: Efficiently computing data-independent memory-hard functions. In: Robshaw, M., Katz, J. (eds.) CRYPTO 2016. LNCS, vol. 9815, pp. 241–271. Springer, Heidelberg (2016). https://doi.org/10.1007/978-3-662-53008-5_9
7. Alwen, J., Blocki, J.: Towards practical attacks on Argon2i and balloon hashing. In: 2017 IEEE European Symposium on Security and Privacy (EuroS&P), pp. 142–157. IEEE, April 2017. http://ieeexplore.ieee.org/document/7961977/
8. Alwen, J., Blocki, J., Pietrzak, K.: Depth-robust graphs and their cumulative memory complexity. In: Coron, J.-S., Nielsen, J.B. (eds.) EUROCRYPT 2017. LNCS, vol. 10212, pp. 3–32. Springer, Cham (2017). https://doi.org/10.1007/978-3-319-56617-7_1
9. Alwen, J., Serbinenko, V.: High parallel complexity graphs and memory-hard functions. In: Proceedings of the Forty-Seventh Annual ACM on Symposium on Theory of Computing - STOC 2015, pp. 595–603. ACM Press, New York (2015). http://dl.acm.org/citation.cfm?doid=2746539.2746622
10. Biryukov, A., Dinu, D., Khovratovich, D.: Argon2: new generation of memory-hard functions for password hashing and other applications. In: 2016 IEEE European Symposium on Security and Privacy (EuroS&P), pp. 292–302. IEEE, March 2016. http://ieeexplore.ieee.org/document/7467361/
11. Boneh, D., Corrigan-Gibbs, H., Schechter, S.: Balloon hashing: a memory-hard function providing provable protection against sequential attacks. In: Cheon, J.H., Takagi, T. (eds.) ASIACRYPT 2016. LNCS, vol. 10031, pp. 220–248. Springer, Heidelberg (2016). https://doi.org/10.1007/978-3-662-53887-6_8
12. Bradley, W.F.: Superconcentration on a pair of butterflies, January 2017. http://arxiv.org/abs/1401.7263
13. Burt, K.: PKCS #5: password-based cryptography specification version 2.0. Technical report (2000). https://tools.ietf.org/html/rfc2898
14. Forler, C., Lucks, S., Wenzel, J.: Catena: a memory-consuming password-scrambling framework. citeseerx.ist.psu.edu/viewdoc/download?https://doi.org/10.1.1.437.9101&rep=rep1&type=pdf
15. Forler, C., Lucks, S., Wenzel, J.: The Catena Password-Scrambling Framework (2015). https://password-hashing.net/submissions/specs/Catena-v5.pdf
16. Lengauer, T., Tarjan, R.E.: Asymptotically tight bounds on time-space trade-offs in a pebble game. Journal of the ACM **29**(4), 1087–1130 (1982). http://portal.acm.org/citation.cfm?doid=322344.322354
17. Percival, C.: Stronger Key Derivation Via Sequential Memory-hard Functions. https://www.bsdcan.org/2009/schedule/attachments/87_scrypt.pdf
18. Pornin, T.: The MAKWA password hashing function specifications v1.1 (2015). http://www.bolet.org/makwa/makwa-spec-20150422.pdf
19. Simplicio, M.A., Almeida, L.C., Andrade, E.R., Dos Santos, P.C.F., Barreto, P.S.L.M.: Lyra2: password hashing scheme with improved security against time-memory trade-offs. https://eprint.iacr.org/2015/136.pdf

20. Wang, D., Cheng, H., Wang, P., Huang, X., Jian, G.: Zipf's law in passwords. IEEE Trans. Inf. Forensics Secur. **12**(11), 2776–2791 (2017). http://ieeexplore.ieee.org/document/7961213/
21. Wang, D., Zhang, Z., Wang, P., Yan, J., Huang, X.: Targeted online password guessing. In: Proceedings of the 2016 ACM SIGSAC Conference on Computer and Communications Security - CCS 2016, pp. 1242–1254. ACM Press, New York (2016). http://dl.acm.org/citation.cfm?doid=2976749.2978339

Privacy (II)

Practical Strategy-Resistant Privacy-Preserving Elections

Sébastien Canard[1], David Pointcheval[2,3], Quentin Santos[1,2,3(✉)], and Jacques Traoré[1]

[1] Orange Labs, Caen, France
quentin.santos@orange.com
[2] DIENS, École normale supérieure, CNRS, PSL University, Paris, France
[3] INRIA, Paris, France

Abstract. Recent advances in cryptography promise to let us run complex algorithms in the encrypted domain. However, these results are still mostly theoretical since the running times are still much larger than their equivalents in the plaintext domain. In this context, Majority Judgment is a recent proposal for a new voting system with several interesting practical advantages, but which implies a more involved tallying process than first-past-the-post voting. To protect voters' privacy, such a process needs to be done by only manipulating encrypted data.

In this paper, we then explore the possibility of computing the (ordered) winners in the Majority Judgment election without leaking any other information, using homomorphic encryption and multiparty computation. We particularly focus on the practicality of such a solution and, for this purpose, we optimize both the algorithms and the implementations of several cryptographic building blocks. Our result is very positive, showing that this is as of now possible to attain practical running times for such a complex privacy-protecting tallying process, even for large-scale elections.

1 Introduction

1.1 Motivation

Practical Cryptography. Homomorphic encryption allows running algorithms in a way that preserves the confidentiality of sensitive data, and thus, in a lot of practical use-cases, the privacy of some individuals. Fully homomorphic encryption permits to treat almost all applications in the encrypted domain, but is today too slow for practical use. Conversely, additively homomorphic encryption (such as in ElGamal and Paillier cryptosystems) is reasonably efficient, but, since an algorithm is, most of the time, not solely a combination of additions, practical uses typically involve a hybrid approach. In this case, part of the process is done in the encrypted domain, but some intermediate results are decrypted, and the final stages are realized in the clear. This approach can give reasonable

J. Lopez et al. (Eds.): ESORICS 2018, LNCS 11099, pp. 331–349, 2018.
https://doi.org/10.1007/978-3-319-98989-1_17

confidentiality while remaining very effective. But, for most of existing practical needs, there is today no possibility to obtain at the same time real-world performances and full confidentiality (without revealing any intermediate value).

Electronic Voting. Electronic voting concerns itself with the problem of giving voters strong guarantees regarding their own privacy, as well as the integrity of the whole election.

Referendums adapt very well to additively homomorphic encryption, since it then suffices to have voters encrypt 1 for "Yes" and 0 for "No", and then tally the ballots using homomorphic addition. It is moreover usually required that each voter provides a cryptographic proof that their ballot contains either 0 or 1 (without revealing which). First-past-the-post voting, where each voter selects a single candidate among several possible ones, and for which the candidate with the most votes wins, can be implemented in a similar fashion (but in less efficient way, since cryptographic proofs become more complicated).

Other voting systems such as Majority Judgment or Single Transferable Vote (STV) offer interesting properties, such as strategy-resistance, but are more complex, especially for the tallying phase. In both examples, one possibility is to homomorphically aggregate all the votes before decryption, and then perform the final steps in the clear. Although this approach is generally acceptable with relation with the confidentiality of the voters, it does reveal information such as the scores of all the candidates. But candidates who were eliminated may not want their exact scores to be known.

As a consequence, we explore in this paper the possibility of running such a voting system in a way that only reveals the winning candidate, or the ordered winners. As we will see, the related work in this domain (with such strong desired confidentiality property) is quite inexistent.

1.2   Related Work

Secure implementations of referendum and first-past-the-post voting have been regularly studied in cryptographic literature. In particular, [DK05] offers a solution for running referendums without revealing the exact count (only whether "Yes" or "No" won) that does not rely on MixNets or on any trusted server. As for strategy-resistant voting systems, [TRN08,BMN+09] explore the case of privacy-preserving STV using a mixing protocol. As far as we know, no such study nor implementation has been done for the Majority Judgment voting system.

1.3   Our Contributions

In this paper, we propose an implementation of the Majority Judgment voting system on a restricted set of logical gates, which we build using the Paillier cryptosystem so as to provide distributed trust, while keeping performance manageable. We then run benchmarks against our Python implementation based on the gmpy2 wrapper library.

$$
\text{Candidates} \begin{cases} \text{Alice} \\ \text{Bob} \\ \text{Charlie} \end{cases} \begin{matrix} + & \leftarrow \text{Grades} \rightarrow & - \\ A & B & C & D & E \\ \begin{pmatrix} 0 & 0 & 1 & 0 & 0 \\ 0 & 1 & 0 & 0 & 0 \\ 0 & 0 & 0 & 1 & 0 \end{pmatrix} \end{matrix} = \mathcal{B}_i
$$

Fig. 1. Single ballot: this voter attributes C to Alice, B to Bob and D to Charlie

We stress that our approach provides strong cryptographic guarantees regarding confidentiality and integrity of all the voters. Additionally, we support multi-seat elections, where several winners can be determined. All this is done without revealing any intermediate value while obtaining real-world practical results since, e.g., for 5 candidates and 1000 voters, the tallying phase works in less than 10 min to give the winner.

Additionally to the real voting application, we think that our work serves to show that it is really possible to use cryptography in a very conservative setting (revealing as little information as possible) while still being very practical (actually revealing the result in reasonable time). We hope it can help bridge the gap that continues to exist between theoretical cryptography (strong guarantees) and industrial practices (high efficiency) and encourage a more widespread use of cryptography to improve users' privacy in many applications.

2 Majority Judgment

2.1 Definition

Principle. Majority Judgment was presented by Michel Balinski and Rida Laraki in [BL07,BL10]: this is a voting mechanism that claims to improve the legitimacy of the elected candidates.

In Majority Judgment, each voter $\mathcal{V}_i$ attributes a grade to each candidate $\mathcal{C}_i$. Grades need not be numbers, but do need to be ordered (with a strict ordering, from the best to the worst grade, such as, e.g., from A to E). For this, the ballot is structured as a matrix where each row represents a candidate and each column represents a grade; the voter writes a 1 in the chosen grade for each candidate and 0 in other cells (See Fig. 1).

After summing all the votes into an Aggregate Matrix A, the median grade (or "majority-grade") of each candidate is computed: the median grade corresponds to the grade for which there are as many votes for worse grades as for better grades. The candidate with the best median grade is elected, or the candidate with the worst median grade is eliminated.

In Fig. 2, Alice and Bob have the same best median grade, C, and Charlie has the worst median grade, E. Charlie is eliminated, but we cannot yet decide the winner (here, all the candidates get the same total number of grades, so values can be seen as ratios).

Solving Ties. As in our above example, it is likely that several candidates get the same median grades. In that case, for these candidates, we consider the grades lower than the median grade and the grades greater than the median grade to make a decision. We construct the Tiebreak Matrix T by aggregating grades to the left and to the right of the median grade, see Fig. 3. To make a decision, the largest of these values is considered. If it pertains to the right column (many low grades), then the corresponding candidate is eliminated. If it pertains to the left column (many high grades), then the corresponding candidate wins.

More formally, from Balinski and Laraki, the result of each candidate can be summed up into a triplet (p, α, q) where α represents the majority-grade, p represents the ratio of votes above the candidate's majority-grade α, and q the ratio of those below. For any two candidates C_A and C_B with corresponding triplets (p_A, α_A, p_B) and (p_B, α_B, q_B), then C_A wins against C_B when one of the following (mutually exclusive) conditions is met:

1. $\alpha_A > \alpha_B$ (better median grade);
2. $\alpha_A = \alpha_B \wedge p_A > q_A \wedge p_B < q_B$ ("stronger"[1] median grade);
3. $\alpha_A = \alpha_B \wedge p_A > q_A \wedge p_B > q_B \wedge p_A > p_B$ (more secure median grade);
4. $\alpha_A = \alpha_B \wedge p_A < q_A \wedge p_B < q_B \wedge q_A < q_B$ (less insecure median grade).

This defines a total ordering on the candidates with high probability. Our goal is to output the names of the candidates according to this ordering.

We now consider a set of voters V_i, of candidates C_i and of authorities A_i (that will perform the counting). Our aim is to propose an implementation of Majority Judgment in the encrypted domain, in order to output the above ordering, but without leaking any additional information. For this purpose, we have to both find the suitable encryption scheme and provide the best possible description of such a voting system, so as to obtain the best possible privacy-preserving achievement for our problem.

Justification. As an electoral system, Majority Judgment gives the voters better incentives to simply vote for their preferred candidates rather than strategically vote for another candidate. For instance, in first-past-the-post voting, voters

$$
\text{Candidates} \begin{cases} \text{Alice} \\ \text{Bob} \\ \text{Charlie} \end{cases}
\begin{array}{ccccc}
+ & \leftarrow & \text{Grades} & \rightarrow & - \\
A & B & C & D & E
\end{array}
\left(\begin{array}{ccccc}
31 & 151 & \mathbf{529} & 254 & 35 \\
21 & 48 & \mathbf{442} & 301 & 188 \\
101 & 7 & 2 & 86 & \mathbf{804}
\end{array} \right) = A
$$

Fig. 2. Aggregate Matrix: each cell represents the number of voters who gave this grade to that candidate; in bold are the candidates' median grades.

---

[1] when $p > q$, the median grade is strong and noted α^+; when $p < q$, weak, noted α^-.

$$\begin{pmatrix} 31 + 151 & 254 + 35 \\ 21 + 48 & 301 + 188 \end{pmatrix} = \begin{pmatrix} 182 & 289 \\ 69 & \mathbf{489} \end{pmatrix} = T$$

Fig. 3. Tiebreak Matrix: candidates with equal median; the **largest value** rejects Bob.

select a single candidate on their ballots, and the candidates who was selected by the most voters wins the election; in this settings, voters are incentivized not to vote for lesser-known candidates, feeling like they are wasting their vote on a candidate with little chance of winning the election. This is partly addressed in two-round systems, where voters are given two opportunities to state their opinions: in the first round, they can vote for their favorite candidate, knowing that they will be able to express their preference between the candidates selected for the second round, who are usually among the most well-known ones.

However, even the two-round system remains imperfect, which translates in a restricted number of parties gathering most of the votes (usually two in the US, three in France). Several ranking systems propose to ameliorate this situation by allowing the voters to explicitly list their favorite candidates, ensuring that their opinion is take into account even when their first choice is eliminated. The most well-known such system is the Single Transferable Vote, also known as Instant-Runoff Voting for single-winner elections. However, this voting system is particularly complex as it requires each individual ballot to be considered potentially several times, usually by hand. Majority Judgment is a more recent proposal for a ranked voting system which allows to aggregate the ballots before counting.

By shifting the incentives of the voters away from strategic voting, such voting systems might improve the legitimacy of political and administrative elections by giving each voter the feeling that their opinion was fully taken into account, and potentially increase the turnout.

2.2   Removing Branching

At first sight, it may seem like an algorithm implementing Majority Judgment would require complex control flow with branching instructions (conditional structures and loops), depending on whether a candidate is eliminated or not. This would incur important overheads when evaluated in the encrypted domain (both branches must be computed). However, it is possible to devise a branchless algorithm without introducing such an important overhead.

Early Elimination of Candidates. The first remark is that we can avoid explicitly checking condition 1, but we can build the Tiebreak Matrix with just the best median grade. In the previous use-case, C is the best median grade (for Alice and Bob), which leads to the following Tiebreak Matrix

$$T = \begin{pmatrix} 31 + 151 & 254 + 35 \\ 21 + 48 & 301 + 188 \\ 101 + 7 & 86 + 804 \end{pmatrix} = \begin{pmatrix} 182 & 289 \\ 69 & 489 \\ 108 & \mathbf{892} \end{pmatrix}$$

Then Charlie gets eliminated, since he holds the highest number on the right column.

More generally, let W and L be candidates such that W wins against L by above condition 1 (e.g. $\alpha_W < \alpha_L$). Let us define p'_L (resp. q'_L) the ratio of votes for L that are better (resp. worse) than α_W (instead of α_L). Since $\alpha_W < \alpha_L$, $p'_L < 1/2 < q'_L$, but we also have $q_W < 1/2$, and thus $q_W < q'_L$. As a consequence, we only need to compute the p' and q' values, defined around the best median grade (rather than each candidate's median grade) and use the following (mutually exclusive) conditions to determine whether candidate $\mathcal{C}_A$ wins against candidate $\mathcal{C}_B$:

2'. $p'_A > q'_A \wedge p'_B < q'_B$;
3'. $p'_A > q'_A \wedge p'_B > q'_B \wedge p'_A > p'_B$;
4'. $p'_A < q'_A \wedge p'_B < q'_B \wedge q'_A < q'_B$.

Building the Tiebreak Matrix T. To build the Tiebreak Matrix T, we need to detect which elements are to the left (resp. right) of the best median grade. For this, we first compute the Candidate Matrix $C = (c_{i,j})$, such that $c_{i,j} = 1$ when column j represents a grade which is better than the candidate's median grade. From the Aggregate Matrix $A = (a_{i,j})$ (with the number of grades for each candidates), we want

$$c_{i,j} = \begin{cases} 1 & \text{if } 2 \times \sum_{k<j} a_{i,k} < \sum_k a_{i,k} \\ 0 & \text{otherwise.} \end{cases}$$

In our use-case, one gets the following Candidate Matrix C, where the zeroes in bold are first in their each line, and correspond to the median grade for each candidate:

$$C = \begin{pmatrix} 1 & 1 & \mathbf{0} & 0 & 0 \\ 1 & 1 & \mathbf{0} & 0 & 0 \\ 1 & 1 & 1 & 1 & \mathbf{0} \end{pmatrix}.$$

Then, we can compute the Grade Vector $G = (g_j)$, such that $g_j = 1$ when column j represents a grade which is greater than the global median grade. We can easily compute $G = (g_j)$ from $C = (c_{i,j})$ since $g_j = \wedge_i c_{i,j}$, where G and C are Boolean matrices, and 0 and 1 respectively represent False and True:

$$G = \begin{pmatrix} 1 & 1 & \mathbf{0} & 0 & 0 \end{pmatrix}.$$

Again, the first zero, in bold, corresponds to the global (the best) median grade.

Once we have this Grade Vector G, we can build the two columns of the Tiebreak Matrix $T = (t_{i,k})$, from the Aggregate Matrix $A = (a_{i,j})$, as:

$$t_{i,1} = \sum_{\substack{j \\ g_j = 1}} a_{i,j} \quad \text{and} \quad t_{i,2} = \sum_{\substack{j \\ g_{j-1} = 0}} a_{i,j}.$$

Note that the second column uses a shifted version of G to filter votes below the median grade. With the integer representation of Boolean, that can be written as $t_{i,1} = \sum_j g_j \times a_{i,j}$ and $t_{i,2} = \sum_j (1 - g_{j-1}) \times a_{i,j}$.

Identifying the Winner. Once we have built the Tiebreak Matrix $T = (t_{i,k})$, it only remains to reveal for each candidate the result of the following explicit Boolean formula, which selects the Winner:

$$w_i = \bigwedge_{\substack{j \\ j \neq i}} \begin{pmatrix} (t_{i,1} > t_{i,2} \wedge t_{j,1} < t_{j,2}) \\ \vee (t_{i,1} > t_{i,2} \wedge t_{j,1} > t_{j,2} \wedge t_{i,1} > t_{j,1}) \\ \vee (t_{i,1} < t_{i,2} \wedge t_{j,1} < t_{j,2} \wedge t_{i,2} < t_{j,2}) \end{pmatrix}$$

Notice that $w_i = 1$ when candidate i beats all the other candidates by either condition 2', 3' or 4', hence the definition for the Winner Vector $W = (w_i)$. Once W has been computed, we search the unique component equal to 1, identifying the elected candidate.

If one wants more than one winner, one can run again the above protocol, after having removed the line of the winner in the Candidate Matrix C. The computation has to be run again to generate G, T, and W, interactively for all the winners.

2.3 Expected Features for Encrypted Scheme

If we assume that the votes are encrypted, running the Majority Judgment algorithm means that we need to use an encryption scheme that allows the following operations (without knowing the decryption key):

- *addition of two plaintexts*, to compute the Aggregate Matrix A and the Tiebreak Matrix T;
- *comparison of two plaintexts*, to compute the Candidate Matrix C and the Winning Vector W;
- *AND/OR Boolean gate between two plaintexts*, to compute the Grade Vector G and the Winning Vector W;
- *multiplication of two plaintexts*, to compute the Tiebreak Matrix T.

Eventually, a distributed decryption of the Winning Vector W would provide the final result.

Notice that the operations required for computing the Tiebreak Matrix T actually only multiply some value by 0 or 1 (i.e. one operand is restricted to $\{0,1\}$, actually a Boolean). Indeed, multiplications are merely a conditional filter on the elements to be summed. We can thus relax our requirement from a full multiplication gate to a "*conditional gate*": $\mathsf{CondGate}(x,y) = x \times y$ for $y \in \{0,1\}$.

If we use an additively homomorphic encryption scheme, addition gives us the logical NOT gate, since $\neg x = 1 - x$ when 0 means False and 1 means True. Then, the conditional gate gives us the AND Boolean gate, as $x \wedge y = x \times y$. Eventually, these two gates let us construct the OR and XOR gates.

In the following, we will thus use an additively homomorphic encryption scheme, together with efficient Multi-Party Computation (MPC) protocols for distributed decryption, distributed evaluation of the conditional gate, and distributed comparison. As we will explain, multi-party computation necessitates in particular the use of some zero-knowledge proofs of correctness of the computed values. In the next section, we then give all the basic cryptographic material we will need for our solution.

3 Cryptographic Tools

3.1 Paillier Encryption Scheme

Our scheme relies on the Paillier encryption scheme [Pai99], for its additively homomorphic property, and the fact that distributed decryption can be efficiently done on arbitrary ciphertexts.

Let p and q be two large safe primes (so that $p = 2p'+1$ and $q = 2q'+1$ where p' and q' are also primes), set $n = pq$, $\varphi = 4p'q'$, $g = 1+n$, and $s = n^{-1} \bmod \varphi$. Then $\mathsf{pk} = (n, g)$ and $\mathsf{sk} = (\mathsf{pk}, s)$. The encryption/decryption algorithms work as follows, for $M \in \mathbb{Z}_n$.

- $\mathsf{Encrypt}(\mathsf{pk}, M)$: pick $r \xleftarrow{\$} \mathbb{Z}_n^*$, return $C = g^M r^n \bmod n^2$;
- $\mathsf{Decrypt}(\mathsf{sk}, C)$: compute $R = C^s \bmod n$, and return $M = \frac{(CR^{-n} \bmod n^2)-1}{n}$.

Indeed, since $g = 1+n$, $C = r^n \bmod n$, we can recover $R = C^s = r \bmod n$ and thus obtain M from $CR^{-n} = g^M = 1 + Mn \bmod n^2$.

This encryption scheme is well-known to be additively homomorphic, but it also allows efficient distributed decryption among the authorities, with a threshold: as explained in [Sho00], one can distribute s using a Shamir Secret Sharing mechanism, modulo $\varphi = 4p'q'$. Since $|n - \varphi| = 2(p' + q') + 1 < n^{1/2}$, a random element in $\mathbb{Z}_\varphi$ follows a distribution that is statistically indistinguishable from a random element in $\{0, \ldots, n-1\}$. Hence, one can choose a random polynomial P of degree $t - 1$ in $\mathbb{Z}_\varphi$ so that $P(0) = s = n^{-1} \bmod \varphi$, and set $s_i = P(i)$ for $i = 1, \ldots, k$, the k authorities. If less than t of these authorities collude, no information leaks about s, while any t of them can reconstruct Δs, where $\Delta = k!$, with

$$\lambda_i^S = \left(\prod_{j \in S \setminus \{i\}} j \right) \times \left(\frac{\Delta}{\prod_{j \in S \setminus \{i\}} (j - i)} \right)$$

since for any set S of t elements, $\sum_{i \in S} \lambda_i^S \cdot s_i = \Delta \cdot P(0) = \Delta \cdot s$. One should remark that the denominator divides $i!(k - i)!$, which in turns divides $\Delta = k!$, as noted in [Sho00]. Hence, λ_i^S is an integer.

Then, each authority $\mathcal{A}_i$ just has to compute $R_i = C^{s_i} \bmod n$, and the simple combination leads to R: with $R' = \prod_{i \in S} R_i^{\lambda_i^S} = C^{\Delta s}$, one has $R'^n = C^\Delta \bmod n$.

But Δ and n are relatively prime and so there exist u and v such that $un + v\Delta = 1$: $(C^u R'^v)^n = C \bmod n$. As a consequence, from the R_i's, anybody can compute

$$R = C^u \times \left(\prod_{i \in S} R_i^{\lambda_i^S} \right)^v \bmod n.$$

Then, any subset of t authorities can compute and publish R, which leads to $M = (CR^{-n} \bmod n^2 - 1)/n$.

This encryption scheme achieves indistinguishability against chosen-plaintext attacks (IND-CPA) under the High-Residuosity assumption, which claims that the following High-Residuosity problem is hard.

High-Residuosity Problem (HR). For an RSA modulus $n = pq$, the challenger chooses a random element $r_0 \xleftarrow{\$} \mathbb{Z}_{n^2}^*$, a random element $R \xleftarrow{\$} \mathbb{Z}_n^*$ and sets $r_1 = R^n \bmod n^2$, and eventually outputs r_b for a random bit b, the adversary has to guess b.

This also holds for the distributed decryption, when the authorities are honest-but-curious. To ensure correctness of the decryption values R_i, each authority $\mathcal{A}_i$ must prove that R_i is the result of the exponentiation of C to the power s_i.

3.2 Zero-Knowledge Proofs

In the following, we will have two kinds of proofs of equality of discrete logarithms: when the order of the group is known, and when the order of the group is not known.

Chaum-Pedersen Protocol [CP93]. Let G be a cyclic group of known order q, and κ the security parameter. To prove knowledge (or just existence) of $x \in \mathbb{Z}_q$ such that $y_1 = g_1^x$ and $y_2 = g_2^x$ for $g_1, g_2, y_1, y_2 \in G$, the prover $\mathcal{P}$ can proceed as follows with a verifier $\mathcal{V}$:

- $\mathcal{P}$ picks $u \xleftarrow{\$} \mathbb{Z}_q$ and sends commitments $t_1 \leftarrow g_1^u$ and $t_2 \leftarrow g_2^u$
- $\mathcal{V}$ sends a challenge $h \xleftarrow{\$} \mathbb{Z}_{2^\kappa}$
- $\mathcal{P}$ returns $w \leftarrow u - hx \bmod q$
- $\mathcal{V}$ checks that $g_1^w = t_1 y_1^{-h}$ and that $g_2^w = t_2 y_2^{-h}$.

This protocol is only known to be zero-knowledge when the verifier is honest. But one can make it non-interactive, in the random oracle model using the Fiat-Shamir heuristic [FS87, PS96].

Fiat-Shamir Heuristic [FS87, PS96]. The challenge can be replaced by the output of hash function (modeled as a random oracle), removing the interaction needed to obtain h, and thus making the proof non-interactive and fully zero-knowledge. Then, one can set $h = H(g_1, g_2, y_1, y_2, t_1, t_2)$, and the verifier can simply check whether $h = H(g_1, g_2, y_1, y_2, g_1^w y_1^h, g_2^w y_2^h)$. The proof just consists of the pair $(h, w) \in \mathbb{Z}_{2^\kappa} \times \mathbb{Z}_q$.

Girault-Poupard-Stern Protocol [GPS06]. After Girault's [Gir91] work, Poupard and Stern [PS98,PS99] studied the proof of knowledge of a discrete logarithm in groups of unknown order. It leads to a similar protocol as above, for the proof of equality of discrete logarithms, but with some margins: to prove knowledge (or just existence) of $x \in \mathbb{Z}_q$, for an unknown $q < Q$ with Q public, such that $y_1 = g_1^x$ and $y_2 = g_2^x$ for $g_1, g_2, y_1, y_2 \in G$, the prover $\mathcal{P}$ can proceed as follows with a verifier $\mathcal{V}$:

- $\mathcal{P}$ picks $u \xleftarrow{\$} \mathbb{Z}_{2^{2\kappa}Q}$ and sends commitments $t_1 \leftarrow g_1^u$ and $t_2 \leftarrow g_2^u$
- $\mathcal{V}$ sends a challenge $h \xleftarrow{\$} \mathbb{Z}_{2^\kappa}$
- $\mathcal{P}$ returns $w \leftarrow u - hx$
- $\mathcal{V}$ checks that $0 < w < 2^{2\kappa}Q$, and both $g_1^w = t_1 y_1^{-h}$ and $g_2^w = t_2 y_2^{-h}$.

Again, to make this proof non-interactive, one can set $h = H(g_1, g_2, y_1, y_2, t_1, t_2)$, and the verifier can simply check whether $h = H(g_1, g_2, y_1, y_2, g_1^w y_1^h, g_2^w y_2^h)$. The proof just consists of the pair $(h, w) \in \mathbb{Z}_{2^\kappa} \times \mathbb{Z}_{2^{2\kappa}Q}$.

Since w can fall outside the correct set, but with negligible probability, the verifier can just verify it, and re-start the proof when w is wrong.

3.3   Proofs of Valid Decryption

During the counting phase, the authorities have to provide a proof that they have properly decrypted some values. We here give some details on that cryptographic tool.

In fact, in the Paillier cryptosystem, the main operation of decryption is to raise the ciphertext to the secret power s_i. Let $C \in \mathbb{Z}_{n^2}^*$ be a ciphertext, $s_i \in \mathbb{Z}_\varphi$ be a secret exponent known to the prover $\mathcal{P}$ only (one authority $\mathcal{A}_i$ in our case); $\mathcal{P}$ must provide $R_i = C^{s_i} \bmod n$, and prove it. For this, one can use the above proof of equality of discrete logarithms, with a reference value $v_i = v^{s_i} \bmod n$, where v is a generator of Q_n, the cyclic group of the quadratic residues in $\mathbb{Z}_n^*$.

Now going to the threshold version, one can thus assume that when each prover/authority receives their secret s_i, the verification value $v_i = v^{s_i} \bmod n$ is published, with a public generator v. Since we need to work in a cyclic group, the prover will prove that the same exponent s_i has been used in

$$R_i^2 = (C^2)^{s_i} \bmod n \quad \text{and in} \quad v_i = v^{s_i} \bmod n.$$

Batch Proofs. We can reduce the cost of this protocol by batching the proofs of valid decryptions, when several decryptions are performed by the same prover on several ciphertexts, as done in [APB+04, Appendix C, pp. 15–16]. For several ciphertexts $(C_j)_j$, $\mathcal{P}$ first publishes the computations $R_j = C_j^s \bmod n$, for all j; then, the verifier $\mathcal{V}$ (or a hash function if using the Fiat-Shamir heuristic), generates a sequence of random scalars $\alpha_j \xleftarrow{\$} \mathbb{Z}_{2^\kappa}$ to build the aggregations $C^* = \prod_j C_j^{\alpha_j} \bmod n$ and $R^* = \prod_j R_j^{\alpha_j} \bmod n$. They should also satisfy $(R^*)^2 = (C^{*2})^{s_i} \bmod n$, which can be proven as above: $\log_v v_i = \log_{C^{*2}} R^{*2}$.

3.4   Proof of Private Multiplication

As explained above in the Majority Judgment description, the tallying process requires multiplication gates which, in the encrypted domain, should be evaluated privately, and in a provable manner. Then, an authority $\mathcal{A}_i$, acting as a prover $\mathcal{P}$, needs to provide a proof of private multiplication, which can be done as follows.

Let $x, y \in \mathbb{Z}_n$ and C_y an encryption of y. Let $\mathcal{P}$ be a prover (an authority in our case) knowing x and C_y. It computes C_z, an encryption of $x \times y \bmod n$, which can be done using private multiplication: $C_z = C_y^x r_z^n$ for $r_z \xleftarrow{\$} \mathbb{Z}_n^*$. Then, $\mathcal{P}$ must provide C_x and C_z to verifier $\mathcal{V}$ and prove that C_x, C_y, C_z are encryptions of some x, y, and z such that $z = x \times y \bmod n$. For this:

- $\mathcal{P}$ draws $u \xleftarrow{\$} \mathbb{Z}_n$, $r_u, r_{yu} \xleftarrow{\$} \mathbb{Z}_n^*$ and sends $C_u = g^u r_u^n \bmod n^2$ and $C_{yu} = C_y^u r_{yu}^n \bmod n^2$ to $\mathcal{V}$;
- $\mathcal{V}$ draws a challenge $e \xleftarrow{\$} \mathbb{Z}_{2^\kappa}$ and sends it to $\mathcal{P}$;
- $\mathcal{P}$ sends $w = u - xe \bmod n$, $r_w = r_u r_x^{-e} \bmod n$ and $r_{yw} = r_{yu} r_z^{-e} \bmod n$ to $\mathcal{V}$;
- $\mathcal{V}$ checks that $C_u = g^w r_w^n C_x^e \bmod n^2$ and $C_{yu} = C_y^w r_{yw}^n C_z^e \bmod n^2$.

This proof can be converted into a non-interactive zero-knowledge proof as above, using the Fiat-Shamir heuristic.

When several proofs have to be conducted in parallel, with the same x and multiple y_i, the above batch proof technique can be applied again, thanks to the linear property of the multiplication: $x \times (\sum_i \alpha_i y_i) = \sum_i \alpha_i (x \times y_i) \bmod n$. Unfortunately, it cannot be applied for independent pairs (x_i, y_i). In consequence, most of the running-time of our implementation is spent computing these proofs and verifying them.

4   Gate Evaluation with Multi-party Computation

We now present how to implement the operations listed in Subsect. 2.3 using MPC protocols.

- Decryption: this is a common operation in MPC protocols, and is also used by the other two protocols below;
- Conditional gate: this can be performed by randomizing the Boolean operand, decrypting it using the previous protocol, and then performing a private multiplication;
- Comparison: this is the most complex operation, which implies to first extract the bits of the operands (using masked decryption), and then performing a bitwise addition (using conditional gates).

As we will see, they can be turned into the malicious setting by additionally providing proofs of correct execution, which will essentially be proofs of equality of discrete logarithms, as already seen for the proof of valid (partial) decryption.

Input: C_x, the encryption of $x \in \mathbb{Z}_n$ and C_y, the encryption of $y \in \{-1, 1\}$
Output: C_z, the encryption of $z = x \times y$
foreach *authority* **do**

> $o \xleftarrow{\$} \{-1, 1\}$
> $C_x \leftarrow C_x{}^o$;   /* homomorphically compute encryption of $x \times o$ */
> $C_y \leftarrow C_y{}^o$;   /* homomorphically compute encryption of $y \times o$ */
> pass C_x, C_y to the next authority

end
$y \leftarrow \mathsf{Decrypt}(C_y)$
assert $y \in \{-1, 1\}$
return $C_z = C_x{}^y$;   /* homomorphically compute encryption of $x \times y$ */

Algorithm 1: CondGate: Conditional gate

4.1 Decryption Gate

As already seen in Subsect. 3.3, one must compute $R = C^s = r \bmod n$ in order to allow full decryption. And this can be performed when s has been distributed using a secret sharing scheme "à la Shamir". We do not detail more, since this just consists on one flow from each authority, even in the malicious setting, with non-interactive zero-knowledge proofs of valid exponentiation (see above).

4.2 Conditional Gate

Schoenmakers and Tuyls introduced the conditional gate in [ST04]. Given $x \in \mathbb{Z}_n$ and $y \in \{-1, 1\}$, this gates computes $x \times y$, which is thus either x or $-x \bmod n$. Although the second parameter is restricted to $\{-1, 1\}$, it is very easy to adapt this into a gate taking $y \in \{0, 1\}$ using the homomorphic property of the Paillier cryptosystem. Thus, it can be used to implement logical AND gates, as well as multiplications by a Boolean.

Conditional Gate. The idea is simply to mask y by a random element in $\{-1, 1\}$ before decrypting it; then, it is easy to compute $x \times y \bmod n$ using private multiplication. To mask y, each authority will in turn multiply it by either -1 or 1. They will also apply the same transformation on x to keep the product unchanged. The algorithm is presented on Algorithm 1, where the decryption of C_y is performed in a distributed way as shown before.

To ensure the security of this gate against malicious adversary, each authority must provide a proof of equality of discrete logarithm o in the exponentiation of C_x and C_y, and verify the proofs of the other authorities before decrypting the final result of the election. Note that, as explained in [ST04], it is not necessary to require proofs that $o \in \{-1, 1\}$ as long as C_y indeed eventually decrypts to $y \in \{-1, 1\}$. However, such proofs may be requested when the condition does not hold, so as to prune misbehaving authorities.

Mapping to $\{0, 1\}$. As said above, the conditional gate can be easily adapted to accept its second operand from $\{0, 1\}$ using the additive property: it allows to

Input: (C_{x_i}), the bitwise encryption of $x \in \mathbb{Z}_n$ and (y_i), the bitwise notation of
$y \in \mathbb{Z}_n$
Output: (C_{z_i}), the bitwise encryption of $z = x + y$
$C_c \leftarrow \mathsf{Encrypt}(0)$;   /* carry */
foreach *index i, from 0 — the least significant bit— ***do**
$\quad\Big|\quad C_{x_i \oplus y_i} \leftarrow C_{x_i} \times C_{y_i} \div C_{x_i}^{2y_i}$;   /* $x_i \oplus y_i = x_i + y_i - 2x_i y_i$ */
$\quad\Big|\quad C_{z_i} \leftarrow C_{x_i \oplus y_i} \times C_c \div \mathsf{CondGate}(C_{x_i \oplus y_i}, C_c)^2$;   /* $(x_i \oplus y_i) \oplus c$ */
$\quad\Big|\quad C_c \leftarrow (C_{x_i} \times C_{y_i} \times C_c \div C_{z_i})^{\frac{n+1}{2}}$;   /* $(x_i + y_i + c - z_i)/2$ */
end
return (C_{z_i})
$\qquad\qquad$ **Algorithm 2:** PrivateAddGate: Private Addition Gate

convert the ciphertext C_y of y into a ciphertext of $2y - 1$. This leads to C_z being a ciphertext of $z = 2xy - x$. Using C_x, the ciphertext of x, one can additively get the ciphertext of $2xy$, which one can multiply by $2^{-1} \bmod n$ to get a ciphertext of xy.

4.3 Greater-Than Gate

Comparing two integers is done by evaluating a classical comparison circuit on their bitwise encryptions (each of their bit encrypted separately). Converting a scalar encryption of an integer into its bitwise encryption is performed by the bit-extraction gate.

Conceptually, the bit-extraction gate works as follows: one first masks the input integer, decrypts the result, encrypts the individual bits of this result, and then applies a binary addition circuit to unmask the bitwise encryption. Note that this binary addition circuit will take the masking operand into its unencrypted form, since it saves several executions of the conditional gate.

Private Addition Gate. The private addition gate is used to unmask an encrypted value. In the following algorithm (Algorithm 2), x_i is known as an encrypted value C_{x_i}, while y_i is a plaintext value. Knowing y_i, we can trivially compute encryptions C_{y_i} for homomorphic operations.

We note that [DFK+06, Section 6, pp. 13–15] offers a constant round circuit for addition (both operands encrypted). However, the constant is 37. Having one operand in the clear let us avoid interactions in line 1 of CARRIES (using private multiplications), bringing this constant down to 36. In contrast, our straightforward private addition gate implies ℓ rounds for up to $2^\ell - 1$ votes. In most practical cases, we expect $\ell < 36$, so using the constant round version is not preferable in our practical use case.

Bit-Extraction Gate. From this private addition gate, Schoenmakers and Tuyls propose a method to extract the bits of an integer encrypted with the Paillier cryptosystem [ST06, LSBs gate]. The general idea is to create a mask

Input: C_x, the encryption of $x \in \mathbb{Z}_n$
Output: (C_{x_i}), the bitwise encryption of x
```
/* C_y is the encryption of y ←$ Z_n, and (C_yi) of the bits yi    */
/* Mask C_x with C_y, decrypt it into z, reencrypt bitwise, unmask */
```
$C_z \leftarrow C_x \div C_y$;   /* $z = x - y$ */
$z \leftarrow \mathsf{DecryptGate}(C_z)$;   /* as relative number in $[-n/2, n/2]$ */
$(C_{x_i}) \leftarrow \mathsf{PrivateAddGate}((C_{y_i}), (z_i))$;   /* $(x_i) = (y_i) + (z_i)$ */
return (C_{x_i})

Algorithm 3: BitExtractGate: Bit Extraction Gate

whose scalar and bitwise encryptions are both known, apply it to the scalar input, and then remove it bitwise after reencryption.

To generate the mask, two more protocols are used to generate encrypted random integers and encrypted random bits. We skip the details of these protocols since they can be executed in the precomputation step. Details can be found in [ST06]. See Algorithm 3.

Greater-Than Gate. Using the conditional gate, we can compare two integers given as bitwise encryptions (C_{x_i}) and (C_{y_i}). For this, we can use the comparison circuit from [ST04], which evaluates $t_{i+1} \leftarrow (1 - (x_i - y_i)^2)t_i + x_i(1 - y_i)$, starting from $t_0 = 0$. See Algorithm 4.

Input: (C_{x_i}), (C_{y_i}) the bitwise encryptions of $x, y \in \mathbb{Z}_n$
Output: $C_{x>y}$, encryption of 1 if $x > y$, and 0 otherwise
$C_t \leftarrow \mathsf{Encrypt}(0)$;   /* temporary result */
foreach *index i, from 0 — the least significant bit— **do***
    $C_{x_i \wedge y_i} \leftarrow \mathsf{CondGate}(C_{x_i}, C_{y_i})$
    $C_a \leftarrow C_1 \div C_{x_i} \div C_{y_i} \times C_{x_i \wedge y_i}{}^2$;   /* $1 - (x_i - y_i)^2$ */
    $C_b \leftarrow \mathsf{CondGate}(C_a, C_t)$;   /* $(1 - (x_i - y_i)^2)t_i$ */
    $C_t \leftarrow C_b \times C_{x_i} \div C_{x_i \wedge y_i}$;   /* $(1 - (x_i - y_i)^2)t_i + x_i(1 - y_i)$ */
end
return C_t

Algorithm 4: GTGate: Greater-Than Gate

We note that [DFK+06] also offers a constant round circuit for comparison. However, the constant is 19, which is not necessarily lower than the number of bits required in our use-case.

5   Implementation

5.1   Encryption of the Ballots

We remind a voter that attributes C to Alice, B to Bob and D to Charlie will cast a ballot as shown on Fig. 1, which consists of a series of 0 and 1, with exactly one 1 per row. To participate in our secure version of an election using Majority Judgment, a voter encrypts their ballot element-wise and provides zero-knowledge proofs that each element is either 0 or 1 (OR-proof), and that there is one 1 per row (for instance, prove that the sum of each row decrypts to 1).

From this, it is easy to assemble the Aggregate Matrix A. A purely additively homomorphic implementation would decrypt A at this point and then proceed in the clear, assuming that aggregating the votes together provides adequate confidentiality. In our implementation however, we implement the approach described in Subsect. 2.2.

5.2 Avoiding Final Logical Gates

Notice that, since we use 0 and 1 to represent our Boolean values, $\bigvee_i x_i \Leftrightarrow \sum x_i \neq 0$ for any Boolean values (x_i). We can apply this remark to avoid evaluating the last part of the Boolean circuit on the negation of w_i:

$$w_i = \bigvee_{j \neq i} \left(\begin{array}{l} \neg(t_{i,1} > t_{i,2} \wedge t_{j,1} < t_{j,2}) \\ \wedge \neg(t_{i,1} > t_{i,2} \wedge t_{j,1} > t_{j,2} \wedge t_{i,1} > t_{j,1}) \\ \wedge \neg(t_{i,1} < t_{i,2} \wedge t_{j,1} < t_{j,2} \wedge t_{i,2} < t_{j,2}) \end{array} \right)$$

Thus, we can instead compute the Losing Vector $L = (\ell_i)$ as

$$\ell_i = \sum_{j \neq i} \left(\begin{array}{l} \neg(t_{i,1} > t_{i,2} \wedge t_{j,1} < t_{j,2}) \\ \wedge \neg(t_{i,1} > t_{i,2} \wedge t_{j,1} > t_{j,2} \wedge t_{i,1} > t_{j,1}) \\ \wedge \neg(t_{i,1} < t_{i,2} \wedge t_{j,1} < t_{j,2} \wedge t_{i,2} < t_{j,2}) \end{array} \right)$$

and test whether $\ell_i = 0$ or not. For this, each authority multiplies it by a secret non-zero value before decryption in order to hide the non-zero values.

5.3 Summary

We reproduce below the full protocol for evaluating Majority Judgment in the encrypted domain (See Algorithm 5). To improve readability, we note $\mathsf{CondGate}(x_i)$ the fact of reducing (x_i) through $\mathsf{CondGate}$ (depth can be reduced by using a binary tree).

To make the protocol secure against malicious adversary, we use cryptographic proofs in the basic gates, as detailed in Subsects. 4.1 and 4.2 and when randomizing ℓ_i. Since all participants will execute the same protocol in parallel, they can reproduce all the other steps and ensure the consistency of the computation. The verifications of these proofs need not be done synchronously, but they must be finished before the final result is decrypted (which actually reveals information).

Remark 1. After candidate $\mathcal{C}_W$ is elected, it is possible to reveal the next candidate by removing the line W of A and repeating the algorithm. This allows for multi-seat elections, but does reveal the order of the elected candidates.

Input: encrypted Aggregate Matrix $(C_{a_{i,j}})$
Output: index of elected candidate
```
/* Candidate matrix ci,j = Σk<j ai,k < ½ × Σk ai,k                      */
```
$$C_{c_{i,j}} \leftarrow \mathsf{GTGate}(\textstyle\prod_k C_{a_{i,k}}, (\prod_{1 \leq k \leq j} C_{a_{i,k}})^2)$$
```
/* Grade vector gj = ∧i ci,j                                            */
```
$$C_{g_j} \leftarrow \mathsf{CondGate}(C_{c_{i,j}})$$
```
/* Tiebreak matrix left column ti,1 = Σj gj × ai,j                      */
```
$$C_{t_{i,1}} \leftarrow \textstyle\prod_j \mathsf{CondGate}(C_{a_{i,j}}, C_{g_j})$$
```
/* Tiebreak matrix right column ti,2 = Σj(1 − gj−1) × ai,j             */
```
$$C_{t_{i,2}} \leftarrow \textstyle\prod_j \mathsf{CondGate}(C_{a_{i,j}}, (C_1 \div C_{g_{j-1}}))$$
```
/* Each assignment maps to an inner parenthesis of li                   */
```
$$C_{p^1_{i,j}} \leftarrow \mathsf{CondGate}(\mathsf{GTGate}(C_{t_{i,1}}, C_{t_{i,2}}), \mathsf{GTGate}(C_{t_{j,2}}, C_{t_{j,1}}))$$
$$C_{p^2_{i,j}} \leftarrow \mathsf{CondGate}(\mathsf{GTGate}(C_{t_{i,1}}, C_{t_{i,2}}), \mathsf{GTGate}(C_{t_{j,1}}, C_{t_{j,2}}), \mathsf{GTGate}(C_{t_{i,1}}, C_{t_{j,1}}))$$
$$C_{p^3_{i,j}} \leftarrow \mathsf{CondGate}(\mathsf{GTGate}(C_{t_{i,2}}, C_{t_{i,1}}), \mathsf{GTGate}(C_{t_{j,2}}, C_{t_{j,1}}), \mathsf{GTGate}(C_{t_{j,2}}, C_{t_{i,2}}))$$
```
/* Losing Vector li = Σj≠i ¬p¹i,j ∧ ¬p²i,j ∧ ¬p³i,j                     */
```
$$C_{\ell_i} \leftarrow \textstyle\prod_{j \neq i} \mathsf{CondGate}(C_1 \div C_{p^1_{i,j}}, C_1 \div C_{p^2_{i,j}}, C_1 \div C_{p^3_{i,j}})$$

foreach *authority* **do**
> $o \xleftarrow{\$} \mathbb{Z}_n$
> $C_{\ell_i} \leftarrow C_{\ell_i}^o$

end
$\ell_i \leftarrow \mathsf{DecryptGate}(C_{\ell_i})$
return unique i such that $\ell_i = 0$

Algorithm 5: Full Protocol

5.4 Optimizations

Batching. As noted previously when discussing the theoretical aspects of zero-knowledge proofs, it is possible to batch certain operations to reduce the total number of modular exponentiations that are performed in the protocol. To take full advantage of this, we have designed our software implementation to batch operations as much as possible. To be more specific, each gate was implemented in a "batch" version, where it receives a list of inputs to process; instead of processing these inputs sequentially, it can group them as much as possible when calling other "batch" gates. At the lowest level are the proofs of valid decryption and the proofs of private multiplication which actually take advantage of this batching.

Pipelining. The multi-party computation gates presented above target theoretical metrics such as a low number of exchanged messages or a low circuit depth. However, during implementation, more practical considerations must also be taken into account.

For instance, during the main loop of the conditional gate, only one authority is active at any given time, since they must wait for the previous authorities to provide them with the inputs. Since this operation is one of the most frequent

	3 candidates	5 candidates
Up to $2^{10} - 1$ voters	4' 26"	09' 53"
Up to $2^{20} - 1$ voters	8' 53"	19' 05"

Fig. 4. Time to tally the ballots for 3 authorities and 5 possible grades, all run on a single computer with two physical CPU cores (i5-4300U)

ones during the execution of the protocol (almost as frequent as decryption), a straightforward implementation would imply that most of the runtime would be spent waiting for input.

However, we can virtually erase idle CPU time by exploiting pipelining: as shown previously, executions the conditional gate can be batched together. Although it is not possible to batch the multiplication proofs used during this operation, we can exploit this. For this, we remark that the order in which the values circulate among the authorities is of no importance. It only matters that each authority has the opportunity to negate each value. Thus, for α authorities, we can split the batch in α sub-batches, give one sub-batch to each authority, and then have the authorities consider each sub-batch in turn. This approach reduces most of the idle time due to the sequential nature of this operation.

5.5 Benchmarks

We implemented this protocol in Python using the gmpy2 library (GMP's powmod is faster than CPython's pow). In contrast to a real-life implementation, we have all communications go through a central point of coordination (but confidentiality and integrity do not rely on it), and we use a simpler secret sharing. Run times are shown in Fig. 4. They should be improved when using several CPU cores for each node, but we are below 20 min for electing one candidate among 5 by more than 1 million of voters! Our implementation can as of now be truly used in a real-world election.

These do not include the encryption (on each voter's computer), verification of the ballots, nor their aggregation into $(C_{a_{i,j}})$ (assumed to be done on-the-fly).

Acknowledgments. This work was supported in part by the European Research Council under the European Community's Seventh Framework Programme (FP7/2007-2013 Grant Agreement no. 339563 – CryptoCloud).

References

[APB+04] Aditya, R., Peng, K., Boyd, C., Dawson, E., Lee, B.: Batch verification for equality of discrete logarithms and threshold decryptions. In: Jakobsson, M., Yung, M., Zhou, J. (eds.) ACNS 2004. LNCS, vol. 3089, pp. 494–508. Springer, Heidelberg (2004). https://doi.org/10.1007/978-3-540-24852-1_36

[BL07] Balinski, M., Laraki, R.: A theory of measuring, electing, and ranking. Proc. Natl. Acad. Sci. **104**(21), 8720–8725 (2007)

[BL10] Balinski, M., Laraki, R.: Majority Judgment: Measuring Ranking and Electing. MIT Press, Cambridge (2010)

[BMN+09] Benaloh, J., Moran, T., Naish, L., Ramchen, K., Teague, V.: Shufflesum: coercion-resistant verifiable tallying for STV voting. IEEE Trans. Inf. Forensics Secur. **4**(4), 685–698 (2009)

[CP93] Chaum, D., Pedersen, T.P.: Wallet databases with observers. In: Brickell, E.F. (ed.) CRYPTO 1992. LNCS, vol. 740, pp. 89–105. Springer, Heidelberg (1993). https://doi.org/10.1007/3-540-48071-4_7

[DFK+06] Damgård, I., Fitzi, M., Kiltz, E., Nielsen, J.B., Toft, T.: Unconditionally secure constant-rounds multi-party computation for equality, comparison, bits and exponentiation. In: Halevi, S., Rabin, T. (eds.) TCC 2006. LNCS, vol. 3876, pp. 285–304. Springer, Heidelberg (2006). https://doi.org/10.1007/11681878_15

[DK05] Desmedt, Y., Kurosawa, K.: Electronic voting: starting over? In: Zhou, J., Lopez, J., Deng, R.H., Bao, F. (eds.) ISC 2005. LNCS, vol. 3650, pp. 329–343. Springer, Heidelberg (2005). https://doi.org/10.1007/11556992_24

[FS87] Fiat, A., Shamir, A.: How to prove yourself: practical solutions to identification and signature problems. In: Odlyzko, A.M. (ed.) CRYPTO 1986. LNCS, vol. 263, pp. 186–194. Springer, Heidelberg (1987). https://doi.org/10.1007/3-540-47721-7_12

[Gir91] Girault, M.: An identity-based identification scheme based on discrete logarithms modulo a composite number. In: Damgård, I.B. (ed.) EUROCRYPT 1990. LNCS, vol. 473, pp. 481–486. Springer, Heidelberg (1991). https://doi.org/10.1007/3-540-46877-3_44

[GPS06] Girault, M., Poupard, G., Stern, J.: On the fly authentication and signature schemes based on groups of unknown order. J. Cryptol. **19**(4), 463–487 (2006)

[Pai99] Paillier, P.: Public-key cryptosystems based on composite degree residuosity classes. In: Stern, J. (ed.) EUROCRYPT 1999. LNCS, vol. 1592, pp. 223–238. Springer, Heidelberg (1999). https://doi.org/10.1007/3-540-48910-X_16

[PS96] Pointcheval, D., Stern, J.: Security proofs for signature schemes. In: Maurer, U. (ed.) EUROCRYPT 1996. LNCS, vol. 1070, pp. 387–398. Springer, Heidelberg (1996). https://doi.org/10.1007/3-540-68339-9_33

[PS98] Poupard, G., Stern, J.: Security analysis of a practical "on the fly" authentication and signature generation. In: Nyberg, K. (ed.) EUROCRYPT 1998. LNCS, vol. 1403, pp. 422–436. Springer, Heidelberg (1998). https://doi.org/10.1007/BFb0054143

[PS99] Poupard, G., Stern, J.: On the fly signatures based on factoring. In: ACM CCS 1999, pp. 37–45. ACM Press, November 1999

[Sho00] Shoup, V.: Practical threshold signatures. In: Preneel, B. (ed.) EUROCRYPT 2000. LNCS, vol. 1807, pp. 207–220. Springer, Heidelberg (2000). https://doi.org/10.1007/3-540-45539-6_15

[ST04] Schoenmakers, B., Tuyls, P.: Practical two-party computation based on the conditional gate. In: Lee, P.J. (ed.) ASIACRYPT 2004. LNCS, vol. 3329, pp. 119–136. Springer, Heidelberg (2004). https://doi.org/10.1007/978-3-540-30539-2_10

[ST06] Schoenmakers, B., Tuyls, P.: Efficient binary conversion for paillier encrypted values. In: Vaudenay, S. (ed.) EUROCRYPT 2006. LNCS, vol. 4004, pp. 522–537. Springer, Heidelberg (2006). https://doi.org/10.1007/11761679_31

[TRN08] Teague, V., Ramchen, K., Naish, L.: Coercion-resistant tallying for STV voting. In: 2008 USENIX/ACCURATE Electronic Voting Workshop, EVT 2008, 28–29 July 2008, San Jose, CA, USA, Proceedings (2008)

Formal Analysis of Vote Privacy Using Computationally Complete Symbolic Attacker

Gergei Bana[1]($\boxtimes$), Rohit Chadha[2]($\boxtimes$), and Ajay Kumar Eeralla[2]($\boxtimes$)

[1] University of Luxembourg, Luxembourg City, Luxembourg
gergei.bana@uni.lu
[2] University of Missouri, Columbia, USA
chadhar@missouri.edu, ae266@mail.missouri.edu

Abstract. We analyze the FOO electronic voting protocol in the provable security model using the technique of Computationally Complete Symbolic Attacker (CCSA). The protocol uses commitments, blind signatures and anonymous channels to achieve vote privacy. Unlike the Dolev-Yao analyses of the protocol, we assume neither perfect cryptography nor existence of perfectly anonymous channels. Our analysis reveals new attacks on vote privacy, including an attack that arises due to the inadequacy of the blindness property of blind signatures and not due to a specific implementation of anonymous channels. With additional assumptions and modifications, we were able to show that the protocol satisfies vote privacy in the sense that switching votes of two honest voters is undetectable to the attacker. Our techniques demonstrate effectiveness of the CCSA technique for both attack detection and verification.

1 Introduction

The FOO protocol was introduced by Fujioka, Okamoto, and Ohta in [1]. It was one of the first protocols for large-scale secure electronic voting. The design was supposed to achieve fairness, eligibility, vote privacy and individual verifiability. Since it's publication, it has been the subject of several attempts to formalize and verify its security properties. The focus of this paper is the formal analysis of vote privacy of FOO, namely, the property that the votes of honest voters cannot be linked to the voters. There are more modern protocols nowadays such as [2,3]. We chose FOO because of its abstract formulation, which make it convenient for symbolic analysis and its numerous phases which makes it prone to attacks.

Gergei Bana was partially supported by the ERC Consolidator Grant CIRCUS (683032) and by the National Research Fund (FNR) of Luxembourg under the PolLux project VoteVerif (POLLUX-IV/1/2016). Rohit Chadha was partially supported by NSF CNS 1314338 and NSF CNS 1553548. Ajay Kumar Eeralla was partially supported by NSF CNS 1314338.

J. Lopez et al. (Eds.): ESORICS 2018, LNCS 11099, pp. 350–372, 2018.
https://doi.org/10.1007/978-3-319-98989-1_18

As far as we are aware of, the FOO protocol was the first electronic voting protocol that was formally specified and analyzed [4]. In the seminal work of Kremer and Ryan [4], both the formalization and analysis of the FOO protocol was carried out in the Dolev-Yao (DY) attacker model using the applied pi-framework [5]. The vote privacy property was the most intricate property analyzed in [4], and Kremer and Ryan were only able to prove vote privacy by hand. Subsequent development in DY verification allowed the proof to carried out automatically [6,7]. As the DY model makes the assumption of perfect cryptography, the question of whether the proof carries over in the provable security model (computational model) remained unanswered.

In this paper, we formally verify vote privacy in the provable security framework, using symbolic verification techniques. In particular, we use the computationally complete symbolic attacker technique for indistinguishability properties introduced by Bana and Comon in [8] (a.k.a. CCSA framework). As far as we know, this is the first formal analysis of FOO protocol in the provable security model. Besides proving vote privacy for FOO, our other aim is to further develop the library of axioms of the CCSA framework and to demonstrate its effectiveness in attack detection and verification.

CCSA technique was first introduced by Bana and Comon in [9] for reachability properties and then for indistinguishability properties in [8]. Since then it has been used to find new attacks to the Needham-Schroeder-Lowe protocol [10,11]; to treat algebraic operations notoriously difficult to reason about in the DY model, such as exponentiation along with it the decisional Diffie-Hellmann property and versions of the Diffie-Hellman key-exchange protocol [12]; to verify unlinkability of RFID protocols [13]; and to analyze key wrapping API's [14]. Automated tool is not yet available for the indistinguishability technique, but work is in progress. In the meantime, we continue developing the library of axioms, and verifying relatively simple protocols by hand.

FOO protocol assumes two election authorities: administrator and collector. The protocol proceeds in three phases: In the first phase, voters prepare their ballots in the form of a trapdoor commitment of their votes and obtain a blind signature on the ballots from the administrator indicating that they are eligible to vote. In the second, voters send their ballots to the collector using an anonymous channel who publishes them on a public bulletin board (BB). In the final phase, each voter verifies the presence of their ballots on the BB and then sends their trapdoor key along with the entry number of their commitment on bulletin board to the collector, again via an anonymous channel. The trapdoor keys are then also added to the bulletin board next to the commitments. After the votes finish, votes are tallied from BB. The creators of the FOO protocol did not specify how the anonymous channels are implemented. In our modeling, we model anonymous channel as a mix-net server [15] which, upon receiving a list of encrypted messages outputs their plaintexts in lexicographic order after decrypting them.

FOO protocol is designed to provide vote privacy even when the administrator and collector are corrupt and our analysis of vote privacy assumes this to be the case. As in [4,16,17], vote privacy is modeled as indistinguishability of two protocol executions: in one, honest voter A votes for candidate v_1 and honest voter B votes for candidate v_2 and in the other, honest voter A votes for candidate v_2 and honest voter B votes for candidate v_1. Observe that, as stated above, FOO protocol does not satisfy vote privacy as the attacker may choose to forward only Alice's trapdoor key in the final phase of the protocol to the mix-net server. We argue that privacy of votes can never be guaranteed for any voting protocol if the attacker allows only one participant to complete the protocol. Hence, our formalization is carefully crafted to avoid these cases.

Our analysis revealed new attacks on the FOO protocol (See Sect. 3.2). The first attack occurs because of an inadequacy of blindness property of blind signatures. Intuitively, blindness [18] means that a dishonest signer who engages in two sessions (parallel or sequential) with an honest user on messages m_0 and m_1 cannot detect which session is for m_0 and which session is for m_1 if the user successfully outputs signatures in *both* sessions. The blindness property, however, does allow the possibility that the attacker can distinguish between the sessions if the user is successful in only one session. In order to prevent this attack, we have to assume that the identities of the candidates are of equal length. This attack does not depend on the implementation of the anonymous channel. The second attack exploits the fact that encryption scheme used by the mix-net server may be length-revealing and hence the length of the encrypted messages to the mix-net server may reveal their senders. In order to prevent this, we have to assume that the signatures obtained on *equal length* messages by executing the blind signature interactive protocol with the *same* signer must be of equal length. The above two attacks lie outside the DY model and hence were not detected in previous works on formal analysis of FOO protocol. A third attack is a DY style replay attack in which messages from the Voting phase can be replayed in the Opening phase. This attack can be prevented by introducing phase numbers in the FOO protocol.

With these additional assumptions, we establish vote privacy of the FOO protocol for one session with two honest voters and one dishonest voter. The proof carries over to n dishonest voters for any fixed n. The proof of vote privacy rests on the blindness property of the blind signature, the computational hiding property of the trapdoor commitments and of IND-CCA2 assumption on the encryption used in the anonymizing mechanism. The proof of vote privacy in the DY model, in contrast, relies only on the blindness property.[1] The commitment hiding property of trapdoor commitments does not play a role in establishing vote privacy in the DY analysis.

Related Work. There have been several attempts at formal analysis of FOO protocol in the DY model (see, for example, [4,6,7]). These analyses assume perfectly anonymous channels. In the computational model, there are several attempts at formalizing vote privacy in electronic voting such as in [16,17,19,20].

---

[1] As evidence, we ran AKiSs [7] on a two-phase variant of the FOO protocol without commitments. The variant satisfies the vote privacy property in the DY model.

Please see [20] for a comparison amongst these definitions. All these definitions apply to single phase voting protocols. Our definition is adapted to FOO-protocol which has three phases. The only other work at formally verifying vote privacy for electronic voting that we are aware of is the mechanized proof of vote privacy for the Helios family of single-phase protocols given in [21]. The inadequacy of the blindness axiom has also been pointed out in [22] who show how any blind signature scheme can be combined with trapdoor commitments to resolve this inadequacy.

2   FOO Voting Protocol and Its Computational Modeling

We briefly recall the electronic voting protocol FOO introduced by Fujioka, Okamoto, and Ohta in [1]. We assume that the reader is familiar with the crypto-graphic primitives of public key encryption, trapdoor commitment schemes and digital signatures schemes. The FOO protocol also uses blind signature schemes. Informally, a blind signature scheme is an interactive protocol that allows a party $\mathcal{U}$ to obtain the signature of a party $\mathcal{S}$ on a message that is obfuscated by $\mathcal{U}$ until $\mathcal{S}$ completes the protocol and $\mathcal{U}$ publishes the signed message. We assume as in [23,24] that the interactive protocol consists of three phases: blinding by $\mathcal{U}$, (blind) signing by $\mathcal{S}$ and unblinding by $\mathcal{U}$. The primitives are described in detail in Sect. 2.2.

The FOO protocol has three roles: voters (V_i), administrator (A), and collector (C). It assumes the existence of anonymous channels. Following Kremer et al. [4], we group the (original) protocol in three phases, Authentication, Voting, and Opening, as described in Fig. 1. In the Figure, $\rightarrow$ means send, $\dashrightarrow$ means send via anonymous channel.

2.1   Anonymous Channel

The creators of FOO did not specify how to implement anonymous channels. We model anonymous communication using a mix-net server which, upon receiving a list of messages encrypted with its public key, checks if they are all distinct, decrypts each message in the list, outputs them in lexicographic order. Hence-forth, we refer to mix-net server as the mixer. In particular, in the Voting phase (resp. Opening phase), the voter encrypts $\langle c_i, \sigma_A(c_i) \rangle$ (resp. $\langle l_i, k_i \rangle$) with the mixer M's public key pk_M. The mixer waits until a certain time during which receives the messages from the voters, checks if all messages received until that time are distinct. If the check succeeds, the mixer decrypts the messages, shuffles the decrypted messages into lexicographic order and outputs them.

2.2   Computational Modeling of the FOO Protocol

As usual, we assume that all agents in the protocol execution, the voters, the administrator, the collector are interactive probabilistic polynomial-time Turing (PPT) machines. Furthermore, the network is controlled by an attacker, which

Authentication :

1 : V_i : computes $c_i := \xi(v_i, k_i)$, a commitment on her vote v_i with trapdoor k_i, $b_i := \chi(c_i, r_i)$,
blinding the ballot c_i with blinding key r_i, and $s_i := \text{sign}_i(b_i)$, a signature on b_i

2 : $V_i \rightarrow A : \langle ID_i, b_i, s_i \rangle$

3 : A : verifies the signature s_i and eligibility (not yet applied for his signature) of V_i

4 : $A \rightarrow V_i : \text{bsign}_A(b_i)$, (blind) signature of A on the blinded ballot b_i

Voting :

5 : V_i : checks if the received message is A's blind signature on b_i; if the check
passes, V_i unblinds the signature and it is denoted by $\sigma_A(c_i)$

6 : $V_i \dashrightarrow C : \langle c_i, \sigma_A(c_i) \rangle$

7 : C : verifies the signature, and adds the received message to Bulletin Board (BB) with label ℓ_i

8 : C : after a certain time, C publishes the BB

Opening :

9 : V_i : finds her ballot on the BB and records its label ℓ_i

10 : $V_i \dashrightarrow C : \langle \ell_i, k_i \rangle$

11 : C : opens the commitments at ℓ_i using the key k_i, and appends $\langle k_i, v_i \rangle$ to
$\langle c_i, \sigma_A(c_i) \rangle$ in the BB, and after a certain time, publishes the new BB

12 : C : checks the validity of the votes, counts them and publishes the result

Fig. 1. FOO Voting Protocol

is also an interactive PPT machine. Each message goes through the attacker, except those that are "published", in which case the message is written directly on each participant's work tape synchronously. The Bulletin Board BB is simply a list of tuples. We assume that the id's ID_i are the same as the voters' public keys used for verifying their digital signatures.

We assume that encryption used in the protocol is *indistinguishable against adaptive chosen cipher text attack*, i.e., satisfies the IND-CCA2 property. The interested reader is referred to [25]. Digital signatures are used in the protocol to ensure that only eligible voters vote and do not play a part in establishing vote privacy. We now present the computational modeling of the commitment and blind digital signature schemes, and their security properties we assume for the verification.

Trapdoor Commitments. A trapdoor commitment scheme allows one party, say V, to commit to a value obfuscating the value it committed to until it is revealed by V with the help of the trapdoor. In general, a commitment scheme satisfies two properties: *binding* and *hiding*. The former property states that the party V cannot change the message once V committed to it while the latter property says that it should be computationally infeasible for any other party to retrieve the message from the commitment unless the V reveals the trapdoor.

Formally, a commitment scheme [25] $\mathcal{C}$ is a triple of algorithms $(KG,$ $Commit, Open)$ such that KG is a PPT algorithm with input 1^η, while $Commit$

and *Open* are PT algorithms such that there is a polynomial $p(\cdot)$ such that for each security parameter η and bit-string m of length at most $p(\eta)$, $Commit(m,k)$ computes the commitment on message m for $k \leftarrow KG(1^\eta)$, and *Open* is a deterministic algorithm such that for all $k \leftarrow KG(1^\eta)$, $Open(Commit(m,k),m,k) = true$. We assume that the commitment schemes are length regular. That is, if m_0 and m_1 are messages of equal length then the commitments of m_0 and m_1 are of equal length [26,27].

The computational hiding property is formalized as a game between a (PPT) attacker and a (honest) challenger. Initially, the attacker generates two messages m_0 and m_1 of *equal length*, which it gives to the challenger. The challenger creates commitments, com_0 and com_1 for m_0 and m_1 with different (secret) commitment keys and sets a *secret* bit b with uniform probability. The challenger then gives the ordered pair (com_b, com_{1-b}) to the attacker who wins if it correctly guesses the value of b. The commitment scheme is said to satisfy the commitment hiding property [25] if the winning probability of the attacker cannot be non-negligibly different from $\frac{1}{2}$.

Blind Digital Signatures. Blind signature schemes were introduced by Chaum [23]. They are small interactive protocols between a user and a signer. Informally, a blind signature scheme is an interactive protocol that allows a party $\mathcal{U}$ to obtain the signature of a party $\mathcal{S}$ on a message that is obfuscated by $\mathcal{U}$ until $\mathcal{S}$ completes the protocol and $\mathcal{U}$ publishes the signed message.

Formally, a blind digital signature scheme [18,24] B is a tuple $(Gen, \langle \mathcal{S}, \mathcal{U} \rangle, verif)$, a PPT key generation algorithm Gen, an interactive algorithm $\langle \mathcal{S}, \mathcal{U} \rangle$ of the PPT singer $\mathcal{S}$ and the PPT user $\mathcal{U}$, and a PT verification algorithm verif, such that for each security parameter η: $Gen(1^\eta)$ outputs a public and private key pair (pk, sk), the joint execution of signer $S(pk, sk)$ and the user $\mathcal{U}(pk, m)$ on the message $m \in \{0,1\}^\eta$ produces an output σ for the user, and the deterministic algorithm $verif(m, \sigma, pk)$ outputs a bit. The algorithm $\mathcal{U}(pk, m)$ may fail to produce an output; in which case $\mathcal{U}$ is said to abort and $\mathcal{U}(pk, m)$ said to be undefined. In that case, we write $\mathcal{U}(pk, m) = \bot$. A blind signature scheme is required to be *complete*, i.e., for all parameter η the following holds: for all messages $m \in \{0,1\}^\eta$, if $(pk, sk) \leftarrow Gen(1^\eta)$ then the joint execution of $S(pk, sk)$ and $\mathcal{U}(pk, m)$ must be defined and the produced output σ should be such that $verif(m, \sigma, pk) = true$.

Blind signatures should also satisfy two security properties, *blindness* and *unforgeability*. Intuitively, unforgeability says a malicious user who engages in ℓ sessions with an honest user should not be able to produce $\ell + 1$ valid message-signature pairs. In the FOO protocol, unforgeability is used to make sure only eligible voters vote. It does not play a role in voting privacy. For this reason, we omit the formalization of unforgeability. The interested reader is referred to [18].

The blindness property [18] on the other hand, is useful in establishing privacy of votes. Intuitively, blindness means that a dishonest signer cannot learn the contents of the message it signed. The blindness property is formalized as a game between a (PPT) attacker acting as the signer and a (honest) challenger.

Initially, the attacker generates two messages m_0 and m_1, which it gives to the challenger. The challenger sets a *secret* bit b with uniform probability. The challenger, acting as the user, then engages in two blind signature sessions with the attacker as the signer; the first is for obtaining signature on m_b and the second is for obtaining signature on m_{1-b}. If the user successfully completes both sessions and obtains signature σ_b, σ_{1-b} then it gives the ordered pair (σ_0, σ_1) to the attacker. Otherwise, it gives the pair $(\perp, \perp)$ to the attacker. The attacker wins if it correctly guesses the value of b. Note that it is important that the challenger gives the pair (σ_0, σ_1) and not (σ_b, σ_{1-b}) (otherwise the attacker will win with probability 1). The blind signature scheme is said to satisfy the blindness property [18] if the winning probability of the attacker cannot be non-negligibly different from $\frac{1}{2}$.

We model the blind signatures using an interactive protocol between the user and the singer in three steps, blinding, blind signing, and unblinding and involving four algorithms, *blind*, *bsign*, *accept*, and *unblind* [23,24]. Before the protocol commences, the signer generates a public key and secret-key pair (pk, sk) and publishes pk. **Blinding:** User computes $b := blind(m, pk, r_b)$ for a message m, using the signer's public key pk, and a random seed r_b, and sends b to the signer. **Blind signing:** The signer computes $\rho := bsign(b, sk, r_s)$ using his own secret key sk and a random seed r_s, and sends it to the user. **Unblinding:** User checks validity of ρ by running $accept(m, pk, r_b, \rho)$. If it outputs false, the user quits the protocol without any output. If it outputs true, the user computes $\sigma = unblind(m, pk, r_b, \rho)$.

3   Vote Privacy for the FOO Protocol

The fundamental idea of vote privacy in the literature is that permutation of votes cast by honest voters cannot be detected by the attacker. There are numerous attempts to formalize this idea such as [19,20]. In the FOO protocol however, unlike the *single-phase* protocols considered therein, the Bulletin Board (BB) is built incrementally in different phases. Hence, we have to adapt the definition of privacy of votes to FOO protocol. We describe our formalization below. We consider only one session.

3.1   Formalization of Vote Privacy

We assume that the attacker controls the network and we allow the administrator and the collector to be corrupt. We require that the flipping of votes of two honest voters should result in computationally indistinguishable runs to any PPT attacker even if he controls all other voters. Under these assumptions however, there is an obvious unavoidable attack. Suppose A votes v_0 and B votes v_1, while in the flipped voting scenario, A votes v_1 and B votes v_0. If the attacker allows the ballots of both A and B to be posted in the Voting phase, but subsequently blocks B's message in the opening phase, then the two situations will be distinguishable. This is because in the first scenario only v_0 vote will appear on the BB, while in the second, only v_1. Therefore, our formalization requires that the scenario with the original votes and with the flipped votes be indistinguishable only when either both voters' votes appear on the BB or neither does.

Accordingly, we require the following two games to be computationally indistinguishable to a PPT attacker. For bit b, let Π_b be the following game between the Attacker and the Challenger simulating two honest voters of the FOO protocol and the mixer but aborting when only one of the commitment keys reach the mixer. The attacker simulates the corrupt administrator, the corrupt collector, and at the end has to guess the value of b:

1. Challenger publishes public keys of A, B, and the mixer, and a list of candidates.
2. Attacker publishes possibly dishonestly generated public keys of other voters, the administrator, and the collector. It then gives Challenger two valid votes v_0 and v_1.
3. Challenger creates the ballots of v_b for A and v_{1-b} for B.
4. Attacker calls one of A or B to authorize vote with administrator.
5. Challenger prepares the corresponding blinded ballot. It sends the corresponding identity, the blinded ballot, and the corresponding signature to the attacker.
6. Attacker creates the possibly fake authorization, sends it back to the voter, and calls for the other voter to carry out the authorization.
7. Challenger prepares the appropriate blinded ballot and sends it to the attacker.
8. Attacker creates and sends again the authorization now for the other voter, and asks either A or B to proceed with sending the ballot.
9. If the corresponding blind signature was accepted, Challenger unblinds it, and sends the signed ballot encrypted with the mixer's public key. Otherwise skips.
10. Attacker makes some computations and sends a message back (which is possibly the unchanged ciphertext sent in the previous step).
11. If the other of A or B's blind signature was accepted, Challenger now unblinds that, sends the signed ballot encrypted with the mixer's public key. Otherwise skips.
12. Attacker makes some computations and sends a message back (which is possibly the unchanged ciphertext sent in the previous step).
13. Attacker also sends the Challenger further possible encrypted signed ballots of the other, possibly corrupted voters.
14. Challenger waits for all the signed encrypted ballots to arrive. It decrypts the signed ballots with the secret key of the mixer, and puts them through the shuffle. Gives the result of the shuffle to the attacker.
15. Attacker creates the bulletin board BB and gives it to the Challenger. Note that the ballots of A and B may or may not appear on the BB. Attacker also specifies which of A or B should move to the next step first.
16. If A (resp. B) was asked to move next, A (resp. B) accepted the blind signature in phase 2 and A's (resp. B's) ballot appears on the bulletin board,

then the Challenger sends A's (resp. B's) $\langle l_i, k_i \rangle$ to the attacker encrypted with the public key of the mixer. Otherwise, the challenger skips this step.

17. Attacker makes some computations and sends a message back (which is possibly the unchanged cipher sent in the previous step).

18. If the other agent accepted the blind signature in phase 2 and its ballot appeared on the bulletin board, then the Challenger sends the other agent's $\langle l_i, k_i \rangle$ to the attacker encrypted with the public key of the mixer. Otherwise, it skips this step.

19. Attacker makes some computations and sends a message back (which is possibly the unchanged cipher sent in the previous step).

20. Attacker may also send other messages of the form $\langle l_i, k_i \rangle$ encrypted.

21. Challenger puts the decrypted messages through the shuffle. If only one of A's or B's commitment key appears, the Challenger aborts. If none of them appear or both of them appear, the Challenger gives the result of the shuffle to the attacker.

22. The attacker outputs 0 or 1.

If in the situation above the probability that the attacker outputs 1 playing game Π_0 is non-negligibly different from outputting 1 playing game Π_1, then the attacker wins the game. Our aim is to show that no PPT attacker can win the above game.

3.2   Attacks on the FOO Protocol

We describe three attacks on the vote privacy for FOO protocol, which we caught with the CCSA technique. We will comment at the beginning of Sect. 4 on how attacks are found in CCSA, and then in Sect. 5.3 on how these specific attacks were found. The first two attacks cannot be captured in the DY model as they cannot be discovered under the assumption of perfect cryptography. Moreover, the first attack is an issue of the original FOO protocol and the standard definition of blindness property; it is not a feature of our implementation of anonymous channels. On the other hand, the second attack appears because our implementation uses CCA secure encryption. The third attack is DY in nature but does not appear in previous DY analyses of the protocol as those analyses assume perfectly anonymous channels.

The first attack exploits an insufficiency in the blindness property. This insufficiency has also been pointed out in [22]. Recall that in the blindness game, a (potentially dishonest) signer engages in two sessions (parallel or sequential) with an honest user on messages m_0 and m_1. If one session successfully completes and the other aborts then the information of which session aborted is not revealed to the attacker. Thus, the blindness property does *not rule out* the possibility that the signer is able to deduce which session corresponded to m_0 and which corresponded to m_1 if one session aborted and the signer knows which session aborted. For example, in the three-step blind signature scheme described above, replace *accept* by *accept'* where $accept'(m, pk, r_b, \rho)$ always returns false if m is of even length and returns the value of $accept(m, pk, r_b, \rho)$ otherwise. The resulting blind signature scheme continues to satisfy the blindness property if the original one does. Now, if m_0 is of even length and m_1 is of odd length, then the session corresponding to message m_0 always aborts and thus the dishonest signer be able to associate the aborted session to m_0.

The first attack on FOO protocol proceeds as follows. Assume that we use the modified blind signature scheme in the FOO protocol and that the candidate choice v_0 is of even length and the choice v_1 is of odd length. Since commitments may reveal the length, it is possible that the commitment of v_0 is also even while of v_1 is odd. Assume that A chooses v_b and Bob chooses v_{1-b}. Vote privacy requires that the attacker not be able to deduce the value of b. In authentication phase, the attacker, acting as the administrator, correctly follows the protocol. The blinding still hides the commitments even though their lengths are different, but according to our modified accept algorithm, the signature on v_0 will be rejected while the one on v_1 will be accepted. Then during the voting phase, only one voter will send its ballot to the administrator. If this voter is A then b must be 1, otherwise b must be 0. Note, this attack is not a feature of our specific implementation of the anonymous channel. Note also that even though the commitments are revealed on the BB, there they appear in the same order on the two sides, so the attack works not because the commitments reveal to the attacker the vote inside, but because one accept may pass, the other may not. Observe also that the attack does not manifest if v_0 and v_1 are of equal length. Indeed, if v_0 and v_1 are of equal length then the property of commitment hiding ensures that an abort by a voter does not reveal information about its intended vote.

The second attack relies on the fact that there is no guarantee on the lengths of the (blind) signatures and that an encryption scheme used may reveal the lengths of the underlying plaintexts. If a length revealing encryption scheme (such as IND-CCA2) is used then the encrypted ballots in the voting phase are different, which allows the attacker to deduce how A and B voted. To *rule out* this attack, we have to assume that the (blind) signatures on equal length messages are of equal length.

Finally, we point out the DY style attack. The attack replays a message in the voting phase of the protocol in the opening phase. Assume that there is a third voter C in addition to A and B. The attacker remembers A's encrypted ballot to the mixer in the voting phase. In the opening phase of the protocol, the attacker forwards the encrypted commitment keys of A and B to the mixer, but replaces C's commitment key by A's encrypted ballot from the voting phase. The mixer checks that the three encryptions are different, decrypts them and outputs them after shuffling them into lexicographic order. The only ballot that appears in the output is A's. The commitment keys of A and B are also part of the output. The attacker can then deduce how A and B voted. In order to prevent this attack, we modify the FOO protocol to *also include phase* numbers inside the encryptions in the voting and opening phases of the FOO protocol. The mixer *must* check that the phase numbers correspond to the current phase in the protocol.

4   Computationally Complete Symbolic Attacker (CCSA)

The CCSA model was introduced by Bana and Comon in [9] with the aim of establishing computational guarantees for symbolic analysis by making the symbolic attacker as powerful as the computational one. We limit our attention in this paper to their indistinguishability framework given in [8]. The CCSA framework is similar to the DY framework in the sense that explicit symbolic adversarial messages are created. The DY framework specifies *all* rules that the attacker can use to create new messages from what he has seen, and the protocol agents use pattern matching to check whether messages coming from the attacker have the correct form. On the other hand, in the CCSA framework, each message from the attacker is modeled by a function f_i applied to the sequence of messages that the attacker has seen thus far. Pattern matching is replaced by applying function symbols on the term coming from the attacker. Limitations on attacker capabilities originating from computational assumptions on the primitives are specified as a set of axioms A in first-order logic based on a single indistinguishability predicate (representing computational indistinguishability of sequences of messages). Computationally, a security property of a protocol Π is formulated as the computational indistinguishability of two protocols Π_1 and Π_2 constructed (depending on the security property) from the original Π.

Verification. In the CCSA framework, the security translates to the validity of the formula obtained by applying the indistinguishability predicate on the list of terms produced by the symbolic execution of Π_1 and Π_2. Hence the security formula obtained this way must be derived as a logical consequence of the axioms A using first-order inference. If the formula is derived and the axioms in A shown to be computationally sound then the protocol Π is computationally secure according to Theorem 1 in [8].

Attack finding. If the security formula cannot be derived then the negation of the security formula is consistent with A and a symbolic attacker model is then obtained. In practice, for the security proof, a proof tree is being built, and some branch cannot be reduced to axioms. For example, often what happens is that it cannot be shown that an attacker message $f_i(\cdots)$ cannot equal a term, that is, the attacker may produce a message that passes some check when it should not. Then from this branch, an Herbrand model can be built on the terms, resulting in a symbolic attack. This symbolic attack then has to be checked to see if it corresponds to a computational attacker or if it originates from having too few axioms in A, as the set of axioms is not complete.

4.1   Syntax

Terms: Let S be a finite set of *sorts* that includes at least the sorts bool and msg. $\mathcal{X}$ is an infinite set of *variable symbols*, each coming with a sort $s \in S$. Terms are built on a set of function symbols $\mathcal{F}$ representing honest computation of primitives, a set of function symbols $\mathcal{G}$ representing attacker's computation, a set of zero-arity function symbols (names) $\mathcal{N}$ representing honest generation of randomness, and a set of variables $\mathcal{X}$. The set $\mathcal{F}$ contains the basic symbols such as $\mathbf{0}$, $\textbf{true}$, $\textbf{false}$, L, $\langle \_, \_ \rangle$, EQ$(\_, \_)$, if $\_$ then $\_$ else $\_$, π_1 and π_2 with the typing rules as follows:

- $\mathbf{0}$: msg representing the empty message.
- $\textbf{true}, \textbf{false}$: bool.
- $\mathsf{L}(\_)$: msg $\rightarrow$ msg. $\mathsf{L}(x)$ represents the length of x in unary.
- $\langle \_, \_ \rangle$: msg $\times$ msg $\rightarrow$ msg representing pairs.
- Polymorphic equality test EQ$(\_, \_)$: $\begin{array}{l} \text{msg} \times \text{msg} \rightarrow \text{bool} \\ \text{bool} \times \text{bool} \rightarrow \text{bool}. \end{array}$
- Polymorphic conditional branching if $\_$ then $\_$ else $\_$: $\begin{array}{l} \text{bool} \times \text{msg} \times \text{msg} \rightarrow \text{msg} \\ \text{bool} \times \text{bool} \times \text{bool} \rightarrow \text{bool}. \end{array}$
- $\pi_1(\_), \pi_2(\_)$: msg $\rightarrow$ msg. π_i represents the i-th projection of a pair

Formulas: As presented in [12], we have for every sequence of sorts $s_1, \ldots, s_n$ a *predicate symbol* that takes $2 \times n$ arguments of sort $(s_1 \times \ldots \times s_n)^2$, which we write as $t_1, \ldots, t_n \sim u_1, \ldots, u_n$. The predicate $t_1, \ldots, t_n \sim u_1, \ldots, u_n$ represents *computational indistinguishability* of the two sequences of terms $t_1, \ldots, t_n$ and $u_1, \ldots, u_n$.

The first-order formulas are built from the above atomic formulas combining the Boolean connectives $\neg$, $\wedge$, $\vee$, and $\rightarrow$, and the quantifiers $\forall$ and $\exists$. The formulas are used to represent both axioms (assumptions) and the security properties of the protocols.

Equational Theory: We use binary relation symbol $=_E$ to indicate equations the function symbols have to satisfy. Note that $=_E$ is not part of the first-order signature. The equations specified by $=_E$ will result in axioms for $\sim$. We assume that the following hold: $\forall x_1, x_2.\ \pi_i(\langle x_1, x_2 \rangle) =_E x_i$, for $i = 1, 2$; $\mathsf{L}(\mathsf{L}(x)) =_E \mathsf{L}(x)$.

Abbreviations: In order to reduce the size of the terms, we shall use the following abbreviations: $\mathsf{not}(b) \stackrel{\text{def}}{\equiv}$ if b then $\textbf{false}$ else $\textbf{true}$, $b_1 \mathbin{\&} b_2 \stackrel{\text{def}}{\equiv}$ if b_1 then b_2 else $\textbf{false}$, b_1 or $b_2 \stackrel{\text{def}}{\equiv}$ if b_1 then $\textbf{true}$ else b_2 and $x = y \stackrel{\text{def}}{\equiv} \mathsf{EQ}(x, y) \sim \textbf{true}$. The abbreviation $\mathsf{EQL}(x_1, x_2) \stackrel{\text{def}}{\equiv} \mathsf{EQ}(\mathsf{L}(x_1), (\mathsf{L}(x_2)))$ modeling length equality test. Finally, the abbreviation $\langle x_1, x_2, x_3 \rangle \stackrel{\text{def}}{\equiv} \langle x_1, \langle x_2, x_3 \rangle \rangle$ encodes triples.

4.2   Semantics

As Bana and Comon defined it in [8], the logic is interpreted over a *computational model*. A computational model $\mathcal{M}^c$ is a particular first-order model in which the domain consists of probabilistic polynomial-time algorithms taking the input 1^η

together with two infinitely long random tapes (ρ_1, ρ_2), where ρ_1 is for honestly generated names, and ρ_2 for adversarial use. We use $[\![\_]\!]$ to denote the semantics of syntactic objects. Once $[\![\_]\!]$ is given on function symbols, and a valuation σ of variables of term t in the domain, the interpretation of t in the domain is defined the usual way and denoted as $[\![t]\!]^\sigma$. Let $[\![t]\!]^\sigma_{\eta,\rho} := [\![t]\!]^\sigma(1^\eta; \rho_1, \rho_2)$. In this model, function symbols in $\mathcal{F}$ representing the cryptographic primitives are interpreted as polynomial-time algorithms and they act on the outputs of the PPT algorithms in their arguments. For example, $[\![\mathsf{EQ}(t_1, t_2)]\!]^\sigma_{\eta,\rho} := 1$ if $[\![t_1]\!]^\sigma_{\eta,\rho} = [\![t_2]\!]^\sigma_{\eta,\rho}$, otherwise it is 0, and $[\![\text{if } t_1 \text{ then } t_2 \text{ else } t_3]\!]^\sigma_{\eta,\rho} := [\![t_2]\!]^\sigma_{\eta,\rho}$ if $[\![t_1]\!]^\sigma_{\eta,\rho} = 1$, and $[\![\text{if } t_1 \text{ then } t_2 \text{ else } t_3]\!]^\sigma_{\eta,\rho} := [\![t_3]\!]^\sigma_{\eta,\rho}$ if $[\![t_1]\!]^\sigma_{\eta,\rho} = 0$. Function symbols in $\mathcal{G}$ representing adversarial computation are interpreted as probabilistic polynomial-time algorithms and they also act on the outputs of the PPT algorithms in their arguments, but they can also use randomness from ρ_2. Each name $n \in \mathcal{N}$ is interpreted as a machine $[\![n]\!]$ which extracts a random word of length $p(\eta)$ (where p is a polynomial globally fixed by $\mathcal{M}^c$) from ρ_1. Different names draw from disjoint parts of the tape ρ_1. The predicate symbol $\sim$ is interpreted as computational indistinguishability of the outputs of the PPT algorithms on the two sides of $\sim$. Interested reader can consult either [8] or [12] for complete definition of this semantics. A formula is computationally valid if it is satisfied in all computational interpretations.

4.3   Computationally Valid Axioms

A core set of valid axioms of the CCSA have been given in [12]. Essentially, these core axioms can be divided into four sets. The first set of axioms reflect the properties of the indistinguishability predicate $\sim$, namely, that it is an equivalence relation and is preserved under projection, permutation and function application. The second set of axioms says that the abbreviation $=$ is a congruence and preserves the equational theory $=_E$. The third set of axioms reflect the properties of the function symbol if_then_else_ such as if **true** then x else $y = x$. Finally, we have a couple of axioms that reflect the *truly* random nature of names such as replacing any name n_1 by a fresh name n_2 yields indistinguishable sequence of terms. The interested reader is referred to [12] for additional details, where several small examples of usage of the axioms are also given.

5   Vote Privacy for the FOO Protocol in CCSA Framework

We assume that the FOO protocol is modified to ensure that the length candidate identities are equal and that the phase identifiers are used in Voting and Opening phases. We will drop the adjective modified in the rest of the section and show how vote privacy can be modeled in CCSA framework. In order to make things simpler, we assume that other than voters A and B, there is only a single other (possibly dishonest) voter. The proof of vote privacy carries over to n dishonest voters for any fixed n.

5.1   Function Symbols and Axioms

In order to formalize the FOO voting protocol in the CCSA framework, we shall include the following (see Table 1) function symbols in $\mathcal{F}$. Please note that each argument in these symbols has sort msg. Each key-generation algorithm and each random seed generation will be represented by a corresponding unary function symbol. When the function symbol is applied to a name n (recall that names represent truly random objects), then the resulting term shall represent a correctly generated key or seed.

Table 1. FOO function symbols with their co-domain sorts (each argument sort is msg)

Commitments	Encryptions	Blind Signatures	Signatures	Other Symbols
		$\bot$: msg		
$k_c(\_)$: msg		$k_b(\_)$: msg		ph_2, ph_3: msg
$com(\_,\_)$: msg	$k_e(\_)$: msg	$r_b(\_)$: msg	$k_s(\_)$: msg	A, B, M: msg
$open(\_,\_,\_)$: msg	$r_e(\_)$: msg	$bsign(\_,\_,\_)$: msg	$r_s(\_)$: msg	C_1, C_2, C_3: msg
	$\{\_\}_\_^\_$: msg	$b(\_,\_,\_)$: msg	$sign(\_,\_,\_)$: msg	$to(\ )$: msg
Shuffling	$dec(\_,\_)$: msg	$ub(\_,\_,\_,\_)$: msg	$ver(\_,\_,\_)$: bool	$V_0(\_)$: msg
$shufl(\_,\_,\_)$: msg		$acc(\_,\_,\_,\_)$: bool		$V_1(\_)$: msg
		$bver(\_,\_,\_)$: bool		$pubkey(\_)$: msg

Commitments. We include a symbol $k_c(\_)$ in $\mathcal{F}$ to represent the key generation algorithm for the commitment schemes defined in Sect. 2.2. $com(x, y)$ is the commitment of x using the key y whereas $open(u, z)$ is the opening of the commitment u using the key z. We assume that, for all x, y, $open(com(x, k_c(y)), k_c(y)) =_E x$.

Encryptions. The symbol $k_e(\_)$ denotes the public-key secret-key pair generation algorithm of encryptions. We define $pk_e(x) \stackrel{\text{def}}{=} \pi_1(k_e(x))$ and $sk_e(x) \stackrel{\text{def}}{=} \pi_2(k_e(x))$, the public encryption key and secret decryption key parts of $k_e(x)$ respectively. In order to formalize the random seed of encryptions, we introduce a symbol $r_e(\_)$ (see Table 1). Encryption of x with random seed z and public key y is denoted as $\{x\}_y^z$ and decryption of x with secret key z is denoted as $dec(x, z)$. We assume that for all x, y, z, $dec(\{x\}_{pk_e(y)}^z, sk_e(y)) =_E x$.

Blind Signatures. We introduce a symbol $k_b(\_)$ to represent a public-verification-key secret-signing-key pair generation algorithm of blind signatures. Once again, $pk_b(x) \stackrel{\text{def}}{=} \pi_1(k_b(x))$ and $sk_b(x) \stackrel{\text{def}}{=} \pi_2(k_b(x))$ represent the public verification key and secret signing key parts of the key $k_b(x)$. We also introduce a symbol $r_b(\_)$ to represent blinding key generation algorithm. The interpretations of the function symbols b, bsign, bver, ub and acc are *blind, blindsign, verify, unblind* and *accept* as defined in Sect. 2.2. $b(x, y, z)$ is the blinding of the message x using the public verification key y and the blinding key z. $\mathsf{bsign}(x, y, r)$ is the (blinded) message x blind-signed with secret blind signing key y and random seed r. $\mathsf{acc}(x, y, z, w)$ is the acceptance check of the blindsign w created for the blinded message $b(x, y, z)$ and $\mathsf{ub}(x, y, z, w)$ its unblinding. $\perp$ represents undefined that is used to model blindness game. Finally, $\mathsf{bver}(x, s, y)$ is the verification of unblinded signature s on the message x with the public verification key y. The co-domains of the symbol acc and bver are bool.

Digital Signatures. In addition to blind signatures, we also need plain digital signatures. As in [12], let $k_s(\_)$ represent generation of a key pair, the public verification key and the secret signing key. $\mathsf{vk}(x) \overset{\text{def}}{\equiv} \pi_1(k_s(x))$ and $\mathsf{ssk}(x) \overset{\text{def}}{\equiv} \pi_2(k_s(x))$ represent the public verification key and secret signing key parts of the key $k_s(x)$. In order to randomize signatures, we introduce a symbol $r_s(\_)$ for random seed generation. $\mathsf{sign}(x, y, r)$ is the message x singed with secret signing key y with a random seed r and $\mathsf{ver}(z, u, y)$ is the verification of signature u on the message z with the public verification key y.

Mixer. We introduce a symbol $\mathsf{shufl}(\_, \_, \_)$ to model the shuffling functionality of mix-nets. $\mathsf{shufl}(x_1, x_2, x_3)$ is the lexicographic ordering of the messages x_1, x_2, and x_3. As we model only three voters, shufl has only three arguments.

Other Function Symbols. We introduce constants ph_2 (resp. ph_3) to represent the Voting (resp. Opening) Phase of the FOO protocol. These symbols are necessary to avoid *replay attacks* in which an attacker can learn honest vote value by forwarding one of the honest voter's message from the Voting Phase to the Opening Phase (see Subsect. 3.2). Constants A and B model the identity of two honest voters and constant M models the identity of the mixer. C_1, C_2, C_3 model the identities of the candidates. (For simplicity, we assume only three candidates.) Finally, the function symbols $\mathsf{to}(\_), \mathsf{V}_0(\_), \mathsf{V}_1(\_), \mathsf{pubkey}(\_)$ are used to model the security game and explained in Sect. 5.2.

Axioms. We present axioms (see Table 2) that formalize the security assumptions on the primitives. The axioms use the notion of *freshness* [8]: For any list of names $\vec{n}$, and a (possibly empty) list of terms $\vec{v}$, $\mathsf{fresh}(\vec{n}; \vec{v})$ is the constraint that the names in $\vec{n}$ are pairwise distinct and that none of the names in $\vec{n}$ occur in $\vec{v}$.

The axiom CompHid models the computational hiding property of the commitments (see Sect. 2.2). Intuitively, the axiom says that if the attacker is presented with commitments on equal length messages but the order of these messages is hidden, then the attacker cannot determine the order if it does not have access to commitment keys. CompHid can be shown to be computationally valid if and only if $[\![k_c(\_)]\!]$, $[\![com(\_,\_)]\!]$, $[\![open(\_,\_)]\!]$ satisfy the computational hiding property.

The axiom BLINDNESS models the blindness property of the blind signatures (see Sect. 2.2). Intuitively, in the blindness game, the dishonest signer attacker is asked to sign two blinded messages (could be of unequal length), but the order of these messages is hidden. Thus, the blinded messages on the two sides of $\sim$ are in reversed order. Moreover, the signer is also allowed to see the unblinded signatures if the user does not abort for either signature. However, in order to hide the order, the unblinded signatures are presented in the same order. BLINDNESS can be shown to be computationally valid if and only if blind signature scheme ($[\![k_b]\!].[\![r_b]\!]$, $[\![b]\!]$, $[\![ub]\!]$, $[\![bsign]\!]$, $[\![acc]\!]$, $[\![bver]\!]$) satisfies the blindness property. The axiom SHUFFLE models the shuffling capability of the mixer. We also require further assumptions on the primitives. In particular, COMMEQL models the assumption that the length of commitments on equal length messages are equal. COMMKEYEQL models the assumption that the length of honestly generated commitment keys are equal. UBNOTUNDEFINED models the assumption that if a user successfully completes the blind signature protocol then then the output is different from $\bot$. UBEQL models the assumption that blind signatures on equal length message are of equal length. PAIREQL models the length regularity of pairing. CANDEQL (resp. PHASEEQL) models the assumptions that candidate identities (resp. phase identities) are of equal length. AGENTDIST (resp. PHASEDIST) models the assumption that identities of honest voters (resp. phase identifiers) are distinct.

Finally, we recall the axiom representing IND-CCA2 property of encryptions from [12]. Let $\vec{t}[x]$ be a list of terms with a single variable x. For a closed term v, let $\vec{t}[v]$ denote the term that we receive from $\vec{t}[x]$ by replacing all occurrences of x by v. Let u, u', u'' be closed terms. Consider the formula

$$\vec{t}[\text{if EQL}(u,u') \text{ then } \{u\}_{\text{pk}(n_1)}^{\text{r}_e(n_2)} \text{ else } u''] \sim \vec{t}[\text{if EQL}(u,u') \text{ then } \{u'\}_{\text{pk}(n_1)}^{\text{r}_e(n_3)} \text{ else } u'']$$

in which $n_1 \in \mathcal{N}$ occurs only as $k(n_1)$, $\text{sk}(n_1)$ only occurs in decryption position (that is, as in $\text{dec}(\_,\text{sk}(n_1))$), and n_2, n_3 do not occur anywhere else. We call the above formula ENC_{CCA2} if for any $t'[x]$ term with x explicitly occurring in $t'[x]$, $\text{dec}(t'[x],\text{sk}(n_1))$ occurs only as, if $\text{EQ}(t'[x],x)$ then $t''[x]$ else $\text{dec}(t'[x],\text{sk}(n_1))$, where $t''[x]$ is not of the form $\text{dec}(t'''[x],\text{sk}(n_1))$. The intuition is that since in the IND-CCA2 game, after encryption, the decryption oracle decrypts only those messages that are different from the encryption, we have to make sure that the decrypted message, $t'[x]$ is different from the encryption, for which x stands. The reader is referred to [12] for additional details.

5.2   Modeling the Vote Privacy Security Game

As defined in [8], the BC technique treats protocols as abstract transition systems. We do not recall the formal definitions, we just apply them to the vote privacy games Π_b for $b = 0, 1$ between the Challenger and the Attacker as defined in Sect. 3.1. The transition system produces the terms of the execution,

Table 2. Axioms that formalize the computational assumptions of the primitives

---

Commitments

Let t_1 and t_2 be two ground terms. Let n_1 and n_2 be names such that $\mathsf{fresh}(n_1, n_2; t_1, t_2)$ holds.

CommEQL: if $\mathsf{EQL}(t_1, t_2)$ then $\mathsf{EQL}(\mathsf{com}(t_1, \mathsf{k_c}(n_1)), \mathsf{com}(t_2, \mathsf{k_c}(n_2)))$ else *true* $=$ *true*

CommKeyEQL: $\mathsf{EQL}(\mathsf{k_c}(n_1), \mathsf{k_c}(n_2)) =$ *true*

CompHid: Let t, t_1, and t_2 be three ground terms and let $\vec{z}$ be a list of ground terms and n_1 and n_2 be names such that $\mathsf{fresh}(n_1, n_2; \vec{z}, t, t_1, t_2)$ holds.

$\quad$ if $\mathsf{EQL}(t_1, t_2)$ $\qquad\qquad\qquad\qquad$ if $\mathsf{EQL}(t_1, t_2)$
$\vec{z}$, then $\langle \mathsf{com}(t_1, \mathsf{k_c}(n_1)), \mathsf{com}(t_2, \mathsf{k_c}(n_2)) \rangle \sim \vec{z}$, then $\langle \mathsf{com}(t_2, \mathsf{k_c}(n_1)), \mathsf{com}(t_1, \mathsf{k_c}(n_2)) \rangle$
$\quad$ else t $\qquad\qquad\qquad\qquad\qquad\quad$ else t

Blind Digital Signatures

Blindness: Let m_0, m_1, t be ground terms and let $\vec{z}$ be a list of ground terms. Let t_0 and t_1 be terms containing two variables x and y. Let n_0, and n_1 be names such that $\mathsf{fresh}(n_0, n_1; \vec{z}, t, m_0, m_1, t_0, t_1)$ holds.

$$\vec{z}, \mathsf{b}(m_0, t, \mathrm{r_b}(n_0)), \mathsf{b}(m_1, t, \mathrm{r_b}(n_1)), u^0 \sim \vec{z}, \mathsf{b}(m_1, t, \mathrm{r_b}(n_0)), \mathsf{b}(m_0, t, \mathrm{r_b}(n_1)), u^1$$

where $u^j = $ if acc_0^j & acc_1^j then p^j else $\langle \perp, \perp \rangle$, $\mathsf{acc}_i^0 = \mathsf{acc}(m_i, t, \mathrm{r_b}(n_i), t_i^0)$

$\mathsf{acc}_i^1 = \mathsf{acc}(m_{1-i}, t, \mathrm{r_b}(n_i), t_i^1), p^j = \left\langle \mathsf{ub}(m_0, t, \mathrm{r_b}(n_j), t_j^j), \mathsf{ub}(m_1, t, \mathrm{r_b}(n_{1-j}), t_{1-j}^j) \right\rangle$

$t_i^j = t_i[x \leftarrow \mathsf{b}(m_j, t, \mathrm{r_b}(n_0)), y \leftarrow \mathsf{b}(m_{1-j}, t, \mathrm{r_b}(n_1))]$, $i, j \in \{0, 1\}$

For $i = 0, 1$, let t, t_1^i, and t_2^i be ground terms. Let n^i be a name with $\mathsf{fresh}(n^i; t, t_1^1, t_1^2, t_2^{1-i})$, such that it occurs in t_2^i, only as $\mathsf{b}(t_1^i, t, \mathrm{r_b}(n^i))$:

UBNotUndefined:

if $\mathsf{acc}(t_1^0, t, \mathrm{r_b}(n^0), t_2^0)$ then $\mathsf{EQ}(\mathsf{ub}(t_1^0, t, \mathrm{r_b}(n^0), t_2^0), \perp)$ else *false* $=$ *false*

UBEQL:

if $\mathsf{EQL}(t_1^0, t_1^1)$ & $\mathsf{EQL}(t_2^0, t_2^1)$ & $\mathsf{acc}(t_1^0, t, \mathrm{r_b}(n^0), t_2^0)$ & $\mathsf{acc}(t_1^1, t, \mathrm{r_b}(n^1), t_2^1)$
then $\mathsf{EQL}(\mathsf{ub}(t_1^0, t, \mathrm{r_b}(n^0), t_2^0), \mathsf{ub}(t_1^1, t, \mathrm{r_b}(n^1), t_2^1))$ $\qquad\qquad$ $=$ *true*
else *true*

Mix-net Server

Shuffle: For any permutation p of $\{1, 2, 3\}$, $\mathsf{shufl}(x_1, x_2, x_3) = \mathsf{shufl}(x_{p(1)}, x_{p(2)}, x_{p(3)})$

Further length regularity

PairEQL: if $\mathsf{EQL}(x_1, y_1)$ & $\mathsf{EQL}(x_2, y_2)$ then $\mathsf{EQL}(\langle x_1, x_2 \rangle, \langle y_1, y_2 \rangle)$ else *true* $=$ *true*

CandEQL: $\mathsf{EQL}(C_i, C_j) =$ *true* for $i, j \in \{1, 2, 3\}$

PhaseEQL: $\mathsf{EQL}(\mathsf{ph}_2, \mathsf{ph}_3) =$ *true*

Distinctness of constants

$\qquad\qquad$ **AgentDist:** $\mathsf{EQ}(A, B) = \mathsf{EQ}(A, M) = \mathsf{EQ}(B, M) =$ *false*

$\qquad\qquad$ **PhaseDist:** $\mathsf{EQ}(\mathsf{ph}_2, \mathsf{ph}_3) =$ *false*

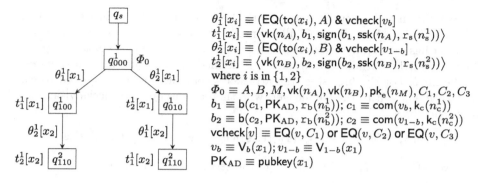

$\theta_1^1[x_i] \equiv (\mathsf{EQ}(\mathsf{to}(x_i), A) \ \& \ \mathsf{vcheck}[v_b]$
$t_1^1[x_i] \equiv \langle \mathsf{vk}(n_A), b_1, \mathsf{sign}(b_1, \mathsf{ssk}(n_A), \mathsf{r_s}(n_s^1)) \rangle$
$\theta_2^1[x_i] \equiv (\mathsf{EQ}(\mathsf{to}(x_i), B) \ \& \ \mathsf{vcheck}[v_{1-b}]$
$t_2^1[x_i] \equiv \langle \mathsf{vk}(n_B), b_2, \mathsf{sign}(b_2, \mathsf{ssk}(n_B), \mathsf{r_s}(n_s^2)) \rangle$
where i is in $\{1, 2\}$
$\Phi_0 \equiv A, B, M, \mathsf{vk}(n_A), \mathsf{vk}(n_B), \mathsf{pk_e}(n_M), C_1, C_2, C_3$
$b_1 \equiv \mathsf{b}(c_1, \mathsf{PK_{AD}}, \mathsf{r_b}(n_b^1)); c_1 \equiv \mathsf{com}(v_b, \mathsf{k_c}(n_c^1))$
$b_2 \equiv \mathsf{b}(c_2, \mathsf{PK_{AD}}, \mathsf{r_b}(n_b^2)); c_2 \equiv \mathsf{com}(v_{1-b}, \mathsf{k_c}(n_c^2))$
$\mathsf{vcheck}[v] \equiv \mathsf{EQ}(v, C_1) \text{ or } \mathsf{EQ}(v, C_2) \text{ or } \mathsf{EQ}(v, C_3)$
$v_b \equiv \mathsf{V}_b(x_1); v_{1-b} \equiv \mathsf{V}_{1-b}(x_1)$
$\mathsf{PK_{AD}} \equiv \mathsf{pubkey}(x_1)$

Fig. 2. Authentication phase of the security game Π_b

on which the indistinguishability predicate is applied. The verification task is to prove that the axioms together with first-order inference rules imply that the execution terms produced by the transition system for $b = 0$ and for $b = 1$ are indistinguishable.

Recall that in addition to honest voters A and B, there is an additional voter only a single other voter. We assume the mixer M is honest, and the administrator as well as the collector are corrupt. Recall that we assume that the names A, B, and M are distinct message constants. We also use distinct names n_A, n_B, n_M for (honest) signing key generations for the voters A, B, and encryption key generation for the Mixer M.

The function symbol to extracts from an incoming message the agent name. This allows the attacker to specify which of A, B, and M should receive the message sent by the attacker. The function symbols V_b, $b \in \{0, 1\}$ extract from an incoming attacker message the candidate choices for the honest voters A and B. The function symbol pubkey extracts from an incoming attacker message the (dishonest) public-key of the attacker.

We present the transition diagram that represents the Authentication Phase of the security game Π_b in Fig. 2. It illustrates all possible moves of the challenger in the authentication phase. At the start of the game, the knowledge of the attacker is initialized and is represented by ϕ_0. The left branch of q_{000}^1 represents the situation where A moves first for authentication followed by B while the right branch simulates the situation that B moves first followed by A. $\theta_i^p[x_j]$s are the bool conditions that the challenger checks upon receiving the message x_j from the attacker before taking the respective transitions. Here p represents the Phase number, i represents the agent that has to move (we use 1 for A, 2 for B and 3 for M) and j represents the message number. Similarly the terms $t_i^p[x_j]$s represent the outputs of the challenger to the attacker which increases attacker's knowledge. When the checks in a transition fail, the transition moves to state q_{exit}, which we omit in transition diagram for clarity. The transition systems for other phases can be similarly defined (see full version of the paper [28]).

We obtain the execution terms from the transition system in the following way. For a given b bit of the Challenger, Φ_i^b lists of terms representing what the attacker has seen up to step i are created according to the rounds of the protocol. Notice that the initialization frame Φ_0 is defined in Fig. 2 and it is independent of the bit b. For the first step, the attacker's computation f_1 is applied to Φ_0, and $f_1(\Phi_0)$ is sent to the Challenger, who then carries out the checks θ_1^1 and θ_2^1, and sends back

$$\phi_1^b := \text{if } \theta_1^1[f_1(\Phi_0)] \text{ then } t_1^1[f_1(\Phi_0)] \text{ else (if } \theta_2^1[f_1(\Phi_0)] \text{ then } t_2^1[f_1(\Phi_0)] \text{ else } \mathbf{0}),$$

and we set $\Phi_1^b \stackrel{\text{def}}{\equiv} \Phi_0, \phi_1^b$. Similarly, in the second step, we have

$$\phi_2^b := \begin{aligned} &\text{if } \theta_1^1[f_1(\Phi_0)] \\ &\text{then (if } \theta_2^1[f_2(\Phi_1^b)] \text{ then } t_2^1[f_2(\Phi_1^b)] \text{ else } \mathbf{0}) \\ &\text{else (if } \theta_2^1[f_1(\Phi_0)] \text{ then (if } \theta_1^1[f_2(\Phi_1^b)] \text{ then } t_1^1[f_2(\Phi_1^b)] \text{ else } \mathbf{0}) \text{ else } \mathbf{0}), \end{aligned}$$

and $\Phi_2^b \stackrel{\text{def}}{\equiv} \Phi_1^b, \phi_2^b$, which is the end of the authentication phase. The other phases are done similarly continuing from Φ_3^b.

Let Φ_m^b be the last frame. In order to establish vote-privacy for the FOO protocol we have to show that the axioms and first-order inference rules imply that $\Phi_m^0 \sim \Phi_m^1$. Then from the soundness theorem of [8], it follows that there is no successful PPT attacker that breaks the security game. We have the following.

Theorem 1. *The modified FOO protocol respects vote privacy for one session with two honest voters and one dishonest voter.*

Proof Sketch: We recall the core axioms FUNCAPP and IFBRANCH from [12]:

FUNCAPP : $\vec{f} \in \mathcal{F} \cup \mathcal{G}, \ \vec{x} \sim \vec{y} \longrightarrow \vec{x}, \vec{f}(\vec{x}) \sim \vec{y}, \vec{f}(\vec{y})$.

IFBRANCH : $\vec{z}, b, x_1, ..., x_n \sim \vec{z}', b', x_1', ..., x_n' \ \wedge \ \vec{z}, b, y_1, ..., y_n \sim \vec{z}', b', y_1', ..., y_n'$
$\longrightarrow$

$$\vec{z}, b, \begin{array}{c} \text{if } b \text{ then } x_1 \\ \text{else } y_1 \end{array}, ..., \begin{array}{c} \text{if } b \text{ then } x_n \\ \text{else } y_n \end{array} \sim \vec{z}', b', \begin{array}{c} \text{if } b' \text{ then } x_1' \\ \text{else } y_1' \end{array}, ..., \begin{array}{c} \text{if } b' \text{ then } x_n' \\ \text{else } y_n' \end{array}.$$

Instead of showing the full security proof, we show how the combination of COMPHID, COMMEQL, UBNOTUNDEFINED and BLINDNESS allows us to fix the inadequacy of the blindness property. The key idea is that as the length of candidate identities are equal, the commitments hide the underlying vote. Thus, the probability that the attacker can cause the blind signature for candidate v_b is accepted but rejected for v_{1-b} is negligibly small. This is formalized in the following Proposition.

Proposition 1. Let v_0, v_1, t be ground terms, let $\vec{z}$ be a list of ground terms. Assume $\mathsf{EQL}(v_0, v_1) = \mathbf{true}$. Let t_0 and t_1 be terms containing two variables x and y. Let n_{b0}, n_{b1}, n_{c0}, n_{c1} be names such that $\mathsf{fresh}(n_{b0}, n_{b1}, n_{c0}, n_{c1}; \vec{z}, t, v_0, v_1, t_0, t_1)$ holds. Suppose that the blind signatures satisfy BLINDNESS and UBNOTUNDEFINED, and commitments satisfy COMPHID and COMMEQL properties. Then

$$\vec{z}, \mathsf{b}(c_0^0[v_0], t, \mathsf{r_b}(n_{b0})), \mathsf{b}(c_1^0[v_1], t, \mathsf{r_b}(n_{b1})), t^0 \sim \vec{z}, \mathsf{b}(c_0^1[v_1], t, \mathsf{r_b}(n_{b0})), \mathsf{b}(c_1^1[v_0], t, \mathsf{r_b}(n_{b1})), t^1$$

$$(1)$$

where $t^0 \equiv$ if acc_0^0 & acc_1^0 then $\langle \langle \mathrm{ub}_0^0[v_0], c_0^0[v_0], \mathrm{k_c}(n_{\mathrm{c}0}) \rangle, \langle \mathrm{ub}_1^0[v_1], c_1^0[v_1], \mathrm{k_c}(n_{\mathrm{c}1}) \rangle \rangle$
$\qquad$ else if acc_0^0 then $\langle \langle \mathrm{ub}_0^0[v_0], c_0^0[v_0], \mathrm{k_c}(n_{\mathrm{c}0}) \rangle, \bot \rangle$
$\qquad\qquad$ else if acc_1^0 then $\langle \bot, \langle \mathrm{ub}_1^0[v_1], c_1^0[v_1], \mathrm{k_c}(n_{\mathrm{c}1}) \rangle \rangle$
$\qquad\qquad\qquad$ else $\langle \bot, \bot \rangle$
$t^1 \equiv$ if acc_0^1 & acc_1^1 then $\langle \langle \mathrm{ub}_1^1[v_0], c_1^1[v_0], \mathrm{k_c}(n_{\mathrm{c}1}) \rangle, \langle \mathrm{ub}_0^1[v_1], c_0^1[v_1], \mathrm{k_c}(n_{\mathrm{c}0}) \rangle \rangle$
$\qquad$ else if acc_1^1 then $\langle \langle \mathrm{ub}_1^1[v_0], c_1^1[v_0], \mathrm{k_c}(n_{\mathrm{c}1}) \rangle, \bot \rangle$
$\qquad\qquad$ else if acc_0^1 then $\langle \bot, \langle \mathrm{ub}_0^1[v_1], c_0^1[v_1], \mathrm{k_c}(n_{\mathrm{c}0}) \rangle \rangle$
$\qquad\qquad\qquad$ else $\langle \bot, \bot \rangle$

$t_i^j = t_i[x \leftarrow \mathrm{b}(c_0^j[v_j], t, \mathbf{r}_\mathrm{b}(\mathrm{b}0))), y \leftarrow \mathrm{b}(c_1^j[v_{1-j}], t, \mathbf{r}_\mathrm{b}(\mathrm{b}1)))], \, i, j \in \{0,1\},$
$c_i^0[v_i] \equiv \mathrm{com}(v_i, \mathrm{k_c}(n_{\mathrm{c}i})) \qquad c_i^1[v_{1-i}] \equiv \mathrm{com}(v_{1-i}, \mathrm{k_c}(n_{\mathrm{c}i}))$
$\mathrm{acc}_i^0 \equiv \mathrm{acc}(c_i^0[v_i], t, \mathbf{r}_\mathrm{b}(n_{\mathrm{b}i}), t_i^0) \quad \mathrm{acc}_i^1 \equiv \mathrm{acc}(c_i^1[v_{1-i}], t, \mathbf{r}_\mathrm{b}(n_{\mathrm{b}i}), t_i^1)$
$\mathrm{ub}_i^0[v_i] \equiv \mathrm{ub}(c_i^0[v_i], t, \mathbf{r}_\mathrm{b}(n_{\mathrm{b}i}), t_i^0) \quad \mathrm{ub}_i^1[v_{1-i}] \equiv \mathrm{ub}(c_i^1[v_{1-i}], t, \mathbf{r}_\mathrm{b}(n_{\mathrm{b}i}), t_i^1)$

The proof idea of the Proposition is the following. Let us further introduce the notation
$$u_i^j[v_{j \oplus i}] \equiv \left\langle \mathrm{ub}_i^j[v_{j \oplus i}], c_i^j[v_{j \oplus i}], \mathrm{k_c}(n_{\mathrm{c}i}) \right\rangle \text{ and } b_i^j[v_{j \oplus i}] \equiv \mathrm{b}(c_i^j[v_{j \oplus i}], t, \mathbf{r}_\mathrm{b}(n_{\mathrm{b}i}))$$
where $\oplus$ is XOR. Then using the axiom IFBRANCH, it is sufficient to show the following equivalences:

$$\vec{z}, b_0^0[v_0], b_1^0[v_1], \mathrm{acc}_0^0 \, \& \, \mathrm{acc}_1^0, \text{ if } \mathrm{acc}_0^0 \, \& \, \mathrm{acc}_1^0 \text{ then } \langle u_0^0[v_0], u_1^0[v_1] \rangle \text{ else } \langle \bot, \bot \rangle$$
$$\sim \vec{z}, b_0^1[v_1], b_1^1[v_0], \mathrm{acc}_0^1 \, \& \, \mathrm{acc}_1^1, \text{ if } \mathrm{acc}_0^1 \, \& \, \mathrm{acc}_1^1 \text{ then } \langle u_1^1[v_0], u_0^1[v_1] \rangle \text{ else } \langle \bot, \bot \rangle$$

which follows from the BLINDNESS, UBNOTUNDEFINED and FUNCAPP; and the equivalences

$$\vec{z}, b_0^0[v_0], b_1^0[v_1], \mathrm{acc}_0^0 \, \& \, \mathrm{acc}_1^0, \text{ if } \mathrm{acc}_i^0 \text{ then } u_i^0[v_i] \text{ else } \bot$$
$$\sim \vec{z}, b_0^1[v_1], b_1^1[v_0], \mathrm{acc}_0^1 \, \& \, \mathrm{acc}_1^1, \text{ if } \mathrm{acc}_{1-i}^1 \text{ then } u_{1-i}^1[v_i] \text{ else } \bot$$

which follow from COMPHID and FUNCAPP. However, the axiom itself is not sufficient, we need the condition that the votes have equal length, otherwise these cannot be proven and an attack is constructed, which is the first attack described in Sect. 3.2.

Of course, in the actual security game, encryptions are sent too where the votes are also in reversed order, and decryptions are done by the mixer. This is dealt with the ENC$_{\mathrm{CCA2}}$ axiom. For the applicability of the axiom, the terms sent have to be rewritten using the equality to introduce cases when the adversarial function symbols on which decryptions are applied are either of the previous encryptions (namely the ones sent by voter A and B), or when they are neither. More precisely, a term of the form $\mathrm{dec}(f(\Phi), \mathrm{sk}(n_1))$, assuming that Φ has say two honest encryptions in them, $\{t\}_{\mathrm{pk}(n_1)}^{r(n)}$ and $\{t'\}_{\mathrm{pk}(n_1)}^{r(n')}$, has to be rewritten as

$$\mathrm{dec}(f(\Phi), \mathrm{sk}(n_1)) = \begin{array}{l} \text{if } \mathrm{EQ}(f(\Phi), \{t\}_{\mathrm{pk}(n_1)}^{r(n)}) \\ \text{then } t \\ \text{else if } \mathrm{EQ}(f(\Phi), \{t'\}_{\mathrm{pk}(n_1)}^{r(n')}) \text{ then } t' \text{ else } \mathrm{dec}(f(\Phi), \mathrm{sk}(n_1)) \end{array}.$$

Thus, when the attacker messages are equal to some encrypted messages sent, the decryptions can be replaced by the plaintext. When they are not equal, then the decryption on the function symbol is kept. Once this is done, the ENC$_{\mathrm{CCA2}}$

axiom can be applied, and the plaintexts inside the encryptions can now be switched as long as they are of equal length. This is why we needed to assume that the unblinding results equal length. Without that assumption we obtain the second attack in Sect. 3.2.

Finally, when the decryptions are applied on the correct previous encryptions, there are still several possibilities for each decryption because a priori the adversary could redirect the same encryption twice. A priori, each decryption will succeed on any of the previous (four) encryptions sent by A and B. To ensure that there is no clash, we made sure that the mixer checks both the phase and that all the decryptions are different. Otherwise we obtain the third attack of Sect. 3.2. □

5.3   Attack Finding

Finally we comment on how we found the attacks presented in Sect. 3.2, which was actually rather simple for this protocol. We illustrate this on the first two attacks. Suppose that we do not require that the lengths of the names of the candidates are the same. At a certain point we arrive at having to verify that the messages sent by the challenger up to point 9 in Sect. 3.1 are equivalent in the two executions with flipped votes. This is the point when one of A or B according to the attacker's choice is supposed to have sent her ballot after having accepted the blind signature. As all the messages in the frames, this on both sides has the form of if c then t_1 else t_2 , where c has all the conditions to get to this point, $t_2 = \mathbf{0}$, and t_1 has the encrypted ballot of either A or B depending on which of them was called first by the adversary, which in turn contains corresponding unflipped vote on one side and the flipped vote on the other side. To show that the two sides are equivalent, we would need to use the IND-CCA2 axiom for encryption, but that is only applicable if the equality of the lengths of the plaintexts are verified. However, without the formula $L(v_1) = L(v_2)$ this cannot be derived, and this gives our second attack through an Herbrand model. The first attack is obtained when we try to verify that the condition c on the two sides are equivalent. This condition contains the acc function symbol applied on the blind signature of v_1 or v_2, flipped on the two sides. The only axiom that is suitable to verify such difference (in the absence of encryption in c) the hiding of the commitment. Note, the blindness axiom can only be applied once both blind signatures were accepted, but at this point we only have one on each branch. The hiding of the commitment on the other hand can only be applied if the lengths are equal. As a result, we can set again $L(v_1) \neq L(v_2)$ and one of the accepts to *true* and the other to *false*, and again an Herbrand model delivers a symbolic attack, which turns out to be a real computational one.

6   Conclusions

We analyzed the FOO electronic voting protocol for vote privacy in the provable security model using the computationally complete symbolic attacker (CCSA) framework. As part of the analysis, we showed that security properties of trap-door commitments and blind signatures can be faithfully translated into axioms in the CCSA framework. We demonstrated that the framework is effective in that it revealed new attacks on the FOO protocol and could be used to prove the modified FOO protocol secure. As part of future work, we plan to investigate expressing and verifying stronger privacy properties of receipt-freeness and coercion-resistance for electronic voting protocols in the CCSA framework. We also plan to investigate automation of the verification tasks.

References

1. Fujioka, A., Okamoto, T., Ohta, K.: A practical secret voting scheme for large scale elections. In: Seberry, J., Zheng, Y. (eds.) AUSCRYPT 1992. LNCS, vol. 718, pp. 244–251. Springer, Heidelberg (1993). https://doi.org/10.1007/3-540-57220-1_66
2. Adida, B.: Helios: web-based open-audit voting. In: Proceedings of the 17th Conference on Security Symposium. SS 2008, pp. 335–348. USENIX Association (2008)
3. Ryan, P.Y.A., Rønne, P.B., Iovino, V.: Selene: voting with transparent verifiability and coercion-mitigation. In: Clark, J., Meiklejohn, S., Ryan, P.Y.A., Wallach, D., Brenner, M., Rohloff, K. (eds.) FC 2016. LNCS, vol. 9604, pp. 176–192. Springer, Heidelberg (2016). https://doi.org/10.1007/978-3-662-53357-4_12
4. Kremer, S., Ryan, M.: Analysis of an electronic voting protocol in the applied pi calculus. In: Sagiv, M. (ed.) ESOP 2005. LNCS, vol. 3444, pp. 186–200. Springer, Heidelberg (2005). https://doi.org/10.1007/978-3-540-31987-0_14
5. Abadi, M., Blanchet, B., Fournet, C.: The applied pi calculus: mobile values, new names, and secure communication. J. ACM 65, 1–41 (2017)
6. Delaune, S., Ryan, M., Smyth, B.: Automatic verification of privacy properties in the applied pi calculus. In: Karabulut, Y., Mitchell, J., Herrmann, P., Jensen, C.D. (eds.) IFIPTM 2008. ITIFIP, vol. 263, pp. 263–278. Springer, Boston, MA (2008). https://doi.org/10.1007/978-0-387-09428-1_17
7. Chadha, R., Cheval, V., Ciobâcă, Ş., Kremer, S.: Automated verification of equivalence properties of cryptographic protocols. ACM Trans. Comput. Log. 17, 1–32 (2016)
8. Bana, G., Comon-Lundh, H.: A computationally complete symbolic attacker for equivalence properties. In: ACM Conference on Computer and Communications Security, pp. 609–620 (2014)
9. Bana, G., Comon-Lundh, H.: Towards unconditional soundness: computationally complete symbolic attacker. In: Degano, P., Guttman, J.D. (eds.) POST 2012. LNCS, vol. 7215, pp. 189–208. Springer, Heidelberg (2012). https://doi.org/10.1007/978-3-642-28641-4_11
10. Bana, G., Adão, P., Sakurada, H.: Computationally complete symbolic attacker in action. In: Foundations of Software Technology and Theoretical Computer Science, pp. 546–560 (2012)
11. Bana, G., Adão, P., Sakurada, H.: Symbolic Verification of the Needham-Schroeder-Lowe Protocol (2012). http://web.ist.utl.pt/pedro.adao/pubs/drafts/nsl-long.pdf
12. Bana, G., Chadha, R.: Verification methods for the computationally complete symbolic attacker based on indistinguishability. Cryptology ePrint Archive, Report 2016/069 (2016). http://eprint.iacr.org/2016/069

13. Comon, H., Koutsos, A.: Formal computational unlinkability proofs of RFID protocols. In: IEEE Computer Security Foundations Symposium, pp. 100–114 (2017)
14. Scerri, G., Stanley-Oakes, R.: Analysis of key wrapping APIs: generic policies, computational security. In: IEEE Computer Security Foundations Symposium, pp. 281–295 (2016)
15. Chaum, D.L.: Untraceable electronic mail, return addresses, and digital pseudonyms. Commun. ACM **24**, 84–90 (1981)
16. Benaloh, J., Tuinstra, D.: Receipt-free secret-ballot elections (extended abstract). In: ACM Symposium on Theory of Computing, pp. 544–553 (1994)
17. Benaloh, J.D.C.: Verifiable Secret-ballot Elections. Ph.D. thesis, Yale University (1987)
18. Juels, A., Luby, M., Ostrovsky, R.: Security of blind digital signatures. In: Kaliski, B.S. (ed.) CRYPTO 1997. LNCS, vol. 1294, pp. 150–164. Springer, Heidelberg (1997). https://doi.org/10.1007/BFb0052233
19. Smyth, B., Bernhard, D.: Ballot secrecy and ballot independence coincide. In: Crampton, J., Jajodia, S., Mayes, K. (eds.) ESORICS 2013. LNCS, vol. 8134, pp. 463–480. Springer, Heidelberg (2013). https://doi.org/10.1007/978-3-642-40203-6_26
20. Bernhard, D., Cortier, V., Galindo, D., Pereira, O., Warinschi, B.: Sok: a comprehensive analysis of game-based ballot privacy definitions. In: IEEE Symposium on Security and Privacy, pp. 499–516 (2015)
21. Cortier, V., Dragan, C.C., Dupressoir, F., Schmidt, B., Strub, P., Warinschi, B.: Machine-checked proofs of privacy for electronic voting protocols. In: IEEE Symposium on Security and Privacy, pp. 993–1008 (2017)
22. Fischlin, M., Schröder, D.: Security of blind signatures under aborts. In: Jarecki, S., Tsudik, G. (eds.) PKC 2009. LNCS, vol. 5443, pp. 297–316. Springer, Heidelberg (2009). https://doi.org/10.1007/978-3-642-00468-1_17
23. Chaum, D.: Blind signatures for untraceable payments. In: Chaum, D., Rivest, R.L., Sherman, A.T. (eds.) Advances in Cryptology, pp. 199–203. Springer, Boston, MA (1983). https://doi.org/10.1007/978-1-4757-0602-4_18
24. Abdalla, M., Namprempre, C., Neven, G.: On the (im)possibility of blind message authentication codes. In: Pointcheval, D. (ed.) CT-RSA 2006. LNCS, vol. 3860, pp. 262–279. Springer, Heidelberg (2006). https://doi.org/10.1007/11605805_17
25. Smart, N.P.: Cryptography Made Simple. Information Security and Cryptography. Springer, Cham (2016). https://doi.org/10.1007/978-3-319-21936-3
26. Damgård, I.B., Pedersen, T.P., Pfitzmann, B.: On the existence of statistically hiding bit commitment schemes and fail-stop signatures. J. Cryptol. **10**, 163–194 (1997)
27. Naor, M.: Bit commitment using pseudorandomness. J. Cryptol. **4**, 151–158 (1991)
28. Bana, G., Chadha, R., Eeralla, A.K.: Formal analysis of vote privacy using computationally complete symbolic attacker. Cryptology ePrint Archive, Report 2018/624 (2018). https://eprint.iacr.org/2018/624

Location Proximity Attacks Against Mobile Targets: Analytical Bounds and Attacker Strategies

Xueou Wang[1]([✉]), Xiaolu Hou[2][iD], Ruben Rios[3][iD], Per Hallgren[4,5],
Nils Ole Tippenhauer[1][iD], and Martín Ochoa[1,6]

[1] Singapore University of Technology and Design (SUTD), Singapore, Singapore
{xueou_wang,nils_tippenhauer}@sutd.edu.sg
[2] Cyber Security Lab, School of Computer Science and Engineering, Nanyang
Technological University, Singapore, Singapore
ho0001lu@e.ntu.edu.sg
[3] Computer Science Department, University of Málaga, Málaga, Spain
ruben@lcc.uma.es
[4] Chalmers University of Technology, Gothenburg, Sweden
[5] Einride AB, Stockholm, Sweden
per.hallgren@einride.tech
[6] Department of Applied Mathematics and Computer Science,
Universidad del Rosario, Bogotá, Colombia
martin.ochoa@urosario.edu.co

Abstract. Location privacy has mostly focused on scenarios where users remain static. However, investigating scenarios where the victims present a particular mobility pattern is more realistic. In this paper, we consider abstract attacks on services that provide location information on other users in the proximity. In that setting, we quantify the required effort of the attacker to localize a particular mobile victim. We prove upper and lower bounds for the effort of an optimal attacker. We experimentally show that a *Linear Jump Strategy* (LJS) practically achieves the upper bounds for almost uniform initial distributions of victims. To improve performance for less uniform distributions known to the attacker, we propose a *Greedy Updating Attack Strategy* (GUAS). Finally, we derive a realistic mobility model from a real-world dataset and discuss the performance of our strategies in that setting.

1 Introduction

Proximity services are a special type of location-based service (LBS) where the user is informed about nearby people of interest and their distance rather than their exact location in an attempt to protect location privacy. To that end, queries are sent to the proximity service including the location of the user, the search radius and possibly some information about the target. Unfortunately, when the exact distance to a user is revealed by the proximity service it is possible to retrieve the exact location of the user. Examples include claims that

© Springer Nature Switzerland AG 2018
J. Lopez et al. (Eds.): ESORICS 2018, LNCS 11099, pp. 373–392, 2018.
https://doi.org/10.1007/978-3-319-98989-1_19

Egyptian authorities leveraged dating apps to track down gay users [6], and others attempted to find locations of Tinder users [19]. Consequently, the need to provide rigorous privacy guarantees in proximity services is evident.

In view of these threats, some effort has been devoted to the development of privacy-preserving proximity testing protocols [8,12,15]. These solutions allow two users to learn whether they are within a certain distance of each other but no further information about their location or distance is revealed to the other user. Some of these protocols rely on a trusted third party to handle users' locations while others get rid of this third party and operate in a decentralized way.

In general, these solutions focus on partially static models, where attackers can change their location freely but victims do not. Capturing the behavior of an optimal attacker in this setting when the victim is static is already hard although some progress has been made in recent years [9,13]. However, this situation is quite unrealistic and motivated us to investigate the expected effort for adversaries to localize users that move in a particular mobility pattern.

Although there has been extensive study in mobility models [2], attack strategies [11,13,19], location privacy protection mechanisms [8,9,18] and location privacy quantification metrics [16,17], there is very limited research on location prediction based on sequential spatio-temporal data using a probabilistic approach. Given that location data acquired from an LBS platform are sequential spatio-temporal data, one can obtain information on the moving patterns/behaviors of the user by analyzing the trajectory dataset. Hence, we are interested in quantifying the effort of an *arbitrary attacker* issuing proximity queries in finding a user under certain models. In other words: *how quickly can an attacker locate a user based on queries to the LBS?*

Our main contributions are as follows:

1. Given any attacker strategy, assuming the victim follows a random walk, we establish a formula for calculating the probability of the attacker finding the location of the victim after any number of queries.
2. We give upper and lower bounds on the minimum number of queries an attacker needs to issue to locate the victim with probability $\frac{1}{2}$ (generalizable to other probabilities). In particular, for a search space of size M and assumptions on victim's initial location and mobility, we show that an optimal attacker needs at most $\frac{M}{2}$ queries to locate a victim with probability $\frac{1}{2}$.
3. We implement the *linear jump* strategy from the proof, and show empirically that its effort falls within the theoretical bounds. We find that for non-uniform initial distributions of victims, the strategy performs worse. To address this, we propose a *greedy updating attacker* strategy.
4. We then use the strategies to estimate attacker effort for more general settings (e.g., limited knowledge known by the attacker, other mobility models).
5. We derive a transition matrix representing real-world mobility patterns from a large dataset [21,22], and show how that mobility pattern influences attacker effort compared to previous results.

The rest of this work is organized as follows. In Sect. 2, we present our mathematical modeling of search spaces and mobility patterns. Section 3 summarizes the problem statement. We present the mathematical analysis for calculating the probability of an attacker locating a victim using location proximity queries in Sect. 4. In Sect. 5, we present our applied linear jumping and greedy attacker strategies, and evaluate them empirically in Sect. 6. Related work and conclusions are discussed in Sects. 7 and 8, respectively.

2   Preliminaries

2.1   Search Domain

In our model, users are able to move in a finite space that can be divided into discrete *locations*. The granularity of the locations is limited by the maximum precision of the positioning device or privacy considerations [5].

Space. We consider two cases. In the one-dimensional case, the search space is divided into n locations, each of which has two adjacent locations, left and right, except for the corners. We call this space $\mathcal{S}^n$. For the two-dimensional case, the search space can be divided into $m \times n$ locations. Each point typically has four adjacent locations, except for the corners. We call this space $\mathcal{S}^M$, with $M = mn$.

Time. We assume discrete time steps $k \in \{0, 1, 2, \dots\}$. In each time step, the user $\mathcal{X}$ can move once. The movement of users is represented as a transition in our model. Let $\mathcal{X}_k$ denote the position of user $\mathcal{X}$ at time k.

Location. A user $\mathcal{X}$ located in the space $\mathcal{S}^M$ at time k is denoted $\mathcal{X}_k$, with $k \in \mathbb{Z}_{\geq 0}$ and $\mathcal{X}_k \in \{0, 1, \dots, M-1\}$. The location of $\mathcal{X}$ at time 0 is called the *initial location of* $\mathcal{X}$. The set of possible values for $\mathcal{X}_{k+1}$ will be determined by the particular mobility pattern of the user.

2.2   Mobility Models

We now describe some common mobility patterns (see Fig. 1) to give a better intuition of our modeling of search spaces and descriptions of entities moving in the search space. We assume an honest user like Bob follows a realistic mobility pattern where subsequent locations are contiguous to each other. We will use mobility patterns and mobility models interchangeably throughout this paper. Two-dimensional search spaces can be projected to a one-dimensional space.

Static Mobility Model. An entity $\mathcal{X}$ that follows a static mobility model starts at a random initial position r in the search space $\mathcal{S}^M$ and does not move afterwards. For example, a person who stays at home or in the office. With a fixed $r \in \mathcal{S}^M$:

$$\mathcal{X}_{k+1} = \mathcal{X}_k, \ \mathcal{X}_0 = r, \ k \in \mathbb{Z}_{\geq 0}$$

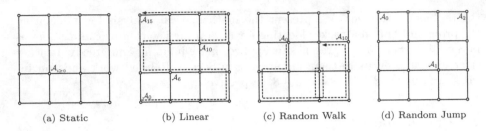

     (a) Static   (b) Linear   (c) Random Walk   (d) Random Jump

Fig. 1. Mobility models

Linear Mobility Model. An entity $\mathcal{X}$ that follows a linear mobility model starts at an arbitrary initial position $\mathcal{X}_0$ within the search space $\mathcal{S}^M$ ($M = mn$ for dimension two and $M = n$ for dimension one) and keeps moving such that the following conditions are satisfied:

1. $\{\mathcal{X}_{iM}, \mathcal{X}_{iM+1}, \ldots, \mathcal{X}_{iM+M-1}\} = \{0, 1, \ldots, M-1\}$ for all $i \in \mathbb{Z}_{\geq 0}$;
2. $\mathcal{X}_{k+1} \in \{\mathcal{X}_k + 1, \mathcal{X}_k - 1\}$ for a one dimensional search space of size n ($k \in \mathbb{Z}_{\geq 0}$).

This model may apply when a person is driving a car on the road.

Random Walk Mobility Model. An entity $\mathcal{X}$ that follows a random walk mobility model starts at a random position and decides its next move uniformly at random from all the positions in its vicinity. Hence the following mathematical expressions hold for a one-dimensional search space of size n (similar expressions can be derived for the two-dimensional case).

$$\Pr\left(\mathcal{X}_{k+1} = \mathcal{X}_k + 1\right) = \Pr\left(\mathcal{X}_{k+1} = \mathcal{X}_k - 1\right) = \frac{1}{2}, \text{ if } 1 \leq \mathcal{X}_k \leq n - 2;$$
$$\Pr\left(\mathcal{X}_{k+1} = 1\right) = 1, \text{ if } \mathcal{X}_k = 0;$$
$$\Pr\left(\mathcal{X}_{k+1} = n - 2\right) = 1, \text{ if } \mathcal{X}_k = n - 1,$$

where $\Pr\left(\cdot\right)$ denotes probability hereinafter. Later, our theoretical probabilistic derivation will start with a random walk mobility model. A person sightseeing or shopping could fit this model.

Random Jump. An entity $\mathcal{X}$ that follows this strategy can arbitrarily move to any other position. In other words, the next position is sampled freshly from a uniform distribution. An attacker, for example, who can fake his/her location as a means to perform attacks, such as trilateration, could be described using the random jump model.

3 Location Proximity Attacks

Based on the modeling of search spaces and possible mobility patterns from Sect. 2, we proceed to give a formal mathematical description of the problem statement for this paper. Afterwards, we will derive general analytical bounds on the expected location effort in dimension one.

3.1   System and Attacker Model

Let Alice ($\mathcal{A}$) be the attacker and Bob ($\mathcal{B}$) be a user whose location is of interest to Alice. Bob uses a LBS that will disclose Bob's presence at location $\mathcal{B}_k$ to other users that claim to be at the same location. Bob (and Alice) can only make one location claim per discrete time step k. Each time k, Bob will move once (and update its location on the LBS), and Alice will thus be able to perform one query to the LBS to verify if Bob is at Alice's claimed location $\mathcal{A}_k$. Alice sends the first query at time $k = 0$, and thus k is the time of the $(k+1)$-th query.

The goal of Alice is to minimize the number of queries that she needs to send to LBS to be able to verify Bob's location. Conversely, Bob does not have a particular goal except to use the service privately. He is not even aware of being tracked. Alice on the other hand is assumed to have a priori information about Bob's probability distribution obtained from past observations, external sources, geographic features of the terrain or a combination thereof. Later in Sect. 6.2, we will discuss a real data example, where the attacker can obtain some information from historical trajectory data of a victim.

While we use a third party LBS in this system model for simplicity, similar scenarios could be constructed if Alice and Bob engage in a privacy-preserving proximity protocol that is initiated by Alice and where the inputs of both of them remain private (e.g., the protocol discussed in [8]).

3.2   Problem Statement and Formalization

We now present our problem statement and the underlying formalization.

Problem Statement. We are interested in finding $k_{O,p}$: the number of queries required by an optimal attacker strategy to locate Bob with probability of at least p. Formally, we define $k_{O,p}$ as follows:

$$k_{O,p} := \min_{\mathcal{A}} k_{\mathcal{A},p}, \qquad (1)$$

with $k_{\mathcal{A},p}$ being the number of steps required by a specific attacker strategy $\mathcal{A}$ to locate Bob with probability $0 \leq p \leq 1$. We can find that number as follows:

$$k_{\mathcal{A},p} := \min\{k : \Pr(E_k) \geq p\},$$

with $\Pr(E_k)$ being the cumulative probability that Bob was located within k steps, that is, $k+1$ queries.

Attacker Strategies. For a fixed attacker strategy $\mathcal{A} = \mathcal{A}_0, \mathcal{A}_1, \ldots$, we are interested in the probability of two events: E_k, and F_j. The event E_k is the event that Alice locates Bob within k steps:

$$E_k := \{\exists i \leq k \text{ s.t. } \mathcal{A}_i = \mathcal{B}_i\}$$

F_j is the event that Alice locates Bob exactly at step j:

$$F_j := \{A_j = B_j\}.$$

Before we can derive the probabilities of those events ($\Pr(E_k)$ and $\Pr(F_j)$), we now show how to compute the probabilistic locations of Bob.

Probabilistic Locations. Consider a search space $\mathcal{S}^M$. We assume the mobility model of Bob can be described by a transition matrix P where each entry of P is a transition probability p_{ij} representing the probability of Bob moving from location i to location j in one step. Furthermore, we assume the probability of Bob moving from location i to location j is the same at any step. More precisely:

$$\Pr(\mathcal{B}_k = j | \mathcal{B}_{k-1} = i) = p_{ij}, \ \forall k \in \mathbb{Z}_{\geq 1} \text{ and } i, j \in \mathcal{S}^M.$$

Thus, it is straightforward to calculate the probability of Bob being at a particular location after k steps by simply taking the kth power of the transition matrix.

Let $B^{(k)}$ ($k \in \mathbb{Z}_{\geq 0}$) be a vector representing the probability of Bob being at each location j ($j \in \{0, 1, \ldots, M-1\}$) after k steps, i.e. $B_j^{(k)} = \Pr(\mathcal{B}_k = j)$. Assume that Bob is at location i after k steps, then $B^{(k+1)}$ ($k \in \mathbb{Z}_{\geq 0}$) can be calculated as follows:

$$B^{(k+1)} = B^{(k)} \cdot P = \begin{pmatrix} 0 & \cdots & \overset{i}{1} & \cdots & 0 \end{pmatrix} \begin{pmatrix} p_{1,1} & p_{1,2} & \cdots & p_{1,M} \\ p_{2,1} & p_{2,2} & \cdots & p_{2,M} \\ \vdots & \vdots & \ddots & \vdots \\ p_{M,1} & p_{M,2} & \cdots & p_{M,M} \end{pmatrix}$$

Upper Bound for $\Pr(E_k)$. By definition,

$$\Pr(E_k) = \Pr(F_0 \cup F_1 \cdots \cup F_k),$$

which gives the following *upper bound* for $\Pr(E_k)$ since the probability of finding Bob at step i is at most equal to the probability of Bob's most likely location at that step:

$$\Pr(E_k) \leq \Pr(F_0) + \Pr(F_1) + \cdots + \Pr(F_k) \leq \sum_{i=0}^{k} \max_j B_j^{(i)}. \tag{2}$$

Note that the above upper bound on $\Pr(E_k)$ holds for any attacker strategy $\mathcal{A}$.

Lower Bound on k. We define

$$k_{lower,p} := \min \left\{ k : \sum_{i=0}^{k} \max_j B_j^{(i)} \geq p \right\}. \tag{3}$$

In view of Eq. 2, $k_{lower,p} \leq k_{O,p}$ is a *lower bound* of $k_{O,p}$.

4 Quantifying Attacker Effort

Next we present the theoretical analysis on the minimal number of steps required by an optimal attack strategy to locate a particular victim. First, we derive the formula for calculating $\Pr(E_k)$ and then we consider the case of a victim following a random walk mobility model. We choose a random walk model to give a rigorous mathematical analysis. In more complex moving patterns, the problem may not have analytical or closed solutions because the transition matrix is indefinable or needs to be recursively updated. Our mathematical derivation will be presented for the one-dimensional case only as we can always project two-dimensions to a one-dimensional space.

4.1 Attacker's Effort Computation

Given the transition matrix P and the vector $B^{(0)}$ of initial position probabilities, $B^{(k)} = B^{(0)}P^k$ gives the probabilities of Bob being at each different position after k steps. More precisely, $B_j^{(k)} = \Pr(\mathcal{B}_k = j)$ is the probability of Bob at position j after k steps.

Let $P_{j_1 j_2}^i$ denote the (j_1, j_2)-entry of the matrix P^i. It gives the probability of Bob going from position j_1 to position j_2 in i steps, i.e. for any $k \in \mathbb{Z}_{\geq 0}$,

$$\Pr(\mathcal{B}_{i+k} = j_2 | \mathcal{B}_k = j_1) = P_{j_1 j_2}^i.$$

Fixing an attacker strategy $\mathcal{A}$, let $\mathcal{A}_i$ denote the position of Alice at step i. For any positive integers $i_1 < i_2$, the probability of Alice locating Bob at both steps i_1 and i_2 is equal to the probability of Bob being at position $\mathcal{A}_{i_1}$ at step i_1 multiplied by the probability of Bob reaching position $\mathcal{A}_{i_2}$ in $i_2 - i_1$ steps, i.e.

$$\Pr(F_{i_1} \cap F_{i_2}) = \Pr(\mathcal{B}_{i_1} = \mathcal{A}_{i_1} \cap \mathcal{B}_{i_2} = \mathcal{A}_{i_2}) \tag{4}$$

$$= \Pr(\mathcal{B}_{i_1} = \mathcal{A}_{i_1})\Pr(\mathcal{B}_{i_2} = \mathcal{A}_{i_2} | \mathcal{B}_{i_1} = \mathcal{A}_{i_1}) = B_{\mathcal{A}_{i_1}}^{(i_1)} P_{\mathcal{A}_{i_1} \mathcal{A}_{i_2}}^{i_2 - i_1}. \tag{5}$$

To get a general formula for $\Pr(E_k)$, we first note

$$\Pr(E_k) = \Pr(F_0 \cup F_1 \cup \cdots \cup F_k) = \Pr((F_0 \cup F_1 \cup \cdots \cup F_{k-1})^c \cap F_k)$$
$$= \Pr(F_0) + \Pr(F_0^c \cap F_1) + \Pr((F_0 \cup F_1)^c \cap F_2) + \cdots$$
$$+ \Pr((F_0 \cup F_1 \cup \cdots \cup F_{k-1})^c \cap F_k)$$
$$= \sum_{0 \leq i \leq k} \Pr((F_0 \cup F_1 \cup \cdots \cup F_{i-1})^c \cap F_i), \tag{6}$$

where F^c is the complement of F, i.e., F_j^c means Alice does not successfully locates Bob at step j. Our GUAS attacker strategy uses this result for aggregate success computation (see Sect. 5.2). From probability theory we can also write

$$\Pr(E_k) = \Pr(F_0 \cup F_1 \cup \cdots \cup F_k)$$
$$= \sum_{m=0}^{k} (-1)^{m+1} \left(\sum_{0 \leq i_1 < \cdots < i_m \leq k} \Pr(F_{i_1} \cap \cdots \cap F_{i_m}) \right). \tag{7}$$

By combining Eq. 4 with Eq. 7, we have the following general formula for $\Pr(E_k)$:

$$\sum_{m=0}^{k} B_{\mathcal{A}_m}^{(m)} \left(1 + \sum_{\ell=1}^{k-m} (-1)^{\ell} \sum_{m < i_1 < i_2 < \cdots < i_\ell \leq k} P_{\mathcal{A}_m \mathcal{A}_{i_1}}^{i_1 - m} \cdots P_{\mathcal{A}_{i_{\ell-1}} \mathcal{A}_{i_\ell}}^{i_\ell - i_{\ell-1}} \right)$$

$$= B_{\mathcal{A}_0}^{(0)} \left(1 - \sum_{i=1}^{k} P_{\mathcal{A}_0 \mathcal{A}_i}^{i} + \sum_{1 \leq i_1 < i_2 \leq k} P_{\mathcal{A}_0 \mathcal{A}_{i_1}}^{i_1} P_{\mathcal{A}_{i_1} \mathcal{A}_{i_2}}^{i_2 - i_1} - \cdots \right)$$

$$+ B_{\mathcal{A}_1}^{(1)} \left(1 - \sum_{i=2}^{k} P_{\mathcal{A}_1 \mathcal{A}_i}^{i-1} + \sum_{2 \leq i_1 < i_2 \leq k} P_{\mathcal{A}_1 \mathcal{A}_{i_1}}^{i_1 - 1} P_{\mathcal{A}_{i_1} \mathcal{A}_{i_2}}^{i_2 - i_1} - \cdots \right) + \cdots + B_{\mathcal{A}_k}^{(k)}. \quad (8)$$

If the attacker strategy is not deterministic, then for one fixed sequence of positions $a_0, a_1, a_2, \ldots, a_k$, $\Pr(E_k | \mathcal{A}_0 = a_0 \cap \mathcal{A}_1 = a_1 \cap \cdots \cap \mathcal{A}_k = a_k)$ is given by

$$\sum_{m=0}^{k} B_{a_m}^{(m)} \left(1 + \sum_{\ell=1}^{k-m} (-1)^{\ell} \sum_{m < i_1 < i_2 < \cdots < i_\ell \leq k} P_{a_m a_{i_1}}^{i_1 - m} P_{a_{i_1} a_{i_2}}^{i_2 - i_1} \cdots P_{a_{i_{\ell-1}} a_{i_\ell}}^{i_\ell - i_{\ell-1}} \right),$$

and we have the following formula for $\Pr(E_k)$

$$\sum_{1 \leq a_0, a_1, \ldots, a_k \leq n} \Pr(\mathcal{A}_0 = a_0 \cap \cdots \cap \mathcal{A}_k = a_k) \cdot \Pr(E_k | \mathcal{A}_0 = a_0 \cap \cdots \cap \mathcal{A}_k = a_k)$$

$$(9)$$

Note that when the attacker strategy is deterministic, for one sequence of positions $a_0, a_1, a_2, \ldots, a_k$ we have $\Pr(\mathcal{A}_0 = a_0, \ldots, \mathcal{A}_k = a_k) = 1$ and we get the formula in (8).

For the next subsection, we assume Bob follows a random walk strategy that can be represented as a Markovian process with transition probabilities p_{ij}, consistent with the provisions of the random walk mobility model in Sect. 2.2. We give our evaluations for the case $p = 0.5$. To simplify the notations, we define

$$k_{\mathcal{A}} := k_{\mathcal{A}, 0.5} = \min\{k : \Pr(E_k) \geq 0.5\},$$
$$k_O := k_{O, 0.5} = \min_{\mathcal{A}} k_{\mathcal{A}},$$
$$k_{lower} := k_{lower, 0.5}.$$

Thus if Alice follows strategy $\mathcal{A}$, $k_{\mathcal{A}}$ (resp. $k_{\mathcal{A}} + 1$) is the number of steps (resp. number of queries) needed for Alice to locate Bob with a probability of at least 0.5. k_O (resp. $k_O + 1$) is the minimum number of steps (resp. minimum number of queries) needed for Alice to locate Bob with a probability of at least 0.5 independently of strategy used. In addition, $k_{lower} \leq k_O$ is a lower bound of k_O.

4.2   Random Walk Example

In this section, we derive upper and lower bounds on k_O by analyzing the matrices $B^{(k)}$. We show that "for a search space of size n, $\lfloor \frac{n}{3} \rfloor - 1 \leq k_O \leq \lfloor \frac{n}{2} \rfloor$"

(see Corollary 1). To achieve this goal, we first estimate the values of $B_j^{(k)}$. For a one-dimensional search space of size n, Bob follows a transition matrix P with initial position vector $B^{(0)}$:

$$B^{(0)} = \left[\frac{1}{n}, \frac{1}{n}, \ldots, \frac{1}{n}\right], \quad P = \begin{bmatrix} 0 & 1 & 0 & \ldots & 0 & 0 \\ \frac{1}{2} & 0 & \frac{1}{2} & \ldots & 0 & 0 \\ 0 & \frac{1}{2} & 0 & \ldots & 0 & 0 \\ \vdots & \vdots & \vdots & \ddots & \vdots & \vdots \\ 0 & 0 & 0 & \ldots & 0 & \frac{1}{2} \\ 0 & 0 & 0 & \ldots & 1 & 0 \end{bmatrix}$$

Then the probabilities of Bob in each position at step i is given by $B^{(i)} = B^{(0)} P^i$:

$$B^{(1)} = \left[\frac{1}{2n}, \frac{3}{2n}, \frac{1}{n}, \ldots, \frac{1}{n}, \frac{3}{2n}, \frac{1}{2n}\right],$$

$$B^{(2)} = \left[\frac{3}{4n}, \frac{1}{n}, \frac{5}{4n}, \frac{1}{n}, \ldots, \frac{1}{n}, \frac{5}{4n}, \frac{1}{n}, \frac{3}{4n}\right],$$

$$B^{(3)} = \left[\frac{1}{2n}, \frac{11}{8n}, \frac{1}{n}, \frac{9}{8n}, \frac{1}{n}, \ldots, \frac{1}{n}, \frac{9}{8n}, \frac{1}{n}, \frac{11}{8n}, \frac{1}{2n}\right],$$

$$B^{(4)} = \left[\frac{11}{16n}, \frac{1}{n}, \frac{5}{4n}, \frac{1}{n}, \frac{17}{16n}, \frac{1}{n}, \ldots, \frac{1}{n}, \frac{17}{16n}, \frac{1}{n}, \frac{5}{4n}, \frac{1}{n}, \frac{11}{16n}\right], \quad (10)$$

We have the following observation:

Lemma 1. *For* $k \in \mathbb{Z}_{\geq 0}$,

$$\begin{cases} \frac{1}{n} \leq B_j^{(k)} \leq \frac{3}{2n} & 1 \leq j \leq n-2 \\ \frac{1}{2n} \leq B_j^{(k)} \leq \frac{3}{4n} & j = 0, n-1 \end{cases}.$$

Proof. We prove the above claims by mathematical induction. For $B^{(0)}$, the claim is true. We assume it is true for $B^{(k)}$, then for $B^{(k+1)}$

1. $2 \leq j \leq n-3$, $B_j^{(k+1)} = \frac{1}{2}\left(B_{j-1}^{(k)} + B_{j+1}^{(k)}\right)$, by induction hypothesis

$$\frac{1}{n} = \frac{1}{2}\left(\frac{1}{n} + \frac{1}{n}\right) \leq B_j^{(k+1)} \leq \frac{1}{2}\left(\frac{3}{2n} + \frac{3}{2n}\right) = \frac{3}{2n}.$$

2. $j = 1, n-2$, $B_1^{(k+1)} = B_0^{(k)} + \frac{1}{2}B_2^{(k)}$, by induction hypothesis

$$\frac{1}{n} = \frac{1}{2n} + \frac{1}{2} \cdot \frac{1}{n} \leq B_2^{(k+1)} \leq \frac{3}{4n} + \frac{1}{2} \cdot \frac{3}{2n} = \frac{3}{2n}; \quad \frac{1}{n} \leq B_{n-2}^{(k+1)} \leq \frac{3}{2n}.$$

3. $j = 0, n-1$, $B_0^{(k+1)} = B_1^{(k)}\frac{1}{2}$, by induction hypothesis

$$\frac{1}{2n} = \frac{1}{2} \cdot \frac{1}{n} \leq B_1^{(k+1)} \leq \frac{1}{2} \cdot \frac{3}{2n} = \frac{3}{4n}; \quad \frac{1}{2n} \leq B_{n-1}^{(k+1)} \leq \frac{3}{4n}.$$

The above bounds on $B_j^{(k)}$ helps us to get upper and lower bounds on k_O. Next we show a lower bound of k_{lower}, which gives a lower bound for k_O.

Proposition 1

$$k_O \geq k_{lower} \geq \left\lfloor \frac{n}{3} \right\rfloor - 1.$$

Proof. By Lemma 1, for any k,

$$\sum_{i=0}^{k} \max_j B_j^{(i)} \leq \frac{3}{2n} \cdot (k+1) = \frac{3k+3}{2n}.$$

If $k < \lfloor \frac{n}{3} \rfloor - 1$, $\sum_{i=0}^{k} \max_j B_j^{(i)} < \frac{1}{2}$. Thus by definition, we must have $k_{lower} \geq \lfloor \frac{n}{3} \rfloor - 1$.

By the definition of k_O, for any given attacker strategy $\mathcal{A}$, $k_O \leq k_{\mathcal{A}}$. Next, we construct a specific attacker strategy $\mathcal{A}_{jp}$ and prove an upper bound for $k_{\mathcal{A}_{jp}}$, to obtain an upper bound for k_O.

Lemma 2. *For any $n \geq 4$, there exists a strategy $\mathcal{A}_{jp}$ such that $k_{\mathcal{A}_{jp}} \leq \lfloor \frac{n}{2} \rfloor$.*

Proof. First we notice that $P_{ij}^{\ell} = 0$ if $j - i > \ell$ due to our construction of the random walk P.

1. Let $n \geq 4$ be even, consider the attacker strategy $\mathcal{A}_{jp}$ with the first $\frac{n}{2}$ positions given by $\mathcal{A}_0 = 0, \mathcal{A}_1 = 2, \mathcal{A}_2 = 4, \ldots, \mathcal{A}_m = 2m, \ldots, \mathcal{A}_{\frac{n}{2}-1} = n - 2$. For all $0 \leq i < j \leq \frac{n}{2} - 1$,
$$\mathcal{A}_j - \mathcal{A}_i = 2(j - i) > j - i.$$
Then for $0 \leq i < j \leq \frac{n}{2} - 1$,
$$\Pr(F_i \cap F_j) = \Pr(\mathcal{B}_i = \mathcal{A}_i \text{ and } \mathcal{B}_j = \mathcal{A}_j) = \Pr(\mathcal{B}_i = \mathcal{A}_i)\Pr(\mathcal{B}_j = \mathcal{A}_j | \mathcal{B}_i = \mathcal{A}_i)$$
$$= B_{\mathcal{A}_i}^i P_{\mathcal{A}_i \mathcal{A}_j}^{j-i} = 0.$$
Together with Lemma 1 we have
$$\Pr\left(E_{\frac{n}{2}-1}\right) = \sum_{i=0}^{\frac{n}{2}-1} \Pr(F_i) = B_0^{(0)} + B_2^{(1)} + \cdots + B_{n-2}^{(\frac{n}{2}-1)} \geq \sum_{i=0}^{\frac{n}{2}-1} \frac{1}{n} = \frac{1}{n}\frac{n}{2} = \frac{1}{2}.$$
Hence $k_{\mathcal{A}_{jp}} \leq \frac{n}{2} - 1$.

2. Let $n \geq 5$ be odd, consider the attacker strategy $\mathcal{A}_{jp}$ with the first $\lfloor \frac{n}{2} \rfloor + 1$ positions given by $\mathcal{A}_0 = 0, \mathcal{A}_1 = 2, \mathcal{A}_2 = 4, \ldots, \mathcal{A}_m = 2m, \ldots, \mathcal{A}_{\lfloor \frac{n}{2} \rfloor} = n - 1$. Similarly we can prove $\Pr(F_i \cap F_j) = 0$ for $0 \leq i < j \leq \lfloor \frac{n}{2} \rfloor$. Together with Lemma 1 we have
$$\Pr\left(E_{\lfloor \frac{n}{2} \rfloor}\right) = \sum_{i=0}^{\lfloor \frac{n}{2} \rfloor} \Pr(F_i) = B_0^{(0)} + B_2^{(1)} + \cdots + B_{n-1}^{(\lfloor \frac{n}{2} \rfloor)}$$

$$\geq \frac{1}{2n} + \sum_{i=0}^{\lfloor \frac{n}{2} \rfloor - 1} \frac{1}{n} = \frac{1}{n}\left(\left\lfloor \frac{n}{2} \right\rfloor + \frac{1}{2}\right) = \frac{1}{2},$$

and hence $k_{\mathcal{A}_{jp}} \leq \lfloor \frac{n}{2} \rfloor$.

Recall the notation:

$$k_{\mathcal{A}} = \min\{k : \Pr(E_k) \geq \frac{1}{2}\}, \qquad k_O = \min_{\mathcal{A}} k_{\mathcal{A}}$$

Corollary 1. *For a one-dimensional search space of size n, $\lfloor \frac{n}{3} \rfloor - 1 \leq k_O \leq \lfloor \frac{n}{2} \rfloor$.*

We used the bounds in Lemma 1 to approximate $\sum_{i=0}^{k} \max_{0 \leq j \leq n-1} B_j^{(i)}$ in Proposition 1. We also derived the lower bound of k_{lower}, which then gave lower bounds on k_O. From Eq. (10), we can see $\max_{0 \leq j \leq n-1} B_j^{(k)}$ decreases when k increases, which means the upper bounds on $B_j^{(k)}$ derived in Lemma 1 can be tightened for larger values of k. Thus we expect the lower bound for k_O in Corollary 1 to be higher than $\lfloor \frac{n}{3} \rfloor - 1$.

Similarly, the upper bound $\lfloor \frac{n}{2} \rfloor$ for k_O was derived through a lower bound on $B_j^{(k)}$. However, from Eq. (10) we see that $B_j^{(k)}$ can achieve higher values than the lower bounds, which suggests that the specific attacker strategy $\mathcal{A}_{jp}$ described in Lemma 2, $k_{\mathcal{A}_{jp}}$ is strictly smaller than $\lfloor \frac{n}{2} \rfloor$. These observations motivate the calculations of exact values of $\sum_{i=0}^{k} \max_{0 \leq j \leq n-1} B_j^{(i)}$ and $k_{\mathcal{A}_{jp}}$, which yield tighter bounds on k_O.

5 Attacker Strategies

In the previous section we derived theoretical bounds for the optimal attacker strategy. Unfortunately, the lower bound estimate does not help to find the optimal strategy. Conversely, the upper bound provides us with a constructive strategy, which we briefly discuss in this section and name it the *Linear Jumping Strategy* (LJS). We also propose a greedy strategy, which we call the *Greedy Updating Attack Strategy* (GUAS), which leverages estimations of Bob's positions to determine next queries.

5.1 Linear Jumping Strategy

The linear jumping strategy sequentially selects every second location in B. Given uniform initial distributions and a random walk mobility model of the victim, it is expected to meet the upper bound cost as discussed in the previous section. The strategy was implemented by us for evaluation on different cases. Algorithm 1 in Appendix A summarizes the implementation in pseudocode. The runtime of LJS is linear in n.

5.2 Greedy Updating Attack Strategy

While we could implement an exhaustive search to find optimal strategies for any given setting, that approach is impractical and computationally expensive. In particular, for n locations, we need to evaluate the $k_{\mathcal{A},p}$ for $n^{\lceil \frac{n}{2} \rceil}$ different strategies (n potential choices per step, we expect to be done within $\lceil \frac{n}{2} \rceil$ steps).

This is infeasible even for moderate values of n. Instead, we introduce a (locally) greedy strategy which is computationally cheaper and allows us to perform simulations on a larger range of settings. We call it the *Greedy Updating Attack Strategy* (GUAS).

Suppose Alice has some assumed initial location of Bob $\tilde{B}^{(0)}$ (for example, Bob's actual initial location distribution $B^{(0)}$), and transition matrix P. At each time step i, Alice keeps her current estimate of Bob's location as $\tilde{B}^{(i)}$. In particular, Alice can use $\tilde{B}^{(i)}$ to keep track of locations she checked previously, and found to be empty. That means that $\tilde{B}^{(i)}$ depends on the actual choices of the attacker, while $B^{(i)}$ just depends on $B^{(0)}$ and P.

In query $(i + 1)$, Alice checks location $\max_j \tilde{B}_j^{(i)}$, that is, the most likely location of Bob at that time[1]. If Alice succeeds, then we are done; if Alice does not find Bob, she updates $\tilde{B}^{(i)}$ by setting the probability of the location checked in the current query to be 0 and re-normalizing $\tilde{B}^{(i)}$ to ensure that $\sum \tilde{B}^i = 1$. Thus, the following values of $\tilde{B}^{(i+1)}$ will be computed under the condition that the victim was not at the location tested in query i and earlier. The algorithm is described as pseudocode in Algorithm 2 in Appendix A. The runtime of the GUAS is quadratic in n: for each of the up to $\lceil \frac{n}{2} \rceil$ queries, we need to find the minimal value of $\tilde{B}^{(i-1)}$ (which is of size n). Thus, we were able to run this strategy for a search space size $n = 2000$ without issues.

In Sect. 6, we evaluate both LJS and GUAS for a random walk transition pattern and a sparse high-dimensional transition matrix derived from a real dataset. For the real dataset, we also investigate the attacker's performance if $\tilde{B}^{(0)} \neq B^{(0)}$, i.e., attacker has no information about victim's initial location distribution.

6   Evaluation

Based on the assumption that the attacker is aware of the victims probability distribution for initial location and the transition matrix, we simulated LJS and GUAS for different values of the initial location of Bob and the transition matrix. In addition, we tested our strategy on a transition matrix derived from a real dataset. All experiments were performed on a Core i3-4005U CPU@1.70 GHz with 8 GB RAM.

6.1   Random Walk Transition Matrix

In this experiment, we used the transition matrix that represents a random walk (i.e., same P as in Sect. 4.2) and performed simulations with various initial distributions for Bob, $B^{(0)}$, and for different search spaces with sizes varying from 100 to 2000. We assume the attacker knows the initial distribution of the victim.

---

[1] Bob's location vector is B^i in Alice's (i+1)-th query, where i starts from 0.

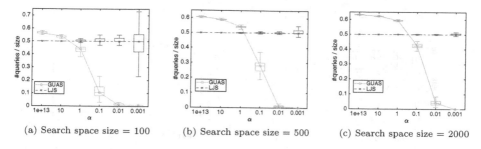

(a) Search space size = 100   (b) Search space size = 500   (c) Search space size = 2000

Fig. 2. GUAS and LJS results for random walk mobility for different search space sizes with success probability of 0.5.

Specifically, we consider space sizes of $100, 500$ and 2000. We run 100 simulations for each of these sizes and represent the initial location probability distribution for $B^{(0)}$ by a Dirichlet distribution with concentration parameter α. With increasing α values, $B^{(0)}$ is *closer* to being uniformly distributed, so a positive α value of almost zero indicates an initial distribution with very high likelihood in one location, and almost zero in all others. The results represent the effort of the attacker to successfully locate Bob with a probability of 0.5 for GUAS and LJS strategies under various initial distributions for $B^{(0)}$ regardless of the search space size. In Fig. 2 we provide a box-plot representation of some representative results (see Table 3 in Appendix B for full results). The upper and lower borders of the box represent the upper and lower quartiles, and the bar in the box is the median. The upper and lower whiskers represent the maximum and minimum number of queries in all simulations, excluding outliers, which are more than 1.5 times beyond the upper and lower quartiles.

We observed that with a large concentration parameter α, which leads to an *almost* uniform distribution of the initial position, LJS achieves the optimal lower bound, while GUAS is unable to do so. With decreasing concentration parameter value, the initial distribution becomes less uniformly distributed. Assuming that the attacker is aware of the exact initial distribution, GUAS becomes more effective for such non-uniform initial distribution. This is true regardless of the size of the search space, as shown in Fig. 2.

6.2   Real-World Mobility Pattern

We also performed simulations with a transition matrix we derived from the T-Drive dataset [21,22] released by Microsoft. The dataset comprises GPS trajectories of 10357 taxis between Feb. 2 and Feb. 8 2008 within the city of Beijing, around 15 million points and a total trajectories distance of sums up to 9 million kilometers. The average sampling interval is around 177 s with a distance of 623 m.

In our simulation, we take a subset of data within the third ring of Beijing. We discretize that area in grid cells of $500\,\text{m} \times 500\,\text{m}$, which corresponds to a lat-long unit of around 0.005. This results in 884 different locations. The area is mapped into a one-dimensional space using the following projection:

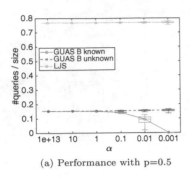
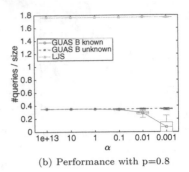

(a) Performance with p=0.5   (b) Performance with p=0.8

Fig. 3. Attack strategies performance on T-Drive dataset for unknown and known initial distributions with success probabilities of 0.5 and 0.8.

$$proj(i,j) = j \times n + i,$$

where (i,j) represents the coordinate of a grid cell in lat-long plane, and n is the total number of partitions in longitude. Based on the aforementioned discretization and projection method, we compute the probability of transitioning from one grid cell to another and build up the aggregated transition matrix, P_{taxi}, in the following way. For each taxi, we check which grid cell the taxi is moving to by reading the data in chronological order on a daily basis. Whenever there is a transit from, say location (or grid cell) x to y, we record this transit. After processing and recording all the transits for the first taxi, we can normalize the resulting matrix and build up a transition matrix only for this taxi. We do this for all the taxis, aggregate all the transition matrices and then normalize them to arrive at P_{taxi}.

Results. We simulated different "true" initial distributions for the victim, and checked on both the cases where the attacker does not know and knows about Bob's initial distribution. If the attacker is unaware of the initial distributions for the victim, she assumes a uniform initial distribution. See Fig. 3a and b for results calculated over 100 simulations. In these cases, the success is determined by how close the victim's distribution is to uniform. While for larger values of α, the attacker's guess is close enough to not decrease performance significantly. If the victim's initial distribution is less random ($\alpha \leq 0.01$), the attacker without knowledge on the initial distribution will perform worse, while the attacker with knowledge on initial B can leverage this in the GUAS strategy to decrease the required number of guesses.

Comparing performance of GUAS and LJS in Fig. 3a and b, we observe that for a less structured/dynamic mobility pattern, which for example could be modeled by some highly sparse transition matrix, GUAS performs better than LJS. Our interpretation of this result is that a realistic transition matrix leads to a set of locations that are significantly more likely than others. For LJS, it does not matter if the attacker knows the initial distribution since LJS does not utilize knowledge on the victim. See Tables 1 and 2 in Appendix B for detailed results.

7   Related Work

An extensive body of research has been devoted to describing and understanding mobility models for mobile ad hoc and other types of networks, such as vehicular networks [3,10]. Typically, these papers describe mobility models where mobile nodes are independent of or dependent on each other, namely entity mobility models or group mobility models. The goal is usually to study the behavior of individual entity mobility models and help researchers decide which model is most suitable. Random mobility models are the models of choice of most authors.

Similarly, other authors have studied the *Rendezvous Problem* [20], which consists of finding an optimal strategy for two or more mobile entities who are unaware of each others' location, to meet. This problem and some slight variations of it has attracted much attention from the research community because of its potential application to many engineering problems like the one we are considering in this paper. However, as far as we are concerned, this problem remains open [1,4]. The main difference between rendezvous search problems and the one we are tackling in this paper is that rather than having two entities trying to find each other, here one of the entities is a victim that might not even aware of the existence of the attacker trying to find him/her.

Another line of work studies the probability for n independent entities to meet while they all follow random walk trajectories in dimension two [7,14]. For $n = 2$, this is related to the special case when Alice chooses a random walk strategy. The difference is that we assume the entities take a step after every fixed length of time interval, while in the aforementioned papers they consider an entity takes a step after a time interval whose length follows a Poisson distribution.

In the realm of location privacy, the effort an attacker needs to locate a victim has been studied in different settings [9,13,16,17]. In [9,13], the focus was on static victim. A particular attacker model was used against moving target in [9]. Although this attacker model was shown to be optimal for a static victim, its efficiency as an attacker model for moving victim was not discussed. This is precisely the focus of our paper.

In [16,17], the focus is on the quantification of users' location privacy by analyzing location-based applications and location-privacy preserving mechanism (LPPM). They assume an obfuscated trace (obtained by an LPPM) of the victim is available to the attacker and the goal of the attacker is to find out the real trace [17] or the real location [16] of the victim. In contrast, in this paper the attacker is only aware of the mobility model of the victim, without any knowledge of the victim's trajectory.

8 Conclusions

In this paper, we have presented a framework to reason about the expected effort of attackers attempting to locate moving targets using proximity testing. We first provide mathematical analysis for asymptotic bounds (on the search space) on the best attacker strategies under a random walk mobility model for the moving victim. We then derive two concrete strategies, and evaluate their performance over a range of parameters. The LJS strategy is found to work well for random walk mobility and close to uniform initial distribution of Bob, while the GUAS strategy requires less queries for less uniform initial distributions of Bob (which are known to the attacker). We then derive a realistic mobility model from a real dataset consisting of spatio-temporal trajectory data, and analyze the performance of our strategies. In that setting, we find that the GUAS strategy consistently requires less than $\frac{N}{6}$ queries ($p = 0.5$), while LJS requires more than $0.75N$, where N is the search space size. Summarizing, we have shown theoretically and practically that (using a strategy suitable to the setting), an attacker is able to locate a victim with 50% probability with at most $\frac{N}{2}$ steps. For example, using GUAS in our Beijing dataset the attacker could localize a victim with 50% probability in 134 steps (6.6 h), within an area of $0.25\,\text{km}^2$.

Proposed Countermeasures. To prevent the demonstrated attack, we propose the following countermeasures: (a) The LBS could probabilistically return a wrong result (e.g., with 20% chance), (b) the LBS could verify that the sequence of attacker's location claims confirms to some assumed transition matrix P (i.e., the likelihood of a claimed trajectory is above some threshold τ), and (c) the LBS could impose limitations on the number of queries or the speed/frequency of queries by the requester. We leave the evaluation of these countermeasures for future work.

Acknowledgements. Xueou was supported by SUTD-ZJU grant ZJUSP1600102. R. Rios was partially funded by the Spanish Ministry of Economy and Competitiveness (TIN2016-79095-C2-1-R, TIN2014-54427-JIN) and the 'Captación de Talento para la Investigación' fellowship from University of Malaga. This work was partly funded by the Swedish Foundation for Strategic Research (SSF) and the Swedish Research Council (VR).

A Pseudocodes of Algorithms

The *Linear Jump Strategy* (LJS) is given as pseudocode in Algorithm 1, and the *Greedy Updating Attacker Strategy* (GUAS) is provided in Algorithm 2.

Algorithm 1. Linear Jumping Strategy (LJS)

Result: Number of queries that Alice needs to perform to locate Bob with
probability of at least 0.5.

Set $success = 0$;

while $i < MAX\_QUERIES$ **do**

$\quad$ $\mathcal{A}_i = 2 * i$; $\qquad\qquad\qquad\qquad$ // linear jumps through B

$\quad$ $success = success + (1 - success) * B_{\mathcal{A}_i}^{(i-1)}$;

$\quad$ **if** $success \geq 0.5$ **then**

$\qquad$ | $\quad$ return i; $\qquad\qquad\qquad$ // Minimal number of steps found

$\quad$ **end**

$\quad$ $B_{\mathcal{A}_i}^{(i-1)} = 0$; $\quad$ // Set this position empty for following calculations

$\quad$ $B^{(i-1)} = \text{normalize}(B^{(i-1)})$;

$\quad$ $B^i = B^{(i-1)} \cdot P$; $\qquad\qquad$ // Bob's location probability in next query

$\quad$ $i = i + 1$;

end

return ERROR ; $\qquad\qquad$ // Attacker was unable to locate Bob within
MAX_QUERIES

Algorithm 2. Greedy Updating Attack Strategy (GUAS)

Result: Number of queries that Alice needs to perform to locate Bob with
probability of at least 0.5.

Initialize $\tilde{B}$, set $success = 0$;

while $i < MAX\_QUERIES$ **do**

$\quad$ $\mathcal{A}_i = \max_j \tilde{B}_j^{(i-1)}$; $\qquad\qquad$ // select maximum likelihood estimate of B

$\quad$ $success = success + (1 - success) * B_{\mathcal{A}_i}^{(i-1)}$;

$\quad$ **if** $success \geq 0.5$ **then**

$\qquad$ | $\quad$ return i; $\qquad\qquad\qquad$ // Minimal number of steps found

$\quad$ **end**

$\quad$ $B_{\mathcal{A}_i}^{(i-1)} = 0$; $\quad$ // Set this position empty for following calculations

$\quad$ $\tilde{B}_{\mathcal{A}_i}^{(i-1)} = 0$; $\qquad\qquad$ // Attacker estimates this position empty

$\quad$ $B^{(i-1)} = \text{normalize}(B^{(i-1)})$;

$\quad$ $\tilde{B}^{(i-1)} = \text{normalize}(\tilde{B}^{(i-1)})$;

$\quad$ $B^i = B^{(i-1)} \cdot P$; // Bob's actual location probability in next query

$\quad$ $\tilde{B}^i = \tilde{B}^{(i-1)} \cdot P$; $\qquad$ // Bob's estimated location probability in next
query

$\quad$ $i = i + 1$;

end

return ERROR; $\qquad\qquad$ // Attacker was unable to locate Bob within
MAX_QUERIES

B   Simulation Results

In Tables 1, 2, and 3 we provide the exact simulation results used for plotting Figs. 2 and 3. In these tables, α is the Dirichlet concentration parameter, size represents the number of locations in the search space and "#Q" stands for number of queries. The mean ("#Q.mean"), standard deviation ("#Q.std"), min ("#Q.min") and max ("#Q.max") are calculated over 100 simulations. The value "$\frac{\#Q.\text{mean}}{\text{Size}}$" represents how the strategy performs under different initial position distributions regardless of the search space size.

Table 1. GUAS performance on T-Drive dataset with known and unknown initial distribution for probability of 0.5 and 0.8.

	α	Size	Unknown					Known				
			#Q.mean	$\frac{\#Q.\text{mean}}{\text{Size}}$	#Q.std	#Q.min	#Q.max	#Q.mean	$\frac{\#Q.\text{mean}}{\text{Size}}$	#Q.std	#Q.min	#Q.max
p = 0.5	1e+13	884	135	0.1527	0	135	135	135	0.1527	0	135	135
	10	884	134.93	0.1526	0.2564	134	135	134.54	0.1522	0.5009	134	135
	1	884	134.83	0.1525	0.5515	134	136	133.24	0.1507	0.6215	132	134
	0.1	884	134.9	0.1526	1.2432	132	138	124.9	0.1413	2.6874	118	129
	0.01	884	135.33	0.1531	3.7526	123	141	78.39	0.0887	21.7004	2	111
	0.001	884	135.25	0.1530	9.028	81	146	3.3	0.0037	7.0245	1	48
p = 0.8	1e+13	884	310	0.3507	0	310	310	310	0.3507	0	310	310
	10	884	310.02	0.3507	0.1407	310	311	310	0.3507	0	310	310
	1	884	310.15	0.3508	0.5573	309	311	308.65	0.3492	0.5573	307	310
	0.1	884	310.32	0.3510	1.2624	307	313	300.34	0.3400	2.6370	293	304
	0.01	884	310.75	0.3515	3.7400	298	317	253.65	0.2869	22.1630	167	287
	0.001	884	310.7	0.3515	9.0403	256	322	76.01	0.0860	70.8871	1	223

Table 2. LJS performance on T-Drive dataset for probability of 0.5 and 0.8

α	Size	p = 0.5					p = 0.8				
		#Q.mean	$\frac{\#Q.\text{mean}}{\text{Size}}$	#Q.std	#Q.min	#Q.max	#Q.mean	$\frac{\#Q.\text{mean}}{\text{Size}}$	#Q.std	#Q.min	#Q.max
1e+13	884	680	0.7692	0	680	680	1561	1.7658	0	1561	1561
10	884	679.98	0.7692	0.1407	679	680	1560.96	1.7658	0.1969	1560	1561
1	884	679.85	0.7691	0.4794	678	682	1560.81	1.7656	0.4191	1559	1561
0.1	884	680.19	0.7694	1.0982	677	682	1560.83	1.7656	0.6522	1558	1562
0.01	884	680.48	0.7698	5.2445	641	687	1560.14	1.7649	5.1247	1517	1564
0.001	884	681.43	0.7708	5.0317	666	689	1560.44	1.7652	4.0310	1544	1566

Table 3. GUAS and LJS results for different search space sizes and Bob's initial distributions with success probability of 0.5

α	Size	GUAS						LJS				
		#Q.mean	$\frac{\text{\#Q.mean}}{\text{Size}}$	#Q.std	#Q.min	#Q.max		#Q.mean	$\frac{\text{\#Q.mean}}{\text{Size}}$	#Q.std	#Q.min	#Q.max
1e+13	100	56.13	0.5613	0.7740	54	58		50	0.5	0	50	50
10	100	53.79	0.5379	0.6860	52	56		50.04	0.5004	0.1969	50	51
1	100	44	0.44	2.5898	33	50		50.43	0.5043	1.1304	47	53
0.1	100	11.5	0.115	4.5115	3	23		50.49	0.5049	3.2114	32	58
0.01	100	1.42	0.0142	0.7272	1	4		50.96	0.5096	10.5523	5	87
0.001	100	1.00	0.01	0	1	1		49.54	0.4954	20.0668	1	95
1e+13	500	302.68	0.6054	2.0345	298	306		250	0.5	0	250	250
10	500	295.32	0.5906	1.7401	290	299		250.1	0.5002	0.3015	250	251
1	500	269.83	0.5397	3.3183	262	277		250.28	0.5006	0.8538	248	252
0.1	500	136.36	0.2727	22.1622	79	186		250.7	0.5014	2.8727	240	260
0.01	500	6.54	0.0131	5.2655	1	25		249.87	0.4997	16.3130	138	290
0.001	500	1.1	0.0022	0.3015	1	2		261.05	0.5221	43.3281	105	456
1e+13	2000	1263.5	0.6318	2.9763	1255	1270		1000	0.5	0	1000	1000
10	2000	1246.38	0.6232	2.9432	1238	1253		1000.1	0.5001	0.3015	1000	1001
1	2000	1186.99	0.5935	5.5405	1173	1202		1000.39	0.5002	0.8978	999	1004
0.1	2000	846.92	0.4235	36.9484	703	952		1000.4	0.5002	3.0218	981	1007
0.01	2000	86.84	0.0434	34.3602	26	245		1001.38	0.5007	6.9787	977	1028
0.001	2000	2.42	0.0012	1.5646	1	10		1010.6	0.5053	59.4701	731	1275

References

1. Alpern, S.: Ten open problems in rendezvous search. In: Alpern, S., Fokkink, R., Gąsieniec, L., Lindelauf, R., Subrahmanian, V. (eds.) Search Theory, pp. 223–230. Springer, New York (2013). https://doi.org/10.1007/978-1-4614-6825-7_14

2. Bai, F., Helmy, A.: A survey of mobility models. Wireless adhoc networks, University of Southern California, USA (2004)

3. Camp, T., Boleng, J., Davies, V.: A survey of mobility models for ad hoc network research. Wirel. Commun. Mob. Comput. **2**(5), 483–502 (2002). https://doi.org/10.1002/wcm.72

4. Chen, L., Bian, K.: The telephone coordination game revisited: from random to deterministic algorithms. IEEE Trans. Comput. **64**(10), 2968–2980 (2015). https://doi.org/10.1109/TC.2015.2389799

5. Cuellar, J., Ochoa, M., Rios, R.: Indistinguishable regions in geographic privacy. In: Proceedings of the ACM Symposium on Applied Computing (SAC), SAC 2012, pp. 1463–1469. ACM, New York (2012). https://doi.org/10.1145/2245276.2232010

6. Culzac, N.: Egypt's police 'using social media and apps like Grindr to trap gay people' (2014). Article on The Independent

7. Gaudillière, A.: Collision probability for random trajectories in two dimensions. Stoch. Process. Appl. **119**(3), 775–810 (2009). https://doi.org/10.1016/j.spa.2008.04.007

8. Hallgren, P.A., Ochoa, M., Sabelfeld, A.: InnerCircle: a parallelizable decentralized privacy-preserving location proximity protocol. In: Proceedings of the Annual Conference on Privacy, Security and Trust (PST), pp. 1–6 (2015). https://doi.org/10.1109/PST.2015.7232947

9. Hallgren, P.A., Ochoa, M., Sabelfeld, A.: MaxPace: speed-constrained location queries. In: Proceedings of IEEE Conference on Communications and Network Security (CNS), pp. 136–144 (2016). https://doi.org/10.1109/CNS.2016.7860479

10. Harri, J., Filali, F., Bonnet, C.: Mobility models for vehicular ad hoc networks: a survey and taxonomy. IEEE Commun. Surv. Tutor. **11**(4), 19–41 (2009). https://doi.org/10.1109/SURV.2009.090403

11. Huang, M.S., Narayanan, R.M.: Trilateration-based localization algorithm using the lemoine point formulation. IETE J. Res. **60**(1), 60–73 (2014)

12. Narayanan, A., Thiagarajan, N., Lakhani, M., Hamburg, M., Boneh, D.: Location privacy via private proximity testing. In: Proceedings of the Network and Distributed System Security Symposium (NDSS) (2011)

13. Polakis, I., Argyros, G., Petsios, T., Sivakorn, S., Keromytis, A.D.: Where's wally?: precise user discovery attacks in location proximity services. In: Proceedings of the ACM Conference on Computer and Communications Security (CCS), pp. 817–828 (2015). https://doi.org/10.1145/2810103.2813605

14. Puchala, Z., Rolski, T.: The exact asymptotic of the time to collision. Electron. J. Probab. **10**, 1359–1380 (2005)

15. Sedenka, J., Gasti, P.: Privacy-preserving distance computation and proximity testing on earth, done right. In: Proceedings of ACM Symposium on Information, Computer and Communications Security (ASIACCS), pp. 99–110 (2014). https://doi.org/10.1145/2590296.2590307

16. Shokri, R., Theodorakopoulos, G., Danezis, G., Hubaux, J.-P., Le Boudec, J.-Y.: Quantifying location privacy: the case of sporadic location exposure. In: Fischer-Hübner, S., Hopper, N. (eds.) PETS 2011. LNCS, vol. 6794, pp. 57–76. Springer, Heidelberg (2011). https://doi.org/10.1007/978-3-642-22263-4_4

17. Shokri, R., Theodorakopoulos, G., Le Boudec, J.Y., Hubaux, J.P.: Quantifying location privacy. In: Proceedings of the IEEE Symposium on Security and Privacy (S&P), pp. 247–262. IEEE Computer Society, Washington, DC (2011). https://doi.org/10.1109/SP.2011.18

18. Shokri, R., Theodorakopoulos, G., Troncoso, C., Hubaux, J.P., Le Boudec, J.Y.: Protecting location privacy: optimal strategy against localization attacks. In: Proceedings of the ACM Conference on Computer and Communications Security (CCS), pp. 617–627. ACM, New York (2012). https://doi.org/10.1145/2382196.2382261

19. Veytsman, M.: How i was able to track the location of any Tinder user, February 2014. http://blog.includesecurity.com/2014/02/how-i-was-able-to-track-location-of-any.html

20. Weber, R.: Optimal symmetric rendezvous search on three locations. Math. Oper. Res. **37**(1), 111–122 (2012). https://doi.org/10.1287/moor.1110.0528

21. Yuan, J., Zheng, Y., Xie, X., Sun, G.: Driving with knowledge from the physical world. In: Proceedings of the 17th ACM SIGKDD International Conference on Knowledge Discovery and Data Mining, pp. 316–324. ACM (2011)

22. Yuan, J., et al.: T-drive: driving directions based on taxi trajectories. In: Proceedings of the SIGSPATIAL International Conference on Advances in Geographic Information Systems, pp. 99–108. ACM (2010)

Multi-party Computation

Constant-Round Client-Aided Secure Comparison Protocol

Hiraku Morita[1]($\boxtimes$), Nuttapong Attrapadung[1], Tadanori Teruya[1],
Satsuya Ohata[1], Koji Nuida[2], and Goichiro Hanaoka[1]

[1] AIST, Tokyo, Japan
{hiraku.morita,n.attrapadung,tadanori.teruya,satsuya.ohata,
hanaoka-goichiro}@aist.go.jp
[2] The University of Tokyo, Tokyo, Japan
nuida@mist.i.u-tokyo.ac.jp

Abstract. We present an improved constant-round secure two-party
protocol for integer comparison functionality, which is one of the most
fundamental building blocks in secure computation.

Our protocol is in the so-called *client-server model*, which is utilized
in real-world MPC products such as Sharemind, where any number of
clients can create shares of their input and distribute to the servers who
then jointly compute over the shares and return the shares of result to
the client. In the *client-aided* client-server model, as mentioned briefly by
Mohassel and Zhang (S&P'17), a client further generates and distributes
some necessary correlated randomness to servers. Such correlated randomness admits efficient protocols since otherwise servers have to jointly
generate randomness by themselves, which can be inefficient.

In this paper, we improve the state-of-the-art constant-round comparison protocols by Damgård et al. (TCC'06) and Nishide and Ohta
(PKC'07) in the client-aided model. Our techniques include identifying
correlated randomness in these comparison protocols. Along the way, we
also use tree-based techniques for a building block, which deviate from
the above two works. Our proposed protocol requires only 5 communication rounds, regardless of the bit length of inputs. This is at least 5 times
fewer rounds than existing protocols. We implement our secure comparison protocol in C++. Our experimental results show that this low-round
complexity benefits in low-latency networks such as WAN.

Keywords: Multi-party computation · Client-server model
Client-aided method · Less-than comparison · Constant rounds
GMW secret sharing

1 Introduction

Multi-party computation (MPC) is a powerful cryptographic tool often used
to achieve privacy-preserving applications such as secure data mining. In general, MPC enables a set of N parties to jointly compute a function, say f, of

© Springer Nature Switzerland AG 2018
J. Lopez et al. (Eds.): ESORICS 2018, LNCS 11099, pp. 395–415, 2018.
https://doi.org/10.1007/978-3-319-98989-1_20

their private inputs. More precisely, the N parties, each holding private input x_i (for $i = 1, \ldots, N$), are able to compute the output $F = f(x_1, \ldots, x_N)$ without having to reveal their private inputs x_i. The security of MPC guarantees that a party i will learn nothing about the others' inputs, namely, x_j for all j not equal to i, except the information that can be derived from the output F and his/her own input x_i.

In this paper, we focus on secret-sharing based MPC [13], as opposed to other approaches such as garbled-circuit [24] or (fully) homomorphic encryption. Comparing among these, secret-sharing based MPC normally admits low computational cost and low bandwidth, while it generally requires more round communications. Constructing *round-efficient* protocols is thus one of the main goals for secret-sharing based MPC.

Secure Comparison Protocols. In this paper, we study integer comparison functionality, which has been considered one of the most fundamental building blocks for MPC since a seminal paper by Yao [24] introduced the Millionaires' problem, which itself is the starting point for researches on MPC. It has many applications that include auctions, machine learning, data clustering, statistical analysis, applications involving sorting, finding minimum/maximum, to name just a few. Secure comparison protocols have many variants (*cf.* [2]); in order to be able to flexibly use them as building blocks in larger applications, it is imperative to consider the variant with *shared inputs and shared output*. More precisely, the inputs to the protocol are shares of x and shares of y, while the output comprises shares of bit b which indicates the result of comparing $x < y$ (note that it is sufficient w.l.o.g. to consider less-than functionality). Throughout the paper, we consider this variant unless stated otherwise.

Despite being such a central functionality, inefficiency of comparison protocols is often a bottleneck for the applications listed above. Such inefficiency inherently stems from the fact that on one hand, applications are *arithmetic* computations; while, on the other hand, computing integer comparison is a *bit string* operation by nature, and protocols that compute such bit decompositions often require $\log n$ rounds, where n is the bit length of inputs.

A breakthrough result was proposed by Damgård et al. [7], who came up with the first secret-sharing based comparison protocol that admits *constant rounds*. Their protocol can be based on any linear secret-sharing based MPC that has multiplication protocol, and require 44 rounds of multiplication protocols (as counted in [15]). When including overall communication such as sharing or revealing phases (see more discussion on this in Sect. 4), in this paper, it can be counted to 79 overall rounds. Nishide and Ohta [15] proposed an improved protocol that has 15 rounds of multiplication protocols, and as counted in this paper, has 28 overall rounds. In this paper, we will improve these constants albeit working in the *client-aided client-server* model.

MPC in the Client-Server Model. In pushing MPC towards real-world usages, the setting of so-called *client-server model* for MPC has recently been largely motivated not only by recent researches including Araki *et al.* [1] but also by commercial-grade MPC products such as Sharemind system by Cybernetica.

Table 1. Comparison of LessThan protocols in the number of rounds, total communication, and estimated total online execution time

Secure LessThan	Round	Total communication* (number of field elements)	Total online time[†] (ms)
Damgård et al. [7]	79	$176n \log n +$ $80n \log \log n + 70n$	5688
Nishide-Ohta [15]	28	$96n + 120 \log n + 4$	2016
Damgård et al. + Client-aided	70	$144n \log n +$ $64n \log \log n + 52n$	5040
Nishide-Ohta + Client-aided	14	$36n + 48 \log n + 7$	1008
Ours	6	$12n^2 + 25$	432
Ours (round reduced)	5	$12n^2 + 301$	360

*For total communication of Damgård et al. [7] and its client-aided version, only dominant terms are shown here (for simplicity). More details can be found in Appendix B.
[†]Total time is estimated in a WAN setting where the network delay is 72 ms.

In such a model, there are N servers and an unbounded number of clients, say t. Each client provides his input x_i by secret-sharing it to the N servers, who will then jointly compute in secure manner over these input shares and return the output $f(x_1, \ldots, x_t)$ to clients.[1] This setting is suitable in real-world business innovation as the MPC engine run by servers can be thought of "as a service". In particular, each client only participates at the input phase and simply waits for the output. A program for client can thus contain only a simple and lightweight computation, namely, the secret sharing procedure, and hence makes it possible to be easily employed (*e.g.*, as a tiny script program in web browsers).

Client-Aided Client-Server Model. In the *client-aided* client-server model, as mentioned briefly by Mohassel and Zhang [14], a client, who distributes shares of its input to servers, further generates and distributes some necessary *correlated randomness* to servers. Such correlated randomness will be used by the N servers for running a protocol among them. This is for the purpose of better efficiency, since otherwise servers would have to jointly generate randomness by themselves, which can be inefficient. The only downside for this model is the restriction that any server is assumed to not collude with the client who generates such correlated randomness; doing so would break security. But this restriction seems reasonable already in the client-server business model, as a server would normally have no incentive to collude to a client.[2]

---

[1] As a side note, this setting can be considered as $(N + t)$-party MPC, where the N parties have no input.

[2] This, however, depends on applications. Nevertheless, in most cases, a company (a server) might have to be worried more about losing its credit if the fact that it colludes with a client to obtain other client's secret is somehow exposed.

1.1 Our Contribution

Our main contribution is an efficient secure comparison (LessThan) protocol in the client-aided client-server model with two servers (and with an unbounded number of clients). It improves upon the state-of-the-art secure comparison protocols that achieve a constant round complexity. We show a comparison for the number of communication rounds in Table 1, which also shows the total communication and an estimated total time for executing a protocol in a WAN setting (see below). The number of overall rounds for our protocol is 5, which is considerably much lower than the previous schemes (at least 5 times fewer rounds than Nishide-Ohta [15], which requires 28 overall rounds). We also implement our secure comparison protocol in C++. Our experimental results show that this low-round complexity benefits in low-latency networks such as WAN (also see below).

Our Techniques. Our protocol is based loosely on the previous protocols of [15], which is, in turn, based on [7]. Our techniques for reducing rounds consist of the following strategies (described only in a high-level overview):

- We first note that [15] uses the LSB (least significant bit) protocol as a building block. While [7,15] can use any linear secret sharing with multiplication protocol, we use a specific secret-sharing scheme, namely, the 2-out-of-2 sharing scheme. Note that such a secret scheme is the base for the original MPC by Goldreich *et al.* [13], which we denote the GMW scheme. This enables us to construct the LSB protocol based on a comparison protocol with *plain inputs* and shared output, called PlainLessThan protocol.
- We then construct a protocol for PlainLessThan by using a tree-based structure called *dyadic range*, similarly to [2]. This has two advantages. First, such a structure admits parallel computations (hence, is suitable for constant-round protocols). Second, each computation is multi-fan-in AND, which we can construct a constant-round protocol.
- We finally construct a constant-round multi-fan-in AND protocol using the protocol proposed also in [7]. This is the point where we utilize the client-aided setting so that the correlated randomness generation phase is entirely computed by a client. We identify the necessary correlated randomness by removing redundancy in [7]. Our client-aided protocol is more sophisticated than the one in [14], which considers correlated randomness for only a simple multiplication protocol (such randomness is called Beaver multiplication triple [3] in the literature); ours is for the whole multi-fan-in AND protocol.

More details for intuition on our building blocks can be found in Sect. 3.

Better Total-Time Efficiency in WAN. While achieving less rounds, our protocol requires larger asymptotic complexity in total communication: ours is $O(n^2)$, versus $O(n \log n)$ and $O(n)$ in [7,15], resp., as shown in Table 1. However, when considering concrete real-world parameters and large-delay networks like WAN (Wide Area Network), this does not matter since the total time for transmitting data of any amount up to its capacity will be roughly the same. More precisely, in WAN, we can set the transmission bandwidth to 9 MB/s and the network delay to 72 ms, as done in [14]. Hence, in one round, we can transmit any amount of data up to $9 \text{ MB/s} \times 72 \text{ ms} = 648 \text{ KB}$, in roughly the same amount of time (72 ms). For our protocol, when considering $n = 32$ bits, the total transmitted data has about $12n^2 + 301 = 12589$ field elements; each element has 32 bits, hence the total data has only 402848 bits (50 KB), which is already less than the capacity of 648 KB. Moreover, the local computation time would contribute only negligible time compared to the network delay (see Sect. 5). Therefore, the total (online) time to run the protocol is indeed simply about the one-round time (72 ms) times the number of rounds, as shown in Table 1. We note also that, thanks to the client-aided method, the offline time is kept small compared to the online time (see Table 2). More details can also be found in Appendix B.

1.2 Related Work

Secure comparison protocols have been widely studied since Yao [24] introduced the Millionaire's protocol. Research on secure comparison protocols have a vast literature, e.g., [4–9, 11, 15, 21, 22, 24], and we would like to point the reader to an excellent survey published relatively recently in 2015 by Veugen et al. [23] for a detailed overview, while we briefly mention some more related ones here. As Veugen et al. [23] pointed out, secret sharing based secure comparisons [6, 11, 15] have an advantage in online phase in comparison with garbled circuit based protocols and homomorphic encryption based protocols. Attrapadung et al. [2] categorized various secure comparison protocols regarding their input/output forms. Damgård et al. [7] proposed a constant-round secure comparison scheme and Nishide-Ohta [15] developed the idea to construct fewer rounds secure comparison protocol, on which our protocol is based. We note that, in this paper, we count the round complexity in a strict sense: the communication rounds of revealing or sharing are also included (while, in most of previous papers, only those of multiplication protocols are counted). See more in Sect. 4. This somewhat leads to more round complexities than those in original papers. In subsequent works to [15], some other optimizations have been introduced based on the assumption that the compared values are restricted to be less than $\frac{p-1}{2}$ [16–18]. (To free up this restriction, the number of rounds would increase.) Reistad [16] claims that the online round complexity is 2; however, the actual round complexity (in our strict counting) seems to be much greater since similar sub-protocols to those in [15] are used. Their main advantage is, nevertheless, the total linear communication. While our focus is on reducing communication rounds to sufficiently small constant, there exist also logarithmic-round secure comparison protocols in literature (e.g., [10, 20]); our sub-protocols in Sect. 3 might be applicable to reduce the communication rounds in these cases too.

2 Preliminaries and Settings

In this section, we introduce notation and terminology. The general notion for a multi-party protocol to *compute* a function f and to *privately compute* a function f in the semi-honest model follows from the standard definition (e.g., [12]).

As a basic terminology throughout the paper, we let p be an odd prime and n be the bit length of p. We represent elements in the prime field $\mathbb{F}_p$ as $\{0, \ldots, p-1\}$.

Syntax for Secret Sharing. An N-out-of-N secret sharing scheme over $\mathbb{F}_p$ consists of two algorithms: Share and Reveal. Share takes as input $x \in \mathbb{F}_p$, and outputs $([\![x]\!]_1, \ldots, [\![x]\!]_N) \in \mathbb{F}_p^N$, where the bracket notation $[\![x]\!]_i$ denotes the share of the i-th party. We denote $[\![x]\!] = ([\![x]\!]_1, \ldots, [\![x]\!]_N)$ as their shorthand. Reveal takes as input $[\![x]\!]$, and outputs x.

Client-Server Model. We describe the setting for secret-sharing based MPC in the client-server model (similarly to *e.g.,* [1]) as follows. We assume that there exists N servers and an unbounded number of clients, say t. We assume that there exists a secure channel between any client and any server, and among any two servers (Note that a secure channel among clients are not needed).

Let S be an N-out-of-N secret sharing scheme over $\mathbb{F}_p$. We say that a protocol Π computes a function $f : \mathbb{A}^t \rightarrow \mathbb{B}$ in the client-server model with a secret sharing scheme S if Π proceeds as follows.

1. In the first pass, each client j (for $j \in [1, t]$) creates shares of its input $a_j \in \mathbb{A}$ as $[\![a_j]\!] = ([\![a_j]\!]_1, \ldots, [\![a_j]\!]_N) \leftarrow \text{Share}(a_j)$. It then distributes $[\![a_j]\!]_i$ to the server i (for $i \in [1, N]$).
2. All the N servers jointly compute f over their shares. More precisely, in this joint protocol, the input from the server i is $([\![a_1]\!]_i, \ldots, [\![a_t]\!]_i)$. Let $b = f(a_1, \ldots, a_t)$. The output for the server i in this joint protocol is the share $[\![b]\!]_i$. We abuse the notation of f and write this protocol as

$$[\![b]\!] \leftarrow f([\![a_1]\!], \ldots, [\![a_t]\!]).$$

3. In the final pass, each server i (for $i \in [1, N]$) returns $[\![b]\!]_i$ to all the clients. Each client can recover b by $\text{Reveal}([\![b]\!])$.

Note that such a protocol setting is a specific case of $(N + t)$-party protocols, where N parties among these do not have input, and t parties among these participate only the first pass (for sending) and the final pass (for receiving). Therefore, the security notion in the semi-honest model follows from the standard notion of private computation (*e.g.,* [12]).

Client-Aided Client-Server Model. The client-aided setting (similarly to [14]) further specializes the above setting by allowing the following:

- A fixed client, w.l.o.g. say client number 1 (but could be any), will additionally send an auxiliary input aux_i to the server i (for all $i \in [1, N]$). The distribution of auxiliary inputs can be done offline or at the same time as the first pass in the client-server model described above. We denote $\text{aux} = (\text{aux}_1, \ldots, \text{aux}_N)$.
- In the joint computation for f, each server i can input its auxiliary input aux_i. We write this protocol as $[\![b]\!] \leftarrow f([\![a_1]\!], \ldots, [\![a_t]\!]; \text{aux})$, where we also often omit explicitly writing aux when the context is clear.

We assume that the client that generates auxiliary inputs is honest and does not collude with any servers. As a remark, this setting can be considered as the trusted initializer model [19] where the "trusted initializer" in our case is one of the t clients.

Our Setting: Two-Server GMW Scheme. In this paper, we consider two servers, that is, $N = 2$. Hence, in particular, we only allow the adversary to corrupt only one server. We use the standard 2-out-of-2 secret sharing scheme defined by

- Share(x): randomly choose $r \in \mathbb{F}_p$ and let $[\![x]\!]_1 = r$ and $[\![x]\!]_2 = x - r$.
- Reveal($[\![x]\!]_1, [\![x]\!]_2$): output $[\![x]\!]_1 + [\![x]\!]_2$.

We note that this is the secret sharing scheme used in the original MPC by Goldreich, Micali, and Widgerson [13], hence we often call it the GMW-style two-party secret sharing scheme. In this scheme, we have protocols for fundamental operations: ADD(x, y) := $x + y$ and MULT(x, y) := xy as follows:

- $[\![z]\!] \leftarrow$ ADD($[\![x]\!], [\![y]\!]$) can be done locally by simply adding its own share on x and on y.
- $[\![w]\!] \leftarrow$ MULT($[\![x]\!], [\![y]\!]$) can be done in various ways. We will use the standard method based on Beaver multiplication triples [3]. Such a triple consists of $\mathsf{aux}_1 = (a_1, b_1, c_1)$ and $\mathsf{aux}_2 = (a_2, b_2, c_2)$ such that $(a_1 + a_2)(b_1 + b_2) = c_1 + c_2$. In particular, we can use the client-aided method to let a client generate and distribute aux_1 and aux_2 to the two servers, respectively.

We abuse notations and write the ADD protocol simply as $[\![z]\!] \leftarrow [\![x]\!] + [\![y]\!]$, and MULT protocols simply as $[\![w]\!] \leftarrow [\![x]\!] \cdot [\![y]\!]$. Note that multiplication with constant c can use the ADD protocol, and we write $c[\![x]\!]$.

3 Our Secure Comparison Protocol

In this section, we present our protocol for computing the less-than comparison functionality, LessThan. It consists of various sub-protocols, which might be of independent interest in their own right, that we also present in this section. These consist of the following.

- MULT*: multi-input multiplication functionality.
- AND*: multi-fan-in AND functionality.
- PlainEqual: equality test functionality with *plain* inputs.
- PlainLessThan: less-than comparison functionality with *plain* inputs.
- WrapAround: a functionality for testing if the addition of the two shares (in the integers, without modulo p) is more than p or not (wrapping around p or not).
- LSB: least-significant-bit functionality.
- HalfTest: a functionality for testing if a (shared) input is less than $p/2$ or not.

We remark that all of these functionality except two have *shared inputs* and *shared output*. (Definitions for each functionality will be provided below.) The only two exceptions are PlainEqual and PlainLessThan, where inputs consist of plain values that are private to each party.

Outline of Our Protocol for LessThan. We will use the functionality for HalfTest to construct LessThan, and LSB to construct HalfTest in exactly the same manner as in [15]. To construct a protocol for LSB, we will use WrapAround, which is then constructed based on PlainLessThan. This is different to the construction of LSB in [15]. Our protocol for PlainLessThan is based on binary tree structure, which admits parallel computation (and hence use small constant rounds of communication). This is somewhat related to the protocol in [2], with the difference that here our protocol uses secret sharing, while [2] uses homomorphic encryption. PlainLessThan uses PlainEqual as a subroutine. PlainEqual then uses the multi-fan-in AND, namely, AND*, as a subroutine. AND* is then based on the multi-input multiplication, namely, MULT*, in a similar manner to [7]. Finally, MULT* is constructed based on using correlated randomness produced by the aiding party.

3.1 Multi-input Multiplication Protocol (MULT*)

We first describe the smallest building block (besides ADD, MULT), namely, the multi-input multiplication functionality, MULT*. Its definition is the computation protocol as follows.

$$([\![c_1]\!], [\![c_2]\!], \ldots, [\![c_\ell]\!]) \leftarrow \mathsf{MULT}^*([\![x_1]\!], \ldots, [\![x_\ell]\!]),$$

where we define $c_i := x_1 x_2 \cdots x_i$ for all $i \in [1, \ell]$.

Intuition/Approach. Our protocol follows the basic mechanism of the protocol for MULT* in [7]. The protocol of [7] lets parties collaborate and produce shares of random elements, say t_j, and its *inverse*, namely, t_j^{-1}. Such procedures are somewhat costly. Our idea is to gather and optimize all these correlated randomness elements in one place and let it be generated by an aiding party. For example, the "chaining" like $q_j := t_{j-1} t_j^{-1}$ will be pre-computed. Moreover, the protocol of [7] can be used for any linear secret sharing scheme with MULT protocol. When using a MULT protocol that uses multiplication triples, the correlated randomness for MULT will become redundant with those t_j, t_j^{-1}. We eliminate these redundancy by generating multiplication triples directly over q_j defined as above, and not an independent randomness.

Correlated Randomness for MULT*. The aiding party locally pre-computes the following:

1. For all $j \in [0, \ell]$, pick $t_j \xleftarrow{\$} \mathbb{F}_p^\times$, and also compute its inverse, t_j^{-1}.
2. For all $j \in [1, \ell]$, define $q_j := t_{j-1} t_j^{-1}$, $z_j := t_0^{-1} t_j$, and also pick $a_j \in \mathbb{F}_p^\times$.
3. Set the correlated randomness for P_1 and P_2 to be the following random shares:

$$\mathsf{CR}_\ell := ([\![a_j]\!], [\![q_j]\!], [\![a_j q_j]\!], [\![z_j]\!])_{i \in [1, \ell]}. \tag{1}$$

Our Protocol for MULT*. We show our protocol for MULT* in Algorithm 1.

Algorithm 1. MULT* Protocol

Functionality: $([\![c_1]\!], [\![c_2]\!], \ldots, [\![c_\ell]\!]) \leftarrow$ MULT*$([\![x_1]\!], \ldots, [\![x_\ell]\!])$.
Input: Arithmetic shared values $[\![x_1]\!], \ldots, [\![x_\ell]\!]$ over $\mathbb{F}_p$ and an integer ℓ.
Auxiliary Input: CR_ℓ in Eq. (1).
Output: $([\![c_1]\!], [\![c_2]\!], \ldots, [\![c_\ell]\!])$ over $\mathbb{F}_p$.
 1: For all $j \in [1, \ell]$, in parallel, compute and reveal

$$[\![x_j]\!] - [\![a_j]\!].$$

   Hence, each party learns $x_j - a_j$.
 2: For all $j \in [1, \ell]$, in parallel, compute and reveal

$$[\![d_j]\!] \leftarrow (x_j - a_j) \cdot [\![q_j]\!] + [\![a_j q_j]\!].$$

   Hence, each party learns $d_j := (x_j - a_j)q_j + a_j q_j = x_j q_j$.
 3: For all $j \in [2, \ell]$, (locally) compute

$$[\![c_j]\!] \leftarrow d_1 \cdots d_j \cdot [\![z_j]\!]. \tag{2}$$

Correctness/Security. The protocol correctness can be shown by verifying Eq. (2), which is indeed correct since $d_1 \cdots d_j \cdot z_j = (x_1 q_1) \cdots (x_j q_j) \cdot t_0^{-1} t_j = x_1 \cdots x_j \cdot (t_0 t_1^{-1}) \cdot (t_1 t_2^{-1}) \cdots (t_{j-1} t_j^{-1}) \cdot t_0^{-1} t_j x_1 \cdots x_j = c_j$. We sketch an argument for security as follows. We observe that the only points where potential information leak may occur are the revealing of $x_j - a_j$ and of $x_j q_j$. However, a_j and q_j are used only once, and hence they act as one-time pad to x_j (additively and multiplicatively, respectively). More precisely, in $x_j q_j$, the value x_j is multiplicatively blinded by t_j^{-1}. Note also that a_j and q_j are available to the parties as shares, hence no information on a_j and q_j leaks either. To prove more formally from this argument in the standard simulator-based notion (*e.g.*, [12]), we just define a simulator that simply simulates the view in the step 1 and 2 of the protocol by random elements. This simulated view is indistinguishable from the real protocol view exactly by the one-time use of a_j and q_j.

A Special Case: Power. For further use, we also define a special case of MULT* where all the inputs x_j are the same, say x. It thus computes powers of an element x. For formality, we write $([\![x]\!], [\![x^2]\!], \ldots, [\![x^\ell]\!]) \leftarrow$ Power$([\![x]\!], \ell)$.

3.2   Multi-fan-in AND (AND*)

We next describe the multi-fan-in AND functionality and a protocol for it below. This is defined by $[\![y_1 \wedge \cdots \wedge y_m]\!] \leftarrow$ AND*$([\![y_1]\!], \ldots, [\![y_m]\!])$.

Intuition/Approach. We construct this protocol based on MULT* (or more precisely, Power) using exactly the approach for *symmetric function* evaluation in [7]. In such a function, the output depends only on the number of 1's in its input. Hence, it can be interpreted as a function with input $\sum_{j=1}^m y_j$. (To exclude it being 0 which is problematic, we will add 1 to it, similarly to [7,15].)

This function can be constructed via Lagrange interpolation. In the case of the multi-fan-in AND functionality, its corresponding interpolated function (with coefficient $c_k \in \mathbb{F}_p$) is defined by

$$p_m(x) = \frac{1}{m!} \prod_{j=1}^{m}(x-j) \bmod p =: \sum_{k=0}^{m} c_k x^k. \tag{3}$$

Our Protocol for AND^*. We show our protocol for AND^* in Algorithm 2.

Algorithm 2. AND^* Protocol

Functionality: $\llbracket y_1 \wedge \cdots \wedge y_m \rrbracket \leftarrow \mathsf{AND}^*(\llbracket y_1 \rrbracket, \ldots, \llbracket y_m \rrbracket)$.
Input: Arithmetic shared values $\llbracket y_1 \rrbracket, \ldots, \llbracket y_m \rrbracket$ over $\mathbb{F}_p$ where $y_j \in \{0,1\}$ for
  all $j \in [1, m]$.
Auxiliary Input: CR_m.
Output: $\llbracket y_1 \wedge \cdots \wedge y_m \rrbracket$ over $\mathbb{F}_p$.
 1: Compute (locally) for $\llbracket x \rrbracket \leftarrow 1 + \sum_{j=1}^{m} \llbracket y_j \rrbracket$.
 2: Compute $(\llbracket x \rrbracket, \llbracket x^2 \rrbracket, \ldots, \llbracket x^m \rrbracket) \leftarrow \mathbf{Power}(\llbracket x \rrbracket, m)$.
 3: Compute (locally) and output $\llbracket v \rrbracket \leftarrow c_0 + \sum_{k=1}^{m} c_k \llbracket x^k \rrbracket$, where the coefficients c_k's are as in Eq.(3).

Correctness/Security. We can verify that $v = y_1 \wedge \cdots \wedge y_m$ as follows: First, the AND function is a symmetric function and thus the output depends only on the value $x := 1 + \sum_{j=1}^{m} y_j$. In particular, we have that

$$y_1 \wedge \cdots \wedge y_m = \begin{cases} 0 & \text{if } x \in [1, m] \\ 1 & \text{if } x = m+1 \end{cases}.$$

The Lagrange interpolation of the polynomial defined on these $m+1$ points are indeed the polynomial in Eq. (3). That is, $y_1 \wedge \cdots \wedge y_m = \sum_{k=0}^{m} c_k x^k$, and hence $v = y_1 \wedge \cdots \wedge y_m$, as required. As for security, it holds straightforwardly since we only call Power as a subroutine.

3.3 Equality Test with Plain Inputs (PlainEqual)

We next describe the equality test functionality with *plain* inputs (and shared output). This is defined by $\llbracket \delta \rrbracket \leftarrow \mathsf{PlainEqual}(x, y)$ where $\delta = 1$ if $x = y$, and $\delta = 0$ otherwise.

Intuition/Approach. We construct this protocol in straightforward way. To confirm equality of x and y, we check if the i-th bit of x, namely x_i, equals the i-th bit of y, namely y_i. Instead of sharing each bit, we let the share of the other party be 0 so as to save communication.[3]

---

[3] This does not leak any private information as long as addition (or subtraction) of shared values is executed soon afterward as in Step 3 of Algorithm 3, where subtraction $1 - \llbracket x_i \rrbracket - \llbracket y_i \rrbracket$ is computed first and then its squared value is computed.

Our Protocol for PlainEqual. We show our protocol for PlainEqual in Algorithm 3.

Algorithm 3. PlainEqual Protocol

Functionality: $[\![\delta]\!] \leftarrow \mathsf{PlainEqual}(x, y)$, where $\delta = 1$ if $x = y$; $\delta = 0$, otherwise.
Input: Cleartexts $x, y \in \mathbb{F}_p$
Output: Arithmetic shared value $[\![\delta]\!]$
1: Parse $x = x_{n-1} \,\|\, x_{n-2} \,\|\, \ldots \,\|\, x_0$.
2: Parse $y = y_{n-1} \,\|\, y_{n-2} \,\|\, \ldots \,\|\, y_0$.
3: P_1 sets $[\![x_i]\!]_1 \leftarrow x_i$ and $[\![y_i]\!]_1 \leftarrow 0$ for $i \in [0, n-1]$.
4: P_2 sets $[\![x_i]\!]_2 \leftarrow 0$ and $[\![y_i]\!]_2 \leftarrow y_i$ for $i \in [0, n-1]$.
5: Compute $[\![v_i]\!] \leftarrow (1 - [\![x_i]\!] - [\![y_i]\!])^2$ for $i \in [0, n-1]$.
6: Compute $[\![\delta]\!] \leftarrow \mathsf{AND}^*([\![v_0]\!], [\![v_1]\!], \ldots [\![v_{n-1}]\!])$.
7: **return** $[\![\delta]\!]$.

Correctness/Security. If $x = y$, the i-th bit of x matches the i-th bit of y, that is, $x_i = y_i$ for $i \in [0, n-1]$, where $x = x_{n-1} \,\|\, x_{n-2} \,\|\, \ldots \,\|\, x_0$ and $y = y_{n-1} \,\|\, y_{n-2} \,\|\, \ldots \,\|\, y_0$ for $x_i, y_i \in \mathbb{Z}_2$. We set $[\![v_i]\!] \leftarrow (1 - [\![x_i]\!] - [\![y_i]\!])^2$ for $i \in [0, n-1]$. This value is 1 if $x_i = y_1$, and 0 otherwise. Now, we obtain that $x = y$ if and only if $v_i = 1$ for all $i \in [0, n-1]$.

$$
\mathsf{AND}^*([\![v_0]\!], [\![v_1]\!], \ldots, [\![v_{n-1}]\!]) = \begin{cases} 0 & \text{if } \sum_{i=0}^{n-1} v_i \in [0, n-1] \\ 1 & \text{if } \sum_{i=0}^{n-1} v_i = n. \end{cases}
$$

As for security, it holds straightforwardly since we only call AND^* as a subroutine.

3.4 Less-Than Comparison with Plain Inputs (PlainLessThan)

We describe the less-than comparison with plain inputs and a protocol for it below. This is defined by $[\![\delta]\!] \leftarrow \mathsf{PlainLessThan}(x, y)$ where the inputs are $x, y \in [0, p-1]$, and the output bit is $\delta = (x < y)$.[4]

Algorithm 4. PlainLessThan Protocol

Functionality: $[\![\delta]\!] \leftarrow \mathsf{PlainLessThan}(x, y)$, such that $\delta = (x < y)$
Input: Cleartext $x \in [0, p-1]$ from P_1, $y \in [0, p-1]$ from P_2
Output: Arithmetic shared value $[\![\delta]\!]$ over $\mathbb{F}_p$
1: P_1 sets $R = [x + 1, 2^n - 1]$.
2: P_1 computes $\{(i, a_i)\} \leftarrow \mathsf{rangeEnc}(R)$; $W_R \leftarrow \{i \mid \exists a \text{ s.t. } (i, a) \in \mathsf{rangeEnc}(R)\}$.
3: P_1 sets $a_j = 2^n - 1$ for all $j \in [0, n]$ s.t. $j \notin W_R$.
4: P_2 computes $\{(i, b_i)\} \leftarrow \mathsf{pointEnc}(y)$.
5: Compute $[\![d_i]\!] = \mathsf{PlainEqual}(a_i, b_i)$ for all $i \in [0, n]$.
6: $[\![\delta]\!] \leftarrow \sum_{i=0}^{n} [\![d_i]\!]$.
7: **return** $[\![\delta]\!]$.

Intuition/Approach. We construct a protocol for PlainLessThan based on binary-tree-based approach called *dyadic range* in a similar manner to [2]. The

---

[4] For a statement C, we denote $(C) = 1$ if C is true, and 0 otherwise;.

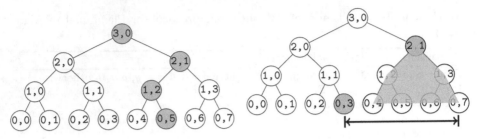

Fig. 1. Example of point encoding for $x = 5$. Here, $\mathsf{pointEnc}(5) = \{(0,5),(1,2),(2,1),(3,0)\}$.

Fig. 2. Example of range encoding for $x = 2$, which defines the range $R = [3,7]$. Here, $\mathsf{rangeEnc}([3,7]) = \{(0,3),(2,1)\}$.

main idea of this tree-based approach is that when the inputs are plain, we can *directly* "encode" them to a data structure that is suitable for comparison in parallel. This encoding method is called *range and point encoding* in [2]. At the core of this approach is the equality test functionality over plain inputs. For this equality test, [2] uses additive homomorphic encryption. On the other hand, we construct this functionality by secret sharing, which is more computationally efficient; this is the main difference to [2]. As described above, our equality test essentially uses multi-fan-in AND as a building block.

Range/Point Encoding. We use a similar terminology from [2], which we recall here. Recall first that n is the bit length of p, that is, $n = \lceil \log_2 p \rceil$. Hence, in particular, $x, y \leq p - 1 < 2^n - 1$. Let $\mathbb{T}_{2^n}$ be a complete binary tree whose leaves correspond to integers from 0 to $2^n - 1$. Let $\mathbb{S}_{2^n}$ be the set of all nodes in the tree $\mathbb{T}_{2^n}$ and a node $w_{i,j}$ represents a pair of its layer and its index: (i,j) for $i \in [0,n]$ and $j \in [0, 2^{n-i} - 1]$. We identify a value $x \in \mathbb{Z}_p$ with a node $(0,x)$. Consider a range $R = [u,v]$ for $0 \leq u \leq v \leq 2^n - 1$. For any range R, a node $w_{i,j} \in \mathbb{S}_{2^n}$ is called a cover node of R if all the descendant leaves of $w_{i,j}$ are in R. We write the set of such nodes as $\mathsf{cover}(R)$. For $w_{i,j} \in \mathbb{S}_{2^n}$ with $(i,j) \neq (n,0)$, let $\mathsf{parent}(w_{i,j})$ be the parent node of $w_{i,j}$. The range and point encodings are then defined as follows. For a range $R = [u,v]$ with $0 \leq u \leq v \leq 2^n - 1$, we let

$$\mathsf{rangeEnc}(R) := \{(i,a_i) \in \mathbb{S}_{2^n} \mid (i,a_i) \in \mathsf{cover}(R), \mathsf{parent}(i,a_i) \notin \mathsf{cover}(R)\}.$$

For a point $x \in [0, p-1]$, we let $\mathsf{pointEnc}(x)$ be the set of all ancestors of a node $(0,x)$ in $\mathbb{T}_{2^n}$ including the node $(0,x)$ itself. An example for point and range encoding is illustrated in Figs. 1 and 2, respectively. The main property is as follows: if for any range R, and any point $x \in [0, p-1]$, we have $|\mathsf{rangeEnc}(R) \cap \mathsf{pointEnc}(x)|$ equals to 1 if $x \in R$, and equals to 0 if $x \notin R$.

Note that we set the range R to reach the furthest to the right, *i.e.*, $v = 2^n - 1$, in our setting, which leads that $\mathsf{rangeEnc}(R)$ has no more than one node in each layer.

Our Protocol for $\mathsf{PlainLessThan}$. We show our protocol for $\mathsf{PlainLessThan}$ in Algorithm 4.

Correctness/Security. Suppose $x < y$. Hence, we have $y \in R = [x+1, 2^n - 1]$. Therefore, by the property of encodings, we have that exactly one element in pointEnc(y) equals to an element in rangeEnc(y). To perform OR over these equality tests for each layer, we simply sum their results up (as in Step 6). Note that, similarly to [2], Step 3 is for creating a dummy for all layers that are not contained in the range encoding of R. We can use the unused value $2^n - 1$ since $x, y < 2^n - 1$. Consequently, the equality tests corresponding to these layers always return false; we need them so that the number of layers to perform equality test will always be the same, namely, $n + 1$ layers (so as to ensure that there will be no additional information on the range R). As for security, it holds straightforwardly since we only call PlainEqual as a subroutine protocol (and note that rangeEnc and pointEnc are local algorithms).

3.5 WrapAround

We now describe a functionality that represents whether a reconstructed share wrap-arounds p. Its definition is as follows:

$$[[y]] \leftarrow \mathsf{WrapAround}([[x]]_1, [[x]]_2),$$

where $y = 1$ if $[[x]]_1 + [[x]]_2 \geq p$ computed over $\mathbb{Z}$, and $y = 0$ otherwise.

Intuition/Approach. In this protocol, P_1 inputs $[[x]]_1 \in \{0, 1, \ldots, p-1\}$, while P_2 inputs $[[x]]_2 \in \{0, 1, \ldots, p-1\}$, and the output is a share $[[y]]$ where

$$y = \begin{cases} 0 & \text{if } [[x]]_1 + [[x]]_2 = x \\ 1 & \text{if } [[x]]_1 + [[x]]_2 = x + p \end{cases}$$

where the sum is over the integers (*i.e.*, not modulo p).

Our Protocol for WrapAround. A protocol for the wrap-around functionality can be done by simply computing $[[y]] \leftarrow 1 - \mathsf{PlainLessThan}([[x]]_1, p - [[x]]_2)$.

Correctness/Security. The correctness holds since $y = 1 \iff [[x]]_1 \geq p - [[x]]_2$. As for security, it holds straightforwardly since we only call PlainLessThan as a subroutine.

3.6 Least Significant Bit

We describe the least significant bit functionality. This is defined by $[[(x)_0]] \leftarrow \mathsf{LSB}([[x]])$ where $(x)_0 := x \bmod 2$ is the LSB of x.

Intuition/Approach. The least significant bit can be evaluated by using LSB of shares and a flag representing a bit flip.

Our Protocol for LSB. Algorithm 5 presents our LSB protocol.

Algorithm 5. LSB Protocol

Functionality: $[\![(x)_0]\!] \leftarrow \mathsf{LSB}([\![x]\!])$

Input: Arithmetic shared value $[\![x]\!]$ over $\mathbb{F}_p$.

Output: $[\![(x)_0]\!]$ over $\mathbb{F}_p$ where $(x)_0 = x \bmod 2$.

1: P_1 locally extracts $b_1 := [\![x]\!]_1 \bmod 2$ and shares $[\![b_1]\!]$. At the same time, P_2 locally computes $b_2 := [\![x]\!]_2 \bmod 2$ and shares $[\![b_2]\!]$.
2: Compute $[\![w]\!] \leftarrow \mathbf{XOR}([\![b_1]\!], [\![b_2]\!]) = [\![b_1]\!] + [\![b_2]\!] - 2[\![b_1]\!] \cdot [\![b_2]\!]$.
3: Compute $[\![v]\!] \leftarrow \mathsf{WrapAround}([\![x]\!]_1, [\![x]\!]_2)$.
4: Output $[\![t]\!] \leftarrow \mathbf{XOR}([\![w]\!], [\![v]\!]) = [\![w]\!] + [\![v]\!] - 2[\![w]\!] \cdot [\![v]\!]$.

Correctness/Security. We can verify that

$$(x)_0 = \begin{cases} ([\![x]\!]_1)_0 \oplus ([\![x]\!]_2)_0 & \text{if } [\![x]\!]_1 + [\![x]\!]_2 = x \\ ([\![x]\!]_1)_0 \oplus ([\![x]\!]_2)_0 \oplus 1 & \text{if } [\![x]\!]_1 + [\![x]\!]_2 = x + p \end{cases}$$

$$= ([\![x]\!]_1)_0 \oplus ([\![x]\!]_2)_0 \oplus \mathsf{WrapAround}([\![x]\!]_1, [\![x]\!]_2).$$

As for security, it holds straightforwardly since we only call WrapAround and **XOR** as subroutines.

Note that this protocol can be run in 4 rounds. Step 1–2 takes 2 rounds, and can be run in parallel with Step 3 (3 rounds). Step 4 takes 1 round. Thus, it is 4 rounds in total, and its total communication is $4n^2 + 5$.

3.7 HalfTest

We describe a functionality that checks if the input is less than half of p as in [15]. This is defined by $[\![z]\!] \leftarrow \mathbf{HalfTest}([\![x]\!])$ where $z = (x < \frac{p}{2})$.

Our Protocol for HalfTest. As in Nishide-Ohta [15], this can be done by

$$[\![z]\!] \leftarrow 1 - \mathsf{LSB}([\![2x]\!]). \tag{4}$$

Correctness/Security. Security holds straightforwardly since we only call LSB as a subroutine.

3.8 Less-Than Comparison

Finally, we describe our less-than comparison functionality and a protocol for it. This is defined by $[\![z]\!] \leftarrow \mathbf{LessThan}([\![x]\!], [\![y]\!])$ where $z = (x < y)$.

Intuition/Approach. As shown in [15], we construct the LessThan protocol using HalfTest as a subroutine.

Our Protocol for LessThan. As shown in Nishide-Ohta [15], when we set $h_x := (x < \frac{p}{2})$, $h_y := (y < \frac{p}{2})$ and $h := (x - y \bmod p < \frac{p}{2})$, the required output can be computed as in the following equality relation:

$$z = h_x(1 - h_y) + (1 - h_x)(1 - h_y)(1 - h) + h_x h_y (1 - h). \tag{5}$$

For formality, we capture this protocol in Algorithm 6.

Algorithm 6. LessThan Protocol

Functionality: $[\![z]\!] \leftarrow$ LessThan$([\![x]\!], [\![y]\!])$
Input: Arithmetic shared values $[\![x]\!]$ and $[\![y]\!]$ over $\mathbb{F}_p$.
Output: Arithmetic shared value $[\![z]\!]$ over $\mathbb{F}_p$ where $z = (x < y)$.
1: Compute $[\![h_x]\!] \leftarrow$ HalfTest$([\![x]\!])$.
2: Compute $[\![h_y]\!] \leftarrow$ HalfTest$([\![y]\!])$.
3: Compute $[\![h]\!] \leftarrow$ HalfTest$([\![x - y]\!])$.
4: Compute $[\![z]\!] \leftarrow [\![h_x]\!] \cdot (1 - [\![h_y]\!]) + (1 - [\![h_x]\!]) \cdot (1 - [\![h_y]\!]) \cdot (1 - [\![h]\!]) + [\![h_x]\!] \cdot [\![h_y]\!] \cdot (1 - [\![h]\!])$.
5: Return $[\![z]\!]$.

Correctness/Security. As for security, it holds straightforwardly since we only call HalfTest as a subroutine.

4 Theoretical Efficiency

The efficiency of our protocol is measured in two aspects: round complexity and total communications. In literature, the round complexity is examined by the chain of multiplication protocols, and the total communication is examined by total invocations of multiplication protocols. However, any procedure that needs communication with other parties are crucial for execution time. Therefore, we count any communication such as "reveal", "send", or "share" as one round, which have been ignored in previous work. Thus, our rigid measurement counts up more rounds than that of previous work. In Table 1, we analyze previous constant-rounds secure comparison protocols from Damgård et al. [7] and Nishide-Ohta [15]. Moreover, we reconsider their protocols in the client-aided model and show that the rounds will be fewer in the model. We also show the result of our 6 rounds secure comparison protocol and its reduced round version.

Damgård et al.'s original secure comparison protocol [7] needs 79 rounds and total communication of $272n \log n + 138n + 22 \log n + 24(\log n)^2 + 24n \log \log n + 12$ field elements, since the protocol consists of two BITS protocols (69 rounds and $136n \log n + 56n + 8 \log n + 12(\log n)^2 + 12n \log \log n + 6$ total communications per BITS) and BIT-LT protocol (13 rounds including 3 rounds for random generation and $26n + 6 \log n$ total communications). Similarly, Nishide-Ohta's original secure comparison protocol [15] needs 28 rounds and total communication of $168n + 36 \log n + 16$, since the protocol consists of 3 LSB protocols (in parallel) and 2 MULT protocols, where LSB is 26 rounds and $32n + 40 \log n$ total communications and MULT is 1 round and 2 total communications.

In the client-aided model, we can omit procedures of generating randomness so that BITS will be 60 rounds and total communications will be $52n \log n + 16n + 5 \log n + 10(\log n)^2 + 10n \log \log n$, while BIT-LT will be 10 rounds and $12n + 5 \log n$ total communications. This let Damgård et al.'s protocol be 70 rounds and $144n \log n + 52n + 64 \log n + 64(\log n)^2 + 64n \log \log n - 6$ total communications. Similarly, LSB will be 12 rounds and $12n + 5 \log n + 3$ total communications in the client-aided model, which makes Nishide-Ohta's

Table 2. Execution times of protocols

Operations	Round	Offline [ms]	Online comp. [us]	Estimated online comm. [ms]	Estimated online total [ms]
ADD	0	–	0.000,10	–	–
MULT$_{pub}$	0	–	0.000,20	–	–
MULT$_{priv}$	1	0.001,355	0.000,10	72	72
MULT* ($\ell = 32$)	2	0.059,558	0.681,70	144	144
Power ($\ell = 32$)	2	0.059,558	0.667,20	144	144
AND* ($m = 32$)	2	0.059,558	1.044	144	144
PlainEqual	3	0.100,386	2.461	216	216
PlainLessThan	3	1.823	63.783	216	216
WrapAround	3	1.823	63.416	216	216
LSB	4	1.821	76.028	288	288
HalfTest	4	1.821	76.424	288	288
LessThan	6	5.574	273.600	432	432

secure comparison protocol 14 rounds and $36n + 15 \log n + 13$ total communications.

Our secure comparison protocol LessThan consists of three HalfTest (more precisely, LSB that is 4 rounds and $4n^2 + 5$ total communications as explained in Sect. 3.6) protocols and a degree-3 polynomial (more precisely, 5 MULT, which has 10 total communications). Naïvely computing the polynomial (without merging the same computations), our protocol has 6 rounds and at most $12n^2 + 25$ total communications.

Further Reducing Rounds. We can combine the step 4 of the LSB protocol and Eqs. (4) to (5) to a degree-6 polynomial. Since each variable is 0 or 1 shared in $\mathbb{Z}_p$, multiplications can be done by AND* protocol in 2 rounds. This results in a LessThan protocol with 5 rounds. The maximum transmitting data amount in one round is within the limitation assumed in our WAN setting. See Appendix A for more details.

5 Experimental Efficiency

In this section, we give performance evaluation of our secure comparison protocol LessThan based on our experiments. For the evaluation, we implement the protocol in C++ programming language using a desktop PC (Xeon E5-2699 v4, 2.20 GHz), Linux Ubuntu 16.04.3 LTS, and a compiler GCC version 5.4.0. Throughout the experiments, we set the prime number $p = 4294967291 = 2^{32} - 5$. Note that our proposed algorithms are independent from the choice of the prime number. Also note that the architecture we used supports 64 bits instruction set, and as shown above, the bit length of p is 32; thus it is unnecessary to use multi-precision arithmetic. To implement our protocol, we do not use assembler, any optimization technique by hand, and any optimized arithmetic software library. We use a special file "`/dev/urandom`" to implement cryptographically secure pseudorandom number generator, and optimizations by the compiler with an option "`-O3`." From this implementation, we evaluate computational time of our protocols, the number of communication rounds, and communication sizes. Based on them, we further estimate the total execution time assuming that the two servers are connected via Wide Area Network (WAN) whose bandwidth and network delay are the same as those in [14] (Namely, we set the bandwidth to be 9 MB/s and the network delay to be 72 ms).

Table 2 shows the execution times of our LessThan protocol and its subroutines. The column of "Offline" represents time for a client to generate multiplication triples and correlated randomness, and the column "Online Comp." represents the computation time of each protocol without communication. The column "Estimated Online Comm." represents the estimated communication time of each protocol by using the assumption described above. Namely, it takes 72 ms per a round. The column "Estimated Online Total" represents the estimated total execution time which is the sum of "Online Comp." and "Estimated Online Comm". For taking the execution times, we set the numbers of inputs of protocols MULT*, Power, and AND* as 32 (*i.e.*, in Algorithm 1, $\ell = 32$, and in Algorithm 2, $m = 32$). We note that in the total execution time, network delay is the dominant factor, and compared to this, influence of computational time and communication size is almost ignorable. Therefore, it is important that the number of communication rounds should be reduced as much as possible when combining a secure comparison protocol to construct concrete applications. For reducing the round complexity, our proposed algorithms can be adopted to the vectorization (*i.e.*, operating on vectors) same as in [14] and batch execution techniques.

Acknowledgement. This work was supported by JST CREST JPMJCR1688.

A   Further Round-Reduced LessThan Protocol

As we mentioned in Sect. 4, our LessThan protocol can be executed in 5 rounds as follows: We can combine the step 4 of the LSB protocol and Eqs. (4) to (5) to a degree-6 polynomial. In particular, this technique breaks down our LessThan to three LSBish protocols (3 rounds and $4n^2 + 3$ total communications) and a degree-6 polynomial F defined below: $F = w + v - w_x w - w_x v - w v_x - v_x v + w_y - w_y w - w_y v - w_x w_y - w_y v_x + v_y - w v_y - v_y v - w_x v_y - v_x v_y + 2(-wv + w_x wv + w_y wv + w_x w_y w + w_x w_y v + w_y wv_x + w_y v_x v + wv_x v + w_x wv_x + w_x v_x v + w_x w_y v_x + wv_y v + w_x wv_y + w_x v_y v + wv_x v_y + v_x v_y v + w_x v_x v_y - w_y v_y + w_y wv_y + w_y v_y v + w_x w_y v_y + w_y v_x v_y) + 4(-w_x wv_x v - w_x w_y wv - w_y wv_x v - w_x w_y wv_x - w_x w_y v_x v - wv_x v_y v - w_x wv_x v_y - w_x v_x v_y v - w_y wv_y v - w_x w_y wv_y - w_y v_x v_y v - w_y wv_x v_y - w_x w_y v_y v - w_x w_y v_x v_y - v_y w_x wv) + 8(w_x w_y wv_x v + w_x wv_x v_y v + w_x w_y wv_y v + w_y wv_x v_y v + w_x w_y wv_x v_y + w_x w_y v_x v_y v) - 16 w_x w_y wv_x v_y v.$

The function F contains 13 degree-2, 26 degree-3, 15 degree-4, 6 degree-5, and 1 degree-6 terms, which can be computed in 2 rounds and 292 total communications. Since each variable is 0 or 1 shared in $\mathbb{Z}_p$, multiplications of the function F can be done by AND^* protocol in 2 rounds. This results in a LessThan protocol with 5 rounds and the total communication is $3(4n^2 + 3) + 292 = 12n^2 + 301$.

Algorithm 7. LSBish Protocol

Functionality: $([\![w]\!], [\![v]\!]) \leftarrow \mathbf{LSBish}([\![x]\!])$
Input: Arithmetic shared value $[\![x]\!]$ over $\mathbb{F}_p$.
Output: $[\![(x)_0]\!]$ over $\mathbb{F}_p$ where $(x)_0 = x \bmod 2$.
1: P_1 locally extracts $b_1 := [\![x]\!]_1 \bmod 2$ and shares $[\![b_1]\!]$. At the same time, P_2 locally computes $b_2 := [\![x]\!]_2 \bmod 2$ and shares $[\![b_2]\!]$.
2: Compute $[\![w]\!] \leftarrow \mathbf{XOR}([\![b_1]\!], [\![b_2]\!]) = [\![b_1]\!] + [\![b_2]\!] - 2[\![b_1]\!][\![b_2]\!]$.
3: Compute $[\![v]\!] \leftarrow \mathsf{WrapAround}([\![x]\!]_1, [\![x]\!]_2)$.
4: Output $([\![w]\!], [\![v]\!])$.

Algorithm 8. LessThan Protocol (described explicitly)

Functionality: $[\![z]\!] \leftarrow \mathsf{LessThan}([\![x]\!], [\![y]\!])$
Input: Arithmetic shared values $[\![x]\!]$ and $[\![y]\!]$ over $\mathbb{F}_p$.
Output: Arithmetic shared value $[\![z]\!]$ over $\mathbb{F}_p$ where $z = (x < y)$.
1: Compute $([\![w_x]\!], [\![v_x]\!]) \leftarrow \mathbf{LSBish}([\![x]\!])$.
2: Compute $([\![w_y]\!], [\![v_y]\!]) \leftarrow \mathbf{LSBish}([\![y]\!])$.
3: Compute $([\![w]\!], [\![v]\!]) \leftarrow \mathbf{LSBish}([\![x - y]\!])$.
4: Compute F by using $\mathbf{AND}$, addition, and multiplication with public value.
5: Return $[\![z]\!]$.

B   Round Complexity and Communication Complexity

In Table 3, we put round complexity and total communications of each protocol from [7,15]. In Table 4, we show round complexity and total communication of our LessThan protocol and its subroutines. These are used for calculating rounds and total communication in Table 1. We note that a more detailed value for total communication of the Damgård et al. [7] protocol is $176n \log n + 70n + 84 \log n + 80(\log n)^2 + 80n \log \log n - 6$ (which is reduced to $144n \log n + 52n + 64 \log n + 64(\log n)^2 + 64n \log \log n - 6$ for the client-aided version).

Table 3. Number of rounds and total communication of each protocol from [7,15]

Protocol	Round	Total comm. (elements)
Unbounded-fan-in OR with ℓ inputs	5	$10\ell - 2$
Prefix OR	11	$10n + 20\log n - 2$
RAN$_2$	3	4
SOLVED-BITS	14	$18n + 20\log n - 1$
BIT-LT	13	$14n + 20\log x - 2$
BIT-ADD	25	$44n\log n - 2n - 4\log n + 20(\log n)^2 + 20n\log\log n$
CARRIES	25	$44n\log n - 2n - 4\log n + 20(\log n)^2 + 20n\log\log n$
PRE$_\circ$	24	$44n\log n - 4n - 4\log n + 20(\log n)^2 + 20n\log\log n$
BITS	69	$88n\log n + 28n + 32\log n + 40(\log n)^2 + 40n\log\log n - 2$
LessThan of [7]	79	$176n\log n + 70n + 84\log n + 80(\log n)^2 + 80n\log\log n - 6$
LSB	26	$32n + 40\log n$
LessThan of [15]	28	$96n + 120\log n + 4$

Table 4. Number of rounds and total communication of our LessThan protocol and its subroutines

Protocol	Round	Total comm. (elements)
MULT$_{\mathsf{priv}}$	1	2
MULT*, Power, AND* (ℓ inputs)	2	2ℓ
PlainEqual	3	$4n$
PlainLessThan, WrapAround	3	$4n^2$
LSB, HalfTest	4	$4n^2 + 5$
LessThan (Implemented in Sect. 5)	6	$12n^2 + 25$
LessThan (1 round reduced)	5	$12n^2 + 301$

One might wonder if the amount of transmitting field elements during any round exceeds the limitation, $i.e.$, $9\,\mathrm{MB/s} \times 72\,\mathrm{ms} = 648\,\mathrm{KB}$. If the amount of transmitting data (elements of $\mathbb{F}_p$) exceeded the limitation, the protocol would need extra rounds to send all the data. In our LessThan protocol, a larger amount of data is needed during executing PlainLessThan protocol, more specifically n PlainEqual protocols in parallel. This protocol sends at most $2n^2$ field elements at one round. This leads to that our LessThan sends at most $6n^2$ field elements, since it run three HalfTest (constructed by WrapAround that has PlainLessThan as subroutine) protocols at once. When p is 32-bit prime, $i.e.$, $n = 32$, our LessThan protocol sends at most $6144 = 6 \times 32^2$ field elements (196608 bits) in one round, which is less than the limitation; 648 KB.

References

1. Araki, T., Furukawa, J., Lindell, Y., Nof, A., Ohara, K.: High-throughput semi-honest secure three-party computation with an honest majority. In: Proceedings of the 2016 ACM SIGSAC Conference on Computer and Communications Security, pp. 805–817 (2016)
2. Attrapadung, N., Hanaoka, G., Kiyomoto, S., Mimoto, T., Schuldt, J.C.N.: A taxonomy of secure two-party comparison protocols and efficient constructions. In: 15th Annual Conference on Privacy, Security and Trust, PST 2017, Calgary, Canada, 28–30 August 2017. IEEE (2017)
3. Beaver, D.: Efficient multiparty protocols using circuit randomization. In: Feigenbaum, J. (ed.) CRYPTO 1991. LNCS, vol. 576, pp. 420–432. Springer, Heidelberg (1992). https://doi.org/10.1007/3-540-46766-1_34
4. Blake, I.F., Kolesnikov, V.: Strong conditional oblivious transfer and computing on intervals. In: Lee, P.J. (ed.) ASIACRYPT 2004. LNCS, vol. 3329, pp. 515–529. Springer, Heidelberg (2004). https://doi.org/10.1007/978-3-540-30539-2_36
5. Blake, I.F., Kolesnikov, V.: Conditional encrypted mapping and comparing encrypted numbers. In: Di Crescenzo, G., Rubin, A. (eds.) FC 2006. LNCS, vol. 4107, pp. 206–220. Springer, Heidelberg (2006). https://doi.org/10.1007/11889663_18
6. Catrina, O., de Hoogh, S.: Improved primitives for secure multiparty integer computation. In: Garay, J.A., De Prisco, R. (eds.) SCN 2010. LNCS, vol. 6280, pp. 182–199. Springer, Heidelberg (2010). https://doi.org/10.1007/978-3-642-15317-4_13
7. Damgård, I., Fitzi, M., Kiltz, E., Nielsen, J.B., Toft, T.: Unconditionally secure constant-rounds multi-party computation for equality, comparison, bits and exponentiation. In: Halevi, S., Rabin, T. (eds.) TCC 2006. LNCS, vol. 3876, pp. 285–304. Springer, Heidelberg (2006). https://doi.org/10.1007/11681878_15
8. Damgård, I., Geisler, M., Krøigaard, M.: Homomorphic encryption and secure comparison. IJACT 1(1), 22–31 (2008)
9. Damgard, I., Geisler, M., Kroigard, M.: A correction to 'efficient and secure comparison for on-line auctions'. Int. J. Appl. Cryptogr. 1(4), 323–324 (2009)
10. David, B., Dowsley, R., Katti, R., Nascimento, A.C.A.: Efficient unconditionally secure comparison and privacy preserving machine learning classification protocols. In: Au, M.-H., Miyaji, A. (eds.) ProvSec 2015. LNCS, vol. 9451, pp. 354–367. Springer, Cham (2015). https://doi.org/10.1007/978-3-319-26059-4_20
11. Garay, J., Schoenmakers, B., Villegas, J.: Practical and secure solutions for integer comparison. In: Okamoto, T., Wang, X. (eds.) PKC 2007. LNCS, vol. 4450, pp. 330–342. Springer, Heidelberg (2007). https://doi.org/10.1007/978-3-540-71677-8_22
12. Goldreich, O.: The Foundations of Cryptography - Volume 2, Basic Applications. Cambridge University Press, Cambridge (2004)
13. Goldreich, O., Micali, S., Wigderson, A.: How to play any mental game or a completeness theorem for protocols with honest majority. In: 1987 Proceedings of the 19th Annual ACM Symposium on Theory of Computing, pp. 218–229 (1987)
14. Mohassel, P., Zhang, Y.: SecureML: a system for scalable privacy-preserving machine learning. In: SP 2017, pp. 19–38 (2017)
15. Nishide, T., Ohta, K.: Multiparty computation for interval, equality, and comparison without bit-decomposition protocol. In: Okamoto, T., Wang, X. (eds.) PKC 2007. LNCS, vol. 4450, pp. 343–360. Springer, Heidelberg (2007). https://doi.org/10.1007/978-3-540-71677-8_23

16. Reistad, T.I.: Multiparty comparison - an improved multiparty protocol for comparison of secret-shared values. In: SECRYPT 2009, pp. 325–330 (2009)
17. Reistad, T.I., Toft, T.: Secret sharing comparison by transformation and rotation. In: Desmedt, Y. (ed.) ICITS 2007. LNCS, vol. 4883, pp. 169–180. Springer, Heidelberg (2009). https://doi.org/10.1007/978-3-642-10230-1_14
18. Reistad, T., Toft, T.: Linear, constant-rounds bit-decomposition. In: Lee, D., Hong, S. (eds.) ICISC 2009. LNCS, vol. 5984, pp. 245–257. Springer, Heidelberg (2010). https://doi.org/10.1007/978-3-642-14423-3_17
19. Rivest, R.L.: Unconditionally secure commitment and oblivious transfer schemes using private channels and a trusted initializer (1999, unpublished manuscript)
20. Schneider, T., Zohner, M.: GMW vs. yao? Efficient secure two-party computation with low depth circuits. In: Sadeghi, A.-R. (ed.) FC 2013. LNCS, vol. 7859, pp. 275–292. Springer, Heidelberg (2013). https://doi.org/10.1007/978-3-642-39884-1_23
21. Schoenmakers, B., Tuyls, P.: Practical two-party computation based on the conditional gate. In: Lee, P.J. (ed.) ASIACRYPT 2004. LNCS, vol. 3329, pp. 119–136. Springer, Heidelberg (2004). https://doi.org/10.1007/978-3-540-30539-2_10
22. Veugen, T.: Encrypted integer division and secure comparison. Int. J. Appl. Cryptol. 3(2), 166–180 (2014)
23. Veugen, T., Blom, F., de Hoogh, S.J.A., Erkin, Z.: Secure comparison protocols in the semi-honest model. J. Sel. Top. Sig. Process. 9(7), 1217–1228 (2015)
24. Yao, A.C.: How to generate and exchange secrets (extended abstract). In: 27th Annual Symposium on Foundations of Computer Science, Toronto, Canada, 27–29 October 1986, pp. 162–167. IEEE Computer Society (1986)

Towards Practical RAM Based Secure Computation

Niklas Buescher[(✉)], Alina Weber, and Stefan Katzenbeisser

Technische Universität Darmstadt, Darmstadt, Germany
`buescher@seceng.informatik.tu-darmstadt.de`

Abstract. Secure multi-party computation (MPC) protocols are powerful privacy enhancing technologies. Yet, their scalability is limited for data intensive applications due to the circuit computation model. Therefore, RAM based secure computation (RAM-SC) has been proposed, which combines MPC with Oblivious RAM (ORAM). Unfortunately, realizing efficient RAM-SC applications by hand is a tedious and error-prone task, which requires expert knowledge in both cryptographic primitives and circuit design. To make things worse, a multitude of ORAMs with different trade-offs has been proposed. To overcome this entry barrier to RAM-SC, we present a two-fold approach. First, we explore all cost dimensions of relevant ORAMs in various deployment scenarios. Second, we present a fully automatized compilation approach from ANSI-C to RAM-SC. The presented compiler analyzes the input source code and extracts relevant information about the usage patterns of all arrays in the code. The results of the analysis are then used to predict the runtime of suitable ORAMs and to identify the ORAM that achieves minimal runtime. Thus, for the first time, RAM-SC also becomes accessible to non-domain experts.

1 Introduction

The continuous grow of data gathering and processing, which is fired by cheap sensors (e.g., in smart phones and wearables), cheap storage costs, and efficient machine learning algorithms, enables many useful applications and powerful online services. However, this data processing is also a huge risk for the individuals privacy, as users of these services become more and more transparent and reveal possibly sensitive data to an untrusted service provider.

Yet, since the 1980's [32,33] it is (theoretically) known that any computation over sensitive data from multiple parties can be performed securely, such that the participating parties do not learn more about the inputs of the other parties from the computation than they can already derive from the output. Consequently, this form of generic secure multi-party computation (MPC) is a powerful privacy-enhancing technology that provides a solution for the aforementioned privacy problems by enabling the computation over sensitive data in untrusted environments. MPC has rapidly developed in recent years, with many new protocols using various different cryptographic primitives, e.g., [1,9,13,32].

© Springer Nature Switzerland AG 2018
J. Lopez et al. (Eds.): ESORICS 2018, LNCS 11099, pp. 416–437, 2018.
https://doi.org/10.1007/978-3-319-98989-1_21

Moreover, many theoretical and practical optimizations, e.g., [3,19,36], made these protocols ready for practice.

Almost all MPC protocols have in common that they compute functionalities in the circuit computation model. Thus, to compute a function f, the function has to be represented as Boolean or Arithmetic circuit C_f. Unfortunately, every random memory access in this model requires a scan of the complete memory, which renders MPC protocols impractical for any data intensive application. To overcome this performance barrier, Gordon et al. [15] proposed the idea of RAM-SC, later refined by Liu et al. [22], which combines MPC with Oblivious RAM (ORAM) [14]. Thus, RAM-SC partially performs the same MPC computations, yet every RAM access is evaluated (more efficiently) using an ORAM protocol. ORAMs obfuscate each RAM access by producing a sequence of physical accesses that is indistinguishable to a random access pattern.

Many ORAMs using a wide range of constructions have been proposed, e.g., [20,24,29], and recently also new or adapted ORAMs optimized for RAM-SC have been presented, e.g., [12], SCORAM [31], Circuit ORAM (C-ORAM) [30], optimized Square-Root ORAM (SQ-ORAM) [37], and FLORAM [11]. Even though RAM-SC is asymptotically more efficient than MPC, it is almost impossible to identify a suitable ORAM that achieves optimal runtime by hand, which can differ by multiple orders of magnitude due to their complex cost models.

For instance, the array size influences the ORAM choice. Namely, all ORAMs have different ranges of use, e.g., SQ-ORAM is very effective for smaller RAMs, whereas C-ORAM is asymptotically the fastest ORAM. Yet, not only the number of accesses is relevant, but also the distinction between the access type: read or write access with private index or public index (i.e., the stored data is still encrypted yet accessed position is known). For example, array accesses with publicly known index can be performed at little cost in FLORAM, but have to be performed with costs similar to an access with private index in C-ORAM. Additionally, the RAM initialization pattern within the program itself influences the RAM-SC runtime. Also, the environment in which the protocol is executed has to be taken into account, as all ORAMs have different communication and computation patterns. This includes the properties of the network connection (bandwidth and latency), but also the computational power of the executing hardware. Concluding, for an optimal ORAM choice it is necessary to consider all aforementioned parameters. Up to know it is a tedious task for a developer to create an efficient RAM-SC program, as this requires an array usage statistic of the input program and in depth knowledge about ORAMs and their deployment costs.

Contribution. To make RAM-SC accessible for non-domain experts, we present an automatized framework that analyzes which ORAMs (if at all) should be used to achieve optimal runtime for a RAM-SC program with a given number of array accesses and a deployment scenario. Moreover, by implementing the framework in the CBMC-GC compiler by Holzer et al. [17], we illustrate a compile-chain from generic ANSI-C code into a RAM-SC program.

In contrast to previous work, such as SCVM [22] and ObliVM [23], which statically decide for or against a single ORAM, our approach is aware of all aforementioned cost dimensions of RAM-SC. Namely, we automatically identify all array accesses (individually for each array in the input code), determine an optimal ORAM choice depending on the access pattern, which includes an optimal selection of ORAM parameters, and automatically partition the code into circuit based computations and ORAM accesses.

For this purpose, we revisit C-ORAM, which is the most efficient tree-based ORAM optimized for MPC, SQ-ORAM, and FLORAM, which both have been developed to outperform C-ORAM for mid-sized arrays, to develop a library with gate-precise costs models. This library allows runtime estimations for arbitrary access patterns, ORAM sizes, and deployment scenarios within seconds, which is multiple orders of magnitude faster than benchmarking all ORAMs in an actual deployment scenario. Moreover, the library can compute multiple different cost metrics, e.g., to determine which ORAM has minimal communication complexity in a given scenario. As a side-product of our studies, we present practical optimizations for all ORAMs that reduce the runtime for each access of up to a factor of two. Furthermore, we present the first extensive study on RAM-SC runtimes for different real world deployment scenarios and show that the use of ORAMs over purely circuit based computations is often only useful for arrays larger than one could assume.

Outline. Preliminaries and related work are described in the next section. We study the different ORAMs and propose optimizations in Sect. 3, before describing the compiler in Sect. 4. Finally, an evaluation of our approach is given in Sect. 5.

2   Preliminaries and Related Work

2.1   Secure Multi-party Computation (MPC)

MPC protocols are cryptographic protocols performed between two or more parties that allow a joint computation of a functionality $f(x_1, x_2, \dots)$ over the private inputs $x_1, x_2, \dots$ of the participating parties $P_1, P_2, \dots$ with guaranteed *correctness* and *privacy*, i.e., the parties do not learn more about the other party's inputs than they could already derive from the observed output. In this work we present our ideas for one of the most researched two-party protocols, namely Yao's garbled circuits protocol [32,33]. Moreover, we focus on the semi-honest (passive) adversarial model, yet remark that many ideas presented in this work can be generalized and transferred to other protocols.

Functionalities in Yao's protocol are expressed as combinatorial Boolean circuits, which consist of a number n of Boolean gates, two sets of input wires and two sets of output wires, one for each party. Boolean circuits for MPC are constructed similarly to circuits in digital hardware design, yet, with the major difference that linear gates (e.g., XOR) are favored over non-linear (e.g., AND) gates. This is because non-linear gates require noticeable more computation and communication to be evaluated in an MPC protocol [19]. Thus, the major goal in circuit design for Yao's protocol is to minimize the number of non-linear gates.

2.2 Oblivious RAM

Oblivious RAM (ORAM), first introduced by Goldreich and Ostrovsky [14], is a cryptographic primitive that allows to obfuscate the access pattern to an outsourced storage to achieve *memory trace obliviousness*. Therefore, each logical access on some virtual address space is translated into a sequence of physical accesses on the memory, which appears to be random to observers, resulting in the security guarantee that two sequences of virtual accesses of the same length produce indistinguishable physical access patterns.

ORAMs are commonly modeled as a protocol between an ORAM client, who is the data owner, and an untrusted ORAM server, who provides the physical storage. Typically, an ORAM construction is comprised of two distinct algorithms, the initialization and the access algorithm. An ORAM has a capacity m, which describes the number of data elements it can store. Moreover, most ORAMs require to store metadata for each data element, which in combination with the element itself is referred to as *block*.

The design goals of standalone ORAM constructions are manifold, e.g., minimizing client side storage, communication or computation costs. Therefore, many optimized ORAMs have been proposed, e.g., [14,20,24,29]. For their combination with MPC (described in Sect. 2.3), a different cost model applies, because the ORAM client has to be evaluated as a circuit. In this work, we study the most efficient known ORAMs for MPC, namely Circuit-ORAM (C-ORAM) [30], optimized Square-Root ORAM (SQ-ORAM) [37], FLORAM [11], and the FLO-RAM variant CPRG (FCPRG) [11]. A description of all ORAMs is given in Sect. A.1.

2.3 RAM Based MPC (RAM-SC)

MPC protocols evaluate functionalities represented as circuits. Circuits allow to express arbitrary computations, yet random memory accesses have to be expressed as a chain of multiplexers of the complete memory, referred to as linear scan (LS). This limits MPC for applications that rely on dynamic memory accesses. Therefore, Gordon et al. [15] proposed to combine MPC protocols with ORAM to enable dynamic memory accesses with sublinear overhead. The authors describe a RAM machine, where the circuit computes an oblivious machine that evaluates instructions and memory accesses. A complete RAM machine is often not necessary, and thus the so-called *RAM-SC* model was later refined by Liu et al. [22] for practical efficiency. Its major concepts are described in the following paragraphs.

First, the parties performing the MPC protocol also act as distributed ORAM server, and the ORAM client is implemented as circuit evaluated by the MPC

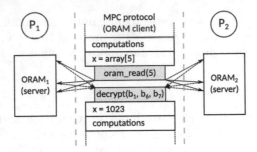

Fig. 1. *Exemplary and simplified illustration of RAM-SC.* A program flow is illustrated that is computed within an MPC protocol, run between two parties P_1 and P_2. At some point, a value is read from an array with virtual index 5. Therefore, a circuit representing the ORAM client functionality is executed that translates the virtual index into multiple physical addresses. These addresses are revealed to both parties, who enter the blocks as input to the MPC protocol.

protocol itself. Thus, both roles are shared between the computing parties. Second, a program is evaluated by interweaving the MPC protocol with oblivious ORAM accesses. Consequently, a RAM-SC program consists of many small protocols that either perform a computation or an ORAM access. This behavior is exemplary illustrated in Fig. 1.

The construction of RAM-SC as described, is very generic because it allows to combine different MPC protocols and ORAMs. We observe that in one RAM-SC program multiple ORAMs of possibly different type can be used, e.g., one ORAM for each array in the input program. Moreover, as in standalone ORAMs, the blocks stored on the ORAM server have to be encrypted. This can be realized by performing an encryption and decryption within a circuit, which requires (even highly optimized) a substantial amount of gates, e.g., 5000 non-linear gates to encrypt a single block of 128 bits AES [4], using a secret sharing scheme, e.g., XOR sharing [11], or by (re-)soldering the existing garbled labels based on the publicly revealed index [37]. In the XOR sharing approach a physical block is read by entering the shares as input to the MPC protocol, which are then recombined within the protocol. Similarly, to write to one or multiple blocks, the MPC protocol outputs one share for each block to every party. When using the soldering approach, the circuit garbler re-uses the existing wire labels but remaps them according the accessed indices reveled to both parties, similar to a multiplexer (array) access with public index. We also remark, that in RAM-SC, the ORAM access type, i.e., read or write, can be revealed to both parties, as the algorithm description is seen as public knowledge. This access type is also referred to as *semi-private access* [11].

Security. RAM-SC provides the same privacy and correctness properties as traditional MPC protocols [15]. As in [15,22] we focus on the semi-honest setting in this work.

Complexity. The computation and communication complexity of a RAM-SC protocol depends on the circuit complexity of the computation, the circuit complexity of the ORAM client, the number of protocol rounds, as well as additional ORAM protocol costs that are performed outside of the MPC protocol. For ORAMs with less than $O(m)$ computations or less than $O(m)$ bandwidth RAM-SC is (asymptotically) more efficient than any circuit based MPC protocol.

Oblivious Data Structures. Related to the work on RAM-SC, is the work on structured memory accesses in MPC. For example, Zahur and Evans [34] as well as Keller and Scholl [18] have studied dedicated data structures, such as oblivious stacks or queues that can outperform the generic ORAM solution for applications with the according access pattern.

2.4   Compilation for MPC and RAM-SC

Jointly with the first practical MPC implementation, Malkhi et al. [25] realized the need for tool support and presented the first compiler for MPC. Subsequently, many compilers for Boolean (and Arithmetic) circuit based MPC have been proposed, e.g., TASTY [16], CBMC-GC [17], or Frigate [26].

The first compiler that combines ORAMs and MPC, named SCVM, has been proposed by Liu et al. [22]. In a follow up work, Liu et al. presented the ObliVM [23] compiler, and also adapted their work to the needs of ORAM supported hardware synthesis [21]. All these compilers translate a domain-specific or annotated language that compiles specially marked arrays into RAM-SC programs using a single ORAM type. Although simplifying the developing effort for RAM-SC, the developer is still required to have expert knowledge in ORAMs. The ObliVC compiler by Zahur and Evans [35] is a recent compiler that allows to jointly compile public and private computations, and has therefore been used to implement ORAM protocols. However, it does not primarily target RAM-SC and therefore does not provide any form of automatization for RAM-SC.

3   Analysis and Optimization of ORAMs for Secure Computation

In order to precisely determine the best suiting ORAM for a RAM-SC application, in this section we revisit the most efficient ORAMs for RAM-SC to establish gate-precise cost models. These models allow the approximation of runtime costs in any RAM-SC deployment, which forms the basis for the optimizing compiler in Sect. 4. Since RAM accesses are basic primitives for any algorithm, they should be optimized to the full extent. Therefore, we also propose gate-level optimizations for all ORAMs. We begin with a description of implementation pitfalls observed in previous implementations, which can lead to inefficient RAM-SC.

3.1   Pitfalls of ORAM Implementations for MPC

ORAMs are complex cryptographic primitives, and thus substantial engineering effort is necessary to translate them in efficient circuit representations as required for RAM-SC. Consequently, the majority of ORAM implementations in MPC is written in high-level languages for MPC and translated using compilers for MPC. Unfortunately, due to the lacking maturity of tools, compilers, and programming paradigms, a straight-forward high-level implementation does not automatically translate into an efficient circuit description. Thus, while revising the ORAMs and their implementations we identified the following inefficiencies and provide hints for future implementations:

Overallocation of Internal Variables. Some MPC compilers use fixed bitwidths for all program variables. For example, leaf identifiers for any tree based ORAM scheme can be represented as bit strings of $\log(m)$ bits. Consequently, for small to medium numbers of elements m, e.g., $m < 2^{32}$, a fixed integer bitwidth of 32 bit, introduces a noticeable overhead in the number of used gates, which also propagates to subsequent (possibly recursive) computations. Therefore, it is preferable to either use optimizing compilers, such as CBMC-GC [17] or to adjust the bitwidth accordingly.

Insufficient Constant Propagation. Constants are not always properly identified and propagated by some compilers, especially between multiple functions, which can result in cascading effects of significant circuit size. This especially concerns temporary variables in conditional blocks, which could be expressed by wires without any gate costs, but are often multiplexed with all other variables in the conditional.

Duplicated Multiplexer Blocks. Conditional blocks are represented by multiplexers on the circuit level. When using `if/else` statements that write the same variable (with different values), some compilers introduce duplicated multiplexer blocks, one for each write. However, both can be merged into a single conditional write, which results in a smaller circuit.

Bound Checking. The most recent MPC ORAM implementations [11,37] perform an inefficient out-of-bounds check for each array access. To prevent misbehavior, the index is masked using a modulo computation, which additionally increases the number of gates. While there is no perfect solution to this problem, as there is no unified error handling approach in MPC, several other and more efficient approaches exist. For example, an MPC compiler that is able to identify out-of-bounds accesses can be used (if possible), a faster masking scheme can be used, or for some schemes the ORAM's size can be increased to the next power of two without a noticeable loss in runtime.

3.2   Circuit Models and Optimized ORAM Construction for MPC

To determine an optimal ORAM choice for RAM-SC, we develop parametrized cost models for all schemes, which are composed of hand-crafted cost models for all circuit building blocks, e.g., conditional swap, adder, or shuffle. Using a modular construction of all ORAM schemes, allows to adapt to future improved building blocks, to recombine different ORAM schemes (e.g., for the recursive position map), and to evaluate different implementation options.

The developed models are based on the papers and their implementations [11,30,37] and precisely consider the number of non-linear gates, the communication complexity (rounds and bandwidth), and auxiliary computation costs, i.e., computations performed outside of secure computation. We use optimal bitwidths for variables and avoid the earlier described pitfalls. Due to the lack of space, we do not elaborate on the created models, but focus on their optimization. We begin with a study of the trivial circuit solution.

Trivial Circuit Solution. Traditionally, MPC compilers translate a dynamic array access into a linear scan (LS) of the complete memory to hide which position was actually accessed. The most efficient MPC circuit construction for LS read is based on a multiplexer tree that bit-wise encodes the accessed index over the stages of the tree. For write accesses a decoder of $m-1$ non-linear gates is used to convert the index to a so called One-Hot Code, where each bit of the decoders' output is connected to a multiplexer, which selects either the element to write or the previous data [7]. In contrast to ORAM schemes, the elements are not shared between the parties but reside inside the garbled circuit. Hence, while LS has a significant circuit size for a growing numbers of elements, it is very efficient in case of networks with high latencies and smaller array sizes, as accesses can be performed in zero rounds and without any initialization.

C-ORAM. C-ORAM [30] is known to achieve almost optimal asymptotic costs, and is thus the best suiting ORAM scheme for larger arrays. Unfortunately, C-ORAM suffers from high initialization costs, as each element has to be initially written in an ordinary ORAM access. Furthermore, C-ORAM is a multi-round protocol, where the number of communication rounds is dominated by the recursive structure of the scheme. Nevertheless, accesses to physical blocks can be performed using the soldering approach (cf. Sect. 2.3), which only requires to transmit the computed public indices.

The most recent implementation of C-ORAM [11] that we are aware has been implemented with OblivC, which neither optimizes the bitwidth of internal variables nor thoroughly eliminates unnecessary multiplexer blocks. This has a significant impact on the number of gates required for the eviction algorithm, where for example variables with bitwidth $\log(\log(m) + 1)$ are sufficient to represent the tree height. Additionally, an inefficient implementation of LS is used. Furthermore, the ReadAndRemove() operation used in all tree ORAMs to read a path, can be optimized such that only the necessary payload and isDummy flag is accessed.

SQ-ORAM. Optimized SQ-ORAM [37] has been proposed to outperform C-ORAM for moderate array sizes, albeit being asymptotically less efficient. For small numbers of elements the circuit complexity is (surprisingly) small, as the major costs stem from the scan of the stash, i.e., the temporary cache, whose publicly known size is of at most $\sqrt{m}$. SQ-ORAM has a substantially more efficient initialization phase in comparison to C-ORAM. Physical blocks are efficiently accessed using the soldering approach. However, similar to C-ORAM, the number of communication rounds depends on the number of recursive position maps, which is in $\log_c(m)$ with c being the packing factor.

The implementation of Square-Root ORAM in Obliv-C was done by the original authors of the paper, is highly optimized, and is, to the best of our knowledge, the most efficient implementation of this scheme. For their construction the same low-level optimizations as described for C-ORAM can be applied, while the LS is already using the most efficient version.

FLORAM. FLORAM is the most recent ORAM scheme for RAM-SC. Based on PIR techniques, $O(m)$ server computations are required per access, however, these are performed outside secure computation and lead to very low communication complexity. For the generation of the FSS, the FLORAM algorithm requires $2 \cdot \log_2(m)$ AES encryptions that have to be computed inside a circuit, which consists of ≈5000 non-linear gates each. Being a constant round protocol, FLORAM has a huge advantage over the other ORAMs in high latency settings. Furthermore, in contrast to other ORAMs, it is possible to efficiently perform semi-private accesses with little costs, as the physical addresses of the elements correspond to the virtual addresses used. The implementation of FLORAM uses inefficient modulo operations to compute the element position inside its 128 bit data blocks, which requires additional 6000 non-linear gates upon each access. This checks can be omitted, when using a packing factor c that is a power of two, which is the case when using standard data types.

FCPRG. The CPRG optimization for FLORAM was proposed to remove the expensive computation of the many AES encryptions within MPC, so that both parties are able to compute the encryptions locally and only input their results into the secure computation for each stage of the FSS tree. Hence, it introduces a trade-off by reducing the computational effort within the MPC protocol, yet turns the constant round protocol into a multi-round protocol with $O(\log_2(m))$ rounds. The implementation of the FCPRG scheme can be optimized in the same manner as the original FLORAM.

Optimal Parameter Selection for Recursive ORAMs. Most ORAM schemes come with a set of parameters that can be selected for every instantiation. For example, while maintaining the same level of security, larger buckets in tree based ORAMs allow to use a smaller stash [31], which influences the resulting circuit complexity and thus RAM-SC runtime. Therefore, for an optimal

ORAM instantiation in RAM-SC it is desirable to identify optimal parameters. These parameters, i.e., bucket size, stash size, number of levels in ORAMs with recursive position maps, and the eviction strategy are (often) constrained by the desired security level, as well as the failure probability (overflow of the stash). Fortunately, for most ORAM schemes, safe parameter ranges for different security configurations have been proposed [29–31]. Within these ranges, we solve the combinatorial optimization problem by exhaustive search over the parameter space, which can be performed in seconds for all schemes.

Although we only described optimizations that lead to constant improvements, in Sect. 5.2 we observe gate reductions up to 70.7% for C-ORAM, 17.9% for SQ-ORAM and up to 35.6% for FCPRG.

4 Automatized RAM-SC

In order to facilitate the broad usage of RAM-SC, we present an automatized compilation approach from ANSI-C to RAM-SC that is able to detect dynamic memory accesses in a high-level input language and that places the corresponding arrays into ORAMs without the need of any interaction, e.g., by annotations, from the programmer.

To achieve this goal, we follow a two-step approach. First, an input code analysis and transformation is performed, that identifies arrays and enumerates array usage statistics. Second, an optimizer is invoked that identifies a suitable scheme for each array in the input code for a selected runtime environment, using the analysis result of the first step, as well as the cost models developed in Sect. 3.

4.1 Input Code Analysis and Transformation

To transform an input source code into a RAM-SC program, a naïve compilation can be performed by iterating over the abstract syntax tree of the input source code and by translating each array and access into an equivalent RAM access. However, this approach leads to very inefficient RAM-SC programs, as not every access requires full memory trace-obliviousness. For example, arrays can also be accessed purely with public indexes or with a mix of public and private indices. Moreover, the number of accesses, as well as the initialization of the array, play an important role for the performance of RAM-SC (cf. Sect. 5.1). Also the order of accesses is of relevance, e.g., in the case of semi-private accesses, the stash size in FLORAM only depends on the number of writes. Therefore, for an optimized compilation it is important to create precise array usage statistics.

We implemented such a more advanced compilation approach for the CBMC-GC [17] compiler, which provides the most powerful symbolic execution (SE), required for the analysis, of all currently available compilers for MPC. For example, CBMC-GC performs a powerful constant propagation, which allows to separate private and semi-private array accesses. Internally, CBMC-GC unrolls the input program and translates it into a single-static assignment form. This form is then used for a SE of the source code. During SE, every expression of the unrolled code is visited and partial evaluation is performed. Therefore, by extending the SE interface for array accesses, it is possible (i) to maintain a list of all allocated arrays, (ii) to track each access, and (iii) to distinguish semi-private and private accesses. This approach allows to create a detailed usage statistic for each array, which consists of array size m, element bitwidth b, an enumeration of all (semi-)private reads and writes, and an initialization pattern. Namely, we distinguish the case that an array is initialized (i) by only one party, (ii) by using only public indices, e.g., by iterating over the array, or (iii) in a random manner purely based on private writes.

To compile a RAM-SC program the existing LS interface, which is CBMC-GC's traditional approach to handle array accesses, is overwritten, such that each array read or write is replaced by input and output wires of the circuit. Using this approach the compiler does not need to be aware of the concept of RAM-SC, as it is only concerned about the computations performed in the circuit model. Consequently, the remaining code is compiled into a circuit using the existing compilation chain of CBMC-GC. This ensures to profit from all implemented gate-level optimizations. To execute a compiled RAM-SC program, the inputs and outputs have to be connected to ORAM client circuits, which are selected in the second compilation step. We remark, that the implementation of the ORAM protocols is outside the scope of this work and mostly an engineering task.

4.2   Optimal ORAM Selection

Given a detailed array access description, an ORAM scheme should be selected that achieves minimal costs, e.g., provides optimal runtime. For a given array description, the compiler computes a model of all ORAM schemes with the help of the ORAM library developed in Sect. 3. Furthermore, for a desired security level and each ORAM scheme, the possible parameter space is identified, i.e., the secure parameter configurations, discussed in Sect. 3.2. Finally, this combinatorial optimization problem is solved by enumerating the complete search space, consisting of all ORAMs and their possible configurations, which is manageable in seconds on commodity hardware. The optimal choice then depends on the desired evaluation metric, which currently is either the runtime or the number of transferred bits. Next, we describe how to predict the runtime in RAM-SC and remark that these ideas can also be transferred to other metrics, e.g., cloud computing costs (cf. [28]), with little engineering effort.

Runtime Estimation. Using the library developed in the previous section, the runtime of all RAM accesses within a RAM-SC program can be estimated efficiently for a computing environment specified by the developer. Namely, taking the type of array usage description and the security parameter κ into account, the library returns a gate count, the number of communication rounds, the number of OTs, and additional local costs, e.g., such as the FSS evaluation for FLORAM. The environment is described by three parameters, i.e., the computational power (as the non-linear gate throughput, the number of OTs that can be performed per second, and the time to evaluate a FSS scheme), the available bandwidth, and the round trip time.

For runtime approximation we assume a computing time that is linear in the number of non-linear gates and the number of OTs, which is a reasonable assumption as in practice both depend on the throughput of the AES-NI hardware extension. Thus, assuming perfect resource allocation and parallel generation of garbled tables and their transmission (known as streaming), the runtime is estimated as the sum of the time until the last gate has been evaluated (assuming a constant garbling throughput) by the circuit evaluator, the time to perform OTs with OT Extension (assuming a constant OT throughput), and number of communication rounds times the latency. The runtime for the circuit initialization can be estimated in a similar manner.

Although simplifying the RAM-SC computation, we observed moderate deviations ($\leq 20\%$) that are decreasing with increasing RAM size, when comparing to experimentally measured runtimes, which is especially acceptable as only the relation between different ORAM schemes is of major relevance.

Optimizing Multidimensional Arrays. Multidimensional arrays can be represented in a single or in multiple (hierarchical structured) ORAMs, where one ORAM scheme is used per dimension. The latter can be more efficient, if one dimension is predominately accessed using static indexes. Therefore, our compiler studies both cases, i.e., using multiple or a singular ORAM separately to identify the optimal choice.

5   Evaluation

We give a threefold evaluation of our approach for automatized RAM-SC. First, we evaluate the parameter space that influences the choice for a suitable ORAM when implementing a RAM-SC application. Second, we study the circuit optimizations presented in Sect. 3.2. Finally, we illustrate the compilation approach introduced in Sect. 4 for an exemplary use case.

Experimental Setup. Our evaluation is based on the runtime estimation, described in the previous section. Assuming a state of the art implementation of Yao's protocol and a commodity CPU, at least 10 million (M) non-linear gates can be garbled per second per core (fixed-key garbling [3]), where two wire labels per non-linear gate have to be transmitted (cf. two halve gates [36]). We use a security level of $\kappa = 80$ bit. Thus, each label has length $\kappa_{gc} = 80$ bit. The computation of XOR is assumed to be for free (free-XOR [19]). Similarly, we assume an efficient OT Extension implementation with a throughput of 10 millions (correlated) OTs per seconds [2]. Two values with length $\kappa_{ot} = 80$ bit have to be transmitted per OT. We remark that in practice, these numbers could be probed in the executing environment for better accuracy, yet also observe that these (conservative) estimates, easily exceed the capacity of a 1 Gbit link. The time to compute base OTs is left of out scope, as these only need to be computed once and have practically negligible costs for any larger RAM-SC application. The computational effort for the local computations in FLORAM are taken from [11], assuming a parallelization onto four cores.

We investigate three exemplary network settings. First, for comparison purposes with [37] we use a data center (DC) setting, a scenario with 1.03 Gbit connectivity a low latency 0.5 ms. Second, a local area network (LAN) scenario, typical for the internal network of a larger company, with a 1 Gbit bandwidth and 5 ms latency is studied. Finally, we study a wide area network (WAN) setting as it can be found in nowadays Internet, i.e., servers located on different continents, with 200 Mbit bandwidth and 50 ms latency.

5.1   RAM-SC Parameter Dimensions

We give a quantitative evaluation of the different parameter dimensions of ORAM schemes. The results of this analysis are given in Fig. 2, where the average ORAM access runtime is shown for different network settings, block sizes b, and number of accesses.

Network Settings. In the first row of Fig. 2, the runtime to perform a typical integer access with $b = 32$ bit for different ORAM sizes m is shown in the three different network settings without considering initialization costs. We observe that for latencies above or equal to 5 ms (LAN), LS is superior to all other schemes for ORAM sizes of up to $m \approx 2^{12}$ elements, afterwards, FLORAM becomes more efficient. The efficiency of LS and FLORAM stems from the fact that they are constant (or zero) round protocols, whereas the other recursive schemes are multi round protocols. SQ-ORAM outperforms the other schemes for a mid-sized RAM sizes, yet its advantages decreases with increasing latency.

Blocksize. The runtime of a single ORAM access without considering initialization costs for three different block sizes, namely $b = 64, 128, 1024$ bit, in the DC setting is shown in the second row. In general we observe that the range of use of all ORAM schemes shifts towards smaller RAM sizes with only marginal changes in their relation to each other. Moreover, with increasing block sizes LS becomes more inefficient, because all blocks are scanned to the full extent for every access.

Number of Accesses and Initialization Amortization. The ORAM schemes have different initialization costs, which have not been considered in the previous analyses. Shown in the last row of Fig. 3 is the total time to initialize a RAM with m values and to perform n accesses afterwards in the DC setting. We observe that LS and FLORAM have none or negligible initialization costs, whereas SQ-ORAM and C-ORAM require a certain number of accesses to amortize their asymptotic costs. In Fig. 3g and h, the amortization of SQ-ORAM's initialization costs is shown, which is achieved with $n \ll m$ accesses. Whereas C-ORAM requires almost $n \approx m$ accesses for its amortization, cf. Fig. 3i, albeit being around 10 times faster per access than the second best ORAM, i.e., FCPRG, with a total amortization time of 2900 days.

Summary. For small blocksizes and elements, LS is the recommendation of choice in any network setting, SQ-ORAM is effective in fast networks and for larger blocksizes, yet has a very short range of use that must be carefully studied before deployment. In all other settings, FLORAM is the most promising ORAM. With its constant rounds and the ability to parallelize the server workload, it is significantly less constrained by the network resources that are often the limiting factor in practice. In fast networks FCPRG slightly outperforms FLORAM, but also has a comparably high round complexity (logarithmic to the power of two, and not logarithmic to the packing factor c, as SQ-ORAM and C-ORAM). We were unable to identify a scenario where C-ORAM amortizes its high initialization costs with less than one month total runtime to outperform FLORAM or FCPRG.

5.2   ORAM Optimizations

We evaluate the ORAM optimizations presented in Sect. 3.2 by comparing the optimized ORAMs with the latest implementation given in [11] in the number of non-linear gates. The resulting circuit sizes are shown for an exemplary single write access for elements of size $b = 32$ bit and different ORAM sizes m in Fig. 3. We observe that the break-even points between different schemes shift. For example, both FLORAM variants outperform LS for a lager number of elements than previously assumed. The improvements of the individual schemes are discussed in the following paragraph.

We observe a difference in form of a factor of two in the number of (non-linear) gates between the optimized LS and the LS based on equality comparators, as it has often been used in the past. This has a noticeable impact on the break-even points with the other ORAM schemes, as LS is more efficient than previously assumed. The difference between the two LS implementations becomes smaller with an increasing block size. The circuit size of C-ORAM is reduced by 40%–70%. Yet, we remark that the difference between the two implementations slightly decreases when increasing m, as all overly allocated resources are decreasingly used. The existing SQ-ORAM implementation is already highly optimized and therefore, only marginal improvements are observed, i.e., for up to $m = 2^{11}$ elements, on average 12.5% non-linear gates are saved. We only observe marginal relative improvements for FLORAM with savings of up to 20.8% in non-linear gates. This is because the majority of FLORAMs circuit consists of already highly optimized AES circuits. This is not the case in FCPRG, where only two AES circuits are used per access and therefore, an improvement of up to 35.7% of non-linear gates is observed.

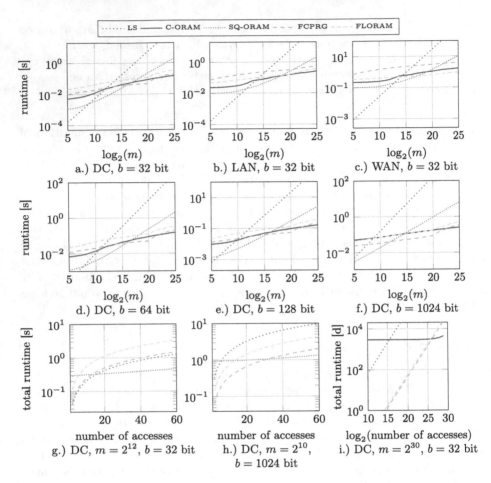

Fig. 2. *Parameter space of RAM-SC.* Illustrated is the runtime of a one or multiple RAM-SC access in seconds (or in days Fig. 3i) for ORAMs of different size m in different configurations.

5.3 Use Case – Dijkstra Shortest Path Algorithm

We illustrate our compilation approach for an exemplary use case that has previously been studied in RAM-SC research, namely Dijkstra's single-source shortest path algorithm [22,23]. One party inputs a set of weighted edges between the nodes in the graph, representing the distances, as a two-dimensional array (INPUT_A_e) and the other party inputs the source and destination node, represented by the indices of the respective nodes. The algorithm (given in Sect. A.2) consists of multiple arrays that are accessed in a semi- and private manner.

In the first step of the compilation, constants are propagated, such that unnecessary array access are removed. Afterwards, the array usage statistic is generated, which is illustrate for $m = 8$ nodes in Table 1. The code uses two

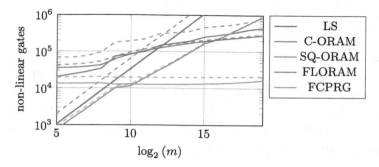

Fig. 3. *Circuit Optimization.* Comparison of the circuit size (in the number of non-linear gates) between the ORAM schemes for RAM-SC in [11], illustrated with dotted lines, and the optimized circuits described in Sect. 3.2, illustrated with solid lines, for one write access of bitwidth $b = 32$ bit and different array sizes m.

one dimensional arrays, namely the (vis) array to store visited nodes and the (dis) array to store the shortest path to the source node, as well as the two dimensional INPUT_A_e array. Shown is the analysis result when separating the two dimensions. The inner dimension of the array is always accessed using a public index, whereas the outer dimension is accessed with private indices only. Moreover, the arrays vis and dis are first written during the algorithm, whereas, the weighted graph is already pre-initialized with values from Party A. In the next compilation step, the statistics are handed to the optimizer, who selects the most suitable scheme for a user chosen deployment scenario. The runtime estimated by the ORAM library in the DC setting for the two most compute intensive arrays is illustrated in Fig. 4 for different graph sizes m. We note that the compiler is only able to compute absolute array usage statistics, yet not parametrized formulas. Therefore, the results are based on multiple compiler runs, one for each size m. Shown is the total runtime in seconds to perform all semi- and private array accesses for the two most efficient ORAM choices for each array. The array dis is best stored as a LS for up to $m = 2^8$ nodes, then SQ-ORAM becomes most efficient. For the INPUT_A_e array, a decomposition in two dimensions l0 and l1 is more efficient the placing it in a single ORAM. For $m \leq 2^9$ a SQ-ORAM representation of INPUT_A_e_l0 is most efficient. Albeit being a small array, the significant blocksize to store the second layer of the array makes LS inefficient. For $m > 2^9$ nodes, FCPRG becomes most efficient.

We observe, that even for simple algorithms, an automatized approach is highly beneficial, as many factors need to be considered when manually selecting ORAMs. In total we observe runtime of more than an hour for a moderately sized array, e.g., 2^{10}.

Table 1. *Exemplary array usage statistics for* $m = 8$. Statistics gathered by the compiler extension after symbolic execution.

Array	m	b	Initialized	Private		Semi-private	
				Read	Write	Read	Write
visited (vis)	8	8	False	0	8	64	8
distance (dis)	8	32	False	106	0	105	72
edges_inner (INPUT_A_e_l0)	8	16	True	0	0	64	0
edges_outer (INPUT_A_e_l1)	8	128	True	8	0	0	0

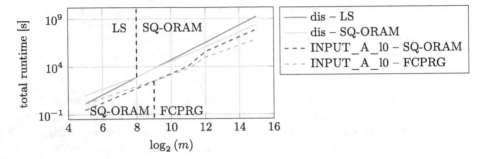

Fig. 4. *Total runtime for all accesses to the arrays* dis *and* INPUT_A_10 *in Dijkstra's algorithm.*

6   Conclusion and Future Work

We conclude our work with two insights. First, further automatization, i.e., tool support, is a necessity for the efficiency and thus the widespread use of RAM-SC. We presented such a tool that compiles RAM-SC programs from ANSI-C, allowing also non-domain experts to profit from RAM-SC. Our approach is also beneficial when deciding whether RAM-SC is sufficient solution for an application or whether dedicated protocols are needed. Second, RAM-SC is only at the verge of being practical. Even in fast networks, RAM accesses create noticeable costs. As it impossible to perform a RAM access faster than the latency, the round complexity becomes a sincere bottleneck in any intercontinental deployment scenario. Consequently, for future work the automatized compilation of oblivious algorithms is promising and also parallel RAM-SC [6,8,27] becomes necessary to overcome the performance barrier of multi-round RAM-SC protocols.

Acknowledgements. We thank all anonymous reviewers for their helpful and constructive comments. This work has been co-funded by the German Federal Ministry of Education and Research (BMBF) and the Hessen State Ministry for Higher Education, Research and the Arts (HMWK) within CRISP and by the DFG as part of project E4 within the CRC 1119 CROSSING, and by the DFG as part of project A.1 within the RTG 2050 "Privacy and Trust for Mobile User".

A   Appendix

A.1   ORAMs for RAM-SC

Circuit ORAM (C-ORAM). C-ORAM by Wang et al. [30] is a derivative of Path ORAM [29], which is the most practical standalone ORAM, and has been optimized for MPC. C-ORAM is a tree-based ORAMs that store m data elements in a binary tree structure of at most $\log_2(m)$ stages and an additional root level called *stash*, which can also be imagined as a cache. Each node in the tree is a smaller ORAM itself, called *bucket ORAM*, that stores multiple blocks. Each data element is randomly mapped to one of the leaf nodes, maintaining the invariant that an element with leaf identifier l is contained in one of the buckets on the path from the root node to leaf l or in the stash. To read or write an element in tree-based ORAMs, the according path from root to the leaf is read, a new leaf identifier for the read element is chosen, and the accessed path is moved to the stash. Moreover, after each access an *eviction* procedure is initiated, which writes blocks from stash into the tree while moving blocks as close as possible to their designated leaves.

For RAM-SC C-ORAM requires a recursive position map, which associates the virtual index of each element with the position in the tree. Henceforth, a tree-based ORAM has several construction parameters, including the size of the bucket ORAMs B, the number of recursive steps r, a packing factor c describing the number of mappings contained in one block of the recursive ORAMs.

Square-Root ORAM (SQ-ORAM). SQ-ORAM was one of the two ORAMs introduced in the seminal paper by Goldreich and Ostrovsky [14] and later optimized for MPC by Zahur et al. [37] SQ-ORAM uses a fundamentally different strategy than Path ORAM. Its core idea is to randomly permute the memory and to periodically refresh this permutation. For m elements, the so-called *permuted memory* has size $m + \sqrt{m}$, Furthermore, a shelter/stash for $\sqrt{m}$ elements is needed. The simulation of a RAM program takes place in so called epochs of $\sqrt{m}$ steps, consisting of three phases: In a first step the memory is obliviously permuted using a permutation π that assigns each element a position in the permuted memory by using random tags assigned to each element. Afterwards, $\sqrt{m}$ virtual accesses can take place, during which the updated values are written to the shelter. As last step of an epoch, the permuted memory is updated according the shelter. To access an element at index v, first the entire shelter is scanned. If the element cannot be found, the permuted memory is accessed to retrieve the element at position $\pi(v)$, otherwise, the element has previously been visited and can thus be found in the shelter, and a dummy access to the permuted memory is performed.

Zahur et al. [37], removed the use of PRFs (needed for the permutation), dummy elements, expensive oblivious sorting algorithms, and identified public metadata. Furthermore, they introduced the usage of recursive maps to compute the mapping between virtual and physical addresses.

FLORAM. FLORAM, recently introduced by Doerner and Shelat [10,11], differs from the other ORAM constructions as it is built from function secret sharing (FSS) introduced by Boyle et al. [5]. FLORAM is a *distributed* ORAM [24], where the data is stored in a secret shared manner (XOR) between two servers. Elements are accessed using Private information retrieval (PIR) techniques, i.e., a short query is evaluated on all elements on the server to extracted the desired element. A point function $f_{\alpha,\beta}(x)$ evaluates to β if $x = \alpha$ and 0 otherwise. Informally, FSS allows to share a distributed point function (DPF) in such a way, that the parties can evaluate the point function on arbitrary input, yet neither learn α nor β. This feature allows the client to send the servers specially crafted queries $q^0(i)$ or $q^1(i)$ using FSS to retrieve or to write an element at index i.

In more detail, FLORAM distinguishes a read-only memory (OROM) and write-only memory (OWOM). Data in both is stored using an XOR sharing, yet in OROM, each share is additionally masked using a PRF with a key known only to the storing party. After a number of write accesses, the OWOM memory is converted into the OROM. This process is referred to as *refresh*. To read an index i, the client shares a DPF that evaluates to 1 on input i. The server evaluates the DPF on all indices, multiplies the result with each associated element share and returns the aggregated result. Writing is performed using a similarly. A conversion between OWOM and OROM is too expensive to be performed after every write access, therefore a stash is used that functions as a cache between refreshes. The stash is scanned when performing read accesses, to identify updated elements.

FLORAM CPRG (FCPRG). FCPRG [11] is an extension to FLORAM. The main client side costs of FLORAM occur for computing the FSS scheme, which requires to compute $2 \cdot \log_2(m)$ PRFs for every access. In MPC the evaluation of the PRFs can render the scheme expensive and therefore, the authors propose to compute the PRFs locally, with the trade-off that $O(\log_2(m))$ interactions between the computing parties are required.

A.2   Code Example – Dijkstra

```
1  #define M 128
2  typedef struct {short m[M][M];} Graph;
3
4  int main (Graph INPUT_A_e, int INPUT_B_s, int INPUT_B_d) {
5    char vis[M]; // inidicates if node has been visitied
6    int dis[M]; // current smallest distance from src to dst
7    for(int i = 0; i < M; i++) {vis[i] = 0; dis[i] = 0;}
8    vis[INPUT_B_s] = 1;
9    for(int i = 0; i < M; i++)
10     dis[i] = INPUT_A_e.m[INPUT_B_s][i];
11
12   for(int i = 0; i < M; i++) {
13     int minj = -1;
```

```
14      for(int j = 0; j < M; j++) {
15        if(!vis[j] && (minj < 0 || dis[j] < dis[minj]))
16          minj = j
17      }
18      vis[minj] = 1;
19      for(int j = 0; j < M; j++)
20        if(!vis[j] &&
21            (dis[minj]+INPUT_A_e.m[minj][j] < dis[j])) {
22          dis[j] = dis[minj] + INPUT_A_e.m[minj][j];
23        }
24    }
25    return dis[INPUT_B_d];
26  }
```

Listing 1.1. *Dijkstra's shortest-path algorithm.* Source code is based on [23] using CBMC-GC's input annotations.

References

1. Araki, T., et al.: Optimized honest-majority MPC for malicious adversaries - breaking the 1 billion-gate per second barrier. In: IEEE S&P (2017)
2. Asharov, G., Lindell, Y., Schneider, T., Zohner, M.: More efficient oblivious transfer and extensions for faster secure computation. In: ACM CCS (2013)
3. Bellare, M., Hoang, V.T., Keelveedhi, S., Rogaway, P.: Efficient garbling from a fixed-key blockcipher. In: IEEE S&P (2013)
4. Boyar, J., Peralta, R.: A small depth-16 circuit for the AES S-box. In: Gritzalis, D., Furnell, S., Theoharidou, M. (eds.) SEC 2012. IAICT, vol. 376, pp. 287–298. Springer, Heidelberg (2012). https://doi.org/10.1007/978-3-642-30436-1_24
5. Boyle, E., Gilboa, N., Ishai, Y.: Function secret sharing. In: Oswald, E., Fischlin, M. (eds.) EUROCRYPT 2015. LNCS, vol. 9057, pp. 337–367. Springer, Heidelberg (2015). https://doi.org/10.1007/978-3-662-46803-6_12
6. Boyle, E., Chung, K.-M., Pass, R.: Oblivious parallel RAM and applications. In: Kushilevitz, E., Malkin, T. (eds.) TCC 2016. LNCS, vol. 9563, pp. 175–204. Springer, Heidelberg (2016). https://doi.org/10.1007/978-3-662-49099-0_7
7. Buescher, N., Franz, M., Holzer, A., Veith, H., Katzenbeisser, S.: On compiling Boolean circuits optimized for secure multi-party computation. FMSD **51**, 308–331 (2017)
8. Buescher, N., Katzenbeisser, S.: Faster secure computation through automatic parallelization. In: USENIX Security (2015)
9. Damgård, I., Pastro, V., Smart, N., Zakarias, S.: Multiparty computation from somewhat homomorphic encryption. In: Safavi-Naini, R., Canetti, R. (eds.) CRYPTO 2012. LNCS, vol. 7417, pp. 643–662. Springer, Heidelberg (2012). https://doi.org/10.1007/978-3-642-32009-5_38
10. Doerner, J., Shelat, A.: Scaling ORAM for secure computation. Cryptology ePrint Archive, Report 2017/827 (2017)
11. Doerner, J., Shelat, A.: Scaling ORAM for secure computation. In: ACM CCS (2017)

12. Gentry, C., Goldman, K.A., Halevi, S., Julta, C., Raykova, M., Wichs, D.: Optimizing ORAM and using it efficiently for secure computation. In: De Cristofaro, E., Wright, M. (eds.) PETS 2013. LNCS, vol. 7981, pp. 1–18. Springer, Heidelberg (2013). https://doi.org/10.1007/978-3-642-39077-7_1

13. Goldreich, O., Micali, S., Wigderson, A.: How to play any mental game or a completeness theorem for protocols with honest majority. In: ACM STOC (1987)

14. Goldreich, O., Ostrovsky, R.: Software protection and simulation on oblivious RAMs. J. ACM **43**, 431–473 (1996)

15. Gordon, S.D., et al.: Secure two-party computation in sublinear (amortized) time. In: ACM CCS (2012)

16. Henecka, W., Kögl, S., Sadeghi, A.R., Schneider, T., Wehrenberg, I.: TASTY: tool for automating secure two-party computations. In: ACM CCS (2010)

17. Holzer, A., Franz, M., Katzenbeisser, S., Veith, H.: Secure two-party computations in ANSI C. In: ACM CCS (2012)

18. Keller, M., Scholl, P.: Efficient, oblivious data structures for MPC. In: Sarkar, P., Iwata, T. (eds.) ASIACRYPT 2014. LNCS, vol. 8874, pp. 506–525. Springer, Heidelberg (2014). https://doi.org/10.1007/978-3-662-45608-8_27

19. Kolesnikov, V., Schneider, T.: Improved garbled circuit: free XOR gates and applications. In: Aceto, L., Damgård, I., Goldberg, L.A., Halldórsson, M.M., Ingólfsdóttir, A., Walukiewicz, I. (eds.) ICALP 2008. LNCS, vol. 5126, pp. 486–498. Springer, Heidelberg (2008). https://doi.org/10.1007/978-3-540-70583-3_40

20. Kushilevitz, E., Lu, S., Ostrovsky, R.: On the (in)security of hash-based oblivious RAM and a new balancing scheme. In: ACM-SIAM SODA (2012)

21. Liu, C., et al.: GhostRider: a hardware-software system for memory trace oblivious computation. In: ACM ASPLOS (2015)

22. Liu, C., Huang, Y., Shi, E., Katz, J., Hicks, M.W.: Automating efficient RAM-model secure computation. In: IEEE S&P (2014)

23. Liu, C., Wang, X.S., Nayak, K., Huang, Y., Shi, E.: ObliVM: A programming framework for secure computation. In: IEEE S&P (2015)

24. Lu, S., Ostrovsky, R.: Distributed oblivious RAM for secure two-party computation. In: Sahai, A. (ed.) TCC 2013. LNCS, vol. 7785, pp. 377–396. Springer, Heidelberg (2013). https://doi.org/10.1007/978-3-642-36594-2_22

25. Malkhi, D., Nisan, N., Pinkas, B., Sella, Y.: Fairplay - a secure two-party computation system. In: USENIX Security (2004)

26. Mood, B., Gupta, D., Carter, H., Butler, K.R.B., Traynor, P.: Frigate: a validated, extensible, and efficient compiler and interpreter for secure computation. In: IEEE EuroS&P (2016)

27. Nayak, K., Wang, X. S., Ioannidis, S., Weinsberg, U., Taft, N., Shi, E.: GraphSC: Parallel secure computation made easy. In: IEEE S&P (2015)

28. Pattuk, E., Kantarcioglu, M., Ulusoy, H., Malin, B.: CheapSMC: a framework to minimize secure multiparty computation cost in the cloud. In: Ranise, S., Swarup, V. (eds.) DBSec 2016. LNCS, vol. 9766, pp. 285–294. Springer, Cham (2016). https://doi.org/10.1007/978-3-319-41483-6_20

29. Stefanov, E., et al.: Path ORAM: an extremely simple oblivious RAM protocol. In: ACM CCS (2013)

30. Wang, X., Chan, T.H.H., Shi, E.: Circuit ORAM: on tightness of the Goldreich-Ostrovsky lower bound. In: ACM CCS (2015)

31. Wang, X.S., Huang, Y., Chan, T.H.H., Shelat, A., Shi, E.: SCORAM: oblivious RAM for secure computation. In: ACM CCS (2014)

32. Yao, A.C.C.: Protocols for secure computations (extended abstract). In: IEEE FOCS (1982)

33. Yao, A.C.C.: How to generate and exchange secrets (extended abstract). In: IEEE FOCS (1986)
34. Zahur, S., Evans, D.: Circuit structures for improving efficiency of security and privacy tools. In: IEEE S&P (2013)
35. Zahur, S., Evans, D.: Obliv-C: a language for extensible data-oblivious computation. Cryptology ePrint Archive, Report 2015/1153 (2015)
36. Zahur, S., Rosulek, M., Evans, D.: Two halves make a whole. In: Oswald, E., Fischlin, M. (eds.) EUROCRYPT 2015. LNCS, vol. 9057, pp. 220–250. Springer, Heidelberg (2015). https://doi.org/10.1007/978-3-662-46803-6_8
37. Zahur, S., et al.: Revisiting square-root ORAM: efficient random access in multiparty computation. In: IEEE S&P (2016)

Improved Signature Schemes for Secure Multi-party Computation with Certified Inputs

Marina Blanton[1(✉)] and Myoungin Jeong[2]

[1] Department of Computer Science and Engineering, University at Buffalo (SUNY), Buffalo, USA
mblanton@buffalo.edu
[2] Department of Mathematics, University at Buffalo (SUNY), Buffalo, USA
myoungin@buffalo.edu

Abstract. The motivation for this work comes from the need to strengthen security of secure multi-party protocols with the ability to guarantee that the participants provide their truthful inputs in the computation. This is outside the traditional security models even in the presence of malicious participants, but input manipulation can often lead to privacy and result correctness violations. Thus, in this work we treat the problem of combining secure multi-party computation (SMC) techniques based on secret sharing with signatures to enforce input correctness in the form of certification. We modify two currently available signature schemes to achieve private verification and efficiency of batch verification and show how to integrate them with two prominent SMC protocols.

Keywords: Signature schemes with privacy · Batch verification
Secure multiparty computation · Certified inputs

1 Introduction

Secure multi-party computation (SMC) deals with protecting confidentiality of private data during computation in distributed or outsourced settings. This is a mature research field with a variety of techniques for securely evaluating arbitrary functions by two or more computational parties who are not permitted to have access to the inputs in the clear. Recent rapid advances in this field significantly reduced SMC overhead, and we are witnessing growing deployment of SMC solutions in practice [3,4,25].

A standard formulation of SMC defines the problem as evaluating some function f on k (≥ 1) private inputs $\mathsf{in}_1, \ldots, \mathsf{in}_k$ from different sources by m (≥ 2) computational parties and producing s (≥ 1) outputs which get revealed to the designated parties. The security objective is that no information about the private data is revealed to any party beyond the agreed upon output (or no information at all if a party receives no output). Standard security definitions

© Springer Nature Switzerland AG 2018
J. Lopez et al. (Eds.): ESORICS 2018, LNCS 11099, pp. 438–460, 2018.
https://doi.org/10.1007/978-3-319-98989-1_22

model the participants as semi-honest (who correctly follow the prescribed computation, but might analyze the messages they receive in the attempt to learn unauthorized information) or malicious (who can arbitrary deviate from the computation in the attempt to learn unauthorized information). Output correctness guarantees must also hold in these respective models. These definitions, however, provide no guarantees with respect to what inputs are entered into the computation. That is, a malicious participant can modify its real input in the attempt to harm security or correctness. For example, the participant can perturb his input in such a way that all output recipients receive incorrect information, but he can compensate for the error and learn the correct result. Or, alternatively, the participant can modify his input in such a way as to learn the maximum amount of information about private data of others', beyond what would be available if the computation was run on truthful inputs ([2] gives an example of this attack in the context of computing with genomic data). These attacks are beyond the scope of standard SMC security models and cannot be mitigated.

In this work, we study enforcement of correct (i.e., truthful) inputs being used in SMC via input certification. That is, at the time of computation initiation, a party supplying input accompanies it by a certificate and proves that the data input into the computation is identical to what has been certified. It goes without saying that the certificate and its verification must maintain data confidentiality. There are many types of data which is generated or can be verified by an authority (such as the government, a medical facility, etc.) who can issue private certification to the user at that time.

The problem of enforcing input correctness via certification has been studied for specific SMC applications (e.g., anonymous credentials [8] or set operations [10, 15]) and, more recently, for general functions [2, 24, 33]. However, all of the efforts we are aware of for the general case have been for secure two-party computation based on garbled circuits (GCs). It is an interesting problem to study because GC evaluation does not naturally combine with signature or certification techniques, but we also believe that this problem deserves attention beyond GCs. For this reason, in this work we treat the problem of input certification in the multi-party setting based on secret sharing.

Because both secret sharing and signature schemes exhibit algebraic structure, the use of signatures appears to be a natural choice in enabling input certification in secret sharing based SMC. We note that, unlike many other conventional uses of signatures, this problem setting requires that signature verification is performed privately, without revealing any information about the signed message to the verifier. Another important consideration is that in many SMC applications the size of the input is large (consider, e.g., genomic data). Because signatures are built using rather expensive public-key techniques, which in the privacy-preserving setting often need to be combined with zero-knowledge proofs, we are interested in improving signature verification time using batch verification of multiple signatures.

In this work we study two types of signatures in the context of this problem: (i) CL-signatures [6, 7] which were designed for anonymity applications and achieve both message privacy and unlinkability of multiples showings of the same signature and (ii) conventional ElGamal signatures [17]. After formulating the necessary security guarantees of private signature verification, we show that signature showing in [7] can be simplified to meet our definition of message privacy and construct a batch verifier for the resulting signature. In the case of ElGamal signatures, we first modify a provably secure ElGamal signature scheme from [29] to achieve private verification and consequently construct a batch verifier for the resulting algorithm. Our batch verifiers use the small exponents technique [1] to randomize multiple signatures to ensure that batch verification can succeed only when all individual signatures are valid.

Another component of this work deals with combining the developed signature schemes with SMC techniques secure in the malicious model. Toward this goal, we identify two prominent constructions of SMC based on secret sharing: (i) Damgård-Nielsen solution [13] of low communication complexity where the number of corrupted parties is below $m/3$ and (ii) SPDZ [14] with a very fast online phase and tolerating any number of corruptions. We show how to modify their input phase to use our signatures with an additional optimization of utilizing a single commitment to multiple signatures instead of using individual commitments.

Finally, we implement our ElGamal-based signature scheme and SPDZ-based use of certified inputs for a varying number of messages (SMC inputs) and show that they result in efficient performance. The techniques are general enough to be applicable to other signature algorithms (such as ElGamal-based DSA and others).

2   Related Work

The only publications on certified inputs for SMC that we are aware of were mentioned above (i.e., techniques for specific applications [8,10,15] and techniques for GCs [2,24,33]). There is also work on using game theory to incentivize rational players to enter their inputs truthfully (see, e.g., [22,31] among others), but such techniques are complementary to this work and can be used for inputs which cannot be feasibly certified.

The first systematic treatment of batch signature verification appeared in [1], although interest in batch verification of signatures and other cryptographic operations in general goes further back. More recent techniques for batch verification include [5,18] among others, although none of them target private verification (defined in Sect. 3.1) which is central to this work.

A related concept is that of aggregate signatures. It allows a number of different signatures to be aggregated into a single short signature to save bandwidth in resource-constrained environments. Aggregate signature schemes were developed for CL signatures on which we build in this work [26]. There are, however, two central differences from our work: (i) aggregate signatures have strictly weaker security guarantees than batch verification [5] because verification of an aggregate signature can succeed even if the individual signatures included in it do not verify, and (ii) message privacy was not considered. Guo et al. [21] use privacy features of CL signatures and construct an aggregate CL signature, but the difference in the security guarantees still stands.

Privacy-preserving signature schemes have been studied in other contexts. Examples include anonymous signatures [32], confidential signatures [16], and pseudorandom signatures [19]. There is a connection between these concepts (especially, confidential signatures) and our notion of signatures with privacy, but these prior concepts provide message confidentiality guarantees only for high-entropy message spaces.

3 Preliminaries

3.1 Definitions

We next describe notation and definitions used in the rest of the paper. A function $\epsilon : \mathbb{N} \to \mathbb{R}_{\geq 0}$ is *negligible* (denoted, negl) if for every positive polynomial $p(\cdot)$ there exists an integer N such that for all $\kappa > N$ $\epsilon(\kappa) < \frac{1}{p(\kappa)}$. The notation $G = \langle g \rangle$ means that g generates group G. We rely on groups with pairings, which we review next.

Definition 1 (Bilinear map). *A one-way function $e : G \times G \to \mathbf{G}$ is a bilinear map if it is:*

- *(Efficient) G and $\mathbf{G}$ are groups of the same prime order q and there exists an efficient algorithm for computing e.*
- *(Bilinear) For all $g, h \in G$ and $a, b \in \mathbb{Z}_q$, $e(g^a, h^b) = e(g, h)^{ab}$.*
- *(Non-degenerate) If g generates G, then $e(g, g)$ generates $\mathbf{G}$.*

We assume that there is a trusted setup algorithm Setup that, on input a security parameter 1^κ, outputs the setup for group $G = \langle g \rangle$ of prime order $q \in \Theta(2^\kappa)$ that has a bilinear map e, and $e(g, g)$ generates $\mathbf{G}$ of order q. That is, $(q, G, \mathbf{G}, g, e) \leftarrow$ Setup(1^κ).

Definition 2 (Signature scheme). *A signature scheme consists of three algorithms:*

- KeyGen *is a probabilistic polynomial-time (PPT) algorithm that, on input a security parameter 1^κ, generates a public-private key pair (pk, sk).*
- Sign *is a PPT algorithm that, on input a secret key sk and message m from the message space, outputs signature σ.*
- Verify *is a deterministic polynomial-time algorithm that, on input a public key pk, a message m, and a signature σ, outputs a bit.*

Security of a signature scheme is defined as difficulty of existential forgery under a chosen-message attack by any PPT adversary, which we provide in Appendix A.

Batch verification [1] is a method for verifying a set of signatures on different messages signed by the same or different signers, which is intended to be more efficient than verifying them independently. In this work, we are primarily interested in batch verification of signatures produced by the same signer. Batch verification is defined as:

Definition 3 (Batch verification of signatures [5]). *Let $\Pi = ($ KeyGen, Sign, Verify$)$ be a signature scheme and κ be a security parameter. Let (pk_1, sk_1), $\ldots$, (pk_n, sk_n) be key pairs of n signers $P_1, \ldots, P_n$ produced by* KeyGen(1^κ) *and $PK = \{pk_1, \ldots, pk_n\}$. Let* Batch *be a PPT algorithm that takes a set of tuples (pk_i, m_i, σ_i) and outputs a bit. Then* Batch *is a batch verification algorithm if the following holds:*

- *If $pk_i \in PK$ and* Verify$(pk_i, m_i, \sigma_i) = 1$ *for all $i \in [1, n]$, then* Batch$((pk_1, m_1, \sigma_1), \ldots, (pk_n, m_n, \sigma_n)) = 1$.
- *If $pk_i \in PK$ for all $i \in [1, n]$ and* Verify$(pk_i, m_i, \sigma_i) = 0$ *for at least one $i \in [1, n]$, then* Batch$((pk_1, m_1, \sigma_1), \ldots, (pk_n, m_n, \sigma_n)) = 1$ *with probability at most $2^{-\kappa}$.*

In our constructions, we rely on *zero-knowledge proofs of knowledge* (ZKPKs) and *commitments*. A ZKPK is a two-party protocol between a prover and a verifier, during which the prover convinces the verifier that a certain statement is true without revealing anything else about the values used in the statement. Informally, a ZKPK should satisfy the following properties: (i) *completeness*: if the statement is true, then an honest verifier will be convinced of the statement's validity after interacting with an honest prover; (ii) *soundness*: if the statement is false, then no cheating prover can convince an honest verifier that the statement is true, except with a negligible probability (in the security parameter); and (iii) *zero-knowledge*: if the statement is true, then no cheating verifier can learn anything other than the fact that the statement is true. We are interested in simple statements over discrete logarithms such as those described, e.g., in [9,11].

A *commitment scheme* allows one to commit to message m in such a way that the commitment reveals no information about m and, given a commitment on m, it is not feasible to open it to a value other than m. In other words, once the value m has been committed to, it cannot be changed and kept private until the user reveals it. These properties are known as hiding and binding. A commitment scheme is defined by Commit and Open algorithms, and we omit their formal specification here. We only note that Commit is a randomized algorithm and for that reason we use notation $com(m, r)$ to denote a commitment to m using randomness r.

As mentioned before, in this work we are interested in signature schemes which allow for private verification of signature validity without revealing any information about the signed message. We refer to such schemes as *signature schemes with privacy* and refer to the corresponding verification process as *private verification* to distinguish it from the conventional signature verification process. This property implies that the signature itself reveals no information about the signed message. In the rest of this subsection, we provide the necessary definitions for signature schemes with privacy. We start by re-defining the traditional formulation of a signature scheme as follows:

Definition 4 (Signature scheme with privacy). *A* signature scheme with privacy *consists of the following polynomial-time algorithms:*

- KeyGen *is a PPT algorithm that, on input a security parameter 1^κ, generates a public-private key pair (pk, sk).*
- Sign *is a PPT algorithm that, on input a secret key sk and message m from the message space, outputs signature σ and optional auxiliary data x_σ.*
- PrivVerify *is a possibly interactive algorithm, in which the prover and the verifier hold a public key pk, the prover has access to m and (σ, x_σ) output by* Sign, *supplies a message encoding x_m and a (possibly modified) signature $\tilde\sigma$ to the verifier, and the verifier outputs a bit.*

With this definition, we allow for two possibilities: either x_σ produced during signing can be used to form x_m used during verification, or x_σ is empty and anyone with access to σ and m can compute a suitable (possibly randomized) x_m for signature verification.

To ensure unforgeability, PrivVerify must verify signature $\tilde\sigma$ similar to the way Verify would and must enforce that the prover knows the message m (encoded in x_m) to which the $\tilde\sigma$ corresponds. Because in this work x_m always takes the form of a commitment to m, $com(m, r)$, we explicitly incorporate this in our security definition.

The security (unforgeability) experiment of a signature with privacy is similar to the conventional definition (see ForgeSig in Appendix A) with two conceptual differences: (i) After producing the challenge pair $(\tilde\sigma^*, x_{m^*})$, the adversary $\mathcal{A}$ is required to prove in zero-knowledge that x_{m^*} corresponds to a message, a signature on which has not been queried before. (ii) The signature forging experiment now invokes modified verification algorithm PrivVerify instead of Verify. The signature is verified against a committed value $x_{m^*} = com(m^*, r)$, but the prover is also required to prove the knowledge of message m^* itself encoded in the commitment. Thus, we obtain the following:

Experiment ForgePrivSig$_{\mathcal{A}, \Pi}(\kappa)$:

1. The challenger creates a key pair $(pk, sk) \leftarrow$ Gen(1^κ) and gives pk to $\mathcal{A}$.
2. $\mathcal{A}$ has oracle access to Sign$_{sk}(\cdot)$. For each message m that $\mathcal{A}$ queries the oracle, m is stored in list $\mathcal{Q}$ and $\mathcal{A}$ learns $(\sigma, x_\sigma) =$ Sign$_{sk}(m)$.
3. The challenger and $\mathcal{A}$ engage in PrivVerify, as part of which $\mathcal{A}$ reveals the challenge pair $(x_{m^*}, \tilde\sigma^*)$. $\mathcal{A}$ proves in ZK that it knows the opening of the commitment $x_{m^*} = com(m^*, r)$ and that $m^* \notin \mathcal{Q}$.
4. Output 1 if PrivVerify returns 1 and all other checks succeed; otherwise, output 0.

To model private verification, we define the following message indistinguishability experiment for a signature scheme with privacy $\Pi =$ (KeyGen, Sign, PrivVerify):

Experiment MesInd$_{\mathcal{A}, \Pi}(\kappa)$:

1. The challenger creates a key pair $(pk, sk) \leftarrow$ KeyGen(1^κ) and gives pk to $\mathcal{A}$.
2. $\mathcal{A}$ has oracle access to Sign$_{sk}(\cdot)$ and learns the algorithm's output for messages of its choice. $\mathcal{A}$ eventually outputs a pair (m_0, m_1).

3. The challenger draws a random bit $b \in \{0, 1\}$. Upon $\mathcal{A}$'s request, it executes $(\sigma_b, x_{\sigma_b}) \leftarrow \mathsf{Sign}_{sk}(m_b)$. It computes x_{m_b} and returns $(\tilde{\sigma}_b, x_{m_b})$ where $\tilde{\sigma}_b$ is derived from σ_b. If x_{m_b} and/or $\tilde{\sigma}_b$ are probabilistic, $\mathcal{A}$ can request multiple encodings $(\tilde{\sigma}_b^{(i)}, x_{m_b}^{(j)})$ for the same signature and $i, j \in \mathbb{N}$. These signature verification queries are repeated the desired number of times.
4. $\mathcal{A}$ eventually outputs a bit b'. The experiment outputs 1 if $b = b'$, and 0 otherwise.

Definition 5 (Private verification). *A signature scheme $\Pi = (\mathsf{KeyGen}, \mathsf{Sign}, \mathsf{PrivVerify})$ is said to achieve* private verification *if for all PPT adversaries $\mathcal{A}$ there is a negligible function* negl *such that* $\Pr[\mathsf{MesInd}_{\mathcal{A},\Pi}(\kappa) = 1] \leq \frac{1}{2} + \mathsf{negl}(\kappa)$.

On the relationship of private verification and proving possession of a signature in zero-knowledge. Prior work on using signatures in privacy-preserving contexts [6,7] allows for proving possession of a signature in ZK. Their definition implies that no information about the signed message is revealed and two instances of proving knowledge of a signature cannot be linked to each other. Our definition of private verification is weaker in the sense that we do not attempt to hide whether the same or different signature is verified at two different times, but fully protect the signed data itself. Unlinkability of signature showings is generally not needed in our application, where a user can use its data (e.g., DNA data) in multiple computations and does not need to hide the fact that the same data was used (which can be determined from the computation itself). Thus, we only protect information about the signed values and this difference allows for faster signature verification while still maintaining the necessary level of security.

When we consequently discuss batch verification of signatures with privacy, we modify the interface of Batch to match that of PrivVerify.

3.2   Signature and Commitment Schemes

In this work, we build on Camenisch-Lysyanskaya signature Scheme A from [7] (CL Scheme A for short), defined as follows:

Key generation: On input 1^κ, execute $(q, G, \mathbf{G}, g, e) \leftarrow \mathsf{Setup}(1^\kappa)$, choose random $x, y \in \mathbb{Z}_q$ and compute $X = g^x, Y = g^y$. Set $sk = (x, y)$ and $pk = (q, G, \mathbf{G}, g, e, X, Y)$.

Signing: On input message $m \in \mathbb{Z}_q$, secret key $sk = (x, y)$ and public key $pk = (q, G, \mathbf{G}, g, e, X, Y)$, choose random $a \in G$ and output $\sigma = (a, b, c) = (a, a^y, a^{x+mxy})$.

Verification: On input message m, $pk = (q, G, \mathbf{G}, g, e, X, Y)$, and signature $\sigma = (a, b, c)$, check whether $e(a, Y) = e(g, b)$ and $e(X, a) \cdot e(X, b)^m = e(g, c)$. If both equalities hold, output 1; otherwise, output 0.

Proof of signature: The prover and verifier have $pk = (q, G, \mathbf{G}, g, e, X, Y)$. The prover also has $m \in \mathbb{Z}_q$ and the corresponding signature $\sigma = (a, b, c) = (a, a^y, a^{x+mxy})$.

1. The prover chooses random $r', r'' \in \mathbb{Z}_q$, computes blinded signature $\tilde{\sigma} = (a^{r''}, b^{r''}, c^{r''r'}) = (\tilde{a}, \tilde{a}^y, (\tilde{a}^{x+mxy})^{r'}) = (\tilde{a}, \tilde{b}, \hat{c})$, and sends it to the verifier.
2. Let $\mathbf{v}_x = e(X, \tilde{a})$, $\mathbf{v}_{xy} = e(X, \tilde{b})$, and $\mathbf{v}_s = e(g, \hat{c})$. The prover and verifier engage in the following ZKPK: $PK\{(\mu, \rho) : \mathbf{v}_x^{-1} = \mathbf{v}_{xy}^\mu \mathbf{v}_s^\rho\}$.
3. The verifier accepts if it accepts the proof above and $e(\tilde{a}, Y) = e(g, \tilde{b})$.

Unforgeability of CL Scheme A is shown under the LRSW assumption [27], while demonstrating the zero-knowledge property of proving possession of a signature uses no additional assumptions other than hardness of discrete logarithm.

We also build on ElGamal signature scheme [17]. Because the original construction allows for existential forgeries, we use its provably secure variant by Pointcheval and Stern [29,30]. The setup assumes an α-hard prime number p for some fixed α, defined as having $p - 1 = qR$ where q is prime and $R \leq |p|^\alpha$. This is necessary for the difficulty of discrete logarithm and is more general than requiring the use of prime order q. This signature scheme uses a hash function H and is shown to be unforgeable in the random oracle model (i.e., H is modeled as a random oracle).

Key generation: On input a security parameter 1^κ, choose a large α-hard prime p and a generator g of $\mathbb{Z}_p^*$. Then choose random $x \in \mathbb{Z}_{p-1}$ and compute $y = g^x \bmod p$. Set $sk = x$ and $pk = (p, g, y)$.

Signing: On input message m, secret key $sk = x$ and public key $pk = (p, g, y)$, choose random $k \in \mathbb{Z}_{p-1}^*$, compute $t = g^k \bmod p$ and $s \equiv (H(m||t) - xt)k^{-1}$ (mod $p - 1$), where $||$ denotes concatenation, then output $\sigma = (t, s)$.

Verification: On input message m, public key $pk = (p, g, y)$, and signature $\sigma = (t, s)$, check whether $1 < t < p$ and $g^{H(m,t)} \equiv y^t t^s$ (mod p). If both conditions hold, output 1; otherwise, output 0.

Lastly, we also utilize well-known Pedersen commitment scheme [28] based on discrete logarithm. The setup consists of a group G of prime order q and two generators g and h. To commit to message $m \in \mathbb{Z}_q$, we choose random $r \in \mathbb{Z}_q$ and set $com(m, r) = g^m h^r$. To open the commitment, the user reveals r. This commitment scheme is information-theoretically hiding and computationally binding (when the discrete logarithm of h to the base g is not known to the user) under the discrete logarithm assumption.

4 Constructions Based on CL Signatures

In this section, we discuss constructions based on CL signatures. We start by demonstrating that CL signatures with protocols satisfy our notion of signatures with privacy and discuss the cost of verifying multiple signatures using that construction. We consequently proceed with simplifying CL Scheme A's verification and construct the corresponding batch verifier. The next section treats ElGamal signatures.

4.1   CL Scheme A

Recall that a signature scheme with privacy is defined as $\Pi = (\mathsf{KeyGen}, \mathsf{Sign},$ $\mathsf{PrivVerify})$. To use CL Scheme A in our context, we leave KeyGen and Sign unmodified, except that KeyGen additionally computes $h = g^u$ for a random $u \in \mathbb{Z}_q$ and stores it in the public key, i.e., $pk = (q, G, \mathbf{G}, g, h, e, X, Y)$. $\mathsf{PrivVerify}$ is realized as follows:

$\mathsf{PrivVerify}$: The prover holds signature $\sigma = (a, b, c)$ on private message $m \in \mathbb{Z}_q$ and both parties hold pk. The prover computes $x_m = com(m, r) = g^m h^r$ using random $r \in \mathbb{Z}_q$ and sends x_m to the verifier. The remaining steps are the same as in the proof of signature in Scheme A above, except that the ZKPK in step 2 is modified to: $PK\{(\mu, \rho, \gamma) : x_m = g^\mu h^\gamma \wedge \mathbf{v}_x^{-1} = \mathbf{v}_{xy}^\mu \mathbf{v}_s^\rho\}$.

Note that the signing algorithm is not modified and in the verification protocol we only extend the ZKPK statement. Because the original proof of signature protocol was shown to be proof of knowledge and the signature was shown to be unforgeable, this scheme satisfied signature unforgeability. We also achieve the private verification property:

Theorem 1. *CL Scheme A above is a signature scheme with privacy.*

Because of space constraints, the proofs of this and most other theorems are provided in the full version.

    To facilitate close comparison of different algorithms, we spell out the computation used in the ZKPK of $\mathsf{PrivVerify}$ above. This will allow us to determine the exact number of operations (such as modulo exponentiations and pairing function evaluations). In this ZKPK, the prover first chooses random $v_1, v_2, v_3 \in \mathbb{Z}_q$, computes $T_1 = g^{v_1} h^{v_3}, T_2 = \mathbf{v}_{xy}^{v_1} \mathbf{v}_s^{v_2}$, and sends T_1, T_2 to the verifier. The verifier chooses a challenge $e \in \mathbb{Z}_q$ at random and sends it to the prover. The prover responds by sending $r_1 = v_1 + em \bmod q$, $r_2 = v_2 + er' \bmod q$, and $r_3 = v_3 + er \bmod q$. Finally, the verifier accepts if $g^{r_1} h^{r_3} = T_1 x_m^e$ and $\mathbf{v}_{xy}^{r_1} \mathbf{v}_s^{r_2} = T_2 \mathbf{v}_x^{-e}$.

    When certified inputs are used in SMC, we need to evaluate the time of signature verification and integration into an SMC protocol. Thus, we consider signature issuance as a one-time cost and concentrate on verification. Then to use this scheme with secure computation, the cost of (independent) private verification of n signatures is $3n$ modulo exponentiations (mod exp) for signature randomization, $2n$ mod exp for creating commitments (n of which are for messages and are thus short), and $10n$ mod exp and $5n$ pairings for proving the knowledge of signatures. This gives us $15n$ mod exp (n of which are short) and $5n$ pairings and serves as the baseline for our comparisons.

4.2   Modified CL Scheme A

We next introduce a simplification to CL Scheme A of the previous subsection to allow for more efficient private verification in the context of SMC. To construct a signature scheme with privacy $\Pi = (\mathsf{KeyGen}, \mathsf{Sign}, \mathsf{PrivVerify})$, we retain KeyGen and Sign algorithms of the previous subsection (i.e., the public key is augmented with h), but modify the verification algorithm $\mathsf{PrivVerify}$ as follows:

$\mathsf{PrivVerify}$: The prover has private message $m \in \mathbb{Z}_q$ and the corresponding signature $\sigma = (a, b, c) = (a, a^y, a^{x+mxy})$; both parties hold $pk = (q, G, \mathbf{G}, g, h, e, X, Y)$.

1. The prover forms a commitment to m as $x_m = com(m, r) = g^m h^r$ using randomly chosen $r \in \mathbb{Z}_q$ and sends x_m to the verifier.
2. The prover chooses random $r' \in \mathbb{Z}_q$, computes randomized signature $\tilde{\sigma} := (a, b, c^{r'}) = (a, b, \tilde{c})$, and communicates it to the verifier.
3. Let $\mathbf{v}_x = e(X, a)$, $\mathbf{v}_{xy} = e(X, b)$, and $\mathbf{v}_s = e(g, \tilde{c})$. The prover and verifier execute ZKPK: $PK\{(\mu, \rho, \gamma) : x_m = g^\mu h^\gamma \wedge \mathbf{v}_x^{-1} = \mathbf{v}_{xy}^\mu \mathbf{v}_s^\rho\}$.
4. If the verifier accepts the proof in step 2 and $e(a, Y) = e(g, b)$, output 1; otherwise, output 0.

In this verification, part of signature randomization is removed, which means that the verifier will be able to link two showings of the same signature together. This change, however, does not affect the unforgeability property of the scheme. The privacy property can be stated as follows:

Theorem 2. *Modified CL Scheme A above is a signature scheme with privacy.*

Proof. Let $\mathcal{A}$ be a PPT adversary attacking our modified CL Scheme A. Recall that $\mathcal{A}$ has the ability to query the signing oracle and obtain signature on messages of its choice. Once $\mathcal{A}$ submits the challenge (m_0, m_1), it will be given pairs $(\tilde{\sigma}_b^{(i)}, x_{m_b}^{(j)})$, where b is a random bit, $\tilde{\sigma}_b^{(i)} = (a, a^y, a^{r_i'(x+m_b xy)}) = (a, b, \tilde{c}^{(i)})$ for random $r_i' \in \mathbb{Z}_q$, and $x_{m_b}^{(j)} = g^{m_b} h^{r_j}$ for random $r_j \in \mathbb{Z}_q$, for any combination of i and j and the number of queries polynomial in κ. In other words, $\mathcal{A}$ has access to a signature with different randomizations (using r_i's) and different commitments to m_b (using r_js for randomness).

Before we proceed with further analysis, note that the ZKPK in $\mathsf{PrivVerify}$ is zero-knowledge and thus does not reveal information about m_b to $\mathcal{A}$. Furthermore, other signatures on m_0 and m_1 that $\mathcal{A}$ can obtain using its access to the signing oracle do not contribute additional information (and use unrelated randomness) and thus do not help in answering the challenge. It thus remains to analyze $\tilde{c}^{(i)}$ and $x_{m_b}^{(j)}$ values. Now note that each $\tilde{c}^{(i)}$ and $x_{m_b}^{(j)}$ are random elements in G because r_i', r_j are chosen uniformly and independently at random. This means that if we modify $\mathcal{A}$'s view to replace m_b in $\tilde{c}^{(i)}$s and $x_{m_b}^{(j)}$s with a random value, this modified view will be identically distributed to that of the original $\mathcal{A}$'s view. In more detail, suppose that we modify the signature scheme to use a random value z instead of the actual message and the commitment is formed consistently to use the same z as well. Let call the resulting scheme Π'. Clearly, we have that $\mathbf{Pr}[\mathsf{MesInd}_{\mathcal{A},\Pi'}(\kappa) = 1] = \frac{1}{2}$. Also, because the views of $\mathcal{A}$ are identical in the security experiments for Π and Π', we obtain that

$|\mathbf{Pr}[\mathsf{MesInd}_{\mathcal{A},\Pi'}(\kappa) = 1] - \mathbf{Pr}[\mathsf{MesInd}_{\mathcal{A},\Pi}(\kappa) = 1]| = 0$. This means that $\mathcal{A}$ cannot learn any information about m_b during verification in Π and the security property follows. $\qquad\square$

When we use this scheme for secure computation, we reduce the randomization cost by $2n$ mod exp. Thus the cost of private verification of n signatures is $13n$ mod exp (n of which are short) and $5n$ pairings.

4.3   Batch Verification of Modified CL Scheme A

The next step is to design batch verification for verifying n signatures. Because for our application we are primarily interested in verifying multiple signatures issued by the same signer (e.g., information about one's genome represented as a large number of individual values), we present batch verification of signatures issued using the same key. We use a version of the small exponent test [1] that instructs the verifier to choose security parameter l_b such that the probability of accepting a batch that contains an invalid signature is at most 2^{-l_b} (e.g., l_b is set to 60 or 80 in prior work).

Batch: The prover holds signatures $\sigma_i = (a_i, b_i, c_i)$ on messages $m_i \in \mathbb{Z}_q$ for $i = 1, \ldots, n$, and both parties hold $pk = (q, G, \mathbf{G}, g, h, e, X, Y)$.

1. The prover forms commitments $x_{m_i} = com(m_i, r_i) = g^{m_i} h^{r_i}$ using randomly chosen $r_i \in \mathbb{Z}_q$ for $i = 1, \ldots, n$ and sends them to the verifier.
2. The prover chooses random $r'_i \in \mathbb{Z}_q$, computes blinded signatures $\tilde{\sigma}_i = (a_i, b_i, c_i^{r'_i}) = (a_i, b_i, \tilde{c}_i)$ for $i = 1, \ldots, n$, and sends them to the verifier.
3. The verifier chooses and sends random $\delta_1, \ldots, \delta_n \in \{0, 1\}^{l_b}$ to the prover.
4. The parties compute $\hat{\mathbf{v}}_x = e(X, \prod_{i=1}^{n} a_i^{\delta_i})$, $\hat{\mathbf{v}}_{xy_i} = e(X, b_i^{\delta_i})$ and $\hat{\mathbf{v}}_{s_i} = e(g, \tilde{c}_i^{\delta_i})$ for $i = 1, \ldots, n$, and engage in the ZKPK: $PK\{(\mu_1, \ldots, \mu_n, \rho_1, \ldots, \rho_n, \gamma_1, \ldots, \gamma_n) : \hat{\mathbf{v}}_x^{-1} = \prod_{i=1}^{n} \hat{\mathbf{v}}_{xy_i}^{\mu_i} \hat{\mathbf{v}}_{s_i}^{\rho_i} \wedge x_{m_1} = g^{\mu_1} h^{\gamma_1} \wedge \cdots \wedge x_{m_n} = g^{\mu_n} h^{\gamma_n}\}$.
5. If this proof passes and $e(\prod_{i=1}^{n} a_i^{\delta_i}, Y) = e(g, \prod_{i=1}^{n} b_i^{\delta_i})$, the verifier outputs 1; otherwise, the verifier outputs 0.

Theorem 3. Batch *above is a batch verifier for Modified CL Scheme A.*

Proof. First, we show that success of PrivVerify on (pk, m_i, σ_i) for all $i \in [1, n]$ implies that Batch also outputs 1 on $pk, (m_1, \sigma_1), \ldots, (m_n, \sigma_n)$. When all PrivVerify output 1, for each $i = 1, \ldots, n$ $\mathbf{v}_x^{-1} = \mathbf{v}_{xy}^{m_i} \mathbf{v}_s^{r_i}$, which is expanded as $e(X, a_i)^{-1} = e(X, b_i)^{m_i} \cdot e(g, \tilde{c}_i)^{r_i}$. Then $e(X, a_i^{\delta_i})^{-1} = e(X, b_i^{\delta_i})^{m_i} \cdot e(g, \tilde{c}_i^{\delta_i})^{r_i}$ for all i and consequently $\prod_{i=1}^{n} e(X, a_i^{\delta_i})^{-1} = \prod_{i=1}^{n} e(X, b_i^{\delta_i})^{m_i} e(g, \tilde{c}_i^{\delta_i})^{r_i}$. Because $\prod_{i=1}^{n} e(X, a_i^{\delta_i}) = e(X, \prod_{i=1}^{n} a_i^{\delta_i})$, we obtain equivalence with $\hat{\mathbf{v}}_x^{-1} = \prod_{i=1}^{n} \hat{\mathbf{v}}_{xy_i}^{m_i} \hat{\mathbf{v}}_{s_i}^{r_i}$.

To show the other direction, assume that Batch accepts. We know that $\tilde{c}_i, a_i, b_i \in G$, thus $\tilde{c}_i = g^{\gamma_i}, a_i = g^{s_i}, b_i = g^{t_i}$ for some $\gamma_i, a_i, b_i \in \mathbb{Z}_q$. Then

$$\hat{\mathbf{v}}_x^{-1} = \prod_{i=1}^{n} \hat{\mathbf{v}}_{xy_i}^{m_i} \hat{\mathbf{v}}_{s_i}^{r_i} = \prod_{i=1}^{n} e(X, b_i^{\delta_i})^{m_i} \cdot e(g, \tilde{c}_i^{\delta_i})^{r_i} = \prod_{i=1}^{n} e(X, g^{t_i \delta_i})^{m_i} \cdot e(g, g^{\gamma_i \delta_i})^{r_i}$$

$$= \prod_{i=1}^{n} e(g, g)^{x t_i \delta_i m_i} \cdot e(g, g)^{\gamma_i \delta_i r_i} = \prod_{i=1}^{n} e(g, g)^{\delta_i (x t_i m_i + \gamma_i r_i)}$$

Because $\hat{\mathbf{v}}_x^{-1} = e(X, \prod_{i=1}^{n} a_i^{\delta_i})^{-1} = e(g^x, \prod_{i=1}^{n} g^{s_i \delta_i})^{-1} = \prod_{i=1}^{n} e(g, g)^{-x s_i \delta_i}$, $e(g, g)^{-x \sum_i s_i \delta_i} = e(g, g)^{\sum_i \delta_i (x t_i m_i + \gamma_i r_i)}$ and consequently $\sum_i x s_i \delta_i + \sum_i \delta_i (x t_i m_i + \gamma_i r_i) \equiv 0 \pmod{q}$. Let us set $\beta_i = x(s_i + t_i m_i) + \gamma_i r_i$, then

$$\sum_{i=1}^{n} \delta_i \beta_i \equiv 0 \pmod{q} \tag{1}$$

Now suppose that Batch returned 1, while for at least one i PrivVerify returns 0 on the corresponding input (pk, m_i, σ_i). Without loss of generality, let $i = 1$. This means that $e(X, a_1)^{-1} \neq e(X, b_1)^{m_1} \cdot e(g, \tilde{c}_1)^{r_1}$ and consequently $\beta_1 = x(s_1 + t_1 m_1) + \gamma_1 r_1 \neq 0$. Because G and $\mathbf{G}$ are cyclic groups of prime order q, β_1 has an inverse α_1 such that $\beta_1 \alpha_1 \equiv 1 \pmod{q}$.

We re-write Eq. (1) as $\delta_1 \beta_1 + \sum_{i=2}^{n} \delta_i \beta_i \equiv 0 \pmod{q}$, and substitute β_1 with α_1^{-1} to obtain $\delta_1 \alpha_1^{-1} + \sum_{i=2}^{n} \delta_i \beta_i \equiv 0 \pmod{q}$. This gives us

$$\delta_1 \equiv -\alpha_1 \sum_{i=2}^{n} \delta_i \beta_i \pmod{q} \tag{2}$$

Let E be an event such that PrivVerify$(pk, m_1, \sigma_1) = 0$, but Batch$(pk, (m_1, \sigma_1), \ldots, (m_n, \sigma_n)) = 1$. Also, let vector $\triangle = (\delta_2, \ldots, \delta_n)$ and $|\triangle|$ denote the number of possible values of $\triangle$. By Eq. (2), when $\triangle$ is fixed, there exists only one value of δ_1 that results in event E happening. In other words, for a fixed $\triangle$ the probability of E given a randomly chosen δ_1 is $\Pr[E \,|\, \triangle'] = 2^{-l_b}$. Thus, we can bound the probability of E for randomly chosen δ_1 by summing over all possible choices of $\triangle$, i.e., $\Pr[E] \leq \sum_{i=1}^{|\triangle|} (\Pr[E \,|\, \triangle] \cdot \Pr[\triangle])$. We obtain $\Pr[E] \leq \sum_{i=1}^{2^{l_b(n-1)}} (2^{-l_b} \cdot 2^{-l_b(n-1)}) = \sum_{i=1}^{2^{l_b(n-1)}} (2^{-l_b n}) = 2^{-l_b}$. $\qquad\square$

As before, we spell out the ZKPK computation in the Batch protocol: The prover chooses random $v_i, v_i', v_i'' \in \mathbb{Z}_q$ and computes $T_i = g^{v_i} h^{v_i''}$ for $i = [1, n]$ as well as $T = \prod_{i=1}^{n} (\mathbf{v}_{xy_i}^{v_i} \mathbf{v}_{s_i}^{v_i'})$, and sends T_is and T to the verifier. After receiving challenge $e \in \mathbb{Z}_q$ from the verifier, the prover responds with $u_i = v_i + e m_i \bmod q$, $u_i' = v_i' + e r_i' \bmod q$, and $u_i'' = v_i'' + e r_i \bmod q$ for all i. The verifier accepts if $g^{u_i} h^{u_i''} = T_i x_{m_i}^e$ for $i = 1, \ldots, n$ and $\prod_{i=1}^{n} (\mathbf{v}_{xy_i}^{u_i} \mathbf{v}_{s_i}^{u_i'}) = T \mathbf{v}_x^{-e}$.

The cost of using this construction for n certified inputs in SMC is n mod exp for signature randomization, $2n$ mod exp for creating commitments (n of which are short), $12n + 1$ mod exp ($3n$ of which are short) and $2n + 3$ pairings for the ZKPK. This gives us $15n + 1$ mod exp ($4n$ of which are short) and

$2n+3$ pairings and significantly reduces the number of pairing operations, which we consider to be the costliest operation, compared to private verification of individual messages.

The way inputs are entered in the SMC constructions considered in Sect. 6, a single commitment to all inputs of a participant is permissible. Thus, instead of using separate commitments for each m_i, we could form a single commitment to n messages $com(m_1, \ldots, m_n, r) = g_1^{m_1} \cdots g_n^{m_n} h^r$ and modify the ZKPK to use it instead of the individual commitments. This reduces the cost of forming commitments to n short and one regular mod exp, and the cost of ZKPK is reduced by $3n - 3$ mod exp (i.e., only one v'' needs to be formed and we compute only one T_i instead of n of them). This gives us the total of $11n + 5$ mod exp ($4n$ of which are short) and $2n + 3$ pairings.

5   Construction Based on ElGamal Signature

In this section, we show how to modify (provably secure) ElGamal signature scheme to achieve private verification and consequently provide a batch verifier for the resulting construction.

5.1   Modified ElGamal Scheme

Our starting point was provably secure ElGamal [29] described in Sect. 3.2. To enable private verification, the idea is to use signatures on commitments to messages instead of on messages themselves. We also modify the setup to work in a group of prime order q, i.e., a subgroup of $\mathbb{Z}_p^*$, instead of entire $\mathbb{Z}_p^*$. This simplifies the design and opens up additional possibilities, without compromising security guarantees. In particular, the small exponent test used for batch verification is not applicable to groups of non-prime order [1]. Our signature scheme $\Pi = (\mathsf{KeyGen}, \mathsf{Sign}, \mathsf{PrivVerify})$ is given as:

KeyGen: On input a security parameter 1^κ, choose a
   group G of large prime order q and its generator g. Then choose random
   $x, u \in \mathbb{Z}_q$ and compute $y = g^x$ and $h = g^u$. Set $sk = x$, $pk = (q, G, g, y, h)$.
Sign: On input message m, secret key $sk = x$ and public key $pk = (q, G, g, y, h)$,
   choose random $k, r \in \mathbb{Z}_q$ and compute $t = g^k$, $x_m = com(m, r) = g^m h^r$,
   and $s \equiv (H(x_m \| t) - xt)k^{-1} \pmod{q}$. The algorithm outputs $\sigma = (t, s)$ and
   $x_\sigma = r$. The recipient computes $com(m, x_\sigma)$ and verifies the signature on
   $com(m, x_\sigma)$.
PrivVerify: The prover has private m and x_σ, the corresponding signature $\sigma = (t, s)$ on x_m, where $x_m = g^m h^{x_\sigma}$, and both parties hold pk. The prover gives
   the verifier σ and x_m and they engage in the following ZKPK: $PK\{(\mu, \gamma) : x_m = g^\mu h^\gamma\}$. If this proof passes and the equality $g^{H(x_m \| t)} = y^t t^s$ holds, the
   verifier outputs 1; otherwise, the verifier outputs 0.

Note that in this scheme the signer chooses g, h and thus will be able to open a commitment $com(m, r)$ to a message different from m (but the users will not be able to do so). If this poses a security risk, h will need to be produced by an independent party or parties so that the signer does not know the discrete logarithm of h to the base g.

This signature scheme remains unforgeable, and we prove it using the standard definition (Definition 6) with ForgePrivSig experiment that accommodates privacy as described in Sect. 3.1. The intuition is that the prover now has a signature on a commitment, but has to demonstrate the knowledge of the commitment opening, i.e., the message itself, and the use of groups of prime order only simplifies the analysis in [29]. We state unforgeability and privacy properties next, with their proofs available in the full version.

Theorem 4. *Modified ElGamal signature scheme is existentially unforgeable against an adaptive chosen-message attack in a random oracle model.*

Theorem 5. *Modified ElGamal scheme is a signature scheme with privacy.*

The ZKPK in this PrivVerify proceeds similar to prior ZK proofs, where the prover chooses $v_1, v_2 \in \mathbb{Z}_q$, computes $T = g^{v_1} h^{v_2}$, and sends T to the verifier. After receiving the challenge e from the verifier, the prover responds by sending $r_1 = v_1 + em \bmod q$, $r_2 = v_2 + er \bmod q$, and the verifier accepts if $g^{r_1} h^{r_2} = x_m^e T$. The cost of using this construction in SMC is 5 mod exp for the ZKPK and 3 for signature verification, giving us 8 mod exp. (If the user does not store commitment x_m, its re-computation is another 1 regular and 1 short mod exp.)

Table 1. Performance of private verification for a single signature and a batch of size n. It is assumed that commitments are stored pre-computed.

Scheme	Single message	Batch with n commitments	Batch with 1 commitment
Modified CL Scheme A	11 mod exp and 5 pairings	$10n + 1$ regular and $3n$ short mod exp and $2n + 3$ pairings	$6n + 5$ regular and $3n$ short mod exp $2n + 3$ pairings
Modified ElGamal	8 mod exp	$6n + 2$ mod exp	$2n + 6$ mod exp

5.2   Batch Verification of Modified ElGamal Signatures

Our batch verifier for the modified ElGamal signature is given next. It uses the same security parameter l_b as before.

Batch: The prover holds commitments $x_{m_i} = com(m_i, x_{\sigma i}) = g^{m_i} h^{x_{\sigma i}}$ on messages $m_i \in \mathbb{Z}_q$ using randomness $x_{\sigma i} \in \mathbb{Z}_q$ and signatures $\sigma_i = (t_i, s_i)$ on x_{m_i} for $i = 1, \ldots, n$. Both parties hold $pk = (q, G, g, y, h)$.
  1. The prover sends signatures σ_i and commitments x_{m_i} to the verifier for $i = 1, \ldots, n$.

2. The prover and verifier engage in the following ZKPK: $PK\{(\mu_1, \ldots, \mu_n, \gamma_1, \ldots, \gamma_n) : x_{m_1} = g^{\mu_1} h^{\gamma_1} \wedge \cdots \wedge x_{m_n} = g^{\mu_n} h^{\gamma_n}\}$. If the proof fails, the verifier outputs 0 and aborts.

3. The verifier chooses $\delta_1, \ldots, \delta_n \in \{0, 1\}^{l_b}$ at random, computes $u_1 = \sum_{i=1}^{n} H(x_{m_i} \| t_i)\delta_i$ and $u_2 = \sum_{i=1}^{n} t_i \delta_i$, and checks whether $g^{u_1} = y^{u_2} \prod_{i=1}^{n} t_i^{s_i \delta_i}$. If the check succeeds, the verifier outputs 1, and 0 otherwise.

Theorem 6. Batch *above is a batch verifier for the modified ElGamal scheme.*

The ZKPK in Batch above consists of n invocations of the ZKPK in modified ElGamal's PrivVerify. Thus, the cost of batch verification of n messages is $5n$ mod exp for the ZKPK and $n + 2$ mod exp for signature verification, or $6n + 2$ mod exp total. (If the commitments are to be re-computed, we add n regular and n short mode exp.)

Now recall that the way messages are input into SMC allows us to use a single commitment to all n messages. For our modified ElGamal this optimization results in great savings because this means that we can use only a single signature. Thus, the signer now issues a signature on $x_m = com(m_1, \ldots, m_n, r)$ and x_σ still contains the randomness r. This significantly simplifies the Batch algorithm above because only 1 signature and 1 commitment are communicated in step 1, step 2 only involves the proof of knowledge of the discrete logarithm representation of x_m, and step 3 consists of verifying a single signature without the use of δ_is. This has significant performance improvement implications, with the cost of step 2 reduced to $2n+3$ mod exp and the overall cost of Batch reduced to $2n + 6$ mod exp (if the commitment is to be re-computed, we add 1 regular and n short mod exp).

Table 1 summarizes performance of our constructions.

6   Using Certified Inputs in Secure Computation

Having described our private verification protocols, we now address the question of integrating them with SMC techniques based on secret sharing in the presence of malicious adversaries. For that purpose, we have chosen two prominent constructions of Damgård and Nielsen [13] and SPDZ [14] and discuss them consequently. These were chosen based on their attractive performance and distinct security guarantees that they provide: when the computation is performed by m parties, the former solution tolerates fewer than $m/3$ corruptions, while the latter can handle any number of corrupt parties. Our solution uses signatures with privacy to guarantee that inputs entered into secure computation are identical to those generated or observed by an authority, but in general certification could take different forms.

As far as security properties go, the privacy guarantees of SMC in the presence of malicious adversaries must hold as in the standard formulation of the problem (see, e.g., [20] for a formal definition). We additionally require that it is not feasible for a participant to enter (certified) inputs into the computation without possessing a signature on them. Because of space considerations, we defer formal definitions and analysis of these properties to the full version of the paper.

In what follows, we denote the computational parties as $P_1, \ldots, P_m$ and assume that they are connected by pairwise secure channels. These constructions use (m, t)-threshold linear secret sharing, and we denote a secret shared version of x by $[x]$.

6.1 Damgård-Nielsen Scalable and Unconditionally Secure Multiparty Computation

The construction of Damgård-Nielsen [13] is unconditionally secure (assuming secure channels) in the presence of at most $t < m/3$ malicious participants. It was the first to achieve unconditional security with communication complexity where the part that depends on the circuit size is only linear in m. The computation proceeds in two stages: offline pre-computation that generates random multiplication triples and other random values and the online phase which is executed once the inputs become available.

As far as input into the computation (during the online phase) goes, let x denote party P_ℓ's input into the secure computation for some ℓ (the same will apply to all other parties holding inputs; participants with input who are not computational parties can be accommodated as well). To secret-share x among the parties, P_ℓ computes $\delta = x + r$, where r is a random value chosen during pre-computation in such a way that the parties hold shares of r $[r]$ and the value of r is known in the clear to P_ℓ (i.e., $[r]$ was opened to P_ℓ). Both the shares $[r]$ and the value r that P_ℓ possesses are guaranteed to be correct in the presence of malicious participants. Then once P_ℓ computes δ, P_ℓ broadcasts it to all parties who compute $[x] = \delta - [r]$ and use $[x]$ in consecutive computation.

To enable the use of certified inputs, we need to modify the above input sharing procedure to guarantee that x that P_ℓ uses in computing δ was indeed certified. Then to ensure that correct x is input into the computation, the parties could compute a commitment to r and verify (in zero-knowledge) that δ corresponds to the sum of r and x. This could be implemented by having the parties broadcast commitments to their shares of r and interpolating them to compute a commitment to r. In that case, reconstructing a reliable commitment to r presents the main challenge because any participant can be malicious. If the input owner P_ℓ is honest, it can verify correctness of commitments from other parties and discard incorrect transmissions. Dealing with malicious P_ℓ, however, is more difficult because P_ℓ can influence through its share the value of r in the commitment which the parties reconstruct. Then because validity of P_ℓ's share cannot be verified, P_ℓ can adjust its share to modify the reconstructed r by the amount it wants to change x from its certified version, getting around the certification process.

To solve the issue, we chose to proceed with directly entering input x into the computation as opposed to supplying the delta. To accomplish this, we utilize one of the building blocks from [13] for dealing consistent shares of a value (which is input x in our case). It has a mechanism for resolving conflicts and upon successful termination provides a set of parties holding consistent shares. We use this set to form a commitments to shares of x and interpolate them to reconstruct a commitment to x.

Because each P_ℓ often enters multiple inputs into the computation, we will associate inputs $x_1, \ldots, x_n$ with party P_ℓ. In what follows, we describe the version with a single commitment to all x_is which allows for improved performance. The case of a single certified input x will follow from that construction. Also, when P_ℓ's inputs are certified by multiple authorities, this procedure is performed for each public key separately. Because the solution uses (Pedersen) commitments, we assume that a group setup (G, q) where the discrete logarithm problem is hard with generators $g_1, \ldots, g_n, h$ is available to the parties. All signature schemes that we considered in this work already use commitments, and therefore we will assume that this setup comes from the public key of the corresponding signature scheme.

In what follows, we use notation $[y]_j$ to denote the jth share of y held by party P_j. As in [13], we assume that operations on secret shares take place in a field $\mathbb{F}$ and secret shares correspond to the evaluation of a polynomial of degree t on different points. For concreteness, we set $\mathbb{F} = \mathbb{F}_p$ for a prime p ($q \gg p$). The computation is then as follows:

Input: The parties collectively hold the public key pk of the certification authority. P_ℓ has private input $x_1, \ldots, x_n$, $c_x = com(x_1, \ldots, x_n, \hat{r})$, and signatures with privacy $\sigma_1, \ldots, \sigma_n$ on $x_1, \ldots, x_n$, respectively.[1]

Output: $[x_1], \ldots, [x_n]$ are available to the parties and their certification has been verified.

1. The parties execute the protocol for P_ℓ to deal consistent shares of $x_1, \ldots, x_n$ and another value α that P_ℓ randomly chooses from $\mathbb{F}_p$ (as specified in Fig. 7 from [13]). If P_ℓ is honest, there are at least $2t + 1$ parties who hold consistent shares of each x_i and we denote this set by S. (Otherwise, the protocol fails and the parties restart it as specified in [13].)
2. P_ℓ broadcasts commitments $com([x_1]_j, \ldots, [x_n]_j, [\alpha]_j) = g_1^{[x_1]_j} \cdots g_n^{[x_n]_j} h^{[\alpha]_j}$ and each $P_j \in S$ verifies that the jth commitment is consistent with its shares.
3. The parties compute interpolation coefficients β_j (in $\mathbb{F}_p$) for each $P_j \in S$ and then compute $c'_x = com(x'_1, \ldots, x'_n, \alpha') = \prod_{P_j \in S} com([x_1]_j, \ldots, [x_n]_j, \alpha_j)^{\beta_j}$. Note that $x_i = \sum_{P_j \in S} \beta_j [x_i]_j$ (in $\mathbb{F}_p$) for each i.
4. P_ℓ computes $\alpha' = \sum_{P_j \in S} \beta_j [\alpha]_j$ (in $\mathbb{Z}_q$) and $x'_i = \sum_{P_j \in S} \beta_j [r_i]_j$, $s_i = \lfloor x'_i/p \rfloor$ (over integers) for $i = 1, \ldots, n$. It creates commitment $c_s = com(s_1, \ldots, s_n, \tilde{r}) = g_1^{s_1} \cdots g_n^{s_n} h^{\tilde{r}}$ and broadcasts it to the other parties.
5. P_ℓ broadcasts $c_x, \sigma_1, \ldots, \sigma_n$ and the parties execute $\mathsf{Batch}(pk, x_1, \sigma_1, \ldots, x_n, \sigma_n)$ with P_ℓ playing the role of the prover.

---

[1] Note that in the case of our modified ElGamal signatures, P_ℓ will hold a single signature on $com(x_1, \ldots, x_n, \hat{r})$.

6. The parties additionally execute $\text{PK}\{(x_1, \ldots, x_n, x_1', \ldots, x_n', s_1, \ldots, s_n, \alpha', \hat{r}, \tilde{r}) : c_x = g_1^{x_1} \cdots g_n^{x_n} h^{\hat{r}} \wedge c_x' = g_1^{x_1'} \cdots g_n^{x_n'} h^{\alpha'} \wedge c_s = g_1^{s_1} \cdots g_n^{s_n} h^{\tilde{r}} \wedge \bigwedge_{i=1}^{n} (x_i' = x_i + s_i p)\}$ where P_ℓ plays the role of the prover.

Because different moduli are used for exponents in G and arithmetic in $\mathbb{F}_p$, to guarantee correctness, we need to compensate for reduction modulo p for field operations. To accomplish that, we interpolate each x_i over integers and thus have that $x_i' = x_i + s_i p$ for some unique integer s_i, which is the relationship that P_ℓ proves in step 6. This computation requires that $|q| > 2t|p|$, which is the case in practice for typical values of q, t, and p (i.e., threshold t is usually low and set to 1–2, $|p|$ is set to accommodate integers of 64 or fewer bits, and $|q|$ is at least in hundreds to guarantee security).

Note that step 6 already includes a PK of the discrete logarithm representation of $com(x_1, \ldots, x_n, \hat{r})$ and thus the same ZKPK in Batch is no longer executed in step 6.

6.2 SPDZ

The second solution that we study is built on SPDZ [14]. This is an SMC protocol that achieves security in the presence of any number of malicious parties $t < m$ (and thus offers stronger security guarantees than the previous solution) and has a fast online phase. This construction enters private inputs into the computation similar to the way [13] did. That is, to secret share input x_i, the input owner P_ℓ uses a random value r_i computed during the preprocessing phase known only to P_ℓ and the parties jointly holding $[r_i]$. P_ℓ then computes and broadcasts $\delta_i = x_i - r_i$ (in $\mathbb{F}_p$) and the players compute $[x_i] = [r_i] + \delta_i$. The difference is that now additive secret sharing (i.e., $(m-1)$-out-of-m) is used instead of threshold secret sharing and each secret-shared value y also uses a secret-shared MAC $\gamma(y)$ in the form of $\alpha(y + \tau)$, where α is a global secret key and τ is public, to authenticate its value. In other words, a secret shared value $[y]$ is represented by each party P_i holding $\langle \tau, [y]_i, [\gamma(y)]_i \rangle$, where $[y]_1 + \ldots + [y]_n = y$ and $[\gamma(y)]_1 + \ldots + [\gamma(y)]_m = \alpha(y + \tau)$. The value of α is opened at the end of secure computation and is used to verify consistency of certain values used during computation, before the parties can learn the result (see [14] for detail).

Unlike the solution considered in Sect. 6.1, we could proceed with the approach where the parties compute the input as $x_i = r_i + \delta_i$, reconstruct a commitment to r_i, and use it to verify the relationship between x_i and r_i. Verification of correct r_i used in the commitment is deferred to the end of the computation where the value of α is opened. Then if the parties determine that the commitment to r_i was correctly formed, they proceed with reconstructing the output. The inputs of the procedure remain unchanged and the computation proceeds as follows:

1. Each P_j (including P_ℓ) chooses random $\alpha_j' \in \mathbb{Z}_q$, sends its shares $[r_1]_j, \ldots, [r_n]_j$ and α_j' to P_ℓ, and also broadcasts $com([r_1]_j, \ldots, [r_n]_j, \alpha_j') = g_1^{[r_1]_j} \cdots g_n^{[r_n]_j} h^{\alpha_j'}$.

2. P_ℓ verifies that $\sum_{j=1}^{m}[r_i]_j = r_i$ (in $\mathbb{F}_p$) for each $i = 1, \ldots, n$ and that the received commitments are consistent with $[r_i]_j$s and α'_js.

3. The parties compute $c'_r = com(r'_1, \ldots, r'_n, \alpha') = \prod_{j=1}^{m} com([r_1]_j, \ldots, [r_n]_j, \alpha'_j)$.

4. Each P_j (including P_ℓ) chooses random $\alpha''_j \in \mathbb{Z}_q$ and broadcasts
$com([\gamma(r_1)]_j, \ldots, [\gamma(r_n)]_j, \alpha''_j) = g_1^{[\gamma(r_1)]_j} \cdots g_n^{[\gamma(r_n)]_j} h^{\alpha''_j}$.

5. The parties compute $c'_\gamma = com(\gamma'_1, \ldots, \gamma'_n, \alpha'') = \prod_{j=1}^{m} com([\gamma(r_1)]_j, \ldots, [\gamma(r_n)]_j, \alpha''_j)$.

6. P_ℓ computes $\delta_i = x_i - r_i$ (in $\mathbb{F}_p$) and broadcasts δ_i for $i = 1, \ldots, n$.

7. P_ℓ computes $\alpha' = \sum_{j=1}^{m} \alpha_j$ (in $\mathbb{Z}_q$) and $r'_i = \sum_{j=1}^{m}[r_i]_j$, $s_i = \lfloor (r'_i + \delta_i - x_i)/p \rfloor$ (over integers) for $i = 1, \ldots, n$. It creates commitment $c_s = com(s_1, \ldots, s_n, \tilde{r}) = g_1^{s_1} \cdots g_n^{s_n} h^{\tilde{r}}$ and broadcasts it to the other parties.

8. P_ℓ broadcasts $c_x = com(x_1, \ldots, x_n, \hat{r}), \sigma_1, \ldots, \sigma_n$ and the parties execute $\mathsf{Batch}(pk, x_1, \sigma_1, \ldots, x_n, \sigma_n)$ with P_ℓ playing the role of the prover.

9. The parties additionally execute $\mathrm{PK}\{(x_1, \ldots, x_n, r'_1, \ldots, r'_n, s_1, \ldots, s_n, \alpha', \hat{r}, \tilde{r}) : c_x = g_1^{x_1} \cdots g_n^{x_n} h^{\hat{r}} \wedge c'_r = g_1^{r'_1} \cdots g_n^{r'_n} h^{\alpha'} \wedge c_s = g_1^{s_1} \cdots g_n^{s_n} h^{\tilde{r}} \wedge \bigwedge_{i=1}^{n} (r'_i = x_i - \delta_i + s_i p)\}$ where P_ℓ plays the role of the prover.

As before, the ZKPK of $x_1, \ldots, x_n, \hat{r}$ is redundant and no longer executed in Batch.

Then once the computation is complete and the value of α is opened (but prior to reconstructing the output of the computation from the shares), the parties perform additional computation and checks:

1. Each P_j sends α''_j and $[\gamma(r_i)]_j$ for $i = 1, \ldots, n$ to P_ℓ.

2. P_ℓ checks that each $com([\gamma(r_1)]_j, \ldots, [\gamma(r_n)]_j, \alpha''_j)$ is consistent with $[\gamma(r_i)]_j$s and α''_j and aborts otherwise.

3. P_ℓ computes $\alpha' = \sum_{j=1}^{m} \alpha_j$ (in $\mathbb{Z}_q$), $\gamma'_i = \sum_{j=1}^{m} [\gamma(r_i)]_j$, $u_i = \lfloor r'_i/p \rfloor$, $w_i = \lfloor \gamma'_i/p \rfloor$ (over integers) for $i = 1, \ldots, n$. P_ℓ creates commitments $c_u = com(u_1, \ldots, u_n, z) = g_1^{u_1} \cdots g_n^{u_n} h^z$, $c_w = com(w_1, \ldots, w_n, z') = g_1^{w_1} \cdots g_n^{w_n} h^{z'}$ and broadcasts them to other parties.

4. P_ℓ proves the following statement $\mathrm{PK}\{r'_1, \ldots, r'_n, \gamma'_1, \ldots, \gamma'_n, u_1, \ldots, u_n, w_1, \ldots, w_n, \alpha', \alpha'', z, z' : c'_r = g_1^{r'_1} \cdots g_n^{r'_n} h^{\alpha'} \wedge c'_\gamma = g_1^{\gamma'_1} \cdots g_n^{\gamma'_n} h^{\alpha''} \wedge c_u = g_1^{u_1} \cdots g_n^{u_n} h^z \wedge c_w = g_1^{w_1} \cdots g_n^{w_n} h^{z'} \wedge \bigwedge_{i=1}^{n} (\gamma'_i = \alpha(r'_i - u_i p + \tau_i) + w_i p)\}$, where
τ_i was the public value in r_i's MAC.

7 Performance Evaluation

Before we conclude, we provide a brief performance evaluation of the developed techniques. We have implemented the modified ElGamal with private verification that uses a single commitment to n messages (and thus a single signature). Additionally, we have implemented SPDZ-based input of certified inputs into SMC using the same signature. All programs were written in C using OpenSSL's elliptic curve implementation with a 224-bit modulus (equivalent to a 2048-bit modulus in the standard setting) and SHA-256 as the hash function. The experiments were run on an 8-core 2.1 GHz machine with a Xeon E5-2620 processor and 64 GB of memory running CentOS using a single thread and the times were averaged over at least 20 executions. The results are given in Table 2.

Table 2. Performance of batch signatures and using certified inputs in SMC.

			Number of messages n						
			1	10	10^2	10^3	10^4	10^5	10^6
Modified ElGamal signatures	Signing verification communication		0.69 ms	0.70 ms	1.0 ms	5.2 ms	56.1 ms	675 ms	8.59 s
			1.8 ms	2.7 ms	12.6 ms	111 ms	1.11 s	12.6 s	134 s
			140 B	392 B	2.84 KB	27.4 KB	274 KB	2.67 MB	26.7 MB
SPDZ-based entering of certified inputs	Input party	Comp.	4.61 ms	8.69 ms	49.5 ms	462 ms	4.63 s	52.9 s	N/A
		Comm.	1.02 KB	2.81 KB	20.7 KB	200 KB	1.95 MB	19.5 MB	195 MB
	Other party	Comp.	5.45 ms	8.90 ms	43.4 ms	393 ms	3.92 s	45.4 s	N/A
		Comm.	232 B	304 B	1.00 KB	8.03 KB	78.3 KB	781 KB	7.63 MB

The table shows the time of Sign, cumulative computation of Batch (the prover and verifier work), and communication amount in Batch (which is $n + 4$ group elements, with a 28-byte group element in our experiments). Recall that the ZKPK of Batch becomes a part of the ZKPK used during entering certified inputs into SMC and is not executed separately then. For the SPDZ-based solution of Sect. 6.2, we used a setup with $m = 3$ computational parties and $|p| = 32$. We report computation time of input party P_ℓ and all other parties (who do identical work) as well as the amount of communication sent by P_ℓ and other parties, respectively. A broadcast message is counted multiple times using direct transmissions to each party and an EC point is counted as 1 group element.

In our construction, P_ℓ does a slightly larger amount of work per input x_i than other parties, which is reflected in Table 2 for large n. When, however, n is small, the constant terms (e.g., batch verification carried out by everyone except P_ℓ) noticeably contribute to the overall time making P_ℓ's time slightly faster. But in all cases, each party's work is not substantially higher than the work of private signature verification itself.

An improvement to SPDZ [12] reports for p near 2^{32} in the malicious model (without certified input) 7.5–134 thousand multiplications per second (for 1 to 50 operations in parallel) during the online phase. This is about 7.5–130 μs per multiplication (including communication), while our work associated with input certification is about 400 μs with on the order of hundred bytes of communication per message, which in not drastically higher than that of an online multiplication (all of which can be improved with parallel execution using multiple cores). For many computations, the number of multiplications is significantly greater than the number of inputs, which means that the cost of computation will exceed that of entering and verifying inputs in our solution. Furthermore, offline work per multiplication triple in SPDZ is significantly higher at 28.7 ms per triple. All of this suggests that the performance of our solution is quite good and is not expected to be the bottleneck in secure computation.

8   Conclusions

In this work, we showed how to modify CL and ElGamal signature schemes to achieve efficient private batch verification for use in SMC with certified inputs and integrate them with two secret-sharing-based protocols. Our results demonstrate that the techniques are efficient even for a large number of inputs and the ideas behind private verification are rather general to have a potential application to other signature schemes.

Acknowledgments. We thank anonymous reviewers for their valuable feedback. This work was supported in part by grant 1319090 from the National Science Foundation (NSF). Any opinions, findings, and conclusions or recommendations expressed in this publication are those of the authors and do not necessarily reflect the views of NSF.

A   Additional Background

Let $\Pi = (\mathsf{KeyGen}, \mathsf{Sign}, \mathsf{Verify})$ be a signature scheme and consider the following experiment:

Experiment $\mathsf{ForgeSig}_{\mathcal{A},\Pi}(\kappa)$:

1. The challenger creates a key pair $(pk, sk) \leftarrow \mathsf{Gen}(1^\kappa)$ and gives pk to $\mathcal{A}$.
2. $\mathcal{A}$ has oracle access to $\mathsf{Sign}_{sk}(\cdot)$. For each message m that $\mathcal{A}$ queries the oracle, m is stored in list $\mathcal{Q}$ and $\mathcal{A}$ learns $\sigma = \mathsf{Sign}_{sk}(m)$. $\mathcal{A}$ eventually outputs a pair (m^*, σ^*).
3. The experiment outputs 1 if both $\mathsf{Verify}_{pk}(m^*, \sigma^*) = 1$ and $m^* \notin \mathcal{Q}$. Otherwise, it outputs 0.

Definition 6 (Security of a signature scheme [23]). *A signature scheme* $\Pi = (\mathsf{Gen}, \mathsf{Sign}, \mathsf{Verify})$ *is* existentially unforgeable under an adaptive chosen-message attack *if for all PPT adversaries* $\mathcal{A}$ *there is a negligible function* negl *such that* $\Pr[\mathsf{ForgeSig}_{\mathcal{A},\Pi}(\kappa) = 1] \leq \mathsf{negl}(\kappa)$.

References

1. Bellare, M., Garay, J.A., Rabin, T.: Fast batch verification for modular exponentiation and digital signatures. In: Nyberg, K. (ed.) EUROCRYPT 1998. LNCS, vol. 1403, pp. 236–250. Springer, Heidelberg (1998). https://doi.org/10.1007/BFb0054130
2. Blanton, M., Bayatbabolghani, F.: Efficient server-aided secure two-party function evaluation with applications to genomic computation. In: PoPET, vol. 4, pp. 1–22 (2016)

3. Bogdanov, D., Jõemets, M., Siim, S., Vaht, M.: How the estonian tax and customs board evaluated a tax fraud detection system based on secure multi-party computation. In: Böhme, R., Okamoto, T. (eds.) FC 2015. LNCS, vol. 8975, pp. 227–234. Springer, Heidelberg (2015). https://doi.org/10.1007/978-3-662-47854-7_14

4. Bogetoft, P., et al.: Secure multiparty computation goes live. In: Dingledine, R., Golle, P. (eds.) FC 2009. LNCS, vol. 5628, pp. 325–343. Springer, Heidelberg (2009). https://doi.org/10.1007/978-3-642-03549-4_20

5. Camenisch, J., Hohenberger, S., Pedersen, M.Ø.: Batch verification of short signatures. In: Naor, M. (ed.) EUROCRYPT 2007. LNCS, vol. 4515, pp. 246–263. Springer, Heidelberg (2007). https://doi.org/10.1007/978-3-540-72540-4_14

6. Camenisch, J., Lysyanskaya, A.: A signature scheme with efficient protocols. In: Cimato, S., Persiano, G., Galdi, C. (eds.) SCN 2002. LNCS, vol. 2576, pp. 268–289. Springer, Heidelberg (2003). https://doi.org/10.1007/3-540-36413-7_20

7. Camenisch, J., Lysyanskaya, A.: Signature schemes and anonymous credentials from bilinear maps. In: Franklin, M. (ed.) CRYPTO 2004. LNCS, vol. 3152, pp. 56–72. Springer, Heidelberg (2004). https://doi.org/10.1007/978-3-540-28628-8_4

8. Camenisch, J., Sommer, D., Zimmermann, R.: A general certification framework with applications to privacy-enhancing certificate infrastructures. In: Fischer-Hübner, S., Rannenberg, K., Yngström, L., Lindskog, S. (eds.) SEC 2006. IIFIP, vol. 201, pp. 25–37. Springer, Boston, MA (2006). https://doi.org/10.1007/0-387-33406-8_3

9. Camenisch, J., Stadler, M.: Proof systems for general statements about discrete logarithms. Technical report 260, Department of Computer Science, ETH Zurich (1997)

10. Camenisch, J., Zaverucha, G.M.: Private intersection of certified sets. In: Dingledine, R., Golle, P. (eds.) FC 2009. LNCS, vol. 5628, pp. 108–127. Springer, Heidelberg (2009). https://doi.org/10.1007/978-3-642-03549-4_7

11. Chaum, D., Pedersen, T.P.: Wallet databases with observers. In: Brickell, E.F. (ed.) CRYPTO 1992. LNCS, vol. 740, pp. 89–105. Springer, Heidelberg (1993). https://doi.org/10.1007/3-540-48071-4_7

12. Damgård, I., Keller, M., Larraia, E., Pastro, V., Scholl, P., Smart, N.P.: Practical covertly secure MPC for dishonest majority – or: breaking the SPDZ limits. In: Crampton, J., Jajodia, S., Mayes, K. (eds.) ESORICS 2013. LNCS, vol. 8134, pp. 1–18. Springer, Heidelberg (2013). https://doi.org/10.1007/978-3-642-40203-6_1

13. Damgård, I., Nielsen, J.B.: Scalable and unconditionally secure multiparty computation. In: Menezes, A. (ed.) CRYPTO 2007. LNCS, vol. 4622, pp. 572–590. Springer, Heidelberg (2007). https://doi.org/10.1007/978-3-540-74143-5_32

14. Damgård, I., Pastro, V., Smart, N., Zakarias, S.: Multiparty computation from somewhat homomorphic encryption. In: Safavi-Naini, R., Canetti, R. (eds.) CRYPTO 2012. LNCS, vol. 7417, pp. 643–662. Springer, Heidelberg (2012). https://doi.org/10.1007/978-3-642-32009-5_38

15. De Cristofaro, E., Tsudik, G.: Practical private set intersection protocols with linear complexity. In: Sion, R. (ed.) FC 2010. LNCS, vol. 6052, pp. 143–159. Springer, Heidelberg (2010). https://doi.org/10.1007/978-3-642-14577-3_13

16. Dent, A.W., Fischlin, M., Manulis, M., Stam, M., Schröder, D.: Confidential signatures and deterministic signcryption. In: Nguyen, P.Q., Pointcheval, D. (eds.) PKC 2010. LNCS, vol. 6056, pp. 462–479. Springer, Heidelberg (2010). https://doi.org/10.1007/978-3-642-13013-7_27

17. ElGamal, T.: A public key cryptosystem and a signature scheme based on discrete logarithms. IEEE Trans. Inf. Theory **31**(4), 469–472 (1985)

18. Ferrara, A.L., Green, M., Hohenberger, S., Pedersen, M.Ø.: Practical short signature batch verification. In: Fischlin, M. (ed.) CT-RSA 2009. LNCS, vol. 5473, pp. 309–324. Springer, Heidelberg (2009). https://doi.org/10.1007/978-3-642-00862-7_21

19. Fleischhacker, N., Günther, F., Kiefer, F., Manulis, M., Poettering, B.: Pseudorandom signatures. In: ASIACCS, pp. 107–118 (2013)

20. Goldreich, O.: Foundations of Cryptography: Volume 2, Basic Applications. Cambridge University Press, Cambridge (2004)

21. Guo, N., Gao, T., Wang, J.: Privacy-preserving and efficient attributes proof based on selective aggregate CL-signature scheme. Int. J. Comput. Math. **93**(2), 273–288 (2016)

22. Halpern, J., Teague, V.: Rational secret sharing and multiparty computation. In: ACM Symposium on Theory of Computing (STOC), pp. 623–632 (2004)

23. Katz, J., Lindell, Y.: Introduction to Modern Cryptography, 2nd edn. Chapman Hall/CRC, Boca Raton (2014)

24. Katz, J., Malozemoff, A.J., Wang, X.: Efficiently enforcing input validity in secure two-party computation. IACR Cryptology ePrint Archive Report 2016/184 (2016)

25. Kreuter, B.: Secure multiparty computation at Google. Real World Crypto (2017). https://www.youtube.com/watch?v=ee7oRsDnNNc

26. Lee, K., Lee, D.H., Yung, M.: Aggregating CL-signatures revisited: extended functionality and better efficiency. In: Sadeghi, A.-R. (ed.) FC 2013. LNCS, vol. 7859, pp. 171–188. Springer, Heidelberg (2013). https://doi.org/10.1007/978-3-642-39884-1_14

27. Lysyanskaya, A., Rivest, R.L., Sahai, A., Wolf, S.: Pseudonym systems. In: Heys, H., Adams, C. (eds.) SAC 1999. LNCS, vol. 1758, pp. 184–199. Springer, Heidelberg (2000). https://doi.org/10.1007/3-540-46513-8_14

28. Pedersen, T.P.: Non-interactive and information-theoretic secure verifiable secret sharing. In: Feigenbaum, J. (ed.) CRYPTO 1991. LNCS, vol. 576, pp. 129–140. Springer, Heidelberg (1992). https://doi.org/10.1007/3-540-46766-1_9

29. Pointcheval, D., Stern, J.: Security proofs for signature schemes. In: Maurer, U. (ed.) EUROCRYPT 1996. LNCS, vol. 1070, pp. 387–398. Springer, Heidelberg (1996). https://doi.org/10.1007/3-540-68339-9_33

30. Pointcheval, D., Stern, J.: Security arguments for digital signatures and blind signatures. J. Cryptol. **13**(3), 361–396 (2000)

31. Wallrabenstein, J.R., Clifton, C.: Equilibrium concepts for rational multiparty computation. In: Das, S.K., Nita-Rotaru, C., Kantarcioglu, M. (eds.) GameSec 2013. LNCS, vol. 8252, pp. 226–245. Springer, Cham (2013). https://doi.org/10.1007/978-3-319-02786-9_14

32. Yang, G., Wong, D.S., Deng, X., Wang, H.: Anonymous signature schemes. In: Yung, M., Dodis, Y., Kiayias, A., Malkin, T. (eds.) PKC 2006. LNCS, vol. 3958, pp. 347–363. Springer, Heidelberg (2006). https://doi.org/10.1007/11745853_23

33. Zhang, Y., Blanton, M., Bayatbabolghani, F.: Enforcing input correctness via certification in garbled circuit evaluation. In: Foley, S.N., Gollmann, D., Snekkenes, E. (eds.) ESORICS 2017. LNCS, vol. 10493, pp. 552–569. Springer, Cham (2017). https://doi.org/10.1007/978-3-319-66399-9_30

SDN Security

Stealthy Probing-Based Verification (SPV): An Active Approach to Defending Software Defined Networks Against Topology Poisoning Attacks

Amir Alimohammadifar[1], Suryadipta Majumdar[1(✉)], Taous Madi[1], Yosr Jarraya[2], Makan Pourzandi[2], Lingyu Wang[1], and Mourad Debbabi[1]

[1] CIISE, Concordia University, Montreal, QC, Canada
{ami_alim,su_majum,wang,debbabi}@encs.concordia.ca
[2] Ericsson Security Research, Ericsson Canada, Montreal, QC, Canada
{yosr.jarraya,makan.pourzandi}@ericsson.com

Abstract. Since a key advantage of Software Defined Networks (SDN) is providing a logically centralized view of the network topology, the correctness of such a view becomes critical for SDN applications to make the right management decisions. However, recently discovered vulnerabilities in OpenFlow Discovery Protocol (OFDP) show that malicious hosts and switches can poison the network view of the SDN controller and consequently lead to more severe security attacks, such as man-in-the-middle or denial of service. Existing solutions mostly rely on passive techniques, which only work for known attacking methods. In this paper, we propose a novel stealthy probing-based verification approach, namely, *SPV*, to detect fake links regardless of the attacking methods used to fabricate them. Specifically, SPV incrementally verifies legitimate links and detects fake links by sending stealthy probing packets designed to be indistinguishable from normal traffic. To illustrate the feasibility of our approach, we implement SPV in an emulated SDN environment using Mininet and OpenDaylight. We further evaluate the applicability and the performance of SPV based on a real SDN/cloud topology. The experimental results show that SPV can respond in near real-time (e.g., less than 120 ms) in both real and emulated environments, which makes SPV a scalable solution for large SDN networks.

Keywords: SDN security · Topology poisoning · Link verification
Active probing

1 Introduction

The Software Defined Networks (SDN) paradigm is gaining momentum as a promising solution with various benefits, such as increasing network resource utilization, simplifying network management, and reducing operating cost [17,

© Springer Nature Switzerland AG 2018
J. Lopez et al. (Eds.): ESORICS 2018, LNCS 11099, pp. 463–484, 2018.
https://doi.org/10.1007/978-3-319-98989-1_23

20, 34]. As the central idea of SDN, i.e., separating the network's control and data planes, brings most of those benefits, it also unavoidably empowers the SDN controllers and increases the dependence of SDN applications on those controllers [20, 34]. Specifically, as the operating system of an SDN network, the SDN controller is responsible for maintaining a logically centralized view of the network, which serves as the basis for many SDN applications to make important network management decisions, such as routing, load balancing, firewalling, and monitoring [15]. The validity of such a view is thus critical for the proper functionalities of the SDN applications, and SDN in general.

However, as the SDN controller discovers changes to its network view by sending out special Link Layer Discovery Protocol (LLDP) packets, malicious switches or hosts can easily poison such a view by either manipulating legitimate LLDP packets or injecting fake LLDP packets. As evidenced by recently discovered vulnerabilities in the OpenFlow Discovery Protocol (OFDP) [18], such attacks may take various forms depending on the capabilities of attackers [4, 8, 10, 16, 32]. To make our discussions more concrete, we first illustrate such attacks through an example.

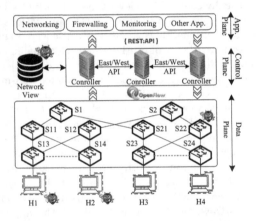

Fig. 1. Topology poisoning attacks in SDN

Motivating Example. Figure 1 illustrates a simple SDN topology which includes two malicious hosts H1 and H2, and a malicious switch S22. We first describe how the SDN controller may discover its network view (i.e., the switches and their links illustrated as solid lines in the figure) and how such a view may be poisoned through attacks.

– **Legitimate topology discovery protocol.** We show how a legitimate run of the topology discovery protocol works to discover a newly added link between switches S12 and S13. First, the controller sends an LLDP packet to all the switches. Each switch is supposed to broadcast this packet to all its ports (except the port connected to the controller). Therefore, switches

S12 and S13 receive a copy of this packet from each other, upon which they add their identity information to the packets and return the packets to the controller. Based on those packets, the controller concludes that there is a new link between the two switches S12 and S13.

- **Attack 1: Relaying LLDP packets using hosts.** According to the topology discovery protocol, a host is supposed to ignore any LLDP packets broadcasted by the switches. However, upon receiving every such packet from switch S13, a malicious host H1 immediately sends it to an accomplice, host H2, through an out-of-band channel. Host H2 then forwards the packet to switch S14, which, unaware of such an ongoing attack, adds its identity information and returns the packet to the SDN controller. Receiving such a packet from S14 tricks the SDN controller into adding the fake (non-existent) link between S13 and S14 into its network view.

- **Attack 2: Injecting fake LLDP packets.** In this attack, upon receiving every LLDP packet from switch S13, a malicious host H1 forges the packet to masquerade itself as switch S13, and sends the forged packet (using an out-of-band channel) to switch S14. The SDN controller is again tricked into believing there exists a link between S13 and S14.

- **Attack 3: Relaying LLDP packets using switches.** This attack involves a compromised switch[1], i.e., S22, to create a fake link between switches S23 and S24. Instead of sending back to the controller, switch S22 forwards the LLDP packet received from S23 to S24. Switch S24 returns this packet to the SDN controller, which results in a fake link between S23 and S24 to be added.

By poisoning an SDN controller's network view, those attacks may open doors to more severe threats, such as man-in-the-middle and DoS attacks [15,16,18]. Most existing works [3,5,10,16] rely on a passive approach that only works for known attacking methods. For example, TopoGuard [16] is a powerful tool that can detect a wide range of attacks on both hosts and links, and it detects the first two attacks above by identifying compromised hosts for unexpectedly sending LLDP packets, and by authenticating the LLDP packets, respectively. However, if the attacker changes his/her methods, e.g., relaying legitimate LLDP packets for the first attack or sending forged LLDP packets for the second from a host, whose connection with a switch is unknown to TopoGuard, then he/she may easily evade the detection. Our key observation is that, such a passive approach can be complemented with an active approach that detects a fake link simply based on its non-existence, regardless of how such a link is fabricated.

In this paper, we propose the first active approach of sending probing packets in a stealthy manner to incrementally verify legitimate links and identify fake links independent of how a fake link is fabricated. Specifically, the probing packets are designed to be stealthy in the sense that they are indistinguishable from normal traffic. We provide detailed methodology and algorithms for both link

---

[1] Note those are software-based switches in SDN/cloud environments which can easily be compromised by malware infections or remote attacks.

verification and packet generation. As a proof of concept, we implement and test our approach based on both emulated (using Mininet [26] network emulator) and real SDN environments using the OpenDaylight [1] SDN controller. Finally, we evaluate both the efficiency and effectiveness of our solution against reactive adversaries using both synthetic and real data.

Our main contributions are as follows.

- To the best of our knowledge, SPV is the first active probing-based solution to SDN topology poisoning attacks, and the first comprehensive solution that works regardless of the attacking methods.
- Our implementation using OpenFlow-based SDN environment demonstrates the practicality of our approach. Moreover, we have designed SPV to be separated from the SDN controller implementation, such that it can be easily adapted to other controller implementations.
- As demonstrated through experiments using both synthetic data and the topology of a real SDN/cloud hosted at one of the largest telecommunication vendors, SPV responds in near real-time (e.g., less than 120 ms) for each new link, which confirms its scalability for large SDN networks.

The rest of the paper is organized as follows. Section 2 introduces SDN and our threat model. Section 3 details our methodology. Section 4 discusses security analysis of SPV. Sections 5 and 6 describe the implementation details and experimental results, respectively. Section 7 gives more discussions. Section 8 discusses the related work, and Sect. 9 concludes the paper.

2   Preliminaries

This section provides a brief overview of SDN, and discusses our threat model.

2.1   Background

SDN Overview. As demonstrated in Fig. 1, SDN adopts a three-layered architecture [14,17]: (i) the application layer (the upper layer in the figure), which consists of different applications that manage the data plane, (ii) the control plane (i.e., SDN controller), and (iii) the data plane, which consists of the forwarding devices and their connecting links. The SDN controller communicates with the application layer and the data plane layer through the northbound and the southbound APIs, respectively. The OpenFlow protocol [13,24] is the most widely used southbound API for SDN [14,17].

SDN Topology Management. Most SDN controller implementations follow the OFDP protocol to send LLDP packets for topology management [16]. To facilitate further discussions, the upper figure in Fig. 2 demonstrates the three basic steps of the OFDP protocol as follows. Step (1): the SDN controller encapsulates an LLDP packet (the format of an LLDP packet is shown in the lower figure in Fig. 2) into a message, and sends it to switch S12. Step (2): the received message instructs switch S12 to advertise the enclosed LLDP packet in all its ports except the port it receives the packet from. Step (3): switches S11 and S13 send back the LLDP packet in an encapsulated message along with their specifications to the SDN controller. Based on the received packets, the SDN controller discovers the link between switches S11 and S12 and the link between switches S12 and S13.

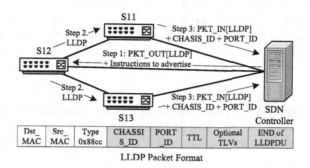

Fig. 2. The OFDP protocol and LLDP packet format

2.2   Threat Model

Similar to existing works [3,5,6,8,16,18], we assume that an adversary may compromise one or more host(s) and/or switch(es) in the network. S/he can send information through the compromised hosts using the out-of-band links, and modify the flows of the compromised switches. Furthermore, s/he is able to distinguish between host-generated packets and SDN control packets. S/he can sniff packets, modify them, and inject them into the network. Consequently, the in-scope threats in our work include all the three types of poisoning attacks mentioned in Sect. 1.

On the other hand, we assume the SDN controller is not compromised and the established control channels between the SDN controller and OpenFlow switches are trusted. Consequently, the attackers can only attempt to distinguish probing packets based on their contents. we also assume the confidentiality and integrity of public-private key pairs that are installed on switches are preserved, and the implementation or specification of switch software remains unmodified.

3   Methodology

This section details our methodology including how to verify a newly added link using probing packets and how to generate the probing packets in a stealthy manner.

3.1   Link Verification

Before SPV can verify a newly added link, it must keep track of updates made to the network view. For this purpose, SPV communicates with the SDN controller via the northbound API in order to be notified about any updates to the network view including link creation (a detailed discussion of the SPV architecture and how it interacts with SDN can be found in the Appendix due to page limitations). Once a new link is created, SPV collects relevant information for generating the probing packet, and prepares necessary flows for sending the packet. Finally, SPV sends the probing packet and, depending on the outcome, it marks the link as either legitimate or fake. In the following, we first build intuitions through an example, and then describe the details of our link verification algorithm.

Example 1. Figure 3 shows a simplified SDN topology with three switches and one SDN controller. We assume switch S12 is malicious and it has created a fake link between switches S11 and S13 (shown by dashed line in Fig. 3) through the aforementioned attack. The following explains how SPV can detect this fake link.

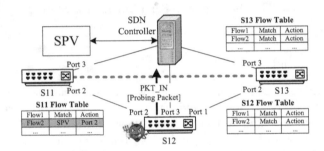

Fig. 3. An example of how SPV verifies a link

- First, since SPV continuously monitors updates to the network topology view, it obtains information about the new link between switches S11 and S13 (noted as S11:Port2-S13:Port2) as soon as it is created.
- Second, SPV generates a probing packet based on the flow tables of switches S11 and S13 (the packet generation will be further elaborated in the next section).
- Third, SPV installs a new flow in the flow table of S11 (shown as a shaded row in the table) stating that the packets matching this flow must be forwarded to S11:Port2, as the link to be verified is S11:Port2-S13:Port2.
- Fourth, SPV sends the probing packet to switch S11, which forwards the packet on its port S11:Port2 due to the matching flow. At this point, if there were indeed a legitimate link, the probing packet would be forwarded to switch S13. However, as the link is fake and S11:Port2 is in fact connected to S12:Port2, switch S12 receives the probing packet instead and it returns the packet to the controller. Clearly, no matter how the fake link is fabricated,

SPV can always detect it, as long it is non-existent in the sense that not all packets will pass through it (we will discuss the effect of dropping packets in Sect. 4) and attackers cannot identify our probing packets (we will explain why S12 cannot identify this probing packet in the next section).

– Finally, once the probing packet is received, SPV discovers that it is sent to the controller from switch S12 instead of switch S13. Therefore, SPV reports link S11:Port2-S13:Port2 to be fake and switch S12 to be compromised.

The ideas illustrated in Example 1 are more formally described in Algorithm 1 and explained below.

Algorithm 1. Link Verification Algorithm

1: **Input:** *links*: Network view of the SDN controller
2: **procedure** UPDATECHECK(network view)
3:     **while** true **do**
4:         newLink=checkUpdtae(network view)
5:         **if** newLink == "NOT NULL" **then**
6:             links = links+newLink
7:             VerificationPreparation(links)
8: **Input:** *links*: List of links to be verified
9: **procedure** VERIFICATIONPREPARATION(links)
10:     **for** each $l \in links$ **do**
11:         $srcSwStat$ = getStat($l.srcSwID$)   ▷ collecting flows for the source switch
12:         $dstSwStat$ = getStat($l.dstSwID$)   ▷ collecting flows for the destination switch
13:         $ProbingPacket$ =generatePacket($srcSwStat, dstSwStat, l$)
14:         SPV_Flow = generateFlow($ProbingPacket.header, l.srcSwID, l.srcSwPort$)
15:         installFlow($SPV\_Flow, l.srcSwID$)   ▷ installing a flow on the source switch
16:         **while** true **do**
17:             **if** sendPacket($ProbingPacket, l.srcSwID, l.srcSwPort$) == "Successful" **then**
18:                 $l.ProbingPacket = ProbingPacket$ ▷ storing the latest $ProbingPacket$
19:                 break
20:         **while** true **do**
21:             $receivedPacket = receivePacket()$
22:             **if** $time \leq threshold$ **then**
23:                 LinkValidation(receivedPacket, receivedPacket.SwID)
24:                 break
25:             **else if** $time > threshold$ **then**
26:                 sendPacket($ProbingPacket, l.srcSwID, l.srcSwPort$)
27: **Input:** RET_PKT: the returned probing packet to SPV via controller
28: **Input:** $SwID$: the switch ID of the probing packet sender to the controller
29: **procedure** LINKVALIDATION($RET\_PKT, SwID$)
30:     **for** each $l \in links$ **do**
31:         **if** $SwID == l.dstSwID$ **then**
32:             $l.Status =$ "Legitimate"
33:         **else if** $SwID \neq l.dstSwID$ **then**
34:             $l.Status =$ "Malicious"
35:             $maliciousSwList.add(SwID)$

Lines 2–6: Tracking Network View Updates. The first step of SPV is to capture every change in the network topology and to maintain a local view of the network state to facilitate efficient processing. As soon as an update is reported, SPV stores the link information and initiates the verification preparation.

Lines 11–13: Generating a Probing Packet. Based on information about the newly added link obtained from the previous step, SPV identifies the source and destination switches of the new link. Then, SPV collects flows and other relevant statistics of these two switches (lines 11–12). Afterwards, it generates a probing packet based on these flows and statistics (the packet generation step is further detailed in Sect. 3.2).

Lines 14–15: Installing Flow to Forward Probing Packet. Utilizing the link information, i.e., link switches and their connecting ports, and the generated probing packet, SPV creates a flow and installs it on the source switch so that this switch can forward the received probing packet on its outgoing port towards the destination switch. Note that the flow is deleted from the switch after a successful round of verification of the given link (omitted from the algorithm).

Lines 16–19: Sending Probing Packets. Once the flow is successfully installed, SPV sends the probing packet to the source switch. SPV keeps sending the packet till the transmission is successful, and then stores the latest probing packet for verification and future packet generation.

Lines 20–26: Receiving Probing Packets. After transmission, SPV waits until it receives the probing packet within a given time threshold. Alternatively, if the packet is dropped for any reason (e.g., an active adversary dropping probing packets purposely), after a certain timeout, SPV re-sends the probing packet to the same switch with randomly chosen time intervals so that an active adversary cannot later predict the probing packets (this defense mechanism of SPV is further discussed in Sect. 4). Upon a successful return of a probing packet, SPV triggers the link validation procedure to verify the returned packet.

Lines 30–35: Validating a Specific Link. Finally, SPV verifies the validity of a link. To this end, SPV first checks the switch ID of the sender switch of the returned packet. If the ID is the same as that of the destination switch of the link to be verified, then the link is a legitimate link. Otherwise, the link is considered fake and the sender switch of the returned packet is considered compromised. There is another possibility (omitted from the algorithm), where the probing packet is not returned to SPV for certain reason, e.g., dropped due to network congestion or an active adversary. In such a case, SPV marks the link as "Not-Validated" and conducts further rounds of verification with randomly chosen time intervals to prevent an active adversary (discussed more in Sect. 4).

3.2   Probing Packet Generation

The link verification method introduced in the previous section critically depends on the fact that attackers cannot effectively distinguish the probing packets from normal traffic. This section details the generation of such stealthy probing packets. Again, we first build intuitions through an example and then present the formal packet generation algorithm with the detailed description.

Example 2. Following Example 1, a stealthy probing packet is generated to validate the link between switches S11 and S13. SPV generates this probing packet as follows.

- First, SPV builds a packet pool by collecting the OFTP_PACKET_IN messages sent from switches towards the SDN controller, which contain a host generated packet inside them (as shown in Table 1 with PKT_TYPE equal to HOST). Each entry of this pool contains different attributes to store useful information about the collected packets (details of such attributes are discussed later in this section).
- Second, upon detecting a new link between switches S11 and S13, SPV prepares a list of candidate packets from the pool in a manner such that none of the packets in the list have traversed through S11 and S13.
- Third, SPV randomly chooses a packet from the list of candidates, forges its header information, and assigns a unique ID to the chosen packet.
- Fourth, SPV calculates a hash value over the unique ID and the timestamp at the moment of packet generation, i.e., Hash(PKT_ID||Timestamp) and uses it as the packet's data field. This generated probing packet is then sent to verify the link between S11 and S13 as explained in Example 1. The packet is also added to the pool, shown as the shaded row in Table 1.

Table 1. An example packet pool

#	PKT_ID	PKT_TYPE	Switch DPID	PKT_IN_hdr	Data_hdr	Data_size	Link_ID	Timestamp
1	-	HOST	S_12	ip:mac	ip:mac	1024	-	-
2	-	HOST	S_13	ip:mac	ip:mac	74	-	-
4	adr341...w34	SPV	-	-	ip:mac	256	Link_1	1522643791
5	-	HOST	S_11	ip:mac	ip:mac	74	-	-
6	dgw213...a78	SPV	-	-	ip:mac	256	Link_3	1522644976

The ideas illustrated in Example 2 are more formally described in Algorithm 2 and explained below.

Lines 4–7: Building the Packet Pool. To build the packet pool, SPV first identifies the attributes shown in Table 1, which are needed for probing packet generation. Second, SPV collects all incoming packets sent to the controller. Third, SPV extracts the header information of each packet and other metadata (e.g., size). Finally, SPV stores the extracted attributes for each packet into the packet pool. Specifically, for each entry in the packet pool, the PKT_ID attribute specifies a unique identifier, which is randomly generated for each probing packet in the pool. The PKT_ID attribute serves as the secret information used for authentication purposes in SPV. The PKT_TYPE attribute can be either "Host" or "SPV", since we collect only these two types of packets. SPV obtains the Switch_DPID attribute of the switch that has sent the packet from the MAC address of the packet sender's switch. The PKT_IN_hdr and Data_hdr attributes contain the headers of the OFTP_PACKET_IN and the host generated packets, respectively. The Link_ID attribute contains the ID of the link that the probing packet has been sent to verify its validity. Finally, the Timestamp attribute shows the timestamp of the probing packet generation.

Lines 12–20: Generating Probing Packets. From the packet pool, SPV first chooses a list of packets which have not traversed through the two switches between which the link to be verified situates to avoid a possible mapping between the probing packet and these reference packets (discussed more in Sect. 4). If there does not exist any previously stored probing packet for this link (meaning that this is the first round of verification for this link), then SPV randomly chooses a packet from the above-mentioned list, and forges the source and destination IP and/or MAC addresses and ports of the packet header. Thus, SPV prevents a compromised switch from identifying probing packets (discussed further in Sect. 4). At this point, a unique ID, i.e., PKT_ID, is assigned to the packet. SPV also calculates the hash value Hash(PKT_ID||Timestamp) and stores it as part of the probing packet's payload to prevent adversaries from forging or replaying probing packets as will be discussed in Sect. 4. This concludes the packet generation. However, if this is not the first round of verification for this link, then SPV fetches the related probing packet from the pool. Afterwards, SPV utilizes the line sweep algorithm [19] (in a similar way as in [23]) to produce the next probing packet for verifying this link so that the header information remains less different (e.g., same subnet) than the previous one(s).

Lines 25–28: Sending Probing Packets. This step is to transmit probing packets towards a given switch at the specific port for the purpose of link verification.

Algorithm 2. Probing Packet Generation Algorithm

1: **Input:** *PKT_IN*: the exchanged packets between switches and the SDN controller
2: **Input:** *SwID*: the switch ID of the packet sender
3: **procedure** PKTCOLLECTOR(PKT_IN, SwID)
4:     **if** $PKT\_IN.payload \neq controlMsg$ **then**
5:         pktPool.add($PKT\_IN, SwID$)
6:         **if** $PKT\_IN.payload == ProbingPacket$ **then**
7:             $LinkVerification.LinkValidation(PKTIN\_SPV, SwID)$

8: **Input:** *srcSwStat*: flows and status of source switch of the link
9: **Input:** *dstSwStat*: flows and status of destination switch of the link
10: **Input:** *link*: the link information
11: **procedure** PKTGEN(srcSwStat, dstSwStat, link)
12:     $pkts = getPktsFromPool(srcSwID, dstSwID)$
13:     **if** $link.ProbingPacket == null$ **then**   ▷ first round of verification
14:         $pkt = selectPkt(pkts)$ ▷ select and forge the header of a random packet
15:         $pkt\_ID = generateID(pkt)$
16:         $pkt.payload = hash(pkt\_ID||Timestamp)$
17:     **else**   ▷ further rounds of verification
18:         $l.ProbingPacket = fetchPacket(pool, link)$
19:         $pkt = lineSweepPktGen(l.ProbingPacket)$
20:     **return** *pkt*

21: **Input:** *PKT*: a packet to be sent
22: **Input:** *SwID*: the switch ID to send the packet to
23: **Input:** *SwPort*: the port number of the switch to send the packet on
24: **procedure** PACKETSENDER(PKT, SwID, SwPort)
25:     **if** NorthBoundAPI.SendPacket($PKT, SwID, SwPort$) == *"Successful"* **then**
26:         **return** *"Successful"*
27:     **else**
28:         **return** *"Unsuccessful"*

---

4   Security Analysis

This section discusses how attackers may attempt to evade SPV and how such attempts are addressed in SPV.

Stealthiness Feature of SPV. The security of SPV relies on the so-called stealthiness feature of a probing packet, meaning the packet cannot be distinguished from other normal host-generated packets traveling through the network. To achieve this, SPV forges its probing packets based on normal host-generated packets (discussed in Sect. 3.2) in a special way. Specifically, a probing packet is designed to have some fields matching those of normal host-generated packets, whereas other fields must not match. For example, when a probing packet is generated based on a reference packet chosen from the candidate pool (detailed in Sect. 3.2), the Eth_Type field and the packet's payload size would both match those of the reference packet, whereas the Src_IP, Dst_IP, Src_MAC, Dst_MAC, Src_Port and Dst_Port fields must not match those of the reference packet. The former ensures that the probing packet would look exactly like a legitimate packet, and the latter prevents a compromised switch from correlating the probing and reference packets based on common source and destinations.

Relaying or Dropping Packets. A malicious switch may be able to identify probing packets, if SPV always sends them immediately after a new link creation. To address this concern, SPV keeps sending probing packets to the same switch with randomly chosen time intervals so that an active adversary cannot predict the probing packets during its further rounds. Alternatively, a malicious switch may evolve by forwarding traffic including SPV packets passing through it hoping that the fake link remains undetected. However, since the probing packets are indistinguishable, the malicious switch may need to forward every single packet traversing the fake link in order to completely evade detection. However, by forwarding all the traffic, the fake link essentially serves the purpose of a true link, which is against the original objective of the attacker. Hence, a more practical adversary might partially forward the traffic within certain time intervals after the link creation, hoping that the probing packet is among those forwarded. We measure the effect of such attacks on SPV in Sect. 6. Moreover, to detect such attacks, one potential solution is to employ the timing channel (i.e., comparing time differences between packets traversing on different links), which is considered as a future work. Finally, a malicious switch may choose to only relay the LLDP packets and drop all other packets including SPV packets. However, such DoS attacks can be more easily detected and such detection is beyond the scope of this work.

Compromising Multiple Adjacent Switches. An attacker may compromise multiple switches adjacent to each other, which, however, may not provide any advantage due to the following. (i) If the compromised switches relay packets independently, then the chance they all happen to relay a probing packet becomes even lower. (ii) Alternatively, if the compromised switches act in coordination, then they essentially become one switch so the chance of relaying a probing packet is the same as with one compromised switch.

Forging or Replaying Probing Packets. A strong adversary may employ malicious switches to mimic the link verification mechanism of SPV by either forging or replaying probing packets, and having them sent back to the SDN controller as if those packets are returned from the other end of the fake link. However, as discussed in Sect. 3.2, SPV addresses this issue by authenticating each received probing packet using a unique hash value over the secret PKT_ID and timestamp, i.e., Hash(PKT_ID||timestamp). Since SPV keeps track of the secret PKT_ID values of all its probing packets, it will not accept any probing packets forged by the adversary. Moreover, the freshness proof (i.e., timestamp) also prevents the adversary from replaying previous probing packets.

Learning Probing Packets. Even though OpenFlow switches by design are not meant to process packet payloads, the presence of soft switches in the network allows an attacker to learn patterns of probing packets by processing the network traffic. For example, if we were to use only the aforementioned hash value as the payload of probing packets, then a compromised switch may process the host-generated packets to measure their payload size in order to distinguish the probing packets. To address this issue, we ensure the payload size of each probing packet is the same as its reference packet by padding dummy data to the aforementioned hash value. Moreover, a strong adversary might keep a history of packets, and leverage learning methods to classify probing packets based on their header information (e.g., source/destination addresses). Therefore, through the line sweeping algorithm, SPV ensures that the header information of probing packets for the same switch remain very close (e.g., in the same subnet).

Injecting Packets by a Malicious Host. A malicious host may inject packets into the network hoping to influence the probing packet generation. However, this attack only works when the following conditions are satisfied: (i) the injected packet is used as the reference packet to generate a probing packet. Since SPV chooses reference packets randomly, this can only be achieved with a considerable amount of injected packets, which may be detected by other security solutions such as IDS, (ii) the owner of the malicious host also has a compromised switch, which is not connected to the same host (since probing packets are never chosen to verify the same switch from where the original packet has been collected), and (iii) the probing packet is sent to verify the connecting links of the same compromised switch, which involves a considerable amount of uncertainty.

5   Implementation

This section describes the implementation details of SPV.

Background. We use OpenDaylight (ODL) [1], which is an open platform for automating large-scale networks [25], as the SDN controller, and implement the data plane using Mininet network emulator [21,26], which is a network emulator that can be used to deploy OpenFlow switches and virtual hosts.

SDN Setup. In this paper, we mainly focus on the SDN controller functionality of ODL by making use of the REST northbound API and OpenFlow southbound

API. In our work, we utilize some of ODL's features such as (a) *odl-restconf*, (b) *odl-l2switch*, (c) *odl-mdsal*, (d) *odl-dlux*, (e) *network-topology* and (f) *packet-processing*. In our setup, we install ODL Carbon release on a virtual machine running a Linux Ubuntu server 16.04 with two Intel(R) Xeon(R) E3-1271 v3 CPUs and 6 GB of RAM. We configure ODL to instruct data-plane switches that join the network to install reactive flows and to forward the newly received packets to the ODL for further instructions. Moreover, proactive flows for LLDP packets (Ether type 0x88cc) is installed upon joining a switch to the network for discovering the network topology. To set up data plane devices, we utilize Mininet 2.2.1 on a separate Linux virtual machine running Ubuntu server 16.04 with two Intel(R) Xeon(R) E3-1271 v3 CPUs and 4 GB of RAM. We utilize OpenFlow version 1.3, since it is the latest supported version by Mininet 2.2.1. The OpenFlow switches in the data plane are chosen to be software based Open vSwitch [33] switches.

SPV's Implementation Details. SPV is mostly implemented in Java. We leverage Scapy [30], a packet manipulation tool, for the purposes of probing packet generation and encoding. We implement the SPV in both single-threading and multi-threading modes to enhance the response time of link verification while verifying multiple links simultaneously. We provide further implementation details of SPV in the following.

SPV communicates with ODL's northbound API for querying the changes in network topology, storing the topology locally, installing flows on data plane switches and performing link verification. More specifically, SPV interacts with ODL's *opendaylight-topology* module to keep track of changes in the data plane network. SPV stores the topology in a tree data structure which consists of links, nodes (e.g., switches and hosts) and their connections along with other useful information, e.g., switch statistics or links' status. SPV verification results are also stored in this tree. To send, sniff, dissect and forge network packets, SPV utilizes Scapy. Also, Scapy is used to generate probing packets, encode them in the Base64 format and send them towards specific links using ODL's northbound API.

6   Experiments

This section first discusses the network topology used in our experiments, and then presents different experimental results.

Network Topology. We consider a fat-tree topology [2], which is one of the mostly used network topologies in nowadays large data centers [35], for our data plane. We vary the switches from five to 40 where the largest topology has eight core switches, 16 aggregate switches and 16 edge switches, which comply with the size of a medium-sized data center to accommodate tens of thousands of servers [2,35]. To further stress the SPV and evaluate its accuracy, we conduct further set of experiments to measure SPV's performance up to for 5,000 link verifications in the network.

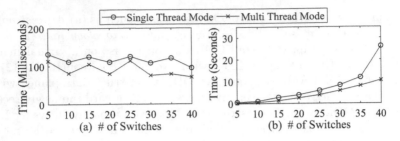

Fig. 4. Time required by SPV to verify (a) a new link and (b) all existing links while varying both the number of switches and number of links in both single and multi-threading modes

The Efficiency of SPV. In the first set of our experiments, we measure the time requirement of SPV. The reported verification time includes the time for performing all steps mentioned in Sect. 3.1. Figure 4(a) depicts the time in milliseconds to incrementally verify a newly added link in both single threading and multi-threading modes while varying the size of the network by increasing the number of switches from five to 40 with a maximum of 96 data-plane links. In this case, the average verification time is 102 ms, which shows the near-real-time nature of SPV to verify a newly added link. Also, the verification time is independent of the size of the network (e.g., number of switches and their connected links). Figure 4(b) shows the time required by SPV to verify a group of links in both single threading and multi-threading modes while varying the size of the network by increasing the number switches from five to 40 with a maximum 96 data-plane links. The verification time for the largest dataset in the single threading mode is 26.1 s. We further improve the verification time by leveraging the multi-threading mode, which reduces the verification time to 10.6 s. Even though the increase in the number of switches in the network results in the increase of verification time for both modes, the increase of the verification time remains almost linear in the multi-threading mode. These results show the practicality of SPV in medium-sized data centers to verify their topology.

Resource Consumption by SPV. The second set of the experiments is to measure the resource consumption (i.e., CPU and memory usage) by SPV. Figure 5 depicts the average CPU and memory usage to verify all existing links in the network by varying the number of switches for single threading mode. More specifically, Fig. 5(a) shows that SPV on average requires about 20% of the CPU, which is a reasonable amount. Figure 5(b) depicts the memory consumption by SPV to verify all existing links for different network sizes. Even though we observe an increase in the memory consumption for larger datasets, it still remains below 2%. Note that, the CPU and memory consumption for verifying a single link is negligible and hence not reported in this paper.

Evaluating SPV Against Different Attacks. The objective of the third set of experiments is to investigate the effect of packet loss, network traffic and the

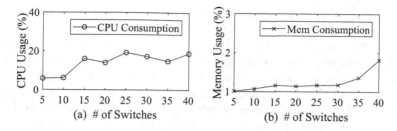

Fig. 5. Average (a) CPU usage and (b) memory usage by SPV to verify all existing links while varying the number of switches up to 40 and the number of links accordingly

packet relay attack on SPV. Figure 6(a) and (b) show the percentage of unverified links in the first round of SPV for 5,000 links in the network while varying the packet loss rate and increasing traffic throughput, respectively. More specifically, Fig. 6(a) depicts that the increase of the packet loss rate, the percentage of the unverified links linearly increases due to the fact that the probing packets may be also lost; however, since the distribution of packet loss rate is among all links in the network, and SPV only deals with one link at a time, the percentage of unverified links are always less than packet loss rate in the network which concludes that our approach is resilient to high packet loss rates in the network. In Fig. 6(b) by increasing the traffic throughput to the maximum allowed bandwidth while keeping the loss rate to 5%, the percentage of unverified links stays almost constant. The reason is that the flow installed by SPV to forward the probing packet, has a higher priority than other flows on a given switch and this fact makes SPV be independent of network congestion and only be dependent on network packet loss rate. To further alleviate this effect, SPV periodically sends probing packets until a link is verified and hence, all of the network links are eventually verified.

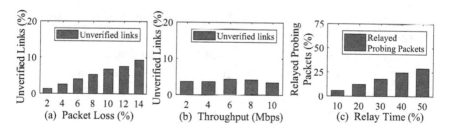

Fig. 6. Evaluating SPV with the presence of attackers in the network that tend to increase packet loss or congest the network by showing percentage of unverified links while varying the (a) packet loss rate (%) and (b) traffic throughput (Mbps), and (c) measuring the percentage of relayed probing packets while varying the percentage of the time that the attacker may relay all the traffic

In this part of the experiments, we measure the percentage of probing packets being affected in the presence of one or multiple malicious switch(es) that forward(s) 10% to 50% of the traffic at different time intervals. The effect of tampering probing packets by an attacker will depict quite similar results, as an attacker cannot distinguish a probing packet from host-generated packets. Figure 6(c) shows that the amount of forwarded probing packets remains less than 30% for the case a malicious switch forwards all the packets in 50% of the time, however, in this experiments we consider the worst case where the malicious switch is not detected until the last round of verification. The resilience of SPV to this attack can be further improved by using different probabilistic functions with different distributions in choosing the time intervals for sending the probing packets.

Applicability of SPV in a Real SDN/Cloud Topology. The objective of our last set of experiments is to validate the applicability of SPV in a real SDN/cloud topology. To this end, we utilize an accessible part of the topology of a real SDN/cloud hosted at one of the largest telecommunication vendors that comprises of OpenStack [27] cloud with 22 compute nodes, each having a software-based OpenFlow switch, to reside thousands of VMs. All 22 OVS switches are connected to each other in a mesh architecture having 231 bidirectional links. Table 2 reports the results obtained based on this real topology and compares them with the results for our largest fat-tree topology. The results illustrate that the verification time for an incremental link verification in the network remains almost constant (i.e., around 100 ms) independent of network topology and its size, and the verification time for all links in the multi-threading mode can rise up to 13 s. Other results presented in Table 2 also indicate a reasonable performance and demonstrate the practicality of our approach in a real-world SDN/cloud.

Table 2. Summary of the experimental results with real SDN/cloud topology

Results	SDN/Cloud mesh	Mininet fat-tree
All link verification time (MT)	13.2052 s	10.6406 s
All link verification time (ST)	134.147 s	26.1725 s
Single link verification time (ST)	100.306 ms	94.8919 ms
CPU consumption (ST)	8.50294%	18.79099%
Memory consumption (ST)	1.81817%	1.81003%

7 Discussion

This section discusses different concerns on SPV.

Exhausting Flow Table Capacity of SDN Switches. There exist several attacks (as described in [22,31]) to exhaust the flow table capacity of SDN switches which may affect the availability by adding new flow rules on those switches. Consequently, these attacks may affect the verification process of SPV by preventing the installation of flow rules related to forwarding the SPV_PKT packets. Even though such flow table overflow attacks are beyond the scope of this paper, existing solutions (e.g., [36]) to address them could be leveraged to avoid any effect on SPV.

Effect of Encrypted Communication Between Control and Data Planes. In case TLS is enabled for secure communications, administrators require to share en/decryption keys of control messages with SPV; which might be a practical assumption for an administrator intending to protect his/her network topology from poisoning attacks. However, if SPV would be implemented within the SDN controller, this explicit sharing of keys is unnecessary.

Implementing SPV within SDN Controller. The rationale behind placing SPV outside of SDN controller is to make it applicable to different implementations (e.g., [11,12,29]) of SDN controller with minimal effort. However, placing SPV within the SDN controller may help to further improve SPV's performance. For example, retrieving control messages or network topology would be much faster in the latter case. However, such design may decrease the overall security of SPV, since with the current design, SPV can be a hardened box/software which is easier to secure.

8 Related Work

This section discusses different categories of related works.

SDN Topology Poisoning Attack Detection Mechanisms. There exist several works (e.g., [3,10,16,32]) targeting SDN topology poisoning attacks. TopoGuard [16,32] proposes an OpenFlow-based SDN controller extension, which checks the legitimacy of switch ports and host migration to prevent host-based topology poisoning attacks. In contrast to SPV, TopoGuard can detect a wider range of attacks on both hosts and links. However, it still adopts a passive approach which means the detection relies on knowledge about the attacking methods used to fabricate the fake links. We consider SPV and TopoGuard complementary solutions due to their different advantages. SPHINX [10] proposes a more generic solution on detecting both known and potentially unknown attacks on network topology. In contrast to our work, SPHINX cannot detect the creation of fake links in the topology, which would falsify the generated flow graphs based on which the data plane verification is performed. In [3], the authors propose an LLDP packets authentication approach based on adding the HMAC of a switch ID and the corresponding port ID to the LLDP packet. Unlike SPV, it cannot handle fake link creation caused by relayed LLDP packets by malicious hosts or switches since it solely depends on HMAC authenticated LLDP packets.

OFDP Security Enhancement Mechanisms. Several works propose variations of the OFDP protocol for SDN security enhancement. Pakzad et al. [28]

propose a modified version of OFDP, namely, OFDPv2, which requires the SDN controller to send only one OFTP_PAKCKET_OUT message containing an LLDP packet to a switch and instructs the switch to advertise the LLDP packet in all its ports, instead of sending an OFTP_PAKCKET_OUT message for every port of each switch. sOFTDP [5] also proposes a variation of the OFDP protocol. The main idea is to transfer the burden of topology discovery from the SDN controller to the data-plane switches. Unlike SPV, both OFDPv2 [28] and sOFTDP [5] do not verify fake link creation.

Active Probing Techniques. Probing techniques are typically used to maliciously infer network specifications (e.g., firewall rules, OpenFlow rules, bandwidth estimation, flow tables usage and capacity, etc.). For instance, in [31], the authors utilize the delay required for flow installation on SDN switches to detect whether a network is an SDN. INSPIRE [23] relies on some senders located inside the network, a receiver deployed outside the network and a line sweep algorithm to select forged probing packets to be sent to the network in order to infer OpenFlow rules. INSPIRE can infer the flow rules installation mode (i.e., proactive or reactive), by measuring the delay between a packet sending time and its reception, then an apriori algorithm is used to discover the rules. In [7], the authors use active probing techniques based on crafted packets to trigger switch-controller communications, then they use round trip time (RTT) and packet-pair dispersion features to infer information about flow rules. The authors in [22] also use probing and RTT measurement to infer the OpenFlow switches' tables capacity and usage along with the flow rules' hard and idle timeouts. They also trigger controller-switch interactions by sending probing packets to infer the processing time of a specific rule. Unlike these works, SPV utilizes network probing as a defensive mechanism to deceive malicious hosts and SDN switches. Similarly to our work, in [9], network probing is used as a defensive technique. Therein, a periodic sampling-based approach is proposed to detect malicious OpenFlow switches in an SDN. Our effort can be seen as complementary to this work since the latter checks the legitimacy of switches but cannot verify the links between them.

9   Conclusion

The correctness of SDN controller view on network topology is known to be critical for making the right management decisions. However, recently discovered vulnerabilities in OFDP protocol show that poisoning network view of the SDN controller may lead to severe security attacks, such as man-in-the-middle or denial of service. In this paper, we proposed SPV, a novel stealthy probing-based approach, to significantly extend the scope of existing solutions, by generating and sending stealthy packets to incrementally verify legitimate links and detect fake links as well as the responsible malicious switches. As a proof of concept of our approach, we implemented SPV in an emulated SDN environment using Mininet and OpenDaylight. Through extensive experiments, we showed that SPV can respond in near real-time (e.g., less than 120 ms), which makes SPV a scalable solution for large SDN networks. We also measured the performance of SPV in a real SDN/cloud hosted at one of the largest telecommunication vendors to validate the applicability of SPV in a real environment. To further improve the accuracy and performance of SPV, considering traversal time of stealthy packets in the link verification procedure and integrating SPV within the SDN controller (for faster processing of control messages or being independent of public/private key sharing) can be considered as potential future work. Also, to enhance the security of SPV against certain attacks such as flow table exhaustion, adapting methods such as [22] could be beneficial. Moreover, the robustness of our packet generation mechanism can be further improved by leveraging machine learning techniques in analyzing network traffic.

Acknowledgements. The authors thank the anonymous reviewers for their valuable comments. This work is partially supported by the Natural Sciences and Engineering Research Council of Canada and Ericsson Canada under CRD Grant N01823.

Appendix

The SPV Architecture. Figure 7 depicts the architecture of SPV including its interactions with SDN. SPV has two major modules: Link Verification and Stealthy Packet Handler. In the following, we describe each module in details.

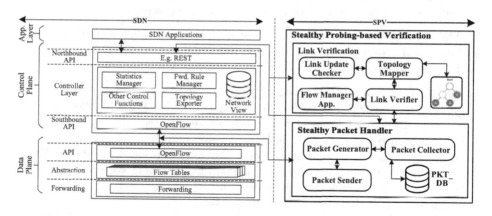

Fig. 7. SDN and stealthy probing-based verification (SPV) architecture

The Link Verification module is responsible for tracking and verifying the data plane changes, by making use of stealthy probing packets, which comprises the following modules.

1. **Link Update Checker.** As the very first step of SPV, the Link Update Checker module is to identify updates in the network through communications with the SDN controller[2] and inform the Link Verification module of any

---

[2] The communication is conducted via northbound API.

changes made to the network. This module is installed from the initialization of the network to verify the network topology incrementally.

2. **Topology Mapper.** This module maintains a tree data structure to locally store the up-to-date topology information provided by Link Update Checker. The tree stores the information of data plane devices, i.e., if it is a host or a switch or a link, along with their specifications, e.g., their status that is up/down, and other useful information such as Device IDs, Port IDs and so on. Also, the tree stores the received updates after verification procedure to maintain the validity status of every switch and their connecting links.

3. **Flow Manager.** This module works as an application to the SDN controller to communicate through the northbound API for querying the flows and statistics of a given switch and installing a given flow on a given switch. This module interacts with the Link Verifier module to perform the above-mentioned functionalities and provide the results.

4. **Link Verifier.** The Link Verifier module interacts with Topology Mapper, Flow Manager Application and Stealthy Packet Handler modules. Based on the input data from the Link Update Checker, the Link Verifier communicates with the Topology Mapper to get the link endpoints, and to query the flows and the statistics of them via the Flow Manager Application module. Also, this module relies on the Stealthy Packet Handler module, more specifically Packet Collector and Packet Generator modules, which are to generate the stealthy probing packets, and Packet Sender, which is responsible to transmit the packets to be traversed through the links to be verified.

The Stealthy Packet Handler is responsible for generating, sending and collecting stealthy probing packets to/from data plane. Details of corresponding modules are discussed below.

1. **Packet Generator.** This module is responsible to generate stealthy probing packets, namely, SPV_PKT packets, with the help of the Packet Collector module upon receiving a request from the Link Verifier module. The generation of stealthy probing packets is performed using two different algorithms (discussed in Sect. 3.2) depending on two possible situations. (i) A link is being verified for the first time, and (ii) a certain link is being verified again, i.e., further rounds of verification for a certain link which is not yet verified, due to the reasons such as loss of SPV_PKT packets.

2. **Packet Collector.** This module collects two types of packets. First, it collects and stores OFTP_PACKET_IN messages, that contain host generated packets in their content, in its local database, namely, PKT_DB, which are later used by Packet Generator. Second, it collects and stores OFTP_PACKET_IN messages that contain SPV_PKT, and reports them to the Link Verifier.

3. **Packet Sender.** This module is to send stealthy probing packets towards the source endpoint switches of the links to be verified. More specifically, the first responsibility of this module is to receive a stealthy probing packet and information of the link to be verified from the Link Verifier module. The second responsibility is to send the received packet to be traversed through the link to be verified by utilizing the SDN controller's northbound API.

References

1. OpenDaylight (2017). https://www.opendaylight.org/
2. Al-Fares, M., Loukissas, A., Vahdat, A.: A scalable, commodity data center network architecture. In: ACM SIGCOMM Computer Communication Review, vol. 38, pp. 63–74 (2008)
3. Alharbi, T., Portmann, M., Pakzad, F.: The (in)security of topology discovery in software defined networks. In: 40th Conference on Local Computer Networks (LCN), pp. 502–505. IEEE (2015)
4. Antikainen, M., Aura, T., Särelä, M.: Spook in your network: attacking an SDN with a compromised OpenFlow switch. In: Bernsmed, K., Fischer-Hübner, S. (eds.) NordSec 2014. LNCS, vol. 8788, pp. 229–244. Springer, Cham (2014). https://doi.org/10.1007/978-3-319-11599-3_14
5. Azzouni, A., Boutaba, R., Trang, N.T.M., Pujolle, G.: sOFTDP: secure and efficient topology discovery protocol for SDN. arXiv preprint arXiv:1705.04527 (2017)
6. Azzouni, A., Trang, N.T.M., Boutaba, R., Pujolle, G.: Limitations of OpenFlow topology discovery protocol. arXiv preprint arXiv:1705.00706 (2017)
7. Bifulco, R., Cui, H., Karame, G.O., Klaedtke, F.: Fingerprinting software-defined networks. In: 23rd International Conference on Network Protocols (ICNP) (2015)
8. Bui, T., et al.: Analysis of topology poisoning attacks in software-defined networking (2015)
9. Chi, P.W., Kuo, C.T., Guo, J.W., Lei, C.L.: How to detect a compromised SDN switch. In: 1st IEEE Conference on Network Softwarization (NetSoft) (2015)
10. Dhawan, M., Poddar, R., Mahajan, K., Mann, V.: SPHINX: detecting security attacks in software-defined networks. In: NDSS (2015)
11. Erickson, D.: Beacon (2013). https://openflow.stanford.edu/display/Beacon/Home
12. Floodlight, P.: Open source software for building software-defined networks (2017). http://www.projectfloodlight.org/floodlight/
13. Foundation, O.N.: OpenFlow switch specification version 1.3.5 (2014). https://www.opennetworking.org/software-defined-standards/specifications/
14. Goransson, P., Black, C., Culver, T.: Software Defined Networks: A Comprehensive Approach. Morgan Kaufmann, Burlington (2016)
15. Gude, N., Koponen, T., Pettit, J., Pfaff, B., Casado, M., McKeown, N., Shenker, S.: NOX: towards an operating system for networks. ACM SIGCOMM Comput. Commun. Rev. **38**(3), 105–110 (2008)
16. Hong, S., Xu, L., Wang, H., Gu, G.: Poisoning network visibility in software-defined networks: new attacks and countermeasures. In: NDSS (2015)
17. Jarraya, Y., Madi, T., Debbabi, M.: A survey and a layered taxonomy of software-defined networking. IEEE Commun. Surv. Tutor. **16**(4), 1955–1980 (2014)
18. Khan, S., Gani, A., Wahab, A.W.A., Guizani, M., Khan, M.K.: Topology discovery in software defined networks: threats, taxonomy, and state-of-the-art. IEEE Commun. Surv. Tutor. **19**(1), 303–324 (2017)
19. Kim, H., Ju, H.: Efficient method for inferring a firewall policy. In: 13th Asia-Pacific Network Operations and Management Symposium (APNOMS) (2011)
20. Kreutz, D., Ramos, F.M., Verissimo, P.E., Rothenberg, C.E., Azodolmolky, S., Uhlig, S.: Software-defined networking: a comprehensive survey. Proc. IEEE **103**(1), 14–76 (2015)
21. Lantz, B., Heller, B., McKeown, N.: A network in a laptop: rapid prototyping for software-defined networks. In: Proceedings of the 9th ACM SIGCOMM Workshop on Hot Topics in Networks, p. 19. ACM (2010)

22. Leng, J., Zhou, Y., Zhang, J., Hu, C.: An inference attack model for flow table capacity and usage: exploiting the vulnerability of flow table overflow in software-defined network. arXiv preprint arXiv:1504.03095 (2015)
23. Lin, P.C., Li, P.C., Nguyen, V.L.: Inferring OpenFlow rules by active probing in software-defined networks. In: 19th International Conference on Advanced Communication Technology (ICACT) (2017)
24. McKeown, N., et al.: OpenFlow: enabling innovation in campus networks. ACM SIGCOMM Comput. Commun. Rev. **38**(2), 69–74 (2008)
25. Medved, J., Varga, R., Tkacik, A., Gray, K.: Opendaylight: towards a model-driven SDN controller architecture. In: 15th International Symposium on a World of Wireless, Mobile and Multimedia Networks (WoWMoM) (2014)
26. Mininet: An instant virtual network on your laptop (or other PC) (2017). http://mininet.org/
27. OpenStack: Open source software for creating private and public clouds (2017). https://www.openstack.org/
28. Pakzad, F., Portmann, M., Tan, W.L., Indulska, J.: Efficient topology discovery in software defined networks. In: 2014 8th International Conference on Signal Processing and Communication Systems (ICSPCS), pp. 1–8. IEEE (2014)
29. POX: The pox controller (2013). https://github.com/noxrepo/pox
30. Scapy: Packet manipulation program (2017). http://www.secdev.org/projects/scapy/
31. Shin, S., Gu, G.: Attacking software-defined networks: a first feasibility study. In: Proceedings of the Second ACM SIGCOMM Workshop on Hot Topics in Software Defined Networking, pp. 165–166. ACM (2013)
32. Skowyra, R., et al.: Effective topology tampering attacks and defenses in software-defined networks. In: Proceedings of the 48th Annual IEEE/IFIP International Conference on Dependable Systems and Networks (DSN 2018), June 2018
33. vSwitch, O.: Production quality, multilayer open virtual switch (2016). http://openvswitch.org/
34. Xia, W., Wen, Y., Foh, C.H., Niyato, D., Xie, H.: A survey on software-defined networking. IEEE Commun. Surv. Tutor. **17**(1), 27–51 (2015)
35. Xia, W., Zhao, P., Wen, Y., Xie, H.: A survey on data center networking (DCN): infrastructure and operations. IEEE Commun. Surv. Tutor. **19**(1), 640–656 (2017)
36. Zhang, M., Bi, J., Bai, J., Dong, Z., Li, Y., Li, Z.: FTGuard: a priority-aware strategy against the flow table overflow attack in SDN. In: Proceedings of the SIGCOMM Posters and Demos, pp. 141–143. ACM (2017)

Trust Anchors in Software Defined Networks

Nicolae Paladi[1]($\boxtimes$), Linus Karlsson[2], and Khalid Elbashir[3]

[1] RISE SICS, Kista, Sweden
nicolae.paladi@ri.se
[2] Lund University, Lund, Sweden
linus.karlsson@eit.lth.se
[3] KTH - Royal Institute of Technology, Stockholm, Sweden
elbashir@kth.se

Abstract. Advances in software virtualization and network processing lead to increasing network softwarization. Software network elements running on commodity platforms replace or complement hardware components in cloud and mobile network infrastructure. However, such commodity platforms have a large attack surface and often lack granular control and tight integration of the underlying hardware and software stack. Often, software network elements are either themselves vulnerable to software attacks or can be compromised through the bloated trusted computing base. To address this, we protect the core security assets of network elements - authentication credentials and cryptographic context - by provisioning them to and maintaining them exclusively in isolated execution environments. We complement this with a secure and scalable mechanism to enroll network elements into software defined networks. Our evaluation results show a negligible impact on run-time performance and only a moderate performance impact at the deployment stage.

1 Introduction

Software Defined Networking (SDN) is a widely used approach to operate network infrastructure in virtualized environments. Separation of forwarding and control logic, a core idea of this model, is often realized by software network elements in a virtualized network infrastructure deployed on commodity hardware. However, by departing from hardware network elements with tightly couped software and hardware often provided by the same vendor [20], SDN broke previous assumptions, outdated best-practices and introduced new vulnerabilities [41, 42]. Scott-Hayward et al. outlined a series of attack vectors that can lead to unauthorized access, data leakage or modification, malicious applications on the network, configuration issues, and a wider collection of system-level security vulnerabilities [49]. This concern applies to both the data plane and the application plane in SDN deployments. On the data plane, related literature describes both potential attacks on SDN in case of a virtual switch compromise [2], partly demonstrated

J. Lopez et al. (Eds.): ESORICS 2018, LNCS 11099, pp. 485–504, 2018.
https://doi.org/10.1007/978-3-319-98989-1_24

in [55]. Malicious applications deployed on the SDN infrastructure are a particular concern in virtualized environments. They affect network security both directly (by intercepting or modifying traffic), or indirectly through horizontal attacks aimed to leak authentication credentials and encryption keys [54].

Earlier research addressed SDN security through additional services [21, 48, 53], formal verification [6] and isolated execution using Intel Software Guard Extensions (SGX) [28,43,44,52], and most popular network element implementation support communication over transport layer security (TLS) [15]. Despite these efforts, the confidentiality and integrity of authentication credentials of network elements in SDN remain unaddressed. In particular, the existing approaches to provision authentication credentials to network elements in SDN are either plain insecure or both insecure and unscalable, requiring manual steps[1] [38]. Moreover, credentials provisioned to network elements in virtualized environments are often stored in plaintext on the file system. Adversaries exploiting vulnerabilities in process and virtualization isolation can access authentication credentials to perform network attacks or impersonate network elements. In this paper, we address two complementary questions: (1) *How can authentication credentials be securely provisioned to software network elements in SDN deployments?* and (2) *How can the TLS context of virtual switches be protected on compromised hosts?*

1.1 Contributions

In this work, we present the following contributions:

- A secure, practical, and scalable mechanism to provision authentication credentials and bootstrap communication between software network elements.
- TLSonSGX[2], a library allowing to maintain authentication credentials and the TLS context exclusively in isolated execution environments.
- A novel approach to restricting the availability of authentication credentials for SDN components to hosts with an attested trusted computing base.
- A first thorough analysis of the performance trade-offs of deploying components of network elements in SGX enclaves.

1.2 Structure

The remainder of this paper is structured as follows. We present the system model and threat model in Sect. 2. Next, we describe the proposed solution in Sect. 3 and its implementation in Sect. 4. We evaluate the approach in Sect. 5, discuss the related work in Sect. 6, outline limitations and future work in Sect. 7 and conclude in Sect. 8.

---

[1] Indeed, the Open vSwitch manual contains phrases as "Write the fingerprint down on a slip of paper and copy sc-req.pem to the machine that contains the PKI structure".

[2] Source code available: https://github.com/TLSonSGX/TLSonSGX.

2   System and Threat Model

We consider an SDN infrastructure deployed on commodity platforms in a distributed system, such as in a cloud platform or a mobile communications network. The infrastructure is managed by the *administrators* of a *network operator*. Physical access to the platforms is restricted and auditable.

System Model. Administrators use *orchestrators* to manage network infrastructure, software components and network services [20]. They deploy network elements on the *data plane, control plane* and *application plane*. The *data plane* consists of hardware or software switches (e.g. Open vSwitch [47]) and communication links between them. The *control plane* consists of a logically centralized *network controller* (e.g. ONOS [7], Floodlight [25]). The network controller manages software switches through protocols such as OpenFlow [34] (to add or remove flows) or OVSDB [46] (to create ports and tunnels); it manages hardware switches through OpenFlow (if supported) or other interfaces, such as NETCONF [17]. The *application plane* comprises *network functions* that implement services such as traffic engineering, monitoring, or caching. A *Virtual Network Function* (VNF) is a virtualisation of a network function [20]. Orchestrators deploy VNFs upon request from the network controller or a tenant. The network controller configures flows and steers traffic to the network functions.

Network elements on the data-, control-, and application planes communicate over two application programming interfaces (APIs). The controller communicates with data plane elements over the *southbound* API, commonly Openflow [8,34,51] and with application plane elements over the *northbound* API.

At deployment time, the orchestrator provisions TLS certificates to network elements during the *enrollment* process. Furthermore, to protect the data within the SDN deployment, the network controller enforces communication over TLS with mutual authentication on both southbound and northbound APIs.

Threat Model. Similar to earlier work on SDN security threats [30,41], we assume physical security of the platforms underlying the SDN infrastructure and correct implementation of cryptographic algorithms and communication security protocols, such as TLS [15]. The adversary has the capabilities of a system administrator with remote access to commodity platforms in the SDN infrastructure. The adversary can intercept, drop and modify packets on the southbound and northbound interfaces. Furthermore, the adversary can run arbitrary network elements in the SDN deployment and elsewhere [20]. The adversary can read the memory of the commodity platforms, exploit vulnerabilities in network elements on the data- and application planes, and circumvent virtualization isolation [2].

3   Solution Space

We next present the approach for provisioning and protecting authentication credentials on the data and application planes of SDN deployments. We first introduce three building blocks to create trust anchors in SDN deployments: Software Guard Extensions (SGX), Trusted Platform Module (TPM) and Integrity Measurement Architecture (IMA).

3.1 Trust Anchors

We use SGX enclaves [1,32,33,61] to create trusted execution environments (TEEs) during operating system execution. We use the TEEs to store authentication credentials and execute cryptographic operations for network elements. SGX enclaves rely on a trusted computing base (TCB) of code and data loaded at enclave creation time, processor firmware and processor hardware. Program execution within an enclave is transparent to the underlying operating system and other mutually distrusting enclaves on the platform. Enclaves operate in a dedicated memory area called the Enclave Page Cache, a range of DRAM that cannot be accessed by system software or peripherals [23,33]. The CPU firmware and hardware are the root of trust of an enclave; it prevents access to the enclave's memory by the operating system and other enclaves. Remote attestation [12] allows an enclave to provide integrity guarantees of its contents [1].

We use TPMs to store platform integrity measurements collected during boot, and attest the integrity of platforms hosting the SDN infrastructure. A TPM is a discrete component on the platform motherboard and its state is distinct from the state of the platform. TPMs provide secure non-volatile storage, cryptographic key generation and use, sealed storage and support (remote) attestation [56]. TPMs assume platform integrity by identifying and reporting the platform state that comprises the hardware and software components [36]. In this context, *trust* is based on the conjecture that a certain behaviour can be expected based on the reported platform state [42]. TPMs can prove the association between a cryptographically verifiable identity and the host platform [56,57].

We use Linux IMA to measure the integrity of the TCB. Linux IMA measures a predefined set of files on the system by hashing their contents and storing the values in a measurement list; it can be configured to detect modifications of files at runtime. To guarantee the integrity of the measurement list, its trust can be rooted in the TPM. The system's trustworthiness can be assessed by a remote appraiser by comparing the measurement list to an expected configuration [12]. We utilize IMA to collect measurements of the network elements on the platform. During the remote attestation of the platform, we use the measurement list to verify the integrity - and implicitly the trustworthiness - of network elements.

3.2 Data Plane

At cloud platform deployment time, an orchestrator deploys and runs virtual switches on the underlying compute resources. To enable network connectivity, the orchestrator instructs virtual switches to add (or delete) ports whenever virtualized execution environments are instantiated or torn down.

Fig. 1. TLSonSGX system design

For a secure deployment, the administrator must ensure both a secure installation of hardware and software, as well as provision the correct initial configuration of the virtual switch instances in the cloud infrastructure. In turn, secure generation of keys and provisioning of certificates is a precondition to ensuring security of the initial deployment configuration. Furthermore, ensuring the integrity of virtual switch binaries and configurations is a precondition for ensuring the run-time security of the deployed instances.

We address this with a new library, **TLSonSGX**, that enables virtual switches to use a cryptographic library running in a TEE (see Fig. 1). TLSon-SGX provides an abstraction layer and a wrapper around the cryptographic library deployed in a TEE, allowing to easily substitute the implementation depending on performance, functionality and licensing aspects. Following this approach, TLS sessions originate and terminate within the TEE and the generated keys and certificates are confined to the TEE, ensuring the confidentiality and integrity of core assets, such as generated keys, certificates and TLS context, even in the event of a host compromise. This, in combination with an infrastructure monitoring system and a file integrity subsystem (such as Linux IMA), prevents the adversary from impersonating data plane network elements [55] and from enrolling additional network elements into the infrastructure.

Secure provisioning of authentication certificates is challenging, especially at scale, and depends on the capability to establish a secure communication channel between the certificate authority (CA) and the target component. Several vendor-specific solutions exist [27,33]. To support the deployment, we introduced a CA with extended functionality to sign certificates for the virtual switches and the SDN controller. CA certificates are provisioned to the virtual switches and the SDN controller in the deployment and are subsequently used for mutual authentication. Beyond secure certificate provisioning, the extended CA verifies the integrity of the virtual switches before signing their certificates. We leverage the remote attestation capability provided by the TPM to verify the TCB integrity on the host platform. The TPM is in this protocol the root of trust that stores and provides a signed quote of the integrity measurements of the virtual switch binary and ancillary libraries, collected by IMA.

3.3 Application Plane

Network elements on the application layer, such as VNFs, must be authenticated and integrity verified prior to enrollment into the SDN infrastructure. As the

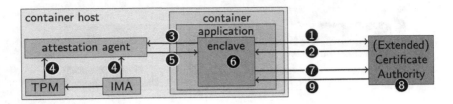

Fig. 2. Enrollment steps in the application layer.

controller requires mutual authentication with all its clients, this ensures that only trustworthy VNFs can communicate with the controller. Similar to the approach above, the TPM is used as a root of trust.

We use SGX enclaves to ensure integrity and confidentiality of the authentication credentials for enrolled VNFs. Storing the credentials in SGX enclaves reduces the attack surface to the enclave TCB and offers an additional layer of protection even in the case of a breach of the platform TCB. We discuss the limitations of this approach in Sect. 6.3.

We next provide an overview of the proposed solution (see Fig. 2). The extended certificate authority (CA) introduced above determines whether or not a VNF configuration is valid, by matching against a list of known good configurations. If a configuration is valid, the CA can also sign certificates. This component can be collocated with the network elements in the deployment, or be deployed and operated by a third party. We assume that the CA root certificate is provided to the SDN controller during initial setup.

At the start of the enrollment protocol, the orchestrator launches an execution environment (such as a bare-metal host, virtual machine or container) with TPM and IMA support. Together, these two mechanisms record both the software and hardware configuration in a measurement log, including the TCB of the VNFs. The measurement log is anchored in the TPM located of the host, allowing the use of the TPM's remote attestation functionality. Note that both a native and a virtualized TPM can be used in this case.

Similar to [62] we use an *attestation agent* running on the container host. This agent proxies the communication between the container and the TPM and IMA. We propose a solution where the attestation agent is only accessible from the container running on the same host. This prevents direct communication between the attestation agent and the CA. To prevent cuckoo attacks [45], the communication passes through the container application and the enclave and ensures that the enclave is running on the same host.

The enrollment phase consists of the following steps (see Fig. 2): Upon initialization of the container and application, the latter requests a nonce from the CA ❶, ❷. Next, the application requests from the attestation agent a quote for the given nonce, together with the IMA measurement list ❸. The agent communicates with the TPM and the IMA to retrieve the data ❹, and returns the data to the application ❺. The enclave generates a new private key and a certificate signing request (CSR) and stores it in the SGX enclave ❻. The application sends the quote, measurement list, and the CSR to the CA **❼**, that verifies the message **❽**. As the measurement list covers both the host system and the container TCB, the integrity of the host and target containers can be validated. If the measurement values match known good configurations, the CA signs the CSR and returns the signed certificate to the enclave **❾**. At this point, the VNF can establish a secure TLS connection with the SDN controller. The proposed solution ensures that only trustworthy VNFs receive valid certificates and can be enrolled in the SDN infrastructure.

4   Implementation

To facilitate adoption and obtain reproducible results, we implemented the proposed solution using common open-source libraries and execution isolation features available on commodity platforms. We used Open vSwitch (OvS), a popular software switch implementation and the Ryu and Floodlight SDN controllers, mainly due to their popularity and simple configuration. In the remainder of this section, we first describe the implementation of TLSonSGX on the data plane. Next, we describe the security mechanisms deployed on the application plane.

4.1   TLSonSGX

The SGX programming model requires that applications deployed in SGX enclaves have an external component that can be called by other processes running on the operating system, and that in turn maps such calls to software in the enclave. This external component is not part of the enclave and its integrity cannot be attested using the SGX integrity attestation mechanisms, thus is considered *untrusted*; in contrast, the code running in the enclave is considered *trusted* once its integrity has been attested. Following the SGX programming model, the untrusted code portion of the TLSonSGX library is a wrapper that maps OpenSSL external methods (used by Open vSwitch) internally into enclave calls (ECALLs). The trusted portion of the code, contained within the SGX enclave, implements the ECALLs by utilizing the SGX trusted TLS library. Support for TLS libraries in SGX varies and evolves continuously; we have chosen the mbed TLS [31] library considering its sufficient support for SGX enclaves.

Considering that authentication keys and certificates are confined to the enclave, we modified OvS to use only a limited set of OpenSSL external methods that we subsequently implemented in TLSonSGX. The OpenSSL library implements three data structures: `SSL_METHOD`, `SSL_CTX`, and `SSL`.

These data structures all contain crucial information for TLS connection security, therefore we create and confine them within the enclave. The objects are passed by the OvS instance via an unmodified API using the external methods we implemented. They are created, confined, and handled inside the enclave during the operation of the virtual switch, and hence discarded and not passed to ECALLs. There is no one-to-one mapping in mbed TLS for these three structures, hence we redefine these structures using mbed TLS primitives (specifically the `mbedtls_ssl_config` and `mbedtls_ssl_context` data structures).

The code in `stream-ssl.c` implements the interface between OvS and the OpenSSL library. We extended the OvS configuration script and `stream-ssl.c` with a new compilation flag, SGX. If the SGX flag is set at compilation time, `stream-ssl.c` will use the TLSonSGX static library instead of the OpenSSL library. Moreover, the sections of `stream-ssl.c` that load keys and certificates from the file system become redundant and are omitted.

4.2 Application Plane

On the application plane, the solution consists of three major components: the network application, the attestation agent, and the certificate authority.

The attestation agent is a service running on the container host, setup to listen to connections from containers running on the same host, as those are the only containers able to request a quote from this host. The attestation agent can return both a copy of the measurement list, and a quote from the TPM. The quotes are made over the appropriate PCR registers to capture the current configuration, together with a nonce to prevent replay attacks. Interfacing with the TPM is implemented using the TrouSerS TSS library [22] on Linux. Using an attestation agent reduced the code base of the containers, since they do not have to interface directly with a TPM or Linux IMA.

Next, the CA fulfills two goals. First, it validates the integrity of the components by validating the quote, and compares the configuration and measurement list to known good values. Second, if the two values match, the CA signs the applications CSR. We implemented this using the OpenSSL C library to create the signature with a pre-configured root certificate. This root certificate is distributed to the SDN controller, allowing it to validate the certificate chain.

The final component is the container application. Using mbed TLS [31], we implemented an application that supports the attestation sequence described earlier, and communicates with both the attestation agent and the CA. Once the attestation sequence is finished, the application can connect to an SDN controller using the credentials generated and confined within the enclave.

5 Evaluation

5.1 Testbed

We evaluated the solution on the testbed described below (see Fig. 3).

Hardware. The host platform is a Lenovo Thinkpad T460s with a dual-core Intel® Core™ i7-6600U CPU clocked at 2.60 GHz with SGX support. VM_1 was created with 1 virtual CPU, and VM_2 with 2 virtual CPUs; both VMs had 4 GB RAM, 30 GB of storage, and used virtio as vNIC. We used Ubuntu 16.04.1 (with OvS and SGX drivers and SDKs) on both the host and VMs. To enable the use of SGX within the VM environment, we created VM_2 using patched versions of QEMU and KVM provided by the SGX project[3] and Intel SGX SDK, v1.8.

---

[3] SGX Virtualization, 01.org/intel-software-guard-extensions/sgx-virtualization.

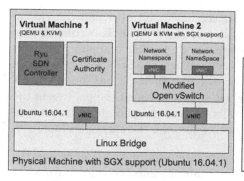

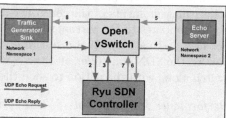

Fig. 3. Testbed architecture   **Fig. 4.** UDP packet path

We enabled hyper-threading on the host platform, yielding 4 logical CPUs. We pinned VM_1 to CPU 2 and VM_2 to CPUs 1 and 3 (same core). In VM_2, we pinned the virtual switch to CPU 1 and the traffic generator/sink and echo server to CPU 2, in order to reduce inter-core communication overhead [50]. However, due to the limited number of cores on the host (2 cores) we were unable to implement strict CPU isolation by dedicating entire cores. In Sect. 5.3 we discuss the potential implications of this.

Software. We used OvS release 2.6.0[4]. In VM_2, we deployed OvS binaries compiled and linked with our TLSonSGX (as explained in Sect. 3.2). We created two network namespaces, each with a port connected to the OvS instance.

The CA uses OpenSSL 1.1.0d for TLS communication with OvS and to sign the OvS and the SDN controller certificates. We used OpenSSL, rather than TLSonSGX for the CA implementation for two reasons: (1) the CA implementation is trusted according to the threat model; and (2) to ensure interoperability between TLSonSGX (on the client side) and OpenSSL (on the server side).

We chose the Ryu SDN open-source controller as it supports TLS communication with OpenFlow switches[5]. It is written in Python and is widely used in research [3] and in commercial products[6].

5.2   Evaluation Targets

SDN Controller Program. In the SDN model, the virtual switch forwards the first packet in a new flow to the SDN controller. The controller replies with a flow table update, the action to be executed by the switch to handle the packet, and the packet itself. The virtual switch handles subsequent packets in the flow according to the newly installed rule in the flow table.

---

[4] Commit 4b27db644a8c8e8d2640f2913cbdfa7e4b78e788.

[5] See Ryu 4.9 Documentation, https://ryu.readthedocs.io/en/latest/tls.html.

[6] See SmartSDN Controller, https://osrg.github.io/ryu-book/.

To exercise the communication between the SDN controller and the virtual switch and to capture latency measurements, we designed the SDN controller as a learning L2 switch, with a MAC address to port number mapping table. To collect measurements of the controller-induced latency, the SDN controller sends no flow updates to the virtual switch (otherwise we would get one measurement per new destination). As a result, the virtual switch sends all the packets in the flow to the SDN controller and the controller returns the packets to the virtual switch along with the action to send the packet through the corresponding port.

Performance Measurements. We are primarily interested in the latency and the time required to generate key pairs and to obtain a signed certificate from the CA. When it comes to latency, the choice of traffic generators was limited to those that can provide latency measurements. Moreover, such measurements require that clocks of both traffic source and sink are synchronized (or co-exist in the same host). Having investigated several traffic generators (qperf[7], pktgen [37], moongen [16], and Click [35]), we chose Click due to its flexibility and versatility.

We implemented a traffic generator and sink using the Click Modular Router. This allows us to measure round trip latency for UDP packets of varying sizes, at a rate of 500 Packets Per Second (pps) using the Click element StoreUDPTimeSeqRecord. Increasing the rate beyond that results in much higher latency variance (see Sect. 5.3).

We deployed the traffic generator and sink in network namespace *(i)* and a UDP echo server in network namespace *(ii)*. The echo server echoes the received UDP packet back to the traffic generator and sink. The two network namespaces communicate through Open vSwitch, as illustrated in Fig. 4. To benchmark the performance, we replicated the measurements in a clone of VM$_2$, using a vanilla QEMU and KVM, with a default Open vSwitch implementation that uses OpenSSL.

5.3 TLSonSGX Performance Evaluation

Keys and Certificate Generation Time. This measurement concerns the time from SSL_library_init invocation in the Open vSwitch until the key pairs and signed certificate are loaded to the enclave's memory. See measurement results in Table 1. There is no corresponding measurement in a vanilla Open vSwitch, since keys and certificates are handled manually [38]. However, as this operation is only executed once when ovs-vswitchd starts, the measurements show that there is little *de facto* overhead introduced by the implementation.

Packet Round Trip Latency. In this section we discuss and analyze the packet round trip latency. The measurements do not include the key generation time; likewise, the time to establish a TLS session is not included, as it must already be established before packets can flow. The TLS session remains active unless one of the two ends (Open vSwitch or SDN controller) terminates the session.

---

[7] See qperf man page.

Table 1. Keys and certificate generation time. 1000 measurements.

Mean	0.344 s
Variance	0.0488
1st Quartile	0.186 s
Median	0.276 s
3rd Quartile	0.434 s

Table 2. Packet rate vs. average CPU utilization.

Packet rate	OpenSSL	TLSonSGX
500 pps	25%	61%
1000 pps	40%	78%
2000 pps	49%	96%

Packet Size. The IP packet size received by the Open vSwitch from the traffic generator is bounded by the Maximum Transmission Unit (MTU) of the network namespace port connected to the Open vSwitch (1500 bytes in our tests). Open vSwitch encapsulates the received packet in an OpenFlow `Packet In` message, adding an 18 bytes header [13], that is in return encapsulated in a TLS record sent from the Open vSwitch to the SDN controller. If the packet sent by the traffic generator is larger than the MTU, then it is fragmented and Open vSwitch handles it as two separate `Packet In` messages to the SDN controller.

The TLS record adds a 5-byte header. Depending on the cipher suite negotiated between the server and the client, a padding field (up to 15 bytes) is added, and the TLS record is appended with a Message Authentication Code (MAC) computed over the data. In the handshake messages exchanged between Open vSwitch and the SDN controller in our tests, the negotiated cipher suite was `ECDHE-RSA-AES256-SHA`, which provides perfect forward secrecy through the use of an Elliptic Curve Diffie-Hellman key exchange [9], while the bulk encryption use 256-bit AES in CBC-mode with SHA-1 for MAC [11].

We measure the latency for increasing packet sizes ranging from 64 bytes up to 1408 bytes (in increments of 64 bytes), including the Ethernet and IP headers (minus the Cyclic Redundancy Check). The upper limit is set to avoid subsequent fragmentation between the Open vSwitch and the SDN controller.

Packet Rate Selection and CPU Utilization. We excluded outliers with a round trip latency over 2.5 ms from the captured data: 5237 outliers when testing OpenSSL and 11622 outliers when testing TLSonSGX, out of 220000 samples for each implementation. We investigated the CPU utilization to identify the cause of the outliers and the order-of-magnitude difference in the outlier numbers between the two implementations. In both implementations, inside the VM, the first vCPU reaches 100% utilization due to the Click packet generation process pinned to it, even at rates lower than 500 pps (i.e., 50, 100, 200 pps). However, the second vCPU, where `ovs-vswitchd` process is pinned, has a higher average CPU utilization when TLSonSGX is used compared to OpenSSL (see Table 2). Increasing the rate beyond 500 pps leads to increasing the second vCPU's utilization and average latency. Thus, we chose 500 pps as a suitable and optimal maximum rate for further measurements and analysis. Using SGX causes increased CPU utilization due to the overhead of transitioning to and from the memory enclave.

Latency and Packet Size. The packet round trip latency measurements are plotted in a boxplot comparing TLSonSGX with the vanilla Open vSwitch with OpenSSL when forwarding UDP packets of a range of sizes (outliers were excluded, as stated above). Figure 5 shows a plot of latency versus packet size.

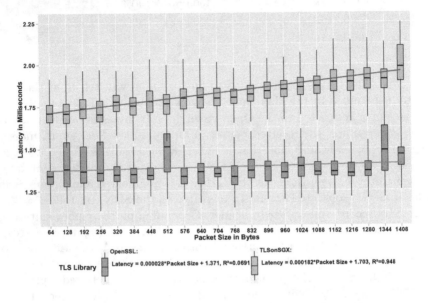

Fig. 5. UDP packet round trip latency vs. packet size

Each box represents the data between first and third quartile, the thick line in the box represents the median. The upper whisker is the minimum value between the data maximum and 3rd Quartile $+ 1.5 * \text{IQR}$, where IQR is the interquartile range. The lower whisker is the maximum value between the data minimum and 1st Quartile $- 1.5 * \text{IQR}$ [18].

A linear regression analysis of means shows that at zero byte TLSonSGX adds an overhead of 0.33 ms compared to OpenSSL. In implementations the latency increases linearly with packet size; we estimate this increase to 28 ns per byte for OpenSSL, and 182 ns per byte for TLSonSGX. While the linear increase is consistent with our expectations (larger packets require more processing time), the increase per byte is higher in TLSonSGX than in OpenSSL (154 ns per byte). This, and the extra cost of 0.33 ms at zero byte are also expected due to the transition overhead to and from the memory enclave.

Once a packet is received at an Open vSwitch port from the network name space, `ovs-vswitchd` triggers `ecall_ssl_write` to encrypt and send the packet to the SDN controller, while checking the SSL state (`ecall_ssl_get_state`) before and after the write ECALL. Since `ovs-vswitchd` uses non-blocking sockets, `ovs-vswitchd` keeps reading and returning from the socket (`ecall_ssl_read`), while comparing the SSL state before and after the read (`ecall_ssl_get_state`). If a negative value is returned (WANT_READ) from `ecall_ssl_read` then it triggers (`ecall_ssl_get_error`) to retrieve the error code which indicates that the read call must be repeated and accordingly continue the loop. If a positive value is returned, there is a response from the controller. The controller will respond with two packets: (1) the original packet itself; (2) the action needed by the switch to forward the packet to the second network name space. The same flow will run during the return trip from the second network name space to the first one.

Table 3. Analysis of packet latency (all measurements are in milliseconds**)

Size (B)	TLSonSGX	OpenSSL	Diff	ecall_ssl_				Total enclave access
				read	write	get_state*	get_error*	
64	1.6500	1.2682	0.3817	0.0047	0.0646	0.0047	0.0043	0.2966
128	1.6667	1.2722	0.3944	0.0048	0.0676	0.0047	0.0043	0.3040
256	1.6820	1.2844	0.3976	0.0049	0.0725	0.0047	0.0043	0.3146
512	1.6852	1.2955	0.3897	0.0049	0.0828	0.0047	0.0043	0.3350
1024	1.6963	1.3145	0.3818	0.0049	0.1022	0.0047	0.0043	0.3740

* `ecall_ssl_get_state` and `ecall_ssl_get_error` are independent of packet size.
** Measurements captured in a different iteration than in Fig. 5.

To analyze and break down the time difference between OpenSSL and TLSon-SGX, we traced the ECALLs indirectly called by `ovs-vswitchd` during the packet's round trip. We measured the time consumed for each ECALL and repeated the measurement 10000 times per packet size. Table 3 lists the mean values for each of the four different ECALLs. The last column in the table shows the sum of all ECALLs times per packet round trip.

We noticed that the duration of `ecall_ssl_write` is longer (and increases with packet size) than that of other ECALLs. This is because `ecall_ssl_write` is the only ECALL that writes from a buffer with a pointer outside the enclave (unprotected memory) to the enclave memory. All other ECALLs do the opposite. According to the manual, ECALLs that pass an external pointer into the enclave are slow, since a buffer is allocated inside the enclave memory[8]. Before copying the contents of the external buffer into the enclave memory, the content and the size of the buffer referenced by the external pointer are verified for every call to prevent overwriting enclave code or data.

Recall from the system model (consistent with a typical SDN deployment) that only the first packet in the flow is sent to the SDN controller. As a result, crafting a small enough first packet (64 bytes) allows to optimize the latency and reduce the time to add the flow rule in the Open vSwitch flow table.

---

[8] Pointer Handling, Intel® Software Guard Extensions SDK, https://software.intel.com/en-us/node/708975.

Table 4. Attestation time in application plane for various stages of the attestation sequence. Stages with execution time <0.010 s removed.

Stage	Mean	Variance	Median
TPM quote	0.332 s	0.000159	0.335 s
Key generation	0.326 s	0.050746	0.266 s
CSR signing	0.011 s	0.000002	0.010 s
Total attestation time	0.686 s	0.050849	0.622 s

5.4 Application Plane Evaluation

In the application plane, we are mostly interested in performance measurement regarding the attestation time. Every time a container is launched, both the container itself and the host it is running on must be attested. In this section, we focus on measuring the attestation time for the proposed application plane design. There are of course other relevant performance aspects, such as time required for the actual TLS connection to the controller, but we refer to previous work for such measurements [19].

The benchmarks were made by repeatedly launching the application which triggers the attestation. We ran 1000 tests, and calculated the mean and median values of the total attestation time (see results in Table 4). As seen from the table, the attestation time is well below one second in the average case. Breaking down the execution time to various stages of the attestation, and presenting those with an execution time of ≥0.010 s, we see that the majority of the attestation time is spent in two different stages: (1) waiting for the TPM chip to generate the quote, and (2) generating the private key within the enclave. Stage (1) is implemented in the TPM chip itself, while stage (2) depends on the size and type of key generated. A 2048-bit RSA key was used for the measurements presented above. We also note that our current implementation is not optimized, and it may be possible to reduce the execution time even further.

6 Related Work

6.1 Isolating Network Elements

Protecting the sensitive code and data of network elements is a topic of active on-going research. Jacquin proposed an architecture that used a hardware root of trust to remotely attest the integrity of virtualization hosts in SDN infrastructure [26]. Furthermore, commodity TEEs were used in case studies on securing network applications [29,52], implemented using OpenSGX, an emulator of SGX [27]. TruSDN is a framework for bootstrapping trust in an SDN infrastructure implemented using OpenSGX [43]. It supports secure provisioning of switches in SGX enclaves, a secure communication channel between switches and SDN controller, and secure communication between endpoints in the network using session keys that are generated per flow and used only during the lifetime of the flow. Similarly, *Trusted Click* [14] explores the feasibility of performing network processing in SGX enclaves.

SCONE enables operators to protect confidentiality and integrity of computation in application containers against an adversary with root access to the container host [4]. SCONE achieves this by deploying containers within SGX enclaves and relies on a `libc` library ported to the SGX environment to reduce performance impact of context switches between SGX enclaves and the underlying OS, at the cost of expanding the TCB.

Our solution addresses both confidentiality of long-term credentials and session keys, as well as integrity of the network element platform. In particular, we enable network elements on remotely attested hosts to protect their communication with the network controller using a TLS library and credentials in a local SGX enclave. This allows us to protect core assets with insignificant performance overhead and minimal changes to network element implementations. Porting entire applications into SGX enclaves - as proposed in the related work above - expands the attack surface to both software vulnerabilities and side-channel attacks. We avoid this by only porting to the enclaves a minimal TCB of the network elements. We reduce the TCB by only confining the TLSonSGX library, credentials, and TLS session information to the enclave.

6.2   Enrolling Network Elements

Incomplete or incorrect network views are an attack vector in SDN deployments [40]. The Secure Network Bootstrapping Infrastructure (SNBI) protocol [39] bootstraps secure communication channels of network elements and controllers and provisions the keys required for secure communication. To enable connectivity to the network devices, SNBI assigns unique IPv6 addresses (based on the unique device identifier) or and bootstraps devices with the required keys. However, the SNBI protocol is not resistant against impersonation attacks on network elements and fails to specify a protocol for software network elements with similar security features. We address the shortcomings of SNBI by attesting the integrity of the trusted computing base of the platforms hosting network elements prior to provisioning authentication credentials; the credentials are stored in a secure enclave and as described in Sect. 4.1, never leave the enclave.

6.3   TLS Implementations for SGX

There are several known TLS libraries ported to SGX enclaves. TaLoS [5] terminates TLS communication inside the container enclave by providing a port of LibreSSL library into SGX and thus maintaining OpenSSL API, including APIs to set private keys and certificates from outside the enclave. In this paper, keys and certificates are maintained inside the enclave and no APIs are exposed to manipulate them. Furthermore, TaLoS was not available at the time of writing.

Initially, mbed TLS was the only available port of a TLS library into SGX in Linux [31]. Intel® [24] and wolfSSL [59] provided a port to Linux in May

2017 and June 2017 respectively. However, none of these three provided an unmodified OpenSSL API that is exposed outside the enclave. Thus, none of the TLS libraries for SGX enclaves expose the required functionality. We implemented TLSonSGX to address the lack of usable implementations. TLSonSGX implements a wrapper around mbed TLS Trusted SGX library that exposes the OpenSSL APIs (that are needed for Open vSwitch TLS operations) outside the enclave.

Popular TLS libraries with support for execution in SGX enclaves (OpenSSL, GnuTLS, mbed TLS, WolfSSL, LibreSSL) are vulnerable to Bleichenbacher attacks [10] and a modified version padding oracle attacks [58] on branch level, cache line level and page level [60]. Such attacks can be mitigated by using the Diffie-Hellman (DH) key exchange instead of RSA-based key exchanges and *Authenticated Encryption with Associated Data* (AEAD) mode for encryption [60]. TLSonSGX is compatible with the mitigation suggested in [60] and can be configured to enforce DH key exchanges and AEAD encryption mode.

7   Limitations and Future Work

We implemented a prototype and tested it using one dual-core laptop and used VMs with SGX support to host the virtual switches, the SDN controller, and network namespaces (See in Sect. 5.1). While this sufficient to demonstrate the feasibility of TLSonSGX and compare it to OpenSSL, the platform choice limited possible performance measurements. Dedicated multi-core platforms, or cloud resources, with SGX support could be used to refine the performance measurements.

The current implementation supports only one virtual switch connecting multiple VMs per physical host, as only one SSL context is created and kept inside the enclave. This can be improved by introducing support for multiple switches per host by extending the library to support multiple SSL contexts. TLSonSGX could also be extended to protect the flow table or OVS database content from tampering by storing them in the enclave.

For keys and certificates to survive host reboots, the enclave could deploy sealing mechanisms to seal the enclave, i.e. encrypt it, export it from the enclave, and store it on the local hard disk. We did not prioritize this, as generating new keys and obtaining a new certificate takes approximately 0.3 s (See Sect. 5.3).

8   Conclusion

Protecting network elements on the data and application planes is essential for the security of SDN deployments and the network isolation between tenants. However, both state of art network elements and the underlying platforms are vulnerable to software attacks, potentially exposing authentication credentials stored in plaintext. To address this, we implement the TLSonSGX library that provides a secure and scalable mechanism for network elements to generate keys and obtain signed certificates, while keeping them secure within a memory enclave. TLSonSGX confines all the TLS connections to the SDN controller within the enclave to ensure that keys, certificates, and session data remain inaccessible outside the enclave. We complement TLSonSGX with additional mechanisms to asses the network element trustworthyness and apply the approach on both data- and application planes.

Our evaluation results show that TLSonSGX does not significantly impact the time to generate credentials and only adds an insignificant overhead when processing the first packet in each flow. TLSonSGX reduces the TLS configuration overhead and improves the security of SDN deployments.

Acknowledgements. This research was conducted within the 5G-ENSURE and COLA projects and received funding from the European Union's Horizon 2020 research and innovation programme, under grant agreements No. 671562 and 731574.

References

1. Anati, I., Gueron, S., Johnson, S., Scarlata, V.: Innovative technology for CPU based attestation and sealing. In: Proceedings of the 2nd International Workshop on Hardware and Architectural Support for Security and Privacy, HASP 2013, p. 10. ACM, June 2013
2. Antikainen, M., Aura, T., Särelä, M.: Spook in your network: attacking an SDN with a compromised OpenFlow switch. In: Bernsmed, K., Fischer-Hübner, S. (eds.) NordSec 2014. LNCS, vol. 8788, pp. 229–244. Springer, Cham (2014). https://doi.org/10.1007/978-3-319-11599-3_14
3. Arbettu, R.K., Khondoker, R., Bayarou, K., Weber, F.: Security analysis of Open-Daylight, ONOS, Rosemary and Ryu SDN controllers. In: 2016 17th International Telecommunications Network Strategy and Planning Symposium (Networks), pp. 37–44, September 2016
4. Arnautov, S., et al.: SCONE: secure Linux containers with Intel SGX. In: Proceedings of the 12th USENIX Conference on Operating Systems Design and Implementation, OSDI 2016, pp. 689–703. USENIX, November 2016
5. Aublin, P.L., et al.: TaLoS: secure and transparent TLS termination inside SGX enclaves. Technical report 2017/5, Imperial College London, March 2017
6. Ball, T., et al.: VeriCon: towards verifying controller programs in software-defined networks. In: Proceedings of the 35th ACM SIGPLAN Conference on Programming Language Design and Implementation, PLDI 2014, pp. 282–293. ACM, June 2014
7. Berde, P., et al.: ONOS: towards an open, distributed SDN OS. In: Proceedings of the 3rd Workshop on Hot Topics in Software Defined Networking, HotSDN 2014, pp. 1–6. ACM, August 2014
8. Bifulco, R., Boite, J., Bouet, M., Schneider, F.: Improving SDN with InSPired switches. In: Proceedings of the Symposium on SDN Research, SOSR 2016, pp. 1–12. ACM, March 2016
9. Blake-Wilson, S., Bolyard, N., Gupta, V., Hawk, C., Moeller, B.: The open vSwitch database management protocol. RFC 4492, IETF, May 2006. http://www.rfc-editor.org/rfc/rfc4492.txt
10. Bleichenbacher, D.: Chosen ciphertext attacks against protocols based on the RSA encryption standard PKCS #1. In: Krawczyk, H. (ed.) CRYPTO 1998. LNCS, vol. 1462, pp. 1–12. Springer, Heidelberg (1998). https://doi.org/10.1007/BFb0055716

11. Chown, P.: Advanced Encryption Standard (AES) Ciphersuites for Transport Layer Security (TLS). RFC 3268, IETF, May 2002. http://www.rfc-editor.org/rfc/rfc3268.txt

12. Coker, G., et al.: Principles of remote attestation. Int. J. Inf. Secur. **10**(2), 63–81 (2011)

13. OpenFlow Switch Consortium: OpenFlow switch specification, v. 1.5.1. Technical report, ONF TS-025, Open Networking Foundation, March 2015

14. Coughlin, M., Keller, E., Wustrow, E.: Trusted click: overcoming security issues of NFV in the cloud. In: Proceedings of the ACM International Workshop on Security in Software Defined Networks & Network Function Virtualization, SDN-NFVSec 2017, pp. 31–36. ACM, March 2017

15. Dierks, T., Rescorla, E.: The Transport Layer Security (TLS) Protocol Version 1.2. RFC 5246, IETF, August 2008. http://www.rfc-editor.org/rfc/rfc3268.txt

16. Emmerich, P., Gallenmüller, S., Raumer, D., Wohlfart, F., Carle, G.: MoonGen: a scriptable high-speed packet generator. In: Proceedings of the 2015 Internet Measurement Conference, IMC 2015, pp. 275–287. ACM, New York (2015)

17. Enns, R., Bjorklund, M., Schoenwaelder, J.: Network configuration protocol (NETCONF). RFC 6241, IETF, June 2011. http://www.rfc-editor.org/rfc/rfc6241.txt

18. Frigge, M., Hoaglin, D.C., Iglewicz, B.: Some implementations of the Boxplot. Am. Stat. **43**(1), 50–54 (1989). http://www.jstor.org/stable/2685173

19. Girtler, D., Paladi, N.: Component integrity guarantees in software-defined networking infrastructure. In: Proceedings of the 2017 IEEE Conference on Network Function Virtualization and Software Defined Networks, NFV-SDN 2017, pp. 292–296, November 2017

20. Group Specification: Network Functions Virtualisation (NFV), Architectural Framework, v. 1.1.1. Technical report, GS NFV 002, European Telecommunications Standards Institute, October 2013

21. Hu, H., Han, W., Ahn, G.J., Zhao, Z.: FLOWGUARD: building robust firewalls for software-defined networks. In: Proceedings of the 3rd Workshop on Hot Topics in Software Defined Networking, HotSDN 2014, pp. 97–102. ACM, August 2014

22. IBM Corp.: TrouSerS: The open-source TCG Software Stack. http://trousers.sourceforge.net/. Accessed 13 Apr 2018

23. Intel: Intel 64 and IA-32 Architectures Software Developer's Manual, Combined Volumes: 1, 2A, 2B, 2C, 2D, 3A, 3B, 3C, 3D and 4. Technical report, 325462-063US, Intel Inc., July 2017

24. Intel Corp.: Intel SGX SSL. https://github.com/01org/intel-sgx-ssl. Accessed 20 July 2017

25. Izard, R.: Floodlight REST API. https://floodlight.atlassian.net/wiki/display/floodlightcontroller/Floodlight+REST+API. Accessed 16 Dec 2016

26. Jacquin, L., Shaw, A.L., Dalton, C.: Towards trusted software-defined networks using a hardware-based integrity measurement architecture. In: Proceedings of the 1st IEEE Conference on Network Softwarization, NetSoft 2015, pp. 1–6, April 2015

27. Jain, P., et al.: OpenSGX: an open platform for SGX research. In: Proceedings of the 2016 Network and Distributed System Security Symposium, NDSS 2016. Internet Society, February 2016

28. Kim, S., Han, J., Ha, J., Kim, T., Han, D.: Enhancing security and privacy of Tor's ecosystem by using trusted execution environments. In: 14th USENIX Symposium on Networked Systems Design and Implementation, NSDI 2017, pp. 145–161. USENIX (2017)

29. Kim, S., Shin, Y., Ha, J., Kim, T., Han, D.: A first step towards leveraging commodity trusted execution environments for network applications. In: Proceedings of the 14th ACM Workshop on Hot Topics in Networks, HotNets-XIV, pp. 7:1–7:7. ACM, November 2015

30. Kreutz, D., Ramos, F., Verissimo, P.: Towards secure and dependable software-defined networks. In: Proceedings of the 2nd ACM SIGCOMM Workshop on Hot Topics in Software Defined Networking, HotSDN 2013, pp. 55–60. ACM, August 2013

31. mbedTLS: TLS for SGX: a port of mbedTLS. https://github.com/bl4ck5un/mbedtls-SGX. Accessed 23 Apr 2018

32. McKeen, F., et al.: Intel software guard extensions (Intel SGX) support for dynamic memory management inside an enclave. In: Proceedings of the 2016 Hardware and Architectural Support for Security and Privacy, HASP 2016, pp. 10:1–10:9. ACM, June 2016

33. McKeen, F., et al.: Innovative instructions and software model for isolated execution. In: Proceedings of the 2nd International Workshop on Hardware and Architectural Support for Security and Privacy, HASP 2013, p. 10:1. ACM, June 2013

34. McKeown, N., et al.: OpenFlow: enabling innovation in campus networks. ACM SIGCOMM Comput. Commun. Rev. **38**, 69–74 (2008)

35. Morris, R., Kohler, E., Jannotti, J., Kaashoek, M.F.: The click modular router. ACM Trans. Comput. Syst. **18**(3), 263–297 (2000)

36. Nyman, T., Ekberg, J.E., Asokan, N.: Citizen electronic identities using TPM 2.0. In: Proceedings of the 4th International Workshop on Trustworthy Embedded Devices, TrustED 2014, pp. 37–48. ACM (2014)

37. Olsson, R.: Pktgen the Linux packet generator. In: Proceedings of the Linux Symposium, Ottawa, Canada, pp. 11–24, May 2005

38. Open vSwitch: Open vSwitch Manual. https://github.com/openvswitch/ovs/blob/master/INSTALL.SSL.rst. Accessed 10 Nov 2017

39. OpenDaylight Community: Secure Network Bootstrapping Infrastructure, October 2017. http://docs.opendaylight.org/en/stable-boron/user-guide/snbi-user-guide.html. Accessed Oct 2017

40. Paladi, N., Gehrmann, C.: Towards secure multi-tenant virtualized networks. In: 2015 IEEE TrustCom/BigDataSE/ISPA, vol. 1, pp. 1180–1185, August 2015

41. Paladi, N.: Towards secure SDN policy management. In: Proceedings of the 8th International Conference on Utility and Cloud Computing, UCC 2015, pp. 607–611, December 2015. https://doi.org/10.1109/UCC.2015.106

42. Paladi, N.: Trust but verify: trust establishment mechanisms in infrastructure clouds. Ph.D. thesis, Department of Electrical Engineering, Lund University, September 2017

43. Paladi, N., Gehrmann, C.: TruSDN: bootstrapping trust in cloud network infrastructure. In: Deng, R., Weng, J., Ren, K., Yegneswaran, V. (eds.) SecureComm 2016. LNICST, vol. 198, pp. 104–124. Springer, Cham (2017). https://doi.org/10.1007/978-3-319-59608-2_6

44. Paladi, N., Karlsson, L.: Safeguarding VNF credentials with Intel SGX. In: Proceedings of the SIGCOMM Posters and Demos, SIGCOMM Posters and Demos 2017, pp. 144–146. ACM, August 2017

45. Parno, B.: Bootstrapping trust in a "trusted" platform. In: Proceedings of the 3rd Conference on Hot Topics in Security, HOTSEC 2008, pp. 9:1–9:6. USENIX, July 2008

46. Pfaff, B., Davie, B.: The open vSwitch database management protocol. RFC 7047, IETF, December 2013. http://www.rfc-editor.org/rfc/rfc7047.txt

47. Pfaff, B., et al.: The design and implementation of open vSwitch. In: Proceedings of the 12th USENIX Symposium on Networked Systems Design and Implementation, NSDI 2015, pp. 117–130. USENIX, May 2015

48. Porras, P., Shin, S., Yegneswaran, V., Fong, M., Tyson, M., Gu, G.: A security enforcement kernel for OpenFlow networks. In: Proceedings of the 1st Workshop on Hot Topics in Software Defined Networks, HotSDN 2012, pp. 121–126. ACM, August 2012

49. Scott-Hayward, S., Natarajan, S., Sezer, S.: A survey of security in software defined networks. IEEE Comm. Surv. Tutor. **18**, 623–654 (2015)

50. Sekar, V., Egi, N., Ratnasamy, S., Reiter, M.K., Shi, G.: Design and implementation of a consolidated middlebox architecture. In: Proceedings of the 9th USENIX Conference on Networked Systems Design and Implementation, p. 24. USENIX Association (2012)

51. Sherwood, R., et al.: Carving research slices out of your production networks with OpenFlow. ACM SIGCOMM Comput. Commun. Rev. **40**, 129–130 (2010)

52. Shih, M.W., Kumar, M., Kim, T., Gavrilovska, A.: S-NFV: securing NFV states by using SGX. In: Proceedings of the 2016 ACM International Workshop on Security in Software Defined Networks & Network Function Virtualization, SDN-NFV Security 2016, pp. 45–48. ACM, March 2016

53. Shin, S., Porras, P.A., Yegneswaran, V., Fong, M.W., Gu, G., Tyson, M.: FRESCO: modular composable security services for software-defined networks. In: Proceedings of the 20th Annual Network & Distributed System Security Symposium, NDSS 2013. Internet Society, February 2013

54. Telecommunication Standardization Sector of ITU: Security requirements and reference architecture for software-defined networking. Technical report, X.1038, International Telecommunications Union, October 2016

55. Thimmaraju, K., et al.: The vAMP attack: taking control of cloud systems via the unified packet parser. In: Proceedings of the 2017 on Cloud Computing Security Workshop, CCSW 2017, pp. 11–15. ACM, New York (2017)

56. Trusted Computing Group: TPM Main Specification Level 2 Version 1.2, Revision 116. Parts 1–3. Technical report, 116_01032011, Trusted Computing Group Inc., March 2011

57. Trusted Computing Group: Trusted Platform Module Library Specification, Family "2.0", Level 00, Revision 01.16. Technical report, 120_01102013, Trusted Computing Group Inc., October 2014

58. Vaudenay, S.: Security flaws induced by CBC padding—applications to SSL, IPSEC, WTLS. In: Knudsen, L.R. (ed.) EUROCRYPT 2002. LNCS, vol. 2332, pp. 534–545. Springer, Heidelberg (2002). https://doi.org/10.1007/3-540-46035-7_35

59. WolfSSL: wolfSSL with Intel SGX on Linux. https://www.wolfssl.com/wolfSSL/Blog/Entries/2017/6/14_wolfSSL_with_Intel_SGX_on_Linux.html. Accessed 20 July 2017

60. Xiao, Y., Li, M., Chen, S., Zhang, Y.: Stacco: differentially analyzing side-channel traces for detecting SSL/TLS vulnerabilities in secure enclaves. arXiv preprint arXiv:1707.03473 (2017)

61. Xing, B.C., Shanahan, M., Leslie-Hurd, R.: Intel software guard extensions (Intel SGX) software support for dynamic memory allocation inside an enclave. In: Proceedings of the 2016 Hardware and Architectural Support for Security and Privacy, HASP 2016, pp. 11:1–11:9. ACM, June 2016

62. Zhu, S.Y., Scott-Hayward, S., Jacquin, L., Hill, R.: Guide to Security in SDN and NFV, 1st edn. Springer, Heidelberg (2017). https://doi.org/10.1007/978-3-319-64653-4

Applied Crypto (II)

Concessive Online/Offline Attribute Based Encryption with Cryptographic Reverse Firewalls—Secure and Efficient Fine-Grained Access Control on Corrupted Machines

Hui Ma[1], Rui Zhang[1,3]($\boxtimes$), Guomin Yang[2], Zishuai Song[1,3], Shuzhou Sun[1,3], and Yuting Xiao[1,3]

[1] State Key Laboratory of Information Security, Institute of Information Engineering, Chinese Academy of Sciences, Beijing 100093, China
r-zhang@iie.ac.cn
[2] Institute of Cybersecurity and Cryptology, School of Computing and Information Technology, University of Wollongong, Wollongong, NSW, Australia
[3] School of Cyber Security, University of Chinese Academy of Sciences, Beijing 100049, China

Abstract. Attribute based encryption (ABE) has potential to be applied in various cloud computing applications. However, the Snowden revelations show that powerful adversaries can corrupt users' machines to compromise the security, and many implementations of provably secure encryption schemes may present undetectable vulnerabilities that can expose secret, e.g., the scheme still works properly even some backdoors have been stealthily engineered on users' machines. Undoubtedly, ABE is also facing the above security threats. Recently, Mironov and Stephens-Davidowitz proposed cryptographic reverse firewall (CRF) to solve the problem. Unfortunately, no CRF-based protection for ABE has been proposed so far due to the complex system model and the extra access structure component. Besides, the encryption scheme in the CRF framework will suffer double computation latency, which is worse for ABE that has already yielded expensive operations. In this paper, we propose a concessive online/offline ciphertext-policy attribute based encryption with cryptographic reverse firewalls (COO-CP-ABE-CRF), which can resist the exfiltration of secret information and achieve selective CPA security. Furthermore, compared with the original scheme without CRF, our scheme reduces the total computation cost by half. Moreover, we develop an extensible library called libabe that is compatible with Android devices, and we implement the prototype on a laptop and a mobile phone. The experimental results indicate that the scheme is efficient and practical.

© Springer Nature Switzerland AG 2018
J. Lopez et al. (Eds.): ESORICS 2018, LNCS 11099, pp. 507–526, 2018.
https://doi.org/10.1007/978-3-319-98989-1_25

1   Introduction

As an innovative cryptographic primitive, attribute based encryption (ABE), that can provide fine-grained access control over encrypted data, has potential to be applied in many cloud-assisted applications, such as Pay TV/Music [1,2], Electronic Medical Record [3,4], audit logs [5,6], and web services [7,8] etc.

However, in the last couple of years, it has become increasingly clear that the practical cryptographic implementation presents many vulnerabilities even the protocol has been proved to be secure in theory. The revelations of Edward Snowden show that powerful actors have remarkable ability to successfully obtain a massive secret information by extraordinary techniques, including embedding backdoors into the public cryptographic standard [9,10] and the pseudorandom generator [11,12], intercepting and tampering with users' hardware deliveries [13]. Meanwhile, many security flaws [14–17] have been reported in widely deployed implementations of cryptographic softwares, which will certainly lead to large-scale security risks. The vulnerabilities of cryptographic implementations are extremely hard to detect in practice, because the implemented protocol still works properly even backdoors have been stealthily engineered without user's knowledge. Unfortunately, ABE is also facing the disturbing and quite real possibility of the above-mentioned compromises, e.g., the adversary tampers the setup algorithm on the private key generator (PKG) to generate some special but functional-maintaining public parameters which can expose the system master secret key or it embeds backdoors into the pseudorandom generator on PKG. This intractable situation motivates us to strengthen the security of ABE when the adversary may arbitrarily tamper with the victim's machine.

Recently, Mironov and Stephens-Davidowitz [18] proposed an innovative concept called cryptographic reverse firewall (CRF) that can strengthen the security to resist inside vulnerabilities such as security backdoors. Informally, a CRF implemented on a trust machine is located between the user's machine and the outside world and is able to intercept and modify the machine's incoming and outgoing messages to provide security protections even if the user's machine has been tampered. Though several CRF-based protections have been proposed for message-transmission protocol [19], key-agreement protocol [19], oblivious transfer protocols [18,20], oblivious signature-based envelope [20] etc., no CRF-based protection for ABE has been proposed so far. To strengthen the security of ABE by applying CRF-based protection, there exist the following serious challenges.

- Dodis et al. [19] proposed that the encryption scheme in the CRF framework should be both key malleable and strongly rerandomizable. While the situation in ABE is somewhat complicated: (1) Unlike the simple system with CRF (e.g., ElGamal), more entities are involved in ABE system and the communication becomes complex, thus the system model should be creatively redesigned to adapt CRF. (2) Since ABE utilizes various access structures to achieve fine-grained access control, it needs careful consideration that whether the property of extra access structure component matches the CRF framework. Therefore, the first challenge is that *how to design ABE with CRF-based protection to resist the exfiltration of secret information?*

- The encryption scheme with CRF always suffers double computation latency due to the rerandomization, which is even worse for ABE that has already yielded the heavy computation cost, largely the pairing and exponentiation operations, which often grow with the complexity of access formula. This is a huge burden for the private key generator (PKG) and users, especially for resource-constrained mobile devices. Therefore, the second challenge is that *how to improve the computation efficiency of ABE in the CRF framework?*

1.1 Our Contribution

Aiming at solving above challenges, we propose a concessive online/offline ciphertext-policy attribute based encryption with cryptographic reverse firewalls (COO-CP-ABE-CRF), which not only resists the exfiltration of secret information from arbitrarily compromised functional-maintaining algorithms, but also improves the computation efficiency of all the algorithms significantly and is suitable for mobile devices. Our contribution is three-fold:

- **Exfiltration Resistance.** We first propose a new system model for ABE in the CRF framework (cf. Fig. 2), where three reverse firewalls are adopted for the PKG, data owner and data consumer respectively. Then, we present a detailed construction, where all the random parameters including the parameters in the LSSS access structure are rerandomized by three reverse firewalls to achieve exfiltration resistance.
- **High Computation Efficiency.** We propose a concessive online/offline attribute based encryption with cryptographic reverse firewalls, where the online computation efficiency of the entities including PKG, data owner, data consumer and reverse firewalls for the PKG and data owner is optimized significantly. Compared with the original scheme without CRF [21], our CRF-based scheme reduces the total computation cost of key generation[1] by half and improves the total computation efficiency of encryption. The data consumer only needs 1 exponentiation to complete the decryption.
- **Compatible Implementation.** We develop an extensible library libabe that is compatible with Android OS. We implement a prototype within libabe on a laptop and a mobile phone. The results indicate the high efficiency and practicability of our methodology. We believe that this library can make ABE a step closer to actual deployment with mobile devices.

1.2 Related Work

Attribute based encryption (ABE) was first introduced by Sahai and Waters under the name fuzzy identity-based encryption [22]. Goyal et al. [6] extended fuzzy IBE to ABE. Up to now, there are two forms of ABE: key-policy ABE (KP-ABE) [6,23–25], where the key is assigned to an access policy and the ciphertext to a set of attributes, and ciphertext-policy ABE (CP-ABE) [26–28], where the

---

[1] It is the total workload of the PKG and the reverse firewall for the PKG.

ciphertext is assigned to an access policy and the key to a set of attributes. A user can decrypt a ciphertext if the set of attributes satisfies the access policy.

Cryptographic reverse firewall (CRF) was first introduced by Mironov and Stephens-Davidowitz [18], they proposed the CRF-based protection for oblivious protocol and presented a generic construction to protect users from data leakage against eavesdroppers via any protocol. Dodis, Mironov and Stephens-Davidowitz [19] considered message transmission protocols in the CRF framework. They proposed a rich collection of solutions in different settings which vary in efficiency, security, and setup assumptions. Moreover, they proposed a generic framework for constructing two-round protocol from rerandomizable encryption schemes. Chen et al. [20] introduced the notion of malleable smooth projective hash function (SPHF) and showed that how to construct CRFs using malleable SPHAs for some widely used cryptographic protocols. However, all the above CRF-based protections are not suitable for ABE due to the more complex system model and the extra components adopted in ABE construction.

2 Preliminary

In this section, we review some definitions of attribute based encryption and cryptographic reverse firewalls.

2.1 Attribute Based Encryption

Definition 1 (Bilinear Groups). *Let* $\mathbb{G}, \mathbb{G}_T$ *be two multiplicative cyclic groups of prime order* p. *Let* g *be a generator of* $\mathbb{G}$ *and* $e : \mathbb{G} \times \mathbb{G} \to \mathbb{G}_T$ *be a bilinear map with the following properties: (1) Bilinearity: for all* $g, h \in \mathbb{G}$ *and* $a, b \in \mathbb{Z}_p^*$, *we have* $e(g^a, h^b) = e(g, h)^{ab}$. *(2) Nondegeneracy:* $e(g, h) \neq 1$ *whenever* $g, h \neq 1_\mathbb{G}$.

Definition 2 (Access Structure [29]). *Let* $\{P_1, \ldots, P_n\}$ *be a set of parties. A collection* $\mathbb{A} \subseteq 2^{\{P_1, \ldots, P_n\}}$ *is monotone for* $\forall B$ *and* C, *if* $B \in \mathbb{A}, B \subseteq C$, *then* $C \in \mathbb{A}$. *An access structure (respectively, monotone access structure) is a collection (respectively, monotone collection) of nonempty subsets of* $\{P_1, \ldots, P_n\}$, *i.e.,* $\mathbb{A} \subseteq 2^{\{P_1, \ldots, P_n\}} \setminus \{\emptyset\}$. *The sets in* $\mathbb{A}$ *are called authorized sets, and the sets not in* $\mathbb{A}$ *are called unauthorized sets.*

Definition 3 (Linear Secret Sharing Schemes (LSSS) [29]). *A secret sharing scheme* Π *over a set of parties is called linear over* $\mathbb{Z}_p$ *if (1) The shares of the parties form a vector over* $\mathbb{Z}_p$; *(2) There exists a matrix* M *with* l *rows and* n *columns called the share-generating matrix for* Π. *There exists a function* ρ *which maps each row of the matrix to an associated party, i.e., for* $i = 1, \ldots, l$, *the value* $\rho(i)$ *is the party associated with row* i. *When we consider the column vector* $v = (s, r_2, \ldots, r_n)$, *where* $s \in \mathbb{Z}_p$ *is the secret to be shared, and* $r_2, \ldots, r_n \in \mathbb{Z}_p$ *are randomly chosen, then* Mv *is the vector of* l *shares of the secret* s *according to* Π. *The share* $(Mv)_i$ *belongs to party* $\rho(i)$.

2.2   Cryptographic Reverse Firewalls

We review the definitions of reverse firewall introduced in [18,20]. We assume that a cryptographic scheme $\mathcal{E}$ satisfies functionality requirement $\mathcal{F}$ and security requirement $\mathcal{S}$. There are two kinds of reverse firewalls, one can access all the public parameters and messages but not the private input or output of entities, another one can access all the public and private input and output of entities.

Definition 4 (Cryptographic Reverse firewall (CRF)). *A cryptographic reverse firewall is a stateful algorithm $\mathcal{W}$ that takes as input its state and a message and outputs an updated state and message. For simplicity, we do not write the state of $\mathcal{W}$ explicitly. For a party P and reverse firewall $\mathcal{W}$, we define $\mathcal{W} \circ P$ as the composed party where $\mathcal{W}$ is applied to the incoming and outgoing messages of P. When the composed party engages in a protocol, the state of $\mathcal{W}$ is initialized to the public parameters. If $\mathcal{W}$ is meant to be composed with a party P, we call it a reverse firewall for P.*

Definition 5 (Functionality-maintaining CRFs). *For any reverse firewall $\mathcal{W}$ and any party P, let $\mathcal{W}^1 \circ P = \mathcal{W} \circ P$, for $k \geq 2$, let $\mathcal{W}^k \circ P = \mathcal{W} \circ (\mathcal{W}^{k-1} \circ P)$. For a scheme $\mathcal{E}$ that satisfies functionality requirement $\mathcal{F}$, we say a reverse firewall $\mathcal{W}$ maintains $\mathcal{F}$ for P in $\mathcal{E}$ if $\mathcal{W}^k \circ P$ maintains $\mathcal{F}$ for P in $\mathcal{E}$ for any polynomial bounded $k \geq 1$. When $\mathcal{F}, P, \mathcal{E}$ are clear, we say $\mathcal{W}$ maintains functionality.*

We use $\hat{P}$ to represent the functionality-maintaining adversarial implementations. For a scheme $\mathcal{E}$ with party P, we write $\mathcal{E}_{P \to \hat{P}}$ to represent the scheme where the role of party P is replaced by party $\hat{P}$.

Definition 6 (Weakly security-preserving CRFs). *For a scheme $\mathcal{E}$ that satisfies security requirement $\mathcal{S}$ and functionality $\mathcal{F}$ and a reverse firewall $\mathcal{W}$, $\mathcal{W}$ weakly preserves $\mathcal{S}$ for P in $\mathcal{E}$ if the scheme $\mathcal{E}_{P \to \mathcal{W} \circ \hat{P}}$ satisfies $\mathcal{S}$. When $\mathcal{E}, \mathcal{F}, \mathcal{S}, P$ are clear, we say that $\mathcal{W}$ weakly preserves security.*

A reverse firewall should also achieve weakly exfiltration resistance which means that no corrupted functionality-maintaining implementation of P can leak information through the firewall. We define a game LEAK that is presented in Fig. 1. The game asks the adversary to distinguish between a tampered implementation and an honest implementation. An exfiltration-resistant reverse firewall therefore prevents an adversary from even learning whether a party has been compromised, let alone leaking information.

Definition 7 (Weakly exfiltration-resistant CRFs). *For a scheme $\mathcal{E}$ that satisfies functionality $\mathcal{F}$ and a reverse firewall $\mathcal{W}$, we say $\mathcal{W}$ is weakly exfiltration-resistant for party P_1 against party P_2 in scheme $\mathcal{E}$, if for any PPT adversary $\mathcal{A}$, $Adv_{\mathcal{A},\mathcal{W}}^{\mathsf{LEAK}}(l) = Pr[\mathsf{LEAK}(\mathcal{E}, P_1, P_2, \mathcal{W}, l) = 1] - \frac{1}{2}$ is negligible[2] in the security parameter l provided that $\overline{P}_1$ maintains $\mathcal{F}$ for P_1.*

---

[2] A function f is negligible if for every $c > 0$ there exists $\lambda_0 > 0$ such that $f(\lambda) < 1/\lambda^c$ for all $\lambda > \lambda_0$.

$$
\boxed{
\begin{array}{l}
\textbf{Proc.LEAK}(\mathcal{E}, P_1, P_2, \mathcal{W}, l) \\
(\overline{P_1}, \overline{P_2}, I) \to \mathcal{A}(1^l) \\
b \xleftarrow{\$} \{0,1\} \\
\text{If } b = 1,\ P^* \leftarrow \mathcal{W} \circ \overline{P_1} \\
\text{Else, } P^* \leftarrow \mathcal{W} \circ P_1 \\
\mathcal{T}^* \leftarrow \mathcal{E}_{P_1 \to P^*, P_2 \to \overline{P_2}}(I) \\
b^* \leftarrow \mathcal{A}(\mathcal{T}^*, st_{\overline{P_2}}) \\
\text{Output } (b = b^*)
\end{array}
}
$$

Fig. 1. The exfiltration resistance security game for a reverse firewall $\mathcal{W}$ for party P_1 in scheme $\mathcal{E}$ against party P_2. $\mathcal{A}$ is the adversary, l the security parameter, $st_{\overline{P_2}}$ the state of $\overline{P_2}$ after the run of the scheme, I valid input for $\mathcal{E}$, and $\mathcal{T}^*$ is the transcript of running scheme $\mathcal{E}_{P_1 \to P^*, P_2 \to \overline{P_2}}(I)$.

3   System Model and Security Model

3.1   System Model

As illustrated in Fig. 2, four different entities are involved in our system: the private key generator (PKG), the public cloud, the data owner (DO) and the data consumer (DC). Moreover, three reverse firewalls are adopted. $\mathcal{W}_{\textbf{PKG}}$ is the reverse firewall for PKG, $\mathcal{W}_{\textbf{DO}}$ is the reverse firewall for the data owner and $\mathcal{W}_{\textbf{DC}}$ is the reverse firewall for the data consumer.

PKG is responsible to generate public parameters and the master secret key.
Data Owner defines access policies and encrypts data under these policies before uploading them to the public cloud.
Public Cloud is deployed to provide cloud data storage service and outsourced decryption service. Users can upload and download the cloud file.
Data Consumer can download any encrypted data of his/her interest from public cloud and try to decrypt the ciphertext.
$\mathcal{W}_{\textbf{PKG}}$ is responsible to rerandomize public parameters and users' secret keys in case that the setup and key generation algorithms of PKG are compromised.
$\mathcal{W}_{\textbf{DO}}$ is responsible to rerandomize the ciphertexts generated by the data owner in case that the encryption algorithm of the data owner is compromised.
$\mathcal{W}_{\textbf{DC}}$ is responsible to rerandomize the conversion key generated by the data consumer in case that the conversion key[3] generation algorithm of the data consumer is compromised.

Let S represent a set of attributes, and (M, ρ) be an access structure. The concessive online/offline ciphertext-policy attribute based encryption with cryptographic reverse firewalls (COO-CP-ABE-CRF) for access structure space $\mathcal{G}$ consists of 15 algorithms:

---

[3] The public cloud can use it to do outsourced decryption.

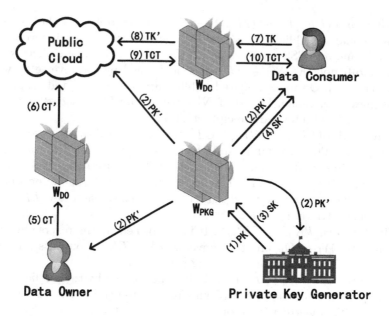

Fig. 2. System model of COO-CP-ABE-CRF

Setup$(\lambda, U) \rightarrow (PK, MSK)$. It is performed by the PKG. On input a security parameter λ and a universe description U, it outputs public parameters PK and a master secret key MSK.

$\mathcal{W}_{\mathbf{PKG}}.\mathbf{Setup}(PK) \rightarrow (PK', f)$. It is performed by the reverse firewall for PKG $\mathcal{W}_{\mathbf{PKG}}$. On input public parameters PK, it outputs updated public parameters PK' and a corresponding random f.

KeyGen.offline$(PK', MSK, N) \rightarrow ISK$. It is performed by PKG. On input updated public parameters PK', a master secret key MSK and a number N that assumes the attribute number, it outputs an intermediate secret key ISK.

KeyGen.online$(PK', S, ISK) \rightarrow SK$. It is performed by the PKG. On input updated public parameters PK', an attribute set S and an intermediate secret key ISK, it outputs a secret key SK.

$\mathcal{W}_{\mathbf{PKG}}.\mathbf{KG.offline}(PK', f, N) \rightarrow ISK'$. It is performed by the reverse firewall for PKG $\mathcal{W}_{\mathbf{PKG}}$. On input the updated public parameters PK', a random f and a number N that assumes the attribute number, it outputs an updated intermediate secret key ISK'.

$\mathcal{W}_{\mathbf{PKG}}.\mathbf{KG.online}(PK', ISK', SK) \rightarrow SK'$. It is performed by the reverse firewall for PKG $\mathcal{W}_{\mathbf{PKG}}$. On input the updated public parameters PK', an updated intermediate secret key ISK' and a secret key SK, it outputs an updated SK'.

Encrypt.offline$(PK', N') \rightarrow IT$. It is performed by the data owner. On input the updated public parameters PK' and a number N' that assumes a maximum bound of N' rows in LSSS structure, it outputs an intermediate ciphertext IT.

Encrypt.online$(PK', IT, m, (M, \rho)) \rightarrow CT$. It is performed by the data owner. On input updated public parameters PK', an intermediate ciphertext IT, a plaintext m and an LSSS access structure (M, ρ), it outputs a ciphertext CT.

$\mathcal{W}_{\mathbf{DO}}$.**Enc.offline**$(PK', N') \rightarrow IT'$. It is performed by the reverse firewall for data owner $\mathcal{W}_{\mathbf{DO}}$. On input updated public parameters PK' and a number N' that assumes a maximum bound of N' rows in any LSSS access structure, it outputs an updated intermediate ciphertext IT'.

$\mathcal{W}_{\mathbf{DO}}$.**Enc.online**$(PK', IT', CT) \rightarrow CT'$. It is performed by the reverse firewall for data owner $\mathcal{W}_{\mathbf{DO}}$. On input updated public parameters PK', an updated intermediate ciphertext IT' and a ciphertext CT, it outputs an updated CT'.

KeyGen.ran$(SK') \rightarrow (TK, RK)$. It is performed by the data consumer. On input an updated secret key SK', it outputs a conversion key TK and the corresponding retrieval key RK.

$\mathcal{W}_{\mathbf{DC}}$.**TKUpdate**$(TK) \rightarrow (TK', \beta)$. It is performed by the reverse firewall for data consumer $\mathcal{W}_{\mathbf{DC}}$. On input a conversion key TK, it outputs an updated conversion key TK' and a corresponding random β.

Decrypt.out$(TK', CT') \rightarrow TCT$ or $\perp$. It is performed by the public cloud. On input an updated conversion key TK' and an updated ciphertext CT', it outputs the transformed ciphertext TCT or $\perp$.

$\mathcal{W}_{\mathbf{DC}}$.**Decrypt**$(TCT, \beta) \rightarrow TCT'$. It is performed by the reverse firewall for data consumer $\mathcal{W}_{\mathbf{DC}}$. On input a transformed ciphertext TCT and a random β, it outputs an updated transformed ciphertext TCT'.

Decrypt.user$(RK, TCT') \rightarrow m$. It is performed by the data consumer. On input a retrieval key RK and an updated transformed ciphertext TCT', it outputs the plaintext m.

Correctness. For the fixed universe description U, the security parameter $\lambda \in \mathbb{N}$, the access structure space $\mathcal{G}$ and the message m, the correctness property requires that for all $(PK, MSK) \in Setup(\lambda, U)$, all $(PK', f) \in \mathcal{W}_{\mathbf{PKG}}.Setup(PK)$, all $S \subseteq U$, all $(M, \rho) \in \mathcal{G}$, all $ISK \in KeyGen.offline(PK', MSK, N)$, all $SK \in KeyGen.online(PK', S, ISK)$, all $ISK' \in \mathcal{W}_{\mathbf{PKG}}.KG.offline$ (PK', f, N), all $SK' \in \mathcal{W}_{\mathbf{PKG}}.KG.online(PK', ISK', SK)$, all $IT \in Encrypt.$ $offline(PK', N')$, all $CT \in Encrypt.online(PK', IT, m, (M, \rho))$, all $IT' \in \mathcal{W}_{\mathbf{DO}}.Enc.offline(PK', N')$, all $CT' \in \mathcal{W}_{\mathbf{DO}}.Enc.online(PK', IT', CT)$, all $(TK, RK) \in KeyGen.ran(SK')$, all $(TK', \beta) \in \mathcal{W}_{\mathbf{DC}}.TKUpdate(TK)$, all $TCT \in Decrypt.out(TK', CT')$, all $TCT' \in \mathcal{W}_{\mathbf{DC}}.Decrypt(TCT, \beta)$, if S satisfies (M, ρ), $Decrypt.user(RK, TCT') \rightarrow m$.

3.2 Security Model

Adversarial Model. In the system, the PKG, the data owner and the data consumer are totally trusted, but the *Setup, KeyGen.offline, KeyGen.online* algorithms run by the PKG, the *Encrypt.offline, Encrypt.online* algorithms run by the data owner and the *KeyGen.ran* algorithm run by the data consumer may be stealthily compromised without the executors' knowledge, because the algorithms will maintain the functionality even malicious backdoors have already been implanted. The public cloud and the reverse firewalls $\mathcal{W}_{DO}, \mathcal{W}_{DC}$ are "honest but curious" [30,31]. More precisely, they will follow the protocol but try to find out as much private information as possible. While the reverse firewall $\mathcal{W}_{PKG}$ should be totally trusted because it has to access every user's secret key. Moreover, all the reverse firewalls are considered as the trust zones that will not be tampered by any outsiders. Next, we will introduce the selective CPA security Game for COO-CP-ABE-CRF.

Init. The adversary $\mathcal{A}$ sends the challenge access policy $\mathbb{A}^*$ and the functionality-maintaining algorithms $Setup^*, KeyGen.offline^*, KeyGen.online^*, KeyGen.$ $ran^*, Encrypt.offline^*, Encrypt.online^*$ to the challenger $\mathcal{C}$.

Setup. $\mathcal{C}$ runs $Setup^*$ to get PK, MSK, then runs $\mathcal{W}_{PKG}.Setup(PK)$ to get the updated PK' and the corresponding random f. $\mathcal{C}$ keeps MSK and f to itself and sends PK' to $\mathcal{A}$.

Phase 1. In this phase, $\mathcal{A}$ can adaptively ask for secret keys for attribute sets $S_1, S_2, \ldots, S_q$. For each query S_i, $\mathcal{C}$ calls $KeyGen.offline^*(PK', MSK, N) \rightarrow$ ISK, $KeyGen.online^*(PK', S_i, ISK) \rightarrow SK_i$, then runs $\mathcal{W}_{PKG}.$ $KG.offline(PK', f, N) \rightarrow ISK_i', \mathcal{W}_{PKG}.KG.online(PK', ISK_i', SK_i) \rightarrow SK_i'$. Next, $\mathcal{C}$ calls $KeyGen.ran^*(SK_i') \rightarrow TK_i$ and runs $\mathcal{W}_{DC}.TKUpdate$ to get TK_i'. At last, $\mathcal{C}$ sends (SK_i', TK_i') to $\mathcal{A}$. The restriction that has to be satisfied for each query is that none of the queried attribute sets satisfies the challenge policy.

Challenge. $\mathcal{A}$ sends two equal-length plaintexts m_0, m_1 to $\mathcal{C}$. $\mathcal{C}$ selects a random bit $b \in \{0, 1\}$ and runs $Encrypt.offline^*(PK', N') \rightarrow$ $IT, Encrypt.online^*(PK', IT, m_b, \mathbb{A}^*)$ to obtain CT_b. Then $\mathcal{C}$ calls $\mathcal{W}_{DO}.Enc.offline(PK', N') \rightarrow IT', \mathcal{W}_{DO}.Enc.online(PK', IT', CT_b) \rightarrow CT_b'$ and sends CT_b' to $\mathcal{A}$.

Phase 2. Same as Phase 1.

Guess. $\mathcal{A}$ outputs the guess $b' \in \{0, 1\}$ for b.

Definition 8. *A COO-CP-ABE-CRF scheme is selective CPA-secure if all probabilistic polynomial time (PPT) adversaries have at most a negligible advantage in the above security game, denote:*

$$\epsilon = |\Pr[b = b'] - \frac{1}{2}| \leq negl(\lambda).$$

4   Concessive Online/Offline CP-ABE with Cryptographic Reverse Firewalls

In this section, we first present a basic construction of concessive online/offline ciphertext-policy attribute based encryption (COO-CP-ABE) which is based on the Rouselakis and Waters's CP-ABE scheme in [21]. Then, we propose the construction of COO-CP-ABE with cryptographic reverse firewalls (COO-CP-ABE-CRF) and give the security proof in the standard model.

4.1 Basic Construction of Concessive Online/Offline CP-ABE

Technique Overview. To improve the computation efficiency, we propose the basic construction of concessive online/offline CP-ABE. For key generation and encryption, if we directly utilize the "connect and correct" technique in online/offline ABE [32], the randomness of ciphertexts and secret keys cannot be all rerandomized in the CRF framework. Thus, we propose the concessive version, which is suitable for the CRF framework but sacrifices a small amount of efficiency. Now, we will introduce the construction.

Setup(λ, U). The PKG chooses a bilinear map $D = (\mathbb{G}, \mathbb{G}_T, e, p)$, where $p \in \Theta(2^\lambda)$ is the prime order of the groups $\mathbb{G}$ and $\mathbb{G}_T$. The attribute universe is consisting of elements in $\mathbb{Z}_p$. It chooses random generators $g, u, h, w, v \in \mathbb{G}$ and picks a random $\alpha \in \mathbb{Z}_p$. It sets the keys as $PK = (D, g, u, h, w, v, e(g,g)^\alpha)$, $MSK = \alpha$.

KeyGen.offline(PK, MSK, N). On input public parameters PK, a master secret key MSK and a number N which assumes the number of attributes, the PKG picks $N+1$ random $r, r_1, r_2, \ldots, r_N \in \mathbb{Z}_p$ and computes $\hat{K}_0 = g^\alpha w^r$, $\hat{K}_1 = g^r$. Then for $i = 1$ to N, it computes $\hat{K}_{i,2} = g^{r_i}$, $\hat{K}_{i,3} = h^{r_i} v^{-r}$. It sets the intermediate secret key $ISK = (\hat{K}_0, \hat{K}_1, \{r_i, \hat{K}_{i,2}, \hat{K}_{i,3}\}_{i \in [1,N]})$.

KeyGen.online(PK, S, ISK). On input public parameters PK, an attribute set $S = \{A_1, A_2, \ldots, A_k\} \subseteq \mathbb{Z}_p$ where $k \leq N$ and an intermediate secret key ISK, the PKG sets $K_0 = \hat{K}_0 = g^\alpha w^r$, $K_1 = \hat{K}_1 = g^r$. Then for $i = 1$ to k, it sets and computes $K_{i,2} = \hat{K}_{i,2} = g^{r_i}$, $K_{i,3} = \hat{K}_{i,3} \cdot u^{A_i r_i} = (u^{A_i}h)^{r_i} v^{-r}$. It sets the secret key $SK = (S, K_0, K_1, \{K_{i,2}, K_{i,3}\}_{i \in [1,k]})$.

KeyGen.ran(SK). On input a secret key SK, the data consumer chooses a random $\tau \in \mathbb{Z}_p$ and computes $K'_0 = K_0^{1/\tau} = g^{\alpha/\tau} w^{r/\tau}$, $K'_1 = K_1^{1/\tau} = g^{r/\tau}$. For $i = 1$ to k, compute $K'_{i,2} = K_{i,2}^{1/\tau} = g^{r_i/\tau}$, $K'_{i,3} = K_{i,3}^{1/\tau} = (u^{A_i}h)^{r_i/\tau} v^{-r/\tau}$. The conversion key is $TK = (S, K'_0, K'_1, \{K'_{i,2}, K'_{i,3}\}_{i \in [1,k]})$, the retrieval key is $RK = \tau$.

Encrypt.offline(PK, N'). On input public parameters PK and the number N' which assumes a maximum bound of N' rows in any LSSS structure, the data owner first picks a random $s \in \mathbb{Z}_p$ and computes $\hat{C} = e(g,g)^{\alpha s}$, $\hat{C}_0 = g^s$. For $j = 1$ to N', choose random $t_j \in \mathbb{Z}_p$ and compute $\hat{C}_{j,1} = v^{t_j}$, $\hat{C}_{j,2} = h^{-t_j}$, $\hat{C}_{j,3} = g^{t_j}$. It sets the intermediate ciphertext $IT = (s, \hat{C}, \hat{C}_0, \{t_j, \hat{C}_{j,1}, \hat{C}_{j,2}, \hat{C}_{j,3}\}_{j \in [1,N']})$.

Encrypt.online$(PK, IT, m, (M, \rho))$. On input public parameters PK, an intermediate ciphertext IT, a plaintext m and an LSSS access structure (M, ρ), where M is an $l \times n$ ($l \leq N'$) matrix, the data owner first picks $\overrightarrow{y} = (s, y_2, \ldots, y_n)^T \in \mathbb{Z}_p^{n \times 1}$ where the random secret s from IT will be shared among the shares. The vector of the shares is $\overrightarrow{\lambda} = (\lambda_1, \ldots, \lambda_l)^T = M\overrightarrow{y}$. It computes $C = \hat{C} \cdot m = e(g,g)^{\alpha s} \cdot m$ and sets $C_0 = \hat{C}_0 = g^s$. For $j = 1$ to l, compute and set

$$C_{j,1} = \hat{C}_{j,1} \cdot w^{\lambda_j} = w^{\lambda_j} v^{t_j}, \quad C_{j,2} = \hat{C}_{j,2} \cdot u^{-\rho(j)t_j} = (u^{\rho(j)}h)^{-t_j}, \quad C_{j,3} = \hat{C}_{j,3} = g^{t_j}.$$

The ciphertext is $CT = ((M, \rho), C, C_0, \{C_{j,1}, C_{j,2}, C_{j,3}\}_{j \in [1,l]})$.

Decrypt.out(TK, CT). On input a conversion key TK for the attribute set S and a ciphertext CT for access structure (M, ρ), if S does not satisfy this access structure, the public cloud outputs $\perp$. Otherwise, it calculates $I = \{i : \rho(i) \in S\}$ and computes the constants $\{\omega_i \in \mathbb{Z}_p\}_{i \in I}$ such that $\sum_{i \in I} \omega_i \cdot M_i = (1, 0, \ldots, 0)$, where M_i is the i-th row of the matrix M. Then it computes

$$A = \frac{e(C_0, K_0')}{\prod_{i \in I}(e(C_{i,1}, K_1') \cdot e(C_{i,2}, K_{j,2}') \cdot e(C_{i,3}, K_{j,3}'))^{\omega_i}} = e(g, g)^{\alpha s / \tau}.$$

where j is the index of the attribute $\rho(i)$ in S (it depends on i). It outputs the partially decrypted transformed ciphertext $TCT = (C = e(g, g)^{\alpha s} m, \; A)$.
Decrypt.user(RK, TCT). On input a retrieval key RK and a transformed ciphertext TCT, the data consumer computes $\frac{C}{A^\tau} = \frac{e(g,g)^{\alpha s} m}{(e(g,g)^{\alpha s / \tau})^\tau} = m$.

Theorem 1. *The basic COO-CP-ABE scheme is selective CPA-secure if the CP-ABE scheme in [21] is selective CPA-secure.*

Proof. The online and offline algorithms in our scheme are executed by the same entity, and the forms of user secret keys SK and ciphertexts CT are identical to those in [21]. Therefore, the modification does not affect the security proof. Moreover, we utilize the key blinding technique in [33]. The proof is simple and similar to [33], thus we omit it.

4.2   Construction of COO-CP-ABE-CRF

Technique Overview. To resist the exfiltration of secret information from arbitrarily compromised functional-maintaining algorithms executed by the PKG, the data owner and the data consumer, we propose the construction of COO-CP-ABE with cryptographic reverse firewalls (COO-CP-ABE-CRF) that is based on the basic construction in Sect. 4.1. In the construction, we introduce three reverse firewalls: $\mathcal{W}_{\mathbf{PKG}}$ (between the PKG and other entities), $\mathcal{W}_{\mathbf{DO}}$ (between the data owner and the public cloud), $\mathcal{W}_{\mathbf{DC}}$ (between the data consumer and the public cloud) to rerandomize the cryptographic keys PK, SK, TK and the ciphertexts CT. To rerandomize the cryptographic keys, we utilize the malleability of keys PK, SK, TK and rewind the updated PK' to the PKG. To rerandomize the ciphertexts, we utilize the homomorphism of the ciphertext [21] and the linear secret sharing schemes (LSSS) [29]. Moreover, we utilize the concessive online/offline technique to optimize the online computation efficiency of the reverse firewalls $\mathcal{W}_{\mathbf{PKG}}, \mathcal{W}_{\mathbf{DO}}$. Now, we present the construction in detail.

System Initialization. The PKG runs $Setup(\lambda, U) \to (PK, MSK)$ and keeps MSK by itself. Before broadcasting PK to other entities, PKG will first send PK to the reverse firewall $\mathcal{W}_{\mathbf{PKG}}$, which runs the following algorithm.
$\mathcal{W}_{\mathbf{PKG}}$.**Setup**$(PK)$. Receiving public parameters PK from the PKG, the reverse firewall $\mathcal{W}_{\mathbf{PKG}}$ picks random $a, b, c, d, e, f \in \mathbb{Z}_p$ and computes $g' = g^a, u' = u^b, h' = h^c, w' = w^d, v' = v^e, \alpha' = \alpha + f, e(g', g')^{\alpha'} = e(g, g)^{\alpha a^2} e(g, g)^{a^2 f} = e(g, g)^{a^2 (\alpha + f)}$. It stores f and broadcasts the updated public parameters $PK' = (D, g', u', h', w', v', e(g', g')^{\alpha'})$ to all the entities including the PKG.

During the key generation phase, the PKG runs $KeyGen.offline(PK',$ $MSK, N) \rightarrow ISK$ (which can be done in the spare time) and $KeyGen.online$ $(PK', S, ISK) \rightarrow SK$, then sends $SK = (S, K_0, K_1, \{K_{i,2}, K_{i,3}\}_{i \in [1,k]})$ to the reverse firewall $\mathcal{W}_{\mathbf{PKG}}$, which does as follows.

Before receiving the user secret key SK, the reverse firewall $\mathcal{W}_{\mathbf{PKG}}$ does some preparation work such as the below algorithm in the spare time.

$\mathcal{W}_{\mathbf{PKG}}.\mathbf{KG.offline}(PK', f, N)$. On input updated public parameters PK', the stored random f and a number N which assumes the number of attributes, the reverse firewall $\mathcal{W}_{\mathbf{PKG}}$ first picks $N + 1$ random $r', r'_1, r'_2, \ldots, r'_N \in \mathbb{Z}_p$ and computes $\hat{K}'_0 = g'^f w'^{r'}$, $\hat{K}'_1 = g'^{r'}$. Then for $i = 1$ to N, it computes $\hat{K}'_{i,2} = g'^{r'_i}, \hat{K}'_{i,3} = h'^{r'_i} v'^{-r'}$. It sets the updated intermediate secret key $ISK' = (\hat{K}'_0, \hat{K}'_1, \{r'_i, \hat{K}'_{i,2}, \hat{K}'_{i,3}\}_{i \in [1,N]})$.

When the secret key SK is arriving, $\mathcal{W}_{\mathbf{PKG}}$ runs the following algorithm.

$\mathcal{W}_{\mathbf{PKG}}.\mathbf{KG.online}(PK', ISK', SK)$. On input updated public parameters PK', an updated intermediate secret key ISK' and a secret key SK, the reverse firewall $\mathcal{W}_{\mathbf{PKG}}$ computes $K'_0 = K_0 \cdot \hat{K}'_0 = g'^{\alpha+f} w'^{r+r'} = g'^{\alpha'} w'^{r+r'}$, $K'_1 = K_1 \cdot \hat{K}'_1 = g'^{r+r'}$. Then for $i = 1$ to k where $k \leq N$, compute

$$K'_{i,2} = K_{i,2} \cdot \hat{K}'_{i,2} = g'^{r_i+r'_i}, \quad K'_{i,3} = K_{i,3} \cdot \hat{K}'_{i,3} \cdot u'^{A_i r'_i} = (u'^{A_i} h')^{r_i+r'_i} v'^{-r-r'}.$$

It sends the updated secret key $SK' = (S, K'_0, K'_1, \{K'_{i,2}, K'_{i,3}\}_{i \in [1,k]})$ to the user.

Data Upload. The data owner calls $Encrypt.offline(PK', N') \rightarrow IT$ (which can be done in the spare time) and $Encrypt.online(PK', IT, m, (M, \rho)) \rightarrow CT$, then sends $CT = ((M, \rho), C, C_0, \{C_{j,1}, C_{j,2}, C_{j,3}\}_{j \in [1,l]})$ to the reverse firewall $\mathcal{W}_{\mathbf{DO}}$, which does as follows.

Before receiving the ciphertext CT, the reverse firewall $\mathcal{W}_{\mathbf{DO}}$ does some preparation work such as the below algorithm in the spare time.

$\mathcal{W}_{\mathbf{DO}}.\mathbf{Enc.offline}(PK', N')$. On input updated public parameters PK' and a number N' which assumes a maximum bound of N' rows in any LSSS structure, the reverse firewall $\mathcal{W}_{\mathbf{DO}}$ first picks another random secret $s' \in \mathbb{Z}_p$ to be shared among the shares. Then pick N' random exponents $t'_1, t'_2, \ldots, t'_N \in \mathbb{Z}_p$ and compute $\hat{C}' = e(g', g')^{\alpha' s'}$, $\hat{C}'_0 = g'^{s'}$. For $j = 1$ to N', compute $\hat{C}'_{j,1} = v'^{t'_j}$, $\hat{C}'_{j,2} = h'^{-t'_j}$, $\hat{C}'_{j,3} = g'^{t'_j}$. It sends the updated intermediate ciphertext $IT' = (s', \hat{C}', \hat{C}'_0, \{t'_j, \hat{C}'_{j,1}, \hat{C}'_{j,2}, \hat{C}'_{j,3}\}_{j \in [1,N']})$.

When the ciphertext CT is arriving, $\mathcal{W}_{\mathbf{DO}}$ runs the following algorithm.

$\mathcal{W}_{\mathbf{DO}}.\mathbf{Enc.online}(PK', IT', CT)$. On input updated public parameters PK', an updated intermediate ciphertext IT' and a ciphertext CT, the reverse firewall $\mathcal{W}_{\mathbf{DO}}$ first sets and picks $\overrightarrow{y'} = (s', y'_2, \ldots, y'_n)^T \in \mathbb{Z}_p^{n \times 1}$ where s' is the same random secret in IT'. The vector of the shares is $\overrightarrow{\lambda'} = (\lambda'_1, \ldots, \lambda'_l)^T = M\overrightarrow{y'}$. Then it computes $C' = C \cdot \hat{C}' = m \cdot e(g', g')^{\alpha'(s+s')}$, $C'_0 = C_0 \cdot \hat{C}'_0 = g'^{s+s'}$. For $j = 1$ to l where $l \leq N'$, compute

$$C'_{j,1} = C_{j,1} \cdot \hat{C}'_{j,1} \cdot w'^{\lambda'_j} = w'^{\lambda_j + \lambda'_j} v'^{t_j+t'_j}, \quad C'_{j,3} = C_{j,3} \cdot \hat{C}'_{j,3} = g'^{t_j+t'_j},$$
$$C'_{j,2} = C_{j,2} \cdot \hat{C}'_{j,2} \cdot u'^{-\rho(j)t'_j} = (u'^{\rho(j)} h')^{-(t_j+t'_j)}.$$

It sends the updated ciphertext $CT' = ((M,\rho), C', C_0', \{C_{j,1}', C_{j,2}', C_{j,3}'\}_{j\in[1,l]})$ to the public cloud.

Data Download. The data consumer first runs $KeyGen.ran(SK') \to (TK, RK)$ and sends $TK = (S, K_0'', K_1'', \{K_{i,2}'', K_{i,3}''\}_{i\in[1,k]})$ to the reverse firewall $\mathcal{W}_{\mathbf{DC}}$, which runs the following algorithm.

$\mathcal{W}_{\mathbf{DC}}.\mathbf{TKUpdate}(TK)$. On input a conversion key TK, the reverse firewall $\mathcal{W}_{\mathbf{DC}}$ chooses a random $\beta \in \mathbb{Z}_p$ and computes $K_0''' = K_0''^{1/\beta} = g'^{\alpha'/\tau\beta} w'^{(r+r')/\tau\beta}, K_1''' = K_1''^{1/\beta} = g'^{(r+r')/\tau\beta}$. Then for $i = 1$ to k, it computes

$$K_{i,2}''' = K_{i,2}''^{1/\beta} = g'^{(r_i+r_i')/\tau\beta}, \quad K_{i,3}''' = K_{i,3}''^{1/\beta} = (u'^{A_i}h')^{(r_i+r_i')/\tau\beta}v'^{-(r+r')/\tau\beta}.$$

It stores β and sends the updated conversion key $TK' = (S, K_0''', K_1''', \{K_{i,2}''', K_{i,3}'''\}_{i\in[1,k]})$ to the public cloud.

Receiving the decryption request from the data consumer, the public cloud runs $Decrypt.out(TK', CT') \to TCT$ and sends $TCT = (C' = e(g',g')^{\alpha'(s+s')}m, A = e(g',g')^{\alpha'(s+s')/\tau\beta})$ to the reverse firewall $\mathcal{W}_{\mathbf{DC}}$, which runs the algorithm.

$\mathcal{W}_{\mathbf{DC}}.\mathbf{Decrypt}(TCT, \beta)$. On input a transformed ciphertext TCT and the stored β, the reverse firewall $\mathcal{W}_{\mathbf{DC}}$ computes $A' = A^\beta = e(g',g')^{\alpha'(s+s')/\tau}$ and sends the updated $TCT' = (C', A')$ to the data consumer.

Receiving the updated transformed ciphertext TCT', the data consumer runs $Decrypt.user(RK, TCT')$ to recover the plaintext m.

4.3 Security Analysis

Theorem 2. *The proposed COO-CP-ABE-CRF is selective CPA-secure and the reverse firewalls for the PKG, the data owner and the data consumer maintain functionality, weakly preserve security, and weakly resist exfiltration if the basic construction of COO-CP-ABE in Sect. 4.1 is selective CPA-secure.*

Proof. We verify that our construction satisfies the following properties.

Functionality Maintaining. The correctness can be easily verified. If the attribute set S of the secret key is authorized, we have that $\sum_{i\in I} \omega_i \cdot (\lambda_i + \lambda_i') = s + s'$. Therefore,

$$
\begin{aligned}
A' &= \frac{e(C_0', K_0''')}{\prod_{i\in I}(e(C_{i,1}', K_1''') \cdot e(C_{i,2}', K_{j,2}''') \cdot e(C_{i,3}', K_{j,3}'''))^{\omega_i}} \\
&= \frac{e(g',g')^{\alpha'(s+s')/\tau\beta} e(g',w')^{(r+r')(s+s')/\tau\beta}}{\prod_{i\in I} e(g',w')^{(r+r')(\lambda_i+\lambda_i')\omega_i/\tau\beta} e(g',v')^{(r+r')(t_i+t_i')\omega_i/\tau\beta}} \\
&\quad \cdot \frac{1}{\prod_{i\in I} e(g',u')^{-\rho(i)(t_i+t_i')(r_i+r_i')\omega_i/\tau\beta} e(g',h')^{-(t_i+t_i')(r_i+r_i')\omega_i/\tau\beta}} \\
&\quad \cdot \frac{1}{\prod_{i\in I} e(g',u')^{(t_i+t_i')(r_i+r_i')A(i)\omega_i/\tau\beta} e(g',h')^{(t_i+t_i')(r_i+r_i')\omega_i/\tau\beta}}
\end{aligned}
$$

$$\cdot \frac{1}{\prod_{i \in I} e(g', v')^{-(r+r')(t_i+t_i')\omega_i/\tau\beta}}$$

$$= \frac{e(g',g')^{\alpha'(s+s')/\tau\beta} e(g',w')^{(r+r')(s+s')/\tau\beta}}{e(g',w')^{(r+r')\sum_{i \in I}(\lambda_i+\lambda_i')\omega_i/\tau\beta}} = e(g',g')^{\alpha'(s+s')/\tau\beta}$$

$$\frac{C'}{A'^\tau} = \frac{C'}{A^{\beta\tau}} = \frac{m \cdot e(g',g')^{\alpha'(s+s')}}{e(g',g')^{\alpha'(s+s')}} = m$$

Weak Security Preservation and Weak Exfiltration Resistance. For any tampered implementation on the PKG, the data owner and data consumer that maintains functionality, we will prove the selective CPA security of our proposed COO-CP-ABE-CRF with tampered algorithms $Setup^*, KeyGen.offline^*$, $KeyGen.online^*$, $KeyGen.ran^*$, $Encrypt.offline^*, Encrypt.online^*$ by proving the indistinguishability between the security game of COO-CP-ABE-CRF and the security game of the basic construction COO-CP-ABE in Sect. 4.1. Additionally, the weak security preservation and weak exfiltration resistance for CRF can be easily proved. Next, we consider the following games:

Game 0. It is identical to the security game of COO-CP-ABE-CRF in Sect. 3.2.

Game 1. Same as *Game 0* except that during the setup phase, PK, MSK are generated by *Setup* in the basic construction, not $Setup^*$ and $\mathcal{W}_{\mathbf{PKG}}.Setup$.

Game 2. Same as *Game 1* except that during *Phase 1* and *Phase 2*, the secret key SK is generated by $KeyGen.offline, KeyGen.online$ in the basic construction, not $KeyGen.offline^*, KeyGen.online^*, \mathcal{W}_{\mathbf{PKG}}.KG.offline$ and $\mathcal{W}_{\mathbf{PKG}}.KG.online$, and the conversion key TK is generated by $KeyGen.ran$ in the basic construction, not $KeyGen.ran^*$ and $\mathcal{W}_{\mathbf{DC}}.TKUpdate$.

Game 3. Same as *Game 2* except that during the challenge phase, the challenge ciphertext CT_b are generated by $Encrypt.offline, Encrypt.online$ in the basic construction, not $Encrypt.offline^*, Encrypt.online^*, \mathcal{W}_{\mathbf{DO}}.Enc.offline$ and $\mathcal{W}_{\mathbf{DO}}.Enc.online$. Actually, *Game 3* is the security game of the basic construction.

Then we prove the indistinguishability between the pairs *Game 0* and *Game 1*, *Game 1* and *Game 2*, *Game 2* and *Game 3* respectively. For the pair *Game 0* and *Game 1*, for any tampered algorithm $Setup^*$, after the post-processing by the reverse firewall $\mathcal{W}_{\mathbf{PKG}}.Setup$, the public parameters PK are uniformly random due to the key malleability, which is identical to the original algorithm *Setup* in the basic construction, regardless of the behavior of $Setup^*$. Thus *Game 0* and *Game 1* are indistinguishable. Since the user secret key SK and the conversion key TK also have key malleability, *Game 1* and *Game 2* are indistinguishable. For the pair *Game 2* and *Game 3*, for any tampered algorithm $Encrypt.offline^*, Encrypt.online^*$, after the post-processing by the reverse firewall $\mathcal{W}_{\mathbf{DO}}.Enc.offline, \mathcal{W}_{\mathbf{DO}}.Enc.online$, the updated ciphertext CT' are uniformly regenerated because the ABE scheme and the linear secret sharing scheme are rerandomizable, which is identical to the encryption algorithm in the basic

Table 1. Efficiency comparison

Operation	[21]	[32]	Ours
Setup	$1\mathrm{Exp} + 1\mathrm{P}$	$1\mathrm{Exp} + 1\mathrm{P}$	$1\mathrm{Exp} + 1\mathrm{P}$
KeyGen.online	$(4y + 3)\mathrm{Exp}$	$3y\mathrm{Exp}$	$y\mathrm{Exp}$
Encrypt.online	$(5l + 2)\mathrm{Exp}$	0	$2l\mathrm{Exp}$
KeyGen.ran	×	×	$(2l + 2)\mathrm{Exp}$
Decrypt.user	$(|I|)\mathrm{Exp} + (3|I| + 1)\mathrm{P}$	$(|I + 1|)\mathrm{Exp} + (3|I| + 2)\mathrm{P}$	$1\mathrm{Exp}$
$\mathcal{W}_{\mathbf{PGK}}.Setup$	×	×	$7\mathrm{Exp} + 1\mathrm{P}$
$\mathcal{W}_{\mathbf{PKG}}.KG.online$	×	×	$y\mathrm{Exp}$
$\mathcal{W}_{\mathbf{DO}}.Enc.online$	×	×	$2l\mathrm{Exp}$
$\mathcal{W}_{\mathbf{DC}}.TKUpdate$	×	×	$(2l + 2)\mathrm{Exp}$
$\mathcal{W}_{\mathbf{DC}}.Decrypt$	×	×	$1\mathrm{Exp}$

‡Exp and P denote a modular exponentiation and a pairing computation, respectively. y, l, and I indicate the number of attributes, the access policy size, and the set that satisfies decryption requirement, respectively.

construction, regardless of the behavior of $Encrypt.offline^*, Encrypt.online^*$. Thus *Game 2* and *Game 3* are indistinguishable. Therefore, we conclude that *Game 0* and *Game 3* are indistinguishable. Since the basic construction is selective CPA-secure, the proposed OO-CP-ABE-CRF is selective CPA-secure.

The selective CPA security of the proposed scheme indicates that the reverse firewalls for PKG, the data owner and data consumer maintain weakly preserve security. The indistinguishability between *Game 0* and *Game 3* indicates that the reverse firewalls for PKG, the data owner and data owner maintain weakly resist exfiltration. Combining all the discussions, we complete the proof.

5   Performance Evaluations

5.1   Theoretical Analysis

The online computation cost of the PKG, the data owner, the data consumer and the reverse firewalls refers to the execution time of *Setup, KeyGen.online, Encrypt.online, KeyGen.ran, Decrypt.user, $\mathcal{W}_{\mathbf{PGK}}.Setup$, $\mathcal{W}_{\mathbf{PKG}}.KG.online$, $\mathcal{W}_{\mathbf{DO}}.Enc.online$, $\mathcal{W}_{\mathbf{DC}}.TKUpdate$, $\mathcal{W}_{\mathbf{DC}}.Decrypt$*. Table 1 compares the number of modular exponentiations and pairing operations in our construction with those in the original scheme [21] and online/offline ABE [32].

For *Setup*, the computation cost of three schemes are the same. For *KeyGen.online*, the efficiency rank is $[21] < [32] < Ours$. The efficiency of our construction is four times that of [21] and three times that of [32]. For *Encrypt.online*, the efficiency rank is $[21] < Ours \ll [32]$. The reason that we propose concessive online/offline technique instead of directly utilizing the technique in [32] is that the randomness of ciphertexts and user secret keys in [32] cannot be all rerandomized, thus we choose to achieve stronger security by sacrificing a small amount of efficiency. For *Decrypt.user*, the efficiency rank is [21] < [32] ≪ *Ours*, the data consumer only needs to do one exponentiation to complete the decryption.

Next, we analyze the efficiency of reverse firewalls. For *Setup*, the overhead of the reverse firewall $\mathcal{W}_{\textbf{PKG}}$ is more than that of the PKG, because $\mathcal{W}_{\textbf{PKG}}$ needs to do the rerandomization. For *KG.online* and *Enc.online*, the reverse firewalls $\mathcal{W}_{\textbf{PKG}}, \mathcal{W}_{\textbf{DO}}$ have the same workload with *KeyGen.online, Encrypt.online* in our construction. For *Decrypt*, the computation cost of $\mathcal{W}_{\textbf{DC}}.TKUpdate, \mathcal{W}_{\textbf{DC}}.Decrypt$ are the same as *KeyGen.ran, Decrypt.user* in our construction. In general, the encryption scheme in the CRF framework will suffer double computation latency during key generation and encryption phase, while the total latency of key generation in our construction is two times less than the original scheme [21], and the total latency of encryption is less than [21]. We remark that our proposed COO-CP-ABE-CRF not only strengthens the security to resist the exfiltration of secret information, but also achieves high computation efficiency.

5.2 Experimental Analysis

To evaluate the practical performance, we develop an extensible library called libabe, which offers essential APIs for implementing ABE schemes. To be compatible with Android OS, libabe is developed by C language and only dependent on Pairing-Based Cryptography (PBC) library [34], thus we can develop the evaluation program on Android OS with Java Native Interface (JNI). The curve that we choose is the 224-bit MNT elliptic curve from PBC. We use a laptop produced by HASEE to act as the PKG, the public cloud and three reverse firewalls, a mobile device produced by XIAOMI plays the part of the data owner and the data consumer. The device configuration is presented in Table 2.

Experiment Setting. We set access policies for *CT*s in the form of (S_1 AND ... AND S_l) to simulate the worst situation. We set 20 distinct access policies with l increasing from 10 to 100, repeat each instance 20 times and take the average value. The time is given in milliseconds. Since the routines of MNT elliptic curve adopt asymmetric groups while the groups in the scheme are symmetric, only a small change needs to be made. Specifically, there are three groups $\mathbb{G}_1, \mathbb{G}_2$ and $\mathbb{G}_T$ and an asymmetric pairing $e : \mathbb{G}_1 \times \mathbb{G}_2 \to \mathbb{G}_T$. Because the time taken to execute operations in $\mathbb{G}_1$ is much less than $\mathbb{G}_2$ in MNT224 elliptic curve group, more operations in the scheme are executed in $\mathbb{G}_1$ rather than $\mathbb{G}_2$.

Computation Time. In Fig. 3, we show *KeyGen.offline Time* and *KeyGen.online Time* of the PKG, *Encrypt.offline Time* and *Encrypt.online Time* of the data owner, *KeyGen.ran Time* and *Decrypt.user Time* of the data consumer, *Decrypt.out Time* of the public cloud, $\mathcal{W}_{\textbf{PKG}}.KG.offline$ *Time* and $\mathcal{W}_{\textbf{PKG}}.KG.online$ *Time* of $\mathcal{W}_{\textbf{PKG}}$, $\mathcal{W}_{\textbf{DO}}.Enc.offline$ *Time* and $\mathcal{W}_{\textbf{DO}}.Enc.online$ *Time* of $\mathcal{W}_{\textbf{DO}}$, $\mathcal{W}_{\textbf{DC}}.TKUpdate$ *Time* and $\mathcal{W}_{\textbf{DC}}.Decrypt$ *Time* of $\mathcal{W}_{\textbf{DC}}$.

Table 2. Device configuration

Type	Configuration	Role	Algorithm
Laptop (HASEE)	Intel Core i7-4710MQ @2.5 GHz, 8 GB RAM, Ubuntu 16.04LTS 64-bit	PKG, $\mathcal{W}_{PKG}$, $\mathcal{W}_{DO}$, $\mathcal{W}_{DC}$, Public Cloud	$Setup$, $KeyGen.offline$, $KeyGen.online$, $Decrypt.out$, $\mathcal{W}_{PKG}.Setup$, $\mathcal{W}_{PKG}.KG.offline$, $\mathcal{W}_{PKG}.KG.online$, $\mathcal{W}_{DO}.Enc.offline$, $\mathcal{W}_{DO}.Enc.online$, $\mathcal{W}_{DC}.TKUpdate$, $\mathcal{W}_{DC}.Decrypt$
Mobile Device (MIX 2)	Qualcomm Snapdragon 835@2.45 GHz, 6 GB RAM, Android 8.0	Data Owner, Data Consumer	$Encrypt.offline$, $Encrypt.online$, $KeyGen.ran$, $Decrypt.user$

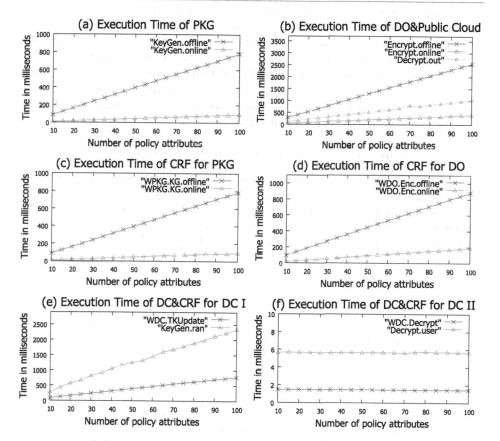

Fig. 3. Experimental results

In Fig. 3(a), *KeyGen.offline Time* is about 47 ms–783 ms while *Key-Gen.online Time* is about 3 ms–93 ms. In Fig. 3(b), *Encrypt.offline Time* on the mobile phone is about 0.15 s–2.55 s while *Encrypt.online Time* on the mobile phone is about 22 ms–386 ms. *Decrypt.out Time* is about 64 ms–1.02 s. In

Fig. 3(e) and (f), *KeyGen.ran Time* on the mobile phone is about 0.14 s–2.33 s and *Decrypt.user Time* on the mobile phone is always about 5.6 ms, which is quite efficient for mobile devices. In Fig. 3(c), $\mathcal{W}_{\mathbf{PKG}}.KG.offline$ *Time* is about 48 ms–781 ms while $\mathcal{W}_{\mathbf{PKG}}.KG.online$ *Time* is about 3 ms–93 ms. In Fig. 3(d), $\mathcal{W}_{\mathbf{DO}}.Enc.offline$ *Time* is about 52 ms–881 ms while $\mathcal{W}_{\mathbf{DO}}.Enc.online$ *Time* is about 8 ms–186 ms. In Fig. 3(e), $\mathcal{W}_{\mathbf{DC}}.TKUpdate$ *Time* is about 46 ms–774 ms. In Fig. 3(f), $\mathcal{W}_{\mathbf{DC}}.Decrypt$ *Time* is always about 1.4 ms.

6   Conclusion

In this paper, we propose a concessive online/offline ciphertext-policy attribute based encryption with cryptographic reverse firewalls, which can resist the exfiltration of secret information. Furthermore, compared with the original scheme without CRF, our scheme reduces the total computation cost by half. Moreover, we develop an extensible library called libabe that is compatible with Android devices, and we implement the prototype on a laptop and a mobile phone. In the future, we will focus on designing more compact system model of ABE in the CRF framework without rewinding PK to PKG.

Acknowledgments. The authors thank anonymous reviewers for their valuable comments, and Wenhan Xu for many helps on the experiments. This work was supported in part by National Natural Science Foundation of China (Nos. 61632020, 61472416, 61772520), Key Research Project of Zhejiang Province (No. 2017C01062), Fundamental theory and cutting edge technology Research Program of Institute of Information Engineering, CAS (No. Y7Z0321102), Australian Research Council Discovery Early Career Researcher Award (No. DE150101116), Scientific Research Plan Project of Tianjin Municipal Education Commission (Grant No. 2017KJ237).

References

1. Wan, Z., Liu, J., Zhang, R., Deng, R.H.: A collusion-resistant conditional access system for flexible-pay-per-channel pay-tv broadcasting. IEEE Trans. Multimed. **15**(6), 1353–1364 (2013)
2. Ning, J., Cao, Z., Dong, X., Liang, K., Ma, H., Wei, L.: Auditable σ-time outsourced attribute-based encryption for access control in cloud computing. IEEE Trans. Inf. Forensics Secur. **13**(1), 94–105 (2018)
3. Zhou, J., Cao, Z., Dong, X., Lin, X.: TR-MABE: white-box traceable and revocable multi-authority attribute-based encryption and its applications to multi-level privacy-preserving e-healthcare cloud computing systems. In: IEEE Conference on Computer Communications, INFOCOM 2015, Kowloon, Hong Kong, 26 April–1 May, pp. 2398–2406 (2015)
4. Li, M., Yu, S., Zheng, Y., Ren, K., Lou, W.: Scalable and secure sharing of personal health records in cloud computing using attribute-based encryption. IEEE Trans. Parallel Distrib. Syst. **24**(1), 131–143 (2013)
5. Ma, H., Zhang, R., Wan, Z., Lu, Y., Lin, S.: Verifiable and exculpable outsourced attribute-based encryption for access control in cloud computing. IEEE Trans. Dependable Secur. Comput. **14**(6), 679–692 (2017)

6. Goyal, V., Pandey, O., Sahai, A., Waters, B.: Attribute-based encryption for fine-grained access control of encrypted data. In: 13th ACM Conference on Computer and Communications Security, CCS 2006, Alexandria, VA, USA, 30 October–3 November, pp. 89–98 (2006)

7. Liu, J.K., Au, M.H., Huang, X., Lu, R., Li, J.: Fine-grained two-factor access control for web-based cloud computing services. IEEE Trans. Inf. Forensics Secur. **11**(3), 484–497 (2016)

8. Zhang, R., Ma, H., Lu, Y.: Fine-grained access control system based on fully outsourced attribute-based encryption. J. Syst. Softw. **125**, 344–353 (2017)

9. James Ball, J.B., Greenwald, G.: Revealed: how US and UK spy agencies defeat internet privacy and security. Guardian Weekly (2013)

10. Perlroth, N., Larson, J., Shane, S.: NSA able to foil basic safeguards of privacy on web. The New York Times, 5 September 2013

11. Dodis, Y., Ganesh, C., Golovnev, A., Juels, A., Ristenpart, T.: A formal treatment of backdoored pseudorandom generators. In: Oswald, E., Fischlin, M. (eds.) EUROCRYPT 2015. LNCS, vol. 9056, pp. 101–126. Springer, Heidelberg (2015). https://doi.org/10.1007/978-3-662-46800-5_5

12. Checkoway, S., et al.: On the practical exploitability of dual EC in TLS implementations. In: Proceedings of the 23rd USENIX Security Symposium, San Diego, CA, USA, 20–22 August 2014, pp. 319–335 (2014)

13. Greenwald, G.: No place to hide: Edward Snowden, the NSA, and the US surveillance state. Macmillan, New York (2014)

14. Vulnerability summary for CVE-2014-1260 (heartbleed), April 2014. http://cve.mitre.org/cgi-bin/cvename.cgi?name=CVE-2014-1260

15. Vulnerability summary for CVE-2014-1266 (goto fail), February 2014. http://cve.mitre.org/cgi-bin/cvename.cgi?name=CVE-2014-1266

16. Vulnerability summary for CVE-2014-6271 (shellshock), September 2014. http://cve.mitre.org/cgi-bin/cvename.cgi?name=CVE-2014-6271

17. Lenstra, A.K., Hughes, J.P., Augier, M., Bos, J.W., Kleinjung, T., Wachter, C.: Public keys. In: Safavi-Naini, R., Canetti, R. (eds.) CRYPTO 2012. LNCS, vol. 7417, pp. 626–642. Springer, Heidelberg (2012). https://doi.org/10.1007/978-3-642-32009-5_37

18. Mironov, I., Stephens-Davidowitz, N.: Cryptographic reverse firewalls. In: Oswald, E., Fischlin, M. (eds.) EUROCRYPT 2015. LNCS, vol. 9057, pp. 657–686. Springer, Heidelberg (2015). https://doi.org/10.1007/978-3-662-46803-6_22

19. Dodis, Y., Mironov, I., Stephens-Davidowitz, N.: Message transmission with reverse firewalls—secure communication on corrupted machines. In: Robshaw, M., Katz, J. (eds.) CRYPTO 2016. LNCS, vol. 9814, pp. 341–372. Springer, Heidelberg (2016). https://doi.org/10.1007/978-3-662-53018-4_13

20. Chen, R., Mu, Y., Yang, G., Susilo, W., Guo, F., Zhang, M.: Cryptographic reverse firewall via malleable smooth projective hash functions. In: Cheon, J.H., Takagi, T. (eds.) ASIACRYPT 2016. LNCS, vol. 10031, pp. 844–876. Springer, Heidelberg (2016). https://doi.org/10.1007/978-3-662-53887-6_31

21. Rouselakis, Y., Waters, B.: Practical constructions and new proof methods for large universe attribute-based encryption. In: ACM SIGSAC Conference on Computer and Communications Security, CCS 2013, Berlin, Germany, 4–8 November, pp. 463–474 (2013)

22. Sahai, A., Waters, B.: Fuzzy identity-based encryption. In: Cramer, R. (ed.) EUROCRYPT 2005. LNCS, vol. 3494, pp. 457–473. Springer, Heidelberg (2005). https://doi.org/10.1007/11426639_27

23. Ostrovsky, R., Sahai, A., Waters, B.: Attribute-based encryption with non-monotonic access structures. In: PACM Conference on Computer and Communications Security, CCS 2007, Alexandria, Virginia, USA, 28–31 October, pp. 195–203 (2007)

24. Lewko, A., Okamoto, T., Sahai, A., Takashima, K., Waters, B.: Fully secure functional encryption: attribute-based encryption and (hierarchical) inner product encryption. In: Gilbert, H. (ed.) EUROCRYPT 2010. LNCS, vol. 6110, pp. 62–91. Springer, Heidelberg (2010). https://doi.org/10.1007/978-3-642-13190-5_4

25. Okamoto, T., Takashima, K.: Fully secure functional encryption with general relations from the decisional linear assumption. In: Rabin, T. (ed.) CRYPTO 2010. LNCS, vol. 6223, pp. 191–208. Springer, Heidelberg (2010). https://doi.org/10.1007/978-3-642-14623-7_11

26. Waters, B.: Ciphertext-policy attribute-based encryption: an expressive, efficient, and provably secure realization. In: Catalano, D., Fazio, N., Gennaro, R., Nicolosi, A. (eds.) PKC 2011. LNCS, vol. 6571, pp. 53–70. Springer, Heidelberg (2011). https://doi.org/10.1007/978-3-642-19379-8_4

27. Bethencourt, J., Sahai, A., Waters, B.: Ciphertext-policy attribute-based encryption. In: IEEE Symposium on Security and Privacy (S&P 2007), Oakland, CA, USA, 20–23 May 2007, pp. 321–334. IEEE (2007)

28. Cheung, L., Newport, C.C.: Provably secure ciphertext policy ABE. In: ACM Conference on Computer and Communications Security, CCS 2007, Alexandria, VA, USA, 28–31 October, pp. 456–465 (2007)

29. Beimel, A.: Secure schemes for secret sharing and key distribution. Ph.D. thesis, Technion-Israel Institute of Technology, Faculty of Computer Science (1996)

30. Li, J., Jia, C., Li, J., Chen, X.: Outsourcing encryption of attribute-based encryption with mapreduce. In: Chim, T.W., Yuen, T.H. (eds.) ICICS 2012. LNCS, vol. 7618, pp. 191–201. Springer, Heidelberg (2012). https://doi.org/10.1007/978-3-642-34129-8_17

31. Li, J., Huang, X., Li, J., Chen, X., Xiang, Y.: Securely outsourcing attribute-based encryption with checkability. IEEE Trans. Parallel Distrib. Syst. 25(8), 2201–2210 (2014)

32. Hohenberger, S., Waters, B.: Online/offline attribute-based encryption. In: Krawczyk, H. (ed.) PKC 2014. LNCS, vol. 8383, pp. 293–310. Springer, Heidelberg (2014). https://doi.org/10.1007/978-3-642-54631-0_17

33. Green, M., Hohenberger, S., Waters, B.: Outsourcing the decryption of ABE ciphertexts. In: 20th USENIX Security Symposium, San Francisco, CA, USA, 8–12 August (2011)

34. Lynn, B.: The stanford pairing based crypto library. http://crypto.stanford.edu/pbc

Making *Any* Attribute-Based Encryption Accountable, Efficiently

Junzuo Lai[1,2(✉)] and Qiang Tang[3]

[1] Ji'nan University, Guangzhou, China
laijunzuo@gmail.com
[2] State Key Laboratory of Cryptology, Beijing, China
[3] New Jersey Institute of Technology, Newark, USA
qiang@njit.edu

Abstract. Attribute-based encryption (ABE) as one of the most interesting multi-recipient public encryption systems, naturally requires some "tracing mechanisms" to identify misbehaving users to foster accountability when unauthorized key re-distributions are taken place.

We give a generic construction of (black-box) traceable ABE which only doubles the ciphertext size of the underlying ABE scheme. When instantiating properly, it yields the first such scheme with constant size ciphertext and expressive access control.

Furthermore, we extend our generic construction of traceable ABE to support authority accountability. This property is essential for generating an un-deniable proof for user misbehaviors. Our new generic construction gives the first black-box traceable ABE with authority accountability, and constant size ciphertext. All properties are achieved in standard security models.

1 Introduction

Attribute-Based Encryption (ABE), first introduced in [12,29], naturally generalizes the concept of identity based encryption (IBE) to support more expressive "identities" as they can be any string. Two major types of attribute based encryption schemes exist: ciphertext-policy attribute based encryption (CP-ABE) [2] and key-policy attribute based encryption (KP-ABE) [12]. In a CP-ABE scheme, each ciphertext is associated with a decryption policy which can be represented using e.g., an access structure or a boolean formula; every user's decryption key is associated with an attribute set which is used to describe the key owner. A user is able to decrypt a ciphertext only if the set of attributes associated with the user's decryption key satisfies the decryption policy associated with the ciphertext. While in a KP-ABE scheme, the situation is reversed, where every ciphertext is associated with a set of attributes and every user's decryption key is associated with an access structure.

Since its introduction, great advancements have been taken place over the years, both on the expressibility of the decryption policy (can be as general as an circuit [8,9]), and on the asymptotic efficiency (e.g., constant size ciphertext).

© Springer Nature Switzerland AG 2018
J. Lopez et al. (Eds.): ESORICS 2018, LNCS 11099, pp. 527–547, 2018.
https://doi.org/10.1007/978-3-319-98989-1_26

Due to its expressibility, attribute based encryption could be very useful in many settings, here we list two typical application scenarios: (i) enforcing access control by encrypting the data with the access control policy, and issuing decryption keys to users according to their attributes. Such mechanism can be used in company internal networks to improve the robustness of their access control functionality. (ii) distributing contents via a cloud or content delivery network. The content provider simply encrypts the data and store the ciphertext in the publicly accessible cloud, then he issues decryption keys for each subscriber according to his subscription package. For instance, a movie producer encrypts two versions of a movie (based on the resolutions, say) m_1, m_2. The decryption policy for the ciphertext corresponding to the standard quality version m_1 (say 720p) is "(status = regular user $\vee$ status = premier user) $\wedge$ age ≥ 18" and the decryption policy for the high resolution version m_2 (say 1080p) is "status = premier member $\wedge$ age ≥ 18". During the subscription, a premier subscriber who paid higher fees can obtain decryption key that allows him to have access to the high resolution version of the movie.

Despite all recent advancements and those potential applications, attribute based encryption schemes still have not been widely deployed in practice. Besides the potential problem of its concrete efficiency, there is another serious accountability problem that needs to be addressed before the deployment of attribute based encryption (at least to the above two application scenarios). We can see that attribute based encryption is a special kind of multi-recipient encryption scheme in which the decryption capability (or the attributes) from different users may overlap. Imagine in the access control example, each employee in a company is assigned with a secret key according to his position (and the corresponding access rights) to get access to the company documents which may contain business secret. A natural key management policy of the company could be "do not share your decryption key to others, especially to outsiders". But there is no way to prevent a "corrupted" employee from doing so. Although an employee may not directly expose her decryption key material, she can still write a decoder program and share a potentially more restricted decoder program to others. When such an unauthorized decoder, which can be used to decrypt ciphertext with certain policies, is noticed, there are multiple key owners might be suspects. Thus identifying the source of such unauthorized sharing is critical for the manager to carry out proper punishments in order to enforce his key management policy. Similar issue arises in the second application scenario that a pirate decoder of movies should be trace back to the misbehaving subscriber.

The first accountability property we will pursue is to enable tracing[1] from an unauthorized decoder to the actual key owner. From the first look, such traceability in ABE schemes seems to be very close to that in traitor tracing schemes [6]. The major difference here is that in a traitor tracing scheme, every user has the same privilege, just finding out one corrupted user is a reasonable goal.

---

[1] We note here that the tracing mechanism we are pursuing in this paper follows a similar vein to the well-known notion of traitor tracing [6], and it is not hard to see that completely preventing the unauthorized leakage is essentially infeasible.

While in the setting of ABE, different user may have different access right, just identifying one corrupted user is not satisfying. For example, in the movie distribution application, the two users, one with attribute "status = premier member" and the other with attribute "status = regular member", collude to produce a pirate decoder that has attribute "status = premier member", but the tracing algorithm may only return the user with attribute "status = regular member", who has less to lose. (Such difference was first pointed out and formalized by Katz and Schroder in [13] in the setting of predicate encryption.) It turns out that trivially combining ABE with a traitor tracing scheme would only achieve above weak traceability and fail for the stronger traceability requirement. (see details at the end of Sect. 3.1). A series of works tried to combine traitor tracing and ABE in a complex way for achieving stronger traceability.

As a result, they will have to use the inefficient ABE schemes or traitor tracing constructions, thus incur large ciphertext overhead (e.g., square root of the number of users [22]); or only support very primitive policy [20], and white-box traceability [23,24]. Instead, in this paper, we demonstrate how to compile *any* ABE scheme to satisfy the stronger traceability. Such flexibility enables us to choose the best possible ABE scheme to remove both hurdles above. In particular, the size of ciphertext can be pushed down to constant.

However, having strong traceability is still not enough for resolving the accountability problem in attribute based encryption. To see this, let us continue with the above example. Suppose one employee is traced from an unauthorized decoder leaked to the competing company by the manager. When the manager shows the result and asks the employ to resign, the employee can confidently deny and claim that the tracing result is not an non-repudiable proof thus cannot be considered as an evidence for her misbehavior (even brought to a court). This is true because attribute based encryption has the key escrow problem that a key generation center is needed to issue the decryption keys. In this case, either a corrupted user who obtains a secret key from the key generation center, or a corrupted key generation center could be responsible.

The above further motivates us to consider the "accountability" on the key generation center so that an un-deniable proof can be established once a misbehaving user is caught. This is a natural generalization of accountable authority identity based encryption proposed in Crypto' 07 [10] in which every identity will correspond to exponentially many keys, and the user picks one of them obliviously. There are also works considering such a notion in ABE [25]. Unfortunately, besides relying on specific ABE construction and inherit all weakness, all those results can only work if the corrupted party (either a key owner or the key generation center) leaks a *well-formed* secret key. This obviously cannot be true in practice as the corrupted party can simply modify the key material and give instructions about how to adapt the decryption algorithm, or even write an obfuscated program so that the actual secret key used is never exposed. What's worse, this condition also puts further restriction on the definition of non-framing property, i.e., a malicious key generation center cannot frame an innocent user. In such a definition, the adversary is only allowed to run key generation protocol for one specific victim. However, in practice, a key generation center can always wait until many keys are issued, and frame one of them.

We also make progress along this line. We further compile our generic traceable CP-ABE scheme to support authority accountability which allows *black-box* tracing, i.e., the tracing algorithm only needs oracle access to an unauthorized decoder, and no artificial restriction is put on the non-framing definition.

1.1 Our Contributions

In this paper, we give a thorough study of accountability problems in attribute based encryption schemes. We give a *generic* construction of traceable ABE schemes and further make them accountable authority. Moreover, the generic construction only doubles the ciphertext size and supports black-box traceability which is *the* standard model for tracing. The benefits of such a generic construction are twofolds:

Practical benefits—if we instantiate the generic construction with an efficient ABE scheme, it gives the *first* constant size ciphertext traceable ABE scheme, also the *first* accountable authority ABE scheme with black-box traceability (still with constant size ciphertext).

Conceptual benefits—there have been various works considering ad hoc methods combining ABE schemes with traitor tracing schemes, which "obfuscate" the essence of traceability in ABE schemes. Our generic construction peels off the complexity of both its construction and analysis, and demonstrate a simple and clear picture about how accountability problems in ABE could be addressed. We use CP-ABE as an example to demonstrate our generic constructions, we note that our technique actually can easily be adapted to KP-ABE schemes. More concretely, our contributions are as follows:

1. We first propose a generic construction of traceable CP-ABE that can compile any CP-ABE to have traceability. The traceability is done in a standard black-box way that the tracing algorithm only need oracle access to the unauthorized (or pirate) decoder. Our construction utilizes a combinatorial object of fingerprinting codes, and expands the attribute set of each user with extra indices represented by the codeword that is assigned to him. If we pick the famous Tardos codes [30], our generic construction only double the ciphertext size of the underlying ABE. An overview comparing the efficiency of our traceable CP-ABE scheme to those of other traceable CP-ABE schemes is given in Table 1.

   We emphasize that such generic construction achieves the strong traceability that the accused traitor not only participates in producing the pirate decoder, but also his attributes are indeed used by the pirate decoder. See Sect. 3 for formal definitions.

2. We then further transform our generic traceable CP-ABE to be authority accountable, which means the key generation center cannot be aware of the user secret key completely, thus an un-deniable proof can be formed if a traitor is caught from a pirate decoder (this is done via a new Judge protocol). The

simple structure of our generic construction of traceable CP-ABE provides us opportunities to upgrade the construction. Inspired by the concept of asymmetric fingerprinting codes, we adapt asymmetric Tardos codes [14] to the setting of accountable authority CP-ABE.

This new generic construction for the first time allows black-box traceability while preserving the efficiency of our traceable CP-ABE. An overview comparing the efficiency of our accountable authority CP-ABE scheme to those of other accountable authority CP-ABE schemes is given in Table 2.

The main challenge in this setting is to ensure no inconsistency between the tracing and the Judge protocol, i.e., an identified traitor will evade the confirmation from the judge. This heavily relies on the security of the asymmetric fingerprinting scheme. We further utilize a technical building block called fingerprinted data transfer for the key generation protocol to ensure that no innocent user can be framed.

Table 1. Comparison of traceable CP-ABE schemes, where "N" denotes the total number of users in the system, and we instantiate our generic construction with the CP-ABE scheme proposed in [27].

Scheme	Large universe	Expressiveness of access structures	Black-box traceability	Ciphertext size
[20]	×	×	√	$O(1)$
[23]	×	√	×	$O(1)$
[24]	√	√	×	$O(1)$
[22]	×	√	√	$O(\sqrt{N})$
Ours	√	√	√	$O(1)$

Table 2. Comparison of accountable authority CP-ABE schemes, where we instantiate our generic construction with the CP-ABE scheme proposed in [27].

Scheme	Large universe	Expressiveness of access structures	Black-box traceability	Ciphertext size
[25]	×	√	×	$O(1)$
[32]	√	√	×	$O(1)$
Ours	√	√	√	$O(1)$

1.2   Related Work

Traceable Attribute Based Encryption. Traceable ABE has been studied in various works [20, 22–24]. To the best of our knowledge, *all* of them consider ad hoc combination of traitor tracing and specific attribute based encryption. In particular, the scheme in [20] only supports access structures having a single AND gate with wildcard. The schemes in [23,24] support only *white-box* traceability, i.e., it only works against malicious users from leaking well-formed decryption keys directly. Later in [22], Liu et al. proposed an expressive black-box traceable CP-ABE, but it incurs large ciphertext size (square root to the total number of users), thus seriously hinders its practicality. Our generic construction does not suffer from any of the above restrictions.

Accountable Authority Attribute Based Encryption. In order to mitigate the key escrow problem and the malicious key delegation problem in CP-ABE, the notion of accountable authority CP-ABE was studied in [25,32]. Both constructions only achieve *white-box* traceability, i.e., requires the adversary to provide a well-formed secret key. [25] further restricts the malicious key generation center to execute key generation protocol with only one target user. This is not only unrealistic, but also excludes the challenge in tracing systems: the collusion problem. Those serious restrictions suggest that the notion of accountable authority ABE has not been understood. Our generic construction makes a step forward.

Accountable Authority Identity Based Encryption. Goyal [10] introduced the notion of A-IBE as an approach to mitigate the key escrow problem in IBE, Subsequently, Goyal et al. [11] proposed a construction having traceability in the full black-box model with large ciphertext size. Libert and Vergnaud [21] proposed an efficient A-IBE scheme, but only is proven traceable in the weak black-box model. Sahai and Seyalioglu [28] presented the first A-IBE scheme which achieves full black-box traceability and adaptive security against dishonest users at the cost of having a linear sized ciphertext. Under non-standard assumptions, Yuen et al. [31] gave an A-IBE scheme with constant-size ciphertext, while has full black-box traceability and adaptive security against dishonest users. Lai et al. [19] proposed the first A-IBE scheme with public traceability, where tracing a decryption box only uses a public tracing key. Recently, Kiayias and Tang [18] gave a generic A-IBE scheme using oblivious transfer, and showed how to modify the generic construction to provide public traceability. However, their technique cannot be trivially extended to ABE setting due to collusion.

Self-enforcement and Proactive Deterring Mechanisms. Self-enforcement was initially proposed in digital signets that leaking a decryption key leads to revealing of some user secret [7]. Later it was systematically studied in enforcing key management policy in public key infrastructure [16], and in deterring copyright infringement [17]. Especially, leveraging the properties of cryptocurrency, [16,17] studied how to realize the deterrence that unauthorized re-distribution of pirate decoder leads to the loss of coins directly. Considering proactive deterring mechanisms in ABE would be interesting open problems.

2   Preliminaries

Basic Notations. If S is a set, then $s \leftarrow S$ denotes the operation of picking an element s uniformly at random from S. Let $\mathbb{N}$ denote the set of natural numbers. If $n \in \mathbb{N}$ then $[n]$ denotes the set $\{1, \ldots, n\}$. Let $z \leftarrow \mathsf{A}(x, y, \ldots)$

denote the operation of running an algorithm A with inputs $(x, y, \ldots)$ and output z. A function $f(\lambda)$ is *negligible* if for every $c > 0$ there exists a λ_c such that $f(\lambda) < 1/\lambda^c$ for all $\lambda > \lambda_c$.

Robust Fingerprinting Code. A *binary fingerprinting code* [15] is a pair of algorithms (Gen, Trace), where Gen is a probabilistic algorithm taking a number n (upper bound on the number of codewords in the system), an optional number $t \in [n] = \{1, \ldots, n\}$ (upper-bound on the detected coalition size), and security parameter ϵ as input and outputs n bit-strings $\mathcal{C} = \{C_1, \ldots, C_n\}$ (called codewords), where $C_i = \mathsf{c}_1^i \ldots \mathsf{c}_\ell^i$ for $i \in [\ell]$ and a tracing key tk. Trace is a deterministic algorithm inputting the tracing key tk and a "pirate" codeword C^*, and outputting a subset $\mathcal{U}_{acc} \subseteq [n]$ of accused users. A code is called *bias-based* [1] if each codeword $C_j = \mathsf{c}_1^j \ldots \mathsf{c}_\ell^j$ is sampled according to a vector of biases $\langle p_1, \ldots, p_\ell \rangle$, where $\forall j \in [n], \forall i \in [\ell], \Pr[\mathsf{c}_i^j = 1] = p_i$, and $p_i \in [0, 1]$.

A fingerprinting code is called $t-$*collusion resistant* (*fully collusion resistant* if $t = n$) if for any adversary $\mathcal{A}$ who corrupts up to t users (whose indices form a set $\mathcal{U}_{cor} \subset \{1, \cdots, N\}$), and outputs a pirate codeword $C^* = \mathsf{c}_1^* \ldots \mathsf{c}_n^*$ (which satisfies the marking assumption, i.e., for each $i \in [\ell], \mathsf{c}_i^* = \mathsf{c}_i^j$ for some $j \in \mathcal{U}_{cor}$),

$$\Pr[\mathcal{U}_{acc} = \emptyset \text{ or } \mathcal{U}_{acc} \not\subseteq \mathcal{U}_{cor} : \mathcal{U}_{acc} \leftarrow \mathsf{Trace}(tk, C^*)] \leq \epsilon$$

This characterizes that the probability that no users are accused or an innocent user is accused is bounded by ε.

A fingerprinting code is $\delta-$*robust* if the pirate code is further allowed to contain the symbol of '?' (not more than $\delta \ell$, where ℓ is the code length) without violating the marking assumption: now for each $i \in [\ell]$, either $\mathsf{c}_i^* = \mathsf{c}_i^j$ for some $j \in \mathcal{U}_{cor}$, or $\mathsf{c}_i^* = $ '?'.

We also recall the Tardos code [30] $F_{nt\epsilon}$ here, it has length $n = 100l^2k$, with $k - \log \frac{1}{\epsilon}$. The Gen algorithm generates a codeword as follows. For each segment index $j \in [\ell]$, it chooses a bias $p_j \in [0, 1]$ according to a distribution μ (see [30] for the definition of μ). Each bias satisfies $\frac{1}{300t} \leq p_j \leq 1 - \frac{1}{300t}$, where t is the collusion size. For each codeword $C = \mathsf{c}_1 \ldots \mathsf{c}_\ell$ outputted by Gen, $\Pr[\mathsf{c}_j = 1] = p_j$, and $\Pr[\mathsf{c}_j = 0] = 1 - p_j$ for all $j \in [\ell]$. Regarding security, there is a Trace algorithm such that, for any coalition of size at most t, with probability at least $1 - \epsilon^{t/4}$ accuses a member of the coalition, while any non-member is accused with probability at most ϵ. Note that Tardos code can be made *robust* if we extend the code length (see [3] for details).

Fingerprinted Data Transfer. Our accountable authority ABE scheme will rely on a more advanced abstraction – fingerprinted data transfer protocol – that was defined in [14]. A fingerprinted data transfer (FDT) (corresponding to a bias-based binary fingerprinting code) involves two parties, a sender S and a receiver R. The sender inputs two biases $p_0, p_1 \in [0, 1]$, four messages $(m_0^0, m_0^1), (m_1^0, m_1^1)$, and a bit $c \in \{0, 1\}$; At the end of the protocol, R outputs $\{m_i^{b_i}\}$ for $i, b_i \in \{0, 1\}$ such that $\Pr[b_i = 1] = p_i$; while S outputs b_c. The fingerprinted data transfer functionality can be expressed as:

$$\mathsf{FDT}[\bot, ((p_0, p_1), (m_0^0, m_0^1, m_1^0, m_1^1), c)] = [(m_0^{b_0}, m_1^{b_1}), b_c], \text{where } \Pr[b_i = 1] = p_i.$$

The security of a fingerprinted data transfer protocol follows the standard simulation based paradigm, for details we refer to Appendix A.1.

3   Generic Construction of Traceable Attribute Based Encryption

In this section, we will discuss our generic construction of traceable CP-ABE scheme. First we present the formal definitions.

3.1   Definition and Security Models

Traceable CP-ABE. Concretely, a traceable CP-ABE scheme consists of the following five algorithms:

Setup(n, λ): The setup algorithm takes as input the number of users n in the system and a security parameter λ, outputs a master secret key msk, a potential tracing key tk and the public parameters mpk.

KeyGen(mpk, msk, i, S_i): The key generation algorithm takes as input the public parameter mpk, the master secret key msk and a set of attributes S_i. It outputs a private decryption key sk_{i,S_i}, which is assigned and identified by a unique index $i \in \{1, \dots, n\}$.

Enc$(mpk, m, \mathbb{A})$: The encryption algorithm takes as input the public parameters mpk, a message m and a decryption policy that is represented by an access structure $\mathbb{A}$. It outputs a ciphertext c.

Dec(sk_{i,S_i}, c): The decryption algorithm m takes as input the public parameters mpk, a private decryption key sk_{i,S_i} and a ciphertext c. It outputs a message m or $\perp$.

Trace$^{D_S}(mpk, tk, S)$ The tracing algorithm takes as input the public parameters mpk, the tracing key tk, and has black-box access to a δ-useful pirate decoder D_S[2] for a set of attributes S. It outputs an index set $I \subseteq \{1, \dots, n\}$ which identifies the set of malicious users.

Security of Traceable CP-ABE. The security of traceable CP-ABE is composed of the standard semantic security and traceability. For the standard semantic security, we refer to Appendix A.2, and here we only define the strong traceability. Intuitively, the goal of the tracing algorithm to identify at least one of the colluder users, and such identified traitor's attributes should be "critical" for the pirate decoder, (also at the same time, no innocent user should be accused). Consider the following *traceability* game (which could be describing either weak traceability and strong traceability):

---

[2] For a non-negligible δ, a pirate decoder D_S for a set of attributes S is δ-useful, i.e. for any message m and any access structure $\mathbb{A}$ which is satisfied by S, if $\Pr[D_S(\text{Enc}(mpk, m, \mathbb{A})) = m] \geq \delta$.

Setup: The challenger runs the Setup algorithm to generate public parameters mpk, tracing key tk, and master secret key msk. It gives mpk to the adversary $\mathcal{A}$ and keeps tk and msk to itself.

Key Query: The adversary adaptively queries the challenger for secret keys corresponding to sets of attributes $S_1, \ldots, S_q$ for users with indices $k_1, \ldots, k_q$. In response, the challenger runs the key generation algorithm and gives the corresponding secret key sk_{k_i, S_i} to the adversary for $1 \le i \le q$.

Output: $\mathcal{A}$ outputs a δ-useful pirate decoder D_S for an attributes set S.

Let $C = \{k_i | 1 \le i \le q\}$ be the indices of the users corrupted by the adversary and I is the indices of the identified traitors, i.e. the output of $\mathsf{Trace}^{D_S}(mpk, tk, S)$. The adversary $\mathcal{A}$ wins the strong traceability game if: (1) $I = \emptyset$, i.e., no one is accused; (2) or $I \not\subseteq C$, i.e., an innocent user is accused; (3) or none of the identified traitors' attributes set includes S as a subset. The meaning of the third condition characterizes that the identified traitors have to contribute to the pirate decoder their actual functional key according to their attributes.

The advantage of an adversary in the game is defined as the probability that $\mathcal{A}$ wins the strong traceability game, where the probability is taken over the random bits used by the challenger and the adversary.

Definition 1. *A traceable CP-ABE scheme is strongly traceable if all polynomial time adversaries have at most negligible advantage in the above game.*

Note that the adversary $\mathcal{A}$ wins the weak traceability game if we only require the adversary the first two conditions. With only such a weaker requirement, it is possible that the identified traitor does not really have the decryption capability as the decoder. Consider the following trivial generic solution: we run an ABE scheme and a traitor tracing scheme in parallel, the encryption algorithm will first split the message m into $m_1 \oplus m_2$ for a randomly chosen m_1, and encrypts m_1 using ABE scheme and m_2 using the encryption algorithm of the traitor tracing scheme. Such trivial construction can already achieve the weak traceability to identify one of the corrupted users due to the property of traitor tracing scheme. However, as these two systems are not tightly bound together, it cannot satisfy the strong traceability: User i who has the attribute S_i and user j who has the attribute S_j can collude to produce a pirate decoder that has attribute S_i, where user i contributes his partial keys of the ABE system and user j contributes his partial keys of the traitor tracing system. In this way, user j will always be identified as a traitor even if he does not have the attributes of the pirate decoder at all, i.e. attribute S_i.

3.2 A Generic Construction from Tardos Codes

Basic Intuition. The above trivial solution shows that the traitor tracing system has to be embedded into the ABE system. While it might be feasible to be based on concrete algebraic structure, from the first look, it is not clear how we can have a generic construction as ABE itself does not offer traceability. We observe that instead of considering combing a traitor tracing scheme with an

ABE, we may go to a lower level to identify some combinatoric objects that could be useful: (1) It enables identifying source with collusion resistance; (2) It can be embedded to the ABE system generically. In particular, we observe that fingerprinting codes do offer such properties simultaneously.

In more detail, in a binary fingerprinting code, everyone is assigned with a bit-string as the codeword. A collusion of corrupted users can pool their codewords together to produce a pirate code (only restricted by the marking assumption, see Sect. 2 above for details). There is a tracing algorithm that can identify a source codeword from such a pirate codeword. Moreover, such traceability can be easily built into multi-recipient encryption schemes (not only for traitor tracing). The crux here is that each codeword is just a bit string, which can be used as index for user to assign keys. In the setting of CP-ABE, we can use such string to select extra dummy attributes, and the encryption policy will expand the original policy to include such dummy attribute. During regular encryption, both ciphertext encrypting the same message regarding both dummy attributes will be present, thus the extra dummy attribute will not influence the original policy. Tracing can be facilitated by feeding two ciphertext carrying different plaintext. Based on the responses, tracer can recover a pirate codeword (that might include '?'). The robust fingerprinting code then can be used to find one corrupted codeword, thus the traitor.

We remark that the marking assumption is enforced simply by the semantic security of the encryption. More importantly, we do not run the tracing system in parallel with ABE, instead, each codeword is entangled with the attributes set, thus the identified traitor's attributes will be needed for the decoder for sure. Next, we present the formal description of the construction and analysis.

Detailed Construction. Let $(\overline{\mathsf{Setup}}, \overline{\mathsf{KeyGen}}, \overline{\mathsf{Enc}}, \overline{\mathsf{Dec}})$ be any CP-ABE scheme, and $(\overline{\mathsf{Gen}}, \overline{\mathsf{Trace}})$ be a robust binary fingerprinting code (e.g. robust Tardos code [3]). Our generic construction of traceable CP-ABE works as follows:

$\mathsf{Setup}(n, \lambda)$: Let $\epsilon = 1/2^\lambda$. Run $\overline{\mathsf{Setup}}(\lambda)$ and obtain $(\overline{mpk}, \overline{msk})$; also run $\overline{\mathsf{Gen}}(n, \epsilon, \delta)$ to obtain $\{W_1, \ldots, W_n\} := \Gamma$, and tracing key tk, where $W_i \in \{0,1\}^\ell$, for $i = 1, \ldots, n$. Choose dummy attributes $\mathtt{Attr}^0, \mathtt{Attr}^1$, and $\{\mathtt{Attr}_i\}$ for $i = 1, \ldots, \ell$, and set

$$mpk = (\overline{mpk}, \mathtt{Attr}^0, \mathtt{Attr}^1, \mathtt{Attr}_1, \ldots, \mathtt{Attr}_\ell), \ msk = (\overline{msk}, \Gamma).$$

$\mathsf{KeyGen}(mpk, msk, S_i)$: Suppose user i has attribute set S_i. For $k = 1, \ldots, \ell$, let $w_k^{(i)} \in \{0,1\}$ be the k-th bit of W_i and $S_{i,k} = S_i \cup \{\mathtt{Attr}^{w_k^{(i)}}\} \cup \{\mathtt{Attr}_k\}$, run

$$\overline{sk}_{S_{i,k}} \leftarrow \overline{\mathsf{KeyGen}}(mpk, \overline{msk}, S_{i,k})$$

Output the private key $sk_{i,S_i} = \{W_i, \overline{sk}_{S_{i,k}}\}_{k \in [\ell]}$.

$\mathsf{Enc}(mpk, m, \mathbb{A})$: Choose a random position $j \in \{1, \ldots, \ell\}$ and set $\overline{\mathbb{A}}_b = \mathbb{A} \wedge \{\mathtt{Attr}_j\} \wedge \{\mathtt{Attr}^b\}$, where $b \in \{0,1\}$. Compute

$$c_0 \leftarrow \overline{\mathsf{Enc}}(\overline{mpk}, m, \overline{\mathbb{A}}_0), \ c_1 \leftarrow \overline{\mathsf{Enc}}(\overline{mpk}, m, \overline{\mathbb{A}}_1)$$

Output the ciphertext $c = (j, c_0, c_1)$.

$\mathsf{Dec}(mpk, sk_{i,S_i}, c)$: Parse the private decryption key sk_{i,S_i} as $(W_i, \{\overline{sk}_{S_i,k}\}_{k \in [\ell]})$, and the ciphertext c as (j, c_0, c_1). If $w_j^{(i)} = 0$, output $\overline{\mathsf{Dec}}(mpk, \overline{sk}_{S_{i,j}}, c_0)$; otherwise (i.e. $w_j^{(i)} = 1$), output $\overline{\mathsf{Dec}}(mpk, \overline{sk}_{S_{i,j}}, c_1)$.

$\mathsf{Trace}^{D_S}(mpk, tk, S)$: On input the public parameters mpk, the tracing key tk, and the claimed attribute set S of the pirate decoder, the Trace algorithm has oracle access to a δ-useful pirate decoder D_S and does the following: For each j in $\{1, \ldots, \ell\}$, proceed as follows:

1. Choose an access policy $\mathbb{A}$, it is only satisfied by the attributes set S and not satisfied by any subset of S.
2. Set $\overline{\mathbb{A}}_b = \mathbb{A} \wedge \{\mathtt{Attr}_j\} \wedge \{\mathtt{Attr}^b\}$, where $b \in \{0, 1\}$.
3. According to δ, choose proper parameter $N = O(\lambda^2 \ln \ell)$ and repeat the procedure of trying decryption for N times: Choose two random message m, compute

$$c_0 = \overline{\mathsf{Enc}}(mpk, m, \overline{\mathbb{A}}_0), c_1 = \overline{\mathsf{Enc}}(mpk, 0, \overline{\mathbb{A}}_1),$$

$$c_0' = \overline{\mathsf{Enc}}(mpk, m, \overline{\mathbb{A}}_0), c_1' = \overline{\mathsf{Enc}}(mpk, m, \overline{\mathbb{A}}_1).$$

Set $c = (j, c_0, c_1)$ and $c' = (j, c_0', c_1')$.
If $D_S(c) = m_0$, set $w_j = 0$;
else if $D_S(c') = m$ for more than $\sqrt{\lambda}$ times, set $w_j = 1$;
else, set $w_j = $ '?'.[3]
4. Set the pirate codeword $W^* = w_1 \ldots w_\ell$, and run the tracing algorithm of the fingerprinting code $\overline{\mathsf{Trace}}(W^*, tk)$ and output the traitor set I.

Security Analysis. First, semantic security is straightforward. The new encryption algorithm is simply run the ABE scheme twice. Furthermore, each ciphertext is encrypted using a more restricted policy. We omit the details for this property.

Next, we discuss why our construction satisfies strong traceability. First, for simplicity, let us consider the case for $\delta = 1$, i.e., the decoder works perfectly on S. Suppose for a position i, if all $w_i^{(j)} = 0$ for $j \in \mathcal{U}_{cor}$ (the corrupted users), then due to the semantic security, D_S will always output the correct decryption, as the tracing ciphertext c now looks indistinguishable from the regular ciphertext, thus we can correctly capture $w_i = 0$. Similarly, if all $w_i^{(j)} = 1$ for $j \in \mathcal{U}_{cor}$, we can see that D_S will never answer m in the first stage of tests and will always answer m in the second stage of tests, and we again correctly captures $w_i = 1$. The complex case is that there are both 0 and 1 for this position i, then the pirate decoder has to make a decision (including not responding, which yields a "?" that can be handled by a *robust* fingerprinting code). If the decoder answers m correctly, we will set $w_i = 0$; otherwise, the Trace algorithm moves to the second stage of tests. Now because c' is identically distributed as a regular ciphertext, according to correctness, D_S will answer correctly and Trace can correctly capture $w_i = 1$.

---

[3] The tracing idea is similar to the tracing mechanism due to Boneh, Naor [4].

To summarize above, the Trace algorithm will always return a pirate code-word that satisfies the marking assumption, i.e., for each $i \in [\ell]$, $w_i = w_i^{(j)}$ for some $j \in \mathcal{U}_{cor}$. Then the traceability of the fingerprinting code scheme ensures $I \neq \emptyset \wedge I \subseteq \mathcal{U}_{cor}$, where I is the indices of the identified traitors, i.e. the output of $\mathsf{Trace}^{\mathsf{D}_S}(mpk, tk, S)$. Last, let us argue that there exist $j \in I$, such that $S_j \subseteq S$. Suppose D_S only uses keys whose attributes do not satisfy the policy $\mathbb{A}$, then it can never decrypt correctly due to semantic security (especially the collusion resistance of ABE itself). As our Trace algorithm takes action mostly based on a correct answer, this means the "useful" keys in the pirate decoder are all those whose attribute set includes S. To put it another way, the pirate codeword captured by the Trace algorithm is actually generated using codewords of those "useful" keys only.

An imperfect decoder can also be addressed by repetition (and also the robustness of the fingerprinting codes). As the pirate decoder D_S satisfies δ-correctness, that means for ciphertext policy that the claimed attribute set S satisfies, the decoder will answer correctly with probability at least δ. It follows that at most for $\delta \cdot n$ positions, D_S stops working, i.e., for δn many positions i, try decryption using D_S by feeding (i, c_0, c_1) do not give meaningful responses, which yields $w_i =$'?'. For other positions, D_S will function properly, and the above analysis still holds.

As the intuition is not too involved and due to space limit, we defer the complete analysis to the full version and we summarize the security as follows:

Theorem 1. *If the underlying CP-ABE* (Setup, KeyGen, Enc, Dec) *is semantically secure, and the fingerprint code* (Gen, Trace) *is δ-robust and fully collusion resistant, then above CP-ABE scheme is semantically secure and strongly traceable.*

4   Enforcing Authority Accountability

4.1   Definitions and Security Models

As we mentioned in the introduction, the main requirement of authority accountability in traceable ABE is for the following reason: suppose user i is identified from a leaked decoder, however there is also possibility that the decoder is leaked by the key generation center. This ambiguity gives malicious users excuses to evade the punishment. Similar to the concept of asymmetric traitor tracing [26] and accountable authority identity based encryption, we consider the following idea: there will be exponentially many keys per user, and the user will choose one of them obliviously. The technical challenge is to still ensure the structure of the keys (fingerprinted) to maintain the tracing capability.

The KeyGen algorithm now becomes an interactive protocol between the key generation center and each user. After a pirate decoder is noticed, the Trace algorithm will return an index set denoting the corrupted users. There will be an extra Judge protocol that is run among the key generation center, a judge and an accused user to decide whether the user is indeed responsible for the leakage of the pirate box. From above description, we see that the difference of an accountable authority ABE is at the KeyGen, Judge protocols, while the other algorithms are the same as those of traceable ABE. For detailed formal definition, we refer to Appendix A.3.

Security of Accountable Authority ABE. Again, semantic security can be easily adapted from standard definitions. Here we focus more on the security regarding traceability. The first one is the same as traceable ABE, at least one malicious user should be identified as in traceable ABE and further accused by the judge. The challenge in this new setting is that the corrupted users may try to arrange in a way that the result of Trace and Judge to be *inconsistent*. It is easy to see that the traceability in this setting simply adds one more requirement that the Judge protocol should at least accuse one user from the Trace output (actually we can achieve a much stronger requirement that the Judge will accuse all malicious traitors identified by Trace algorithm). We refer formal definition of traceability in Appendix A.3.

The second property is that innocent user cannot be framed by a key generation center, in this way, an accused user will have no excuse to deny. Consider the following non-framing game:

Setup: The adversary $\mathcal{A}$ plays the role of a malicious key generation center, generates mpk, msk and sends mpk to the challenger $\mathcal{C}$.

Key Generation: The adversary and the challenger engage in the KeyGen protocol to generate secret keys for all users. In particular, $\mathcal{A}$ selects attribute sets $S_1, \ldots, S_n$ and generate secret keys for those attribute sets. The challenger will receive secret keys $sk_{S_1}, \ldots, sk_{S_n}$, and the adversary will receive the tracing key tk.

Output: The adversary outputs a decryption box D_S for an attributes set S.

Let I be the indices of the identified traitors, i.e. the output of $\mathsf{Trace}^{D_S}(mpk, tk, S)$, and I' will be the confirmed traitor indices after the Judge protocol. The adversary $\mathcal{A}$ wins the non-framing game if $I' \neq \emptyset$.

Definition 2. *An accountable authority CP-ABE scheme is non-framable if all polynomial time adversaries have at most negligible advantage in the above game.*

Remark 1. Previous work [25,32] considered only white-box traceability, thus in the non-framing game, they also have to specify one single target and only allows the adversary to run KeyGen for this single user. This essentially excludes the main challenge of traceability in the multi-recipient encryption—to defend against collusion. What's worse, this restricts adversary's power too much. As a malicious key generation center, she can obviously output the pirate decoder after issuing keys to multiple, even to all users in the system. Instead, our model removes all those restrictions and tries to capture more realistic scenarios. We also remark that we did not consider here to allow the adversary to issue decryption queries after the key generation phase [11]. We leave this as an open problem.

4.2 Generic Construction of Accountable Authority CP-ABE

Basic Intuition. As illustrated above, the basic idea is that each user will be corresponding to exponentially many secret keys, and the user will choose one of them obliviously. However, note that in our generic construction of traceable ABE, secret key of each user is with special structure and selected according to a fingerprinting code. Suppose we extend the length of the fingerprinting code, then this dummy part can correspond to many keys for one user, and this part could be oblivious to the key generation center. The major technical challenge is to achieve traceability and non-framing property simultaneously. We now draw support from the idea of an asymmetric fingerprinting.

Let us recall the main properties and building blocks of an asymmetric fingerprinting. Suppose we are using the famous Tardos codes [30], which is a bias based codes. In the asymmetric setting [14], the length of the codeword is doubled. The basic requirements are that the authority is only aware of half of the codeword, and the user is not aware of where exactly are the locations that the authority knows the corresponding codeword bits. To facilitate such a goal, a fingerprinted data transfer protocol for the bias based codes was designed [14]. After the protocol, the user will obtain a codeword (or corrected fingerprinted data) with length 2ℓ, and each bit (or the corresponding data) will be distributed according to the bias. And the authority will obtain half of the codeword obliviously according to his choice of locations. Following the security analysis of [14], we can run the original tracing algorithm of Tardos codes to identify traitors. While the judge, using the other half of the codeword, will confirm the accusation. One note we would like to emphasize is that in order to ensure the consistency during the revealing phase to the judge, each party should store the transcripts from the other, and force the other party to open correctly if a judge needs to get involved. We refer detailed protocol to [14].

Now let us look at how to upgrade our traceable ABE to support authority accountability. The key generation center first prepares the corresponding 2ℓ keys for each user (those keys are also based on the extended attribute set). Then using the biases of Tardos codes and the keys as data, the key generation center and the user execute a fingerprinted data transfer protocol as the KeyGen protocol. When a pirate decoder is noticed, the authority will run the tracing algorithm of Tardos codes using the half-codes and the bias as the tracing key. This will yield a set of colluders. If a user i claimed non-guilty, the Judge protocol will be initiated. The idea is to mimic the judge in the (asymmetric) Tardos codes setting. The user and the authority has to supply the judge with the corresponding fingerprinted data transfer protocol transcripts. The judge checks the validity of the fingerprinted data transfer protocol transcripts and uses the other half of the codeword to confirm the accusation.

Detailed Construction. Let $(\overline{\mathsf{Setup}}, \overline{\mathsf{KeyGen}}, \overline{\mathsf{Enc}}, \overline{\mathsf{Dec}})$ be a CP-ABE system. We also use a fingerprinted data transfer system FDT regarding robust Tardos code as a major building block. Our generic construction of accountable authority CP-ABE works as follows:

Setup(λ): It first runs $\overline{\mathsf{Setup}}(\lambda)$ to obtain $(\overline{mpk}, \overline{msk})$. Let ℓ be the code length of robust Tardos code. For each $j \in [2\ell]$, choose bias $p_j \in [0,1]$ according to the distribution defined by Tardos code. Pick a bitstrings $v \in \{0,1\}^\ell$ uniformly at random, and choose dummy attributes $\mathtt{Attr}^0, \mathtt{Attr}^1, \mathtt{Attr}_i$ for $i = 1, \ldots, 2\ell$. Initialize a set $\mathcal{W} = \emptyset$, and set the tracing key $tk = (\{p_j\}_{j \in [2\ell]}, v, \mathcal{W})$. Set

$$mpk = (\overline{mpk}, \mathtt{Attr}^0, \mathtt{Attr}^1, \{\mathtt{Attr}_i\}_{i \in [2\ell]}), \quad msk = (\overline{msk}, \{p_j\}_{j \in [2\ell]}, v)$$

and output the public parameters mpk.

KeyGen($\cdot$): This is a protocol between the key generation center and the user. The key generation center inputs mpk, msk, S_k, and the user inputs mpk, S_k, where S_k is an attribute set.

The key generation center parses the master secret key msk as $(\overline{msk}, \{p_j\}_{j \in [2\ell]}, v)$, and write v as $v_1 \ldots v_\ell$ where $v_i \in \{0,1\}$ is the i-th bit of v for $i \in [\ell]$. For each $i \subset [2\ell]$ and $b \in \{0,1\}$, let $S_{k,i}^b = S_k \cup \{\mathtt{Attr}_i\} \cup \{\mathtt{Attr}^b\}$, and run

$$\overline{sk}_{S_{k,i}}^b \leftarrow \overline{\mathsf{KeyGen}}(\overline{mpk}, \overline{msk}, S_{k,i}^b)$$

Then, for each $i \in [\ell]$, the authority and the user runs the fingerprinted data transfer protocol (FDT), where the authority inputs two biases p_{2i-1}, p_{2i}, four messages $(\overline{sk}_{S_k, 2i-1}^0, \overline{sk}_{S_k, 2i-1}^1), (\overline{sk}_{S_k, 2i}^0, \overline{sk}_{S_k, 2i}^1)$, and a bit v_i.

At the end of the protocol, the user obtains $\overline{sk}_{S_k, 2i-1}^{w_{2i-1}}, \overline{sk}_{S_k, 2i}^{w_{2i}}$ where $w_{2i-1}, w_{2i} \in \{0,1\}$ and $\Pr[w_{2i-1} = 1] = p_{2i-1}, \Pr[w_{2i} = 1] = p_{2i}$, and the authority obtains the bit w_{2i-1+v_i} denoted as $\bar{w}_i$. Note that the fingerprinted data transfer may already contain the necessary committing or zero-knowledge proof steps to ensure both parties to follow the protocol.

The user's private key is set as $sk_{S_k} = (w = w_1 \ldots w_{2\ell}, \{\overline{sk}_{S_{k,i}}^{w_i}\}_{i \subset [2\ell]})$.

The authority uses the half-codeword $\bar{w} = \bar{w}_1 \ldots \bar{w}_\ell$ (which is part of the user codeword) to identify the user, and adds the codeword $\bar{w}$ to the set $\mathcal{W}$, which is used to store the half-code of all the users.

Enc($mpk, m, \mathbb{A}$): Choose a random position $j \in \{1, \ldots, 2\ell\}$ and set $\overline{\mathbb{A}}_b = \mathbb{A} \wedge \{\mathtt{Attr}_j\} \wedge \{\mathtt{Attr}^b\}$, where $b \in \{0,1\}$. Compute

$$c_0 \leftarrow \overline{\mathsf{Enc}}(\overline{mpk}, m, \overline{\mathbb{A}}_0), \quad c_1 \leftarrow \overline{\mathsf{Enc}}(\overline{mpk}, m, \overline{\mathbb{A}}_1)$$

Output the ciphertext $c = (j, c_0, c_1)$.

Dec(mpk, sk_{S_k}, c): Parse the private decryption key sk_{S_k} as $(w = w_1 \ldots w_{2\ell}, \{\overline{sk}_{S_{k,i}}^{w_i}\}_{i \in [2\ell]})$, and the ciphertext c as (j, c_0, c_1). If $w_i = b$, output

$$\overline{\mathsf{Dec}}(\overline{mpk}, \overline{sk}_{S_{k,i}}^b, c_b).$$

Trace$^{D_S}(mpk, tk, S, \delta)$: The Trace algorithm has only oracle access to a pirate decoder D_S. Parse the master secret key msk as $(\overline{msk}, \{p_j\}_{j \in [2\ell]}, v = v_1 \ldots v_\ell)$. Let $T = \{2i - 1 + v_i\}_{i \in [\ell]}$ be the subset of locations that the key generation center knows the half-code of the user. For each $j \in T$, run the Trace algorithm of our traceable ABE scheme in Sect. 3 and output a set I of traitor indices.

Judge(·) This is a protocol among the key generation center, an identified traitor i who does not commit guilty and the judge. The key generation center is with input (mpk, msk, D_S, tk), the user is with input (mpk, sk_{S_k}), and the judge is with input (mpk, D_S).

1. The user first reveals the complete codeword of her, and prove its correctness according to the FDT protocol transcript.
2. The key generation center sends the judge the set $T = \{2j - 1 + v_j\}_{j \in [\ell]}$ of locations that the key generation knows the half-code of the user, and proves its validity to the FDT protocol transcripts.
3. The judge then runs the Trace algorithm on the locations of $[2\ell] - T$ (i.e., the set $\{2j - v_j\}_{j \in [\ell]}$) via oracle access to D_S, and obtains another half pirate codeword. Then the judge runs a slightly different tracing algorithm for the underlying Tardos fingerprinting code to decide whether user i is accused for this half of the pirate codeword (see [14] for details), output 1 if yes.
4. If the judge outputs 1 in the above step, the user will be accused; otherwise, the user will not be accused.

Remark 2. During the protocols, to enforce each party to be honest, we carried zero-knowledge proofs at various steps. However, there are several simple optimizations from [14]. As it is enough to demonstrate the idea here, we omit the details and refer to [14] for optimizations. Furthermore, [14] even achieved group accusation, i.e., *all* identified traitors can be confirmed by the judge.

Security Analysis. Semantic security is straightforward as in the traceable ABE case. Now let us take a closer look at the traceability and non-framing properties.

Regarding traceability, compared with that in the traceable ABE, there are two more chances for a malicious user to evade tracing. The first is during the key generation protocol, whether the user can obtain information about keys she is not supposed to know, or reveal incorrect information about half of her codeword. It is easy to see that this cannot happen due to the (sender) security of the fingerprinted data transfer protocol. The second is whether the malicious user can cause inconsistency during the Trace and Judge phases. We note here that as we can extract both halves of the codeword out, this problem essentially reduces to the property of the underlying Tardos fingerprinting code. Fortunately, this property of Tardos code was formally demonstrated in [14]. The last is during the Judge protocol to fool the judge about her complete codeword, the soundness of the proofs in those steps ensures that this cannot happen.

Regarding non-framing property, there are only a few places that the malicious key generation center can cheat. The first is in the key generation protocol, there is more information leaked to the key generation center (KGC) than half of the codeword chosen according to the locations by KGC. This can be prevented by the security of the (receiver) security of the FDT protocol. The second is during the Judge protocol, again, the proofs are easily verifiable.

We remark that the FDT protocol satisfies the standard simulation security, thus the composition lemma [5] can be applied and we can replace such functionality as an oracle during the analysis.

With the above security intuitions, and due to page limit, we defer detailed security proof to the full version, and we summarize the security as follows:

Theorem 2. *If the underlying CP-ABE* ($\overline{\mathsf{Setup}}, \overline{\mathsf{KeyGen}}, \overline{\mathsf{Enc}}, \overline{\mathsf{Dec}}$) *is semantically secure, and the fingerprint code* ($\overline{\mathsf{Gen}}, \overline{\mathsf{Trace}}$) *is δ-robust and fully collusion resistant, and the fingerprinted data transfer protocol satisfies the simulation security, then above CP-ABE scheme is semantically secure, strongly traceable and non-framable.*

Acknowledgement. We are grateful to the anonymous reviewers for their helpful comments. The work of Junzuo Lai was supported by National Natural Science Foundation of China (No. 61572235), and Guangdong Natural Science Funds for Distinguished Young Scholar (No. 2015A030306045). Qiang Tang was partially supported by NSFC Fund for Oversea Chinese Scholars (No. 61728208).

A   Omitted Definitions

A.1   Simulation Based Security of Fingerprinted Data Transfer

If a protocol satisfies the following properties, we say that it securely implements fingerprinted data transfer.

Correctness: The receiver will obtain ($m_0^{b_0}, m_1^{b_1}$), satisfying that $\Pr[b_i = 1] = p_i$ for $i = 0, 1$. The sender will receive b_c with probability 1.

Receiver Security: The joint distribution of sender's view and the outputs in a real the protocol can be simulated by the inputs and outputs of the sender alone together with the ideal outputs of the functionality. That is, $\forall PPT$ semi-honest sender $\mathcal{S}$, $\exists$ PPT $\mathcal{S}'$, s.t., $VIEW_{\mathcal{S}} \circ OUTPUT$ is computationally indistinguishable from $\mathcal{S}'([(p_0, p_1), (m_0^0, m_0^1, m_1^0, m_1^1), c], b_c) \circ (m_0^{b_0}, m_1^{b_1}, b_c)$.

Sender Security: The joint distribution of receiver's view and the outputs in a real protocol can be simulated by the inputs and outputs of the receiver alone, together with the ideal outputs. That is, $\forall PPT$ semi-honest receiver $\mathcal{R}$, $\exists$ PPT $\mathcal{R}'$, s.t., $VIEW_{\mathcal{R}} \circ OUTPUT$ is computationally indistinguishable from $\mathcal{R}'(m_0^{b_0}, m_1^{b_1}) \circ (m_0^{b_0}, m_1^{b_1}, b_c)$. (here we assume the bits of the codeword $\{b_i\}$ are publicly recoverable from $\{m_i^{b_i}\}$.)

A.2   Semantic Security of Traceable ABE

Semantic Security Game. The game between a challenger and an adversary proceeds as follows:

Setup. The challenger runs the Setup algorithm to generate public parameters mpk, tracing key tk and master secret key msk. It gives mpk to the adversary and keeps tk and msk to itself.

Query Phase 1. Proceeding adaptively, the adversary can repeatedly query the challenger for secret keys corresponding to sets of attributes. In response, the challenger runs the key generation algorithm and gives the corresponding secret key to the adversary.

Challenge. The adversary submits two equal length messages m_0, m_1 and a challenge access structure $\mathbb{A}^*$ such that none of the queried attributes sets in **Query Phase 1** satisfies the challenge access structure $\mathbb{A}^*$. The challenger flips a random coin $\beta \in \{0, 1\}$, and runs $\mathsf{Enc}(mpk, m_\beta, \mathbb{A}^*)$ to get the challenge ciphertext c^*. The resulting c^* is given to the adversary.

Query Phase 2. The adversary continues to adaptively issue private key queries as **Query Phase 1** with the restriction that the adversary can not issue queries on sets of attributes which satisfy the access structure $\mathbb{A}^*$.

Guess. Finally, the adversary $\mathcal{A}$ outputs a guess $\beta' \in \{0, 1\}$. The adversary wins if $\beta' = \beta$.

The advantage of $\mathcal{A}$ in this game is defined as $|\Pr[\beta' = \beta] - \frac{1}{2}|$, where the probability is taken over the random bits used by the adversary $\mathcal{A}$ and $\mathcal{C}$.

Definition 3. *A traceable CP-ABE scheme is semantically secure if all polynomial time adversaries have at most negligible advantage in the above game.*

A.3   Accountable Authority CP-ABE

Concretely, an accountable authority CP-ABE scheme consists of the following five algorithms:

Setup. The setup algorithm takes as input a security parameter λ, outputs a master secret key msk, the tracing key tk and the public parameters mpk.

KeyGen. This is an interactive protocol between the key generation center and a user. The common input to key generation center and the user are the public parameters mpk and the attributes set S of the user. The private input to key generation center is the master secret key msk. At the end of the protocol, the user receives a private key sk_S, which is assigned and identified by a unique index.

Enc. The encryption algorithm takes as input the public parameters mpk, a message m and an access structure $\mathbb{A}$. It outputs a ciphertext c.

Dec. The decryption algorithm m takes as input the public parameters mpk, a private decryption key sk_S and a ciphertext c. It outputs a message m or $\bot$.

Trace. The tracing algorithm takes as input the public parameters mpk, the tracing key tk, and has black-box access to an δ-useful pirate decoder D_S for a set of attributes S. It outputs an index set I which identifies the set of malicious users.

Judge. This is an interactive protocol among the key generation center, a user who does not commit guilty and the judge. The common input to the key generation center, the user and the judge are the public parameters mpk and a δ-useful pirate decoder D_S. Additionally, the key generation center is with input the tracing key tk, and the user is with input his/her private key sk_S. At the end of the protocol, the judge decides whether the user is acquitted.

Traceability in Accountable Authority ABE. Consider the following (strong) traceability game:

Setup: The challenger runs the Setup algorithm to generate public parameters mpk, tracing key tk, and master secret key msk. It gives mpk to the adversary $\mathcal{A}$ and keeps tk and msk to itself.

Key Query: The adversary adaptively queries the challenger for secret keys corresponding to sets of attributes $S_1, \ldots, S_q$ for users with indices $k_1, \ldots, k_q$. In response, the challenger runs the key generation algorithm and gives the corresponding secret key to the adversary for $1 \leq i \leq q$.

Output: $\mathcal{A}$ outputs a δ-useful pirate decoder D_S for an attributes set S.

Let $C = \{k_i | 1 \leq i \leq q\}$ be the indices of the users corrupted by the adversary and I is the indices of the identified traitors, i.e. the output of $\mathsf{Trace}^{D_S}(mpk, tk, S)$. The adversary $\mathcal{A}$ wins the strong traceability game if (1) $I = \emptyset$, i.e., no one is accused; (2) or $I \not\subseteq C$, i.e., an innocent user is accused; (3) or none of the identified traitors' attributes set includes S as a subset; (4) Judge algorithm does not accuse any of the member in C.

The advantage of an adversary in the game is defined as the probability that $\mathcal{A}$ wins the strong traceability game, where the probability is taken over the random bits used by the challenger and the adversary.

Definition 4. *An accountable authority CP-ABE scheme is strongly traceable if all P.P.T adversaries have at most negligible advantage in the above game.*

References

1. Amiri, E., Tardos, G.: High rate fingerprinting codes and the fingerprinting capacity. In: SODA, pp. 336–345 (2009)
2. Bethencourt, J., Sahai, A., Waters, B.: Ciphertext-policy attribute-based encryption. In: IEEE Symposium on Security and Privacy, pp. 321–334 (2007)
3. Boneh, D., Kiayias, A. Montgomery, H.W.: Robust fingerprinting codes: a near optimal construction. In: DRM, pp. 3–12 (2010)
4. Boneh, D., Naor, M.: Traitor tracing with constant size ciphertext. In: CCS, pp. 501–510 (2008)
5. Canetti, R.: Security and composition of multiparty cryptographic protocols. J. Cryptol. 13(1), 143–202 (2000)
6. Chor, B., Fiat, A., Naor, M.: Tracing traitors. In: Desmedt, Y.G. (ed.) CRYPTO 1994. LNCS, vol. 839, pp. 257–270. Springer, Heidelberg (1994). https://doi.org/10.1007/3-540-48658-5_25
7. Dwork, C., Lotspiech, J.B., Naor, M.: Digital signets: self-enforcing protection of digital information (preliminary version). In: STOC, pp. 489–498 (1996)
8. Garg, S., Gentry, C., Halevi, S., Sahai, A., Waters, B.: Attribute-based encryption for circuits from multilinear maps. In: Canetti, R., Garay, J.A. (eds.) CRYPTO 2013. LNCS, vol. 8043, pp. 479–499. Springer, Heidelberg (2013). https://doi.org/10.1007/978-3-642-40084-1_27
9. Gorbunov, S., Vaikuntanathan, V., Wee, H.: Attribute-based encryption for circuits. In: STOC, pp. 545–554 (2013)

10. Goyal, V.: Reducing trust in the PKG in identity based cryptosystems. In: Menezes, A. (ed.) CRYPTO 2007. LNCS, vol. 4622, pp. 430–447. Springer, Heidelberg (2007). https://doi.org/10.1007/978-3-540-74143-5_24

11. Goyal, V., Lu, S., Sahai, A., Waters, B.: Black-box accountable authority identity-based encryption. In: ACM Conference on Computer and Communications Security, pp. 427–436 (2008)

12. Goyal, V., Pandey, O., Sahai, A., Waters, B.: Attribute-based encryption for fine-grained access control of encrypted data. In: ACM Conference on Computer and Communications Security, pp. 89–98 (2006)

13. Katz, J., Schröder, D.: Tracing insider attacks in the context of predicate encryption schemes. In: ACITA (2011)

14. Kiayias, A., Leonardos, N., Lipmaa, H., Pavlyk, K., Tang, Q.: Communication optimal tardos-based asymmetric fingerprinting. In: Nyberg, K. (ed.) CT-RSA 2015. LNCS, vol. 9048, pp. 469–486. Springer, Cham (2015). https://doi.org/10.1007/978-3-319-16715-2_25

15. Kiayias, A., Pehlivanoglu, S.: Encryption for Digital Content. Advances in Information Security, vol. 52. Springer, Heidelberg (2010). https://doi.org/10.1007/978-1-4419-0044-9

16. Kiayias, A., Tang, Q.: How to keep a secret: leakage deterring public-key cryptosystems. In: ACM CCS 2013, pp. 943–954 (2013)

17. Kiayias, A., Tang, Q.: Traitor deterring schemes: using bitcoin as collateral for digital contents. In: ACM CCS 2015, pp. 231–242 (2015)

18. Kiayias, A., Tang, Q.: Making *any* identity-based encryption accountable, efficiently. In: Pernul, G., Ryan, P.Y.A., Weippl, E. (eds.) ESORICS 2015. LNCS, vol. 9326, pp. 326–346. Springer, Cham (2015). https://doi.org/10.1007/978-3-319-24174-6_17

19. Lai, J., Deng, R.H., Zhao, Y., Weng, J.: Accountable authority identity-based encryption with public traceability. In: Dawson, E. (ed.) CT-RSA 2013. LNCS, vol. 7779, pp. 326–342. Springer, Heidelberg (2013). https://doi.org/10.1007/978-3-642-36095-4_21

20. Li, J., Huang, Q., Chen, X., Chow, S.S.M., Wong, D.S., Xie, D.: Multi-authority ciphertext-policy attribute-based encryption with accountability. In: ASIACCS, pp. 386–390 (2011)

21. Libert, B., Vergnaud, D.: Towards black-box accountable authority IBE with short ciphertexts and private keys. In: Jarecki, S., Tsudik, G. (eds.) PKC 2009. LNCS, vol. 5443, pp. 235–255. Springer, Heidelberg (2009). https://doi.org/10.1007/978-3-642-00468-1_14

22. Liu, Z., Cao, Z., Wong, D.S.: Blackbox traceable CP-ABE: how to catch people leaking their keys by selling decryption devices on eBay. In: ACM Conference on Computer and Communications Security, pp. 475–486 (2013)

23. Liu, Z., Cao, Z., Wong, D.S.: White-box traceable ciphertext-policy attribute-based encryption supporting any monotone access structures. IEEE Trans. Inf. Forensics Secur. 8(1), 76–88 (2013)

24. Ning, J., Cao, Z., Dong, X., Wei, L., Lin, X.: Large universe ciphertext-policy attribute-based encryption with white-box traceability. In: Kutyłowski, M., Vaidya, J. (eds.) ESORICS 2014. LNCS, vol. 8713, pp. 55–72. Springer, Cham (2014). https://doi.org/10.1007/978-3-319-11212-1_4

25. Ning, J., Dong, X., Cao, Z., Wei, L.: Accountable authority ciphertext-policy attribute-based encryption with white-box traceability and public auditing in the cloud. In: Pernul, G., Ryan, P.Y.A., Weippl, E. (eds.) ESORICS 2015. LNCS, vol. 9327, pp. 270–289. Springer, Cham (2015). https://doi.org/10.1007/978-3-319-24177-7_14

26. Pfitzmann, B., Schunter, M.: Asymmetric fingerprinting. In: Maurer, U. (ed.) EUROCRYPT 1996. LNCS, vol. 1070, pp. 84–95. Springer, Heidelberg (1996). https://doi.org/10.1007/3-540-68339-9_8

27. Rouselakis, Y., Waters, B.: Practical constructions and new proof methods for large universe attribute-based encryption. In: CCS, pp. 463–474 (2013)

28. Sahai, A., Seyalioglu, H.: Fully secure accountable-authority identity-based encryption. In: Catalano, D., Fazio, N., Gennaro, R., Nicolosi, A. (eds.) PKC 2011. LNCS, vol. 6571, pp. 296–316. Springer, Heidelberg (2011). https://doi.org/10.1007/978-3-642-19379-8_19

29. Sahai, A., Waters, B.: Fuzzy identity-based encryption. In: Cramer, R. (ed.) EUROCRYPT 2005. LNCS, vol. 3494, pp. 457–473. Springer, Heidelberg (2005). https://doi.org/10.1007/11426639_27

30. Tardos, G.: Optimal probabilistic fingerprint codes. J. ACM **55**(2), 10:1–10:24 (2008)

31. Yuen, T.H., Chow, S.S., Zhang, C., Yiu, S.M.: Exponent-inversion signatures and IBE under static assumptions. Cryptology ePrint Archive, Report 2014/311 (2014). http://eprint.iacr.org/

32. Zhang, Y., Li, J., Zheng, D., Chen, X., Li, H.: Accountable large-universe attribute-based encryption supporting any monotone access structures. In: Liu, J.K.K., Steinfeld, R. (eds.) ACISP 2016. LNCS, vol. 9722, pp. 509–524. Springer, Cham (2016). https://doi.org/10.1007/978-3-319-40253-6_31

Decentralized Policy-Hiding ABE
with Receiver Privacy

Yan Michalevsky[1,2(✉)] and Marc Joye[3]

[1] Anjuna Security, Palo Alto, CA, USA
yanm2@cs.stanford.edu
[2] Stanford University, Stanford, CA, USA
[3] NXP Semiconductors, San Jose, CA, USA

Abstract. Attribute-based encryption (ABE) enables limiting access to encrypted data to users with certain attributes. Different aspects of ABE were studied, such as the multi-authority setting (MA-ABE), and policy hiding, meaning the access policy is unknown to unauthorized parties. However, no practical scheme so far provably provides both properties, which are often desirable in real-world applications: supporting decentralization while hiding the access policy. We present the first practical decentralized ABE scheme with a proof of being policy-hiding. Our construction is based on a decentralized inner-product predicate encryption scheme, introduced in this paper, which hides the encryption policy. It results in an ABE scheme supporting conjunctions, disjunctions and threshold policies, that protects the access policy from parties that are not authorized to decrypt the content. Further, we address the issue of receiver privacy. By using our scheme in combination with vector commitments, we hide the overall set of attributes possessed by the receiver from individual authorities, only revealing the attribute that the authority is controlling. Finally, we propose randomizing-polynomial encodings that immunize the scheme in the presence of corrupt authorities.

1 Introduction

Attribute-based encryption (ABE), first proposed by Sahai and Waters [25], addresses the need to provide fine-grained access control to data according to some policy. In contrast to traditional public-key encryption, data is encrypted not under a public key associated with the identity of the intended recipient, but rather under a set of attributes that can be possessed by one or more entities.

This concept falls into the more general paradigm of *functional encryption* (FE) [6,24]. In functional encryption, a setup algorithm produces a matching pair of public/secret keys (mpk, msk). The master public key mpk enables anyone to encrypt data and the master secret key msk enables its holder to issue functional keys—for example, a secret key sk_f for a certain function f. Given a ciphertext $ct = \mathsf{Encrypt}(mpk, x)$ of some message x, anyone who has sk_f can obtain $f(x)$. An important subclass of functional encryption is *Predicate Encryption* (PE) [7,16], and in particular *Inner-Product Predicate Encryption*

© Springer Nature Switzerland AG 2018
J. Lopez et al. (Eds.): ESORICS 2018, LNCS 11099, pp. 548–567, 2018.
https://doi.org/10.1007/978-3-319-98989-1_27

(IPPE), where data can be accessed if and only if the ciphertext ct and the key sk satisfy a certain predicate $P(sk, ct)$ (namely, orthogonality).

To illustrate ABE, suppose we want to encrypt data stored on the university server such that it is accessible to anyone who "is a *network administrator, or a university student* and is taking the class *Introduction to Cryptography*". In single-authority ABE, an authority associated with the university can be in charge of verifying a user's identity and providing a key that certifies all her attributes. However, it is often impractical to rely on a single authority to verify and certify all possible attributes. Consider this example: different university departments are in charge of protecting their own data independently, while also being supported by the IT department. In this case a policy can be "is *network administrator* or *computer science department staff*". The university IT and the computer science department are, in this case, two independent authorities that verify and issue keys for their own attributes.

Multiple works addressed this issue, starting with the ones by Chase [9], Chase and Chow [10], and Müller *et al.* [18] on multi-authority ABE, and following with a decentralized ABE scheme by Lewko and Waters [17]. This last construction enables to encrypt a ciphertext under a general access structure, while the corresponding secret keys are issued by independent authorities that do not need to communicate with each other, or with any central authority, and only refer to common parameters generated by a one-time trusted setup. Another construction with similar properties is by Okamoto and Takashima [20].[1]

Those schemes, however, do not address the often desirable property of hiding the encryption policy. Attribute-hiding means that the ciphertext policy is protected and remains unknown under inspection of the ciphertext. There is a weaker notion, called *weakly attribute-hiding*, which guarantees that the policy is hidden from anyone but a party that is capable of decrypting the ciphertext; *i.e.*, information about it is leaked only upon successful decryption. It is important to be able to hide the access policy since it can contain sensitive meta-data. One example is messaging or emails addressed to a group of users with certain attributes. In addition to protecting the content we may want to hide the target group. In the full paper, we show that an adversary can reveal the encryption policy in Lewko-Waters' scheme, even when it is not explicitly given. While it is yet to be studied whether there is a policy inference attack on the scheme in [20] or whether it can be proved to be weakly attribute-hiding for inner-products, the paper neither claims, nor proves this property. In this work we set out to provide this important property in a decentralized setting.

While we previously illustrated the use of decentralized ABE with a simple toy example, it has practical real-world applications. Prior work on multi-authority ABE mentions supporting multiple authorities authorizing access to DRM-protected content [18], where hiding the policy is important to protect meta-data that can reveal potentially sensitive information about the content.

---

[1] The full version of a paper published in *PKC 2013* is mainly concerned with decentralized attribute-based signatures; however, it proposes a decentralized ABE scheme in Appendix E.

To mention another example, ABE has recently been explored in the context of access-control for blockchains [22,23]. Indeed, in a blockchain setting, both decentralization and policy protection are desirable. Attribute-based encryption or signatures can be an extension of the naïve multi-signature implementations in early blockchain-based crypto-currencies like Bitcoin [19], while policy-hiding can serve to preserve the recipient's privacy.

Our Contributions. We propose a decentralized, policy-hiding ABE scheme that supports several very useful classes of access policies. To the best of our knowledge, this is the first practical scheme with a proof of the attribute-hiding property. We instantiate ABE from a decentralized inner-product predicate encryption for which we provide a construction and a proof of security in the random oracle model, under the k-linear assumption. The decryption procedure of the underlying inner-product predicate scheme is very efficient, and requires only two pairing operations. Based on it, we devise attribute-hiding multi-authority ABE schemes supporting conjunctions, disjunctions, hidden-vector encryption, and threshold policies. On top of that, we add receiver privacy, by preventing individual authorities from knowing the full set of attributes possessed by the recipient when issuing keys.

Achieving security for a decentralized inner-product PE is not trivial since corrupt authorities can assist an adversary to satisfy the predicate by issuing illegitimate keys for specific vector elements. We mitigate it by proposing secure policy encodings. This contribution is of independent interest, as it can be applied to any decentralized PE scheme, and is not particular to the construction used in this paper. It is important to note that while [16] proposes several policy encodings in terms of inner-product predicates, it is a single-authority scheme that does not face the problems that arise in a decentralized setting with some corrupt authorities. Our policy encodings specifically address this challenge, and as such constitute a novel contribution.

Decentralization of a PE scheme, that is naturally single-authority, comes at a certain price, and our scheme has two drawbacks: the first is that we require each authority to publish a Diffie-Hellman public key that is visible to other authorities, and the second is that a change of attributes on the receiver's side requires requesting new keys from all participating authorities and not only from the one that controls the changed attribute. However, those are affordable in an on-line setting where requesting a new key for an unchanged attribute may only require presenting a certificate (or key) that has been previously obtained from the authority.

Paper Structure. In Sect. 2, we briefly present required preliminaries and state our computational assumptions. In Sect. 3, we formally define decentralized inner-product predicate encryption and the corresponding security game. Section 3.3 describes an important enhancement to the key request procedure, which relieves the receiver from disclosing all its attributes to each authority. Section 4 explains how to turn the decentralized inner-product predicate encryption into an attribute-hiding ABE scheme. In Sect. 5, we address the presence of corrupt authorities, colluding with the adversary, by introducing randomizing-polynomial encodings. We formally define the security game in this new setting, and suggest several encodings that immunize the underlying predicate encryption scheme from corrupt authorities. Finally, we state related prior work and outline related open problems.

2 Background and Preliminaries

2.1 Inner-Product Predicate Encryption

In a *predicate encryption* scheme, access to encrypted data is controlled by a certain predicate defined over the attributes included in the ciphertext policy. In particular, in *inner-product predicate encryption*, ciphertexts and secret keys are associated with vectors. In order to decrypt, the secret key has to be associated with a vector that is orthogonal to the vector associated with the ciphertext. The works of Katz *et al.* [16] and Chen *et al.* [11] are examples of such cryptosystems.

2.2 Pairing Groups

Let $\mathcal{G}$ be an algorithm that on input a security parameter λ generates three groups $\mathbb{G}_1 = \langle g_1 \rangle$, $\mathbb{G}_2 = \langle g_2 \rangle$ and $\mathbb{G}_T$ of prime order p, admitting a pairing $\hat{e} \colon \mathbb{G}_1 \times \mathbb{G}_2 \to \mathbb{G}_T$ that has the following properties:

1. Bilinearity: for all $a, b \in \mathbb{Z}$, $\hat{e}(g_1{}^a, g_2{}^b) = \hat{e}(g_1, g_2)^{ab}$;
2. Non-degeneracy: $\hat{e}(g_1, g_2) \neq 1$.

We write $(p, \mathbb{G}_1, \mathbb{G}_2, \mathbb{G}_T, \hat{e}) \leftarrow \mathcal{G}(1^\lambda)$. Groups $\mathbb{G}_1$ and $\mathbb{G}_2$ are called the source groups while $\mathbb{G}_T$ is called the target group.

2.3 Complexity Assumptions

The *Symmetric External Diffie-Hellman (SXDH)* assumption states that the DDH assumption holds in both source groups $\mathbb{G}_1$ and $\mathbb{G}_2$. Formally, we have:

Assumption 1 (SXDH). *Given $(p, \mathbb{G}_1, \mathbb{G}_2, \mathbb{G}_T, \hat{e}) \leftarrow \mathcal{G}(1^\lambda)$, there exists no polynomial-time distinguisher that can decide with a non-negligible advantage between the distributions $\mathscr{D}_0 = (g_1, g_2, g_1{}^a, g_1{}^b, g_1{}^{ab})$ and $\mathscr{D}_1 = (g_1, g_2, g_1{}^a, g_1{}^b, g_1{}^r)$ where $a, b, r \xleftarrow{\$} \mathbb{Z}_p$, and symmetrically, exchanging the roles of $\mathbb{G}_1$ and $\mathbb{G}_2$, between the distributions $\mathscr{D}_0 = (g_1, g_2, g_2{}^a, g_2{}^b, g_2{}^{ab})$ and $\mathscr{D}_1 = (g_1, g_2, g_2{}^a, g_2{}^b, g_2{}^r)$.*

The SXDH assumption can be weakened using higher-rank matrices [13]. It is useful to introduce some notation. For $a_1, a_2, \ldots, a_k \xleftarrow{\$} \mathbb{Z}_p{}^*$, consider

$$\mathbf{A} = \begin{pmatrix} a_1 & 0 & \cdots & 0 \\ 0 & a_2 & & 0 \\ \vdots & & \ddots & \\ 0 & 0 & & a_k \\ 1 & 1 & \cdots & 1 \end{pmatrix} \in \mathbb{Z}_p{}^{(k+1) \times k} \quad \text{and} \quad \mathbf{a}^\perp = \begin{pmatrix} a_1{}^{-1} \\ a_2{}^{-1} \\ \vdots \\ a_k{}^{-1} \\ -1 \end{pmatrix} \in \mathbb{Z}_p{}^{(k+1)}.$$

Then, $\mathbf{A}^\mathsf{T} a^\perp = \mathbf{0}$. We let $\mathfrak{D}_k(\mathbb{Z}_p)$ denote the distribution induced by the previous sampling.

Assumption 2 (k-**Lin in** $\mathbb{G}_1$). *Given* $(p, \mathbb{G}_1, \mathbb{G}_2, \mathbb{G}_T, \hat{e}) \leftarrow \mathcal{G}(1^\lambda)$, *there exists no polynomial-time distinguisher that can decide with a non-negligible advantage between the distributions* $\mathcal{D}_0 = (g_1, g_2, g_1{}^\mathbf{A}, g_1{}^{\mathbf{A}s})$ *and* $\mathcal{D}_1 = (g_1, g_2, g_1{}^\mathbf{A}, g_1{}^z)$ *where* $(\mathbf{A}, a^\perp) \xleftarrow{\$} \mathfrak{D}_k(\mathbb{Z}_p)$, $s \xleftarrow{\$} \mathbb{Z}_p{}^k$, *and* $z \xleftarrow{\$} \mathbb{Z}_p{}^{k+1}$.

The k-Lin assumption in $\mathbb{G}_2$ is defined similarly. By abuse of language, the k-Lin assumption will refer to the k-Lin assumption in both $\mathbb{G}_1$ and $\mathbb{G}_2$.

3   Decentralized Inner-Product Predicate Encryption

Our goal is supporting a multi-authority setting, where keys for different attributes can be requested from n independent authorities, that do not need to communicate with each other or with a central authority. In inner-product predicate encryption, keys are issued by a central authority, given a vector v, to eligible parties. We decentralize the key generation algorithm, such that key-parts are issued separately for different vector elements v_i, by n independent authorities. Without loss of generality, we assume that authority i issues keys for attribute number i. Those key-parts are then combined to form a secret key corresponding to the vector $v = (v_1, \ldots, v_n)$.

For simplicity, we first construct a scheme that is weakly attribute-hiding in the absence of corrupt authorities. It is mostly useful as a stepping-stone, to understand how, in combination with special policy encodings, it becomes secure in the presence of corrupt authorities.

Definition 1. *A decentralized inner-product predicate encryption scheme consists of a tuple of PPT algorithms,* (Setup, AuthSetup, KeyGen, Encrypt, Decrypt), *such that*

- Setup *takes as input the security parameter* λ *and outputs the master public parameters* pp.
- AuthSetup *takes as input the public parameters* pp *and the authority index* i, *and outputs the authority's secret key* SK_i *and public key* PK_i.
- KeyGen *takes as input the master public parameters* pp, *the authority index* i, *its secret key* SK_i, *the public parameters* $\{PK_j\}_{j \neq i}$ *of other authorities, a user's global identifier* GID *and the attribute vector* v, *and outputs a secret key part* $sk_{i,\mathsf{GID},v}$.
- Encrypt *takes as input the master public parameters* pp, *the public parameters of the authorities* $\{PK_i\}$, *the ciphertext policy vector* x *and a message* M *in the message space, and outputs a ciphertext* ct.
  We express it as $ct \xleftarrow{\$} \mathsf{Encrypt}_{pp}(x, M)$.
- Decrypt *takes as input the collection of obtained secret keys* $\{sk_{i,\mathsf{GID},v}\}_{i=1}^n$ *and the ciphertext* ct, *and outputs either the message* M *or the special symbol* $\perp$.
  We express it as $M \leftarrow \mathsf{Decrypt}(\{sk_{i,\mathsf{GID},v}\}, ct)$.

For correctness we require that for all $pp, \boldsymbol{x}, \boldsymbol{v}, sk_{i,\mathsf{GID},v}$:

$$\mathsf{Decrypt}\left(\{sk_{i,\mathsf{GID},v}\}_{i=1}^n, \mathsf{Encrypt}_{pp}(\boldsymbol{x}, M)\right) = \begin{cases} M & \text{if} \langle \boldsymbol{x}, \boldsymbol{v} \rangle = 0 \\ \bot & \text{otherwise} \end{cases}$$

with all but negligible probability.

Definition 2 captures security in the absence of corrupt authorities.

Definition 2. *A decentralized inner-product predicate encryption scheme is weakly attribute-hiding, with respect to a set of attributes Σ, if for all PPT adversaries $\mathcal{A}$, the advantage of $\mathcal{A}$ in winning the following game against a challenger $\mathcal{S}$ is negligible in the security parameter:*

1. *$\mathcal{S}$ runs Setup to generate pp and hands it to $\mathcal{A}$.*
2. *$\mathcal{S}$ runs AuthSetup(pp, i) for each authority i, and gives $\{PK_i\}$ to $\mathcal{A}$.*
3. *$\mathcal{A}$ may request keys for vectors $\boldsymbol{v}$, indicating possession of attributes in Σ. In response, $\mathcal{S}$ gives $\mathcal{A}$ the corresponding keys $sk_{i,\mathsf{GID},v}$ produced by $\mathsf{KeyGen}_{pp}(i, SK_i, \mathsf{GID}, \boldsymbol{v})$. GID is the global identifier of the requesting user; its role is explained in Sect. 3.1.*
4. *$\mathcal{A}$ outputs two policy vectors $\boldsymbol{x_0}, \boldsymbol{x_1}$ and two equal-length messages M_0, M_1. $\mathcal{S}$ checks that none of the previously queried attribute vectors $\boldsymbol{v}$ are orthogonal to $\boldsymbol{x_0}$ or $\boldsymbol{x_1}$; i.e., $\langle \boldsymbol{x_0}, \boldsymbol{v} \rangle \neq 0 \wedge \langle \boldsymbol{x_1}, \boldsymbol{v} \rangle \neq 0$ for all previously requested $\boldsymbol{v}$. The challenger chooses a random bit b and gives $\mathcal{A}$ the ciphertext $ct \xleftarrow{\$} \mathsf{Encrypt}_{pp}(\boldsymbol{x_b}, M_b)$.*
5. *$\mathcal{A}$ may request more keys for vectors $\boldsymbol{v}$ as they are not orthogonal to $\boldsymbol{x_0}, \boldsymbol{x_1}$.*
6. *$\mathcal{A}$ outputs a bit b' and wins if $b' = b$.*

The advantage of $\mathcal{A}$ is defined as $adv(\mathcal{A}) - \left| \Pr[b = b'] - \frac{1}{2} \right|$.

Note 1. The way attribute possession is encoded in the vector $\boldsymbol{v}$ is explained further, when we discuss instantiations of ABE schemes using predicate encryption.

Definition 3 captures security in the presence of corrupt authorities. Here, the adversary does not know $\boldsymbol{x_0}, \boldsymbol{x_1}$ explicitly, as opposed to Definition 2. It provides the policies in the form of a boolean formula, or a threshold t-out-of-n over a set of admissible attributes, or a matching pattern, etc.

Definition 3. *We define a game between an adversary $\mathcal{A}$ and a challenger $\mathcal{S}$:*

1. *$\mathcal{S}$ picks a random bit $b \in \{0, 1\}$ and outputs the public parameters pp.*
2. *$\mathcal{A}$ outputs the set of corrupt authorities $\mathcal{A}^*$, and provides $\mathcal{S}$ with their public parameters.*
3. *$\mathcal{S}$ runs AuthSetup for each one of the non-corrupt authorities, and gives the public parameters to $\mathcal{A}$.*
4. *$\mathcal{A}$ outputs two policies π_0, π_1 and two equal-length messages M_0, M_1. The policies require attributes controlled by non-corrupt authorities, and must agree on the attributes controlled by the corrupt authorities $\mathcal{A}^*$.*

5. $\mathcal{S}$ outputs a challenge ciphertext $ct \xleftarrow{\$} \mathsf{Encrypt}_{pp}(\boldsymbol{x_b}, M_b)$, where $\boldsymbol{x_b}$ is the encoding vector of policy π_b.
6. $\mathcal{A}$ generates key requests for the different authorities. $\mathcal{S}$ checks that the set of attributes, controlled by the authorities for which a non-zero key has been requested, cannot satisfy either of the two policies π_0, π_1.
7. $\mathcal{A}$ outputs a guess b'. If $b' = b$ it wins the game.

Definition 4 (Security). *The scheme is secure (against static corruption of authorities) if any PPT adversary $\mathcal{A}$ has only negligible advantage in winning the game in Sect. 3 against a challenger $\mathcal{S}$.*

3.1 Collusion Prevention and Protection Against Corrupt Authorities

A fundamental requirement from an ABE scheme is to prevent collusion between users. Let u_1 and u_2 be two users, possessing sets of key-parts K_1, K_2. K_1 contains key-parts that enable obtaining a secret key to any $\boldsymbol{v_1} \in V_1$, and K_2 contains key-parts that enable obtaining a secret key to any $\boldsymbol{v_2} \in V_2$. u_1 and u_2 must not be able to mix their key-parts in a way that gives them a secret key to a new vector $\boldsymbol{v}$ such that $\boldsymbol{v} \notin V_1$ and $\boldsymbol{v} \notin V_2$. For example, to enforce the policy "*is a university student, and taking Introduction to Cryptography,*" it is not enough to secret share the message, and encrypt it under the public-keys of the two authorities. Otherwise, two users having only one of the attributes each, can collude to decrypt the ciphertext. Therefore, all works on multi-authority ABE, including ours, address collusion prevention as one of the main challenges.

Prior works on multi-authority ABE [9,10,17] assign a global identifier (GID) to each user. It is used to associate every secret key with an identity by incorporating it into the decryption keys issued by the authorities. In our setting, it is not sufficient to restrict combination of keys to the same GID. Depending on the policy encoding, we may have to ensure that keys are issued for a well-formed attribute-vector $\boldsymbol{v}$. For instance, in a threshold scheme, if a corrupt authority issues a key for a value $v_i > 1$, the user may be able to decrypt despite not having sufficient attributes to satisfy the policy. For our basic scheme, we require the user to supply its attribute vector $\boldsymbol{v}$ when requesting a key, and tie the issued keys to the tuple $(\mathsf{GID}, \boldsymbol{v})$. This imposes the already mentioned requirement, on part of the receiver, to update keys when attributes change.

We use hash functions $\mathsf{H}_1(\mathsf{GID}, \boldsymbol{v}), \ldots, \mathsf{H}_{k+1}(\mathsf{GID}, \boldsymbol{v})$, modeled as random oracles, to map $(\mathsf{GID}, \boldsymbol{v})$ to random elements. This ensures that different authorities issue keys that correspond to some common parameter. As we show in Sect. 3.3, we can replace the attribute vector with a commitment. The binding property, in composition with the random oracle, guarantees that the authorities issue keys for a common attribute vector. This modular combination enables us to extend the scheme with receiver privacy, without changing the core construction or its proof of security.

Note that it does not prevent corrupted authorities from computing a key for a different value than that appearing in $\boldsymbol{v}$. However, in the absence of corrupted authorities, it prevents an adversary from obtaining a key to an invalid attribute vector, as well as collusion between multiple adversaries.

Minimal Trust Requirement. Given a set of l attributes (and l corresponding controlling authorities), we require one special authority (we refer to it as the $l+1$ authority) to be trusted to issue keys only for $v_{l+1} \neq 0$. Note that the authority does not get to learn the policy, or the paylod. This requirement becomes clear once we explain the way policies are encoded. It also ensures that no keys for $\boldsymbol{v} = \boldsymbol{0}$ are ever issued.

3.2   Construction

We build on the elegant predicate encodings framework by Chen and Wee [12], and the single-authority ZIPE scheme by Chen *et al.* [11]. They use dual-system groups instantiated with prime-order bilinear groups, based on the k-linear computational hardness assumption. In particular, the choice of $k = 1$ corresponds to the External Diffie-Hellman (XDH) assumption, and choosing $k = 2$ corresponds to the decision-linear (DLIN) assumption. Essentially, we achieve decentralization by substituting the randomness, chosen by the sender in their framework, with a publicly computable hash function, modeled as a random oracle, that can be computed by all parties. We also introduce masking terms that force the receiver to combine the key parts received from various authorities, prior to using them in any way. We use a random oracle $\mathcal{H} \colon \mathbb{G}_2 \times \{0,1\}^{\lambda} \times \mathbb{Z}_p^{l+1} \to \mathbb{Z}_p^{k+1}$, to generate masking terms that depend on a combination of an authority, the GID, and the attribute vector $\boldsymbol{v}$ (or a commitment to it). It is a simple way to ensure that the receiver cannot use the key parts obtained from the different authorities prior to combining them as specified in the construction. It implies a requirement for certain minimal coordination between authorities. Each one of them publishes a Diffie-Hellman public key, visible to the others. In this sense, our scheme misses the desirable property of full-decentralization, that doesn't require any coordination between authorities whatsoever beyond referring to common public parameters published on setup.

The scheme is as follows:

- Setup(λ): On input a security parameter λ, the algorithm outputs (p, $\mathbb{G}_1$, $\mathbb{G}_2$, $\mathbb{G}_T$, $\hat{e}$). Let g_1, g_2 be two generators of $\mathbb{G}_1, \mathbb{G}_2$ respectively. It picks a random matrix $\mathbf{A} \in \mathbb{Z}_p^{(k+1) \times k}$ and a random matrix $\mathbf{U} \in \mathbb{Z}_p^{(k+1) \times (k+1)}$, and publishes the public parameters

$$pp = \left\{ g_1, g_2, g_1^{\mathbf{A}}, g_1^{\mathbf{U}^{\mathsf{T}} \mathbf{A}} \right\}.$$

- AuthSetup(pp, i): The algorithm samples a random matrix $\mathbf{W_i} \in_p^{(k+1) \times (k+1)}$, a vector $\boldsymbol{\alpha}_i \xleftarrow{\$} \mathbb{Z}_p^{k+1}$ and a random $\sigma_i \in \mathbb{Z}_p$. The authority stores the secret key $SK_i = \{\mathbf{W_i}, \boldsymbol{\alpha}_i, \sigma_i\}$ and publishes the public key

$$PK_i = \left\{ g_1^{\mathbf{W_i}^{\mathsf{T}} \mathbf{A}}, \hat{e}(g_1, g_2)^{\boldsymbol{\alpha}_i^{\mathsf{T}} \mathbf{A}}, y_i = g_2^{\sigma_i} \right\}.$$

- Encrypt$_{pp}(\{PK_i\}, \boldsymbol{x}, m)$: Let $\boldsymbol{x} = (x_1, \ldots, x_n) \in \mathbb{Z}_p{}^n$. The algorithm chooses a random vector $\boldsymbol{s} \in \mathbb{Z}_p{}^k$ and outputs the ciphertext $\boldsymbol{C}$ consisting of the components

$$C_0 = g_1{}^{\mathbf{A}\boldsymbol{s}} \qquad C_i = g_1{}^{(x_i \mathbf{U}^{\mathsf{T}} + \mathbf{W_i}^{\mathsf{T}})\mathbf{A}\boldsymbol{s}}$$
$$C' = m \cdot \prod_{i=1}^{n} \hat{e}(g_1, g_2)^{\boldsymbol{\alpha}_i{}^{\mathsf{T}}\mathbf{A}\boldsymbol{s}} = m \cdot \hat{e}(g_1, g_2)^{\boldsymbol{\alpha}^{\mathsf{T}}\mathbf{A}\boldsymbol{s}}$$

where $\boldsymbol{\alpha} = \sum_{i=1}^{n} \boldsymbol{\alpha}_i$.

- KeyGen$_{pp}(\{PK_i\}, SK_i, \mathsf{GID}, \boldsymbol{v})$: The authority takes the public keys of all other authorities, and computes a masking value $\boldsymbol{\mu}_i \in \mathbb{Z}_p$

$$\boldsymbol{\mu}_i = \sum_{j=1}^{i-1} \mathcal{H}(y_j{}^{\sigma_i}, \mathsf{GID}, \boldsymbol{v}) - \sum_{j=i+1}^{n} \mathcal{H}(y_j{}^{\sigma_i}, \mathsf{GID}, \boldsymbol{v}).$$

It is easy to check that $\sum_{i=1}^{n} \boldsymbol{\mu}_i = \mathbf{0}$.

We use $\mathsf{H}_1(\mathsf{GID}, \boldsymbol{v}), \ldots, \mathsf{H}_{k+1}(\mathsf{GID}, \boldsymbol{v})$ to generate $g_2{}^{\boldsymbol{h}}$ where $\boldsymbol{h} \in \mathbb{Z}_p{}^{k+1}$. Note that the exponent $\boldsymbol{h}$ is unknown and is defined implicitly by the hash functions. We denote

$$\mathsf{H}(\mathsf{GID}, \boldsymbol{v}) = \big(\mathsf{H}_1(\mathsf{GID}, \boldsymbol{v}), \ldots, \mathsf{H}_{k+1}(\mathsf{GID}, \boldsymbol{v})\big)^{\mathsf{T}}.$$

The algorithm outputs the key $sk_{i, \mathsf{GID}, v}$ which consists of

$$K_i = g_2{}^{\boldsymbol{\alpha}_i - v_i \mathbf{W_1}\boldsymbol{h} + \boldsymbol{\mu}_i}.$$

- Decrypt$_{pp}(\{sk_{i, \mathsf{GID}, v}\}, \boldsymbol{C}, \boldsymbol{v})$: Compute

$$\hat{e}\big(C_0, \textstyle\prod_{i=1}^{n} K_i\big) \cdot \hat{e}\big(\textstyle\prod_{i=1}^{n} C_i{}^{v_i}, \mathsf{H}(\mathsf{GID}, \boldsymbol{v})\big) = \hat{e}(g_1, g_2)^{\boldsymbol{\alpha}^{\mathsf{T}}\mathbf{A}\boldsymbol{s}}$$

and recover the message by computing

$$C' / \hat{e}(g_1, g_2)^{\boldsymbol{\alpha}^{\mathsf{T}}\mathbf{A}\boldsymbol{s}} = m.$$

Correctness. Let $\boldsymbol{C} = \big(C_0, \{C_i\}_{i=1}^{n}, C'\big)$ and $\{K_i := sk_{i, \mathsf{GID}, v}\}_{i=1}^{n}$ be as described above. Then

$$\hat{e}\big(C_0, \textstyle\prod_{i=1}^{n} K_i\big) \cdot \hat{e}\big(\textstyle\prod_{i=1}^{n} C_i{}^{v_i}, \mathsf{H}(\mathsf{GID}, \boldsymbol{v})\big)$$
$$= \hat{e}\big(g_1{}^{\mathbf{A}\boldsymbol{s}}, g_2{}^{\sum_{i=1}^{n} \boldsymbol{\alpha}_i - v_i \mathbf{W_1}\boldsymbol{h} + \boldsymbol{\mu}_i}\big) \cdot \hat{e}\big(g_1{}^{\sum_{i=1}^{n} v_i(x_i \mathbf{U}^{\mathsf{T}} + \mathbf{W_i}^{\mathsf{T}})\mathbf{A}\boldsymbol{s}}, g_2{}^{\boldsymbol{h}}\big)$$
$$= \hat{e}(g_1, g_2)^{\boldsymbol{\alpha}^{\mathsf{T}}\mathbf{A}\boldsymbol{s} - \sum_{i=1}^{n} v_i \boldsymbol{h}^{\mathsf{T}}\mathbf{W_i}^{\mathsf{T}}\mathbf{A}\boldsymbol{s}} \cdot \hat{e}(g_1, g_2)^{\langle \boldsymbol{x}, \boldsymbol{v} \rangle \boldsymbol{h}^{\mathsf{T}}\mathbf{U}^{\mathsf{T}}\mathbf{A}\boldsymbol{s} + \sum_{i=1}^{n} v_i \boldsymbol{h}^{\mathsf{T}}\mathbf{W_i}^{\mathsf{T}}\mathbf{A}\boldsymbol{s}}$$
$$= \hat{e}(g_1, g_2)^{\boldsymbol{\alpha}^{\mathsf{T}}\mathbf{A}\boldsymbol{s}} \cdot \hat{e}(g_1, g_2)^{\langle \boldsymbol{x}, \boldsymbol{v} \rangle \boldsymbol{h}^{\mathsf{T}}\mathbf{U}^{\mathsf{T}}\mathbf{A}\boldsymbol{s}}.$$

If $\langle \boldsymbol{x}, \boldsymbol{v} \rangle = 0$, we obtain $\hat{e}(g_1, g_2)^{\boldsymbol{\alpha}^{\mathsf{T}}\mathbf{A}\boldsymbol{s}}$ and can recover the message.

Note 2. Looking at the key format it is easy to see why this construction, in general, requires the masking terms μ_i, and why their generation requires taking v as input. Without it, an adversary can ask for keys corresponding to $v_i = 0$ for $\forall i = 1..n$, obtaining g_2^α. That, in turn, enables to decrypt any ciphertext by pairing with C_0. By examining the vector v, and tying the generated key to it, the authorities ensure that the adversary doesn't obtain a key to an all-zeros vector $(v = 0)$.

It also becomes clear why we need to trust the $l+1$ authority to refuse issuing keys for $v_{l+1} = 0$. If that would have been the case, an adversary colluding with a corrupt i-th authority would request keys from all other authorities presenting $v = e_i$ in the request, while in fact obtaining a key for $v_i = 0$ from the corrupt authority. A sketch of the security proof for this construction is provided in Appendix B, and a formal proof of security is provided in the full paper.

3.3   Improving Receiver Privacy

So far, the receiver has to provide its attribute vector v to each authority it requests a key from. As a result, the authority learns not only whether the user has the attribute which it controls, but also all other attributes it possesses. This is an apparent violation of the user's privacy in a decentralized setting.

We propose an enhancement that provides this additional privacy protection. While we want to ensure consistency of the keys issued by different authorities, and some properties of the vector they were issued for, we can avoid providing v in the clear. We satisfy consistency and privacy using commitments. Proving possession of attributes and certain properties of v is done by partial openings.

First, we propose to provide a vector $c \in \mathbb{Z}_p^n$, consisting of one-bit Pedersen commitments [21] to the values $\{v_i\}_{i=1}^n$, instead of v itself, when requesting a key. This method is useful when we do not use randomizing-polynomial encodings (discussed in Sect. 5) in the ciphertext, relying on honest authorities. In this case, valid receiver attribute vectors are binary, consisting of 0 and 1 elements, and authorities need to verify this property. This property is enforced by one-bit Pedersen commitments, with each element checked by a different authority. For encodings that require the receiver to request keys for arbitrary values, generalized Pedersen commitments can be used. In both cases, the input to the hash is the sequence of commitments.

Second, we propose to reduce the communication between the receiver and the authority by compressing the commitment vector into a single value using an accumulation technique. Catalano and Fiore [8] defined and constructed a *Vector Commitment* scheme. It enables committing to an ordered sequence of values, and later on opening the commitment in a certain position, proving that no other value would have resulted in the previously supplied commitment. This is called *position-binding*. The authors propose two different constructions—one based on the Computational Diffie-Hellman assumption (CDH), and another one based on the RSA assumption. Both constructions result in a constant size commitment. A formal definition of a VC scheme and of the position-binding property is provided in Appendix A.

We use it to hide the set of receiver attributes (v) from the authorities, while guaranteeing that only key parts issued for the same v can be combined to a valid key. Concretely, we use the vector commitment C as an input to the hash functions $H_1, \ldots, H_{k+1}$. To request a key from authority i, the receiver send C, along with an opening in position i. The authority verifies the proof, and generates the key using $H(GID, C)$. Former security guarantees are maintained by the fact that the commitment is binding, while attribute-privacy is achieved by the fact that the commitment is hiding. We note that applying this enhancement for threshold schemes is impossible in the presence of corrupt authorities, that are willing to issue keys for $v_i > 1$.

Application to Our Scheme. The modified Setup algorithm of our ABE scheme uses VC.Setup in order to generate the public parameters for the vector commitments. Prior to requesting keys, the user executes VC.Commit to produce a commitment to v. Upon requesting a key-part from authority i, it executes VC.Open to produce a proof for the values at the i-th position, and supplies C and P_i along with the key request. The authority runs VC.Verify to verify the proof against the commitment C, and uses $H(GID, C)$ to generate the key.

Security. We argue that an adversary cannot mix-and-match keys issued for different attribute vectors. Since the commitment to the vector (using either of the proposed methods) is binding, the adversary is unable, with high-probability, to find two inputs that would yield the same commitment. Therefore, every different attribute vector results in a different input to the random oracle that is used by KeyGen to generate the keys K_i.

4   Decentralized Policy-Hiding ABE

We use the constructed inner-product predicate encryption to build policy-hiding multi-authority ABE. The naïve encodings are simple, assuming the authorities are trusted to issue keys as specified below. In the following, we explain how the sender encodes the policy, and how the receiver issues key requests to the authorities.

We begin with describing how to build an attribute-based encryption from inner-product predicate encryption. We use an inner-product predicate encryption scheme as a building block, and demonstrate encodings for conjunctions, threshold policies, and hidden-vector encryption (HVE).

Exact Threshold ABE. Let $A = \{1, \ldots, l\}$ be the enumeration of all supported attributes. Let S be the subset of attributes in the ciphertext policy. Let S' be the subset of attributes possessed by a party attempting to decrypt the ciphertext. We require that it would be possible for a party to decrypt the ciphertext if it possesses exactly t of those attributes; *i.e.*, if $|S \cap S'| = t$.

We instantiate a $l+1$ dimensional inner-product predicate encryption scheme. To encrypt a messages under such policy we construct a vector $x \in \mathbb{Z}_p^{l+1}$ as follows

1. Set the first l entries such that $x_i = \begin{cases} 1 & i \in S \\ 0 & i \notin S \end{cases}$.

2. Set the $l + 1$ entry to $-t$; i.e., $x_{l+1} = -t \pmod{p}$

and output the ciphertext $CT_x = \mathsf{Encrypt}_{PK}(x, M)$. To obtain a decryption key for the attributes in S', the receiver constructs a vector $v \in \mathbb{Z}_N^{l+1}$ as follows

1. Set the first l entries such that $v_i = \begin{cases} 1 & i \in S' \\ 0 & i \notin S' \end{cases}$.

2. Set the $l + 1$ entry to 1; i.e., $v_{l+1} = 1$.

and execute $\mathsf{GenKey}(v)$ to obtain SK_v. Since $|S \cup S'| = t$ we have exactly t matching entries with the value 1 that cancel out with $-t$, yielding $\langle x, v \rangle = 0$, thereby satisfying the predicate and enabling decryption.

This encoding is only secure in the absence of corrupt authorities. An adversary, that does not have enough required attributes to satisfy the policy, may collude with a corrupt authority and ask it to provide it with a key for a value $v_i > 1$ such that $\langle v, x \rangle = 0$. In Sect. 5 we suggest another, less straightforward encoding, that immunizes the scheme against corrupt authorities that are willing to generate keys for arbitrary values.

Threshold ABE. A general threshold algorithm requires $l - t + 1$ invocations of the exact threshold decryption in the worst case, or $O(l)$ invocations if t is small compared to l. The receiver starts with the subset of its first t attributes, denoted S'_t and constructs the corresponding vector v_t. It requests the corresponding secret key, and attempts decryption. If decryption fails, it knows that it did not hit the exact threshold of common attributes. It adds another attribute, forming the set S'_{t+1}, and constructs the corresponding vector v_{t+1}. Once again, it requests the corresponding secret key and attempts to decrypt. It continues until it hits the exact threshold, or until all possessed attributes are included.

Corrupt Authorities. Matters become more complicated in the presence of corrupt authorities colluding with the adversary. In case the encryption policy includes an attribute controlled by a corrupted authority, the adversary can use it to issue a secret key for any value v_i and break the naïve construction.

Let us consider a threshold-policy t-out-of-n, and let the sender include attribute i in the ciphertext policy; i.e., $x_i = 1$. If the adversary has some prior knowledge that this attribute is included in the ciphertext policy, it can request a key component corresponding to $v_i = t$. Then it combines it with key components corresponding to $v_j = 0$ for all $j \neq i$ and the key component corresponding to the threshold entry $v_{l+1} = 1$. In the inner product, $\sum_{i=1}^{l} x_i v_i = t$ and $x_{l+1} v_{l+1} = -t$ cancel out, resulting in $\langle x, v \rangle = 0$ and thus successful decryption despite not possessing enough attributes. The attack stems from the ability to request key components for arbitrary inputs.

The $l + 1$ authority has to be honest since it controls the threshold setting. If this authority is corrupt, it can issue a secret key component corresponding to a lower (or a zero) threshold - a condition that is much easier (or trivial) for the adversary to satisfy.

In Sect. 5, we propose a threshold encoding that is secure in the presence of corrupt authorities. However, this scheme, while more restrictive, requires linear decoding time, and in certain cases may be preferable to the scheme in Sect. 5.

Conjunctions. Conjunctions are an important class of policies that state that the receiver must possess a certain set of attributes in order to decrypt the message. They are one of the most useful policies in real-world scenarios, since access policies would often specify a combination of several properties that the receiver must have. Suppose we have a total set of attributes Σ, indexed from 1 to l, and we require possession of a subset S. We encode it as a vector $\boldsymbol{x} \in \mathbb{Z}_p^{l+1}$ as follows:

1. Set the first l entries such that $x_i = \begin{cases} r_i \overset{\$}{\leftarrow} \mathbb{Z}_p & i \in S \\ 0 & i \notin S \end{cases}$.

2. Set the $l+1$ entry to $-\sum_{i=1}^{l} r_i \pmod{p}$.

Given the receiver's set of attributes R, the vector $\boldsymbol{v}$ is set as follows:

1. Set the first l entries such that $v_i = \begin{cases} 1 & i \in R \\ 0 & i \notin R \end{cases}$.

2. Set the $l+1$ entry to 1.

We set the elements corresponding to attributes in S to random values, and the last element to minus their sum. Thus, an inner-product with a vector that has 1-s in all indices corresponding to the required attributes, yields 0, resolving the policy, as illustrated below:

v_1	v_2	v_3	...	v_l	v_{l+1}
1	1	0	...	0	1

$\cdot$

x_1	x_2	x_3	...	x_l	x_{l+1}
r_1	r_2	0	...	0	$-(r_1 + r_2)$

$= 0$

Note that in this case the encoding itself immunizes the scheme against corrupted authorities. Normally, an honest authority should only issue keys for values $v_i = 0$ or $v_i = 1$, indicating absence or possession of attribute i. However, a corrupt authority can provide an adversary with a key issued for an adversarially chosen value v_i, in an attempt to satisfy the policy without actually having all necessary attributes. By encoding the required attributes using randomly sampled r_i-s over a large field, we provide information theoretic security against an attempt to craft a key by adversarially picking a value v_i that would result in a zero inner-product. Security of this encoding is captured by Definition 3. It readily follows from the probability that the adversary correctly guesses which value it should craft to cancel out the last entry, which is negligible ($\frac{1}{p}$).

In Appendix C, we provide another example of a secure encoding for Hidden-Vector Encryption [7].

5   Randomizing-Polynomial Encodings

We propose encoding policies using polynomials with random coefficients as a way to protect the scheme against corrupt authorities that extend the adversary's degrees of freedom in obtaining keys. Specifically, a corrupt authority i enables the adversary to obtain a key-part K_i corresponding to an arbitrary value v_i, instead of being limited to 0 or 1.

By weak attribute-hiding, the adversary cannot infer the vector $\boldsymbol{x}$ used to encode the access policy. The sender generates a randomized multivariate polynomial P expressing the policy, and sets x_i to its coefficients, and $x_{l+1} = \pm P(0, \ldots, 0)$, depending on the policy type.

The receiver does not know the polynomial, and in order to obtain 0 it has to evaluate P at $(0, \ldots, 0)$. It requests keys from the authorities for either 0 (when it doesn't have the corresponding attribute), or some non-zero value depending on the type of encoded policy (in case it has the attribute). The $l + 1$ authority is special in that it only issues a key for $v_{l+1} = 1$. Attempting reconstruction using any other coefficients would result in a non-zero inner-product with high probability. In the following, we specify concrete encodings and receiver procedures for several useful access policies.

5.1   Examples of Encodings for Different Policies

Threshold Policy. Let S be the set of attributes that are considered admissible by the sender (out of the total l attributes), and $n = |S|$. To implement a threshold policy t-out-of-n ($n \leq l$), the sender samples t random coefficients $a_i \xleftarrow{\$} \mathbb{Z}_p$ that define a monic polynomial $P(x)$ of degree t:

$$P(x) = x^t + a_{t-1}x^{t-1} + \cdots + a_1 x + a_0 \quad (\mathrm{mod}\ p)$$

The sender generates n shares of P at publicly known points $\{z_i : i \in S\}$ and sets

$$x_i = \begin{cases} P(z_i) & i \in S \\ 0 & i \notin S \end{cases} : \forall i = 1..l \quad \text{and} \quad x_{l+1} = -P(0) = -a_0$$

For example, a ciphertext policy vector can be

x_1	x_2	x_3	...	x_l	x_{l+1}
$P(z_1)$	$P(z_2)$	0	...	$P(z_l)$	$-P(0)$

The receiver computes Lagrange polynomials λ_i at 0, using $\{z_i\}$ corresponding to a subset of t attributes in its possession, and requests the corresponding keys from the attribute authorities:

$$v_i = \begin{cases} \lambda_i & i \in S \\ 0 & i \notin S \end{cases} : \forall i = 1..l \quad \text{and} \quad v_{l+1} = 1.$$

The decryption procedure effectively performs Lagrange interpolation in the exponent, over the shares encoded in the ciphertext. If decryption fails, we form another subset of t attributes, recompute the Lagrange polynomials and request the corresponding keys, and retry decrypting. The receiver repeats this until it succeeds, or until it used all attributes in its possession. A receiver that is not able to decrypt does not learn the set of admissible attributes S. A drawback of this method, is that it requires attempting $O\binom{l}{t} \leq l^t$ attribute subsets. It is polynomial in the overall number of attributes, and exponential in the threshold parameter. Hence, it is practical for small thresholds.

CNF and DNF Formulas. Boolean CNF and DNF formulas can be represented by multivariate polynomials. We illustrate it with a simple example using three attributes A_1, A_2 and A_3. Any policy over this attribute set can be expressed using a polynomial in three variables x, y, z. In the general CNF case, the polynomial can have the terms xyz, xy, xz, yz, x, y, z and a free coefficient. Some terms may have a zero coefficient. For example, consider the CNF formula $(A_1 \lor A_2) \land A_3$, which can be expressed as

$$P(x, y, z) = r_1(x - 1)(y - 1) + r_2(z - 1) = r_1 xy - r_1 x - r_1 y + r_2 z + (r_1 - r_2)$$

The corresponding ciphertext policy vector is given by

x_1	x_2	x_3	x_4	x_5	x_6	x_7	x_8
x	y	z	xyz	xy	xz	yz	$P(0, \ldots, 0)$
$-r_1$	$-r_1$	r_2	0	r_1	0	0	$r_1 - r_2$

Regular authorities, controlling actual attributes, are responsible for issuing the keys corresponding to the terms x, y and z. In addition, special authorities are responsible for issuing keys corresponding to the cross-terms xyz, xy, xz, yz and the free coefficient. The authority corresponding to the free coefficient only issues keys for $v_{l+1} = 1$. The trusted authorities, given $\boldsymbol{v}$, enforce that the values requested for the cross-terms are consistent with those requested for x, y and z.

The policy above can be written in its DNF form, namely $(A_1 \land A_3) \lor (A_2 \land A_3)$, which can be expressed as

$$P(x, y, z) = [r_1(x - 1) + r_3(z - 1)] \cdot [r_2(y - 1) + r_3(z - 1)]$$

and encoded in a similar manner to the CNF representation.

Note that the encodings for CNF and DNF formulae can be seen as a randomized version of the encodings in [16]. Also, note that the authorities responsible for the cross-terms learn sensitive information about the attributes possessed by the receiver. To verify the values requested for the the cross-term, these authorities need to see the relevant inputs. It is possible to improve receiver privacy using commitments to the input values, and a zero-knowledge proof of the requested value being equal to the output of the corresponding boolean circuit. However, the cross-term value itself reveals considerable information and narrows down the solution space for possibile inputs.

5.2   Security of Randomizing-Polynomial Encodings

Essentially, security of randomizing-polynomial encodings relies on the negligible probability $(\frac{1}{p})$ that the adversary crafts an attribute vector v' that is different from a valid attribute-vector satisfying the policy. With overwhelming probability, this reduces to the security of the underlying basic scheme. The formal proof of security is the same as for conjunctions and HVE, and is given in the full paper.

6   Related Work

ABE in a multi-authority setting was initially studied by Chase [9], who proposed to to prevent collusion by incorporating a global user identifier into the key-generation procedure. Further improvements were proposed by Müller et al. [18] and Chase and Chow [10]. A fully decentralized scheme was proposed by Lewko and Waters [17]. Those constructions do not hide the encryption policy.

Agrawal et al. constructed an inner-product PE [2] and a Fuzzy-IBE [1] based on the learning-with-errors assumption (LWE). Lattice-based constructions often naturally hide the encryption policy, and it would be interesting to construct a decentralized scheme, based on LWE. Katz et al. introduce a zero-inner-product PE scheme that is fully-hiding [16], meaning the policy remains hidden even for a receiver who can decrypt the ciphertext.

The notion of vector commitments is related to cryptographic accumulators, first introduced by Benaloh and de Mare [4]. Accumulators are compact representations of a set of values, enabling to verify that a given element was used to compute the representation. As an alternative to the VC scheme we used, vector commitments can also be constructed using commitments to polynomials [15], by setting the polynomial coefficients to the vector elements.

Wichs and Zirdelis [27] and Goyal et al. [14], independently introduced Lockable Obfuscation for Compute-and-Compare programs, based on LWE. A corollary of lockable obfuscation is a transformation of any ABE scheme into one that is weakly attribute-hiding. However, it requires obfuscating a circuit corresponding to the decryption procedure of the underlying ABE scheme. This is highly impractical for the currently known multi-authority ABE schemes, and is not nearly as efficient as our direct construction. However, it is worth mentioning that those constructions theoretically solve the problem of decentralized policy-hiding ABE in a setting where the authorities don't need to know each other at all, and only refer to common public parameters.

Okamoto and Takashima constructed a decentralized ABE scheme, where the authorities do not need to be aware of one-another [20]. Their work claims payload-hiding, but not policy-hiding, and it is left to be studied whether their decentralized scheme can be proven weakly-hiding for the case of inner-product policies. In addition, our scheme enjoys a ciphertext that is at least two times shorter in the number of group elements, and a decryption algorithm that involves only two pairings instead of a number proportional to the vector size. Our scheme, however, requires the authorities to publish public keys that are visible to the other authorities, whereas the scheme in [20] does not require any coordination between authorities except for referring to the same public parameters.

7 Conclusion

We address the problem of decentralized attribute-hiding attribute-based encryption. Starting off the work of Chen *et al.* [11], we constructed a decentralized inner-product predicate encryption scheme. We use it to instantiate a decentralized ABE scheme that hides the ciphertext policy, and show that, in the presence of corrupted authorities, it is not enough to prove security of the underlying PE scheme, but also to properly encode policies. We provide encodings for multiple useful policies. Finally, we propose an extra measure to protect receiver privacy, by using commitments to the attribute vector.

A   Vector Commitments

A vector commitment scheme consists of the following algorithms:

- VC.Setup$(1^\lambda, n)$: On input security parameter λ and the vector size n, output the public parameters pp which implicitly define the message space $\mathcal{M}$.
- VC.Commit$_{pp}(v)$: On input the public parameters and a sequence of values $v = (v_1, \ldots, v_n)$, where $v_1, \ldots, v_n \in \mathcal{M}$, output a commitment string C and auxiliary information aux. The auxiliary information is simply a vector of the underlying hiding per-element commitments.
- VC.Open$_{pp}(v, i, \text{aux})$: Run by the committer (that requests the keys in our setting) to produce a proof P_i that v is the i-th committed value.
- VC.Verify$_{pp}(C, v, i, P_i)$: Outputs *true* only if P_i is a valid proof that C was created to a sequence of values $v_1, \ldots, v_n$ s.t. $v_i = v$.

Definition 5 (Position-Binding). *A vector commitment scheme* VC *is position-binding if* $\forall i = 1, \ldots, n$ *and for every efficient adversary* $\mathcal{A}$, $\mathcal{A}$ *has negligible probability of producing a tuple* (C, v, v', i, P, P') *where* $v \neq v'$ *s.t.*

$$\text{VC.Verify}_{pp}(C, v, i, P) \wedge \text{VC.Verify}_{pp}(C, v', i, P').$$

While position-binding ensures that only key-parts issued for the same vector v can be combined to obtain a functional decryption key, we require the vector-commitment scheme to be hiding. Note that the vector commitment scheme is hiding only when composed with a standard commitment scheme to generate a hiding commitment for each element, that are in turn input to the vector commitment scheme. As suggested in [8], we combine the generic VC scheme with a hiding commitment scheme. Depending on whether valid attribute vectors contain only 0 and 1 or arbitrary values, we can use Pedersen's one-bit commitment scheme [21] or generalized Pedersen commitments.

B   Proof Sketch for the Scheme in Sect. 3

We define a sequence of games, starting with the actual scheme and ending up with a challenge ciphertext that encodes a random message using a random predicate vector. We argue that the games are indistinguishable to the adversary, concluding that the scheme is attribute-hiding. The transition between the hybrids is based on switching to "semi-functional" keys, and a "semi-functional" challenge ciphertext that cannot be decrypted using those keys, and looks uniformly random to the adversary.

A semi-functional ciphertext is one where instead of $A s$ in the exponent, we have a random vector $z \in \mathbb{Z}_p^{k+1}$. A semi-functional key is one where α is replaced by $\alpha + a^{\perp} \hat{t}$ ($\hat{t} \in \mathbb{Z}_p$ and $h = \mathbf{B} r$, where $r \in \mathbb{Z}_p^k$). It is easy to check that a semi-functional key cannot decrypt a semi-functional ciphertext. That, in turn, enables to switch from a game where an actual message m is encrypted under an actual policy vector x, to one where a random message m' is encrypted under a random policy vector $x^{\star}$. This sequence is similar to the one in the proof of the weak attribute-hiding scheme in [11], with certain additions, modifications and reordering of games.

For simplicity, we use the fact that the terms $g_2^{\mu_i}$ are random in $(\mathbb{G}_2)^n$, in the adversarial view, as long as there are at least 2 honest authorities, unless canceled by summation in the exponent. In fact, the key combining is similar to the technique for privacy-preserving aggregation, as proposed by Shi et al. [26]. We can therefore refer to their security proof to justify this step. Barthe et al. [3] also used a similar technique in their privacy-preserving aggregation protocol. A tighter security reduction, linear in the number of adversarial queries, can be achieved using Smooth Projective Hash Functions (SPHF), as in [5].

As a result, K_i are only useful as a product $K - \prod_{i=1}^n K_i$. Therefore, we prove the security of a scheme where the challenger computes K directly and hands it to the adversary, since it can always split it to n random shares in $\mathbb{G}_2$. It is easy to show that if there is an efficient adversary $\mathcal{A}$ that wins the game in Definition 2 against $\mathcal{S}'$, $\mathcal{S}'$ can use it to win the modified game against $\mathcal{S}$. When $\mathcal{A}$ requests a key for (GID, i, v), $\mathcal{S}'$ asks $\mathcal{S}$ for a key for the whole vector v, splits it to random multiplicative shares, and serves the correct share to $\mathcal{A}$. It can later use the other shares for subsequent requests corresponding to the same GID and v. It is therefore enough to prove security of this modified game.

C   Hidden-Vector Encryption

Hidden-Vector Encryption (HVE) was first introduced by Boneh and Waters [7]. Given a set of attributes Σ, let $\Sigma_* = S \cup \{*\}$, and the HVE predicate is

$$P_{a_1,\dots,a_l}^{hve}(x_1,\dots,x_l) = \begin{cases} 1 & \forall i : a_i = x_i \vee a_i = * \\ 0 & \text{otherwise.} \end{cases}$$

Simply put, this is a pattern matching on an input, where $a_i = *$ denotes a wildcard ("don't care"), indicating that at position i, the input vector is allowed to have an arbitrary value. For l attributes, we need to use vectors of size $l+1$. The ciphertext policy vector is constructed by sampling l random values $r_i \xleftarrow{\$} \mathbb{Z}_p$, and setting

$$x_i = \begin{cases} r_i & X_i \neq * \\ 0 & X_i = * \end{cases} : \forall i = 1..l \qquad \text{and} \qquad x_{l+1} = -\sum_{i=1}^{l} r_i X_i \pmod{p}.$$

The receiver attribute vector is given by

$$v_i = \begin{cases} a_i & i \in S \\ 0 & i \notin S \end{cases} : \forall i = 1..l$$

where S is the set of attributes possessed by the receiver, and $v_{l+1} = 1$.

As in the encoding for conjunctions, this encoding is secure even in the presence of corrupt authorities. The proof of security is similar to the one for conjunctions.

References

1. Agrawal, S., Boyen, X., Vaikuntanathan, V., Voulgaris, P., Wee, H.: Functional encryption for threshold functions (or fuzzy IBE) from lattices. In: Fischlin, M., Buchmann, J., Manulis, M. (eds.) PKC 2012. LNCS, vol. 7293, pp. 280–297. Springer, Heidelberg (2012). https://doi.org/10.1007/978-3-642-30057-8_17
2. Agrawal, S., Freeman, D.M., Vaikuntanathan, V.: Functional encryption for inner product predicates from learning with errors. In: Lee, D.H., Wang, X. (eds.) ASIACRYPT 2011. LNCS, vol. 7073, pp. 21–40. Springer, Heidelberg (2011). https://doi.org/10.1007/978-3-642-25385-0_2
3. Barthe, G., Danezis, G., Grégoire, B., Kunz, C., Zanella-Beguelin, S.: Verified computational differential privacy with applications to smart metering. In: 2013 IEEE 26th Computer Security Foundations Symposium (CSF), pp. 287–301. IEEE (2013)
4. Benaloh, J., de Mare, M.: One-way accumulators: a decentralized alternative to digital signatures. In: Helleseth, T. (ed.) EUROCRYPT 1993. LNCS, vol. 765, pp. 274–285. Springer, Heidelberg (1994). https://doi.org/10.1007/3-540-48285-7_24
5. Benhamouda, F., Joye, M., Libert, B.: A new framework for privacy-preserving aggregation of time-series data. ACM Trans. Inf. Syst. Secur. 18(3), 10:1–10:21 (2016)
6. Boneh, D., Sahai, A., Waters, B.: Functional encryption: definitions and challenges. In: Ishai, Y. (ed.) TCC 2011. LNCS, vol. 6597, pp. 253–273. Springer, Heidelberg (2011). https://doi.org/10.1007/978-3-642-19571-6_16
7. Boneh, D., Waters, B.: Conjunctive, subset, and range queries on encrypted data. In: Vadhan, S.P. (ed.) TCC 2007. LNCS, vol. 4392, pp. 535–554. Springer, Heidelberg (2007). https://doi.org/10.1007/978-3-540-70936-7_29
8. Catalano, D., Fiore, D.: Vector commitments and their applications. In: Kurosawa, K., Hanaoka, G. (eds.) PKC 2013. LNCS, vol. 7778, pp. 55–72. Springer, Heidelberg (2013). https://doi.org/10.1007/978-3-642-36362-7_5
9. Chase, M.: Multi-authority attribute based encryption. In: Vadhan, S.P. (ed.) TCC 2007. LNCS, vol. 4392, pp. 515–534. Springer, Heidelberg (2007). https://doi.org/10.1007/978-3-540-70936-7_28

10. Chase, M., Chow, S.S.M.: Improving privacy and security in multi-authority attribute-based encryption. In: Al-Shaer, E., Jha, S., Keromytis, A.D. (eds.) ACM CCS 2009, pp. 121–130. ACM Press, November 2009

11. Chen, J., Gay, R., Wee, H.: Improved dual system ABE in prime-order groups via predicate encodings. In: Oswald, E., Fischlin, M. (eds.) EUROCRYPT 2015. LNCS, vol. 9057, pp. 595–624. Springer, Heidelberg (2015). https://doi.org/10.1007/978-3-662-46803-6_20

12. Chen, J., Wee, H.: Dual system groups and its applications – compact HIBE and more. Cryptology ePrint Archive, Report 2014/265 (2014). http://eprint.iacr.org/2014/265

13. Escala, A., Herold, G., Kiltz, E., Ràfols, C., Villar, J.L.: An algebraic framework for Diffie-Hellman assumptions. J. Cryptol. 30(1), 242–288 (2017)

14. Goyal, R., Koppula, V., Waters, B.: Lockable obfuscation. In: 58th FOCS, pp. 612–621. IEEE Computer Society Press (2017)

15. Kate, A., Zaverucha, G.M., Goldberg, I.: Constant-size commitments to polynomials and their applications. In: Abe, M. (ed.) ASIACRYPT 2010. LNCS, vol. 6477, pp. 177–194. Springer, Heidelberg (2010). https://doi.org/10.1007/978-3-642-17373-8_11

16. Katz, J., Sahai, A., Waters, B.: Predicate encryption supporting disjunctions, polynomial equations, and inner products. J. Cryptol. 26(2), 191–224 (2013)

17. Lewko, A., Waters, B.: Decentralizing attribute-based encryption. In: Paterson, K.G. (ed.) EUROCRYPT 2011. LNCS, vol. 6632, pp. 568–588. Springer, Heidelberg (2011). https://doi.org/10.1007/978-3-642-20465-4_31

18. Müller, S., Katzenbeisser, S., Eckert, C.: Distributed attribute-based encryption. In: Lee, P.J., Cheon, J.H. (eds.) ICISC 2008. LNCS, vol. 5461, pp. 20–36. Springer, Heidelberg (2009). https://doi.org/10.1007/978-3-642-00730-9_2

19. Nakamoto, S.: Bitcoin: a peer-to-peer electronic cash system. Consulted, pp. 1–9 (2008). http://s.kwma.kr/pdf/Bitcoin/bitcoin.pdf

20. Okamoto, T., Takashima, K.: Decentralized attribute-based signatures. Cryptology ePrint Archive, Report 2011/701 (2011). http://eprint.iacr.org/2011/701

21. Pedersen, T.P.: Non-interactive and information-theoretic secure verifiable secret sharing. In: Feigenbaum, J. (ed.) CRYPTO 1991. LNCS, vol. 576, pp. 129–140. Springer, Heidelberg (1992). https://doi.org/10.1007/3-540-46766-1_9

22. Rahulamathavan, Y., Phan, R.C.W., Rajarajan, M., Misra, S., Kondoz, A.: Privacy-preserving blockchain based IoT ecosystem using attribute-based encryption. In: IEEE International Conference on Advanced Networks and Telecommunications Systems, Odisha, India, December 2017

23. Roberts, F.: UK/India consortium explore blockchain for healthcare IoT security. https://internetofbusiness.com/consortium-blockchain-iot-security/

24. Sahai, A., Waters, B.: Slides on functional encryption. PowerPoint presentation (2008). http://www.cs.utexas.edu/~bwaters/presentations/files/functional.ppt

25. Sahai, A., Waters, B.: Fuzzy identity-based encryption. In: Cramer, R. (ed.) EUROCRYPT 2005. LNCS, vol. 3494, pp. 457–473. Springer, Heidelberg (2005). https://doi.org/10.1007/11426639_27

26. Shi, E., Chan, T.H.H., Rieffel, E.G., Chow, R., Song, D.: Privacy-preserving aggregation of time-series data. In: NDSS 2011. The Internet Society, February 2011

27. Wichs, D., Zirdelis, G.: Obfuscating compute-and-compare programs under LWE. In: 58th FOCS, pp. 600–611. IEEE Computer Society Press (2017)

Author Index

Printed in the United States
By Bookmasters